# THE TERROR CONSPIRACY REVISITED

Copyright © 2011 Jim Marrs

Published by The Disinformation Company Ltd.
111 East 14th Street, Suite 108
New York, NY 10003
Phone: +1.212.691.1605
Email: books@disinfo.com
www.disinfo.com

All rights reserved. No part of this book may be reproduced, stored in a database or other retrieval system, or transmitted in any form, by any means now existing or later discovered, including without limitation mechanical, electronic, photographic or otherwise, without the express prior written permission of the publisher.

Library of Congress Control Number: 2011935974

ISBN: 978-1934708-63-7

eISBN: 978-1934708-74-3

Printed in USA

10 9 8 7 6 5 4 3 2 1

Distributed in the USA and Canada by:
Consortium Book Sales and Distribution
Toll Free: +1.800.283.3572
Fax: +1.800.351.5073
www.cbsd.com

The opinions and statements made in this book are those of the author; the publisher has not verified any of his statements, theories or conclusions and no warranty or fitness is implied. The publisher shall have no liability or responsibility to any person or entity with respect to any loss or damage arising from the information contained in this book or from the use thereof or reliance thereon.

# THE TERROR CONSPIRACY REVISITED:

What Really Happened On 9/11,
And Why We're Still Paying The Price

JIM MARRS

disinformation®

# TABLE OF CONTENTS

QUOTES YOU HAVE NOT HEARD IN THE MAINSTREAM MEDIA .. VII

INTRODUCTION .................................... XII

PART I – THE EVENTS OF SEPTEMBER 11, 2001 ............ 1
  A Chronology Of Events........................... 1
  Unresolved Questions Abound ..................... 6
  What Did President Bush Know, And When? ................ 12
  Did War Games Aid The Terrorists? ..................... 15
  Who Authorized The Bin Laden Evacuation? ................. 23
  What About The Hijackers Themselves? ................... 25
  What Really Happened At The Pentagon? ................. 44
  Explosions At The World Trade Center ..................... 57
  Firefighters Thought The Fires Were Controllable. ............. 76
  Advanced Technology At The World Trade Center? ........... 85
  What Caused The Collapse Of WTC Building 7? ............. 101
  Tracks Of Foreknowledge ............................. 111
  The FBI Couldn't, Or Wouldn't, Connect The Dots ........... 126
  Missed Opportunities At The CIA....................... 142
  Selling Stocks Short Indicates Foreknowledge................. 155
  What About Israeli Foreknowledge?...................... 165
  Were The Hijacked Planes Remotely Controlled? ............. 179
  What About The Cell Phone Calls?...................... 193
  What Really Happened To Flight 93?.................... 199
  Remote Viewers Look At 9/11 .......................... 217
  The Official 9/11 Inquiry: Another Warren Commission? ....... 221

## PART II – WAR FOR OIL AND DRUGS ........................ 245
    The Central Asian Gas Pipeline ........................... 250
    Afghan Action Was Planned Long Ago .................... 253
    Wag The Dog In Iraq? ..................................... 260
    Cheney's Dealings In Iraq ................................. 277
    Iraqis And The Murrah Federal Building Bombing ........ 284
    Ancient Technology In Baghdad? ......................... 290
    US Complicity In The World Drug Trade .................. 297
    Bin Laden, The Made-To-Order Enemy ................... 306
    Bin Laden Replies ......................................... 311
    The Bin Laden Family And Friends ....................... 321

## PART III – THE 9/11 BACKLASH ............................ 341
    A History Of Unconstitutional Actions .................... 349
    Posse Comitatus Ignored ................................. 354
    A Questionable Military Record ........................... 362
    Creating Homeland Security .............................. 367
    Was George Orwell Right About 1984? ................... 378
    Tom Ridge And The Phoenix Program .................... 385
    Homeland Security At Work .............................. 389
    Enter The Patriot Act ..................................... 400
    The Patriot Act At Work .................................. 405
    Internment Camps In Place .............................. 419
    Big Brother's Technology ................................. 426
    Governing By Secrecy And Decree ....................... 437
    The Shadow Government Knows ........................ 447

## PART IV – HISTORICAL PRECEDENTS ...................... 451
    The Reichstag Fire ....................................... 452
    Pearl Harbor .............................................. 455
    The Gulf War ............................................. 459

Would Americans Allow Attacks On Americans? .............465
War As An Economic Stimulus.............................468
The Mass Media..........................................476
A Dismal Foreign Policy Record..........................487
Manufactured Enemies....................................494
The Hegelian Dialectic..................................496
What Do We Know Now?....................................499

**SOURCES** .............................................**514**

**APPENDIX – THE PENTAGON ATTACK PAPERS** ..............**553**
Seven Hours in September: The Clock that Broke the Lie

**INDEX**................................................**584**

## QUOTES YOU HAVE NOT HEARD IN THE MAINSTREAM MEDIA

"In the course of our investigation into the national response to the attacks, the 9/11 Commission staff discovered that the official version of what had occurred [the morning of September 11, 2001]—that is, what government and military officials had told Congress, the Commission, the media, and the public about who knew what when—was almost entirely, and inexplicably, untrue."
–John Farmer, senior counsel to the National Commission on Terrorist Attacks Upon the United States (the official 9/11 Commission)

"If the war on terror is real then the first thing that would have happened within a matter of weeks after 9/11 would have been we'd have closed the borders off. You have no national security if your borders are not secure...The official story of 9/11 is the dog that doesn't hunt."
–Col. Ronald D. Ray, US Marine Corps (ret.) and former deputy assistant secretary of defense under the Reagan Administration

"Scholars and professionals...have established beyond any reasonable doubt that the official account of 9/11 is false and that, therefore, the official 'investigations' have really been cover-up operations."
–Lt. Col. Robert Bowman, PhD, US Air Force (ret.)

"Your countrymen have been murdered and the more you delve into it the more it looks as though they were murdered by our government, who used it as an excuse to murder other people thousands of miles away."
–Lt. Col. Shelton F. Lankford, US Marine Corps (ret.)

"I am 100% convinced that the attacks of September 11, 2001 were planned, organized, and committed by treasonous perpetrators that have infiltrated the highest levels of our government....Those of us in the military took an oath to 'support and defend the Constitution of the United States against all enemies, foreign and domestic'...it is our duty to expose the real perpetrators of 9/11 and bring them to justice, no matter how hard it is, how long it takes, or how much we have to suffer to do it. We owe it to those who have gone before us who executed that same oath, and who are doing the same thing in Iraq and Afghanistan right now. Those of us who joined the military and faithfully executed orders that were given us had to trust our leaders. The violation and abuse of that trust is not only heinous, but ultimately the most accurate definition of treason!"
–Lt. Colonel Guy S. Razer, US Air Force fighter pilot, and former instructor at the USAF Fighter Weapons School

"It is as a scientist that I have the most trouble with the official government conspiracy theory, mainly because it does not satisfy the rules of probability or physics."
–Lt. Col. Karen U. Kwiatkowski, PhD, US Air Force (ret.)

"No aircraft hit the Pentagon. Totally impossible! You couldn't make the turns with a 757. You couldn't fly it in over the highway. You couldn't fly it over the light poles. You couldn't even get it that close to the ground because of turbulence."
–Major Douglas Rokke, PhD, US Army (ret.)

"When one starts using his own mind, and not what one was told, there is very little to believe in the official story...[I] have experience flying low altitude, high speed aircraft. I could not have done what these beginners did. Something stinks to high heaven!"
–Commander Ralph Kolstad, TOPGUN pilot, US Navy (ret.)

"We analyzed the data and announced our conclusion on March 26, 2007, that 'The information provided by the NTSB does not support *The 9/11 Commission Report* of American Airlines Flight 77 impact with the Pentagon.'"
–Rob Balsamo, commercial airline pilot, co-founder of Pilots for 9/11 Truth

"I most certainly and honestly believe, that sometime in the near future, it will become common knowledge that the events of 9/11 were an 'inside job' designed, engineered and committed by a very large and 'in control' rogue element within our United States federal government."
–Glen Stanish, commercial airline pilot

"The Pentagon was not hit by a Boeing 757. A Boeing 757 did not crash in Shanksville, PA."
–Captain Gordon Price, retired commercial pilot

"[W]hat we saw happen on that morning of September 11, 2001, was the result of a highly-compartmentalized covert operation to bring about a fascist coup in this country."
–Alan N. Sabrosky, PhD

"No Boeing 757 ever crashed into the Pentagon. No Boeing 757 ever crashed at Shanksville....And no Arab hijacker, ever in a million years, ever flew into the World Trade Center. And if you got 30 minutes I'll tell you exactly why he couldn't do it the first time."
–John Lear, retired commercial airline pilot

"...an airplane that weighs 100 tons all assembled is still going to have 100 tons of disassembled trash and parts after it hits a building. There was no wreckage from a 757 at the Pentagon."
–Captain Russ Wittenberg, retired commercial pilot

"I know from my experience that it would have been highly improbable that even a seasoned American test pilot, a military test pilot, could have flown a T-category, aircraft like the 757, into the first floor of the Pentagon because of a thing called 'ground effect.'"
–Captain Fred Fox, retired commercial airline pilot

"My research into 9/11 raised many red flags, but ultimately pointed to a type of covert operation, used time and time again in history, known as a 'false flag'...an act of aggression meant to appear as though it was carried out by your enemies... Even if I'd had no other reason to investigate, my airlines family deserved an honest account of the attack. I might add that we also deserve this because 9/11 has been used against us ever since, kin a running nightmare of contrived bankruptcy, draconian working conditions and hostile management."
–Philip Marshall, veteran airline captain and former covert operations pilot

"*The 9/11 Commission Report* is fatally flawed. The major conclusions of *The 9/11 Commission Report*—the official, conspiracy theory—are false."
–Enver Masud, engineer and author

"[A]ll three World Trade Center high-rise buildings, the Twin Towers and Building 7 were destroyed not by fire as our government has told us, but by controlled demolition with explosives."
–Richard Gage, founding member of Architects & Engineers for 9/11 Truth

"In my opinion, the building WTC 7 was, with great probability, professionally demolished."
–Jörg Schneider, professor emeritus, Institute for Building & Construction

"I have 'known' from day-one that the buildings were imploded and that they could not and would not have collapsed from the damage caused by the airplanes that ran into them."
–Daniel B. Barnum, architect, FAIA

"[S]ymmetrical collapse is strong evidence of a controlled demolition. A building falling from asymmetrical structural failure would not collapse so neatly, nor so rapidly."
–David A. Johnson, architect, PhD, FAICP

"Obviously it [WTC 7] was the result of controlled demolition and scheduled to take place during the confusion surrounding the day's events."
–Jack Keller, PhD, agricultural and irrigation enginner

"In my opinion the building WTC 7 was, with great probability, professionally demolished."
–Hugo Bachmann, PhD

"The [North Tower] building was designed to have a fully loaded 707 crash into it. That was the largest plane at the time. I believe that the building probably could sustain multiple impacts of jetliners because this structure is like the mosquito netting on your screen door."
–Frank A. DeMartini, architect and WTC construction manager

"I looked at the drawings, the construction and it couldn't be done by fire. So, no, absolutely not...This is controlled demolition...A team of experts did this."
–Danny Jowenko, proprietor, Jowenko Explosieve Demolitie BV

"We have found solid scientific grounds on which to question the interpretation put upon the events of September 11, 2001 by the office of the president of the United States of America and subsequently propagated by the major media of western nations."
–A. K. Dewdney, PhD, 9/11 scientific investigator

"Despite the absence of any visible fire at the time of collapse, the government report alleges WTC Building 7 is the first and only steel-framed high-rise building in the history of mankind to collapse simply as the result of a fire."
–David L. Griscom, research physicist, Scholars for 9/11 Truth & Justice

"Truth, ethics and professionalism are completely lacking in the official aftermath and investigations surrounding the 9/11 disasters. Unfortunately we went to war predicated on lies, sustained in lies, and perpetuated in lies."
–Hamid Mumin, PhD., geologist and engineer

"This is the first time, and this is the worst disaster, but this is the first time that families have been attempted to be silenced through a special fund,...I found that the airlines approached members of Congress and the Senate to get their bailout and their immunity and their protection starting on 9/11."
–Mary Schiavo, JD, former professor of aviation

"On the basis of photographic and video evidence as well as related data and analyses, I provide thirteen reasons for rejecting the official hypothesis, according to which fire and impact damage caused the collapse of the Twin Towers and WTC 7, in favor of the controlled-demolition hypothesis."
–Steven Jones, PhD, former professor of physics

"All the proffered evidence that America was attacked by Muslims on 9/11, when subjected to critical scrutiny, appears to have been fabricated."
–David Ray Griffin, professor emeritus, philosopher, author

"When you grow up in the United States, there are some bedrock principles that require concerted effort to discard. One is the simplest: that our leaders are good and decent people whose efforts may occasionally warrant criticism but never because of malice or venality...But one grows up....And with the lawyer's training comes the reliance on evidence and the facts that persuade...After a lot of reading, thought, study, and commiseration, I have come to the conclusion that the attacks of 9/11 were, in their essence, an inside job perpetrated at the highest levels of the US government."
–William Veale, retired public defender, former instructor of criminal trial practice, Boalt Hall School of Law, University of California, Berkeley

"I taught stand down and false-flag operations at the national war college, I've taught it with all my operatives so I knew exactly what was done to the American public...[9/11] was called a stand down, a false flag operation in order to mobilize the American public under false pretenses....it was told to me even by the general on the staff of [former Deputy Secretary of Defense Paul] Wolfowitz. I will go in front of a federal committee and swear on perjury who the name was of the individual so that we can break it open."
–Steve Pieczenik, PhD, deputy assistant secretary of state under Presidents Nixon, Ford and Carter

# INTRODUCTION

*"Quis custodiet ipsos custodies?"*

(*Who will guard the guards themselves?*)

— Roman poet Juvenal, *Satires*, VI. 347

2011 marks the 10th anniversary of the attacks of September 11, 2001 (9/11), an event that opened a new page in American history for better or worse.

The attacks brought the United States a new era of centralized government and control over its population with enactment of the Patriot Act and the Military Commissions Act, the founding of the Department of Homeland Security, not to mention the ongoing occupations of Iraq and Afghanistan.

Yet, the official explanation of the 9/11 attacks still raises more questions than there are answers.

Certainly, we had the official conspiracy theory of that day—namely, that 19 suicidal Middle Eastern Muslim terrorists—their hearts full of hatred for American freedom and democracy—used small box cutters to hijack four airliners, all of whose transponders were turned off about the same time. Two were crashed into the Twin Towers of New York City's World Trade Center and a third into the Pentagon, near Washington,

D.C.. A fourth airliner reportedly crashed in western Pennsylvania after passengers attempted to overcome the hijackers. Adding some disbelief to this surreal scenario, the whole complex Mission Impossible operation, which defeated a $40 billion-a-year defense system, was blamed on inexperienced Arab student pilots said to be under the direction of a devout Muslim cleric from Saudi Arabia using cell phones and a portable computer in a cave in Afghanistan.

President George W. Bush, speaking to the UN General Assembly on November 10, 2001 stated, "Let us never tolerate outrageous conspiracy theories concerning the attacks of September the 11th, malicious lies that attempt to shift the blame away from the terrorists themselves, away from the guilty." He was right. There is an outrageous conspiracy theory that is poisoning our nation. It is called the official version of 9/11. Facts and evidence which contradict the official version of 9/11 have been skillfully kept from the public by a compliant and sycophantic corporate mass media. Yet this same information, readily available from numerous Internet sources, is so blatant and self-evident that it is incomprehensible that more Americans are not aware of it.

For about 15 years following the assassination of President John F. Kennedy on November 22, 1963, no one spoke publicly about it. It was considered ill mannered to discuss the assassination in polite company. It was only after the revelations of the Church Committee and the House Select Committee on Assassinations in the 1970s that Kennedy's murder became an acceptable topic of conversation. America has been going through a similar period of denial and silence concerning the crimes of 9/11.

Anyone who doubts that what we have all been told about 9/11 is simply wrong must consider the words of John Farmer, the senior counsel to the National Commission on Terrorist Attacks Upon the United States, better known as the 9/11 Commission, the official US government's investigative body of the attacks.

On the second page of his 2009 book *The Ground Truth: The Story Behind America's Defense on 9/11*, Farmer wrote, "In the course of our investigation into the national response to the attacks, the 9/11 Commission staff discovered that the official version of what had occurred [the morning of September 11, 2001]—that is, what government and military officials had told Congress, the commission, the media, and the public about who knew what when—was almost entirely, and inexplicably, untrue."

Untrue. Is that plain enough? If not, Farmer clarified himself a bit further on by writing how "the public had been seriously misled about what occurred during the morning of the attacks ... at some level of the government, at some point in time ... there was an agreement not to tell the truth about what happened."

So the conspiracy theory that was fed to the American public by duplicitous officials and a compliant corporate mass media is untrue. What then is the truth? The one undeniable truth of 9/11 is that the American public has not been told the truth even 10 years after the events. Yet the fallout of the attacks continues to mold our foreign policy as well as our society.

No one can doubt that the tragic attacks of 9/11 were the result of a conspiracy, heretofore a term disparaged by the mass media when connected to any past event in America—whether the JFK assassination, CIA drug running, or the deaths of church members in Waco.

On September 11, 2001, media contempt for the word conspiracy was swept away in the attacks on the United States. This major tragedy could not be blamed on a lone deranged individual. The question now became who precisely was behind this conspiracy to kill Americans, a question that the US government has so far failed to answer adequately, instead merely offering a theory that continues to be shredded by a growing number of doubters.

If the official conspiracy theory sounds far-fetched or just too convenient, a closer look at the events of 9/11 reveals an even more disturbing number of unanswered questions. This also holds true for the aftermath of the event, in which the Bush administration used their predetermined 9/11 conspiracy theory as a pretext for curtailing the cherished liberties of Americans.

As pointed out by thoughtful students of history, one must not be distracted by the *how* of an event but instead should focus on the *who* and the *why*. Accumulate the facts, though often contradictory, and then concentrate on the overall process by which these events transpired. In other words, consider the overview and try to think like a good police detective: Who benefited from this crime? Who had the means, the motive, and the opportunity—not only to devise such attacks, but to circumvent normal security measures and hinder any objective investigation?

Such reasoning brings knowledge, and it is said that knowledge is power.

Many ardent 9/11 researchers have focused on specific and even technical aspects of that event—the melting temperature of structural steel, the size of the Pentagon's hole, etc.—but at some point one must back off and look at the broad overview and search for deeper meanings.

The information within this book should empower Americans who long for such a wider framework and who are ready for some straight talk about the many factual anomalies, conflicting claims, and unanswered questions that still surround the horrific attacks of September 11, 2001 as well as its aftermath.

Indeed, it was the provocation of the attacks of 9/11 that provided the underlying justification for all that followed—the hurried passage of the Patriot Act, increases in the defense and intelligence budgets, the invasion and occupation of Afghanistan and Iraq, the creation of the Department of Homeland Security, the justifications for torture at secret prisons, the warrantless wiretapping of Americans, the centralization of power around the presidency, growing surveillance of the population, and the general stifling of dissent in a nation that claims to be free.

A wider framework for understanding the post-9/11 era is also offered by the Bush administration. It's called the "War on Terrorism," yet the dictionary definition of terrorism is "organized intimidation," simply a tactic of terrorists. Following the Japanese attack on Pearl Harbor, would President Roosevelt have declared a "War on Naval Aviation"? Yet Americans have been warned by Vice President Dick Cheney and others that this global war against a vague concept will last for many years, even decades, a mark already reached in 2011.

Knowledge concerning facts about 9/11 should have been available to be public within months of the tragedies—but it seems that freedom of the press, at least within the United States, belongs only to those who own the presses, , or, in the case of the electronic media, to those corporations that own the media networks and channels.

To those of us who follow the shadowy side of America's national life, the events of 9/11 immediately raised red flags of warning. Just one day after 9/11, I posted my initial thoughts in a piece on the Internet. Here is an excerpt:

## WHO'S TRULY BEHIND THE ATTACK ON AMERICA?

Many people have compared the horrendous terrorist attack on New York's World Trade Center and the Pentagon in Washington to the attack on Pearl Harbor in 1941. It is an apt comparison, though not for the reasons most people think.

For true students of history, it is now beyond dispute that certain high-ranking officials in Washington, D.C. knew in advance of the Japanese intention to attack the US fleet in Hawaii, yet did nothing to prevent it.

Must the citizens of the United States wait another 50 years to learn that the 9/11 terrorist attack was allowed to take place just like Pearl Harbor? Could such an appalling scenario possibly be true?

Simple countermeasures against such an attack now seem apparent. For example, if the airlines would assign just one armed plainclothes security man to each flight, this tragedy may have been averted since apparently the hijackers were armed only with knives or other type blades. So, how were they able to overpower a plane load of people and, more importantly, gain access to the cockpits? Who taught them to fly jumbo jets?

As in the case of the assassination of President John F. Kennedy, the key to understanding the event lies not in who actually committed the violence but rather who was able to strip away the normal security protection.

Government and airline officials knew immediately that planes had been hijacked, yet no interceptors appeared in the air until after the attacks were completed. Who stripped away the normal security protection of America on 9/11?

At least in this most recent case, the government cannot blame the attack on a lone deranged individual, some Lee Harvey McVeigh. They must deal with a full-blown conspiracy, even though authorities were quick to point the finger at Osama bin Laden. Any investigation of bin Laden must look beyond the man, to his backers and financiers.

The trail of the terrorists will most probably become murky, with plenty of accusations for all concerned. But one thing appears quite clear, the tragic events of 9/11 play right into the hands of persons with an agenda aimed at eroding American liberties and sovereignty.

After decades of bloated and misused defense budgets, there are now calls for doubling our defense allocation. In a time of rising recognition that the CIA is an agency never sought by the public and one which has brought so much condemnation on this nation, there are now cries for doubling its size and budget. If the chief security officer for a large company fails to protect one of its most prized assets, is he more likely to be fired or have his pay doubled?

Watch for more anti-terrorist legislation to further shred the US Constitution.

As we all scramble to deal with the effects of terrorism, are we in danger of losing our few remaining individual liberties?

Also, consider that we are distracted from a faltering economy (the current crisis may require more federal financial controls), a plummeting public opinion of George W. Bush and surging energy prices.

Would leaders allow a public disaster to happen with an eye toward advancing their agendas? It's happened before... in Nero's burning Rome, Germany's gutted Reichstag, at Pearl Harbor and again at the Gulf of Tonkin.

While we should grieve for our losses, we must keep our heads. When the emotions of the moment run hot, we must remain cool and thoughtful so that we can find who is truly behind this attack on America.

I believe the basic questions and issues raised in this posting are as valid today as in September 2001.

And I didn't stop there. Within two months of 9/11, I had gathered a vast amount of material, much of which appears in this book (along with lots of new information) and presented it as a proposal to my publisher, HarperCollins of New York, under the title, *The War on Freedom*.

I was told that emotions were too high and the content too "hot" for immediate publication. Foot dragging on the book deal continued until mid-2002. At that time, several employees of the FBI and CIA had come forward to testify that they had tried to warn superiors of an impending terrorist attack. The attitude toward my book proposal softened and I signed a contract to publish the book, along with a nice advance.

Working feverishly throughout the summer of 2002, I produced a manuscript by my October deadline. My editor was elated with the work and predicted it would sell more than a million copies (not to brag, but based on sales of my earlier books, this was not at all implausible).

The wheels of major publishing grind slowly and it was not until early 2003 that the book received a legal review. I had already been sent a copy of the cover and publication was just a few weeks away. The legal review, or vetting, is a process in which legal counsel verifies the source material and checks for anything that might cause a legal problem. This hurdle was passed and the last words from the attorney were, "You have satisfied me."

Within two days, however, I was informed that a senior officer who had not even read it had canceled the book. The only justification given was that the officer "did not want to upset the families of 9/11 victims." This was obviously a specious argument as it was agitation by 9/11 victims' families that resulted in the belated creation of the 9/11 Commission in late 2002, and in 2006 more than 600 families filed lawsuits and complaints against both Saudi Arabia and senior members of the Bush administration.

Under normal circumstances, if a book must be canceled for legal reasons, the author is required to return any payments made in advance. In this case, I was paid the remainder of the entire advance and the rights returned to me. This was an indication that the cancellation of the book was nothing less than sheer censorship, although the identity of the censor was not clear. The senior officer undoubtedly was merely following orders from even higher authority.

"Why would they want to prevent people from learning truths about 9/11 even if those truths were discomfiting to the public and embarrassing to government authorities?" I asked myself, still believing that I lived in a nation which valued free speech.

I proceeded to self-publish *The War on Freedom*, albeit with a very limited distribution, and the book's reception was uniformly good despite the small circulation. Part I of that book was later published and distributed by a small California press under the title of *Inside Job*. *The Terror Conspiracy* replaced *Inside Job* in 2006 and included the three original parts of *The War on Freedom*. It was greatly updated and expanded in the light of events and discoveries since 2002.

As readers kept expressing astonishment at these earlier books, I realized that the knowledge gleaned from a study of published matter, both in print and on the Internet, was indeed painting a dark picture of the persons and forces behind today's current events. I also came to see that some force existed which did not want this information available to the general public. It would certainly upset the carefully constructed "official" explanations for the horrors of 9/11.

Today is a new day. Despite the disinterest of the corporate mass media, the authorized story of 9/11 has been all but discredited in the eyes of an increasingly aware population, thanks to the dedicated work of scores of journalists and private researchers, other professionals, the rapidly growing "9/11 Truth" movement, courageous government whistleblowers and even some revelations from official inquiries.

After actor Charlie Sheen publicly questioned the official government 9/11 conspiracy theory, a CNN QuickVote in 2006 showed four-fifths of respondents agreed with Sheen. Out of 41,449 respondents, 84 percent said they agreed with the idea that the US government covered up the real events of the 9/11 attacks.

As of this 2011 updated edition, we now know that:

- Even members of the official 9/11 Commission have question the conclusions of their own commission. A 2006 *Washington Post* story stated, "Some staff members and commissioners of the Sept. 11th panel concluded that the Pentagon's initial story of how it reacted to the 2001 terrorist attacks may have been part of a deliberate effort to mislead the commission and the public rather than a reflection of the fog of events on that day, according to sources involved in the debate. Suspicion of wrongdoing ran so deep that the 10-member commission, in a secret meeting at the end of its tenure in summer 2004, debated referring the matter to the Justice Department for criminal investigation, according to several commission sources." In the same article, senior counsel

Farmer stated, "I was shocked at how different the truth was from the way it was described. The tapes told a radically different story from what had been told to us and the public for two years. ...This is not spin. This is not true." Even Commission Co-Chairman Thomas Kean voiced the same suspicions of deceit, saying, "We to this day don't know why NORAD [North American Aerospace Defense Command] told us what they told us. It was just so far from the truth...."

- A wide variety of standard defense mechanisms designed to prevent such an attack systematically failed on 9/11. Especially notable are the atypical failures which occurred simultaneously within the Federal Aviation Administration (FAA), the National Military Command Center (NMCC) and the North American Aerospace Defense Command (NORAD), all charged with protecting US airspace.
- Interceptor jets were not scrambled for more than 30 minutes after it was obvious that four airliners had gone off course and were presumably hijacked. In the case of Flight 77, which reportedly slammed into the Pentagon, an hour and 45 minutes elapsed with no interception.
- Missile batteries designed to protect Washington, D.C. failed to stop the strike on the Pentagon, one of the world's most protected structures; and fighter jets on constant alert at Andrews Air Force Base just 12 miles away were never scrambled.
- Several war game exercises, involving both the FAA and NORAD, were being played out on the morning of September 11, 2001, which may have facilitated the attacks. Yet, there has been little or no mention of these exercises by either the major media or the 9/11 Commission.
- President Bush proceeded with a "photo op" at a Florida elementary school even after he and his aides knew that three planes had been hijacked. He lingered in and around the classroom for nearly 20 minutes after being informed that a second plane had struck the World Trade Center (WTC) and that America was at war.
- Not one steel-framed building in history has collapsed solely

due to fire. The free-fall speed collapse of the Trade Center towers, with attendant melted steel and powdery (microparticlized) dust, exhibited all the characteristics of a controlled demolition.
- Just such a controlled demolition apparently occurred about 5 p.m. that same day when, according to the owner of the WTC complex, the 47-story Building 7 was "pulled," collapsing in only eight seconds into its foundation.
- Vital evidence, including the WTC buildings' structural steel, was destroyed through rapid removal and destruction by US government officials with no meaningful investigation.
- An eight-mile-long debris trail indicated that Flight 93 was destroyed in the air rather than in the Pennsylvania crash reportedly caused by an onboard struggle between the hijackers and passengers.
- More than a dozen countries tried to warn US authorities that an attack on American soil was imminent, some only days before the events.
- A growing number of whistleblowers within the federal government have pointed to evidence that various agencies were well aware of the possibility of attack but were prevented from mounting investigations by senior officials.
- In 2005, the public learned of a secret Pentagon intelligence operation codenamed "Able Danger." The officers within this unit had identified Mohamed Atta as a potentially dangerous member of al Qaeda a full year before the 9/11 attacks.
- Far from being a reaction to 9/11, the US invasions of Afghanistan and Iraq were the culmination of longstanding plans, which only awaited a provocation such as 9/11.
- The official explanations for the invasion of Iraq, such as the need to capture weapons of mass destruction, have proven false while the public release of the Downing Street memo proved that senior US officials were well aware of the weakness of this argument more than six months prior to hostilities in Iraq.
- Within a few hours after the 9/11 events, the FBI released

names and photos of the suspected hijackers although later many of those named turned up alive in the Middle East.
- Also within hours of the attacks, FBI agents were scouring the houses, restaurants and flight schools the alleged perpetrators had frequented. If no one had foreknowledge of the hijackers or their activities, how did the FBI know where to look?
- Far from ordering a full and objective investigation to determine who was responsible for the 9/11 tragedies, the Bush administration dragged its feet and actually took actions to impede a swift and truthful probe into the events of that day. It was nearly two years after the events that mounting pressure from the public led by the families of 9/11 victims finally forced the creation of an investigatory commission. But this commission's final report left most of the questions of these 9/11 families unanswered.
- No one in government has been reprimanded or even scolded for what we are told was the greatest intelligence failure in US history. In fact, the very agencies which failed the nation watched their budgets increase dramatically.
- No person in government, except former National Security Council Counterterrorism Chief Richard A. Clarke, has felt the need to apologize to the American people for the 9/11 security failure.
- President Bush himself declined to apologize for the 9/11 tragedy to either the American public or to victim's families during an April 2004, press conference despite being presented with the opportunity to do so at least four times.

This is merely a short list of the many unanswered questions, anomalies and puzzles concerning the 2001 attacks, all of which will be dealt with in some detail in this book.

The paucity of answers from official sources to these questions has prompted the growth of a nationwide 9/11 Truth movement that has resulted in hundreds of websites, dozens of books and films, and numerous citizens' inquiry conferences. In 2006, a group of academics came together to form Scholars for 9/11 Truth. This collection of more than 50 credentialed scholars and experts was spearheaded by Brigham Young

University physics professor Steven E. Jones, who made headlines when he charged that the World Trade Center collapsed because of "pre-positioned explosives." In 2009, his allegation was substantiated by a peer-reviewed scientific paper in Europe.

"We believe that senior government officials have covered up crucial facts about what really happened on 9/11," stated Scholars for 9/11 Truth in a statement announcing its formation. "We believe these events may have been orchestrated by the administration in order to manipulate the American people into supporting policies at home and abroad."

Key members of the group include Jones, University of Minnesota Duluth distinguished McKnight professor of philosophy Jim Fetzer, former director of the US "Star Wars" space defense program Robert M. Bowman and Texas A&M Professor Emeritus Morgan Reynolds.

Reynolds, former director of the Criminal Justice Center at the National Center for Policy Analysis headquartered in Dallas, was also the chief economist for the Labor Department during the first George W. Bush administration. In mid-2005, Reynolds undoubtedly shocked his former Bush associates when he publicly declared the official story of the collapse of the World Trade Center towers "bogus" and said evidence more clearly indicated that the buildings were brought down by controlled demolition.

A collective paper by these scholars asked, "Did the Bush administration know in advance about the impending attacks that occurred on 9/11, and allow these to happen, to provoke pre-planned wars against Afghanistan and Iraq? These questions demand immediate answers."

They went on to declare that they were stunned to learn that the government has brought but one indictment against an alleged perpetrator (Zacarias Moussaoui) and, to the best of their knowledge, has not reprimanded anyone in positions of responsibility for incompetence or dereliction of duty. They also concluded the official conspiracy theory—that nineteen Arab hijackers under control of one man in the wilds of Afghanistan brought this about—is unsupportable by the evidential data. They even indicated that there are good reasons for suspecting that video tapes officially attributed to Osama bin Laden are not genuine.

The group also found the government's own investigations of 9/11 to be "severely flawed." For example, they pointed out that the 9/11 Commission was directed by Philip Zelikow, who had served on the National Security Council's team for the transition between the Clinton and Bush II administrations, and was the co-author of a book with then-National Security Advisor Condoleezza Rice. A man with close ties to the White House and a senior member of the administration's foreign policy team could hardly be expected to conduct an objective and impartial investigation. Their studies further pointed out that that *The 9/11 Commission Report* is filled with omissions, distortions, and factual errors. The official report, for example, entirely ignored the collapse of WTC7, a 47-story building, which was hit by no airplanes, was only damaged by a few small fires, and yet collapsed seven hours after the attack.

Also in 2006, yet another former government official broke ranks by questioning the collapse of the Twin Towers and WTC7. Paul Craig Roberts served as former Assistant of the Treasury in the Reagan administration and was the man credited with the success of "Reaganomics."

A former *Wall Street Journal* editor and currently an Internet columnist, Roberts wrote, "Many patriotic readers have written to me expressing their frustration that fact and common sense cannot gain a toehold in a debate guided by hysteria and disinformation. Other readers write that 9/11 shields Bush from accountability. They challenge me to explain why three World Trade Center buildings on one day collapsed into their own footprints at free fall speed, an event outside the laws of physics except under conditions of controlled demolition. They insist that there is no stopping war and a police state as long as the government's story on 9/11 remains unchallenged.

"They could be right. There are not many editors eager for writers to explore the glaring defects of *The 9/11 Commission Report*. One would think that if the report could stand analysis, there would not be a taboo against calling attention to the inadequacy of its explanations. We know the government lied about Iraqi WMD [weapons of mass destruction], but we believe the government told the truth about 9/11."

Other concerned citizens went so far as to file lawsuits against the Bush administration for complicity in the 9/11 attacks.

One was attorney Stanley G. Hilton, a Republican who had served as chief of staff to Senator Robert Dole (R-KS), who in late 2004 filed a suit on behalf of 400 9/11 victims' family members against top administration officials, including President Bush.

The suit charges that administration officials "all conspired with the government of Saudi Arabia prior to 9/11/01 to knowingly finance, encourage, recruit, permit, and aid and abet, certain individuals to carry out the 9/11/01 attacks on the World Trade Center and Pentagon, in order to orchestrate a contrived, stylized and artificial second Pearl Harbor event for the purpose of galvanizing public support for their military adventure agenda in the Middle East, and in order to persuade congress to enact their repressive patriot acts I and II for the purpose of suppressing political dissent inside the US."

To newsmen, Hilton was even more to the point, stating that al Qaeda is simply a CIA creation and that "[t]his was a government-ordered operation." Citing documents in his possession, Hilton said, "[Bush] personally authorized the attacks. He is guilty of treason and mass murder."

Hilton claimed he had gained information from top military officers, FBI agents and others who asserted that high-ranking government officials were complicit in the attacks of 9/11, which were carried out under the cover of disaster drills and war games, under the command of Vice President Cheney, a former secretary of defense under President George Herbert Walker Bush. He said participants were bound by official gag orders but indicated they would testify if subpoenaed.

Despite what Hilton claimed was a threat by a federal judge, he persisted in prosecuting the $7 billion suit. The case was dismissed in January 2005, by US District Court of Northern California Judge Susan Illston under an unusual ruling citing the "doctrine of sovereign immunity," which has nothing whatsoever to do with the facts of a case but rather the old English contention that the "sovereign [King]" is exempt from lawsuits.

Critics of this ruling said apparently the judge reasoned that US citizens do not have the right to hold a sitting President accountable for anything, even if the charges include premeditated mass murder and premeditated acts of high treason.

A California appeals court refused to hear Hilton's case and even refused to allow him to file a brief outlining the case for government complicity in the 9/11 attacks.

Such serious accusations and the inability to get them into court, coupled with the ever-growing wealth of information pertaining to 9/11 has prompted many honest people from all across the political spectrum to conclude that the tragic attacks of 9/11 were indeed an *inside job*. Indeed, one professional poll in 2004 showed that nearly 50 percent of New Yorkers, the site of the initial attacks, believe this to be the case.

You see, one does not have to actively participate in a crime to be part of it. The employee who becomes an accomplice by knowingly unlocking the rear door to a business is just as guilty as the burglars who loot the building later that night

This is called an *inside job*. It happens all the time in criminal activity.

At a minimum, 9/11 was criminal activity that officials at the highest level allowed to further their own purposes. But far worse, the evidence in the record provided here can lead to the conclusion that an element within the US government, perhaps aided by at least one foreign power, actually orchestrated the 9/11 attacks.

Whatever the case, the attacks of 9/11 were without doubt some of the most monstrous crimes in history. It is my hope that this book will continue to motivate the American public to seek out and bring to justice the real perpetrators behind the horrors that chilled the world on September 11, 2001, and which have led to an aftermath that is putting the future freedom of America in jeopardy.

That fateful day, speaking from Barksdale Air Force Base in Louisiana, President Bush proclaimed, "Make no mistake, the United States will hunt down and punish those responsible for these cowardly acts."

So, to pursue the persons responsible for the attacks of 9/11 is neither fantasizing nor being unpatriotic. It is merely acting on the pledge of former President George W. Bush.

Jim Marrs

# PART I – THE EVENTS OF SEPTEMBER 11, 2001

*"The perpetuation of the untrue official version remains a betrayal of every citizen who demanded a truthful answer to the simple question: What happened?"*

—John Farmer,
senior counsel to the 9/11 Commission

This inquiry begins with a brief look at the timeline of the tragic events of 9/11. This independent timeline is based on the best factual information available, not on the "official" timeline that has been shown to be inaccurate and even misleading.

## A CHRONOLOGY OF EVENTS

At 6:30 a.m. on September 11, 2001, employees at the North American Aerospace Defense Command (NORAD) begin work, already alerted that a week-long series of war game exercises with the overall title "Vigilant Guardian" would command their attention that day. The event was designed to pose an "imaginary crisis" in the form of an "air defense exercise simulating an attack on the United States," according to later news reports. But we now know that these exercises provided the distraction and confusion necessary for the real air attacks of that day to succeed.

Furthermore, at a time when there were complaints that some airlines were canceling flights that were not full to save money, the craft involved on 9/11 carried a suspiciously low number of passengers.

Sometime between 7:45 a.m. and 8:10 a.m. that day, American Airlines Flight 11 and United Airlines Flight 175 were hijacked. By 8:15, air traffic controllers knew that they were obviously off course. Flight 11, a Boeing 767 with 92 persons on board out of a possible 351, had taken off from Boston's Logan International Airport en route to Los Angeles. Flight 175, another Boeing 767 carrying 65 passengers out of a possible 351, also departed from Logan to Los Angeles.

During that same time frame, American Flight 77, a Boeing 757 with 64 passengers out of a possible 289, took off from Dulles International Airport in Washington destined for Los Angeles, while United Flight 93, a Boeing 757 with 45 passengers out of a possible 289, headed for San Francisco from Newark Airport at 8:42 a.m., after a long delay.

According to the independent timeline presented here, at about 8:40 a.m., the Northeast Air Defense Sector (NEADS) of NORAD was alerted to the hijackings of Flights 11 and 175 by the Federal Aviation Administration (FAA) and, according to a NORAD statement, two F-15 jet fighters were scrambled from the Otis Air National Guard Base in Falmouth, Massachusetts. Taking the initial call was Tech. Sgt. Jeremy Powell, a member of the Air National Guard at NEADS. "Hi. Boston [controller here], we have a problem here," Powell was told by Boston Flight Control. "We have a hijacked aircraft headed toward New York, and we need you guys to, we need someone to scramble some F-16s or something up there, help us out." Powell's reply was: "Is this real-world or exercise?"

Moments after 8:55 a.m., it was known to the FAA that four airliners had been hijacked—an unprecedented occurrence.

At 8:46 a.m., Flight 11 struck the north face of the 110-story North Tower of the World Trade Center (WTC) at the 96th floor. Also at this time, the two F-15s from Otis took to the air, after earlier warnings of a hijacking and waiting for several critical minutes for take-off orders. They quickly were directed to New York City.

At 8:47 a.m., despite having its transponder tracking beacon turned off by the hijackers, air traffic controllers could see that American Flight 77 had reversed course somewhere over West Virginia and was moving back toward the East Coast.

At 9:03 a.m., with the hesitant evacuation of the WTC towers proceeding amidst fear and confusion, United Flight 175 careened into the southeast corner of the South Tower at the 80th floor, sending a massive ball of burning fuel into the air over lower New York City. The F-15s were reported as being seventy-one miles away. According to official sources, the jets arrived over New York City at 9:10 a.m., seven minutes too late.

A short time after 9:03 a.m., Secretary of Defense Donald Rumsfeld joined in on an emergency teleconference of top government officials being run out of the White House that included counterterrorism chief Richard A. Clarke, acting chairman of the joint chiefs Richard Myers, and FAA head Jane Garvey. Despite the 9/11 Commission's claim that no one could locate Rumsfeld until approximately 10:30 a.m. that morning, the record shows that Rumsfeld—the military's top civilian official—was on the teleconference by as early as 9:05 a.m., along with the top official of the FAA. (See appendix for further details on this point.)

Nonetheless, according to the timeline presented in *The 9/11 Commission Report*, FAA authorities failed to the inform NORAD and NEADS about three of the four hijackings until *after* these planes had crashed (i.e., Flight 175 into the second World Trade Center tower at 9:03 a.m., Flight 77 into the Pentagon at 9:32 a.m., and Flight 93 in Pennsylvania at 10:06 a.m.).

At 9:06 a.m., President Bush is attending a photo op in Sarasota, Florida at Booker Elementary School in a second grade classroom. His chief of staff, Andrew Card, enters the room and whispers into his ear, "A second plane hit the other tower, and America's under attack." Bush looks perplexed.

Between 9:06 and 9:16 a.m., with both WTC towers burning and terrified occupants leaping to their deaths, President Bush reads *My Pet Goat* to second graders for nearly ten minutes. Apparently, he never considered simply getting up, stating, "I'm sorry children, I have some presidential business to conduct," and walking out to defend his country.

By 9:20 a.m., Transportation Secretary Norman Mineta arrives at the emergency operations bunker under the east wing of the White House. Vice President Cheney had already been rushed to this location by the Secret Service, according to several witnesses. When Mineta arrives, Cheney and others are engaged in the emergency teleconference indicated above. He witnesses Vice President Cheney being told by an aide that an airplane is headed toward Washington from only 50 miles away. *The 9/11 Commission Report* ignores this eyewitness account by Mineta and others, and instead asserts that Cheney did not reach the White House bunker until about 10 a.m.

At 9:30 a.m., two F-16 fighters are scrambled from Langley Air Force Base (AFB) in Hampton, Virginia, heading toward Washington, D.C., in an attempt to intercept incoming Flight 77. But according to numerous authoritative sources, this pair of interceptors is ordered to fly at about a quarter of its top possible speed, as were the F-15s dispatched from Otis.

At 9:31 a.m., President Bush, speaking from the schoolhouse in Florida, declared the disaster in New York an apparent terrorist attack.

At 9:32 a.m. rather than at the official time of 9:37 a.m.—according to veteran military journalist Barbara Honegger, author of the special Appendix in this book—a flying object crashes into the west side of the steel-reinforced concrete and limestone Pentagon, penetrating three of its five rings of offices. A hot debate continues over what actually struck the Pentagon and exactly when. If it is true that Flight 77 actually did hit the Pentagon at 9:32 a.m., anyone concerned with the fact that their tax money supports a half trillion yearly defense budget should be appalled that this flight was allowed to wander over northeastern airspace unmolested for over an hour and that automated defense missile batteries failed to react. Also at about this moment, a bomb or bombs reportedly go off at the same location in the west side of the Pentagon as the location of the crash of a flying object. (See the Appendix.)

At 9:35 a.m., what official sources claim to be American Flight 77, but which may have been a reconnaissance fighter jet that was dispatched just after the impact on the Pentagon, begins making a complicated 270-degree spiral turn while descending seven thousand feet in the direction of the Pentagon.

By 9:48 a.m., key officials of the White House and the Capitol were evacuated and taken to secure but undisclosed locations. One minute later, in an unprecedented action, the FAA ordered all airline flights across the nation grounded. Air traffic controllers, who moments before appeared paralyzed by the confusion over the hijacked planes, were able to accomplish this nationwide grounding activity with unprecedented alacrity.

As early as 9:50 and no later than 10:00 a.m., according to numerous mainstream sources, President Bush had issued a shoot-down order that was transmitted to the military and was intended to apply to any remaining hijacked planes. This would have included Flight 93. With no supporting evidence, the 9/11 Commission claims that this order was not given until 10:25 a.m.

Shortly after 10 a.m., the South Tower of the World Trade Center collapsed, covering lower Manhattan with tons of asbestos-filled ash, dust, smoke, and debris.

At 10:06 a.m., United Flight 93, also with transponder turned off or disabled, crashed in western Pennsylvania about eighty miles southeast of Pittsburgh near Shanksville after passengers reportedly used back-of-the-seat radio phones to report that they intended to fight the hijackers.

This event was followed about twenty-three minutes later by the collapse of the WTC North Tower, the upper floors of which had been burning for about an hour and a half and much longer than the South Tower.

By noon, there were closings at the United Nations, Securities and Exchange Commission, the stock markets, some skyscrapers in several cities and even some large tourist attractions such as Walt Disney World, Mount Rushmore, the Seattle Space Needle, and St. Louis's Gateway Arch.

At 1:04 p.m., President Bush proclaimed, "Make no mistake, the United States will hunt down and punish those responsible for these cowardly acts." But until the April 2006 conviction of Zacarias Moussaoui, who, while admitting to being a member of al Qaeda, denied any involvement in the 9/11 attacks, there were no convictions of any terrorist involved in the 9/11 attacks. The proclaimed architect of the attacks, Osama bin Laden, was finally reported "killed" almost a decade later.

At 5:25 p.m. the 47-story Salomon Brothers (Building 7 of the WTC) suddenly collapsed despite the fact it was not hit by aircraft nor suffered major fire—a rather strange occurrence usually ignored in the official accounts until brought to the attention of the public by independent researchers. Inexplicably, both CNN and the BBC reported the collapse of the building about 30 minutes prior to the incident. BBC reporter Jane Standley on a live broadcast stated the building had collapsed even as it was pictured standing in the New York skyline behind her. About an hour and a half following the collapse of Building 7, disaster relief crews began moving into the area searching for survivors and removing debris.

It should be noted that this timeline is not sacrosanct as there are unresolved conflicts between times reported by the Federal Aviation Administration (FAA), North American Aerospace Defense Command (NORAD), *The 9/11 Commission Report*, and the independent research cited in this book. A 2006 *Washington Post* article co-authored by the 9/11 Commission's senior counsel John Farmer stated, "Some staff members and commissioners of the Sept. 11 panel concluded that the Pentagon's initial story of how it reacted to the 2001 terrorist attacks may have been part of a deliberate effort to mislead the commission and the public rather than a reflection of the fog of events on that day, according to sources involved in the debate. Suspicion of wrongdoing ran so deep that the 10-member commission, in a secret meeting at the end of its tenure in summer 2004, debated referring the matter to the Justice Department for criminal investigation, according to several commission sources….I was shocked at how different the truth was from the way it was described. The tapes told a radically different story from what had been told to us and the public for two years.…This is not spin. This is not true."

Only a truly independent inquiry possessing subpoena power will ever be able to resolve these and a myriad of other factual discrepancies. This book provides essential support to such an effort which is still to come.

[*Editor's note to researchers*: a very detailed timeline information may be found at www.cooperativeresearch.org. Also, for a useful graphic depiction of some of the various 9/11 issues covered in this book, search the Internet for the documentary *Loose Change*.]

## UNRESOLVED QUESTIONS ABOUND

As previously noted, the 9/11 attacks have prompted a lengthy list of disturbing questions, most of which have never been satisfactorily answered despite official government pronouncements and several inquiries.

For example, the "New Jersey widows" who co-founded the 9/11 Family Steering Committee (FSC), along with many other 9/11 family members, made this charge very clear at a July 21, 2005 press conference convened at the National Press Club on the occasion of the first anniversary of the 9/11 Commission's final report. In their opening statement, they declared that the commission had ignored "approximately 70 percent" of their concerns, while also suppressing important evidence and whistleblower testimony that challenged the official story. It will be remembered that the 9/11 Commission was formed only after 18 months of intense lobbying by the FSC, and that the FSC's list of questions were initially considered to be the "road map" for the work of the commission.

Many unanswered questions concern the collapses of the towers at the World Trade Center (WTC). But due to the premature and illegal cleansing of Ground Zero, these crucial issues may never be definitively answered. These questions include the controversy concerning how fires in only upper stories could have brought down steel-frame buildings; the unprecedented speed of their collapse; the cause of their apparent pulverization into fine dust; multiple reports of bombs in the buildings; and the mystery surrounding the collapse of Building 7, which was not hit by hijacked planes nor subjected to intense fires.

In the course of this inquiry, it will become clear that many other pieces of evidence have been systematically withheld, ignored, or even destroyed, raising additional unanswered suspicion. Years of foot-dragging and unnecessary secrecy by the Bush administration, widely documented in the mainstream press, also hampered independent and official inquiries into unanswered questions.

Throughout this difficult process, unanswered questions about the failure of US intelligence also lingered in the minds of critics of the official story. How could an obviously sophisticated terrorist plan that likely involved scores of persons collaborating over many years escape the notice of our intelligence services, especially the FBI and CIA? The fact is, it didn't. Following 9/11, the American public was to learn again and again that a great deal was already known about the alleged plot within the intelligence community—but simply not acted upon, or directly suppressed. Mild admissions of incompetence have been made in official hearings, but a great deal of additional evidence of wrongdoing and missteps by these agencies has still not entered mainstream discourse.

And what about the question of accountability? Was 9/11 simply a case of bungling incompetence by surprised and confused officials, as the official account would have us believe? To many thoughtful people, it is unsettling that *not one* individual within the federal government or military has been fired or even reprimanded for the many obvious government missteps of that day. Indeed, many of those responsible for failures were actually promoted. Many have interpreted this lack of discipline as evidence that government actions on 9/11 were not missteps at all.

John Farmer, chief counsel of the 9/11 Commission, however, was among those who chose to see the success of the attacks as evidence of a total failure of the system. "What failed in the history of 9/11 and in the Katrina crisis was not an individual department head or two, but government itself." And perhaps most important of all is this crucial question: Why did there appear to be such a systematic failure of response on the part of our air defense authorities? NORAD successfully scrambled interceptors within 15 minutes of an alert 129 times in 2000. This was done 67 times between September 2000 and June 2001. Yet on September 11, 2001, they failed to accomplish this practiced task four times that morning!

Both American Flight 11 and United Flight 175 were known to be off course by 8:15 a.m., yet NORAD was not notified for almost twenty minutes. Why the long delay? It then required another fifteen minutes before jet interceptors were ordered off the ground at Otis AFB, entailing a total delay of more than thirty minutes—according to independent chronologies. Even so, we now know that the F-15s still had enough time to reach the World Trade Center in time to intercept Flight 175 before it hit the second tower. Simple calculations using NORAD's own numbers reveal that the fighters were flying at far less than their top speeds.

But even more disconcerting than the aforementioned fatal delays, and the intended or unintended destruction of evidence, is this disturbing fact: The US military had almost an hour-and-a-half lead time to protect Washington after learning that four airliners had been hijacked. Yet no jet interceptors were launched from nearby Andrews AFB where two squadrons of jet fighters are specifically assigned to protect the Pentagon and the White House. Instead, F-16s were dispatched from the more distant Langley AFB, and for some reason flew at an estimated one-fourth of their top speed of 1875 mph, as had also occurred with the F-15s earlier dispatched toward New York. Curiously, none of the sophisticated anti-aircraft batteries adjacent to the Pentagon or in the Washington area were activated. These installations are set to fire automatically if any aircraft approaches the Pentagon that is not sending out a "friendly" signal from its transponder.

The fighter jets scrambled on 9/11 did not arrive in time for a visual check of the hijacked planes' cockpits, even though such jet intercepts of wayward flights are a routine occurrence. For example, in October 1999, when golf pro Payne Stewart's Learjet went off course due to a failure of the plane's oxygen system, the Air Force announced that two F-15s from Eglin Air Force Base, Florida, intercepted the plane within twenty-four minutes after it had lost contact with air traffic controllers, and followed it until it crashed after running out of fuel. In 2001, a private plane that merely passed too close to the Bush ranch in Texas was immediately ordered to land. "It happens all the time," noted investigative journalist William Thomas in a definitive essay on the issue of the 9/11 interceptors. "Between September 2000 and June 2001, the Pentagon launched fighters on sixty-seven occasions to escort wayward aircraft."

The air traffic controllers who actually handled the hijacked flights on 9/11 may have been able to give a clearer picture of what really happened in the hand off to NORAD and other authorities. In fact, according to the inspector general of the Department of Transportation, at least six of the controllers had made tape recordings that day describing their experiences. Incredibly, an FAA quality-assurance manager destroyed these tapes, without making any copies or even a transcript. According to an article in the May 6, 2004 *New York Times* by Matthew L. Wald, the manager told investigators he had destroyed the tape because he thought its production was contrary to FAA policy, which calls for written statements, and because he felt that the controllers "were not in the correct frame of mind to have properly consented to the taping" due to stress.

What could explain such failures? "It seems evident that...the commission has not succeeded in removing grounds for suspicion that the US military had issued stand-down orders for 9/11," concluded author David Ray Griffin in his book *The 9/11 Commission Report: Omissions and Distortions*, a landmark analysis of the 9/11 Commission's report. Griffin is a distinguished author, philosopher, and theologian who taught at California's Claremont School of Theology until his forced retirement believed by many due to his public statements on 9/11.

UNRESOLVED QUESTIONS ABOUND

And what about the war game exercises on that day? The now indisputable record shows that multiple war games and exercises were underway simultaneously with the attacks, and thus might have been the true cause of failure of our air defenses. One former sergeant with the Army's Central Command stated several wargame exercises were underway that morning, including one in which a hijacked commercial airliner was deliberately crashed into one of the World Trade Center towers. He also said false images representing hijacked planes were place on the FAA radar scopes as part of the exercise. Such wargame exercises, which obviously would have contributed to the confusion of that morning, were deemed merely Internet rumors for more than a year and only substantiated after US Counterterrorism Chief Richard A. Clark authored a 2004 book entitled *Against All Enemies* in which he confirmed multiple wargame exercises on 9/11.

And there are more questions: What are the odds that four transcontinental flights on two major airlines—American Flights 77 and 11 and United Flights 175 and 93—would have 78, 74, 81, and 84 percent of their seats empty, respectively, on September 11, 2001? This came at a time when many airlines were trying to save money by overbooking and canceling flights that were not full. Although any airline policy pertaining to canceled flights has not been made public, researchers Mark Hansen and Jing Xiong of the University of California at Berkeley in 2010 demonstrated that such curtailing of nonprofitable fights was continuing after 9/11. After looking at 8,269 airline flight disruption records, they found under-booked flights are at greater risk of cancellation as are any flights that carries the minimum number of people the airline must rebook. They also found that planes were more likely to be canceled on heavily traveled and redundant routes, such as those of the American and United flights on 9/11.

How could TV personality Barbara Olson have been the source of information on the hijacking of Flight 77 when, during the Moussaoui trial, FBI officials testified that only one call was made by Olson and this was an "unconnected call" which reached no one? So, according to the FBI, Theodore "Ted" Olson received no call from his wife, who was the sole source of the information that hijackers had used "knives and box cutters" to take control of Flight 77.

And how did the terrorists obtain top-secret White House and *Air Force One* codes and signals, one of the excuses for hustling President Bush

## PART I – THE EVENTS OF SEPTEMBER 11, 2001

from Florida to Louisiana and finally to Nebraska on September 11?

At 9:00 a.m. that day, just about the time Flight 175 slammed into the South Tower of the WTC, Secret Service agents in Washington received this chilling message: *"Angel* is next." It was chilling because "Angel" was that day's top secret code for Air Force One. Someone had access to our most sensitive codes. Within minutes Vice President Dick Cheney was hurried from his seat in front of a television down to the president's nuclear-bombproof emergency operations center, while the White House was evacuated.

The warning was transmitted in that day's top-secret White House code, indicating that whoever was behind the ongoing attacks had access to the highest level of security codes, only known to the Secret Service. It meant that whoever had the codes could track and accurately pinpoint the president's plane and/or transmit fraudulent messages.

After several days of investigation, the picture grew even darker. Someone had penetrated the National Security Agency's (NSA) Echelon surveillance system. In fact, the perpetrators appeared to have more electronic capability than even the NSA, including the use of "steganography," technology that allows its user to bypass Echelon and other electronic monitoring by hiding messages randomly in otherwise innocent digital files such as music, online advertisements, email headers or even Internet pornography. Such buried messages leave no trace of their presence. The idea that someone had access to such high-level codes provoked speculation that there were "moles," deep-cover secret agents, within the US government. It also meant that whoever was behind the attacks had access to our latest and most sophisticated electronic technology. Was this evidence of an inside job?

Access to high-level secret codes; "moles" within the government; foreknowledge of war-game exercises which disrupted normal air defenses; the lack of a rapid and decisive response to the hijackings; a systemic lack of response to numerous pre-9/11 warnings; no one fired or reprimanded over the series of security failures. Could all this be attributed to random chance or simply bad luck?

Why was Osama bin Laden never charged with the crimes of 9/11? In June 2006, FBI Chief of Investigative Publicity Rex Tomb confirmed what critics of the official 9/11 story had been saying all along when he told Ed Haas, a writer for the *Muckraker Report*, "The reason why 9/11 is not mentioned on Osama bin Laden's Most Wanted page is because the FBI has no hard evidence connecting bin Laden to 9/11."

Questions still abound regarding the attack on the Pentagon. Since Flight 77 supposedly was flown directly into the Pentagon where it exploded, why was it reported that many small pieces of the aircraft were found on the Pentagon's lawn and even out over a nearby highway? If it disintegrated outside the Pentagon why is there nothing that looks like a Boeing 757 on the Pentagon lawn? If it disintegrated either inside or outside the Pentagon where did the small pieces of debris come from and what caused the hole in the C-ring?

A key member of the 9/11 Family Steering Committee, Mindy Kleinberg, summed up the frustration of many about so many unanswered questions in her testimony before the 9/11 Commission during its first public proceedings in early 2003. "Is it luck that aberrant stock trades were not monitored?" Kleinberg asked, referring to the widespread reports of possible insider trading in the week leading up to September 11 indicating specific prior knowledge of the attacks.

"Is it luck when 15 visas are awarded based on incomplete forms? Is it luck when Airline Security screenings allow hijackers to board planes with box cutters and pepper spray? Is it luck when Emergency FAA and NORAD protocols are not followed? Is it luck when a national emergency is not reported to top government officials on a timely basis?

"To me luck is something that happens once. When you have this repeated pattern of broken protocols, broken laws, broken communication, one cannot still call it luck..."

## WHAT DID PRESIDENT BUSH KNOW, AND WHEN?

Despite the government's systematic failure to respond to the 9/11 attacks themselves, reaction *after the fact* came so swiftly that it lent support to the disconcerting idea that planning for such a reaction had been made months before. Perhaps the most remarkable and puzzling instance of this apparent foreknowledge is the actual behavior of President Bush himself.

About ten minutes after the North Tower of the WTC was struck, Bush arrived at an elementary school in Sarasota, Florida, for a photo op with grade school kids. CNN had already interrupted broadcasting to tell of the strike two minutes after it happened, yet reportedly Bush remained unaware until he was briefed shortly after arriving at the school. Or was he?

Yet on more than one occasion Bush said he saw the first plane strike the WTC North Tower. "I was sitting outside the classroom waiting to go in and I saw an airplane hit the tower—the TV was obviously on, and I used to fly myself, and I said, 'There's one terrible pilot.'" The oddity here is that no video of the strike on the North Tower was available until that evening, when a French camera team revealed that they had accidentally filmed the hit while shooting a documentary in Manhattan.

Could Bush have confused the real strike with something he saw in a past drill or perhaps via an unpublicized private broadcast? This possibility was hinted at when Vice President Cheney, during an interview with *Meet the Press* on September 16, 2001, said, "The Secret Service has an arrangement with the FAA. They had open lines after the World Trade Center was..." He ended his statement and moved on to other matters. If Bush indeed witnessed the first strike, why have all later official versions of the school events stated otherwise?

Bush told the school principal that "a commercial plane has hit the World Trade Center and we're going ahead and...do the reading thing anyway." Bush then entered the classroom at about the same time as the second plane struck the WTC South Tower. Moments later, then-Chief of Staff Andrew Card entered the front of the room and whispered to Bush, alerting him that a second plane had struck and that this was clearly a terrorist attack. To the later amazement of many, Bush calmly continued his interaction with the second-graders—even as the rest of country watched terrorist mayhem consume lower Manhattan, and while two additional hijacked planes remained in the air over American territory.

In an effort to address criticism of Bush's lack of immediate action, Card later altered the time frame by telling newsmen that after he informed the president of the second strike, "Not that many seconds later the president excused himself from the classroom." It is now known, however, and supported by video tapes of the photo op, that Bush remained in the classroom until 9:16 a.m.—that's 12 minutes or more than *seven hundred* seconds after Card's notification.

WHAT DID PRESIDENT BUSH KNOW, AND WHEN?

Adding to this puzzling behavior on the part of the nation's commander-in-chief is the fact that his Secret Service detail surely must have realized the danger to the president inherent in a large-scale terrorist attack. Yet, Bush was allowed to finish his chat with the elementary students and calmly leave the school after making general comments to the media. He also left by the same motorcade and along the originally planned route even after officials were alerted that White House security codes had been compromised. *Air Force One* then left Florida with no military jet escort—disconcertingly odd behavior considering the potential danger to the president.

One would expect that in an event as momentous as 9/11, there would be a full and complete record of the movements of the chief executive. But this is not the case. In the feverish frantic climate in the wake of the 9/11 attacks no one was prepared to challenge the official record of Bush's actions—or lack thereof—after leaving the school.

Dissenters from the party line in the media soon found themselves out of work. The television shows of Bill Maher and Phil Donahue were suspended after they made remarks concerning 9/11 and a columnist for the *Texas City Sun* was fired after writing that Mr. Bush, instead of returning to Washington on the day of attacks, was "flying around the country like a scared child, seeking refuge in his mother's bed after having a nightmare."

Such reactions prompted an editorial in the *Washington Post* to opine, "Yes, newspapers and universities and television stations have a right to be spineless. But they will be judged in time by how robustly they resist a climate of intolerance. It is not a show of strength to come down hard on dissent, even in times of war. It is, rather, America's strength to encourage contrarian viewpoints and tolerate distasteful remarks, especially when political discourse matters."

What did the president know, and when? Was the threat to *Air Force One* an attempt to terrorize the president himself? "The guess here is that Bush knew far less than many of his most severe critics might surmise," wrote Webster Griffin Tarpley, a veteran journalist, lecturer, and author of *9/11 Synthetic Terror*. "Bush's crime was not the crime of knowing everything in advance; it was rather the crime of not knowing what he should have known, and then compounding that by capitulating, by turning the US government and policy in the direction demanded by the terror plotters...Students who build their work around the thesis that 'Bush Knew' are on treacherous ground."

Later in his book, Tarpley observed, "[T]he typical model of a Bush presidency is that of a weak and passive executive who comes into office with few ideas beyond the basic desire to rule and to appoint rich cronies to key posts, and who sits in the White House waiting for his networks to tell him what it is he must do. These impulses, naturally, are mediated through the handlers of the White House palace guard. But here lies the danger: when Bush was running for office, it was widely conceded by his supporters that their candidate was a moron, but a moron who would hire the best advisers available, who would guide him through the crises of his presidency. In this sense, both Bush presidencies were oligarchical presidencies, with the chief magistrate in fact functioning as the front man for a committee.

"The events of 9/11 showed the grave danger of such an oligarchical presidency: what happened if the advisors turned out to be traitors, misfits, or absent, as they did on 9/11: the presidency itself was paralyzed and incapable of acting, as occurred during the dark eternity of horror the world experienced as Bush busied himself with reading *My Pet Goat*."

## DID WAR GAMES AID THE TERRORISTS?

US military war games did take place on the very day—in fact the very hour—of the actual 9/11 attacks. Indeed, it appears likely that plans for staging a variety of war game exercises were designed to be so distracting that they may well have contributed to the success of the actual strikes. Equally startling has been the revelation that some of these exercises involved scenarios in which terrorists fly hijacked planes into buildings.

The existence of such exercises remained a secret for nearly a year after 9/11 and then was dismissed as an Internet hoax for several more months. But as many as a half-dozen 9/11 war game exercises have since been acknowledged by the government.

*The 9/11 Commission Report* relegated any discussion of the war game exercises to a footnote on page 458 where, while timidly admitting that

NORAD "was scheduled to conduct a military exercise, Vigilant Guardian," the report actually argued that the military response on 9/11 "was, if anything, expedited by the increased number of staff at the sectors and NORAD..." Apparently they reasoned that increased staff and the foresight of wargaming an attack actually aided in the slow response of that morning. Many Americans still don't know of the exercises and many more relegate them to a side issue in 9/11. However, more astute researchers see the pre-planned war game exercises as integral to the success of the attacks.

To begin with, the powerful but little publicized National Reconnaissance Office (NRO) had scheduled a test exercise for the morning of September 11, 2001. The scenario was that of a corporate jet, crippled by mechanical failure, crashing into one of the four towers of the NRO headquarters building in Chantilly, VA, which is about four miles from Washington's Dulles International Airport. No actual planes were to be used in the exercise, but plans called for evacuating most of the three thousand NRO employees.

The exercise, later described as a "bizarre coincidence," was the brainchild of CIA officer John Fulton, chief of the NRO's strategic gaming division. In 2002, an announcement for a Department of Homeland Security conference noted the exercise with the comment, "On the morning of September 11, 2001, Mr. Fulton and his team...were running a pre-planned simulation to explore the emergency response issues that would be created if a plane were to strike a building. Little did they know that the scenario would come true in a dramatic way that day."

The exercise was canceled when the first plane struck the World Trade Center less than an hour before the test was to begin. All NRO employees, except for certain essential personnel, were sent home for the day, according to NRO officials.

The NRO exercise, astounding in its timing, apparently was either part of—or concurrent with—*an even larger* set of war games being played out by NORAD's northeast sector, the region that included the three 9/11 crash sites in New York, Washington, D.C., and Pennsylvania. This was confirmed by then-NSC Counterterrorism Chief Richard A. Clarke. In his 2004 book *Against All Enemies*, while narrating his experiences during a video teleconference in the White House Situation Room on the morning of 9/11, Clarke writes: "I turned to the Pentagon screen. 'JCS, JCS [Joint

Chiefs of Staff]. I assume NORAD has scrambled fighters and AWACS. How many? Where?'"

Acting Chairman of the Joint Chiefs Air Force Gen. Richard B. Myers then responded, "We're in the middle of Vigilant Warrior, a NORAD exercise, but...Otis has launched two birds toward New York. Langley is trying to get two up now. The AWACS [Airborne Warning and Control System aircraft] are at Tinker [AFB] and not on alert."

Lt. Col. Robert Marr, commanding the Northeast Air Defense Sector (NEADS), upon also receiving notification from Boston regarding the possible hijacking of American Flight 11, asked: "Part of the exercise?" He was then told the hijacking was real. Lt. Col. Dawne Deskins, a NORAD airborne control and warning officer, also received word from Boston regarding the possible hijacking. She immediately thought, "It must be part of the exercise."

It has also been reliably reported that the war game exercises included not only real military aircraft posing as hijacked planes but that perhaps as many as two dozen false aircraft images placed in the FAA's monitors—were in use. Such false images may account for the rumors that day that as many as eight or more aircraft were hijacked.

Army Sgt. Lauro "LJ" Chavez, who participated in the war games exercises as a member of the US Central Command headquarters staff in Florida, said false images called "inputs" representing several hijacked aircraft were placed on radar screens creating confusion over what was real. Chavez, a computer specialist, also stated this was the first military exercise that he had ever participated in that was classified "Top Secret." Chavez dropped several bombshells in his account of that day—he noted that Vice President Dick Cheney had become the first civilian to take command of NORAD only weeks before 9/11 and that the war game exercises included a scenario in which a hijacked commercial airliner was crashed into one of the World Trade Center towers. "What are the odds this could happen for real?" Chavez quoted astonished command center staffers as asking. He also said when some officers began asking why no jet interceptors were in the air, a superior officer stated that Cheney had issued a "stand-down" order.

A stand-down order is not to be confused with a shoot-down order. NORAD's chief of air defense operations, Lt. Col. William E. Glover, Jr.,

DID WAR GAMES AID THE TERRORISTS?

had telephoned Maj. Gen. Larry Arnold, commander of the Continental US NORAD Region at Tyndall AFB, FL, telling him that Cheney had authorized a shoot down of any threatening aircraft in the Washington area. "We created a free-fire zone over the nation's capital," Arnold later reported. "Anyone airborne who did not immediately turn away from the center of town, or who did not land, could be shot down."

Adding to the problem of false radar images, journalist William B. Scott pointed out the enormity of simply trying to locate hijacked aircraft from amongst the thousands of radar contacts. He said, "In essence, [FAA] technicians were half-blind, trying to separate hijacked airliners from thousands of skin-paint returns. At the time, more than 4,000 aircraft were airborne over the nation, most in the northeast sector, which monitors half a million square miles of airspace." The FAA command center was reporting as many as 11 aircraft either not in communication with FAA facilities, or flying unexpected routes. The confusion mounted.

In addition to the NRO, the Pentagon drills and the false "inputs" creating confusion, by several reliable accounts noted these war game exercises also included "Northern Vigilance," which sent fighter interceptors deep into Canada in response to a Russian exercise in the Arctic and northern Pacific; "Vigilant Guardian," which may have included scenarios based on a hijacked airplane; "Vigilant Warrior," believed to have been the "aggressor" component of Vigilant Guardian; "Northern Guardian," another portion of the Vigilant Guardian exercise; "Amalgam Virgo," an exercised specifically dealing with hijacked airplanes used as weapons (Amalgam 01 began in June 2001 may have ended by 9/11 but Amalgam 02 was already in the planning stages); and "Tripod II," a biological warfare exercise mentioned by Mayor Rudolph Giuliani that may explain the arrival of the Federal Emergency Management Agency (FEMA) National Urban Search and Rescue Team in New York the night before the 9/11 attacks and confusion in New York on the day of the attacks.

Author Barbara Honegger, noting the obvious lack of timely response to the 9/11 attacks—especially at the Pentagon—suggested, "This is beyond comprehension over the nation's capital unless some previous piece of information or mental set led them to assume the Pentagon plane could not be a terrorist vehicle, or at least confuse them as to whether it was or not. If those looking on from inside the Pentagon as 9/11 unfolded believed Flight 77 was, or might be, part of a counter-terror exercise set for that very morning, it would explain the otherwise incomprehensible delay, almost to the point of paralysis, in effectively scrambling interceptors."

Honegger, well-known for her 1989 book *October Surprise* that revealed the elder Bush's role in a covert deal with Iranian terrorists that ensured the election of Ronald Reagan in 1980, noted that if in fact the 9/11 attacks were enabled by homegrown war games, this might explain why the leak by a congressional investigation (to be examined later) of a September 10, 2001, NSA intercept message is reported to have upset Vice President Cheney so much.

That message reportedly was between hijack leader Mohamed Atta and the purported attack mastermind, Khalid Sheikh Mohammed. It stated, "The Match is about to begin. Tomorrow is zero hour."

"'Match,' of course, is what you would expect if the speakers were referring to his discovery of the date that the US government had selected to conduct its counter-terror exercises—one that was about to turn very real when the terrorists piggybacked their long-planned plot onto it," said Honegger. "[G]iven the context in which all this finally begins to make sense, Atta was merely communicating to his boss, or vice versa, the date that the US government exercise was to take place. Bin al-Shibh, Atta, and Mohammed didn't choose the date. The US government did."

The NSA phone intercept makes it clear that the hijackers knew when to coordinate their attack with the war games. How could they have obtained this vital yet top-secret information unless through some source within the government? In the Appendix to this book, Honegger provides a detailed scenario for how the hand-off of the "match" information to Atta may have taken place.

Journalist Webster Tarpley saw within the war games, particularly Amalgam Virgo, something sinister. "Here was an exercise which included many of the elements which were put into practice on 9/11. Amalgam Virgo thus provided the witting putschists with a perfect cover for conducting the actual live fly components of 9/11 through a largely non-witting military bureaucracy. Under the cover of this confusion, the most palpably subversive actions could be made to appear in the harmless and even beneficial guise of a drill."

## DID WAR GAMES AID THE TERRORISTS?

The release of news concerning such exercises certainly gives lie to the numerous public statements of President Bush, National Security Adviser Condoleezza Rice, FBI Director Robert Mueller, and others who stated, at times under oath, that the government never considered that terrorists might use airplanes as weapons.

If the idea that war game exercises both explained the lack of initial response on 9/11 as well as put to lie the oft-stated question by Bush administration officials that they could not have known terrorists might use aircraft as weapons, in early 2005 this issue grew even hotter. The *American Free Press* reported that the US Army had planned just such a scenario—in 1976!

Timothy McNiven, a US Defense Dept. contract operative, revealed that his military unit conceived of a mock terrorist attack on the World Trade Center as part of a 1976 exercise. "[A]s I watched the Twin Towers really collapse on the morning of September 11, I realized I was watching the very same thing we devised in 1976," McNiven said.

McNiven, who successfully passed a polygraph "lie detector" test in regard to his story as well as naming about 40 individuals who took part in the planning, said in 1976 he was with C Battery, Second 81st Field Artillery stationed in Strasbourg, Germany, when the unit was ordered to concoct the "perfect terrorist plan" using the World Trade Center towers as their target. The congressionally commissioned project reportedly was to identify security lapses and alert lawmakers to needed legislation. McNiven's group came up with a plan in which Middle Eastern terrorists would hijack commercial airliners using plastic box cutters to bypass security, then level the towers by crashing the planes into them. He said the team's leader, Lt. Michael Teague, was specifically ordered by his superiors to use the World Trade Center towers as the terrorist target.

"Why have I spent every waking hour trying to bring this story to the American people?" McNiven asked during an interview. He said he told his superior officer that if the towers were ever brought down in the manner in which his group had foreseen, he would go public with the story. Initially, he said he was ordered never to talk about the 1976 plan and was even physically beaten for speaking about it. He said a week or so later, in a strange turn of events, he was given a direct order that if the Twin Towers were ever attacked as in the 1976 study, he was to do everything he could to bring this story to the public. "I have no idea why they changed their minds," he said, "but I was then emphatically told that this order was never to be rescinded—never—because those who would rescind it, would be the very same people who turned against the American people."

Do the war games provide sufficient evidence of an inside job? "I think the people who planned and carried out those exercises, they're the ones that should be the object of investigation," said Dr. Robert M. Bowman, Lt. Col., USAF (ret.). Bowman flew 101 combat missions in Vietnam and was a recipient of the Eisenhower Medal, the George F. Kennan Peace Prize, the President's Medal of Veterans for Peace, the Society of Military Engineers Gold Medal (twice), six Air Medals, and dozens of other awards and honors. His PhD is in Aeronautics and Nuclear Engineering from Caltech and he is considered one of the country's foremost experts on National Security. In the 1970s, Bowman worked on the then-secret Star Wars space defense system but left the program when he realized it was designed for offensive warfare against the old Soviet Union.

Bowman said that the entire chain of military command may have been unaware of what was taking place and were used as tools by the people pulling the strings behind the attack. "If I had to narrow it [a 9/11 conspiracy] down to one person...I think my prime suspect would be Dick Cheney," said Bowman in an April 2006, radio interview. He added that reaction to the 9/11 attacks, such as the Patriot Act has "...done more to destroy the rights of Americans than all of our enemies combined."

But if Cheney is a key conspirator as Bowman claims, how was the apparent subterfuge of the war game exercises put into place?

One speculation points to yet another piece of evidence of gaming scenarios. It was learned that as far back as November 3, 2000, the Military District of Washington's Command Emergency Response Training unit conducted a scenario entitled The Pentagon Mass Casualty Exercise, which simulated the crash of an airliner into the courtyard of the Pentagon.

According to an email message sent by a NORAD officer in September 2001, and published by the nonprofit watchdog group, Project Government Oversight, "The NORAD exercise developers wanted an event having a terrorist group hijack a commercial airliner (foreign carrier) and fly it into the Pentagon. Joint Staff action officers rejected it as unrealistic."

"What do you want to bet that, when the April 2001, hijacked-plane-into-Pentagon NORAD war game script writer was turned down, that he took his idea to Cheney or one of Cheney's people, who then took it as their own..." mused Honegger, "...and on September 11, the same scenario that had been turned down in April was embedded in NORAD's own game, 'Vigilant Guardian'?"

Few people realize to what extent Cheney was in a commanding position to know all aspects of the international terrorist structure and particularly America's terrorist attack planning scenarios. On May 9, 2001, four months prior to the attacks, the Bush administration had launched an effort to address the problem of terrorism. President Bush created a new Office of National Preparedness (ONP) within the Federal Emergency Management Agency (FEMA) and named Vice President Dick Cheney to head a special task force to study terrorism and guide FEMA's antiterrorism operations. His position in the counterterrorism effort of the federal government was therefore central—especially so if one considers his previous experience as secretary of defense during the first Bush administration.

Practically speaking, Dick Cheney was in a virtual command-and-control position during the actual events of 9/11, argues Mike Ruppert in *Crossing the Rubicon*. We've already noted that Cheney was rushed to the White House Presidential Emergency Operations Center, (located in a bunker under the east wing of the White House) just after the second plane had hit the WTC, and was directing activities of the government from this secure location while President Bush was being whisked around the country on *Air Force One*.

Cheney's terrorism task force was scheduled to produce antiterrorism recommendations for Congress by October 1, 2001, too late to make a difference. Of course, by that time, the nation was well into the new War on Terrorism. During much of 2001 prior to 9/11, Cheney also was in charge of another crucial task force, this one reviewing national energy policy. This panel later became the center of controversy, when California's escalating power woes indicated that corporate energy executives had unduly influenced national policies. Cheney's task force never turned over its internal papers, despite a lawsuit over this refusal that made its way up to the Supreme Court. Some observers have argued that smoking-gun documents related to 9/11—and revealing a motive involving an invasion of Iraq for the sake of oil—may be hidden in the records that Cheney has refused to make public. But what *has* been revealed is the fact that Cheney met at least six times with officials of the failed energy company Enron.

## WHO AUTHORIZED THE BIN LADEN EVACUATION?

Two days after the attacks, Bush emphatically pledged, "The most important thing is for us to find Osama bin Laden. It is our number one priority and we will not rest until we find him."

Yet as the weeks passed, this position grew more ambivalent. Towards the end of December, speaking at his Crawford, Texas ranch, Bush ruminated, "...he [bin Laden] is not escaping us. This is a guy, who, three months ago, was in control of a county [sic]. Now he's maybe in control of a cave. He's on the run. Listen, a while ago I said to the American people, our objective is more than bin Laden. But one of the things for certain is we're going to get him running and keep him running, and bring him to justice. And that's what's happening. He's on the run, if he's running at all. So we don't know whether he's in cave with the door shut, or a cave with the door open—we just don't know...."

By March 2002, Bush admitted, "I don't know where bin Laden is. I have no idea and really don't care. It's not that important. It's not our priority." In response to a question from newsmen about bin Laden's whereabouts, Bush responded, "I am truly not that concerned about him." This same indifferent attitude apparently did not extend to the bin Laden family.

While hundreds of people around the world were rounded up and arrested by national authorities in the wake of the 9/11 attacks and the public denied the right to fly, about 140 Saudis—including two dozen members of Osama bin Laden's own family—were allowed to fly by private jet to a reunion in Washington and then on to Boston. According to *The New Yorker*, the bin Ladens grouped in Boston, from where they eventually were flown out of the country once the FAA reinstated overseas flights. And this curious operation was carried out even as Osama bin Laden was being fingered as the undoubted perpetrator of the attacks.

Initially dismissed as an Internet rumor or an urban legend, the reports of the bin Laden family flight were confirmed in an October 2003

*Vanity Fair* interview with Richard A. Clarke, who had resigned earlier that year as chief of the Counterterrorism Security Group of the NSC. Clarke said that he did not recall who requested approval for the flight, but thought it was either the FBI or the State Department. "Someone brought to us for approval the decision to let an airplane filled with Saudis, including members of the bin Laden family, leave the country," he said. "So I said, 'Fine, let it happen.'"

Although both the *Tampa Tribune* and the *New York Times* reported that the Saudis were shepherded to their flights by FBI agents, bureau officials denied such reports. The Saudi flights, which came from ten American cities, including Los Angeles, Washington, D.C., and Houston, ended up in Boston where two jumbo jets flew the group to Saudi Arabia in mid-September 2001.

None of the Saudis were seriously interrogated by anyone. "We were in the midst of the worst terrorist act in history and here we were seeing an evacuation of the bin Ladens..." groused Tom Kinton, director of aviation at Boston's Logan International Airport. "I wanted to go to the highest levels in Washington," he told *Vanity Fair* but realized that the operation had the blessing of top federal officials.

Equally disturbing was the accusation of Senator Bob Graham, former chairman of the Senate Intelligence Committee, who in 2004 accused the Bush White House of covering up evidence that might have linked Saudi Arabia to the Sept. 11 hijackers. This charge came following FBI officials refusal to allow investigators for the congressional 9/11 inquiry and the 9/11 Commission to interview an informant, Abdussattar Shaikh, an FBI informant who was landlord in San Diego of two Sept. 11 hijackers. Graham termed the letter from an FBI official stating "the administration would not sanction a staff interview with the source [Shaikh]," a "smoking gun" which proved "The reason for this cover-up goes right to the White House." Republicans unsurprisingly termed such accusation "bizarre conspiracy theories," and Saudi officials said they were unsubstantiated and reckless.

"How was it possible that, just as President Bush declared a no-holds-barred global war on terrorism that would send hundreds of thousands of US troops to Afghanistan and Iraq, and just as Osama bin Laden became Public Enemy No. 1 and the target of a worldwide manhunt, the White House would expedite the departure of so many potential witnesses, including two dozen relatives of the man behind the attack itself?" mused *Vanity Fair* writer Craig Unger.

Numerous bin Laden family members flew out of the US from Logan International on September 18, 2001. The very next day, White House speech writers were formulating President Bush's stirring call for a war on terrorism while at the Pentagon plans were being drawn up for this war to include Iraq. No one yet has pinpointed the authority behind this incredible evacuation, although it is clear this authority must have had control over both the FBI and the FAA.

The sheer fact that someone with authority over the FBI and FAA allowed the family of the chief suspect in the 9/11 attacks to fly with impunity, when the rest of America was grounded, failed to set off alarm bells in both the media and the public.

## WHAT ABOUT THE HIJACKERS THEMSELVES?

Lending support to the contention that al Qaeda has been overblown as a monolithic terrorist network is a lengthy series of disturbing questions concerning that organization as well as the 9/11 hijackers themselves. Further, there is the apparent obfuscation of facts in the official government account of this issue. To initiate a war, there first must be a perceived enemy. America's great enemy today is supposedly still Osama bin Laden's al Qaeda network, but even this is under suspicion.

"There are people within the US intelligence community who doubt that the hijacker list from 9/11 has much truth in it," said one unnamed intelligence source quoted by investigative reporter and publisher Jon Rappoport, who has built up many sources in his more than 20 years experience. "They see it as a more-or-less invented list. They know that if you start with men showing false passports (or no passports) to get on four planes on 9/11, you can't assemble a correct list of nineteen suspects within a few days—especially since all those men are presumed dead and missing, untraceable.

"Al Qaeda is being used as a term to convince people that these terrorists are all connected in a vast, very well-organized network that is global in reach, that has a very sophisticated and far-flung communication setup, that issues orders from the top down to cells all over the world. There are a number of people inside the US intelligence agencies who know this is a false picture. They know that false intelligence is being assembled in order to paint a picture which is distorted, so that the American people will have a single focus on one grand evil enemy."

Supporting this claim is the fact that not one of the accused hijackers' names appeared on the passenger lists made public by American or United Airlines. In fact, as many as seven of those named as the culprits in the attacks were soon found alive and well in the Middle East. These included Saudi pilot Waleed al-Shehri, identified by the US Justice Department as one of the men who crashed American Flight 11 into the WTC. But a few days later, Waleed al-Shehri contacted authorities in Casablanca, Morocco, to proclaim that he was very much alive and played no part in the attacks. Another man identified as one of the hijackers of Flight 11, Abdulaziz al-Omari, also turned up alive in the Middle East, telling BBC News that he lost his passport while visiting Denver, Colorado. Actually two turned up, as yet another Abdulaziz al-Omari surfaced in Saudi Arabia very much alive and telling newsmen, "I couldn't believe the FBI put me on their list. They gave my name and my date of birth, but I am not a suicide bomber. I am here. I am alive. I have no idea how to fly a plane. I had nothing to do with this."

Yet another man identified as one of the hijackers of United Flight 93, Saeed al-Ghamdi, was reported alive and well and working as a pilot in Saudi Arabia. "You cannot imagine what it is like to be described as a terrorist—and a dead man—when you are innocent and alive," said al-Ghamdi, who was given a holiday by his airline in Saudi Arabia to avoid arrest. At least three other named 9/11 hijackers surfaced to proclaim their innocence in the attacks but none of this was widely reported in the US corporate mass media.

In October 2004, the BBC broadcasted in the UK a documentary entitled *The Power of Nightmares: The Rise of the Politics of Fear*, a three-hour documentary that challenged the Bush administration's stated concept of al Qaeda as a multi-faceted globespanning octopus of terrorism. The documentary raised questions such as:

- Why did the Bush administration, after rounding up hundreds of suspected terrorists and using torture during interrogation,

failed to produce any hard evidence of al Qaeda activities?
- Of the 664 suspected terrorists detained in Britain, why have only 17 been found guilty of crimes? Why have none of these men been proven to be members of al Qaeda?
- Why did the Bush administration prompted so much frightening speculation over "dirty" radioactive bombs when experts have stated that public panic over such devices will kill more people than any radioactivity caused by one?
- Why did Defense Secretary Donald Rumsfeld claim on *Meet the Press* in 2001 that al Qaeda controlled massive high-tech cave complexes in Afghanistan, when none were later found following the military invasion?

While it is undeniable that groups of disaffected terrorists do exist, this BBC documentary nevertheless convincingly argued that "the nightmare vision of a uniquely powerful hidden organization waiting to strike our societies is an illusion. Wherever one looks for this al Qaeda organization, from the mountains of Afghanistan to the 'sleeper cells' in America, the British and Americans are chasing a phantom enemy."

*Los Angeles Times* political columnist Robert Scheer said that this documentary makes "a powerful case that the Bush administration, led by a tight-knit cabal of Machiavellian neoconservatives, has seized upon the false image of a unified international terrorist threat to replace the expired Soviet empire in order to push a political agenda." He pointed out that everything we know about al Qaeda comes from only two sources, both with a vested interest in maintaining the concept of a well-financed and deeply entrenched enemy—the terrorists themselves and military and governmental intelligence agencies. "Such a state of national ignorance about an endless war is, as *The Power of Nightmares* makes clear, simply unacceptable in a functioning democracy," Scheer wrote.

In Britain it has been suggested that al Qaeda is not even a real organization, but rather a computer list of Arab freedom fighters or terrorists available for hire. British commentator Robin Cook, who served as foreign secretary from 1997–2001 and as leader of the House of Commons from 2001–2003, has suggested that "Bin Laden...was armed by the CIA and funded by the Saudis to wage jihad against the Russian occupation of Afghanistan. Al Qaeda, literally 'the database,' was originally the com-

WHAT ABOUT THE HIJACKERS THEMSELVES?

puter file of the thousands of Mujahideen who were recruited and trained with help from the CIA to defeat the Russians."

On Thursday, August 10, 2006, British authorities announced they had thwarted a terrorist plot to simultaneously blow up several commercial aircraft bound for the United States using explosives smuggled in carry-on baggage. Carry-on luggage was banned in Britain as well as nearly all forms of liquid except for baby formula.

British officials said 21 persons had been arrested in connection with the bombing plot but declined to identify any of them, only stating that they "appear to be of Pakistani origin." They said the suspects were "homegrown," but it was not clear if the suspects were all British citizens. US Homeland Security Chief Michael Chertoff immediately said the plot had all the "earmarks" of an al Qaeda operation but admitted it was too early in the investigation to reach any conclusions. Yet, it was not too early for authorities to say they had caught the main suspects.

News of the plot caused tightened security procedures at all airports, not only in Britain but also the United States. US air carriers said that while carry-on luggage was still allowed, no liquids, including toothpaste, could be carried onto aircraft. And news of the plot dominated the news channels, distracting from the aggression in the Middle East, the slumping US economy and the growing public awareness of government complicity in the 9/11 attacks.

Interestingly enough, both British Prime Minister Tony Blair and President George W. Bush were both out of pocket when this conspiracy was announced. Blair was vacationing in the Caribbean and Bush was on vacation at his ranch in Crawford, Texas. Chertoff, who seemed to have more information on the bombing attempts than the British officials who presumably briefed him on the case, said the plotters were in the final stage of planning. "We were really getting quite close to the execution phase," he said. No one else in a position of authority and knowledge would speak on the record due to "the sensitivity of the situation," according to the Associated Press.

On ABC News television, former Counterterrorism Chief Richard Clarke reminded viewers that this was a "carbon copy" of the 1995 planned terrorist attack formulated by al Qaeda in the Philippines. These plotters also proposed crashing hijacked airliners into the World Trade Center, a fact conveniently forgotten when Bush officials claimed no one could have suspected such an event prior to 9/11. He also mentioned the broken plot in Miami in June 2006, where seven men were arrested and accused of plotting to bomb Chicago's Sears Tower. Clarke said that British intelligence is "very good" and, in fact, had infiltrated the terrorist "sleeper cells." "What is the full dimension of the attack?" asked Clarke. Many think this is the true question. Who is truly behind these "homegrown" terrorists?

In the Miami case, it was an FBI informant posing as a representative of al Qaeda, just as the British intelligence agents in the current case. The seven young men arrested in this FBI "sting" operation were all from Miami's Liberty City, one of the poorest ghettoes in the US. No weapons, explosives or other paraphernalia was found. All evidence in the case came from "the al Qaeda representative," according to the government's indictment—who, of course, was the FBI informant. Chicago Police Superintendent Phil Cline stated, "There was never any credible threat to the Sears Tower at all." Even FBI Deputy Director John Pistole agreed that "this group was more aspirational than operational."

In May, 2006, Pakistani immigrant Shahawar Matin Siraj was found guilty in New York City of plotting to blow up the Herald Square subway station. Court evidence indicated this "plot" was based entirely on suggestions from an FBI informant, who taunted the defendant with photographs of Abu Ghraib torture victims and demanded to know how, as a Muslim, he could fail to take action. Two years ago, in Albany, New York, the FBI recruited a Pakistani immigrant to ensnare two other immigrants in a fictitious scheme to help a non-existent person buy a weapon for a fake terrorist plot. The immigrant was promised leniency on minor fraud charges in exchange for his cooperation.

In view of these obvious spurious provocations coupled with growing suspicions among the public that the 9/11 attacks themselves were either allowed or orchestrated by elements within the US Government, Clarke's rhetorical question becomes even more significant—"What is the full dimension of the attack?" As in any good crime detection, one must ask, "Who benefits from the crime? Who has the means, motive and opportunity to conduct this crime?"

One good terrorist strike does not necessitate others. The deaths of 9/11 were enough to convince the public that terrorism was abroad in

## WHAT ABOUT THE HIJACKERS THEMSELVES?

the land. Further fatalities are not needed to further diminish individual liberties, just the continued threat of such. This can easily be arranged by government agent provocateurs. For example, say a Pakistani working for British intelligence convenes a group of Pakistanis already bitter about the discrimination they face in Britain. They are taught by the agent to mix chemicals to make explosives and there is much planning to sneak the explosives onto airliners. Then, the trap is sprung and the terrorist threat is thwarted by our brave and vigilant intelligence organizations.

Security everywhere is tightened, liberties further constrained, government budgets increased and everyone is happy except perhaps for the poor patsies who spend the rest of their life in prison trying to figure out how their great revolutionary plan went wrong.

When these acts of terrorism are announced, we should all demand truthful answers to questions such as: Which individual initiated the terrorists' plans? Who did this individual truly represent? Who supplied the funds for the terrorists' activities and where did such funds originate?

Ironically, even supposed enemies are often two sides of the same coin. Author Thom Hartmann pointed out that both the hawks in America and Muslim terrorists operate from similar ideologies—though the specifics may differ, both groups believe the end justifies the means and that people must be frightened into accepting religion and nationalism for the greater good of morality and a stable state.

The day following 9/11, FBI Director Robert Mueller announced some astonishingly swift police work. "We have, in the last twenty-four hours, taken the [passenger] manifests and used them in an evidentiary manner. And have successfully, I believe, identified many of the hijackers on each of the four flights that went down," he told newsmen. Sounding like a 1940s police detective, Mueller added, "We will leave no stone unturned to find those responsible for the tragedies." Yet, at the same time, Mueller acknowledged that the list of named hijackers might not contain their real names.

An obvious set of questions arises from this scenario: If they used aliases, how did the FBI identify them so quickly? How did the FBI learn the names of five of the hijackers and obtain their photographs the day of the attacks? And where did agents obtain the names and locations of businesses and restaurants used by the hijackers by that same afternoon?

"It was proved that five of the names included in the FBI list had nothing to do with what happened," announced Saudi Arabia's foreign minister Prince Saud al-Faisal, after meeting with President Bush on September 20, 2001. Mueller acknowledged within days of the attacks that the identities of the hijackers were in doubt but this gained little notice in the rush to publicize the culprits. Despite initially saying he was "fairly confident" that the published names of the hijackers were correct, Mueller later admitted, "The identification process has been complicated by the fact that many Arab family names are similar. It is also possible that the hijackers used false identities."

Since Saudi Arabia's foreign minister claimed five of the proclaimed hijackers were not aboard the death planes and in fact are still alive, and a sixth man on that list was reported to be alive and well in Tunisia, why are these names still on the FBI list? These same names were used in the final report of the 9/11 Commission with no attempt to clarify the name confusion. In fact, its report goes into considerable detail throughout its pages about the supposed sinister activities of these men, apparently oblivious that numerous mainstream media sources such as the Associated Press and the BBC had long ago established that they were not on the flights. Very soon after the attacks, the stunning news that many of the accused hijackers were in training at American flight schools hit the headlines.

In September 2002, during testimony before a joint congressional committee, Kristin Breitweiser, whose husband, Ronald, died at the WTC, asked a most pertinent question about this admitted fact, a question that continues to go unanswered. She cited a *New York Times* article the day after the strikes stating that FBI agents arrived at flight schools within hours to gather biographies on the terrorists. "How did the FBI know where to go a few hours after the attacks?...Were any of the hijackers already under surveillance?" She asked. Or were they already known to the authorities, thanks to some agency's database?

One obvious lead ignored by the FBI but pursued by investigative reporter Daniel Hopsicker concerns two flight schools at the tiny Venice Airport at the retirement community of Venice, Florida, where three of the four accused 9/11 pilots learned to fly. "Florida is the biggest 9/11 crime scene that wasn't reduced to rubble," noted Hopsicker. "But it hasn't been treated that way. And no one has offered any reason why.

## WHAT ABOUT THE HIJACKERS THEMSELVES?

"Both flight schools were owned by Dutch nationals. Both had been recently purchased, at about the same time. A year later terrorists began to arrive, in numbers greater than we have so far been told. All of this must be just a freak coincidence, according to the FBI."

Hopsicker also noted that government officials claimed that the Arab terrorists came to the United States for flight training because it was less expensive, yet, according to aviation experts, they actually paid more than double the cost of training elsewhere.

Hopsicker said he confirmed that within hours of the 9/11 attacks, a military C-130 Hercules transport plane arrived at the Venice airport where a rental truck loaded with the records of Huffman Aviation—one of the flight schools reportedly used by the hijackers—was driven onto the craft and airlifted to Washington escorted by Florida Gov. Jeb Bush.

We've noted that none of the accused hijackers' names appear on any of the passenger lists. Additionally, there was also a discrepancy of thirty-five names between the published passenger lists and the official death toll on all four of the ill-fated flights. The published names—none with Arabic-sounding names—did not match the total listed for the number of people on board. Why the discrepancy?

To add to this mystery, Dr. Thomas R. Olmsted, a psychiatrist and former navy line officer, filed a Freedom of Information Act request with the Armed Forces Institute of Pathology (AFIP), which had responsibility for identifying all victims in the Pentagon reportedly killed by the crash of Flight 77. Only after the start of the Iraq invasion did Dr. Olmsted finally receive his accounting. "No Arabs wound up on the morgue slab," noted Dr. Olmsted. "However...*additional* [emphasis in the original] people not listed by American Airlines sneaked in. I have seen no explanation for these extras." The airline listed fifty-six persons on Flight 77 yet the AFIP listed sixty-four bodies as passengers on the plane. "And they did not explain how they were able to tell 'victims' bodies from 'hijacker' bodies," added Dr. Olmsted.

Plenty of disturbing questions surround the story of alleged Flight 77 pilot—Hani Hanjour. It is widely known that this young Saudi had a history of great difficulties in his efforts to learn to fly. As late as August 2001, he was unable to demonstrate enough piloting skills to even rent a Cessna 172. Among other news sources on this subject, *Newsday* revealed the following remarkable facts about Hanjour: "At Freeway Airport in Bowie, MD, 20 miles west of Washington, flight instructor Sheri Baxter instantly recognized the name of alleged hijacker Hani Hanjour when the FBI released a list of 19 suspects in the four hijackings. Hanjour, the only suspect on Flight 77 the FBI listed as a pilot, had come to the airport one month earlier seeking to rent a small plane.

"However, when Baxter and fellow instructor Ben Conner took the slender, soft-spoken Hanjour on three test runs during the second week of August, they found he had trouble controlling and landing the single-engine Cessna 172. Even though Hanjour showed a federal pilot's license and a log book cataloging six hundred hours of flying experience, chief flight instructor Marcel Bernard declined to rent him a plane without more lessons." Yet, Hanjour, who was not permitted to rent a Cessna, according to the official story, reportedly piloted a huge Boeing 757 in a 7,000-feet spiraling dive within two minutes, leveled the craft at tree-top level and smashed into the west wall of the Pentagon, a performance that even seasoned pilots would find difficult.

Nila Sagadevan, a pilot and aeronautical engineer in an article posted on the *Veterans Today* website, wrote, "A common misconception non-pilots have about simulators is how *easy* it is to operate them. They are indeed relatively easy to operate if the objective is to make a few lazy turns and frolic about in the *open sky*. But if the intent is to execute any kind of a maneuver with even the least bit of precision, the task immediately becomes quite daunting. And if the aim is to navigate to a specific geographic location hundreds of miles away while flying at over 500 mph, 30,000 feet above the ground the challenges become virtually impossible for an untrained pilot."

He pointed out that after the improbable feat of Hani Hanjour being able to physically overpower Flight 77's captain and first officer, Charles F. Burlingame and David Charlesbois, he then was faced with this situation: "If Hanjour looked straight ahead through the windshield, or off to his left at the ground, at best he would see, 35,000 feet—7 miles—below him, a murky brownish-gray-green landscape, virtually devoid of any significant surface detail, while the aircraft he was now piloting was moving along, almost imperceptibly and in eerie silence, at around 500 mph (about 750 feet every second). In a real-world scenario, with this

WHAT ABOUT THE HIJACKERS THEMSELVES?

kind of 'situational *non*-awareness', Hanjour might as well have been flying over Argentina, Russia, or Japan—he wouldn't have had a clue as to where, precisely, he was…Seeing nothing outside, Mr. Hanjour would be forced to divert his attention to his instrument panel, where he'd be faced with a bewildering array of instruments—nothing like he had seen in a Cessna 172. He would then have to very quickly interpret his heading, ground track, altitude, and airspeed information on the displays before he could even figure out where in the world he was, much less where the Pentagon was located in relation to his position. After all, before he can crash into a target, he has to first find the target."

Sagadevan said, "A discussion on ground effect energy, vortex compression, down-wash reaction, wake turbulence, and jet-blast effects are beyond the scope of this article.…Let it suffice to say that it is physically impossible to fly a 200,000-lb airliner 20 feet above the ground at 400 mph."

After denigrating the official theory of lightly-trained Muslim terrorists being able to miraculously pilot three jumbo airliners into three buildings, Sagadevan explained, "The writers of the official storyline expect us to believe, that once the flight deck crews had been overpowered, and the hijackers 'took control' of the various aircraft, their intended targets suddenly popped up in their windshields as they would have in some arcade game, and all that these fellows would have had to do was simply aim their airplanes at the buildings and fly into them. Most people who have been exposed only to the official storyline have never been on the flight deck of an airliner at altitude and looked at the outside world; if they had, they'd realize the absurdity of this kind of reasoning."

Danielle O'Brien, one of the Dulles air traffic controllers, had this to say about Flight 77: "The speed, the maneuverability, the way [the pilot] turned, we all thought in the radar room, all of us experienced air traffic controllers, that it was a military plane." This assessment may indeed have been correct, as is revealed in the Appendix to this book.

Numerous puzzling stories have also emerged about the so-called mastermind of the hijackers, Mohamed Atta. Atta reportedly left behind in his parked car two suitcases containing incriminating documents, including Atta's passport, driver's license, his last will, a copy of the Koran, flight simulation manuals for Boeing aircraft and a note to other hijackers. But why even take suitcases on a suicide mission? And if the suitcases were camouflage to present the appearance of a normal tourist, why did he leave them behind?

CNN reported on September 16, 2001: "In New York, several blocks from the ruins of the World Trade Center, a passport authorities said belonged to one of the hijackers was discovered a few days ago, according to city Police Commissioner Bernard Kerik. That has prompted the FBI and police to widen the search area beyond the immediate crash site." What happened to the passport and this story? Both seemed to have disappeared.

The discovered passport has been widely reported to have belonged to Mohamed Atta but actually was said to have been in the name of Satam al Suqami, supposedly the pilot of Flight 11 which reportedly was consumed within the North Tower after striking it dead on. The "black box" flight recorders on both WTC planes, designed to withstand crashes, were said to have been damaged beyond recognition and all of the concrete of the actual buildings was reduced to very fine dust. So how is that a paper passport can be fortuitously found intact on the ground blocks from the WTC? Some suspicious researchers smelled planted evidence.

Even stranger was the story told by the father of a 9/11 flight victim. Joseph Iskandar, a 73-year-old native of Lebanon who immigrated to the US in 1980, told of receiving four credit cards that had belonged to his son, Waleed, a passenger on American Flight 11. In an interview, Iskandar recalled, "When I returned to Ground Zero for the first anniversary of 9/11, I was told by some men that they had found four of Waleed's credit cards, all in good condition. They never told me how they found it or where but just sent me the cards." Iskandar, who never questioned the identity of the men or the legitimacy of the cards, added, "Waleed used to keep his credit cards in his wallet and although it was a bit unusual considering the devastating crash, I just considered it to be a miracle from God. I then took the cards and they are included in a memorial at his burial site." The cards—an ATM card and frequent flyer cards from American, Delta and United Airlines—were mailed to his home several weeks following his encounter with the men at Ground Zero.

In yet another odd occurrence of recovered 9/11 property, journalist Greg Szymanski reported that 9/11 first responder Capt. Jim Ingledue of the Virginia Beach Fire Department found a completely unblemished California ID card, driver's license and wedding ring of one of the Flight 77

WHAT ABOUT THE HIJACKERS THEMSELVES?

passengers amidst the devastation and rubble at the Pentagon. "Passenger Suzanne Calley's husband, Frank, of San Martin, CA, verified the return of his wife's items, but like Iskandar didn't question or even seek verification of the credibility of the evidence," wrote Szymanski, who quoted Ingledue as saying, "I remember thinking it was highly unusual and strange to find a perfectly intact ID card amidst all that devastation. When we arrived at the Pentagon, we were advised to turn over any personal effects or possible evidence immediately over to the FBI. I kept this bit of evidence with me a little longer, I don't know why, but I guess I thought it was strange to find an ID in perfect shape when everything else around me was devastated."

Author David Ray Griffin quoted an unnamed high-level intelligence source as saying what was on many people's minds, "Whatever trail was left was left deliberately—for the FBI to chase." Like the suitcase issue, the paper passport found in the World Trade Center debris led many researchers to suspect planted evidence. But who would plant such evidence and for what purpose?

At least one homegrown plot directed by the government as a provocation against Americans may have been uncovered soon after 9/11 itself.

Late on Saturday, May 11, 2002, an astute deputy sheriff in Jacksonville, FL, stopped a speeding late-model pickup truck. The deputy was amazed to find the truck's driver dressed all in black, wearing a pistol in a shoulder holster and plastic pads on his elbows and knees. In the truck also were large knives, a 12-gauge shotgun, shotgun and pistol ammunition, four ammo magazines, a six-volt battery, duct tape, speaker wire and parts of an explosive device. He was further amazed to find the suspect was a soldier from Fort Stewart, GA.

He arrested Army Specialist Derek Lawrence Peterson. The arresting officer recognized Peterson's truck as one seen earlier parked near the main gate of a nearby Florida Power and Light station. Tracking footprints from where the truck had been parked, investigating officers discovered an explosive device beneath power lines. The 27-year-old soldier explained he was practicing night reconnaissance tactics. A spokesman for Fort Stewart confirmed that Peterson had been stationed there for about a month with B Company, 1st Battalion, 64th Armored Division.

If Peterson was simply an idiot that somehow made it into the Army, one would expect widespread news coverage to demonstrate how seriously authorities were taking attempted bombings. On the other hand, if Peterson was carrying out some undisclosed covert military orders, one would expect the incident to be hushed up. The soldier was held in a Jacksonville jail without visitors in lieu of $5 million bail. Somebody was taking this case quite seriously, yet there was no national news coverage of this incident at a time of heightened fear and excitement over terrorist incidents and the initial court hearing for Peterson was postponed. A recemt Internet search on this incident turned up no new information or any resolution of this bizarre case.

In what almost appeared to be an instant replay of the Derek Lawrence Peterson saga, in September 2010, sheriff's deputies in Effingham County, GA, arrested three men in the early morning hours near Georgia Power's Plant McIntosh on Old Augusta Road. The arrest came after an alert Department of Natural Resources ranger reported a suspicious vehicle near the power station. Deputies discovered a machete, shovel, wire cutters and ski masks in the men's 1995 Nissan Ranger.

Arrested were Evgeniy Luzhetskiy from Kazakhastan and Nail Idiatullin and Rustem Ibragimov of Russia. All three said they lived in Charleston, SC. The three were charged with possession of tools during the commission of a crime and handed over to a Joint Terrorism Task Force. David Ehsanipoor, a spokesman for the sheriff's department, said the trio was released after questioning by task force members. "They did all have visas that allowed them to be here and are supposed to be leaving the country soon," said Ehsanipoor. Some conspiracy researchers wondered if the three also were undergoing training at Fort Stewart.

The story of the infamous "underwear bomber" of 2010, which will be detailed later, reads like an act of provocation. And consider the case of the man who tried to stop the first World Trade Center bombing as an historical precedent for agents provocateurs.

According to the *New York Times*, in 1992 and early 1993 an FBI informant named Emad Salem was involved with Middle Eastern terrorists connected to Osama bin Laden. They were developing a bomb for use against New York's World Trade Center. Salem, a 43-year-old former Egyptian Army officer, wanted to substitute a harmless powder for the explosive but his plan to thwart the attack was blocked by an FBI official who apparently did not want to expose the inside informant. The attack was allowed to pro-

WHAT ABOUT THE HIJACKERS THEMSELVES?

ceed. The February 26, 1993 explosion in the WTC resulted in six deaths, more than 1,000 casualties and damage in excess of a half billion dollars.

Salem said he wanted to complain to FBI headquarters in Washington but was dissuaded from doing so by another FBI agent. Salem said the agent told him, "I don't think that the New York [FBI] people would like the things out of the New York office to go to Washington, D.C." It was also reported that the FBI repeatedly attempted to lay blame for the attack on the UN Mission from Sudan.

"[I]n 1992 and 1993, the New York City FBI informant and agent provocateur Emad Salem repeatedly tried to implicate the Sudanese UN mission in his own 'Islamic terror cell' World Trade Center bomb plot conspiracy," noted author Webster Griffin Tarpley. "Here we see how a false-flag terror cell 'sheep-dips' [covers up the true background of] its dupes [and brings them] into contact with a target, which then becomes the object of a police investigation, and possibly later of military attack."

Tarpley also pointed out that when authorities searched the apartment of El Sayyid Nosair, suspected of the 1990 assassination of New York City Rabbi Meir Kahane, they found training manuals from the Army Special Warfare School at Fort Bragg and copies of teletypes going to the secretary of the Army and the Joint Chiefs of Staff. "Clearly, [Nosair] had a source in a sensitive position in the US military…" Tarpley wrote, adding that this "source" may indeed have been Nosiar's controller.

In light of media stories concerning agents provocateurs, a discovered passport, a Koran left behind, flight school materials, and even "suicide" notes, why did FBI director Robert Mueller in an April 19, 2002 speech before the Commonwealth Club in San Francisco declare that the hijackers "left no paper trail"?

Further suspicions were aroused concerning how the WTC fires could destroy airliner "black boxes" yet leave a paper passport undamaged in mid-2003 when two New York firefighters, Nicholas DeMasi and Mike Bellone self-published a book in which they contradicted the official announcement that no flight or cockpit recorder "black boxes" were found at the WTC. Footnote 76 of Chapter One in *The 9/11 Commission Report*, states, "The CVR's [Cockpit Voice Recorders] and FDR's [Flight Data Recorders] from American 11 and United 175 were not found…"

A spokesman for the National Transportation Safety Board, Ted Lopatkiewicz told the *American Free Press* that such recorders are designed to withstand the tremendous impact and heat of plane crashes. "I can't remember another case [in] which we did not recover the recorders."

DeMasi and Bellone, both now retired from the FDNY, claimed to have found three of the four reddish-orange white-striped boxes while riding an all terrain vehicle at Ground Zero with three federal agents. Bellone said federal agents were adamant about not talking about their find. "They confronted me and told me not to say anything," he recalled. "I said, 'Give me one good reason.' When they couldn't, I told them I wouldn't shut up about it...I can tell you this, though, it was all very strange. I worked on the spaceship *Columbia* cleanup, and you known when something important is found and when something is not." He added that he did not catch the FBI agents' names but added, "They had on their FBI jackets [and] I'm sure I could pick them out of a lineup or recognize their pictures."

Both firemen said several other firefighters witnessed the recovery of the data recorders but were ordered into silence by federal agents. DeMasi and Bellone published their story in a book entitled *Behind the Scene: Ground Zero* in August 2003, but no one contacted them about their claims except reporter William Bunch of the *Philadelphia Daily*.

Questions also arose regarding the behavior of the identified hijackers. On the night before the attacks, according to the *Boston Globe*, four of the suspected hijackers called several escort services asking how much it would cost to acquire prostitutes for the night. Other news sources stated that other suspects spent time in bars and strip clubs in Florida, New Jersey, and Las Vegas. Heavy drinking and a search for hookers by some of the hijackers sound more like mercenaries carousing before a mission than pious religious fundamentalists about to meet their maker.

According to journalist Daniel Hopsicker, stripper Amanda Keller was the girlfriend of Mohamed Atta while he was in the USA. She told of Atta's cocaine use as well as shadowy contacts with foreign nationals while living in Florida. Hopsicker was amazed that Keller's tale of sex, drugs and hijackers was not picked up and ballyhooed by the sensation-seeking mass media.

Hopsicker also was astounded that no one in government seemed concerned or interested in facts he discovered linking Atta and other 9/11

WHAT ABOUT THE HIJACKERS THEMSELVES?

hijackers in Florida to an underworld of international drug smuggling. In his book *Welcome to Terrorland: Mohamed Atta & the 9-11 Cover-Up in Florida*, Hopsicker quoted former Assistant Attorney General Michael Chertoff as telling a Senate Banking Committee, "Frankly, we can't differentiate between terrorism and organized crime and drug dealing."

More discrepancies: Why did the seat numbers of hijackers given by a phone call from flight attendant Madeline "Amy" Sweeney to Boston air traffic control not match the seats occupied by the men the FBI claimed were responsible?

And why did news outlets describe the throat cutting and mutilation of passengers on Flight 93 with box cutters when *Time* magazine on September 24 reported that one of the passengers called home on a cell phone to report, "We have been hijacked. They are being kind."?

In the days following September 11, many major media pundits correctly pointed out that a ragtag bunch of fanatics could not have successfully pulled off the large-scale and well-coordinated attacks by themselves. They must have had the sponsorship of some state, they argued. It was this rationale that provided the foundation argument for the subsequent attacks on Afghanistan and Iraq.

One captured al Qaeda chief may have provided a startling answer to the question of who actually provided state sponsorship for the 9/11 attacks—most likely working hand-in-hand with cosponsors in the US as well as other US-connected foreign intelligence agencies including the Israeli Mossad and/or the Pakistani ISI (i.e., the Mossad and the ISI being the central intelligence agency equivalent in each country).

This "smoking gun" case links al Qaeda directly to Saudi Arabia. It came to light in late March 2002, with the capture of Abu Zubaydah in a middle-class suburb of the Pakistani city of Faisalabad. On April 2, 2002, White House spokesman Ari Fleischer described Zubaydah as the most senior member of al Qaeda captured to that point and stated, "He will be interrogated about his knowledge of ongoing plans to conduct terrorist activities. This represents a serious blow to al Qaeda."

But instead it appears to have been a serious blow to the Saudis. According to a new book by Gerald Posner entitled *Why America Slept*, Zubaydah turned out to be tightly connected with ranking Saudis, including members of the royal family.

Posner, a noted debunker of JFK assassination conspiracies, supported the official version of pre-9/11 intelligence failures in this new book, arguing that despite all the tax dollars spent, federal agencies simply couldn't connect the dots. Posner has admitted being close to friendly CIA sources, which make his ensuing revelations that much more shocking.

According to Posner, when attempts to pry information out of Zubaydah with drugs and torture failed, the al Qaeda chief was flown to an Afghan facility remodeled to look like a Saudi jail cell. Two Arab American special forces operatives, disguised as Saudis, then confronted Zubaydah. The idea was to scare him into revealing al Qaeda secrets. Recall that al Qaeda reportedly detests the Saudi royalty.

Yet, when faced by the faked Saudi interrogators, Zubaydah expressed relief rather than fear, according to Posner. He seemed genuinely happy to see them and offered them telephone numbers for ranking Saudi officials. One number was for Saudi Prince Ahmed bin Salman bin Abdul Aziz, a westernized nephew of Saudi King Fahd and an equestrian whose horse, War Emblem, won the 2002 Kentucky Derby. Zubaydah said Prince Aziz would vouch for him and give the interrogators instructions. The disguised Americans were shocked to find the unlisted Saudi numbers were valid.

The Saudi Arabian-born al Qaeda leader then proceeded to outline his Saudi connections. He explained that one such contact in Saudi Arabia was intelligence chief Prince Turki al-Faisal bin Abdul Aziz, who met with Osama bin Laden in 1991 and agreed to provide bin Laden with funds in exchange for his pledge not to promote a jihad war in Saudi Arabia. He said his royal Saudi contacts operated through Pakistani Air Marshal Mushaf Ali Mir, a man with close ties to Muslims inside Pakistan's Inter-Services Intelligence (ISI). The ISI has long been suspected of providing al Qaeda with arms and supplies. And according to Posner, this convoluted pipeline was blessed by the Saudis. Zubaydah went on to claim that 9/11 did nothing to change the relationships between the Saudis, Pakistanis, and al Qaeda. He claimed that while both Prince Ahmed and Mir knew in advance of the attacks, they did not know the specific targets. They also would have been hesitant to reveal their secret agreements.

Posner also noted that not long after Zubaydah's revelations were passed along to the Saudis, the men mentioned by Zubaydah all died

## WHAT ABOUT THE HIJACKERS THEMSELVES?

within days of each other. Prince Ahmed died of a heart attack at age 43 on July 22, 2002, while two princes, Sultan bin Faisal bin Turki al-Saud and Fahd bin Turki bin Saud al Kabir both were killed in car wrecks within a week of each other. Pakistani Air Marshal Mir died in a plane crash during clear weather. Posner, known for his anti-conspiracy rhetoric, told *Time* the deaths, most convenient to anyone desiring to keep the Saudi–Pakistani–al Qaeda axis hidden, "may in fact be coincidences."

Despite this remarkable information tying al Qaeda to Saudi royals and Pakistani intelligence published in a major US news magazine, very little of such coverage has made its way to the American public.

Bin Laden even had followers within the US military, as evidenced by court records of a former Fort Bragg, North Carolina, sergeant who gathered top-secret materials for more than two years.

Ali A. Mohamed, from 1987 until his arrest in 1989, served for a time at the John F. Kennedy Special Warfare Center and School. Mohamed, who once served as a major in the Egyptian army's special operations forces, was trained at the officer's course for Green Berets at Fort Bragg in 1981. At about that same time, he joined the terrorist group Islamic Jihad, responsible for the 1981 assassination of Egyptian president Anwar Sadat and later became a close adviser to bin Laden. He also tried unsuccessfully to join the CIA but did become a source of information for the FBI, according to Larry Johnson, a former CIA agent and director of counter-terrorism at the State Department during the first Bush administration.

The FBI found documents, believed to have come from Mohamed, in the possession of one of the men convicted in the 1993 WTC bombing. Included were top secret papers belonging to the Joint Chiefs of Staff and the commander in chief of the Army's Central Command. One former special forces officer said, "There is no doubt that his proximity, in hindsight, was very harmful," adding, "Does this hurt our efforts now? Absolutely." It must be recalled that Osama bin Laden as well as many of his al Qaeda operatives are Saudis. And this makes for a very troublesome aspect to the War on Terrorism.

To understand the problem, one must keep in mind the fact that the United States, and perhaps most of the industrialized world, is immeasurably dependent on the eight major oil fields of Saudi Arabia. Loss of even a significant portion of this petroleum could mean unthinkable consequences to the economy of both America and the world. And control over this crucial strategic resource is concentrated in one ruling family, a family line with longstanding and well-documented ties to major players in the oil industry, especially the Bush family.

Contradicting widely circulated news reports, *The 9/11 Commission Report* acknowledged, "…bin Laden did not fund al Qaeda through a personal fortune and a network of businesses in Sudan. Instead, al Qaeda relied primarily on a fund-raising network developed over time…particularly in Saudi Arabia."

A study of history reveals that the Nazi-oriented Muslim Brotherhood was a progenitor of today's al Qaeda terrorist organization, which is mere a database of Muslim mercenaries available to whoever pays the tab. The connection between the Muslim fanatics and Nazis, according to former Justice Department investigator and Nazi-hunter John Loftus, began with Muslim Brotherhood founder Hassan al-Banna, who formed a group of Egyptian youth dedicated to social reform and Islamic morals in the 1920s. "Al-Banna formed this nationalist group called the Muslim Brotherhood. Al-Banna was a devout admirer of Adolf Hitler and wrote to him frequently. So persistent was he in his admiration of the new Nazi Party that in the 1930s, al-Banna and the Muslim Brotherhood became a secret arm of Nazi intelligence," said Loftus, who had unprecedented access to secret US government and NATO intelligence files. "The Arab Nazis had much in common with the new Nazi doctrines. They hated Jews; they hated democracy; and they hated the Western culture. It became the official policy of the Third Reich to secretly develop the Muslim Brotherhood as the fifth Parliament, an army inside Egypt. When war broke out, the Muslim Brotherhood promised in writing that they would rise up and help General Rommel and make sure that no English or American soldier was left alive in Cairo or Alexandria."

After World War II, the Muslim Brotherhood and its German intelligence handlers were wanted for war crimes. Following arrests in Cairo, they were turned over to the British Secret Service, who hired them to fight against the infant state of Israel in 1948. "Only a few people in the Mossad know this, but many of the members of the Arab armies and terrorist groups that tried to strangle the infant state of Israel were the Arab Nazis of the Muslim Brotherhood," said Loftus. "What the British did then, they

## WHAT ABOUT THE HIJACKERS THEMSELVES?

sold the Arab Nazis to the predecessor of what became the CIA. It may sound stupid; it may sound evil, but it did happen. The idea was that we were going to use the Arab Nazis in the Middle East as a counterweight to the Arab communists. Just as the Soviet Union was funding Arab communists, we would fund the Arab Nazis to fight against [them]. And lots of secret classes took place. We kept the Muslim Brotherhood on our payroll.

"But the Egyptians became nervous. [Egyptian President Gamal] Nasser ordered all of the Muslim Brotherhood out of Egypt or be imprisoned, and we would execute them all. During the 1950s, the CIA evacuated the Nazis of the Muslim Brotherhood to Saudi Arabia. Now when they arrived in Saudi Arabia...[one] student was named Osama bin Ladin. Osama bin Ladin was taught by the Nazis of the Muslim Brotherhood who had immigrated to Saudi Arabia."

It was from these Saudi Brotherhood members that the CIA in 1979 drew fanatics to send to Afghanistan to fight the Soviets. "We had to rename them," said Loftus. "We couldn't call them the Muslim Brotherhood because that was too sensitive a name. Its Nazi cast was too known. So we called them the Maktab al-Khidamat Mujahideen, the MAK...we left this army of Arab fascists in the field of Afghanistan."

But the Saudis didn't want the fanatics to return so they paid bribes to Osama bin Ladin and his al Qaeda followers to stay out of Saudi Arabia.

"There are many flavors and branches, but they are all Muslim Brotherhoods....So the Muslim Brotherhood became this poison that spread throughout the Middle East and on 9/11, it began to spread around the world," concluded Loftus, adding that current CIA members themselves don't know this history. "[T]he current generation CIA are good and decent Americans and I like them a lot. They're trying to do a good job, but part of their problem is their files have been shredded. All of these secrets have to come out."

## WHAT REALLY HAPPENED AT THE PENTAGON?

At the Pentagon, again the official story initially seemed plausible—a third hijacked airliner, Flight 77, was flown into America's military command center creating a fire that killed more than 185 persons and caused a section of the west wall to collapse. But, as with the rest of the 9/11 account, the closer one looks, the more mysterious becomes the event.

Even the exact time of the attack has been modified several times. Pentagon spokespersons first reported the explosion at 9:48 a.m. Over the intervening months, this time was lowered to 9:37 a.m., as stated in *The 9/11 Commission Report*. Neither of these times comes close to what appears to be the correct time of 9:32 a.m., as determined by witnesses at the scene. Multiple battery-operated wall clocks in the west corridors of the Pentagon, including the heliport near the west wall, were stopped by a violent event between 9:31 and 9:32 a.m. Military affairs journalist Barbara Honegger taped a 2002 statement from then-White House counsel Alberto Gonzales in which he stated, "The Pentagon was attacked at 9:32." This timing is critical because it appears that some events connected to the Pentagon strike occurred both before and after the now-official time of 9:37 a.m.

The continuing controversy over the Pentagon attack is the result of a simple lack of decisive evidence. One can hardly doubt that there must have been ample evidence at the actual crime scene, and so, the primary problem is that most of this evidence was removed by a variety of suspicious official actions in the wake of the attack. These include the seizing of security videos, the contents of which have never been made public, the immediate and rapid mop-up of the crime scene and the destruction of, or suppression of, nearly all the physical evidence inside the building in the days and weeks following the attack. These "pre-emptive" actions left researchers with only two types of evidence: a small number of eyewitness accounts, and post-crash photographs taken by witnesses by happenstance. Thus, although the best current theories of what happened at the Pentagon are not entirely reliable, the preponderance of the remaining evidence still casts grave doubt on the official story.

Immediately, it was noticed the lack of airplane debris at the supposed crash site. CNN's senior Pentagon correspondent Jamie McIntyre, only minutes following the Pentagon blast, reported, "From my close up inspection there's no evidence of a plane having crashed anywhere near the Pentagon....The only pieces left that you can see are small enough that you could pick up in your hand. There are no large tail sections, wing sections, fuselage—nothing like that anywhere around which would indicate that the entire plane crashed into the side of the Pentagon....It wasn't till about 45 minutes later…that all of the floors collapsed."

McIntyre's account was supported by Arlington County Fire Chief Ed Plaugher, who acknowledged that few pieces of aircraft were in evidence, just "some small pieces of aircraft…there's no fuselage sections and that sort of thing." Further support came from Maj. Gen. Albert Stubblebine, former commander of the Army's Intelligence and Security Command, who stated, "I don't know exactly what hit it [the Pentagon], but I do know, from the photographs that I have analyzed and looked at very, very carefully, it was not an airplane," and by NORAD commander, Maj. Gen. Larry Arnold, who had ordered one of his jet fighters to fly low over the west side of the Pentagon moments after the attack. According to Arnold, the pilot reported that there was no evidence a plane had struck the building.

Then there was the case of April Gallop, who served in the Network Infrastructure Services Agency as an administrative specialist inside the Pentagon's west side when it was struck on 9/11. Gallop was preparing to take her infant son to day care when an explosion rocked the building. "I thought it was a bomb," Gallop recalled. "I was buried in rubble and my first thought was for my son. I crawled around until I found his stroller. It was all crumpled up into a ball and I was then very afraid. But then I heard his voice and managed to locate him. We crawled out through a hole in the [west] side of the building. Outside they were treating survivors on the grassy lawn. But all the ambulances had left, so a man who was near the scene stepped up, put us in his private car, and drove us to the hospital. The images are burned into my brain."

Gallop, initially described by the military as a "hero," was awarded the Purple Heart for injuries sustained at the Pentagon. She said while in the hospital, men in suits visited her more than once. "They never identified themselves or even said which agency they worked for. But I know they were not newsmen because I learned that the Pentagon told news reporters not to cover survivors' stories or they would not get any more stories out of there. The men who visited all said they couldn't tell me what to say, they only wanted to make suggestions. But then they told me what to do, which was to take the [Victim Compensation Fund] money and shut up. They also kept insisting that a plane hit the building. They repeated this over and over. But I was there and I never saw a plane or even debris from a plane. I figure the plane story is there to brainwash people."

In 2008, Gallop's California attorney William Veale filed a civil suit in the US Southern District Cort of New York against former Secretary of Defense Rumsfeld, Vice President Cheney and former US Air Force General Richard Myers, acting chairman of the Joint Chiefs on 9/11. The suit, which demanded a jury trial, alleged the defendants participated in a conspiracy to facilitate the terrorist attacks by not warning those inside the Pentagon, contributing to injuries she and her two-month-old son, Elisha, incurred.

In a news release, Veale stated, "The ex-GI plaintiff alleges she has been denied government support since then, because she raised 'painful questions' about the inexplicable failure of military defenses at the Pentagon that day, and especially the failure of officials to warn and evacuate the occupants of the building when they knew the attack was imminent." He added, "What they don't want is for this to go into discovery. If we can make it past their initial motion to dismiss these claims, and we get the power of subpoena, then we've got a real shot at getting to the bottom of this. We've got the law on our side."

However, attorney Gerald A. Sterns of San Francisco law firm Sterns & Walker, which has specialized in representing victims of air crashes as well as major suits against the US Government, told Stephen C. Webster of *RAW Story*, "However we may feel about these individuals, and what impact [their story may have] had on the United States, we fear [Ms. Gallop] will be very disappointed in trying to address issues or obtain answers through the judicial process." Sterns' premonition proved correct when on March, 15, 2010, federal District Court Judge Denny Chin dismissed her case, stating, "Gallop's claims are factually baseless—indeed, because they are fanciful, fantastic and delusional."

The judge's reasoning followed the circular logic of those in denial of any alternative version to the official 9/11 story by arguing, "Even assuming the factual allegations of the complaint are true, Gallop's claims are not plausible. It is simply not plausible that the vice president of the United States, the secretary of defense, and other high-ranking officials conspired to facilitate terrorist attacks that would result in the deaths of thousands of Americans." So, even if it's true, if just not believable. It should be pointed out that beliefs are not facts. "I don't believe that" is not a legitimate argument.

WHAT REALLY HAPPENED AT THE PENTAGON?

A further rebuke to Gallop's case was made by a relative of the Bush family. Judge Chin's decision was appealed and reached the 2nd Circuit Court of Appeals where on April 27, 2011, Chin's ruling was upheld. On the three-judge panel denying Gallops appeal was Judge John Mercer Walker Jr., a first cousin of former President George Herbert Walker Bush and first cousin once removed of former President George W. Bush. Despite this clear conflict of interest, a motion to remove Walker from the case was denied. Gallop's attorney said the appeals court's decision without considering the facts of the case was analogous to an "indictment in a liquor store hold-up without mentioning the guy walking in with a gun."

Adding support to Gallop's account of no all-consuming fire at the Pentagon are photographs taken at the scene which clearly show undamaged computers, chairs, tables and filing cabinets exposed at the location of the west wall's collapse. Yet, according to the official account, the fire was so intense that it completely melted the Boeing 757 aircraft, in an immense fireball rising through the debris adjacent to this exposed office material.

Eyewitness accounts gave credence to the idea that a bomb, or bombs, may have gone off at the Pentagon about the same time that some sort of flying vehicle slammed into the same part of the building.

"A bomb had gone off. I could smell the cordite. I knew explosives had been set off somewhere," stated witness Don Perkal. Another witness, John Bowman, said, "Most people knew it was a bomb." "It smelled like cordite, or gun smoke," recalled Gilah Goldsmith while Mike Slater said, "I knew it was a bomb or something."

As reported by Honegger, many people in the Pentagon at the time of the attack believed a bomb or bombs had exploded inside the building. She reported that, oddly enough, multiple teams of K-9 bomb-sniffing dogs with handlers in camouflage were seen just outside the Pentagon about at 7:30 a.m. on September 11, 2001. One Army officer said he had never seen the bomb dogs there before or since 9/11. One early Associated Press story stated that the Pentagon had been attacked by a "booby-trapped truck."

The idea of bombs placed in the Pentagon may have focused on the objectives of the attack. An explosion destroyed the secretary of defense's hardened basement Counterterrorism Command Center. "Did the attackers know where the [war game] exercises were being run and intentionally took it out?" questioned Honegger. "If so, they would have eliminated the one place frantic officials could call to ask details of the 'game' scenarios, to try to find out what was real and what was just the games that morning." It should also be noted that the Pentagon attack killed many of the accountants and auditors who would have been tasked with tracking the missing $2.3 trillion mentioned by Rumsfeld the day before.

In a January 29, 2002 article entitled "The War on Waste," CBS News quoted Secretary of Defense Donald Rumsfeld as admitting that, "according to some estimates we cannot track $2.3 trillion in transactions." On September 10, 2001, Secretary of Defense Rumsfeld had held a press conference to announce the problem. According to CBS News, Rumsfeld said that, "the money wasted by the military poses a serious threat. In fact, it could be said it's a matter of life and death."

CBS then got to the punch line: "Rumsfeld promised change but the next day—Sept. 11—the world changed and in the rush to fund the War on Terrorism, the war on waste seems to have been forgotten."

Resource Services Washington, an office of the Army that had only recently reoccupied the west wing of the Pentagon, lost 34 of its 45 employees on 9/11. Most were civilian accountants, bookkeepers and budget analysts, the very people who would have been responsible for tracking the missing trillions. Another large segment of victims were in the Pentagon's Navy Command Center, a command-and-control facility on the first floor of the Pentagon's D-Ring.

Of further interest is the fact that Navy Lt. Kevin Shaeffer, the only survivor of the 30 persons killed in the Navy Command Center that day, after recovering from serious burns, was hired as a professional staff member of the 9/11 Commission, tasked with determining what happened in the Pentagon. "Had the Command Center not been destroyed it surely would have been able to provide the highest levels of our Navy leadership with updates as to exactly what was occurring," Shaeffer later told a Navy publication. Following the attacks of 9/11, all mention of the missing trillions dwindled to nothing in the corporate mass media.

To paint a better overall picture of what may have happened inside the Pentagon, one can join the photographic evidence by those who happened to be near the event. Unlike the World Trade Center, unaffected witnesses were around the Pentagon, some with digital cameras. One such was Steve Riskus, a 24-year-old computer worker, who said he saw the craft pass over him and strike a lamppost before plunging into the Pentagon. He immediately began snapping photographs from less than 200 yards away and later that day posted his photos on a newly acquired website. His photos, along with others not controlled by the government, caused major problems for the later official version of the Pentagon crash.

They depicted a clean green lawn in front of the damaged wall, which contradicted the official claim that the plane hit the ground before entering the building. They also showed one highway lamppost knocked down but not others nearby it well within range of the plane's wingspan.

One website even posted numerous official photos of the Pentagon crash and challenged viewers to find any trace of the aircraft. Interestingly enough, years after 9/11 neither the mass media nor the FBI had taken any notice of Riskus's pictures or the questions being raised. It is well worth noting here that the FBI confiscated all the security videos in the vicinity of the crash within minutes; somewhat later, the Pentagon released a mere five frames from one of these videos, which show a barely discernible object slamming into the building followed by a huge fireball.

The major mystery in regard to the Pentagon crash centers on what exactly happened to American Flight 77, a Boeing 757 carrying a mere 64 passengers. According to official sources, the entire plane was consumed inside the walls of the Pentagon.

To date, no one had produced any photographs of Boeing 757 fuselage, jet engines, seats, luggage, or other recognizable debris. Even the familiar photo of a small piece of red and white painted fuselage on the Pentagon lawn has been called into question because it does not appear in the very first photos of that area. This one small piece of red, white, and silver metal widely distributed by the major news media has never been firmly identified as coming from a Boeing 757. This now-famous mystery item, categorized as a fake by some foreign press, simply does not appear in any of the pictures taken within the first half hour of the Pentagon attack. Many researchers believe this evidence was planted at a later time.

Several photos of what appears to be part of a jet engine cannot be matched with the 757 engine, but more like that of a missile jet engine.

The initial version of the official story claimed that Flight 77 was entirely consumed by fires raging inside the Pentagon. But this version was called into question when the FBI announced it was able to identify passengers by their fingerprints. The fires were hot enough to incinerate metal airplane parts but not hot enough to destroy human tissue?

This non sequitur resulted in FBI spokesman Chris Murray later announcing, "The pieces of the plane are stocked in a warehouse and they are marked with the serial numbers of Flight 77."

Murray's announcement seemed reasonable, as after any major air disaster, every fragment of the aircraft is re-assembled to learn the cause and prevent any reoccurrence. But then this prompts the question: In addition to all the other suppressed evidence at the scene, why has no one within the government produced any photograph of the wreckage of Flight 77? Although such photographs could not prove where the wreckage came from, wouldn't this put an end to the theories regarding no plane hitting the Pentagon?

Then there are the startling problems with the holes in the Pentagon. The Boeing 757 has a normal wingspan of 124 feet, 10 inches. The official version of the Pentagon crash states that a 757 entered the building at a 45-degree angle. This angle would increase the wingspan to 177 feet. Note that the overall height of a 757 is 44 feet, 6 inches and the exterior body width is 12 feet, 6 inches. Yet the hole in the Pentagon cited as the entry point, photographed before the walls collapsed, was only between 15 and 20 feet wide, barely enough to accommodate the width of the craft's body. And the hole's height was less then two stories or about 20 feet, *less than half the height of the 757*. Even after the walls collapsed shortly after 10 a.m., the gaping hole in the building was still not large enough to accommodate the Boeing 757's wingspan. Oddly, no evidence of any kind of the plane's wings or tail were found outside the building, other than the small piece of metal mentioned earlier.

Francois Grangier, a French aviation accident investigator, hoping to defend the official version, studied the Pentagon crash carefully but was forced to conclude, "I think the trajectory as far as one can make it out today rules out an impact against the façade...What is certain when one looks at the photo of this façade that remains intact is that it's obvious the plane did not go through there. It's like imagining that a plane of this size could pass through a window and leave the frame still standing."

Just as strange were photographs depicting what officials said was the exit hole caused by the plane as it completed its penetration of the Pentagon. This hole, located on the inside of the building's fourth ring, is barely more than eight feet high; it shows only slight scorching at the top and even unbroken window panes immediately above it. It is most peculiar that the front of a Boeing 757, lacking density in its aluminum-sheathed nose, could have survived the penetration of four hardened concrete walls, while leaving no known remnants behind. The official story claims that 1500-degree heat caused by the crash was intense enough to immolate the entire plane and occupants. One wonders why the walls to either side of this exit hole are not scorched.

One possible explanation for both the smallness of the craft and the hole blasted in the wall of the Pentagon came from Samuel Danner, a 53-year-old electrical engineer for Amtrak and a pilot since age 16.

In an interview with reporter Christopher Bollyn made public on several Internet sites, Danner said he stopped his car on the shoulder of the highway when he saw a craft approaching the Pentagon. He also saw "a bunch of guys" standing outside the Pentagon looking through binoculars. Danner said he got a good view of the craft as it approached and that it definitely was not a Boeing 757. "No way," said Danner. "It was like a humpback whale..." He described this craft as having one engine on the backside with a V-shaped tail and no windows that he could see. He said it was very quiet and going about 400 miles per hour. Overhead, Danner said he saw another airplane, which he now believes may have controlled the craft that hit the Pentagon. Following an explosion at the Pentagon, Danner ran to help. He said he saw no bodies from the craft and no wreckage from a Boeing 757. He did smell cordite [an explosive] and saw a three-foot single engine on the ground.

From Danner's description it would appear the craft may have been a Global Hawk drone aircraft used by the US military for reconnaissance missions. It has been noted that two Global Hawk unmanned vehicles were missing from the military's inventory at the time of Pentagon attack. See the chapter entitled "Were the Hijacked Planes Remotely Controlled?"

Danner said he was later diagnosed with lymphoma cancer which he believes may have resulted from exposure to depleted uranium (DU) used in a missile fired just ahead of the Global Hawk craft. Depleted uranium is used by the US military to penetrate hardened targets such as bunkers and concrete emplacements. It has been claimed that traces of DU were found at the Pentagon and photographs taken later that day do depict workers wearing protective gear. Danner said his observations that day had been "bugging" him and that he decided to speak publicly after seeing one of the numerous videos challenging the official story of the 9/11 attacks.

While several witnesses, such as Army Captain Lincoln Liebner, said they distinctly saw an American Airlines jetliner coming toward the Pentagon swiftly and at low altitude, others were not so certain.

Steve Patterson, who worked from his home in Pentagon City, told the *Washington Post* that day, he saw a "silver commuter jet" fly past the window of his 14th-floor apartment about 150 yards away. He said it was approaching from the west about 20 feet off the ground and appeared to be a small commuter plane. "The airplane seemed to be able to hold between eight or twelve persons," Patterson said.

A 33-year-old network engineer at the Pentagon, Tom Seibert, said, "We heard something that made the sound of a missile, then we heard a powerful boom."

On Sept. 11, 2001 *USA Today* employee Mike Walter excitedly told CNN, "A plane, a plane from American Airlines. I thought, 'That's not right, it's really low.' And I saw it. I mean, it was like a cruise missile with wings." Much later Walter changed his story emphatically stating that he saw the plane strike the building and its wings folded back which explained the small hole. However, video made from Walter's viewing poin on North Hwy 27 show that a line of trees blocks the line of sight.

Dulles air traffic controller Danielle O'Brien told ABC News, "The speed, the maneuverability, the way that he turned, we all thought in the radar room, all of us experienced air traffic controllers, that that was a military plane. You don't fly a 757 in that manner. It's unsafe."

O'Brien's perceptions were accurate. For whatever plunged toward the Pentagon—reportedly starting 7,000 feet above the ground—was piloted in such a way that it dropped in a downward spiral, forming an almost complete circle in just more than two minutes. This is an extremely difficult maneuver for the even the most experienced pilot. We've already noted that it is exceedingly unlikely that the Haji Hanjour, the alleged hijacker pilot of Flight 77, could have accomplished this miracle of piloting.

The speed, maneuverability, and the high-pitched scream of the jet coupled with the smallness of the hole prompted many researchers to suggest that what struck the Pentagon was nothing less than some sort of winged missile painted to resemble an American Airlines plane.

Could this be why Defense Secretary Donald Rumsfeld inadvertently mentioned a "missile" when describing the Pentagon attack to *Parade* magazine? In an October 2001 interview, Rumsfeld was quoted as saying, "It is a truth that a terrorist can attack any time, any place, using any technique and it's physically impossible to defend at every time and every place against every conceivable technique. Here we're talking about plastic knives and using an American Airlines flight filed with our citizens, and the missile to damage this building [the Pentagon] and similar (inaudible) that damaged the World Trade Center."

Supporting the hypothesis of a missile attack are the recent discoveries by Honegger that NORAD commander, Maj. Gen. Larry Arnold, had ordered one of his interceptors to buzz the west side of the Pentagon moments after the attack. attack. As previously mentioned, the pilot reported, he could see no evidence that a plane had struck the building.

"The likely reason the Pentagon has refused to lower the currently-official time of Flight 77 impact from 9:37 to 9:32—the actual time of the first explosions there—is that they decided to pretend the blip represented by Arnold's surveillance jet approaching just before 9:37 was Flight 77," Honegger concluded. "As the Official Cover Story claims that the alleged 9:37 impact was the only Pentagon attack that morning, and by the time Arnold's surveillance jet arrived on the scene the violent event had already happened, the Pentagon cannot acknowledge the earlier 9:32 attack time without revealing that there was an attack on the building prior to impact."(See Appendix for more details.)

Then there are the disturbing statements, noted earlier, of another high government official. Testifying under oath before the 9/11 Commission in mid-2003, Transportation Secretary Norman Mineta gave a revealing account of his experiences on the morning of 9/11. After joining Vice President Cheney and others in the White House Presidential Emergency Operating Center shortly after the South Tower of the WTC had been struck, at about 9:20 a.m., Mineta recalled: "During the time that the airplane was coming in to the Pentagon, there was a young man who would come in and say to the Vice President, 'The plane is 50 miles out.' 'The plane is 30 miles out.' And when it got down to 'the plane is 10 miles out,' the young man also said to the Vice President, 'Do the orders still stand?' And the Vice President turned and whipped his neck around and said, 'Of course the orders still stand! Have you heard anything to the contrary?' Well at the time, I didn't know what all that meant...[This was the] flight that came into the Pentagon..."

Asked if these "orders" were to shoot down the errant airliners, Mineta responded, "Well, I don't know that specifically. I do know that the [interceptor] airplanes were scrambled from Langley or from Norfolk, the Norfolk area, and so I did not know about the order specifically other than to listen to that other conversation...Subsequently, I found that out."

Commission vice chairman Lee Hamilton then asked, "But there were military planes in the air in position to shoot down commercial aircraft?" "That's right," replied Mineta. "The planes had been scrambled, I believe from Otis, at that point." The strange conversation between Cheney and the "young man" as related by Mineta prompts several puzzling questions. What were these orders? And if the orders were to shoot down captured airliners as later stated by the White House, why weren't they carried out?

And, if fighter jets could not reach the Pentagon in time, what about the antiaircraft missile batteries in place around Washington—indeed, just adjacent to the Pentagon itself? Such batteries are automatically activated whenever an aircraft enters restricted airspace without sending out a "friendly" transponder code signal.

Amazingly enough, the final report of the commission, in order to construct its official story, entirely omitted Secretary of Transportation Norman Mineta's testimony given to the commission itself that Cheney and others in the underground shelter were aware at least by 9:20 a.m. that an aircraft was approaching the Pentagon. Despite evidence to the contrary from Mineta and other eyewitnesses, the commission would have us believe that no one in the US military knew that Flight 77 was incoming toward the Pentagon until a few minutes before the official time of the impact, 9:37 a.m., a disputed time.

In fact, the commission goes further, even claiming against all the evidence that Cheney did not reach this underground shelter until nearly 10 a.m. that morning. In his study of *The 9/11 Commission Report*, David Ray Griffin states that this denial "is probably the feature of the 9/11 Commission's case that is the most patently false."

## WHAT REALLY HAPPENED AT THE PENTAGON?

While researchers have hunted fruitlessly for a stand-down order issued from within the administration to explain the lack of effective response on 9/11, it may be that such orders were much more mundane—a simple matter of slightly changing standard NORAD procedures.

Prior to June 2001, under Department of Defense directives, while the secretary of defense retained approval authority for the release of military jets to support civil air authorities, they also provided that "Nothing in this Directive prevents a commander from exercising his or her immediate emergency response authority..." and that "Requests for an immediate response (i.e., any form of immediate action taken by a DoD Component or military commander to save lives, prevent human suffering, or mitigate great property damage under imminently serious conditions) may be made to any Component or Command. The DoD Components...may initiate informal planning and, if required, immediately respond as authorized in DoD Directive 3025.1 (reference (g))." In other words, in the event of an air emergency, local commanders could initiate a response pending later approval of the secretary of defense.

This all changed on June 1, 2001, with the issuance of Chairman of the Joint Chiefs of Staff Instruction [CJCSI] 3610.01A. Under the heading, "Aircraft Piracy (Hijacking) of Civil and Military Aircraft," this document states, "the NMCC [National Military Command Center] is the focal point within the Department of Defense for providing assistance. In the event of a hijacking, the NMCC will, with the exception of immediate responses as authorized by referenced, *forward requests for DoD assistance to the Secretary of Defense for approval* [emphasis added]."

"Secretary of Defense [Donald] Rumsfeld is personally responsible for issuing intercept orders," surmised Internet writer Jerry Russell. "Commanders in the field are stripped of all authority to act...it is now clear that [any 'stand-down' order] was implemented through a routine administrative memo."

Of course, if Flight 77 did not hit the Pentagon, even more questions arise. What happened to the plane and its passengers? Did it cross into Washington air space before a missile was sent into the Pentagon? Was it ditched into the Atlantic as suggested by some? Was a missile or plane guided from an external location as will be discussed later?

All such conjecture could be ended by simply showing the public the wreckage of the aircraft. But 10 years on, no such photos have been forthcoming.

Finally, there is the question of motive. Why would anyone want to risk attacking the Pentagon, undoubtedly the world's strongest and most protected structure? Some particularly conspiratorial researchers have suggested that the Pentagon was struck to satisfy more than one agenda—first, the most casualties suffered were the accountants and auditors who would have been tasked to account for the missing $2.3 trillion and secondly, an attack on the Pentagon would have successfully deflected any suspicion of military involvement in the planning and execution of the 9/11 attacks.

It might be mentioned here that the Pentagon's undersecretary of defense and comptroller during the time of the missing trillions was Dov Zakheim. According to *Online Journal* associate editor Jerry Mazza, Zakheim carries dual citizenship with both the United States and Israel, is an ordained rabbi and a member of the Council on Foreign Relations. Zakheim also served as CEO of SPS International, part of System Planning Corporation, a defense contractor majoring in electronic warfare technologies, which included remote-controlled aircraft systems including the Flight Termination System (FTS) technology that could remotely capture an airliner's on-board computer and guide it to a crash or landing regardless of the desires of the crew or hijackers. He was a co-author of the Project for the New American Century's position paper, *Rebuilding America's Defenses*, which stated a "new Pearl Harbor" was necessary for galvanizing the American public into accepting the neo-con's agenda for the Middle East.

Intriguing connections such as Zakheim's along with myriad unanswered questions continued to grow in the wake of the 9/11 tragedies, with the strange case of the Pentagon attack being among the most puzzling of all. Even many researchers within the 9/11 truth community continue to disagree on the interpretations of the few useful facts available.

## EXPLOSIONS AT THE WORLD TRADE CENTER

The public might know more of what really happened to the World Trade Center if the New York Police Department and New York Fire Department had been allowed to do their jobs. But, as with the JFK assassination, their work was taken from them by federal officials, who immediately closed off the crime scene and shut out both the public and local authorities from their consultations. People were even arrested for taking photographs of Ground Zero.

The FBI took charge of the criminal investigation while the little-understood Federal Emergency Management Agency (FEMA), an agency created and controlled by the president, took responsibility for determining what happened to cause the collapse of the Twin Towers. FEMA seemed determined to haul away the evidence, even before a full and impartial investigation could be made. Such premature destruction of evidence was called into question by Bill Manning, editor of the 125-year-old firemen's publication *Fire Engineering* in its January 2002 issue.

"For more than three months, structural steel from the World Trade Center has been and continues to be cut up and sold for scrap," wrote Manning. "Did they throw away the locked doors from the Triangle Shirtwaist Fire? Did they throw away the gas can used at the Happyland Social Club Fire? Did they cast aside the pressure-regulating valves at the Meridian Plaza Fire? Of course not. But essentially, that's what they're doing at the World Trade Center.

"For more than three months, structural steel from the World Trade Center has been and continues to be cut up and sold for scrap. Crucial evidence that could answer many questions about high-rise building design practices and performance under fire conditions is on the slow boat to China, perhaps never to be seen again in America until you buy your next car."

Challenging the theory that the Twin Towers collapsed as a result of crashed airplanes and fires, Manning added, "*Fire Engineering* has good reason to believe that the 'official investigation' blessed by FEMA and run by the American Society of Civil Engineers (ASCE) is a half-baked farce that may already have been commandeered by political forces whose primary interests, to put it mildly, lie far afield of full disclosure.

"Except for the marginal benefit obtained from a three-day, visual walk-through of evidence sites conducted by the ASCE investigation committee members—described by one close source as a 'tourist trip'—no one's checking the evidence for anything. The destruction and removal of evidence must stop immediately," Manning declared.

In that same issue, a number of fire officials, including a retired deputy chief from New York's fire department, called on FEMA to "immediately impanel a 'World Trade Center Disaster Review Panel' to coordinate a complete review of all aspects of the World Trade Center incident."

These fire officials noted that the WTC disaster was the largest loss of firefighters ever at one incident; the second largest loss of life on American soil; the first total collapse of a high-rise during a fire in United States history; and the largest structural collapse in recorded history.

"Now, with that understanding, you would think we would have the largest fire investigation in world history," they wrote. "You would be wrong. Instead, we have a series of unconnected and uncoordinated superficial inquiries...Ironically, we will probably gain more detailed information about the destruction of the planes than we will about the destruction of the towers. We are literally treating the steel removed from the site like garbage, not like crucial fire scene evidence." Complaints from the federal investigating team of engineers supported these accusations.

Citing delays by federal agencies and incomplete information, the twenty-six member team of ASCE engineers that was formed to study the collapse of the WTC towers finally produced a 296-page report by early May 2002. But even as the report was issued, team leader and structural engineer Dr. W. Gene Corley told Congress there were still many questions left unanswered by his study. "We didn't have time and resources," Corley complained. It should be noted that in 1995, Corley was selected to lead a Building Performance Assessment Team investigating the bombing of the Alfred P. Murrah Federal Building in Oklahoma City, a tragedy, which has also generated much controversy and speculation among conspiracy researchers.

Corley said his team didn't have enough data to create a computer model of the interior damage caused by the aircraft, nor could they model the spread of the fires. The team also griped that federal agencies feuded over funding and to whom the team should be reporting.

The team never had access to 911 emergency calls, which could have helped determine exactly what happened in the minutes prior to the collapse of the buildings, and—this can not be emphasized enough—they confirmed reports that much of the structural steel was removed from the site, cut up, and sold as scrap before they had a chance to examine it.

The team could not even obtain a complete set of building plans until early in 2002. Then they found that floor supports were attached to exterior columns by strong welds and not, as initially believed and widely reported, relatively small bolts.

The hurried and superficial nature of the FEMA inquiry was evident in the conclusion of its report: "With the information and time available, the sequence of events leading to the collapse of each tower could not be definitively determined." Corley did say the team learned just enough to know that more answers were desperately needed to design protective measures for similar structures that might be future terrorist targets.

Another valid issue was raised by Dr. Judy Wood, who noted, "The Twin Towers together had an estimated 30,000 computers for nearly 50,000 workers. So, 45,000 filing cabinets would not be an unreasonable estimate. It is reported that 200 complete bodies were recovered out of the nearly 3,000 victims, which is about 1/15th. At the same ratio, we would expect 3,000 complete filing cabinets of the 45,000 should have survived intact. Yet only one shrunken filing cabinet was reportedly found."

The quest for more answers coupled with congressional outrage over the obstacles thrown in front of Corley's engineering team prompted President Bush to pledge $16 million for a follow-up study by the National Institute of Standards and Technology (NIST). NIST's National Construction Safety Team (NCST), after more than a year of administrative and organizational activity, finally announced in early 2004 that a draft report on the World Trade Center disaster might be "realistic and achievable" by September 2004. The final reported was issued only in November 2008.

A good portion of the NIST team's effort went to study the February 20, 2003, West Warwick, Rhode Island, nightclub fire, which claimed one hundred lives and apparently their $16 million budget was taxed. In an initial report to Congress in December 2003, the group complained of the "recurring problem" of insufficient staff for on-site inspections and subsequent research and tests. "The scale and complexity of the current World Trade Center disaster has strained NIST's existing resources," they reported.

They did, however, recommend the creation of a NIST Building and Fire Research Laboratory with a permanent staff funded for $2 million, the establishment of a safety team investigation reserve fund for another

$2 million, the establishment of a program to "familiarize local and state investigating authorities about the NCST Act, and a "research program investigating the factors affecting human decision making and evacuation behavior during emergencies in buildings."

The report echoed complaints from the FEMA engineering team by stating the group's major challenges were lack of data ("through most of 2003, significant gaps existed in the data collection related to almost all of the project areas.") and the future need to deploy safety teams immediately to an incident for the collection of physical evidence and witness testimony. The NIST inquiry also declined to hear testimony from New York firemen or building engineers despite repeated efforts on their part to contact the panel.

Therefore, the large gaps left in the official record of the WTC collapses have been forced to be filled in by others. Perhaps the best information that we now have about the collapses of the towers comes from independent researchers—most notably from a growing list of courageous scientists and academics noted earlier, whose names can be found listed at the website Scholars for 911 Truth, Scholars for 9/11 Truth & Justice as well as Architects & Engineers for 9/11 Truth.

Observers have long noted that the physical characteristics of the collapses of the two towers were almost identical. That has permitted physicist and pioneer critic of the official story, Jim Hoffman, to compile the list below that describes principal features of the destruction of both towers. These observations are based on intensive independent study of the surviving evidence, as contrasted with the "official" explanation of a gravity collapse caused by fire. One can easily see that critical mysteries about the towers' collapse remain unsolved, in large part due to the destruction of evidence and the under-funded inadequate investigations that followed.

1. *The cores of the towers were obliterated and the perimeter walls were shredded.* According to Hoffman, "there is no gravity collapse scenario" or probable explanation by fire that can account for the complete leveling of the 47 massive columns that comprised the towers' cores, or the ripping apart of their sturdy perimeter walls. But if not, what scenario does explain this?

2. *Nearly all the concrete was pulverized in the air, so finely that it blanketed parts of lower Manhattan with inches of dust.* In a gravity collapse, according to Hoffman, "there would not have been enough energy to pulverize the concrete until it hit the ground, if then." With regard to this observation, the crucial unanswered question becomes: How then was it possible for the non-metallic components of the buildings to turn to dust as fine as flour—and further, which begin to appear so massively at the very outset of the collapse? Independent scientists cited by Hoffman in a highly technical paper have shown that the energy required for the pulverization of this much concrete and for the stupendous expansion of the dust clouds is as much as "100 times greater than could have been produced from each tower's gravitational potential energy" (i.e., mass times height).
3. *Parts of the towers were thrown up to 500 feet laterally.* Hoffman: "The downward forces of a gravity collapse cannot account for the energetic lateral ejection of pieces." But what forces caused these lateral explosions?
4. *Explosions were visible before many floors had collapsed.* "But in the South Tower collapse," writes Hoffman, "energetic dust ejections are first seen while the top is only slightly tipping, not falling." Compression pressure therefore cannot account for this ejected dust. Numerous eye-witness reports of explosions in the buildings have already been recounted.
5. *The towers' tops mushroomed into thick dust clouds much larger than the original volumes of the buildings.* "Without the addition of large sources of pressure beyond the collapse itself," claims Hoffman, "the falling building and its debris should have occupied about the same volume as the intact building." Some observers compared these pyroclastic clouds with those seen in nuclear explosions.
6. *The tops of the towers fell at nearly the rate of free fall, in less than fifteen seconds.* "We've examined this previously. These astounding rates of fall, according to Hoffman's technical explanation, "indicate that nearly all resistance to the

downward acceleration of the tops had been eliminated ahead of them. The forms of resistance, had the collapses been gravity-driven, would include: the destruction of the structural integrity of each storey; the pulverization of the concrete in the floor slabs of each storey, and other non-metallic objects; and the acceleration of the remains of each storey encountered either outward or downward. There would have to be enough energy to overcome all of these forms of resistance and do it rapidly enough to keep up with the near free-fall acceleration of the top."

The issue of the cause of the collapse of the towers has become so salient that one wealthy American activist, Jimmy Walter, has offered a one million dollar reward to anyone who can prove that explosives were not used in the World Trade Center. Walter has gained notoriety and headlines by his efforts—costing him millions—to educate ordinary Americans and Europeans about the possibility that 9/11 is an inside job.

Concerns over the validity of the free-fall scenario based on fires in the buildings were echoed by former Bush I administration official Morgan Reynolds, a Texas A & M professor emeritus of economics, who was also former chief economist for the Department of Labor and former director of the Criminal Justice Center at the National Center for Policy Analysis. Reynolds is also a leading member of scholarsfor911truth.org.

"Only professional demolition appears to account for the full range of facts associated with the collapses of WTC 1 (North Tower), WTC 2 (South Tower), and the much-overlooked collapse of the 47-story WTC Building 7 at 5:21 p.m. on that fateful day," wrote Reynolds. He added, "Controlled demolition would have required unimpeded access to the WTC, access to explosives, avoiding detection, and the expertise to orchestrate the deadly destruction from a nearby secure location. Such access before 9/11 likely depended on complicity by one or more WTC security companies." His detailed analysis of both the World Trade Center collapses and the Pentagon strike may be found at www.lewrockwell.com/reynolds/reynolds12.html.

Reynolds also speculated on why WTC Building 7 was brought down later on 9/11. "Why would the killers destroy WTC 7, especially since a collapse would arouse suspicion in some quarters?" he asked. "A logical if unproven theory is that the perpetrators used Mayor Giuliani's sealed OEM [Office of Emergency Management] 'bunker' on the 23rd story of WTC 7 to conduct the Twin Tower implosions and then destroyed the building and evidence to cover up their crimes, just as a murderer might set his victim's dwelling ablaze to cover up the crime (one in four fires is arson). Giuliani's 'undisclosed secret location' was perfect because it had been evacuated by 9:45 a.m. on 9/11, it enabled unmolested work, provided a ringside seat, was bullet- and bomb-resistant, had its own secure air and water supply, and could withstand winds of 160 mph, necessary protection from the wind blasts generated by collapsing skyscrapers."

The professor also joined the chorus of criticism leveled at FEMA officials for the rapid removal of WTC debris which prevented later study. "The criminal code requires that crime scene evidence be saved for forensic analysis but FEMA had it destroyed before anyone could seriously investigate it," stated Reynolds. "FEMA was in position to take command because it had arrived the day before the attacks at New York's Pier 29 to conduct a war game exercise, 'Tripod II,' quite a coincidence. The authorities apparently considered the rubble quite valuable: New York City officials had every debris truck tracked on GPS and had one truck driver who took an unauthorized one-and-a-half hour lunch fired."

Responding to the question of why controlled demolitions have never been considered by the official government investigations of 9/11, Reynolds said, "If demolition destroyed three steel skyscrapers at the World Trade Center on 9/11, then the case for an 'inside job' and a government attack on America would be compelling."

Several experts and numerous independent observers, including news anchors, viewed did the destruction of the World Trade Center towers as more more like a controlled implosion than terrorist-caused destruction. Former wrestler and Minnesota Governor Jesse Ventura, host of a popular cable show entitled *Conspiracy Theory*, in 2008 stated, "I did watch the film of Building 7 going down and in my opinion, there is no doubt that that building was brought down with demolition." It is important to note that Ventura formerly served as a member of the Navy SEAL's Underwater Demolition Team, extensively trained in the use of explosives.

On the morning of the 9/11 attacks, CBS's Dan Rather, in an interview with Jerome Hauer, then director of the Office of Public Health Preparedness, "Based on what you know, and I recognize we're dealing with so few facts, is it possible that just a plane crash could have collapsed these buildings, or would it have required the, sort of, prior positioning of other explosives in the, uh, in the buildings? I mean, what do you think?" Hauer responded with a concise explanation which matched that of the subsequent official explanation, "No, I, uh, my sense is just the velocity of the plane and the fact that you have a plane filled with fuel hitting that building, uh, that burned, uh, the velocity of that plane, uh, certainly, uh, uh, had an impact on the structure itself, and then the fact that it burned and you had that intense heat, uh, probably weakened the structure as well, uh, and I think it, uh, was, uh, simply the, uh, the planes hitting the buildings, and, and causing the collapse."

It might be noted that until 2000 Hauer was director of Rudy Giuliani's Office of Emergency Management and a managing director of Kroll Associates, then in charge of security for the World Trade Center complex. It was in his capacity as a public health official that Hauer advised the Bush White House to begin taking the anti-anthrax drug Cipro more than a week prior to the anthrax mail attacks that followed the events of 9/11.

Both North and South Towers had 47 core columns made of steel with 236 steel columns around the outer perimeter, for a total of 566 columns. Explosives would have been required at each column to bring down the building by conventional controlled demolition. This would not have been a small undertaking.

Such questions concerning the collapse of the towers also were immediately advanced by experts in demolition and firefighting, only to die away in the subsequent media blitz of "official" pronouncements. Many people, experts and laymen alike, also asked why the South Tower collapsed first when it was not as extensively damaged as the North Tower, which burned for almost an hour and a half before its collapse?

Numerous sources have claimed that bombs rather than the planes caused the collapse of the World Trade Center towers.

Van Romero, vice president for research at the New Mexico Institute of Mining and Technology and a former director of the Energetic Materials Research and Testing Center said televised images of the collapse of the WTC towers suggested that explosives were used to create a controlled demolition.

"My opinion is, based on the videotapes, that after the airplanes hit the World Trade Center there were some explosive devices inside the buildings that caused the towers to collapse," Romero told the *Albuquerque Journal* on September 11, 2001.

Romero, who ironically was in the Washington area during the 9/11 attacks attempting to gain government funding for defense research at his school, said the collapse of the WTC was "too methodical" to be the chance result of airplanes colliding with the structures. He said it appeared more like the controlled implosions used to demolish old buildings.

"It could have been a relatively small amount of explosives placed in strategic points," he said, adding that the detonation of bombs within towers is consistent with common terrorist strategy. "One of the things terrorist events are noted for is a diversionary attack and secondary device. Attackers detonate an initial, diversionary explosion that attracts emergency personnel to the scene, then detonate a second explosion," he explained.

Within 10 days, Romero reversed himself, telling the *Albuquerque Journal* that following conversations with "other experts" he came to understand that "Certainly the fire is what caused the building to fail." He did concede that the final collapse may have been caused when fire reached an electrical transformer or other source of combustion within the building, leaving open the question of explosions. There was no word of whether or not New Mexico Tech received its federal funding requests although in 2010 the school now provides provide counterterrorism training to firemen, policemen, and first responders in courses entitled "Incident Response to Teroristic Bombings" and "Prevention and Response to Suicide Bombing Incidents."

Many have wondered about the witnesses who claimed to have heard multiple explosions within the buildings. One such witness was the head of WTC security, John O'Neill, who stated shortly before he himself became a victim that he had helped dig out survivors on the 27th floor before the building collapsed. Since the aircraft crashed into the 80th floor, what heavily damaged the 27th floor?

Another of those mentioning bombs was Louie Cacchioli, a fifty-one-year-old fireman assigned to Engine 47 in Harlem. "We were the first ones in the second tower after the plane struck," recalled Cacchioli. "I was taking firefighters up in the elevator to the twenty-fourth floor to get in position to evacuate workers. On the last trip up a bomb went off. We think there were bombs set in the building." The fireman became trapped in an elevator but managed to escape with the use of tools.

Cacchioli claimed he was misquoted. In later years, he cooperated with the editors of Popular Mechanics who published *Debunking 9/11 Myths: Why Conspiracy Theories Can't Stand Up to the Facts*, and gave guided tours of Ground Zero.

But FDNY Auxiliary Lt. Paul Isaac, Jr. also mentioned bombs, telling Internet reporter Randy Lavello that New York firemen were very upset by what they considered a cover-up in the WTC destruction. "Many other firemen know there were bombs in the buildings," he said, "but they are afraid for their jobs to admit it because the higher-ups forbid discussion of this fact." Isaac, who was stationed at Engine 10 near the WTC in the late 1990s, said the higher-ups included the FDNY's antiterrorism consultant, James Woolsey, a former CIA director. "There were definitely bombs in those buildings," Isaac added.

Other firemen also supported the idea of multiple explosions in the towers. Their testimonies came from 503 oral histories recorded by the New York Fire Department in late 2001. The tapes were of both fire personnel and emergency medical workers. The city had refused to release the tapes until ordered to do so by the New York Court of Appeals acting on a suit filed jointly by the *New York Times* and several 9/11 victims' families. They were publicly released in August 2005, only lightly covered by the mass media and remain largely unknown to most Americans. In these unpublicized histories, more than 100 New York firemen reported multiple explosions at the Word Trade Center. None of these persons were mentioned in *The 9/11 Commission Report*.

Comments in these tapes, some of which were edited, related to the possibility of controlled demolitions in the WTC. These included:

FDNY Captain Dennis Tardio: "I hear an explosion and I look up [at the South Tower]. It is as if the building is being imploded from the top floor down, one after another, boom, boom, boom."

New Jersey Fire Police Officer Sue Keane: "[I]t sounded like bombs going off [in the South Tower]. That's when the explosions happened…I knew something was going to happen…It started to get dark, then all of a sudden there was this massive explosion…[In the North Tower] another explosion. That sent me and the two firefighters [with her] down the stairs...I can't tell you how many times I got banged around. Each one of those explosions picked me up and threw me...There was another explosion and I got thrown with two firefighters out onto the street."

FDNY Battalion Chief John Sudnik: "[W]e heard a loud explosion or what sounded like a loud explosion and looked up and I saw Tower Two start coming down."

FDNY EMS Paramedic Daniel Rivera, "At first I thought it was—do you ever see professional demolition where they set the charges on certain floors and then you hear, 'Pop, pop, pop, pop, pop'? That's exactly what—because I thought it was that. When I heard that frigging noise, that's when I saw the building coming down."

FDNY Assistant Commissioner Stephen Gregory: "I thought...before... [Tower] No. 2 came down that I saw low-level flashes...Lieutenant Evangelista...asked me if I saw low-level flashes in front of the building and I agreed with him because I...saw a flash, flash, flash...[at] the lower level of the building. You know, like when they demolish a building, how when they blow up a building, when it falls down? That what I thought I saw."

FDNY Captain Karin Deshore: "Somewhere around the middle of the World Trade Center, there was this orange and red flash coming out. Initially, it was just one flash...Then this flash just kept popping all the way around the building and that building had started to explode. The popping sound and with each popping sound it was initially an orange and then a red flash came out of the building and then it would just go all around the building on both sides as far as I could see. These popping sounds and the explosions were getting bigger, going both up and down and then all around the building."

FDNY Deputy Commissioner Thomas Fitzpatrick: "We looked up at the [South Tower]...All we saw was a puff of smoke coming from about two-thirds of the way up...It looked like sparkling around one specific layer of the building...My initial reaction was that this was exactly the way it looks when they show you those [building] implosions on TV."

FDNY Firefighter Christopher Fenyo: "At that point [the collapse of the South Tower], a debate began to rage because many people had felt that possible explosives had taken out 2 World Trade and officers were gathering companies together and the officers were debating whether or not to go immediately back in or to see what was going to happen with 1 World Trade [the North Tower] at that point. The debate ended pretty quickly because 1 World Trade came down."

Survivor Teresa Veliz, manager for a software development company, was on the 47th floor of the North Tower when it was struck. "I got off [the elevator], turned the corner and opened the door to the ladies' room. I said good morning to a lady sitting at a mirror when the whole building shook. I thought it was an earthquake. Then I heard those banging noises on the other side of the wall. It sounded like someone had cut the elevator cables. It just fell and fell and fell."

Veliz reached ground level with a coworker when the South Tower collapsed, knocking them down. In near total darkness, she and the coworker followed someone with a flashlight. "The flashlight led us into Borders bookstore, up an escalator and out to Church Street. There were explosions going off everywhere. I was convinced that there were bombs planted all over the place and someone was sitting at a control panel pushing detonator buttons. I was afraid to go down Church Street toward Broadway, but I had to do it. I ended up on Vesey Street. There was another explosion. And another. I didn't know which way to run."

Ross Milanytch watched the horror at the WTC from his office window on the 22nd floor of a building a couple of blocks away. "[I saw] small explosions on each floor. And after it all cleared, all that was left of the buildings, you could just see the steel girders in like a triangular sail shape. The structure was just completely gone," he said.

John Bussey, a reporter for the *Wall Street Journal*, watched the collapse of the South Tower from the ninth floor of the newspaper's office building. "I...looked up out of the office window to see what seemed like perfectly synchronized explosions coming from each floor.... One after the other. From top to bottom, with a fraction of a second between, the floors flew to pieces."

WNYC Radio's Beth Fertig was on the scene and reported, "It just descended like a timed explosion—like when they are deliberately bringing a building down...It was coming down so perfectly that in one part of my brain I was thinking, 'They got everyone out, and they're bringing the building down because they have to.'"

Fox 5 News in New York City, shortly after 10 a.m. on September

11, videotaped a large white cloud of smoke billowing near the base of the South Tower. The commentator exclaimed, "There is an explosion at the base of the building…white smoke from the bottom…something has happened at the base of the building…then, another explosion. Another building in the World Trade Center complex…"

This view was supported by Steve Evans, a reporter for the BBC, who was in the South Tower at the time of the attacks. "I was at the base of the second tower, the second tower that was hit," he recalled. "There was an explosion—I didn't think it was an explosion—but the base of the building shook. I felt it shake…then when we were outside, the second explosion happened and then there was a series of explosions.… We can only wonder at the kind of damage—the kind of human damage—which was caused by those explosions, those series of explosions."

The most compelling testimony came from Tom Elliott, who was already in his office at Aon Corp. on the 103rd floor of the WTC South Tower before the planes struck. Elliott said he was at his computer answering emails when a bright light startled him shortly before 9 a.m. A rumble shook the building and he could see flames accompanied by dark smoke that appeared to be crawling up the outside of the building. He also felt heat coming through the windows. Strangely, there were no alarms.

"I don't know what's happening, but I think I need to be out of here," Elliott recalled thinking to himself. Elliott and two others began walking down the building's stairwell when they ran into a few others. The absence of more people and the lack of alarms made them feel they had prematurely panicked.

He recalled that as his small group reached the 70th floor, they heard the announcement that the building was secure and there was no need to evacuate. "Do you want to believe them?" one woman said to Elliott. "Let's go!" He followed the woman down the stairs. After descending three more floors, Flight 175 crashed into the South Tower. An article in the *Christian Science Monitor* described what happened next:

"Although its spectacularly televised impact was above Elliott, at first he and those around him thought an explosion had come from below. An incredible sound—he calls it an 'exploding sound'—shook the building, and a tornado of hot air and smoke and ceiling tiles and bits of drywall came flying up the stairwell."

"In front of me, the wall split from the bottom up," Elliott said. He said people in the stairwell panicked and tried to flee upward until some men pointed out that the only escape was downstairs. By about 9:40 a.m., Elliott managed to stumble out of the South Tower and make his way to his roommate's office in Midtown, where he broke down sobbing upon learning of the tower's collapse.

Elliot's description of explosions below the buildings are supported by others, such as FDNY EMS Lieutenant Bradley Mann who told of the ground shaking before each tower collapsed. "Shortly before the first tower came down, I remember feeling the ground shaking. I heard a terrible noise, and then debris just started flying everywhere. People started running," said Mann in the oral history tapes. After returning to the area, he noted, "[W]e basically had the same thing—the ground shook again, and we heard another terrible noise and the next thing we knew the second tower was coming down."

Then there are the accounts of engineers working below ground level. Mike Pecoraro told *The Chief Engineer* magazine he was working in the 6th sub-basement of the North Tower when the lights flickered. This was followed by a loud explosion. Pecoraro and a coworker made their way up to a C level machine shop but found it "gone." "There was nothing there but rubble," recalled Pecoraro. "We're talking about a 50-ton hydraulic press—gone!"

Working their way upwards to a parking garage, the pair found it too was destroyed. "There were no walls, there was rubble on the floor, and you can't see anything," Pecoraro recalled. Ascending two more levels to the tower's lobby, they were astonished to find more debris including a 300-pound steel and concrete fire door wrinkled up "like a piece of aluminum foil." By now, Pecoraro was convinced that a bomb had gone off in the building.

"When I walked out into the lobby, it was incredible," Pecoraro recalled. "The whole lobby was soot and black, elevator doors were missing. The marble was missing off some of the walls. 20-foot section of marble, 20 by 10 foot sections of marble, gone from the walls. The west windows were all gone. They were missing. These are tremendous windows. They were just gone. Broken glass everywhere, the revolving doors were all broken and their glass was gone. Every sprinkler head was going off. I am thinking to myself, how are these sprinkler heads going off? It takes a lot of heat to set off a sprinkler head. It never dawned on me that there was a giant fireball that came through the air of the lobby." He said much later he heard the accounts of jet fuel spilling down the elevator shaft, blowing off all the elevator doors and flames rolling through the lobby.

The lobby of the North Tower was so unrecognizable that many people streaming down the stairs seeking to escape the building bypassed the lobby and had to be directed back up. After moving with other building personnel to the South Tower where he helped evacuate the building, Pecoraro made a dramatic and hazardous escape when the tower collapsed.

Pecoraro's experiences in the basement all occurred prior to the tower's collapse. Yet, according to the official story, there had been only the airplane strike about 95 floors above them.

Adding details that support Pecoraro's account of explosions in the basement was William Rodriguez. President Bush and others hailed him as a hero at the time for his rescue efforts on 9/11. It was widely reported that Rodriguez had adeptly guided rescue workers and had single-handedly saved a number of lives. He was the last person to escape as the North Tower collapsed. But when Rodriguez later went public, it was with a very different account of the WTC tragedy.

Rodriguez had worked for the New York and New Jersey Port Authority for about twenty years. In 2001, he was in charge of maintenance for three stairwells in the North Tower.

Arriving at 8:30 a.m. on September 11, Rodriguez went to the maintenance office located on the first sub-level, one of six sub-basements beneath ground level. There were a total of fourteen people in the office at this time. As he was talking with others, there was a very loud, massive explosion that seemed to emanate from between sub-basements B2 and B3. There were twenty-two people on B2 sub-basement who also felt and heard that first explosion.

At first he thought it was a generator that had exploded. "When I heard the sound of the explosion, the floor beneath my feet vibrated, the walls started cracking and everything started shaking," said Rodriguez. Seconds later there was another explosion way above, which made the building oscillate momentarily. This, he was later told, was a plane hitting the 90th floor.

Upon hearing about the plane, Rodriguez started heading for the loading dock to escape the explosion's fire. When asked later about those first explosions he said: "I would know if an explosion was from the bottom or the top of the building." He was clear about hearing explosions both before and after the plane hit the tower.

Rodriguez said a fellow worker, Felipe David, came into the office. "He had been standing in front of a freight elevator on sub-level 1 about 400 feet from the office when fire burst out of the elevator shaft, causing his injuries. He was burned so badly from the basement explosion that flesh was hanging from his face and both arms." Rodriguez led David outside to safety but returned to the building after hearing screaming inside.

Water from the fire sprinklers from all of the floors had gone into the elevator shaft and there were people trapped below who were in danger of drowning. Rodriguez was able to lower a long ladder into the shaft to enable their escape.

Rodriguez held one of the five master keys that opened all of the stairwell doors at each of the floors in the 110-story building. The other four key holders, though trained for emergencies, had already left the building. Firemen from New York City Unit Six arrived. Each fireman, in addition to protective clothing, had about 70 pounds of equipment. Rodriguez led the firemen up stairwell B.

Reaching the 27th floor, firemen were becoming exhausted from the weight of their equipment. Ascending the stairs, Rodriguez as well as the firemen heard explosions from the 20th through the 30th floor. Chunks of the building fell around them and they could literally hear the building coming down. The firemen continued to climb and give aid.

On the 33rd floor, Rodriguez found the air thick with smoke. Grabbing some dust masks from a maintenance office, he was able to help a woman to evacuate. While on that floor, Rodriguez said he heard what sounded like the movement of heavy equipment and furniture on the 34th floor. This puzzled him because he knew that floor had been closed due to a construction project.

Rodriguez accompanied firefighter to the 39th floor where he was told to turn back. As he began his descent he heard the plane hit the South Tower. Racing through the wrecked lobby, Rodriguez took cover under a fire truck where he was later discovered. After receiving first aid, he joined the effort to find survivors. Rodriguez spent hours giving closed-door testimony before the 9/11 Commission, yet his eyewitness account does not appear anywhere in the 576 page report and in 2010, he posted a link to the commission archives—which indicated his testimony was marked "restricted" and "secret."

He also tried to talk to investigators for the National Institute of Standards and Technology (NIST) but was ignored. "I contacted NIST...four times without a response," he recalled. "Finally, [at a public hearing] I asked them before they came up with their conclusion...if they ever considered my statements or the statements of any of the other survivors who heard the explosions. They just stared at me with blank faces and didn't have any answers."

He also said he contacted the FBI but they never followed up. The media also seemed uninterested. Rodriguez said CNN spent most of a day filming and interviewing him at his home but, when the interview aired, it was severely edited. Rodriguez said one reporter not so subtly warned him to keep quiet or he could be in jeopardy. "You do not know who you are dealing with!" he was told. His response was, "I am living on borrowed time since I probably should be dead anyway."

In late 2004, Rodriguez filed suit in a Philadelphia federal court under the provisions of the Racketeer Influenced and Corrupt Organizations (RICO) Act, naming George Bush, Dick Cheney, Donald Rumsfeld and others as being complicit in the 9/11 attacks. Rodriguez claims that top officials either planned the attacks or had foreknowledge of the attacks and permitted them to succeed for the purpose of exploiting a "New Pearl Harbor" in order to launch wars against Afghanistan and Iraq. The lawsuit entitled *Rodriguez v. Bush, et al.*, Civil Action No. 04 CV 4952, was filed in the US District Court in Philadelphia on October 22. (For details on the lawsuit, see www.911forthetruth.com)

"If what the government has told us about 9/11 is a lie," said Rodriguez explaining why he chose to file suit against government officials, "somebody has to take action to reveal the truth. If suing President Bush is what I have to do to accomplish that, so be it."

Rodriguez's account has been corroborated by José Sanchez, who was in the workshop on the fourth sub-level. Sanchez said that he and a coworker heard a big blast that "sounded like a bomb," after which "a huge ball of fire went through the freight elevator."

Foreign news accounts also noted testimony regarding explosions. A story in the London *Guardian* said that, "police and fire officials were carrying out the first wave of evacuations when the first of the World Trade Center towers collapsed. Some eyewitnesses reported hearing another explosion just before the structure crumbled. Police said that it looked almost like a 'planned implosion.'"

A CNN video of the scene at the WTC showed smoke boiling up from the street level prior to the collapse of the towers, apparently from the eight-story WTC Building 6, more popularly known as the Customs House building. Nothing of significance had struck street level at that time. Did the billowing smoke come from a premature detonation?

Due to a delayed broadcast, there was some initial confusion about just when the smoke began. However, CNN's Public Affairs Department confirmed that the video footage of an apparent explosion at ground level was made at 9:04 a.m., just one minute after Flight 175 struck the South Tower and long before either tower collapsed.

Asked what might have caused the smoke seen in the video, the CNN archivist replied, "We can't figure it out." Later, arguments were made that CNN's time code was wrong and that the billowing smoke was simply dust from the collapsing South Tower.

Lending support to the idea that Building 6 was ravaged by a separate explosion were photos depicting a very noticeable huge circular hole with deep crater blasted from this building which was not hit by airplanes and still standing after the towers collapsed.

According to news reports, the FEMA team of engineers commissioned to investigate the WTC tragedy was barred from entering the Customs House building. FEMA officials reported that because the structure was considered "very dangerous," there was "no data collection" from Building 6. Yet, the FEMA report blithely stated, "Building Five was the only building accessible for observation [by the team of engineers]...the observations, findings and recommendations are assumed to be applicable to all three buildings." A spokesman for the Export-Import Bank of the United States confirmed the 9:04 time of the blast but said all of the eight hundred or so employees of the Customs House building had already been evacuated after the WTC North Tower was struck.

Other occupants of the building, which included the Customs Service, the Departments of Commerce, Labor, and Agriculture and the Bureau of Alcohol, Tobacco and Firearms, declined to explain either the early blast or the massive crater at the center of the Customs House ruins. No explanation for this explosion or crater has been forthcoming.

But if there were bombs in the towers, how did they get there? What kind were they? What is powerful enough to bring down a 110-story steel and concrete skyscraper? The public was left with the official explanation that high-temperature fires caused by burning jet fuel and office furnishings melted 47 internal structural steel beams, causing the towers to drop into their own foundations.

## FIREFIGHTERS THOUGHT THE FIRES WERE CONTROLLABLE

An audiotape of New York firefighters at the scene, unpublicized until mid-2002, indicated that fire officials managed to reach the 78th floor of the South Tower—very near the crash scene, which was at the 80th floor—and seemed convinced that the fire was controllable.

The tape was briefly mentioned by the *New York Times* but was kept from the public by the US Justice Department, which claimed it might be needed in the trial of the "twentieth hijacker," Zacarias Moussaoui, even though Moussaoui was in custody at the time of the attacks. The audiotape was a recording of radio transmissions made on the morning of September 11, 2001. The tape reportedly was discovered two or three weeks after 9/11 in offices of the Port Authority of New York and New Jersey at WTC Building 5. Apparently, Port Authority personnel were monitoring and recording the New York Fire Department (FDNY) channel.

Two fire officials mentioned by name in the tape were Battalion Chief Orio J. Palmer and Fire Marshal Ronald P. Bucca, both of whom perished when the South Tower collapsed along with 343 other firefighters, the greatest single loss of firefighters in one incident in history. According to the *Times* article, both firemen "showed no panic, no sense that events were racing beyond their control....At that point, the building would be standing for just a few more minutes, as the fire was weakening the structure on the floors above him. Even so, Chief Palmer could see only two pockets of fire and called for a pair of engine companies to fight them."

Transcripts released on the Internet provided this statement, "Battalion Seven...Ladder 15, we've got two isolated pockets of fire. We should be able to knock it down with two lines. Radio that, 78th floor numerous 10-45 Code Ones."

As noted by reporter Christopher Bollyn, "The fact that veteran firefighters had a 'coherent plan for putting out' the 'two pockets of fire,' indicates they judged the blazes to be manageable. These reports from the scene of the crash provide crucial evidence debunking the government's claim that a raging steel-melting inferno led to the tower's collapse."

Supporting Chief Palmer's description of only small fires in the South Tower are survivors Stanley Praimnath, Donovan Cowen and Ling Young. Praimnath, on the 81st floor, recalled, "The plane impacts. I try to get up and then I realize that I'm covered up to my shoulder in debris. And when I'm digging through under all this rubble, I can see the bottom wing starting to burn, and that wing is wedged 20 feet in my office doorway." Cowen was in an open elevator at the 78th floor sky-lobby. She recalled, "We went into the elevator. As soon as I hit the button, that's when there was a big boom. We both got knocked down. I remember feeling this intense heat. The doors were still open. The heat lasted for maybe 15 to 20 seconds I guess. Then it stopped." Young was in her 78th floor office and related, "Only in my area were people alive, and the people alive were from my office. I figured that out later because I sat around in there for 10 or 15 minutes. That's how I got so burned."

Government pronouncements and hired experts claimed temperatures in the area of these three witnesses were hot enough to cause the trusses of the South Tower to fail, yet these eye-witnesses stated temperatures were cool enough for them to walk away.

Additionally, a number of experts have disputed the claim that melting structural steel brought down the Twin Towers.

Kevin R. Ryan was a site manager for Environmental Health Laboratories in South Bend, IN, a subsidiary of Underwriters Laboratories Inc. (UL), the giant product safety testing firm. In 2003, Ryan wrote to Frank Gayle, deputy chief of the Metallurgy Division of the National Institute of Standards and Technology's (NIST) Material Science and Engineering Laboratory, challenging the theory that burning jet fuel weakened the towers' structural steel causing them to fall.

In this communication, Ryan wrote, "As I'm sure you know, the company I work for certified the steel components used in the construction of the WTC buildings...the samples we certified met all requirements...the results of these tests appear to indicate that the buildings should have easily withstood the thermal stress caused by pools of burning jet fuel."

Ryan went on to question the conclusions of "experts," including Dr. Hyman Brown, who have claimed that the towers collapse was caused by structural steel melting at temperatures of 2,000 degrees Fahrenheit.

Reiterating that his company had certified the steel to withstand temperatures of 2,000 degrees for several hours, Ryan wrote, "I think we can all agree that even un-fireproofed steel will not melt until reaching red-hot temperatures of nearly 3,000°F. Why Dr. Brown would imply that 2,000°F would melt the high-grade steel used in those buildings makes no sense at all."

"This story just does not add up," Ryan concluded. "If steel from those buildings did soften or melt, I'm sure we can all agree that this was certainly not due to jet fuel fires of any kind, let alone the briefly burning fires in those towers. That fact should be a great concern to all Americans. Alternatively, the contention that this steel did fail at temperatures around 250°C suggests that the majority of deaths on 9/11 were due to a safety-related failure. That suggestion should be of great concern to my company."

Although Ryan made it clear that he was speaking only for himself, not his company, his employers' reaction was decisive. On November 22, 2004, the *South Bend Tribune* carried this headline, "South Bend firm's lab director fired after questioning federal probe." UL officials denied any testing of the WTC steel and said Ryan was terminated because his letter was written "without UL's knowledge or authorization."

But the cat was out of the bag as Ryan's letter had reached the hands of several organizations questioning the official 9/11 story. Dan Kubiak, then-executive director of 911truth.org, a national organization of activists and researchers, said Ryan's firing was "unfortunate for the country and it's particularly tragic for him, but inspiring as hell."

"The way things are working in the country right now, it's only going to be citizens like this who take their professional knowledge and sense of personal integrity and put it ahead of the strange status quo, that we will see truth and justice [come] out of the system."

Another puzzling anomaly of the World Trade Center building collapses concerns pools of molten steel, which were recorded under the towers as well as Building 6 up to five weeks after September 11, 2001. Thermal imaging aerial photos showed large pools of hot molten steel in the basement of the three buildings, indicating temperatures of up to 2,000 degrees Fahrenheit.

Mark Loizeaux, president of Controlled Demolition, Inc., of Phoenix, Arizona, who consulted on removing the WTC debris, confirmed that these "hot spots" of molten steel were found as many as five weeks after the collapse when rubble was removed from the elevator shafts seven levels down. These pools of melted metal were also mentioned by Peter Tully, president of Tully Construction, one of four contractors hired to remove debris. Interestingly enough, WTC Building 7, which may have been brought down by explosives, does not show any heat signatures in the thermal imaging photos.

Loizeaux speculated that steel-melting fires were generated by "paper, carpet and other combustibles packed down the elevator shafts by the towers as they 'pancaked' into the basement." Since construction steel's melting point is about 2,800 degrees Fahrenheit, other experts disputed this idea, saying that due to the lack of oxygen, such debris would have been only a smoldering pile.

Speculating further, Loizeaux told the *American Free Press*, "If I were to bring the towers down, I would put explosives in the basement to get the weight of the building to help collapse the structure." Subterranean explosives could explain the "hot spots" discovered under the rubble. Considering the total destruction, reports from survivors and firemen, and the seismic shocks just prior to the collapse, many people believed that Loizeaux's description was exactly what happened on September 11, 2001.

It is worth noting that Controlled Demolition, Inc. is the same company that hurriedly removed the rubble of the Murrah Federal Building in Oklahoma City following the explosion there in 1996. Both there and at the WTC, crucial structural evidence was removed before any independent examination or investigation.

FIREFIGHTERS THOUGHT THE FIRES WERE CONTROLLABLE

Further strong evidence of ground explosions causing the WTC collapses came from seismographs at Columbia University's Lamont-Doherty Earth Observatory in Palisades, New York, twenty-one miles north of the WTC. Just prior to the collapse of the Twin Towers, seismic equipment recorded two "spikes," indicating large bursts of energy that shook the ground beneath the WTC towers just *before* their collapse.

Columbia's seismic equipment recorded a 2.1-magnitude ground shock during the ten-second collapse of the South Tower and a 2.3 quake during the eight-second collapse of the North Tower. However, the strongest shocks, or "spikes," on the data recorder both occurred at the beginning of the tower's collapse, well before falling material struck the ground. The two spikes were more than twenty times the amplitude of the other seismic shock waves associated with the collapsed buildings. One seismologist said the 1993 truck bomb at the WTC did not even register on seismographs; that massive explosion did not cause detectable shock waves through the ground.

"New York seismometers recorded huge bursts of energy, which caused unexpected seismic 'spikes' at the beginning of each [tower] collapse. These spikes suggest that massive underground explosions may have literally knocked the towers off their foundations, causing them to collapse," reported the *American Free Press* in September 2002.

Seismologist Arthur Lerner-Lam, director of Columbia's Center for Hazards and Risk Research, added to this by saying, "During the collapse, most of the energy of the falling debris was absorbed by the towers and the neighboring structures, converting them into rubble and dust or causing other damage—but not causing significant ground shaking." Asked about the two unusual shocks, Lerner-Lam was noncommittal. "This is an element of current research and discussion. It is still being investigated," he told the media.

Compounding the mystery of the seismic spikes and the witnesses who claimed to have heard multiple explosions prior to the fall of the towers is the question of the free-fall speed of the collapse. The South Tower, which was struck second but fell first, collapsed within 10 seconds. The North Tower collapsed in only eight seconds. It has been estimated that any object, a hammer for example, dropped from the roof of either tower would free fall to the ground in 9 seconds. It should also be noted that the collapse of WTC Building 7, which according to much evidence was brought down by a controlled demolition, took 8 seconds, approximately the same time as both towers.

Noting the near free-fall speed of the towers' collapse, many researchers have asked, "How could simply falling debris crush one hundred steel and concrete floors?" Officials at NIST initially attempted to argue that Building 7 did not collapse at free-fall speed but later, faced with the hard data, were forced to admit that at least the top 18 floors did drop at free-fall or even greater speed.

Pools of molten steel still registering intense heat weeks after the incident, seismic "spikes" just prior to the collapse of the buildings, the free-fall speed of the buildings' collapse, the pulverization of cement walls—none of this can be adequately explained by airplane crashes and fires alone, much less falling masonry and steel.

There was no initial consensus explanation for the towers collapse since none of the engineers hired by FEMA inspected or tested the steel before it was hauled away for salvage.

"I am not a metallurgist," explained Dr. W. Gene Corley, head of the FEMA engineer team, who admitted his group was not allowed to make a close study of the WTC steel girders.

Corley himself seemed unconvinced that burning jet fuel was the sole cause of the towers' collapse. In the executive summary of the "World Trade Center Building Performance Study," he wrote, "…absent other severe loading events such as a windstorm or earthquake, the buildings could have remained standing in their damaged states until subjected to some significant additional load." He then explained that fires must have constituted this "significant additional load."

"The large quantity of jet fuel carried by each aircraft ignited upon impact into each building. A significant portion of this fuel was consumed immediately in the ensuing fireballs. The remaining fuel is believed either to have flowed down through the buildings or to have burned off within a few minutes of the aircraft impact. The heat produced by this burning jet fuel does not by itself appear to have been sufficient to initiate the structural collapses," he stated.

But Corley explained that secondary fires, involving office supplies and furniture ignited by the burning jet fuel "induced additional stress-es into the damaged structural frames while simultaneously softening and weakening these frames." "This additional loading and the resulting damage were sufficient to induce the collapse of both structures," the FEMA-sponsored study concluded.

But a growing number of people, including experts, have questioned this conclusion.

After all, it has been pointed out, no independent investigation was funded and the $600,000 allocated by FEMA for the WTC study included the cost of hiring their selected experts plus the cost of printing their report. Additionally, Corley and his group were barred from independent visits to Ground Zero and were not able to examine any steel for almost a month after 9/11. Even then, they only examined 150 pieces of steel out of millions, with no way of knowing where they originated.

By the time the FEMA team called for "further investigation and analysis" in its report of May 2002, Ground Zero had been scraped clean of all debris.

According to FEMA's "Building Performance Assessment," temperatures at the crash site—only two floors above Chief Palmer and Marshal Bucca—were as high as 1,700–2,000 degrees Fahrenheit, so intense as to melt the structure's steel frame girders.

Assuming FEMA's temperature estimates are correct, the interiors of the towers became furnaces capable of casting aluminum and glazing pottery. Yet the firemen were able to work for an extended period of time in close proximity and believed the fires they encountered were manageable. Furthermore, photographic blowups depicting the jagged gash in the North Tower just before its collapse clearly show survivors peering out through the hole made by the airplane.

"The sooty smoke and the black holes [seen in photographs of the towers prior to their collapse] cannot be dismissed as interesting aspects of the fires, nor as problems with the photography," said researcher and author Eric Hufschmid. "Rather, they are signs that the air flow was so restricted that the only significant fires were near broken windows. The fires in both towers were probably coating the [structural] columns with soot rather than heating the columns to a high temperature."

Citing a severe fire in Philadelphia's Meridian Plaza in 1991, Hufschmid noted, "The Meridian Plaza fire was extreme, but it did not cause the building to collapse. "The fire in the South Tower seems insignificant by comparison to both the Meridian Plaza fire and the fire in the North Tower. How could the tiny fire in the South Tower cause the entire structure to shatter into dust after fifty-six minutes while much more extreme fires did not cause the Meridian Plaza building to even crack into two pieces?" The fact still remains that no other high-rise buildings have ever collapsed due to a fire of any size, or of any length—let alone in under one hour.

"The official theory of the collapse, therefore, is essentially a fire theory, so it cannot be emphasized too much that fire has *never* caused large steel-frame buildings to collapse—never, whether *before* 9/11, or *after* 9/11, or anywhere in the world *on* 9/11 except allegedly New York City—*never*," declared David Ray Griffin.

To see how ludicrous is the claim that the short-lived fires in the towers could have induced structural collapse, we can compare them with some other fires. In 1988, a fire in the First Interstate Bank Building in Los Angeles raged for 3.5 hours and gutted 5 of this building's 62 floors, but there was no significant structural damage. In 1991, a huge fire in Philadelphia's One Meridian Plaza lasted for 18 hours and gutted 8 of the building's 38 floors, but, said the FEMA report in 1991, although "[b]eams and girders sagged and twisted...under severe fire exposures..., the columns continued to support their loads without obvious damage." In Caracas in 2004, a fire in a 50-story building raged for 17 hours, completely gutting the building's top 20 floors, and yet it did not collapse. And yet we are supposed to believe that a 56-minute fire caused the WTC South Tower to collapse. Unlike the fires in the towers, moreover, the fires in Los Angeles, Philadelphia, and Caracas were hot enough to break windows. On February 12, 2005, the 32-story Windsor building in Madrid, Spain, made of steel-reinforced concrete, burned for almost a full day. Fire completely engulfed the upper ten stories of the building. Although the fire apparently caused the collapse of the top floor spans surrounding the still-standing core structure of the ten uppermost floors, fear that the structure would totally collapse like the Twin Towers proved unfounded. The structure remained intact.

And yet we are supposed to believe that a 56-minute fire caused the WTC South Tower to collapse. Unlike the fires in the towers, moreover, the fires in Los Angeles, Philadelphia, and Caracas were hot enough to break windows.

Another important comparison is afforded by a series of experiments run in Great Britain in the mid-1990s to see what kind of damage could be done to steel-frame buildings by subjecting them to extremely hot, all-consuming fires that lasted for many hours. FEMA, having reviewed those experiments, said: "Despite the temperature of the steel beams reaching 800–900°C (1,500–1,700°F) in three of the tests…, no collapse was observed in any of the six experiments"

These comparisons bring out the absurdity of NIST's claim that the towers collapsed because the planes knocked the fireproofing off the steel columns. Fireproofing provides protection for only a few hours, so the steel in the buildings in Philadelphia and Caracas would have been directly exposed to raging fires for 14 or more hours, and yet this steel did not buckle. NIST claims, nevertheless, that the steel in the South Tower buckled because it was directly exposed to flames for 56 minutes.

It was also considered peculiar that both towers dropped within fifteen seconds, essentially free-fall speed. Wouldn't the lower floors have held the weight even if only momentarily?

Massachusetts Institute of Technology Materials Professor Thomas Eager explained to PBS's *NOVA* that the WTC fires were so massive that they caused the total collapse of 47 core steel-reinforced columns as well as 236 exterior columns. "If it [fire] had only occurred in one small corner, such as a trashcan caught on fire, you might have had to repair that corner, but the whole building wouldn't have come crashing down," explained Eager. "The problem was, it was such a widely distributed fire, and then you got this domino effect."

He described this domino effect as caused by the failure of angle clips, steel brackets that held the floor trusses between the inner core columns and the exterior columns. "Once you started to get angle clips to fail in one area, it put extra load on the other clips, and then it unzipped around the building on that floor in a matter of seconds," said Eager.

Eager's explanation suffers from the fact that neither tower had fires covering the entire floor and the fact that cross trusses would have prevented, or at least slowed, the "unzipping" effect of the angle clips. His explanation also fails to address the speed of the towers' collapse. Even if one can accept that each floor did not impede the collapsing ones above it, there is no explanation for what shattered the outer walls and inner core columns, threw debris hundreds of feet away from the buildings, and turned most of the concrete to pulverized dust.

Rather than come up with an explanation of how a limited hydrocarbon fire that burned for a short time could have weakened the 47 core steel-reinforced columns in each of the two towers sufficiently for a free-fall collapse, *The 9/11 Commission Report* simply omitted this fact, and instead depicts the interior of the towers as "a hollow steel shaft, in which elevators and stairwells were grouped."

According to David Ray Griffin, the commission avoided the "embarrassing problem" of the massive steel interior columns by simply denying their existence, "thereby demonstrating enormous ignorance or telling an enormous lie."

## ADVANCED TECHNOLOGY AT THE WORLD TRADE CENTER?

World Trade Center Building 4 was nine stories tall. After its collapse following the 9/11 attacks, there was left a debris pile of three stories. Compare this ratio of building to debris with the two 110-story WTC towers, both of which left a mere six stories of debris.

About 10,000 tons of debris was hauled away from Ground Zero every day following 9/11, according to Kathy Dawkins with the public information office for the NYC Department of Sanitation. By the end of October, 2001, more than 400,000 tons of debris have been removed. By the official end of the clean up in the summer of 2002, an estimated 1.6 million tons of debris had been removed.

Yet, the Twin Towers were estimated to have weighed approximately 3.6 billion tons. Serious researchers question what happened to two billion tons of debris and where were the massive chunks of concrete normally found at a building collapse?

With the WTC towers turned to powdered ash and the twisted beams and metal quickly hauled away, no one can ever be certain as to this disappearance or its cause but some interesting theories have been advanced. Some are as far out as space-based electromagnetic weapons or a particle beam device reportedly being developed at Brookhaven National Laboratory on Long Island, well within range of the WTC.

One speculative theory is that explosive charges were placed in the towers back in the 1960s to prevent a catastrophe such as 9/11 from causing them to fall over on neighboring buildings, magnifying the destruction. No proof of this has been established. Explosive experts discount this theory, stating that explosives could not have remained effective after an extended period of time. A similar theory postulates that charges were placed in the buildings following the 1993 bombing for the reason stated above.

The idea that explosives were planted in the buildings gained traction after Ben Fountain, a financial analyst who worked on the 47th floor of the South Tower, told *People* magazine that in the weeks preceding 9/11 there were numerous unusual and unannounced "drills" in which sections of both towers as well as Building 7 were evacuated for "security reasons." These drills could have provided a perfect cover for persons planting explosives. "How could they let this happen?" wondered Fountain. "They knew this building was a target. Over the past few weeks we'd been evacuated a number of times, which is unusual. I think they had an inkling something was going on."

Another South Tower worker, Scott Forbes, said that every floor above the 50th floor had no electricity for about 36 hours the weekend before 9/11. He added that during these "power downs," he witnessed strangers in overalls with reels of wiring working inside his building. "Seeing so many strangers who didn't work at the WTC was unusual," commented Forbes. Scott, like so many others, tried to tell what he knew to both authorities and the 9/11 Commission but was ignored.

Reporting in *The American Reporter*, an electronic daily newspaper, Margie Burns noted that President Bush's younger brother, Marvin P. Bush, was a principal in a company called Securacom that provided security for the World Trade Center, United Airlines, and Dulles International Airport. The company, Burns noted, was backed by KuwAm, a Kuwaiti-American investment firm. CEO of Securacom was Wirt Walker III, a cousin to the Bush family.

Securacom has since changed its name to Stratesec, but is still backed by KuwAm. Marvin Bush, who did not respond to repeated interview requests from *The American Reporter*, is no longer on the board of either company and has not been linked with any terrorist activities. According to its present CEO, Barry McDaniel, the company had an ongoing contract to handle security at the World Trade Center "up to the day the buildings fell down." Stratesec was dropped from the American Stock Exchange in July 2002 due to financial problems.

Many people lost their lives in the collapse of the Twin Towers because the public address system advised workers to return to their desks. Researchers wondered who exactly ordered the broadcast over the loudspeakers in the South Tower as workers were trying to evacuate, "Remain calm, damage is in Tower One. Return to your desks." Minutes later the towers collapsed unexpectedly.

By 2010, more than 1,200 architectural and engineering professionals along with 9,000 other supporters, including architecture and engineering students, had joined a group called Architects & Engineers for 9/11 Truth and had signed a petition demanding Congress initiate a new and truly independent investigation. The group claimed the *Twin Towers' destruction exhibited all of the characteristics of destruction by explosives.*

These included: the destruction proceeded through the path of greatest resistance at nearly free-fall acceleration; the improbable symmetry of debris distribution; more than 100 first responders reported explosions and flashes; multi-ton steel sections were ejected laterally; the mid-air pulverization of some 90,000 tons of concrete and metal decking; the massive volume of expanding pyroclastic-like clouds; the 1,200-foot-diameter debris field with no "pancaked" floors remaining; the several tons of molten metal found under all three high-rises even after several weeks; the lack of precedent for a steel-framed high-rise collapse due to fire and evidence of explosives found in dust samples.

One of the first to publicly advance the allegation that explosives were used to bring down the towers was Professor Emeritus Steven E. Jones, a physicist at Brigham Young University in Utah. Jones stirred controversy in the 1980s with his research on "cold fusion" (today known as muon-catalyzed fusion to avoid confusion of the term).

In 2005, Jones again drew the ire of authorities by suggesting that the speed and symmetry of the tower collapses, the eyewitness reports of explosions down low in the buildings, partially vaporized beams, molten metal in the basements and the fact that no modern high rise structure framed with steel had ever collapsed from fire, Jones said this evidence suggested a controlled demolition possibly through the use of thermite or a derivative.

Although much derided in the media at the time and even pressured into retiring from his position at BYU in late 2006 following a paid leave ordered by school officials, Jones was vindicated in 2009 with the publication of an article entitled "Active Thermitic Material Discovered in Dust from the 9/11 World Trade Center Catastrophe." This was published in the scientific publication *The Open Chemical Physics Journal*. Jones, one of the paper's authors, was joined by Niels H. Harrit, of the University of Copenhagen's Chemistry Department; Jeffrey Farrer and Daniel Farnsworth of BYU's Department of Physicis and Astronomy; Kevin R. Ryan with the 9/11 Working Group; Frank M. Legge of Logical Systems Consulting in Perth, Australia; Gregg Roberts of Architects & Engineers for 9/11 Truth; James R. Gourley of the International Center for 9/11 Studies; and Bradley R. Larsen of S & J Scientific Co. in Provo, UT.

In their paper, the authors laboriously record the methodology used to arrive at their conclusions. They detail how samples were taken from Ground Zero, explaining that "One sample was collected by a Manhattan resident about ten minutes after the collapse of the second WTC Tower, two the next day, and a fourth about a week later. The properties of these chips were analyzed using optical microscopy, scanning electron microscopy, X-ray energy dispersive spectroscopy, and differential scanning calorimetry [DSC]."

Their findings? "We have discovered distinctive red/gray chips in all the samples we have studied of the dust produced by the destruction of the World Trade Center. Examination of four of these samples, collected from separate sites, is reported in this paper. These red/gray chips show marked similarities in all four samples...The red material contains grains approximately 100 nm across which are largely iron oxide, while aluminum is contained in tiny plate-like structures. Separation of components using methyl ethyl ketone demonstrated that elemental aluminum is present. The iron oxide and aluminum are intimately mixed in the red material. When ignited in a DSC device the chips exhibit large but narrow exotherms occurring at approximately 430 °C, far below the normal ignition temperature for conventional thermite. Numerous iron-rich spheres are clearly observed in the residue following the ignition of these peculiar red/gray chips. The red portion of these chips is found to be an unreacted thermitic material and highly energetic."

Thermite is a pyrotechnic used primarily by the military and demolition firms. It is made from compositions of metal powder—usual aluminum—and metal oxide to produce short-lived bursts of extremely high temperatures capable of slicing through hardened material such as steel beams.

According to the scientific paper's researchers, "Commercially available thermite behaves as an incendiary when ignited, but when the ingredients are ultra-fine grain and are intimately mixed, this 'nano-thermite' reacts very rapidly, even explosively, and is sometimes referred to as 'super-thermite.'" Such super-thermite is known as thermate.

The paper stated that all their data "suggest that the thermitic material found in the WTC dust is a form of nano-thermite, not ordinary (macro-) thermite." In trying to determine if such nano-thermite could have been available in 2001, the researchers found the 221st National Meeting of the American Chemical Society held during April 2001 in San Diego featured a symposium on Defense Applications of Nanomaterials. One presentation was entitled "Nanoenergetics: an emerging technology area of national importance." Citing research going back at least 10 years, it was noted that "all of the military services and some DOE and academic laboratories have active R & D programs aimed at exploiting the unique properties of nanomaterials that have potential to be used in energetic formulations for advanced explosives..."

*The Open Chemical Physics Journal* paper concluded "that the red layer of the red/gray chips we have discovered in the WTC dust is active, unreacted thermitic material, incorporating nanotechnology, and is a highly energetic pyrotechnic or explosive material."

In what many felt was an example of the global and powerful pressure being exerted on professionals who align themselves with alternative views of 9/11, the editor-in-chief of *The Open Chemical Physics Journal*, Professor Dr. Marie-Paule Pileni, director of the Mesoscopic & Nanometric Materials Laboratory of the *Institut Universitaire de France*, resigned her position in April 2009, and disavowed the paper on active thermitic material. "They have printed the article without my permission," Pileni wrote in response to a query regarding the article. "I did not know that the article had appeared. I cannot accept this, and therefore I have written Bentham [Science Publishers] that I resign from all activities with them...I cannot accept that this topic is published in my journal. The article has nothing to do with physical chemistry or chemical physics, and I could well believe that there is a political viewpoint behind its publication. If anyone had asked me, I would say that the article should never have been published in this journal. Period."

"Political" seemed to be the key word, for while Pileni raised the possibility of the article based on a political viewpoint, she did not dispute either its methodology or its conclusions. She did indicate that the scope of the paper was outside of her expertise, although a search of her background showed extensive connections with defense industry research involving chemical research, experimental nanosciences, physical chemistry, and nanometrics.

"It surprises me, of course, and it is regrettable, if it discredits our work," said Niels Harrit, one of the paper's authors. "But her departure doesn't change our conclusions, for it is a purely personnel related thing she is angry about. I still believe that we have carried out chemical physics, and if there is something wrong with our study, she is welcome to criticize us for it."

Further proof that a form of thermite was used to destroy the buildings came with the revelation that sulfur, which reduces the melting point of iron by producing a "eutectic" mixture, meaning a low temperature combination of materials. Such a mixture results in holes in structural steel resembling Swiss cheese. The *New York Times* called such pieces of melted steel "perhaps the deepest mystery uncovered in the investigation." FEMA documented such "inter-granular melting, rapid oxidation, and sulfidation" of steel members yet offered no explanation for this phenomena which required temperatures far greater than caused by office fires or even jet fuel.

Various scientific researchers state that the sulfur most likely came from thermate. Civil engineer Jonathan Cole explained that sulfur is added to thermite to make thermate. Some scientists speculated that the holed steel resulted from the burning of a combination of gypsum board, jet fuel and office materials. "Scientists and engineers have urged the National Institute of Standards and Technology (NIST) to perform experiments to determine the source of the sulfur. But despite spending over $20,000,000 NIST failed to do any experiments or provide a working theory," he wrote.

So, Cole conducted his own experiment by filling a steel beam with normal building materials, including wallboard, diesel fuel, and aluminum to see if burning it in fire would reproduce the holed steel found at the WTC. It did not. In fact, after burning in an intense fire for more than a day and a half, the steel beam was not even distorted. Cole had proven what NIST could, or would not, even after spending $20 million of taxpayers money—that burning office materials, including jet fuel, could not produce the sulfur and punctures seen on WTC steel. But thermate could. Cole's compelling experiment may be viewed at www.ae911truth.org/news/41-articles/321-ae911truth-engineer-does-forfree-what-nist-couldnt-for-millions.html.

Despite the qualifications of these men and the fact that *The Open Chemical Physics Journal* article was peer-reviewed for accuracy and attention to scientific methods, the corporate mainstream mass media in the United States has consistently failed to report their findings. Many Americans, in response to the allegation that explosives were involved in the WTC destruction, have asked, "Where is the proof?" Is this the proof of explosives at the World Trade Center? The poor public may never know since this scientific, peer-reviewed paper has yet to come to their attention thanks to the lack of reporting.

The fact that the Twin Towers exploded into vast clouds of pulverized concrete, hurling massive steel beams and assemblies up to 500 feet in all directions indicating they were destroyed with much more energy than a conventional demolition—perhaps two orders of magnitude more. This means it is possible that something even more powerful and esoteric than nano-thermite may have been in use. One scary scenario being put forth by some 9/11 researchers is that the the anomalies of the WTC destruction, including the onset of thyroid and blood cell cancers in first responders may be the result of nuclear technology.

Although the vast majority of the American population does not know about them, knowledgeable experts acknowledge that small micro- or mini-nuclear devices exist. Military training films of the 1950s demonstrate the use of nuclear cannon shells, no larger than conventional shells. The media for some years has warned of old Soviet Russian "suitcase" nukes gone missing in the wake of the collapse of communism. With 21st century technology it is now possible to construct nuclear devises no larger than a baseball.

Dr. Peter Leitner, author of "Decontrolling Strategic Technology, 1990–1992," explained how nuclear technology could be advanced in secret when he told the congressional Joint Economic Committee on April 28, 1998, "As the planet shows no sign of nearing the point where nuclear weapons are banned, it is reasonable to assume that current or aspiring nuclear weapons states will vigorously attempt to acquire high-performance computers to advance their nuclear programs with a degree of covertness hitherto impossible to achieve."

Some researchers have theorized that just such exotic new nuclear devices, in the form of shaped charges to focus the direction of the blast, were used to evaporate the 47 steel columns at the core of the WTC towers. They also point to the following observations as substantiating the nuclear theory:

- The underground puddles of molten steel found weeks after 9/11.
- The inability of water to cool the dirt at Ground Zero.
- The missing core columns (vaporized?).
- The spreading of sand at Ground Zero and the washing of steel, both common characteristics of radiation contamination.
- The extreme security measures to keep both the media and the public from Ground Zero.
- The transformation of solid concrete into gaseous clouds of dust.
- The mid-air disintegration of steel beams as caught on video that day.
- The complete disappearance of human bodies not to mention nearindestructible objects such as elevator doors, toilets and sinks, heavy furniture, metal filing cabinets and large machinery including a 50-ton hydraulic press.
- Floor fragments found fused together.
- The multiple blast waves and fireballs described by survivors.
- The evidence of extremely high temperatures as evidenced by twisted steel beams.
- The discovery of small iron microspheres providing evidence

# PART I – THE EVENTS OF SEPTEMBER 11, 2001

of the vaporization of steel.
- The pyroclastic clouds observed over both towers that mimicked an atomic blast.
- The compactness of the Ground Zero debris.
- The multiple descriptions of bright flashes of light during the collapse of both towers.

New York Fire Department EMT Patricia Ondrovic was at the WTC about 45 minutes before the towers dropped. When the South Tower began to collapse, Ondrovic said, "I didn't know what was happening, but there was a loud 'roar'—lots of crashing sounds. I was attempting to put my stretcher back into the vehicle. The ground was shaking and I saw a sea of people, mostly the various agencies on scene, fire, police, EMS, all running towards me. I had no idea what they were running from, but I decided I'd be ahead of them and just started running west towards the river. As I was running, parked cars were blowing up and some were on fire, the street was cracking a bit as well....I remember [car] parts flying off—I think I got hit with a car door. I remember they were also on fire, but I don't specifically recall the movie type fireball, but there was a loud bang as the door flew off the one car I was running past....I tried to run into the lobby of 6 World Trade, but there were federal police—maybe 4 to 6 of them—standing in the open doorways. As I tried to run in, they wouldn't let me, waving me out, telling me 'you can't come in here, keep running.' As I turned to start running west again, I saw a series of flashes around the ceiling of the lobby all going off one-by-one like the [Christmas] lights that 'chase' in pattern. I think I started running faster at that point."

Ondrovic also told of an incident which seemed to indicate interference with electronics might have been involved in the WTC destruction. "[A]t one point there was a loud 'buzzing' sound and none of the EMS radios worked for maybe 30 seconds. We all used Motorola radios and I believe our repeaters were on top of the towers, so when the tower came down our radios failed. I tried to use my cell phone, but that too did not work." Could this radio disruption been caused by an electromagnetic pulse (EMP) associated with a nuclear blast?

Paramedic Robert Ruiz, in December 2001 described his ordeal. Ruiz said he barely escaped the destruction of the South Tower by ducking into a doorway. He described the ground around him shaking before the building collapse began. Could this be evidence of a nuclear device detonating in the lower levels of the tower? Ruiz, who wrapped his shirt around his head to protect against the choking dust, recalled, "I was trapped there. Like things weren't bad enough already, the car that's parked right on that corner catches on fire. I don't mean a little fire, the entire thing. Don't ask me how. The entire car caught on fire. You would think maybe just a motor part or just the engine part. But this entire car just goes up in fire."

One prolific blogger, calling himself "The Anonymous Physicist," described in detail how a nuclear bomb will emit a great flux of gamma rays. "These will ionize (expel electrons from) surrounding air molecules. The electrons' behavior is such that a coherent electromagnetic wave front moves outward. This has been named an Electromagnetic Pulse, or EMP. An EMP will adversely affect any metallic objects that it intersects as it reaches them. A high voltage and current will be induced into the metal, which can cause circuitry, or any metallic parts to melt, catch fire, or explode. Just what an EMP will do to a metallic object is determined in part by the intensity of the EMP, distance to the object, angle, intervening shielding, and other factors. The intensity of an EMP from a nuke is determined by the strength/yield of the nuke, altitude of detonation, its type and design. In general, the smaller the nuke, the smaller the strength and effective range of the EMP it will produce. A multi-megaton nuke exploded in the upper atmosphere can cause a continent-wide EMP. A micro-nuke would yield an EMP of only some fraction of a mile. Possibly only a couple of blocks depending on where it was detonated, shielding etc."

This writer pointed to witness testimony such as that of Mike Pecoraro, Patricia Ondrovic and Robert Ruiz as evidence of effects explainable only by an EMP pulse generated by a small nuclear device. He noted that an EMP pulse results in massive sparking of electrical cables and connectors leading to fires and explosions.

Two well-known 9/11 researchers, Morgan Reynolds and Judy D. Wood, also noted the evidence of an EMP pulse, noting "Electrical outage over a wide area with repairs taking over three months, suggesting EM pulses." To further support the idea of EMP use, it should be noted that there were reports of many cell phones becoming inoperative near the WTC buildings.

Wood is a former professor of mechanical engineering specializing in experimental stress analysis, structural mechanics, and the materials characterization of biomaterials and composite materials. A member of the Society for Experimental Mechanics (SEM), she co-founded its SEM's Biological Systems and Materials Division, and received her doctorate degree in materials engineering science from the Department of Engineering Science and Mechanics at Virginia Tech in Blacksburg, Virginia.

Wood noted that the World Trade Center was protected from the waters of the Hudson River by an underground foundation ring or "bathtub" constructed into bedrock seven stories below the surface of lower Manhattan. This enclosure, sometimes called the "slurry wall," protected the foundation of the Twin Towers as well as other WTC buildings. The strange fact that this wall was largely undamaged is credited with saving lower Manhattan Island from devastating flooding. According to *New York Times* reporter Dennis Overbye, "To the relief of the engineers, there is no evidence that the 70-foot-deep retaining wall around the basements has been damaged or breached, although the collapse of the towers left one section perilously unsupported."

"How did the bathtub avoid significant damage despite a million tons of WTC material supposedly slamming into it?" asked Wood. "Even if no material directly hit the bathtub, serious seismic impacts on bedrock would have damaged walls, wall corners and tunnels under WTC leading under the Hudson River because of motion similar to that caused by an earthquake. The bathtub was not built to withstand such colossal impact, we may be assured, because New York is not an active seismic zone. Although a disputed number, each tower weighed an estimated 500,000 tons and the official story insists airplane damage and fires caused each tower to collapse symmetrically into its own footprint. No bathtub structure could remain unscathed after a mountain of quarter-mile high material was dropped on it twice. The intact bathtub appears to contradict the official theory of a gravity-driven collapse in which virtually the entire weight of the Twin Towers would crash into the bathtub."

Other evidence of more than a simple building collapse involved at the WTC involved vehicles scorched on only one side, upside down cars, cracked sidewalks and even dozens of damaged parking meters, all some distance from the WTC complex. An estimated 1,400 vehicles from cars to fire trucks were scorched and their tires melted away, including many as far away as the FDR Drive, about seven blocks from the WTC.

In 2003, Wood stated, "I have been collecting data over the last year and a half or so and I have found these distinct and unusual characteristics, which I have given names such as 'fuming' and 'toasted' cars—I have even noticed flipped cars in some pictures. In some cases, the flipped cars are sitting next to trees that are fully covered with leaves." This prompted the question, "If the flipping of the cars was caused by big explosions or 'wind' from the towers coming down, how did the leaves stay on the trees?"

Aerospace and chemical engineer T. Mark Hightower agreed that something was at work other than a simple building collapse due to fire. "Some have speculated that an EMP caused the devastation to these vehicles," said Hightower. "Whatever the case, the destruction resulted from much more than a common office fire. There are technologies in existence beyond anything the general public knows about."

Joel Meyerowitz, in his 2006 coffee table book of photographs of New York and Ground Zero entitled *Aftermath*, depicted a bent and burnt parking meter and wrote, "I often wondered, as I walked along Barclay Street, what it was that did this to the parking meters. There were at least eight of them, all leaning over the sidewalk at a thirty-degree angle, their bodies charred and their plastic faces melted away."

It has been argued that the use of a small thermonuclear device might also explain the melting of the 47 super-strong steel interior girders, many too thick even for thermite. Aside from the blast effect, peripheral damage to cars and parking meters and electromagnetic interference, there were other indications of the use of small nuclear devices that did not necessarily produce large amounts of radioactivity.

One was the extremely loud rumbling heard even prior to the towers collapse. FDNY Lt. Robert Larocco recalled, "Anyway, just to describe to you the collapse of the South Tower coming down, I really wasn't aware there was a full collapse. I thought it might have been just a localize collapse. It was the loudest noise I've ever heard in my life. It was in both ears. Kind of like those rockets that they launch the space shuttles with, it was like I had one going off in each ear. When I thought it was the loudest noise I ever heard, every second it was just increasing getting louder and louder and louder."

Then there were the people who remembered waves of heat and even fireballs. But these were much more than simply rolling flames. Felipe David working for Aramark Corp. tending vending machines in a basement of the North Tower recalled, "That day I was in the basement in sub-level 1 sometime after 8:30 a.m. Everything happened so fast, everything moved so fast. The building started shaking after I heard the explosion below; dust was flying everywhere and all of a sudden it got real hot. I threw myself onto the floor, covered my face because I felt like I was burned. I sat there for a couple of seconds on the floor and felt like I was going to die, saying to myself 'God, please give me strength.' When I went in, I told them it was an explosion," David, with his skin hanging in tatters may have been the person helped to safety by William Rodriguez.

Skin dripping off the body was mentioned by several 9/11 victims. Gamma ray radiation can cause a person to just feel heat, then pain and then the skin will be damaged. The skin may be vaporized, charred or left hanging.

Shirley Hoofard was a 38-year-old Red Cross worker in the Dallas area on 9/11. Hoofard was ordered to New York to begin working with victims and their families. She also was ordered not to reveal any information to the media or the public. "It was very difficult to deal with," she recalled. "The only way I got through it was to shut down. I didn't think or feel. I just did what I did. By the middle of January [2002] I said 'I have to go home.'" But she could not get out of her mind what some of the victims told her. "Several victims told me they saw people engulfed in a fireball and disintegrating. One man said he was at work when he heard a loud noise and at the far end of the cubicles he saw a man running toward him with a fireball coming after him. The running man just exploded, flying into pieces...I heard stories like that from people from both towers....I don't know the physics but at what temperature does a human vaporize?"

Wood and Reynolds were joined by John Hutchinson in their suspicion that a novel directed energy weapon may have been used to demolish the Twin Towers. They said such a weapon incorporated novel technology developed during the Missile Defense or "Star Wars" program. They theorized that such a directed energy weapon caused molecular dissociation, or disintegration, of the physical material making up the World Trade Center towers creating nanoparticles.

Hutchison is a Canadian scientist who has been experimenting with energenic "field effects" for nearly 30 years in an attempt to duplicate the work of Nikola Tesla. He applied the term the "Hutchison Effect" to a collection of phenomena noticed during experiements with radio frequencies and electrostatic sources. These results include "levitation of heavy objects, fusion of dissimilar materials such as metal and wood...anomalous melting (without heating) of metals without burning adjacent material, spontaneous fracturing of metals (which separate by sliding in a sideways fashion), and both temporary and permanent changes in the crystalline structure and physical properties of metal samples."

Asked about the ongoing dirt removal and hosing down at the WTC complex for weeks after 9/11, Hutchison commented in one interview, "I think there is an ongoing reaction or 'infection.'" Wood noted that after damage done to the nearby Bankers Trust Building was repaired, it was still decided to demolish the building down. She said this action indicated there is may have been continuing reaction there. "Rusting beams in the Bankers Trust Building and in the temporary PATH train station also suggest ongoing reactions too," she added.

However, much criticism has been leveled against the energy weapon scenario including "a scientific critique" by James R. Gourley with the International Center for 9/11 Studies, who wrote that the energy weapon concept is "not a scientifically sound hypothesis."

But one fact that Gourley and other skeptics failed to notice was the unusual rise of radiation-linked cancers among 9/11 first responders. By 2006, there were 400 diagnosed cancers in the WTC responders. More than 75 of these involved blood cell cancers, commonly seen in radiation victims. Other diagnosed cancers included thyroid, tongue and throat, testicular, brain, breast, prostate, and other soft tissue tumors. More than a half dozen physicians and epidemiologists confirmed that these cancers were caused by exposure to debris at Ground Zero, commonly referred to as "the Pile."

It must not be forgotten that only seven days after 9/11, the then-EPA Administrator Christine Todd Whitman, announced, "We are very encouraged that the results from our monitoring of air-quality and drinking-water conditions in both New York and near the Pentagon show that the public in these areas is not being exposed to excessive levels of asbestos or other harmful substances. Given the scope of the tragedy from last week, I am glad to reassure the people of New York...that their air is safe to breathe and the water is safe to drink."

The rising incidence of blood cell cancers prompted Kristen Lombardi to write in the *Village Voice*, "In many ways, these illnesses suggest the slow but deteriorating health issues that faced the atomic-bomb survivors of Hiroshima and Nagasaki, where thousands died in the years and decades that followed the United States' use of nuclear weapons." Reminiscent of Hiroshima survivors, by 2010 more than 900 first responders on 9/11 had died of various causes, the most prevalent being cancer.

In 2001, NYPD Detective Gary White was a hailed a hero for his work at Ground Zero. Nine years later, he was fighting for compensation and his life, taking a daily dose of 15 medications amid mounting medical bills for illnesses not covered by the police department which claimed they are not linked to 9/11. "It's totally across the page," said White, describing his medical problems. "Carcinoma, sarcoma, gall bladder cancer, liver cancer."

Another first responder with throat cancer, John Devlin, in 2010 also was seeking compensation for medical bills exceeding $1 million. "We do so much overseas," lamented Devlin. "And I'm not saying don't do it. We're a powerful nation. We should lead by example. But we're not leading by example here when you turn your backs on the 9/11 emergency responders."

Dr. Ed Ward, who has argued the nuclear device option for the 9/11 destruction, stated, "There is one thing and only one thing that can cause all these cancers and problems—*radiation* [emphasis in original]." He also noted the above-average level of tritium found at Ground Zero.

Eight scientific researchers in an April 2002 paper presented at the Symposium on Radioanalytical Methods at the Frontier of Interdisciplinary Science, admitted to elevated tritium levels at Ground Zero. However, they blamed the presence of this radioactive isotope on aircraft gauges and signs along with weapons with tritium gun-sights within WTC government offices (including the BATF), police handguns and even tritium watches worn by victims. They concluded that the tritium was "well below the levels of concern to public exposure."

"The 'well below levels of concern to human exposure' and 'seven times less than the EPA limit' of tritium in the environment are in actuality 27 to 35 times higher than should have been found in one sample, and 21 to 28 times higher than should have been found in the other sample. In spite of this fact it was deemed that no other testing was needed," argued

Dr. Ward.

He also pointed to the fact that the US military possessed small nuclear devices, including ones termed minimum residual radiation (MRR), as far back as the 1950s and announced their availability for civilian demolition work. Older veterans might recall atomic shells fired from regular cannons. More than 35 years ago, physicist Samuel Cohen, the inventor of the neutron bomb, proposed that a low-yield neutron bomb could be constructed so as to focus its energy. So it is well within reason to believe that a small nuclear shaped charge, one in which the blast effect could be channeled in a certain direction, could certainly have been used to vaporize the 47 interior steel girders of the Twin Towers, relieving the 110 floors of any support.

Other theories considered by most to be outlandish, such as "Star Wars" space weapons, holographic airplanes and other exotic technology, may contain some substance as discussed in a later section entitled "Ancient Technology in Baghdad?" Of course, if explosives—whether nuclear devices, "Star Wars" energy weapons and/or thermite—were used to demolish the towers, then someone must have had foreknowledge of this fact.

Apparently New York Mayor Rudolph Giuliani did get word of what was coming. The next morning, he explained to ABC's Peter Jennings that he was in the Mayor's Emergency Management Command Center on the 23rd floor of Building 7 at the WTC. He said, "We were operating out of there when we were told that the World Trade Center was going to collapse and it did collapse before we could get out of the building." Giuliani's recollection of advanced warning was echoed in the testimony of New York Emergency Medical Technician Richard Zarrillo, who provided an oral account of his actions on 9/11 on October 25, 2001.

After rushing into Manhattan after the North Tower was struck, Zarrillo found himself running down Vesey Street "stepping over airplane pieces, several bodies and what not."

Less than 10 minutes after entering WTC Building 7 at the location of the Mayor's Office of Emergency Management (OEM) Command Center, Zarrillo said a representative from OEM came into the main room and said they needed to evacuate the building; that a third plane was inbound and the buildings might collapse.

After leaving the building, Zarrillo met a fire chief who told him there was no third plane but that they needed to re-establish their OEM site. Zarrillo soon found himself alone on Vesey Street. He tried to warn some responders to get out, that the buildings might collapse.

"As I was walking towards the fire command post, I found Steve Mosiello. I said, 'Steve, where's the boss? I have to give him a message.' He said, 'What's the message?' I said the buildings are going to collapse; we need to evac everybody out. With a very confused look, he said, 'Who told you that?' I said I was just…at OEM. OEM says the buildings are going to collapse; we need to get out.

"He [Mosiello] escorted me over to Chief [Peter] Ganci. He said, 'Hey, Pete, we got a message that the buildings are going to collapse. His reply was, 'Who the fuck told you that?' Then Steve brought me in with Chief Ganci, Commissioner Feehan, Steve…I believe Chief Turi was initially there. I said, 'Listen, I was just at OEM. The message I was given was that the buildings are going to collapse; we need to get our people out. At that moment, this thunderous, rolling roar came down and that's when the building came down, the first tower came down"

But how could anyone have known about the collapse in advance? Who warned Giuliani of the impending collapse and who warned EMT Zarrillo? What exactly was going on at the OEM so that one of its representatives knew the towers were about to fall?

Even more peculiar than the rapid collapse of the Twin Towers was the sudden and unexplained collapse of WTC Building 7, which apparently had suffered damage only from falling debris that caused minor fires.

## WHAT CAUSED THE COLLAPSE OF WTC BUILDING 7?

The 47-story Salomon Brothers Building, better known now as WTC Building 7, was an oddity to begin with, as it housed two New York electrical substations, which existed there prior to construction of the building. These substations housed ten transformers, 35 feet tall by 40 feet wide. Additionally, as noted, Mayor Giuliani's Emergency Command Center was located there along with three 500 kW generators for emergency power. Both the command center and other operations in the building stored an estimated 42,000 gallons of diesel fuel for auxiliary generators. Of special interest is the fact that some of that power may have been used by the CIA, Department of Defense, or Secret Service, all of which had offices in Building 7.

Shortly after 4 p.m. on September 11, six hours after the collapse of the South Tower, firemen turned their attention to Building 7 after someone reported small fires. But the fires were surprising since firemen had been ordered out of the building at 11:30 a.m. that morning. At 5:25 p.m. the 47-story structure suddenly collapsed into its footprint, causing very little damage to adjacent structures—the Verizon Building and the US Post Office.

Although no real explanation of the collapse has been offered, it has been reported that the small fires grew larger, reached the stored fuel and started a conflagration so intense it melted the steel frame of the building causing it to crumple. Researcher Eric Hufschmid dismissed this version by noting, "Every photo taken of Building 7 shows only a few tiny fires in only a few windows, and only tiny amounts of smoke were produced," he said. "I would think that a fire of the magnitude necessary to collapse a steel building would have set fire to a lot of the office furniture, carpeting, and other flammable objects. This in turn would have caused a lot of flames to be visible in a lot of windows. I also suspect that such a large fire would have caused many windows to shatter. How could an incredible fire burn in the building without any photos showing evidence of large flames or tremendous plumes of smoke?"

Craig Bartmer, a NYPD officer on 9/11, walked around Building 7 shortly before it fell. He recalled, "I saw a hole. I didn't see a hole bad enough to knock a building down, though…Yeah there was definitely fire in the building, but I didn't hear any…I didn't hear any creaking, or…I didn't hear any indication that it was going to come down. And all of a sudden the radios exploded and everyone started screaming 'get away, get away, get away from it!'…It was at that moment…I looked up, and it was nothing I would ever imagine seeing in my life. The thing started pealing in on itself…Somebody grabbed my shoulder and I started running, and the shit's hitting the ground behind me, and the whole time you're hearing 'boom, boom, boom, boom, boom.' I think I know an explosion when I hear it…Yeah it had some damage to it, but nothing like what they're saying...Nothing to account for what we saw...I am shocked at the story we've heard about it to be quite honest."

Thomas Sullivan, a controlled demolition expert who was forced to leave Controlled Demolition Inc. after business dried up in the fear following the 9/11 attacks, also believed Building 7 was intentionally demolished. Sullivan said he knew the destruction of Building 7 was a classic controlled implosion on the day it occurred. Asked to explain how such a demolition could have been conducted, Sullivan explained, "Looking at the building it wouldn't be a problem—once you gain access to the elevator shafts...then a team of expert loaders would have hidden access to the core columns and beams. The rest can be accomplished with just the right kind of explosives for the job. Thermite can be used as well."

When questioned why detonation cords laying all over the building would not have been noticed, Sullivan replied, "Remote wireless detonators have been available for years. Look at any action movie—and of course the military has them. The reason most contractors don't use them is that they are too expensive—but in a project with a huge budget it would be no problem. As for the casings—everyone in the industry.... would know that RDX explosive cutter charges are completely consumed when they go off—nothing is left. And in the case of thermite cutter charges, that may also be the case. Thermite self-consuming cutter charge casings have been around since first patented back in 1984."

Sullivan explained that the careful placement of charges—focused and precise—is a fey factor in a controlled demolition. "We are not talking about setting off a bomb here," he said. "The amount and type of explosives is an art and collateral damage can often be completely avoided."

But, beyond the obvious indications of controlled demolition, there were more strange aspects to the collapse of Building 7.

Barry Jennings was deputy director with the Emergency Services Department of the New York City Housing Authority. Along with Michael Hess, a founding partner and senior managing director of Giuliani Partners LLC, Jennings went to Mayor Giuliani's Office of Emergency Management's (OEM) Emergency Command Center (EOC) in Building 7 on 9/11 prior to the collapse of the Twin Towers only to find it empty.

"Upon arriving into the OEM EOC, we noticed that everybody was gone. I saw coffee that was on the desk, the smoke was still coming off the coffee, I saw half-eaten sandwiches," Jennings recalled. Jennings and Hess descended stairs trying to leave the building. "When we reached the 6th floor the landing that we were standing on gave way, there was an explosion and the landing gave way, I was left there hanging, I had to climb back up and walk back up to the 8th floor...The explosion was beneath me....so when the explosion happened it blew us back....both buildings (the Twin Towers) were still standing.

"I was trapped in there for several hours, I was trapped in there when both buildings came down—all this time I'm hearing all kinds of explosions, all this time I'm hearing explosions....For me to see what I saw was unbelievable." Jennings said eventually firemen arrived and led him and Hess out of Building 7. Crossing Building 7's shattered lobby, the firemen kept telling him not to look down. Jennings was horrified to see that "we were stepping over people and you can tell when you're stepping over people." Jennings' description of stepping over bodies and multiple explosions within WTC 7 prior to the collapse of the Twin Towers contradicts official statements claiming no fatalities inside Building 7.

Unlike the Twin Towers, which collapsed from the top down, Building 7 collapsed from the bottom up, the classic form of a typical building demolition. In fact, this might have indeed been the case.

In September 2002, during a PBS documentary entitled *America Rebuilds*, WTC leaseholder Larry Silverstein had this to say about Building 7: "I remember getting a call from the, er, fire department commander, telling me that they were not sure they were going to be able to contain the fire, and I said, 'We've had such terrible loss of life, maybe the smartest thing to do is pull it. And they made that decision to pull and we watched the building collapse." The term "pull" is industry slang for the controlled demolition of a structure as voiced by a New York fire commander who told TV news of "pulling" the heavily damaged WTC Building 6.

Some years later as spokesperson for Silverstein Properties Inc. tried to explain that all Silverstein meant was to "pull" the firemen out of the building. Is explanation did not fly with knowledgeable researchers since all firemen had been withdrawn from Building 7 that morning.

Inadvertently adding fuel to this fiery issue was Jeffrey Scott Shapiro of Fox News, who in 2010, after lambasting the 9/11 Truth Movement as "nothing more than a paranoid, delusional pack of lies," revealed startling information based on his memory of that day. "...I remember watching all 47 stories of Building 7 suddenly and silently crumble before my eyes. Shortly before the building collapsed, several NYPD officers and Con Edison workers told me that Larry Silverstein, the property developer of One World Financial Center was on the phone with his insurance carrier to see if they would authorize the controlled demolition of the building—since its foundation was already unstable and expected to fall," recalled Shapiro, who argued, "To dispute the conventional historical account is intellectually dishonest and nonsensical. I know this because I was working as a journalist for Gannett News at Ground Zero that day, and I remember very clearly what I saw and heard."

Despite this dismissal of conspiracy theories, Shapiro went on to say that he did confirm through the New York City Board of Education and the FBI reports of rumors circulating in the New York City Arab-American community about a possible attack on Manhattan and that a Brooklyn high school student predicted the collapse of the World Trade Center five days before it happened.

So, at least according to Shapiro, building owner Silvestein joined conspiracy theories in contemplating the controlled demolition of Building 7. Some iconoclastic researchers have suggested that rather than seek permission for such destruction, Silverstein may in reality have been merely checking to make sure his insurance would pay off following a controlled demolition.

And the oddities and strangeness continued.

Kurt Sonnenfeld, director of broadcast operations for the FEMA's National Emergency Response Team and its official videographer, was sent to Ground Zero on 9/11. After filming for a month and producing 29 tapes, he left for Argentina without turning in his tapes claiming, "What I saw at certain moments and in certain places...is very disturbing!"

While in Argentina, Sonnenfeld wrote of his experiences in a book published there entitled *El Perseguido* (*'The Persecuted'*). While the public was banned from Ground Zero, Sonnenfeld was permitted unrestricted access and his video was "sanitized" and made available to the world's TV news networks. Tapes that reveal things contrary to the official government version of events remain in his possession. Sonnenfeld claimed that because of his knowledge and tapes, he was falsely accused of a crime and pursued through several countries by US government agents.

"Personally, I wasn't forced to leave the United States, and I certainly did not 'flee,'" explained Sonnenfeld in a 2009 interview. "At the time I was still fairly oblivious to what was actually brewing against me. I hadn't connected the dots yet; so that when I left in early 2003 I had every intention of returning. I came to Argentina for a short respite; to try to recuperate after all that had happened to me. I traveled here freely, with my own passport, using my own credit cards. But because of an incredible series of events, I have since been forced into exile, and I haven't been back."

He said the events included suffered false accusations for "crimes" that never happened, abusive imprisonment and torture as a result of those accusations, as well as "outrageous calumnies" against his reputation, the ransacking of his office and home, death threats, kidnap attempts and "several other violations of civil and human rights as denounced by numerous international accords." The US government in 2005 requested his extradition but this was denied by an Argentine federal judge. In 2007, the Supreme Court of Argentina turned down a US appeal, citing fabrications in the original extradition order. Due to this plus the fact that Sonnenfeld and his family continued to be the object of harassment and surveillance, they were placed under constant police protection.

Asked what the US government might be so concerned about, Sonnenfeld replied, "There were many things, in hindsight, that were disturbing at Ground Zero. It was odd to me that I was dispatched to go to New York even before the second plane hit the South Tower, while the media was still reporting only that a 'small plane' had collided with the North Tower—far too small of a catastrophe at that point to involve FEMA. FEMA was mobilized within minutes, whereas it took ten days for it to deploy to New Orleans to respond to Hurricane Katrina, even with abundant advance warning! It was odd to me that all cameras were so fiercely prohibited within the secured perimeter of Ground Zero, that the entire area was declared a crime scene and yet the 'evidence' within that crime scene was so rapidly removed and destroyed. And then it was very odd to me when I learned that FEMA and several other federal agencies had already moved into position at their command center at Pier 92 on September 10th, one day before the attacks!

"We are asked to believe that all four of the 'indestructible' black boxes of the two jets that struck the Twin Towers were never found because they were completely vaporized, yet I have footage of the rubber wheels of the landing gear nearly undamaged, as well as the seats, parts of the fuselage and a jet turbine that were absolutely not vaporized. This being said, I do find it rather odd that such objects could have survived fairly intact the type of destruction that turned most of the Twin Towers into thin dust. And I definitely harbor some doubts about the authenticity of the 'jet' turbine, far too small to have come from one of the Boeings.

"What happened with Building 7 is incredibly suspicious. I have video that shows how curiously small the rubble pile was, and how the buildings to either side were untouched by Building 7 when it collapsed. It had not been hit by an airplane; it had suffered only minor injuries when the Twin Towers collapsed, and there were only small fires on a couple of floors. There's no way that building could have imploded the way it did without controlled demolition. Yet the collapse of Building 7 was hardly mentioned by the mainstream media and suspiciously ignored by the 9/11 Commission."

Sonnenfeld explained that in addition to federal offices of the Secret Service, the Department of Defense, FBI, Internal Revenue Service, Securities and Exchange Commission, and Office of Emergency Management's "Crisis Center" were all housed within Building 7. After September 11, it was revealed that Building 7 had contained the largest clandestine domestic station of the CIA outside of Washington, D.C.

One of the most surprising aspects of Sonnenfeld's story concerned what was under WTC Building 6. "There was no underground parking level at 7 World Trade Center. And there was no underground vault," he explained. "Instead, the federal agencies at Building 7 stored their vehicles, documents and evidence in the building of their associates across the street. Beneath the plaza level of the US Customs House [Building 6] was a large underground garage, separated off from the rest of the complexes underground area and guarded under tight security. This was where the various government services parked their bomb-proofed cars and armored limousines, counterfeit taxi cabs and telephone company trucks used for undercover surveillance and covert operations, specialized vans and other vehicles. Also within that secured parking area was access to the sub-level vault of Building 6.

## WHAT CAUSED THE COLLAPSE OF WTC BUILDING 7?

"When the North Tower fell, the US Customs House [Building 6] was crushed and totally incinerated. Much of the underground levels beneath it were also destroyed. But there were voids. And it was into one of those voids, recently uncovered, that I descended with a special Task Force to investigate. It was there we found the security antechamber to the vault, badly damaged. At the far end of the security office was the wide steel door to the vault, a combination code keypad in the cinder-block wall beside it. But the wall was cracked and partially crumbled, and the door was sprung partially open. So we checked inside with our flashlights. Except for several rows of empty shelves, there was nothing in the vault but dust and debris. It had been emptied. Why was it empty? And when could it have been emptied?

"Building 6 was evacuated within twelve minutes after the first airplane struck the North Tower. The streets were immediately clogged with fire trucks, police cars and blocked traffic, and the vault was large enough, 15 meters by 15 meters—by my estimate, to necessitate at least a big truck to carry out its contents. And after the towers fell and destroyed most of the parking level, a mission to recover the contents of the vault would have been impossible. The vault had to have been emptied before the attack...it's apparent that things of importance were taken out of harm's way before the attacks. For example, the CIA didn't seem too concerned about their losses.

"And Customs at first claimed that everything was destroyed. That the heat was so intense that everything in the evidence safe had been baked to ash. But some months later, they announced that they had broken up a huge Colombian narco-trafficking and money-laundering ring after miraculously recovering crucial evidence from the safe, including surveillance photos and heat-sensitive cassette tapes of monitored calls. And when they moved in to their new building at 1 Penn Plaza in Manhattan, they proudly hung on the lobby wall their commissioner's citation plaque and their big round US Customs Service ensign, also miraculously recovered, in pristine condition, from their crushed and cremated former office building at the World Trade Center."

Sonnenfeld said he was not alone in his observations at Ground Zero and that he and others discussed what they had seen among themselves. "...I hope that they will come forward, but I'm sure they have strong apprehensions as to what will happen to them if they do....People are gripped by fear. Everybody knows that if you question US authority you will have problems in some way or another. At minimum you will be discredited and dehumanized. Most likely you'll find yourself indicted for something completely unrelated, like tax evasion—or something even worse, as in my case."

Asked if he wasn't fearful of being branded a "conspiracy nut," Sonnenfeld responded, "Sometimes it seems to me that the 'nuts' are those who hold to what they've been told with an almost religious fervor despite all of the evidence to the contrary—the ones who won't even consider that there was a conspiracy. There are so many anomalies to the 'official' investigation that you can't blame it on oversight or incompetence. I am familiar with the scientists and qualified professionals [who offer opinions differing from the official story], and their findings are convincing, credible, and presented according to scientific protocol—in stark contrast to the findings of the 'official' investigation. In addition, numerous intelligence agents and government officials have now come forward with their very informed opinions that the 911 Commission was a farce at best or a coverup at worst. My experience at Ground Zero is but one more piece of the puzzle."

Another genuine oddity concerning the sudden loss of Building 7 was the fact that the collapse was broadcast by both CNN and the BBC almost a half hour before it occurred! As mentioned earlier, when BBC reporter Jane Standley reported that the Salomon Brothers building had collapsed, it could clearly be seen still standing in the city skyline behind her on the live broadcast.

Richard Porter, a spokesperson for BBC, naturally denied any notion of conspiracy or foreknowledge. "We're not part of a conspiracy. Nobody told us what to say or do on September 11th. We didn't get told in advance that buildings were going to fall down. We didn't receive press releases or scripts in advance of events happening," stated Porter in a BBC press release. However, he added, "We no longer have the original tapes of our 9/11 coverage (for reasons of cock-up, not conspiracy)." One of the biggest news stories in history and through bungling, they no longer have the original tapes. This rivals the destruction of the original moon landing tapes by NASA in shortsightedness, if indeed that's what it is.

The idea that a modern 47-story steel building can totally collapse

WHAT CAUSED THE COLLAPSE OF WTC BUILDING 7?

strictly due to fire is something outside of normal experience, yet no serious investigation was undertaken.

In fact, FEMA's 2002 WTC Building Performance Study offered this muddled explanation for the loss of Building 7: "…[WTC 7's] loss of structural integrity was likely a result of weakening caused by fires on the 5th to 7th floors. The specifics of the fires in WTC 7 and how they caused the building to collapse remain unknown at this time.

"Although the total diesel fuel on the premises contained massive potential energy, the best hypothesis has only a low probability of occurrence. Further research, investigation and analyses are needed to resolve this issue." In plain English: *We don't really know what caused the collapse and our best guess has a low probability of having occurred.*

In August 2008, NIST released its "Final Report on the Collapse of World Trade Center Building 7." As with the Warren Commission and the 9/11 Commission before it, the NIST report was built upon the impressive number of men and women who contributed their names and credentials. These included the property owner Larry Silverstein.

Following four "disclaimers," including a caution that no part of this report could be used in any legal proceedings, this report, in its "leading hypothesis," again argued that debris raining from the Twin Towers caused fires in Building 7 which led to its total, symmetrical "progressive" collapse. The report said "the breakdown of connections and/or beams resulted in damage to at least one of the critical columns supporting a large-span floor bay on the east side of the building or below floor 13. This was the initiating event of the collapse." It also stated there were no deaths or serious injuries suffered at Building 7.

Utilizing a computer program called SHAMRC, the NIST investigators programmed in six scenarios to determine if controlled demolition could explain the building's demise. Based on the perceived lack of windows broken out or massive blast heard due to explosives, the NIST investigators decided that "no demolition-type blast" caused the collapse. Due to arguments that Building 7 collapsed at near-free-fall speed, the NIST report did admit that the top 18 floors of the north face fell at "40 percent greater than computed free-fall time."

Addressing the argument that there was no "no demolition-type blast" at Building 7, demolition expert Thomas Sullivan stated, "With any implosion there is never just one big explosion but rather waves of smaller explosions—not unlike the percussion section in a symphony—as each loaded floor is progressively set off." When asked if there is any chance that fire of normal office materials could have been responsible for the smooth, symmetrical, free-fall acceleration of building 7 as stated by the NIST report, Sullivan retorted, "Not a chance."

By 2010, there was still no explanation for the collapse of Building 7 that satisfied the members of Architects & Engineers for 9/11 Truth. Furthermore, their attempts to gain access to the NIST's Building 7 collapse-analysis data have been rebuffed. "Most troubling is the reason given for denial," wrote retired NASA flight research engineer Dwain Deets for *OpEdNews*. "The Director of NIST has determined that release of the information *might jeopardize public safety* [emphasis in original]. This reasoning is outrageous. If anything, not releasing the information might jeopardize public safety."

"[I]s there not anyone interested in bringing accountability and justice to players within the military/industrial complex?" asked Deets. "Profits abound from the War on Terror, all justified by the events of September 11, 2001. Many who have studied the available evidence feel the collapse of Building 7 is the Achilles' heel in that day's events. Doesn't that at least warrant a new investigation of the Building 7 collapse? The ramifications would be so massive if it was found that the prior investigation was a fraud. It could bring into question the whole basis of the War on Terror itself."

And if Building 7 was "pulled" by demolition, why is it so far-fetched to consider that the towers were felled the same way? Perhaps there are more reasonable explanations for modern buildings to collapse into nothing but dust, but no one will ever know for certain due to the destruction of evidence and lack of a rigorous and honest investigation.

Perhaps the most expedient way to deal with the mystery of the loss of WTC 7 was exemplified by the government's 9/11 Commission. Its final report deals with the collapse by simply omitting any mention of it.

## TRACKS OF FOREKNOWLEDGE

Following the horrendous attacks of 9/11 President Bush stated, "Had I known that the enemy was going to use airplanes to kill on that fateful morning, I would have done everything in my power to protect the American people." His statement flies in the face of numerous examples of foreknowledge of an attack, including the use of hijacked airliners. Other US leaders said we should avoid "finger pointing" to place blame, ye advance warnings were too numerous and specific to do otherwise.

During 2001, the United States spent $30 billion on intelligence gathering plus an additional $12 billion aimed specifically at counterterrorism. This total of $42 billion exceeds most nations' total gross national product, yet Americans were told that none of its two-dozen alphabet intelligence agencies had any inkling that we were about to be attacked.

Information available today seriously disputes this claim. It was in fact disputed within days of the attacks by people both in and outside the government.

One recent example came in 2009 when a 9/11 Commission document placed in the National Archives reveals that just two days before 9/11, a NORAD exercise as part of the "Vigilant Guardian" war games involved a scenario of terrorists hijacking a London to New York airliner and detonating an on-board bomb to rain debris over the city.

Questions as to why there had been no warning came quickly. The day after the attacks, Congressional Research Service antiterrorism expert Kenneth Katzman was quoted as saying, "How nothing could have been picked up is beyond me."

But something must have been picked up. How else to explain the fact that the State Department on September 7, 2001, issued a worldwide caution to Americans that they "may be the target of a terrorist threat from extremist groups with links to Osama bin Laden's al Qaeda organization...Such individuals have not distinguished between official and civilian targets. As always, we take this information seriously. US government facilities worldwide remain on heightened alert."

As months passed, more and more evidence accumulated until it became overwhelmingly clear that persons within the federal government were forewarned of terrorist attacks, including the use of airplanes against buildings. Even congressional researchers determined that US intelligence agencies had received at least twelve warnings of coming offensive action by terrorists. And, as will be seen, this is a low figure.

By April 2002, leaks in the news media damaging to the official explanation, plus public clamor for an investigation of the 9/11 attacks, prompted congressional leaders to agree to a joint investigation by both the Senate and House Intelligence committees. The charter of the Joint Inquiry into Intelligence Community Activities before and after September 11, 2001—known as the JICI—was to be limited in scope, with authorization only to review intelligence failures and recommend corrections.

The JICI got off to a rocky start when retired CIA Inspector General Britt Snider, the staff director for the JICI, resigned under pressure from committee members who believed his close connection to CIA director George Tenet might interfere with an impartial investigation.

Amid numerous difficulties and delays, the unusual joint hearings that were scheduled for June 2002 did not convene until late September. "Are we getting the cooperation we need? Absolutely not," charged the senior Republican on the Senate Intelligence Committee, Senator Richard Shelby of Alabama. Florida Democratic Senator Bob Graham echoed Shelby's complaint, saying the Bush administration told them they can "only talk to the top of the pyramid."

"Well, the problem is, the top of the pyramid has a general awareness of what's going on in the organization, but if you want to know why Malaysian plotters were not put on a watch list...you've got to talk to somebody at the level where those kinds of decisions were made." Graham referred to a preliminary report, which pointed out that two of the hijacking suspects, Khalid al-Midhar and Nawaf al-Hazmi, lived openly in San Diego even after being observed in a Malaysia meeting with known terrorists.

Bush and Cheney had long opposed any independent investigation of the 9/11 attacks, claiming it would impede the War on Terrorism by leading to leaks of security measures and tying up personnel needed in the war.

But with the revelations of irregularities in investigations by government agencies that came to light in the spring and summer of 2002, Congress was finally moved to get the JICI funded and operational. "The attacks of September 11...highlighted a failure of national policy to respond to the developments of a global terror network implacably hostile to American interests," thundered Senator John McCain, who, along with Senator Joseph Lieberman, cosponsored the bill to fund the independent commission. Legislation authorizing the creation of the ten-person panel, armed with subpoena power and a $3 million budget, was approved by the Senate in a 90 to 8 vote late in September 2002.

The run-up to the actual hearings illustrated the need to strengthen the JICI's charter, including the need for subpoena power.

According to a story in the *Los Angeles Times* in May 2002, "Small teams of investigators have been at the Justice Department and the CIA, gathering documents and conducting interviews. They have come back with a litany of complaints about tactics they say are designed to slow their progress and restrict their access to documents and potential informants, sources said."

Research was quickly coming to light making it clear that from 1998 onward, both the CIA and FBI had received ever-increasing warnings concerning al Qaeda using hijacked aircraft to attack targets within the United States. Despite the serious nature of this evidence, the Bush administration continued to stonewall and hamper the congressional investigation, even launching an investigation of the investigators.

This occurred after word leaked to the public in June 2002 that communications in Arabic intercepted by the National Security Agency on September 10, 2001 contained phrases such as "Tomorrow is zero hour" and "The match is about to begin." As noted earlier, this made it seem likely that the hijackers were privy to the war game exercises scheduled for the following day, evidence of an inside job.

The FBI swung into action. But instead of going after the authors of the notes indicating foreknowledge, they went after the persons on the joint committee who leaked the information.

Even as White House spokesman Ari Fleischer was calling the notes "alarmingly specific," bureau agents were asking committee members to take lie detector tests regarding the leaks. The *Washington Post* reported that nearly all of the thirty-seven members of the joint committee were questioned. Some members declined to take the lie detector tests, citing constitutional separation of powers and the unreliability of such tests.

Eleanor Hill, the new staff director of the JICI, spoke out about advance notice of the attacks passed to ranking leaders. She noted that a briefing for "senior government officials" in July 2001 specifically warned that Osama bin Laden "will launch a significant terrorist attack against US and/or Israeli interests in the coming weeks. The attack will be spectacular and designed to inflict mass casualties against US facilities or interests. Attack preparations have been made. Attack will occur with little or no warning." She said it was unknown if President Bush received specific information regarding the possibility of airliners being used as flying bombs because the director of the CIA would not declassify the information.

Hill, who wrote a report described as preliminary, said it was based on a review of 400,000 government documents and testimony taken during four months of closed-door hearings. Hill stated that while investigators found no specific warning of the 9/11 attacks, collectively the warnings "reiterated a consistent and critically important theme: Osama bin Laden's intent to launch terrorist attacks inside the United States."

Even a survey of mainstream sources shows that warnings of a domestic attack had been coming in for some time—and with increasing frequency right up to 9/11.

For example, in December 2000, the Congressional Advisory Panel to Assess Domestic Response Capabilities for Terrorism Involving Weapons of Mass Destruction issued a report stating, "We are impelled by the stark realization that a terrorist attack on some level within our borders is inevitable."

One clear warning came as early as eight years before the 9/11 attacks in the form of a book written by Yossef Bodansky, director of the US House Task Force on Terrorism and Unconventional Warfare.

In his book, *Target America: Terrorism in the US Today*, Bodansky detailed the airfields in Iran and North Korea where Muslim terrorists trained and noted, "According to a former trainee in Wakiland [Iran], one of the exercises included having an Islamic Jihad detachment seize (or hijack) a transport aircraft. Then, trained air crews from among the terrorists would crash the airliner with its passengers into a selected target."

Wiretaps on suspected al Qaeda terrorists in Italy as far back as 2000 also gave indications of plans for a major attack on the United States involving airplanes and airports. "This will be one of those strikes that will never be forgotten..." was the comment recorded from Abdelkader Mahmoud Es Sayed, an Egyptian accused of being a ranking al Qaeda member in Italy and a man convicted of the 1997 massacre of fifty-eight tourists at Luxor, Egypt. Es Sayed also mentioned danger in airports and flying.

In another taped conversation on January 24, 2001, a Tunisian terrorist spoke about fake identification papers to Es Sayed and asked, "Will these work for the brothers who are going to the United States?" Es Sayed also stated the war against the enemies of Islam would be fought "with any means we can combat them, using…airplanes. They won't be able to stop us even with their heaviest weapons."

According to the *Los Angeles Times*, several US officials said they were unfamiliar with the wiretap messages but "one Justice Department official noted that a small cadre of US intelligence agents might have been privy to them." What is most enlightening about these Italian wiretaps is not that they evinced foreknowledge—they were too vague to be considered a precise warning—but that they gave indication of the many and varied alerts coming into the United States as well as the fact that many foreign intelligence services were monitoring al Qaeda cells.

Spain got in on the act. In August 2001, the voice of an unidentified man in London was taped speaking with the head of a Madrid terrorist cell. The man said he had entered the field of aviation and was taking flying lessons.

Such warnings were not lost on the British. It was revealed in June 2002, that British intelligence chiefs warned the Prime Minister less than two months before September 11 that Osama bin Laden and al Qaeda were in "the final stages" of preparing a terrorist attack in the West. It was stated that this prediction was based not only on reports from MI6 but also from the cabinet office Joint Intelligence Committee, which included representatives from the American CIA and NSA.

According to a report on MSNBC, just two weeks before the 9/11 attacks, a radio station in the Cayman Islands received an unsigned letter warning of a major attack against the United States involving airliners. It was reported that US government officials went to investigate but no further information was forthcoming. As will be seen, the Cayman Islands are an offshore banking haven to many factions, including the CIA and international bankers.

Even the much-disparaged Taliban apparently tried to give us warning.

According to a story posted September 7, 2002, by Independent Digital, an aide to then-Taliban Foreign Minister Wakil Ahmed Muttawakil tried to warn US authorities weeks prior to the 9/11 attacks. Muttawakil, unhappy with the glut of foreign Arab militants in Afghanistan, told his aide he was concerned over the prospect of US military action against his country. He was quoted as saying, "The guests are going to destroy the guest-house."

The aide, unidentified for his own safety by the British publication, said Muttawakil was shocked in the summer of 2001 to learn of a coming attack from fundamentalist Islamic leader Tahir Yildash. "At first, Muttawakil wouldn't say why he was so upset," explained the aide. "Then it all came out. Yildash had revealed that Osama bin Laden was going to launch an attack on the United States. It would take place on American soil and it was imminent. Yildash said Osama hoped to kill thousands of Americans." The aide said he first traveled across the Pakistan border to meet with American consul general David Katz late in July 2001. "They met in a safe house belonging to an old Mujahideen leader who has confirmed to the *Independent* that the meeting took place," reported the news outlet. Katz declined to discuss the matter.

Next, Muttawakil sent the aide to the Kabul offices of the United Nations, where he again issued his warning.

Apparently, since the aide failed to make it clear that he was sent by Foreign Minister Muttawakil, both American and United Nations officials thought his warning more propaganda from the warring factions within Afghanistan and did nothing.

Similar warning signs came from the Far East. In 1995, when Manila authorities answered a fire call they discovered bomb-making materials in the apartment of Ramzi Yousef, later convicted for his role in the 1993 WTC bombing. Yousef escaped but another suspected al Qaeda member, Abdul Hakim Murad, was taken into custody.

Murad told his interrogators that Ramzi had a plan to hijack a commercial airliner in the United States and crash it into CIA Headquarters or the Pentagon. Philippine investigators also found evidence that Ramzi's plan, code-named "Project Bojinka," also involved targeting the White House, the Sears Tower in Chicago, the Transamerica Tower in San Francisco, and the World Trade Center. The plans for Bojinka must have been known at the highest levels of government, which makes a mockery of later claims that no one could have imagined that hijacked airliners could be used as deadly missiles.

Apparently Muslim fanatics had already attempted to put Ramzi's plan into effect. On Christmas Eve 1994, four men thought to be connected to bin Laden's terrorist network hijacked Air France Flight 8969 bound from Algiers to Paris. The plane landed in Marseilles, where the hijackers demanded that it be loaded with explosives and extra fuel. Their plan, apparently to crash the craft into the Eiffel Tower, was derailed when commandos stormed the plane and killed all four hijackers.

Warnings had continued to pour in from the Philippines, a hotbed of terrorist activity. According to the *Manila Times*, Philippine defense and police intelligence officers warned American authorities of an alliance between Abu Sayyaf (ASG) terrorists there and the al Qaeda network. The paper said American officials ignored the warnings until September 11, 2001.

The report went on to describe a 1994 meeting between ASG cofounder Edwin Angeles and WTC bombing mastermind Ramzi Yousef that included convicted Oklahoma City bombing accomplice Terry Nichols, who was married to a Philippine national. The topics of discussion were terrorist targets. The Murrah Federal Building in Oklahoma City was mentioned as well as another attack on the World Trade Center.

It seemed everyone from the Chinese to our own FBI tried to warn Washington authorities that an attack was imminent, yet nothing was done. Chinese military officers wrote about just such an attack as occurred on 9/11 three years before the fact. In a military manual entitled "Unrestricted Warfare," People's Liberation Army colonels Qiao Liang and Wang Xiangsui noted, "Whether it be the intrusions of [computer] hackers, *a major explosion at the World Trade Center, or a bombing attack by bin Laden* [emphasis added], all of these greatly exceed the frequency bandwidth understood by the American military…"

A CIA translation of this Chinese manual was published on September 11, 2002, the one-year anniversary of the attacks. The manual is a recipe book of unorthodox methods for weaker nations to humble America. It discusses multilevel attacks on America's social, political, and economic systems using strategies involving computer hackers, the infiltration of illegal immigrants, stock market manipulation, and even the use of weapons of mass destruction.

The Chinese leadership, and particularly its military chiefs, has long viewed the United States as their principal enemy, a fact that has been marginalized by both the US Congress and the corporate mass media due to the close business and trade relations between the nations.

Exactly one month following the 9/11 attacks, China was quietly approved as a member of the World Trade Organization (WTO) after fifteen years of negotiation. It was a move that had previously prompted many and widespread protests due to that Asian nation's abysmal human rights record. This time, with Americans in shock over the 9/11 attacks, little notice was given to this action, which brought a new market of 1.3 billion persons into the world trading system.

With the heightened security resulting from the attacks, there was no opportunity for demonstrations against this WTO action. According to CNN, WTO ministers meeting in the Persian Gulf state of Qatar were protected by a US helicopter gunship and naval vessels, and were inside a cordon that included more than two thousand US Marines.

The addition of China to the WTO was hailed as a boost for American business by US Trade Representative Robert Zoellick, a member of the Council on Foreign Relations, the Trilateral Commission and an attendee of the secretive Bilderberg meetings of globalists. Critics said the addition of China might bring on even more trade disputes, a warning which proved prescient. In 2010, disputes with China continued to escalate, the most recent in June, when the US Commerce Department announced that it would impose steep countervailing and anti-dumping duties against imports of Chinese steel grating. WTO director general Mike Moore declared China's entry into the trade organization "a major historic event," yet there was minimal publicity in the United States.

Even the Russians seemed to be aware that something big was coming. Dr. Tatyana Koryagina, a senior research fellow for the Institute of Macroeconomic Research under the Russian Ministry of Economic Development and reportedly close to President Putin's inner circle, predicted that an "unusual catastrophe" would strike the United States in late August 2001. Her prediction appeared in a *Pravda* story published on July 12, 2001.

"The US has been chosen as the object of financial attack because the financial center of the planet is located there. The effect will be maximal. The strike waves of economic crisis will spread over the planet instantly and will remind us of the blast of a huge nuclear bomb."

Asked about the discrepancy of dates in a later interview, Dr. Koryagina explained, "I did not make a serious mistake. Indeed, between 15 and 20 August, the dollar started trembling under the pressure of multiple bad news about the US and economy. And within weeks, the Manhattan skyscrapers fell down.

"As a result, a significant part of the world financial network was paralyzed. This strike was aimed at destabilization and destruction of America and (in domino fashion) all the countries making countless billions of dollars." She advised Russian citizens not to invest in American dollars.

She also said the 9/11 attacks were not the work of nineteen terrorists but a group of extremely powerful private persons seeking to reshape the world. This group, she added, has assets of about $300 trillion, which it will use to legitimize its power and create a new world government.

Many persons have taken Dr. Koryagina's comments very seriously when considering both her credentials and her knowledge of Russia's close contacts with nations identified with terrorism, such as Iraq, Iran, Syria, Libya, and North Korea.

As reported by the *Washington Times* on September 28, 2001, "US intelligence agencies have uncovered information that Russian criminal groups have been supplying Osama bin Laden and his al Qaeda terrorist network with components for chemical, biological and nuclear weapons."

Arabic sources too seemed to have been able to discern that bin Laden was preparing to launch a major attack. In mid-2002, Egyptian president Hosni Mubarak revealed that his intelligence service warned US officials about a week before the 9/11 attacks that bin Laden's organization was in the last stages of preparing a major operation against an American target.

Mubarak said Egyptian intelligence chiefs tried unsuccessfully to thwart the operation using an unnamed agent who had penetrated the al Qaeda network. They passed the information regarding this penetration to US intelligence between March and May 2001, he said, adding, "We informed them about everything."

An American intelligence official told the *New York Times* that they had received no such warning but Mubarak said he was informed that security at the US embassy in Cairo was tightened just before the attacks. Mubarak's interview with the *Times* apparently was the first time that a foreign leader admitted that an intelligence service had penetrated the al Qaeda terrorist network.

The *Times* writers noted dryly, "At a minimum, Mr. Mubarak's account adds detail and drama to a list of warnings about potential terrorist attacks that American intelligence fielded in the days, weeks and months before September 11."

Within hours of the attacks Abdel-Barri Atwan, editor of the London newspaper *al-Quds al-Arabi*, told Reuters News Service, "Osama bin Laden warned three weeks ago that he would attack American interests in an unprecedented attack, a big one... Personally we received information that he planned very, very big attacks against American interests. We received several warnings like this."

Although Atwan said he did not notify the authorities of this warning because he did not take it seriously, it begs the question: if a London newspaper knew of impending attacks, why not the American intelligence services? An article in the June 23, 2001, issue of *Airjet Airline World News* noted another Arabic source as claiming that "a big surprise" was expected in coming weeks.

A reporter from Arabic satellite television channel MBC who had recently met with bin Laden was quoted as saying, "A severe blow is expected against US and Israeli interests worldwide...There is a mobilization among the Osama bin Laden forces. It seems that there is a race of who will strike first. Will it be the United States or Osama bin Laden?"

Another source for a warning may have been an Iranian being held in Germany at the time of the 9/11 attacks. According to the German newspaper *Neue Presse*, prior to 9/11 the man asked to contact American authorities to warn them of an imminent attack. It was reported that when the man told the Secret Service that he was facing deportation from Germany, they hung up on him. On September 14, 2001 US agents finally interrogated the man.

Closer to home, in a 1993 letter to the *New York Times*, the Middle Easterners who bombed the World Trade Center in that year made it plain that they would try again. Their letter read:

> We, the fifth battalion in the LIBERATION ARMY, declare our responsibility for the explosion on the mentioned building. This action was done in response for the American po-

litical, economical, and military support to Israel the state of terrorism and to the rest of the dictator countries in the region.

Our demands are:
1. Stop all military, economical, and political aid to Israel.
2. All diplomatic relations with Israel must stop.
3. Not to interfere with any of the Middle East countries' interior affairs.

If our demands are not met, all of our functional groups in the army will continue to execute our missions against the military and civilian targets in and out the United States.

For your own information, our army has more than hundred and fifty suicidal soldiers ready to go ahead.

The terrorism that Israel practices (which is supported by America) must be faced with a similar one. The dictatorship and terrorism (also supported by America) that some countries are practicing against their own people must also be faced with terrorism.

The American people must know that their civilians who got killed are not better than those who are getting killed by the American weapons and support.

The American people are responsible for the actions of their government and they must question all of the crimes that their government is committing against other people. Or they—Americans—will be the targets of our operations that could diminish them.

The conspirators also drafted a second letter, which was later recovered from an erased file on a computer disc seized from Ayyad's office. This second letter, which the conspirators apparently did not send, proclaimed that the World Trade Center bomb did not do as much damage as had been intended, because their "calculations were not very accurate this time." They warned, however, that they would be more precise in the future and would continue to target the World Trade Center if their demands were not met.

Following his 1995 arrest in Pakistan, Ramzi Yousef was more specific. He clearly stated that the conspirators had intended for the bomb to topple one of the towers and hoped that it would crash into the other, bringing them both down and killing one quarter of a million people.

One of the strangest items indicating foreknowledge of the attacks came in the form of registered Internet domain names. Two highly suggestive domain names—attackontwintowers.com and worldtradetower-attack.com—were registered more than a year before the 9/11 attacks. Since the registration was allowed to elapse, no one knows who registered the names.

Neil Livingston, who heads Global Options LLC, a Washington-based investigation and counterterrorism firm, said, "It's unbelievable that they [the registration company whose name was withheld] would register these domain names, probably without any comment to the FBI. If they did make a comment to the FBI, it's unbelievable that the FBI didn't react to it." Incredibly, other domain names registered prior to the 9/11 tragedy included attackamerica.com, horrorinamerica.com, horrorinnewyork.com, nycterroriststrike.com, pearlharborinmanhattan.com, worldtradecenter929.com, worldtradetowerstrike.com, and terroristattack2001.com.

Even from a cursory search of September 11 reports, it would appear as though many people had some inkling of what was to come. As recounted by author Russ Kick, a veteran New York police investigator said that numerous Arab Americans in New York heard about the coming attacks. The officer said the number of leads were so overwhelming that it was difficult to tell who had heard about the attacks from a secondhand source and who had heard it from someone who may have been a participant. A Brooklyn detective was quoted as saying that "a serious and major priority" investigation was made into why so many Middle Easterners failed to show up for work at the World Trade Center on September 11. According to a former US military intelligence officer who arrived in New York on the morning of September 11, 2001, just prior to the attacks he had difficulty in getting a taxi. Once he found one, his driver told him that most of the Arab cab drivers had called in sick that day and that the taxi system was down to nearly half strength.

Even certain school kids seemed to have foreknowledge, according to Kick. A Dallas suburb fifth-grader told his teacher on September 10, "Tomorrow, World War III will begin. It will begin in the United States and the United States will lose."

Another school kid in Jersey City, home of several of the accused hijackers, told friends to stay away from lower Manhattan on the morning of September 11. One week before the attacks, a Brooklyn high school freshman pointed at the WTC towers and told his class, "Do you see those two buildings? They won't be standing there next week."

There are even telltale signs that some prominent politicians and government officials within the United States had some warning of the September atrocities.

San Francisco mayor Willie Brown was scheduled to fly to New York on the morning of September 11, 2001. But at about 10 p.m. the evening of September 10, he received a phone call at home advising him to be cautious about traveling by air. Brown would only say that the call came from "my security people at the airport," but the warning was clear: don't travel by air. He said the call "didn't come in any alarming fashion, which is why I'm hesitant to make an alarming statement." Brown was preparing to leave for the airport the next morning when instead he joined millions of other Americans in viewing the destruction on TV.

One San Francisco official noted that the FAA routinely issues security notices but added that none had been received in the days before September 11. No one has yet discovered who sent the after-hours warning to Brown. *Newsweek* reported on September 24, 2001, that on September 10 "a group of top Pentagon officials suddenly canceled travel plans for the next morning, apparently because of security concerns."

On July 28, 2001, then-Attorney General John Ashcroft left Washington on a fishing trip to Missouri but it was not on a commercial airliner. CBS news correspondent Jim Stewart reported that Ashcroft had suddenly begun flying only on government-chartered jets in response to what an FBI spokesman called a "threat assessment" by the bureau. Ashcroft was advised to travel only by private jet for the remainder of his term under FBI guidelines.

Former Attorney General Janet Reno and all but the secretaries of Interior and Energy in the Bush administration had flown by commercial airliners. Asked about this sudden change in policy, Ashcroft said, "I don't do threat assessments myself and I rely on those whose responsibility it is in the law enforcement community, particularly the FBI. And I try to stay within the guidelines that they've suggested I should stay within for those purposes."

But perhaps most extraordinary was a comment attributed to a member of Congress. During live coverage of the 9/11 attacks, National Public Radio congressional correspondent David Welna was describing the evacuation of the Capitol. He reported, "I spoke with Congressman Ike Shelton—a Democrat from Missouri and a member of the Armed Services Committee—who said that just recently the director of the CIA warned that there could be an attack—an imminent attack—on the United States of this nature. So this is not entirely unexpected."

Perhaps the most baffling and amazing example of what seemed to be exact foreknowledge of what was to come concerned a TV program. On March 4, 2001, more than six months before the 9/11 attacks, TV screen writer and producer Chris Carter, best known for his immensely popular series *The X-Files*, aired the pilot for an *X-Files* spin-off entitled *The Lone Gunmen*. This pilot starred the three computer nerds who helped Fox Mulder in *The X-Files* series. The first program was entitled "Twin Towers" and the plot concerned a conspiracy within the military-industrial complex to seize a commercial airliner using computer-capture, remote-control technology and fly it into one of the World Trade Center towers, all under the cover of war game exercises. The attack would be blamed on Middle East terrorists and the purpose was to start a war against terrorism to increase budgets and government control.

Students of 9/11 saw an eerie similarity between the real events and Carter's screenplay. Much has been written about Carter's contacts with their insider knowledge of secret government programs and technology. Actor Dean Haglund, who portrayed one of the Lone Gunmen, said filming of the "Twin Towers" segment was done in March 2000, about a year and a half before the 9/11 attacks. He said the writers were eclectic in their reading and knowledge and most probably were simply "picking up on what was already out there."

All of the above information stands in sharp contrast to often-repeated Bush administration assertions that no one in government could have imagined an attack by terrorists using hijacked airliners as weapons.

Secretary of Defense Donald Rumsfeld himself admitted, "there were lots of warnings" in an interview with *Parade* magazine. A transcript of his interview was released by the Department of Defense on October 12,

2001. And even then-CIA Director George Tenet had testified to the JICI that by the end of summer, 2001, "the system was blinking red."

As if all of this was not enough, it is now also clear that the Federal Bureau of Investigation itself had numerous advance warnings of what was to come.

## THE FBI COULDN'T, OR WOULDN'T, CONNECT THE DOTS

Even with its extensive use of an electronic eavesdropping system originally named "Carnivore," and despite specific reports from FBI field offices that directly pointed to the imminent attacks, the top tier of the FBI couldn't seem to piece together the available information. In some cases "probable cause" data was presented to FBI Headquarters (FBIHQ) that would have led any reasonable person to conclude that Middle Eastern terrorists were working diligently on plans to attack the United States by hijacking airplanes. Or, perhaps reasonable persons at the FBI weren't allowed come to such conclusions.

Just six days after the 9/11 tragedy, FBI director Robert Mueller stated, "There were no warning signs that I'm aware of that would indicate this type of operation in the country." Clearly contradicting his statement is the suppressed evidence from FBI investigations held at the Phoenix, Minneapolis, Oklahoma City, and Chicago field offices that came to light in the mainstream media in the months following the attacks, not to mention the reports cited in the last section of this book. One can add to this the August 6, 2001, President's Daily Brief report, soon to be examined, that was revealed during the hearings of the 9/11 Commission.

The Carnivore electronic monitoring system created so much consternation from persons concerned with individual rights and privacy that it is now called simply DCS-1000 (Digital Collection System). According to some press reports, the FBI in early 2005 mostly abandoned the use of Carnivore for commercially available software, such as NarusInsight. In at least one instance, Carnivore actually prevented the bureau from gaining information on a suspected terrorist.

In May 2002, the Electronic Privacy Information Center acquired FBI memos under the Freedom of Information Act, which showed that a bureau wiretap in the year 2000 aimed at an unnamed suspect was ineffective because a low-level FBI technical person destroyed the information.

According to David Sobel, general counsel for the center, "The FBI software not only picked up the emails under the electronic surveillance of the FBI's target...but also picked up emails on non-covered targets." One of the obtained memos showed that an FBI supervisor explained, "The FBI technical person was apparently so upset [about intercepting unauthorized emails] that he destroyed all the email take."

The FBI had previously issued assurances that Carnivore could only capture a narrow field of information authorized by a court order. "This shows that the FBI has been misleading Congress and the public about the extent to which Carnivore is capable of collecting only authorized information," Sobel said.

Sobel also discovered that, when Chief Judge Royce Lamberth—heading the special, and mostly secret, Foreign Intelligence Surveillance Court (FISC), which reviews national security wiretaps—found out that in 2000 the FBI had been misrepresenting information in their requests for eavesdropping, an investigation was ordered forcing many FBI wiretaps to be shut down. This disciplinary action foreshadowed the Bush administration's later use of warrantless NSA wiretaps that entirely bypassed the FISC, which came to light in 2006.

Despite the problems with their Carnivore system and bungled wiretaps, many agents within the bureau were actively working on the problem of terrorism by other means.

Perhaps the most knowledgeable person within the FBI on Middle Eastern terrorism in general and Osama bin Laden in particular was John O'Neill. In 1995 O'Neill was promoted to head the FBI's counterterrorism section and began working out of FBI headquarters in Washington, D.C. One of his initial jobs was the capture of Ramzi Yousef, then a key suspect in several acts of terror including the 1993 bombing of the World Trade Center. Through the late 1990s, O'Neill, according to Lawrence Wright writing in the *New Yorker*, became "the bureau's most committed tracker of Osama bin Laden and his al Qaeda network of terrorists."

But O'Neill came to believe that his superiors did not carry the same zeal against terrorism as he did. "John had the same problems with bureaucracy as I had," said Richard A. Clarke in a 2002 magazine interview. Clarke had served as White House coordinator for counterterrorism since the George H. W. Bush administration in the late 1980s. "The impatience really grew in us as we dealt with the dolts who didn't understand."

Despite the 1996 defection of Jamal Ahmed al-Fadl, a long-sought al Qaeda terrorist, and his subsequent detailing of the network to both the CIA and FBI, the State Department refused to list al Qaeda as a terrorist network. Even with O'Neill's growing ire over perceived indulgence of terrorists by higher authorities and his contentious personality, he was hired to the post of special agent in charge of the National Security Division in New York City. Here he created a special "al Qaeda desk" and worked doggedly to pinpoint Osama bin Laden. O'Neill, one of the top-level terrorism experts within the FBI, knew well who and what he was up against. "Almost all of the groups today, if they choose to, have the ability to strike us here in the United States," O'Neill said in a 1997 Chicago speech.

By the summer of 2001, O'Neill had been passed over for promotion and was growing weary of fighting his superiors on the issue of terrorism. Adding to his disillusionment was O'Neill's experience trying to conduct an investigation of the bombing of the USS *Cole* destroyer, which had been severely damaged by a small boat filled with explosives operated by two suicide bombers.

O'Neill, commanding about three hundred heavily armed FBI agents, claimed his investigation was being hampered by everyone from Yemen president Ali Abdullah Saleh to US ambassador Barbara Bodine. The FBI force believed they were never given the authority they required to conduct a strenuous investigation.

"... O'Neill came home feeling that he was fighting the counterterrorism battle without support from his own government," noted Wright in the *New Yorker*. When he tried to return to Yemen in early 2001, O'Neill was refused entry. "The last two years of his life, he got very paranoid," writer Lawrence Wright was told by Valerie James, a close friend of O'Neill's. "He was convinced there were people out to get him."

In the end, it appears it was his old archenemy, Osama bin Laden—or perhaps more precisely bin Laden's covert handlers in the US government—who got him.

By the summer of 2001, events and O'Neill's career were coming to a head. Someone had leaked information on some of O'Neill's bureau gaffes to the *New York Times* and information on terrorism was pouring into government agencies. "Something big is going to happen," he told a friend. "It all came together in the third week of June," recalled Clarke. "The CIA's view was that a major terrorist attack was coming in the next several weeks." Clarke said orders to beef up security were passed to the FAA, the Coast Guard, Customs, the INS, and the FBI.

But O'Neill had had enough. By August 23, he had retired from the FBI and accepted a job paying twice his bureau pay—as chief of security for the World Trade Center. Conspiracy researchers could not help but note the irony that America's leading counterterrorism expert—the one man who would have known of the true activities, plans and backers of Osama bin Laden and his al Qaeda network—died at the WTC on 9/11.

John O'Neill was not the only FBI agent to see definite warning signs. In mid-2002 twelve-year FBI veteran Robert G. Wright Jr. charged the bureau's counterterrorism efforts were ineffective and "not protecting the American people." Going further, Wright charged that FBI superiors had derailed investigations that could have prevented the 9/11 attacks, even claiming the bureau had evidence that the World Trade Center was a possible target.

Wright already had excellent credentials as an FBI agent fighting terrorists. His own investigation initiated in 1998 resulted in the seizure of financial assets of one Yassin Kadi of Chicago, who has since been identified as one of the chief money launderers connected to Osama bin Laden. He then launched an investigation into money laundering by other terrorists within the United States only to have his probe terminated by higher authorities.

On May 9, 2002, Wright, who worked out of Chicago, called a news conference in Washington to publicly accuse the bureau of gross negligence in investigating terrorists in America, despite orders from FBI director Robert Mueller for him to stay home and stay quiet. At the same time he filed a lawsuit against the bureau in Washington's US District Court accusing the bureau of violating his First Amendment rights by prohibiting him from speaking out about FBI wrongdoing.

He charged senior bureau officials "intentionally and repeatedly thwarted and obstructed" his own efforts to root out terrorists and that they prevented his attempts to file cases that could have broken up their operations. In the press conference, Wright revealed that he has been given written orders not to disclose what he knew—either in speech or in writing—and that he was threatened in writing with disciplinary action, civil suits, revocation of security clearances, and even criminal prosecution.

"I love America, and likewise I love the FBI, particularly its purpose and mission," agent Wright told newsmen, echoing the thoughts of many bureau personnel. "However, the mission has been seriously jeopardized to the point where American lives have been needlessly lost." "Knowing what I know," Wright added, "I can confidently say that until the investigative responsibilities for terrorism are transferred from the FBI, I will not feel safe."

As might be expected by now, *The 9/11 Commission Report* makes no mention of Wright and his attempt to reveal the truth about Bureau officials blocking terrorist investigations. Wright's suit was filed just one day after Congress berated the FBI for failing to vigorously act on a July 2001 recommendation from its Phoenix field office that aviation schools should be checked for Middle Easterners seeking flight training.

Counterterrorism experts in Phoenix were concerned after noting that several Middle Eastern men were seeking information on airport operations, security, and flight training. One wrote in a memo to Washington, "FBIHQ should discuss this matter with other elements of the US intelligence community and task the community for any information that supports Phoenix's suspicions."

The memo was written by Phoenix Special Agent Kenneth J. Williams and noted, "Osama bin Laden and Al-Muhjiroun supporters [were] attending civil aviation universities/colleges in Arizona." FBI officials merely passed the memo, which actually pointed to bin Laden by name, along to about a dozen of its offices for "analysis." There was no follow up on this lapse by the 9/11 Commission.

Arizona also became a focus for former "black ops" pilot Philip Marshall. In his book entitled *False Flag 9/11*, Marshall wrote, "…from several old Iran-Contra sources I began hearing about a hush-hush airport used by the government contractor and mercenary outfit Blackwater [now Xe Services LLC], to train covert, special operations flight crews. I soon learned that major flight training had been conducted in the middle of the night with military and civilian airplane in top-secret fashion. Blackwater is one of several operators that use the very airport I had run across [in his research]—Pinal Airpark, a secluded desert facility near the town of Marana, Arizona, and near the former home of Saudi Arabian pilot Hani Hanjour, the hijacker pilot of American 77. I discovered that over 80 perfectly airworthy commercial airliners are scattered around the airport and heavily guarded by a mercenary army with covert Saudi ties. The opportunities are perfect to 'borrow' a Boeing for unlimited and undocumented air training in the dedicated practice range over the desert. The means and the opportunity to slip hijackers in for training were all in place."

One former FBI agent, Gary Aldrich, described the bureau's top management as "incompetent lunkheads and deadheads." Aldrich too said many opportunities to stop the attack were missed. Aldrich blamed Bill and Hillary Clinton for the breakdown of the FBI as well as other federal agencies. He said the Clinton's blatant disregard for national security procedures made the government weak and vulnerable and that they showed more concern for political opponents than foreign enemies.

According to several FBI sources, when the Clinton administration arrived, emphasis in the bureau shifted from antiterrorism to investigating militias, white supremacists, anti-abortion groups and other "right-wing" extremists. "When I left [the FBI] in 1998, domestic terrorism was the number one priority," said retired agent Ivan C. Smith, former head of the analysis, budget, and training sections of the FBI's National Security Division. "And as far as I know, it was still a higher priority than foreign terrorism on September 11."

With the arrival of the Clintons, FBI probes were aimed at local militias, right-wing organizations, the fledgling Patriot movement—everywhere except at foreign terrorists. Veteran agents said some forty boxes of evidence gathered in the 1993 World Trade Center bombing were never analyzed, including almost ten boxes of material from the Philippine side of the investigation. The Clinton-era disinterest in foreign terrorism was not limited to the FBI. Commerce Department officials told reporter Paul Sperry they were ordered to "sanitize" a Y2K counterterrorism report by removing mention of Islamic threats. Only "right-wing" groups were included in the report.

But on March 23, 2004, Richard A. Clarke, former counterterrorism czar under Clinton and Bush, told CNN's *Inside Politics* a different story about the Clinton administration's terrorism strategy. "I would argue that for what had actually happened prior to 9/11, the Clinton administration was doing a great deal," Clarke said. "In fact, so much that when the Bush people came into office, they thought I was a little crazy, a little obsessed with this little terrorist bin Laden. Why wasn't I focused on Iraqi-sponsored terrorism?" In their appearances before the 9/11 Commission in March 2004, Clarke and former Clinton-era officials defended the Clinton record on al Qaeda, claiming that it was the Bush people and especially Bush's FBI and CIA that dropped the ball immediately after the new administration entered the White House.

Mere negligence or incompetence cannot explain the obvious moves by both the Clinton and early Bush administrations to block any meaningful investigations into foreign terrorism. Many theories have been advanced for this odd behavior, including an argument that no one in high authority wanted to incur the anger of the oil-producing states or even that deep probes might have brought to light deep-rooted business and banking connections. It should also be noted that many of the officials within both the Clinton and early Bush administrations were ranking members of globalist organizations such as the Council on Foreign Relations and the secretive Bilderberger group. These high-level connections have prompted some researchers to suspect that overlapping conspiracies may have taken place regardless of party affiliation.

By mid-2002, even FBI director Robert Mueller was forced to acknowledge that the FBI had missed many "red flags," including the Chicago investigations and the Phoenix memos as well as two from the Oklahoma City office. There, FBI agents and one FBI pilot reported "large numbers" of Middle Eastern men receiving flight training at local airports and warned this activity might be related to "planned terrorist activity."

The revelations of FBI misconduct prompted an unusual two-hour press conference in late May 2002 in which a defensive Mueller told reporters, "There was not a specific warning about an attack on a particular day. But that doesn't mean there weren't red flags out there, there weren't dots that should have been connected to the extent possible." Mueller even admitted that he had misspoken in fall 2001 when he denied the existence of any pre-9/11 attack warnings.

Mueller outlined his plan to reorganize the FBI, which consisted primarily of shifting agents from the War on Drugs to the War on Terrorism and to create a new Office of Intelligence headed by a CIA analyst. Many observers saw this plan as an attempt to merge the FBI and CIA into a terrorist-fighting force that would only bring more centralized authority to Washington. This same plan—to combine the worst of two worlds—was later duplicated in the Homeland Security Department legislation.

One government informant, a self-confessed Florida con man named Randy Glass, said he worked undercover for the bureau for more than two years and learned specifically that the World Trade Center Twin Towers were to be the target of terrorists. Hoping to lessen a prison term for a conviction of defrauding jewelry wholesalers out of $6 million, in 1998 Glass contacted federal agents and said he could set up illegal arms deals. Aided by veteran Bureau of Alcohol, Tobacco and Firearms agent Dick Stoltz, Glass began to arrange deals with a variety of persons. He claimed he had acquired heavy weapons such as Stinger and TOW missiles stolen from military facilities.

Business was good but none of the deals seemed to work out until Glass contacted a Pakistani-born New Jersey deli owner. This man helped arrange arms deals with Pakistanis who claimed contacts to Pakistani intelligence, the Taliban, and even Osama bin Laden. Many hours of tapes were made of their meetings.

However, during the lengthy and detailed maneuvering to arrange the financing in early 2001, the Pakistanis grew suspicious and left the country. Only the deli owner and one other man were arrested. The other man pled guilty to trying to sell weaponry and was sentenced to thirty months in jail, while the deli owner went free and his court records were sealed from the public.

ATF agent Stoltz said cases against the men were hampered by the fact that government prosecutors had to remove references to Pakistan in court filings because of diplomatic concerns. Internet Commentator Allan P. Duncan took note of this case and wrote: "Between the Fall of 1998 and June 2001, a group of Middle Eastern men living in New Jersey is caught on tape in an ATF weapons sting conspiring to buy millions of dollars of weapons including components for nuclear bombs. Three years after the operation ended, all of the people involved in the deal are free.

## THE FBI COULDN'T, OR WOULDN'T, CONNECT THE DOTS

"Federal agents who worked on the case were frustrated because it was handled as a criminal case instead of a counterterrorism case. In an in depth look at 'Operation Diamondback' I reveal that one of the suspects who was accused of skimming millions of dollars from a fraudulent HMO to offshore accounts where the money allegedly went to finance terrorism, was defended in the HMO case by a lawyer who later became the assistant attorney general in charge of the Criminal Division, under John Ashcroft. The lawyer, Michael Chertoff, was in his position as assistant attorney general when Operation Diamondback ended and his client was never arrested even though an intelligence document claimed he and his brother in Egypt had links to Osama bin Laden. "Is this why the ATF operation was handled as a criminal case and not a terrorism case by the federal government?"

One of the men Glass taped was the brother of New Jersey neurologist Dr. Magdy Elamir [real name: Magdy El Sayed El Amir] who also said he wanted radioactive materials. Dr. Elamir owned an HMO which was under investigation following a foreign intelligence source accusation that more than $15 million had been siphoned from Elamir's HMO and sent to bin Laden's al Qaeda terrorist network.

"So at this point we now have information that Dr. Magdy Elamir along with his brother Mohamed El Amir have ties to Osama bin Laden and yet neither one of them is arrested. Randy Glass says in fact that federal agents told him to drop the matter," wrote Duncan.

Chertoff, who participated as a lawyer in two of the investigations into the death of Clinton administration official Vincent Foster, was named in 2005 by President Bush to head the Department of Homeland Security, an odd choice considering Chertoff's actions in the Diamondback operation.

This case took a step closer to the 9/11 attacks when Glass told news reporters that on one occasion in 1999 he met with one of the Pakistanis in the Tribeca Grill in Manhattan. "At the meeting, [he] said Americans are the enemy and they would have no problem blowing up this entire restaurant because it is full of Americans," Glass recounted. "As we left the restaurant, [he] turns and says, 'those towers are coming down.'" The man was indicating the World Trade Center.

But perhaps the most provocative evidence of governmental foreknowledge came from the man who led the prosecution in President Bill Clinton's 1998 impeachment in 1998 as the chief investigative counsel for the judiciary committee in the US House of Representatives.

Chicago attorney David Schippers, who by mid-2002 was representing Wright and other disgruntled FBI employees, said in a late October 2001 interview that he had been approached by FBI agents a month and a half prior to the 9/11 attacks. The agents revealed that they had knowledge that lower Manhattan was to be the object of a terrorist attack using airplanes as flying bombs and they wanted to prevent this. They were seeking legal advice because their FBI superiors had ordered them off the case and threatened them with the National Security Act if they spoke out. Schippers said he tried in vain to warn Attorney General John Ashcroft.

"[A]gain I used people who were personal friends of John Ashcroft to try to get him. One of them called me back and said, 'All right, I have talked to him. He will call you tomorrow morning.' This was like a month before the bombing. The next morning I got a call. It wasn't from Ashcroft. It was from somebody in the Justice Department...He said, 'We don't start our investigations at the top. Let me look into this and I will get back to you.' As I sit here today [October 10, 2001], I have never heard from him." Once again, no mention of this incident or even the name of David Schippers, a very prominent Republican attorney, can be found anywhere in *The 9/11 Commission Report*.

Schippers echoed FBI Agent Aldrich's charge that national security precautions were stripped away during the Clinton administration. Speaking of his attempts to warn authorities, Schippers said, "I tried the House, I tried the Senate, I tried the Department of Justice. I didn't go to the FBI because I know there is a roadblock there and I didn't go to the Justice Department until Ashcroft got in there because I know there are roadblocks out there. These are the very same people who put up roadblocks on the attack against the terrorists under Clinton, they are still there. They still constitute, almost like a moat, between the people with the information and the people who should hear the information..."

One particularly damning indictment of both the bureau and the Bush administration came in 2004 when a woman hired as a translator for the FBI revealed that senior US officials knew of al Qaeda's plans to attack targets with aircraft months in advance of 9/11. She claimed that the proper handling of intelligence flowing into the FBI could have prevented the 9/11 attacks and that Condoleezza Rice's statement to the 9/11 Commission regarding no foreknowledge of the attacks was an "outrageous lie."

Sibel Edmonds, a Turkish-American, then 32, explained in a 2004 radio interview, "I started working for the Bureau immediately after 9/11 and I was performing translations for several languages: Farsi, Turkish, and Azerbaijani. And I do have top-secret clearance. And after I started working for the Bureau, most of my translation duties included translations of documents and investigations that actually started way before 9/11.

"The most significant information that we were receiving did not come from counterterrorism investigations, and I want to emphasize this. It came from counter-intelligence, and certain criminal investigations, and issues that have to do with money laundering operations.

"During my work there I came across some very significant issues that I started reporting in December of 2001 to the mid-level management within the FBI. They said to basically leave it alone, because if they were to get into those issues it would end up being a can of worms. And after I didn't see any response from this mid-level bureaucratic management I took it to higher levels all the way up to [Assistant Director] Dale Watson and Director Mueller. And, again, I was asked not to take this any further and just let it be. And if I didn't do that they would retaliate against me.

"At that point, which would be around February 2002, they came and they confiscated my computer, because, they said, they were suspecting that I was communicating with certain Senate members and taking this issue outside the Bureau. And, at that point, I was not. They did not find anything in my computer after they confiscated it. And they asked me to take a polygraph as to the allegations and reports I'd made. I volunteered and I took the polygraph and passed it without a glitch. They have already confirmed this publicly."

In March 2002, Edmonds was fired by the FBI for reporting shoddy work and security breaches to her supervisors that could have prevented those attacks. She remains under two court gag orders that forbid her from testifying in court or mentioning the names of the people or the countries involved. After her firing, Edmonds took her information to the Senate Judiciary Committee, which requested an investigation by the Department of Justice Inspector General's office. Today, the findings of this investigation have not been made public, citing concerns of "national security." Furthermore, at least four attempts to bring Edmonds' gag order into court were rejected with no explanation.

Finally, on Tuesday, July 6, 2004, Judge Reggie Walton dismissed her case. "Under his ruling, I, an American citizen, am not entitled to pursue my 1st and 5th Amendment rights guaranteed under the Constitution of the United States," lamented Edmonds. "The vague reasoning cited, without any explanation, is to protect 'certain diplomatic relations for national security.' Judge Walton reached this decision after sitting on this case with no activity for almost two years. He arrived at this decision without allowing my attorney and I any due process: NO status hearing, NO briefings, NO oral argument, and NO discovery [emphasis in the original]. He made his decision after allowing the government attorneys to present their case to him, privately, in camera, ex parte; we were not allowed to participate in these cozy sessions. Is this the American system of justice we believe in? Is this the due process we read about in our civics 101 courses? Is this the judicial branch of our government that is supposed to be separate from the other two branches in order to protect the people's rights and freedom?

"This court decision by itself would have been appalling and alarming enough, but in light of all other actions taken against my case for the past two years it demonstrates a broken system, a system abused and corrupted by the current executive, a system badly in need of repair."

"This [suppression of her case] was mainly for the reason of accountability," Edmonds said. "As you know... to this day, not a single person has been held accountable [for the failures of 9/11]. And certain issues, yes, they were due to a certain level of incompetence. But there were certain other issues—you know they keep talking about this 'wall,' and not having communication. I beg to differ on that, because there are certain instances where the Bureau is being asked by the State Department not to pursue certain investigations or certain people or certain targets of an investigation—simply citing 'diplomatic relations.' And what happens is, instead of targeting those people who are directly related to these illegal terrorist activities, they just let them walk free."

It should be pointed out in this connection that according to multiple knowledgeable sources, the State Department has been under the control of the Council on Foreign Relations (CFR) since before World War II. Ranking CFR members filled both the Clinton and Bush administrations. "I have seen several top targets for these investigations of these terrorist activities that were allowed to leave the country," Edmonds continued. "I'm not talking about weeks, I'm talking about months after 9/11...I can tell you that there is so much involvement, that if they did let this information out, and if they were to hold real investigations...we would see several significant high level criminal prosecutions in this country. And that is something that they are not going to let out. And, believe me; they will do everything to cover this up." It would appear that Edmonds' words were prophetic. Despite her three and a half hours of testimony to the 9/11 Commission, there was only one reference to her in a footnote buried on page 473 of their 567-page report. Far from mentioning any of her serious charges, the note merely indicated the need for "quality control" of FBI translations.

In a scathing letter to 9/11 Commission Chairman Thomas Kean after the report was issued, Edmonds noted several incidents that indicated advance knowledge of the 9/11 attack within the FBI and added, "...I must assume that other serious issues I am not aware of were in the same manner [as her testimony] omitted from your report. These omissions cast doubt on the validity of your report and therefore on its conclusions and recommendations."

The muzzling of Sibel Edmonds at the highest levels of the federal government prompted US Senators Patrick Leahy (D-VT) and Charles Grassley (R-IA) to write then-Attorney General John Ashcroft stating, "...we fear that the designation of information as classified in some cases [such as Sibel Edmonds] serves to protect the executive branch against embarrassing revelations and full accountability...Releasing declassified versions of these reports, or at least portions or summaries, would serve the public's interest, increase transparency, promote effectiveness and efficiency at the FBI, and facilitate congressional oversight."

Due to what has been described as persecution, in August 2004, Edmonds founded the National Security Whistleblowers Coalition, a group that by 2010 counted more than 50 former and current US government officials from more than a dozen agencies who had gone public to address weaknesses within US security agencies.

It is now clear that still other bureau employees also tried to send warnings upstairs regarding the flight training of terrorists but got nowhere. In August 2001, the FBI arrested Zacarias Moussaoui, the so-called 20th hijacker, after a Minnesota flight school warned the bureau that Moussaoui appeared to be the type of person who might fly a plane loaded with fuel into a building. FBI Special Agent Harry Samit followed up by writing more than one memo to superiors stating that Moussaoui, a French citizen of Moroccan descent, was the type of individual to take a plane and hijack it, perhaps even fly it into the World Trade Center. He also noted that Moussaoui told a flight instructor that he only wanted to learn to maneuver a Boeing 747 but did not need to learn how to land it.

CBS's *60 Minutes II* reported on May 8, 2002, that a ranking French jurist and terrorist expert had also sent a report on Moussaoui, a French citizen, to the FBI weeks before 9/11. US authorities denied there was anything in the report to alert them. One FBI supervisor even questioned the French report, asking how many men named Zacarias Moussaoui must live in France. When informed that there was only one listed in Paris, the supervisory special agent continued to stall any action.

Meanwhile, FBI attorneys turned down or blocked repeated requests from their agents in the Minneapolis field office to search Moussaoui's computer and apartment. If they had, they would have found numerous small knives, jumbo-jet pilot manuals, the names of flight schools and other clues that might have sounded an alarm. As a result of all this inaction, Moussaoui was simply held on immigration charges until after 9/11 when FBI agents finally were able to make their search. They recovered incriminating financial records linking Moussaoui to al Qaeda, flight simulators, and information on crop dusters.

Moussaoui, who in 2006 was sentenced by a jury to life imprisonment without parole, was known as the "twentieth hijacker" based on the theory that he was to replace an original "twentieth hijacker," Ramzi bin al-Shibh, a former roommate of Mohamed Atta, who reportedly sent $14,000 to Moussaoui. Al-Shibh, who also was unable to gain entry into the United States, was arrested in Pakistan in late September 2002. Moussaoui and al-Shibh were the only two men in custody believed to be directly involved in the 9/11 attacks.

The feds were further embarrassed in 2002 when government prosecutors left forty-eight classified documents, summaries of FBI interviews, with Moussaoui. They were later found in searches of Moussaoui's Alexandria, Virginia, jail cell. Moussaoui eventually pled guilty to six charges in connection with the 9/11 attacks and was sentenced to life in a maximum security prison in 2006, to the disappointment of prosecutors seeking the death penalty. Previously, he had been thrown out of court more than once for creating a scene and reportedly shouting, "I am al Qaeda!"

FBI Special Agent Hamit, who arrested Moussaoui prior to the 9/11 attacks, caused a brief sensation during the penalty phase of the trial when he stated in court that his superiors in the bureau were guilty of "criminal negligence and obstruction" for blocking his attempts to learn if Moussaoui was part of a group planning to hijack aircraft in the United States. Samit said under cross-examination, "They [FBI superiors] obstructed it." He said this was a calculated management decision "that cost us the opportunity to stop the attacks."

Such top-side interference in the Moussaoui case briefly made headlines in the late spring of 2002 with the publication of a scathing thirteen-page letter from FBI special agent and Minneapolis chief division counsel Coleen M. Rowley to Director Robert Mueller. In her May 21 letter, Rowley, a twenty-one-year veteran of the bureau, described a top-heavy FBI management bureaucracy riddled with "many who were failures as street agents" and "careerists" who placed advancing their own careers over integrity and truth.

"I know I shouldn't be flippant about this, but jokes were actually made that the key FBIHQ personnel had to be spies or moles like Robert Hanssen [an FBI agent arrested in 2001 and now serving a life sentence after being convicted of spying for the Russians], who were actually working for Osama bin Laden, to have so undercut Minneapolis's effort…

"I have deep concerns that a delicate and subtle shading/skewing of facts by you and others at the highest levels of FBI management has occurred and is occurring in an effort to avoid or minimize personal and/or institutional embarrassment on the part of the FBI and/or perhaps even for improper political reasons," she told Mueller. She added, "I'm hard pressed to think of any case which has been solved by FBIHQ personnel and I can name several that have been screwed up!"

Rowley, after hearing the news media continually quote Director

Mueller as saying the bureau would have taken action if only they had had advance warning of the attacks, sent a message informing him of the intelligence sitting in the Minneapolis files. She said when the same denials of knowledge continued, she and other agents again attempted to inform Mueller of the facts.

"Finally, when similar comments were made weeks later we faced the sad realization that the remarks indicated someone, possibly with your approval, had decided to circle the wagons at FBIHQ in an apparent effort to protect the FBI from embarrassment and the relevant FBI officials from scrutiny," Rowley wrote the director.

She also pointed out that the only difference between incidents when informed FBI agents were denied a search warrant on Moussaoui and when one was approved was the fact of the 9/11 attacks, events that certainly could not be swept under the rug.

Rowley was one of many persons who pointed out the fact that FBI headquarters personnel "were privy to many more sources of intelligence information than field division agents." Despite this fact, she said, "key FBIHQ personnel whose job it was to assist and coordinate with field division agents on terrorism investigations continued to, almost inexplicably, throw up roadblocks and undermine Minneapolis's by-now desperate efforts to obtain a FISA [Foreign Intelligence Surveillance Act] search warrant, long after the French Intelligence Service provided its information and probable cause became clear."

Even after the 9/11 attacks had occurred, Rowley said higher authorities still would not untie their hands. Taking a call from a bureau superior just after the attacks had begun, Rowley said she told him in light of the attacks it would be the "hugest coincidence" if Moussaoui were not involved with the terrorists. Her superior replied that coincidence was the right term; it was just that and the Minneapolis office should not do anything without headquarters' permission because "we might 'screw up' something else going on elsewhere in the country."

Rowley's insightful and damning critique of FBI inefficiency in light of the 9/11 attacks prompted widespread, though brief, mass media coverage. Now a well-known federal whistleblower, Rowley was among three women in 2002 selected as a "Person of the Year" by *Time* magazine. Yet, her testimony to the 9/11 Commission was not made public, and she was relegated to one fleeting footnote on page 557 in its report. One Internet columnist noted that the Bush administration took advantage of the cover of the "Rowley firestorm" to announce the rescission of some of the government's meager rules against indiscriminate domestic spying, rules prompted by the many abuses of the FBI during the 1960s.

Steve Perry with *CounterPunch*, a biweekly newsletter, commented that the Bush team defused Rowley's revelations by choosing that time to announce plans to reorganize the entire intelligence apparatus. Such a move would be time consuming and require much preparation, yet the administration requested no funding for its proposal. According to Perry, this tactic indicated that the timing of the announcement may indeed have been meant to distract attention from Rowley's accusations.

It might also be added that any failures at the FBI cannot be laid off on lower level agents and supervisors. In August 2001, Attorney General Ashcroft, apparently more concerned with the long-lost War on Drugs and pornography, had turned down a bureau request for $50 million to beef up its counterterrorism efforts. All critical information flowing upward within the FBI routinely ended at the desks of Director Mueller and his boss, Ashcroft, both of whom worked closely with President Bush in the period leading up to the events of 9/11.

## MISSED OPPORTUNITIES AT THE CIA

By all accounts the CIA also received a large share of the pre-attack warnings. By some accounts the agency intentionally blocked access to critical information—or worse, may have been covertly setting up "terrorist" patsies for later service in false-flag activities.

Like the FBI, the CIA has its own electronic eavesdropping satellite and computer system, noted earlier, called "Echelon." This system tracks international telephone calls, faxes and email messages all around the world. It was so secret that the government would neither confirm nor deny its existence until 2001. According to a study by the European Union, Echelon accumulates electronic transmissions like a vacuum cleaner using keyword search software in conjunction with massive computer data banks.

The Echelon system, headquartered in the United States with the National Security Agency at Fort Meade, Maryland, has caused protests in several nations, excluding the United States whose population rarely sees any news concerning this powerful global wiretapping system.

In 2000, French prosecutor Jean-Pierre Dintilhac ordered his country's counterintelligence agency to see if Echelon was being used to steal foreign business secrets, to spy on citizens, and to see if it was "harmful to the vital interests of the nation." The Italian Parliament also opened inquiries into Echelon, saying, "The scope is not military." According to a German newspaper, the *Frankfurter Allgemeine Zeitung*, the Echelon spy system provided both US and Israeli intelligence services warning of the impending terrorist attacks at least three months before the fact. The newspaper reported that Echelon, with its 120 satellites, has been used extensively by Israeli intelligence to monitor Arab terrorist groups.

Largely unreported in the American media was a story that Osama bin Laden himself was overheard telling his stepmother on September 9, 2001, "In two days you're going to hear big news and you're not going to hear from me for a while." This telephone interception, publicly attributed to a "foreign intelligence service," undoubtedly was the product of Echelon. Yet apparently no one in America's defense establishment was alerted to bin Laden's "big news."

The CIA also had another high-tech weapon in their arsenal for use against terrorists. The "Predator," an unmanned surveillance aircraft system consisting of four aircraft, a ground control station (GCS), a primary satellite link communication suite and 55 people. Predator drones had been used under the Clinton administration to track the movements of Osama bin Laden. There had even been talk of using the craft to unleash Hellfire missiles on the al Qaeda leader.

Following the attacks of 9/11, such talk turned into action. An armed Predator was used to attack a convoy of sport utility vehicles in Afghanistan thought to be carrying al Qaeda leaders on February 7, 2002. On November 3, 2002, the CIA used a Hellfire missile fired from a Predator to attack a car in Yemen, killing Qaed Senyan al-Harthi, an al Qaeda leader thought to be responsible for the USS *Cole* bombing. Reportedly, this was the first direct US strike in the War on Terrorism outside Afghanistan.

About a year later, an RQ-1 Predator was used to attack a remote village in the southern Ghazni Province of Afghanistan thought to be the hideout of Taliban supporters. Nine children and a 25-year-old man were killed in the strike, which failed to kill the intended target. Afghanistan's president Hamid Karzai stated that he was "profoundly shocked" by the CIA attack and demanded closer coordination with Afghan authorities on all future military strikes. By 2005, the CIA's use of unmanned Predators was becoming more effective. Haitham al-Yemeni, an al Qaeda explosives expert from Yemen, was killed in a village in northwest Pakistan by a Predator again firing a Hellfire missile. On December 3, 2005, a Predator reportedly killed ranking al Qaeda chief Abu Hamza Rabia while sleeping in Haisori, Pakistan. Four others were also killed. On January 13, 2006, several Predators rained missiles on the Pakistani village of Damadola thought to contain al Qaeda's second-in-command Ayman al-Zawahiri. The CIA drone planes reportedly fired 10 missiles killing 18 civilians, including five women and five children.

Because Predators, in production since at least 1995, carries an infrared camera capable of identifying the heat signature of a human body from an altitude of 10,000 feet, the the remote-controlled craft has been coveted by law enforcement. In 2005, the craft was sought to aid in Hurricane Katrina rescue efforts but was not certified by the FAA to fly within US civilian airspace. This was corrected on May 18, 2006, when the FAA granted a certificate of authorization. Some police departments, such as in Houston, Texas, were experimenting with drones in 2010.

There is enticing evidence that ties Osama bin Laden directly to the CIA back at the time the agency was funding and training fighters against the Soviets in Afghanistan. While it has been widely acknowledged that the CIA helped found and fund the al Qaeda network during the Soviet invasion of Afghanistan, the agency steadfastly denied any direct dealings with bin Laden. Despite these denials, there is considerable evidence of prior CIA and Bush family involvement with the bin Laden family going back several decades as will be described later. Many researchers believe the CIA groomed Osama bin Laden for years in preparation for some future need.

For example, one Internet source claimed that bin Laden, under the name Tim Osman, actually was brought to the United States in the late spring of 1986 for a meeting with government agents at the Hilton Hotel in Sherman Oaks, California. Former FBI senior special agent Ted L. Gunderson confirmed this meeting and said he was one of the attendees.

Gunderson said he was contacted by a "top figure" in the Reagan administration and asked to meet with Afghan insurgents to "see what we might do to help them." The four men at the hotel meeting, according to Gunderson, were himself, a quiet Tim Osman (bin Laden), computer expert Michael Riconosciuto, a CIA scientific "asset" with connections in the arms business, and a man identified as Ralph Olberg, who was purchasing weapons on behalf of the Afghan Mujahideen.

Gunderson said conversation during the hour-and-a-half meeting was mostly between Olberg and Riconosciuto while Osman/bin Laden "sat silent in a corner of the room." He added that he was unaware of what, if any, deal was sealed during the meeting but that he is "certain in my own mind" that arrangements were made to provide arms for bin Laden and the Arab fighters. Gunderson's guess has been proven true as it is a historic fact that the CIA supplied both arms and training for bin Laden's fighters in Afghanistan. It should be noted, however, that Gunderson's credibility has been questioned.

According to a former staffer of Republican senator David Durenberger, Olberg was a man often seen in the senator's office during the Reagan years talking about the plight of the Afghan people.

Riconosciuto, also tight with Republican bigwigs, had been involved in the development of the PROMIS software initially planned for use against criminals and terrorists. But this promising software soon turned into a scandal when its creator charged that US government officials, including then-Attorney General Bill Casey, had stolen the software and used it to create a "back door" into computers in both foreign governments and domestic corporations. It was also alleged that the stolen software was used for insider trading including that which preceded the 9/11 attacks as described in the next section. Osama bin Laden is suspected of using the PROMIS software to elude captors and to spy on his enemies.

But by the mid-1990s, the Soviets were out of Afghanistan, the Saudis were our oil friends and, with the exception of certain counterterrorism units, little notice was taken of Osama bin Laden. The CIA, like their brethren in the FBI, apparently became somewhat complacent at the lower levels thanks to the near constant stream of tips, warnings, and

MISSED OPPORTUNITIES AT THE CIA

information. Workers not actively involved in counterterrorism took a cue from their superiors and never got too serious about terrorism.

And it wasn't as if prior warnings had all proven false. Almost a year before the deadly 1998 bombings of the US embassies in Kenya and Tanzania, an al Qaeda member had warned CIA officials of the coming attacks. The informant's information was dismissed as unreliable and nothing was done.

Though admittedly vague, there was even a warning in a September 1999 National Intelligence Council (NIC) report, which foresaw events similar to the 9/11 attacks. This NIC report, entitled "Sociology and Psychology of Terrorism: Who Becomes a Terrorist and Why?" was prepared by about a dozen senior intelligence officers. The NIC was attached to the CIA. "Suicide bomber(s) belonging to al Qaeda's Martyrdom Battalion could crash land an aircraft packed with high explosives (C-4 and semtex) into the Pentagon, the headquarters of the Central Intelligence Agency (CIA) or the White House," stated the report, which was issued exactly two years before 9/11.

"This information was out there," noted Robert L. Worden, chief of the Federal Research Division, which prepared the report from open sources, "certainly to those who study the in-depth subject of terrorism and al Qaeda."

In January 2000, Malaysian security agents conducted surveillance of al Qaeda operatives meeting in Kuala Lumpur at the behest of the CIA. One of the operatives was Khalid al-Midhar, named by the FBI as one of the 9/11 hijackers. It was determined that al-Midhar had a multiple-entry visa to the United States. CIA agents also found that al-Midhar was traveling with a Saudi, Nawaf al-Hazmi, who had previously entered the United States. Neither man was placed on the State Department "watch list" until August 23, 2001, far too late to prevent their participation in the 9/11 attacks.

Endnote 44 to Chapter 6 of *The 9/11 Commission Report* described a CIA cable entitled "Activities of Bin Ladin Associate Khalid [al-Midhar] Revealed." This cable stated that on January 4, 2000, the passport containing a visa for travel to the United States belonging to Khalid, named as one of the hijackers of Flight 77, was photocopied and sent to CIA headquarters. However, this evidence of a known al Qaeda terrorist in the US was not shared with the FBI until August 2001, after a CIA desk officer instructed the FBI agent detailed to the bin Laden unit at the CIA not to send along this information. A few hours later, this same desk officer distributed a cable within the agency that this information had been shared with the bureau, though she later admitted that she did not personally share the information nor could identify who told her it had been shared.

Another example of CIA incompetence, if that's what it was, can be found in the case of Khalid Sheikh Mohammed, who, since the capture of Abu Zubaydah in Pakistan in the spring of 2002, was considered the highest-ranking member of the al Qaeda network still at large, as well as a primary planner of the 9/11 attacks.

Mohammed was so highly placed in bin Laden's organization that the joint congressional committee looking into intelligence failures in the fall of 2002 took special notice of him. But they were so stymied by restrictions on classified material that they could only refer to Mohammed as a "key al Qaeda leader," even though the man was identified as a terrorist chief as far back as 1995.

The joint committee criticized the CIA's handling of Mohammed's case, stating, "there was little analytic focus given to him and coordination amongst intelligence agencies was irregular at best." One US intelligence official disputed this charge but admitted to a *New York Times* reporter, "We had identified him as a major al Qaeda operative before September 11."

Such mishandling continued after 9/11 when it was reported that Mohammed was captured on March 1, 2003, following a nighttime shootout in Rawalpindi, Pakistan. US officials expressed jubilation over the arrest but their celebration faded swiftly as questions arose. Witnesses did not agree with the official account and foreign media speculated that Mohammed may have been misidentified, killed at an earlier date, or might even still be on the loose. Oddly, despite these doubts, Khalid Sheikh Mohammed—supposedly now in US custody and a key informant to the US government—is cited more frequently than any other insider as a crucial source for the narrative of *The 9/11 Commission Report*. In fact, by author Griffin's count, Khalid Shaikh Mohammed is cited 272 times in the report, despite the fact that no corroborating evidence has ever been provided as to the fact of his capture, or even the veracity of his testimony to the government. Such reliance on an unvetted source was reminiscent of the 2010 film *Green Zone*, starring Matt Damon as a Army warrant officer who comes to realize that the bogus intelligence he was given about Iraq's weapons of mass destruction came solely from a US official, who had actually been told by a ranking Iraqi general that there were no WMDs as far back as the Gulf War.

Author Mike Ruppert even went so far as to name Khalid Sheikh Mohammed as one of the top-level al Qaeda chieftains who may have actually been double agents—trained, funded and continuing to work for the CIA. "[Khalid Sheikh Mohammed and others] worked to further an agenda originating out of Washington, strongly influenced by Tel Aviv, rather than out of some ill-defined Muslim hatred of the US," Ruppert wrote.

Mohamed Atta, the accused chief hijacker, was also named by Ruppert as a double agent secretly working for US intelligence. Atta reportedly was under surveillance by US military intelligence agents who had identified him as an al Qaeda ringleader more than a year prior to his visit to the United States for flying lessons.

This astounding fact, only made public in mid-2005, came from a highly classified anti-terrorism program named "Able Danger" formed under the US Special Operations Command (SOCOM) in October 1999. The Able Danger team specifically targeted al Qaeda for investigation. In 2000, a year before to the 9/11 attacks, the Able Danger team identified Mohamed Atta and three other named 9/11 hijackers as possible members of an al Qaeda cell.

This revelation appeared to contradict government claims that no one in US intelligence had identified Atta as a terrorist before 9/11, although it is unclear if senior government officials were given information regarding Atta in either the Clinton or early Bush administrations.

What is clear is that this case of forewarning was presented to the 9/11 Commission who chose not to mention it in their report. It is also noteworthy that in an unprecedented action, General Pete Schoomaker, one of the officers in charge of Able Danger, was brought out of retirement and made Army chief of staff in 2003. In 2006, a report from the Pentagon's Inspector General's Office claimed there had been no pre-9/11 identification of Atta by Able Danger and that those who claimed otherwise were simply mistaken. There was no mention of Able Danger in *The 9/11 Commission Report*.

Upset over claims by 9/11 Commission members that they had not been given critical information concerning Able Danger and its capabilities, Pennsylvania Rep. Curt Weldon in the summer of 2005 wrote to the former chairman and vice-chairman of the 9/11 Commission reminding them that commission staffers had received two briefings on Able Danger, once in October 2003, and another in July 2004. "The impetus for this letter is my extreme disappointment in the recent, and false, claim of the 9/11 commission staff that the commission was never given access to any information on Able Danger," wrote Weldon. "The 9/11 commission staff received not one but two briefings on Able Danger from former team members, yet did not pursue the matter."

Commission Vice-Chairman Lee Hamilton said staff workers indicated that they could not recall being briefed on Able Danger and that no mention of the program was included in their report because the commission had no "information that the United States government had under surveillance or had any knowledge of Mohamed Atta prior to the attacks."

"[Able Danger] Team members believed that the Atta cell in Brooklyn should be subjected to closer scrutiny, but somewhere along the food chain of administration bureaucrats and lawyers, a decision was made in late 2000 against passing the information to the FBI," Weldon stated in his letter to the commission. If the Able Danger intelligence on Atta and his al Qaeda ties was available in 2000, it would be critical to determine who then blocked this information from going to the FBI. But, as usual, there was no investigative follow-up to this information, so damning to official denials of foreknowledge, and which seemed to point to the possibility that Atta was being protected by US intelligence.

In 2010, one of the Able Danger team members, Lt. Col. Anthony A. Shaffer, the winner of a Bronze Star medal for his leadership against the Taliban, published a book entitled *Operation Dark Heart*. In his book, Shaffer, who had retired from the DIA, provided further details on Able Danger as well as his experiences in Afghanistan. He said while serving undercover in Afghanistan, he met with Philip Zelikow, the executive director of the 9/11 Commission, and personally alerted Zelikow to the activities of Able Danger and the fact that they had identified Atta a year prior to the 9/11 attacks. He added that this information was met with "stunned silence," but that nothing of this was mentioned in the commission's report.

In an action reminiscent of Nazi book burnings, Defense Department officials bought and then destroyed nearly 10,000 copies of Shaffer's book, effectively censoring the first printing. This book destruction cost the taxpayers $47,000, according to Fox News. Lt. Col. April Cunningham told CNN the book contained intelligence secrets and might harm national security. It also might have called public attention to the fact that Mohamed Atta and his gang were known to the government a year before the 9/11 attacks.

David Wise, author of *The Invisible Government* and other books on US intelligence, recalled that the CIA attempted to pull this same ploy on him back in 1964 but were confounded by Random House publisher Bennett Cerf who said he would be happy to sell the first printing to the CIA but would then just print more. "Their clumsy efforts to suppress the book only made it a bestseller," quipped Wise.

"The whole premise smacks of retaliation," said Shaffer, whose loss of his security clearance prompted an irate letter from Rep. Christopher Shays, chairman of the Subcommittee on National Security, Emerging Threats and International Relations, who said this action was misuse of the security system. Shaffer quipped, "Someone buying 10,000 books to suppress a story in this digital age is ludicrous." Later in 2010, Shaffer along with five other witnesses to the Able Danger program, told Fox News that investigators for the Inspector General's office looking into Able Danger distorted their statements and attempted to guide their comments and even intimidate them. The whole controversy only served to add support to those who alleged that Atta and his team were known to the US military and that 9/11 was indeed an inside job.

US surveillance of Atta was even reported in European publications long before the Able Danger issue arose. As early as 2001, the German magazine *Focus* reported that US agents, referred to as FBI in some accounts and CIA in others, monitored Atta from January to May 2000 after he was seen buying large quantities of chemicals thought to be used for making bombs. According to the article, the US agents never informed German authorities of Atta's presence or of any suspicions about him.

One of the most outrageous accounts of CIA pre-9/11 activity actually involved Osama bin Laden. One month after the attacks, the French daily *Le Figaro* reported that bin Laden had been treated at an American hospital in the Arab emirate of Dubai in July 2001, and while there was visited by a local CIA agent. According to this report, bin Laden was flown from the Quetta airport in Pakistan to Dubai, where he was admitted to the American hospital located between the Al-Garhoud and Al-Maktoum bridges. He was taken to the urology department for treatment of a kidney infection. The article stated that bin Laden had had mobile kidney dialysis equipment shipped to his hideaway in Pakistan as far back as early 2000.

Furthermore, it went on to say that during his stay at the hospital, between July 4 and 14, bin Laden received visits from family members and prominent Saudis and Emiratis. "During the hospital stay, the local CIA agent, known to many in Dubai, was seen taking the main elevator of the hospital to go to bin Laden's hospital room," stated the *Le Figaro* article, adding, "A few days later, the CIA man bragged to a few friends about having visited bin Laden. Authorized sources say that on July 15th, the day after bin Laden returned to Quetta, the CIA agent was called back to headquarters." Bin Laden, with both a price on his head and eligible for execution under a last-minute order from outgoing president Bill Clinton, nevertheless was allowed to fly without hindrance from Dubai by private jet on July 14.

The article also reported that in late August, customs agents in Dubai notified both American and French authorities of the arrest of Djamel Beghal. Under interrogation, Beghal said he had been ordered to bomb the US embassy in Paris by al Qaeda leader Abu Zubaydah in Afghanistan. "According to Arab diplomatic sources as well as French intelligence, very specific information was transmitted to the CIA with respect to terrorist attacks against American interests around the world, including US soil," stated the French piece. While this story made the rounds in the European media, nothing but a few scattered Internet reports circulated in the United States. In Europe, CIA officials denied the story.

The Dubai story is either true or false. If it is false, the American public needs to know this, so that such untruths can be stopped and not distract from anti-terrorism efforts. If it is true, then the American people need to know that their own CIA let the world's most wanted man walk away unmolested two months prior to the deadly 9/11 attacks. Yet no major American media organization apparently could spare one good reporter to travel to Dubai to check with the hospital staff and others to confirm the story.

The story of the CIA and bin Laden in Dubai is reinforced by a story in the December 23, 2001, edition of the *Washington Post*, which reported that the CIA had recruited a team of Afghan agents to track bin Laden's movements in their country beginning in early 1998. This effort continued right up until September 11, 2001. According to the paper, these agents sent the CIA daily reports on bin Laden's whereabouts but agency officials often dismissed the information because it sometimes conflicted with other intelligence information.

CIA foreknowledge was also obliquely admitted in April 2002 by its own deputy director, James L. Pavitt. In a speech to the Duke University Law School Conference, Pavitt was simultaneously trying to excuse his agency's failure to prevent 9/11 while touting its efficiency. "We had very, very good intelligence of the general structure and strategies of the al Qaeda terrorist organization. We knew and we warned that al Qaeda was planning a major strike. There is no question about that," Pavitt told his audience. His speech later was posted on the CIA's website.

Yet Pavitt tried to echo the administration's claim that there was not enough specific intelligence to prevent the 9/11 attacks. He added that within days of the attacks CIA operatives were "on the ground" operating in Afghanistan. "None of this came easy," he explained. "You cannot learn Pashtun overnight and you can't truly understand the complexities of tribalism, regionalism and personalism in Afghanistan by reading the newspaper or a learned book. My people learned about this by years of study and years of practice often in difficult, hostile and, yes indeed, on the ground in Afghanistan itself.

"If you hear somebody say, and I have, the CIA abandoned Afghanistan after the Soviets left and that we never paid any attention to that place until September 11th, I would implore you to ask those people how we were able to accomplish all we did since the Soviets departed. How we knew who to approach on the ground, which operations, which warlord to support, what information to collect. Quite simply, we were there well before the 11th of September."

In early 2005, the results of an internal CIA investigation were made public. In a report by CIA Inspector General (IG) John Helgerson, former Agency officials, particularly former intelligence chief George Tenet and former deputy director of operations James L. Pavitt, were criticized for the failure to foresee the 9/11 attacks. Both Tenet and Pavitt had resigned from the CIA in the summer of 2004. The IG's report was requested by Congress in December 2002, when it asked "whether and to what extent personnel at all levels should be held accountable" for failure to prevent or stop the attacks. Oddly, Tenet had recently been awarded the Presidential Medal of Freedom by President Bush in a special ceremony at the White House on December 14, 2004.

In this connection it is worth remembering that senior government officials had received this report on Osama bin Laden in July 2001, also quoted earlier: "Based on a review of all-source reporting over the last five months, we believe that [bin Laden] will launch a significant terrorist attack against US and/or Israeli interests in the coming weeks. The attack will be spectacular and designed to inflict mass casualties against US facilities or interests. Attack preparations have been made. Attack will occur with little or no warning."

Even President Bush was fully briefed during this time frame. On July 5, 2001, President Bush received a briefing at his Crawford, Texas, ranch that mentioned the possibility of an airline hijacking as a domestic threat. This information was not made public until nearly nine months after the attacks.

But the most startling revelation of Bush's foreknowledge regarding the attacks did not come until 2004. For nearly two years the Bush administration had attempted to block public access to some of President Bush's President's Daily Brief reports (PDB). Prior to 2005, the PDB was prepared by the CIA. After much legal wrangling, the 9/11 Commission finally obtained these reports in 2004. One in particular, the PDB for August 6, 2001, makes it clear why someone did not want this report made public. The threat, as detailed in this briefing report, was both clear and imminent.

The PDB headline read "Bin Laden Determined To Strike in US". Items detailed in the report, which will be examined later, included the desire of bin Laden to strike Washington; that al Qaeda had support members including US citizens training for attacks; and that bin Laden had wanted to hijack US aircraft in 1998.

The PDB report added that "FBI information since that time [1998] indicates patterns of suspicious activity in this country consistent with preparations for hijackings or other types of attacks, including recent surveillance of federal buildings in New York."

Yet, despite these warnings, when four jetliners went off course on the morning of September 11, there was little or no immediate reaction.

Thomas H. Kean, chairman of the 9/11 Commission, admitted to the possibility that the attacks could have been prevented but saw no design in the voluminous evidence of foreknowledge. "My feeling is a whole number of circumstances, had they been different, might have prevented 9/11," Kean said during a TV network interview. "They involve everything from how people got into the country to failures in the intelligence system."

This picture of missed opportunities to stop the 9/11 attacks was darkened further in early 2005 when the Bush administration released a declassified 120-page report to the National Archives detailing how the FAA had received 52 intelligence reports between April and September 2001, warning of impending attacks. This report, blocked by the Bush administration until more than five months after the release of *The 9/11 Commission Report*, mentioned both bin Laden and al Qaeda by name and the possibility of hijacked aircraft being used as weapons.

Major airports were warned in the spring of 2001 of the possibility that "the intent of the hijacker [may not be] to exchange hostages for prisoners, but to commit suicide in a spectacular explosion…"

The report, only declassified in late January 2005, still contained "heavy redactions" in some areas. It provided more heat in the struggle between the administration and the FAA. The FAA came under attack in the 9/11 Commission's final report for reported failures on September 11, 2001. The 2005 report stated that FAA officials were "lulled into a false sense of security," although it did note that then-FAA Administrator Jane F. Garvey told 9/11 commissioners "that she was aware of the heightened threat during the summer of 2001" but that other senior aviation officials, airline officials and veteran pilots were not.

The 2005 report quoted extensively from FAA circulars distributed to some airports although many of these references were blacked out.

Despite the FAA circulars and a barrage of information on the Internet and in the foreign press, the corporate mass media failed to respond until mid-2002, when complaints from CIA and FBI agents and certain members of Congress became too loud to ignore. Even then, they danced around the subject of all the missed clues and cues.

"Because Bush has long insisted he had no inkling of the attacks, the disclosures [in 2002] touched off a media stampede in a capital long deprived of scandal. The fact that the nation's popular war president might have been warned a little over a month before September 11—and that the supposedly straight-talking Bushies hadn't told anyone about it—opened up a serious credibility gap for the first time in the War on Terror," wrote *Newsweek* writers Michael Hirsh and Michael Isikoff.

Inflated budgets, further centralization of intelligence functions, and adding more intelligence and law enforcement manpower will add nothing to the search for true national security until the American people demand an honest accounting concerning how our government behaved before and during the 9/11 attacks. The record clearly shows that there was a great deal of foreknowledge of what was to come and even covert contact with the alleged hijackers, yet very little commitment at the highest level to stopping the attacks—in fact, considering the hindrance of investigations in both the Clinton and early Bush administrations, there appeared to be a willingness to allow them to happen.

## SELLING STOCKS SHORT INDICATES FOREKNOWLEDGE

Studying recent financial history, one gets the distinct idea that when an event is planned by elite insiders that will dramatically affect the stock market, some greedy individuals with inside connections cannot resist the temptation to profit from such events.

In 1963, in the wake of the assassination of President John F. Kennedy, the New York Stock Exchange recorded a record $21 billion advance, making for the largest single-day rise in the history of the market. It was estimated that the short selling of stock earned unidentified speculators more than $500 million.

Similar suspicious stock trades were reported following the 9/11 attacks. These activities, which implied foreknowledge of the attacks, were loudly trumpeted in the mass media at the time. However, within weeks, this incredible story of high-level profiteering based on the short selling of certain stocks dropped off the corporate mass media's radar screen never to be heard from again.

The evidence of widespread short selling of airline stocks and other forms of insider trading just prior to September 11, 2001 is compelling. Just as there is growing evidence that many insiders had foreknowledge of these attacks, there are clear indications that some used this prior knowledge—not only to profit directly from the deaths of thousands of people—but to do so with the assurance that they would not be caught in such evil machinations. They would also have to have been in a position to know that the attacks would succeed.

Elementary logic also indicated that direct involvement of al Qaeda terrorists in such insider trading was highly unlikely. The idea that Osama bin Laden or al Qaeda leaders would telegraph their intentions through easily tracked stock trades before their attack is implausible, to put it mildly.

Selling stocks short involves having your broker sell shares you don't yet own at a set price to a given buyer, while betting—or perhaps knowing—you can actually acquire them later at a lower price and supply them to the buyer at the set price within a prescribed short time. If you "bet" right, the difference in price is your profit. This form of derivative is risky and you can lose at this game, but you can also win big, especially if you have foreknowledge of an event which will impact the market. Historically, if short selling precedes a traumatic event, it is considered to be an indication of foreknowledge.

Although strictly denied by the US government, it is widely known that the CIA uses the PROMIS computer software to routinely monitor stock trades—in real time—as a possible warning sign of a terrorist attack or suspicious economic behavior. We can safely infer that the CIA could have known in virtual real time, from such trading data alone, that the 9/11 attack was imminent and that it would involve two specific airlines. It also follows that they should also have been able to pinpoint the inside traders through the electronic trail.

It was initially reported by the Israeli Herzliya International Policy Institute for Counterterrorism, a think tank involving former Israeli intelligence officers, that insiders made nearly $16 million profit by short-selling shares in American and United Airlines, the two airlines that suffered the hijackings, as well as the investment firm of Morgan Stanley, which occupied twenty-two floors of the WTC.

According to many other sources, the scandal was much greater even than this. Phil Erlanger, the founder of a Florida firm that tracks short selling and options trading, estimated that traders made off with billions rather than millions of dollars in profit by short selling stocks they knew would tumble in the aftermath of the WTC and Pentagon attacks.

Andreas von Bülow, a former member of the German Parliament and ranking member of the German secret service, estimated profits made by insider traders at $15 billion. CBS offered a far more conservative figure when it reported on Sept 26, 2001, that, "at least seven countries are dissecting suspicious trades that may have netted more than $100 million in profits."

A small FBI scandal indicated that foreknowledge may have prompted bureau agents to seek profit from the attacks. Five persons, including a former and a current agent, were charged in May 2002, with using confidential government information to manipulate stock prices and extort money from businesses.

In indictments brought in Brooklyn, San Diego stock adviser Amr Ibrahim Elgindy was accused of bribing FBI agent Jeffrey A. Royer to give him information on publicly traded companies. Royer, who had worked for the FBI between 1996 and 2000, subsequently left the bureau and went to work for Elgindy's firm, Pacific Equity Investigations. Another FBI agent, Lynn Wingate, was also indicted, accused of passing information to Royer and helping to track investigations of Elgindy through FBI computers. Elgindy reportedly supported Muslim refugees in Kosovo.

According to Assistant US Attorney Kenneth Breen, Elgindy tried to sell $300,000 in stock on September 10, 2001, and told his broker the market was about to drop. Breen saw this as evidence of foreknowledge of the 9/11 attacks. However, higher officials claimed there was no hard evidence of such foreknowledge or that Elgindy had obtained insider information from his FBI contacts.

SELLING STOCKS SHORT INDICATES FOREKNOWLEDGE

Elgindy's father, Ibrahim Elgindy, founded a consortium of Muslim organizations in Chicago and spearheaded a 1998 protest on behalf of Muhammad A. Salah, whose assets were seized after US investigators linked Salah to Palestine's radical Hamas organization.

A week after the September 11 attacks, the London *Times* reported that the CIA had asked regulators for the Financial Services Authority in London to investigate the suspicious sales of millions of shares of stock just prior to the terrorist acts. It was hoped that the business paper trail might lead to the terrorists. The *Times* said market regulators in Germany, Japan, and the United States all had received information concerning the short selling of insurance, airlines, and investment banking stocks, all of which fell sharply in the wake of the attacks.

City of London broker and analyst Richard Crossley noted that certain parties had sold shares in unusually large quantities beginning three weeks before the assault on the WTC and Pentagon. Crossley stated that on the Friday preceding the attacks, more than 10 million shares in the US investment bank Merrill Lynch were sold, compared with 4 million on a normal trading day. "What is more awful than [the perpetrators] should aim a stiletto blow at the heart of Western financial markets?" he added. "But to profit from it. Words fail me."

Stock market regulators in Germany also reported suspicious short selling just prior to September 11.

In the United States, there was an unusually high volume of five-year US Treasury note purchases made just prior to 9/11. *The Wall Street Journal* on October 2, 2001, noted, "Five-year Treasury notes are among the best investments in the event of a world crisis, especially one that hits the US." "This could very well be insider trading at the worst, most horrific, most evil use you've ever seen in your entire life, or this would be one of the most extraordinary coincidences in the history of mankind, if it was a coincidence," said Bloomberg Business News writer Dylan Ratigan.

What are the specifics? Just prior to the 9/11 attacks, there were an unusually high number of "put" options purchased for the stocks of AMR Corp. and UAL Corp., the parent firms of American and United Airlines. A put option gives the bearer the right to sell at a specified price before a certain date. Just like short selling, placing a put option is betting that the stock will fall in price.

According to pioneer 9/11 researcher and former LA police detective Michael Ruppert, between September 6 and 7, 2001, the Chicago Board of Options Exchange reported 4,744 put options on UAL but only 396 call options. On September 10, there were 4,516 put options placed on American Airlines compared to only 748 calls. (Calls reflect the belief that the stock will increase in worth.) American's 6,000 percent jump in put options on the day before the attacks was not matched by any other airlines.

"No similar trading in any other airlines occurred on the Chicago Exchange in the days immediately preceding Black Tuesday," Ruppert said in an October 2001 interview. "That means that someone had advance knowledge that only the stocks of these two airlines would be adversely impacted. Had it just been an industry-wide slump, then you would have seen the same kind of activity on every airline, not just these two."

There were other questionable stock trades made just prior to 9/11. According to Ruppert, Morgan Stanley Dean Witter & Co., which occupied twenty-two floors of the WTC, witnessed the purchase of 2,157 put options during the three trading days before the 9/11 attacks as compared to 27 per day prior to September 6. Merrill Lynch & Co., which also had offices on twenty-two floors of the WTC, had 12,215 one-month put options bought during four trading days prior to 9/11 compared to the normal 252 contracts per day.

"I saw put-call numbers higher than I've ever seen in 10 years of following the markets, particularly the options markets," John Kinnucan, a principal of the independent telecommunications research firm Broadband Research, told the Associated Press.

Alex Popovic, vice president of the Investment Dealers Association of Canada, in early October 2001 confirmed that the US Securities and Exchange Commission had provided a list of thirty-eight companies for scrutiny whose shares had been traded suspiciously but said their review need not be limited to those firms listed. "One shouldn't be wearing blinders when looking at that sort of thing," Popovic told the Associated Press.

Earlier, this same commitment to an opened-ended investigation was voiced by SEC chairman Harvey Pitt, who stated his agency's "No. 1 priority" was to pursue the possible trading by people associated with the terrorists.

Interestingly enough, one of the thirty-eight companies was Vornado

SELLING STOCKS SHORT INDICATES FOREKNOWLEDGE

Realty Trust, a New Jersey-based firm that earlier in 2001 lost a bid to lease the World Trade Center complex from its owner, the Port Authority of New York, to real estate developer Larry A. Silverstein. By early 2003, Silverstein was still in court fighting insurers over whether or not the two planes that struck the WTC constituted one or two separate attacks. Leaseholder Silverstein argued that there were two strikes, which entitled him to a $7.1 billion total payment, $3.55 billion for each attack.

In fact, by adhering to the old journalist creed of "Follow the Money," it is instructive to consider who profited most from the destruction of the WTC structures. On July 24, 2001, Silverstein Properties and Westfield America took out a 99-year lease on the World Trade Center. The total cost of the lease was $3.2 billion. However, by September 11, 2001, the leaser, the Port Authority of New York and New Jersey, had only received an initial payment of about $125 million. In the one-and-a-half months after signing the new lease, Securacom, a firm whose directors included President George W. Bush's younger brother Marvin and his cousin, CEO Wirt Walker III, was engaged to provide security services for the World Trade Center as well as Dulles International Airport and United Airlines, two other entities involved on 9/11. Insurance, including a stipulation that payments would be made in the event of terrorist attack, was arranged through global carriers such as Swiss Re and the German giant Allianz. Following negotiations, Silverstein was finally awarded a total of $4.6 billion for his $125 million investment, accruing a tidy $4,475,000,000 profit. It has been reported that the Port Authority at some point repaid the initial $125 million.

By the end of 2001, stories of profiting on terrorism had vanished. Apparently none of the suspicious put-option transactions could be traced to bin Laden, so this news item quietly dropped from sight—or, perhaps more accurately—was quietly removed from sight, despite the official investigations that were ongoing behind the scenes by the SEC, the FBI, and foreign securities regulators, as was later acknowledged in *The 9/11 Commission Report*. But, if the suspicious trading could not be linked to bin Laden, who was at the end of the investigative trail? Many people wondered if it tracked back to American firms or intelligence agencies. This appears to be the case.

According to the *San Francisco Chronicle*, "[A] source familiar with the

United trades identified Deutsche Bank Alex. Brown, the American investment banking arm of German giant Deutsche Bank, as the investment bank used to purchase at least some of these options."

But this story got worse. The UK's *Independent* reported on October 15, 2001: "To the embarrassment of investigators, it has also emerged that the firm used to buy many of the 'put' options...on United Airlines stock was headed until 1998 by 'Buzzy' Krongard, now executive director of the CIA. "Until 1997, Mr Krongard was chairman of Alex. Brown Inc., America's oldest investment banking firm. Alex. Brown was acquired by Bankers Trust, which in turn was bought by Deutsche Bank. His last post before resigning to take his senior role in the CIA was to head Bankers Trust—Alex. Brown's private client business, dealing with the accounts and investments of wealthy customers around the world." Beginning in 1998, Krongard was counselor to CIA director George Tenet and on March 26, 2001, he was appointed executive director of the CIA.

As chairman of Alex. Brown, Krongard was a man with long-standing and close ties to the financial world. Moving up through the ranks of Alex. Brown, Krongard was elected chief executive officer in 1991 and then chairman of the board in 1994. With the merging of Alex. Brown and Bankers Trust Corp. in 1997, Krongard served as vice chairman of the board until joining the CIA. Bankers Trust was acquired by Deutsche Bank in 1999, becoming the single largest bank in Europe.

Krongard also served as chairman of the Securities Industry Association. A native of Baltimore, he received degrees from Princeton University and the University of Maryland's law school and served as an infantry officer in the Marine Corps. Although Krongard resigned from the CIA with the arrival of CIA Director Porter Goss in September 2004, he nevertheless was a key connection between Blackwater security consulting and the CIA. According to Jeremy Scahill, author of *Blackwater: The Rise of the World's Most Powerful Mercenary Army*, Krongrad was instrumental in obtaining one Blackwater's first security contracts.

"Understanding the interrelationships between CIA and the banking and brokerage world is critical to grasping the already frightening implications of [these] revelations," commented author Michael Ruppert.

Krongard indeed was just the latest of many prominent Americans connected to both the CIA and Wall Street power. These include Clark

Clifford (who was a key player in gaining legitimacy for BCCI, a bank which collapsed in scandal), John Foster Dulles and Allen Dulles (Allen oversaw the failed Bay of Pigs invasion and sat on the Warren Commission, and both Dulles brothers were involved with the Bush-Nazi connection detailed later), William Casey (who moved to the agency after a stint as chairman of the Securities and Exchange Commission), David Doherty (former CIA general counsel, now vice president of the New York Stock Exchange), former president George Herbert Walker Bush (now a paid consultant to the international Carlyle Group, which lists among its clients the bin Ladens), John M. Deutch and Nora Slatkin (Deutch, a former CIA director, and his former executive director Slatkin are both now connected to Citibank and Citigroup) and Hank Greenberg (once nominated as CIA director, then chairman of AIG Insurance representing the third largest pool of investment capital in the world. (He is no longer with AIG and is embroiled in a bitter legal battle over the circumstances of his dismissal.)

As detailed in *Rule by Secrecy*, the CIA historically has been top heavy with members of the Wall Street elite who desire to advance their globalist agenda. It also operates a number of front companies which themselves deal in stocks and bonds.

Again it should be noted that the CIA's PROMIS computer software that is used to track real-time trades in world stock markets should have alerted the Wall Street/CIA elites to all this unusual stock trading and perhaps even of the pending 9/11 attacks.

The PROMIS software had been developed by a computer program designer named Bill Hamilton, who took his work to the federal government only to have the sophisticated software stolen by President Ronald Reagan's attorney general, Ed Meese. This software, which seemed a promising weapon in tracking criminals and illegal money, was turned into an Orwellian program that integrates databases worldwide, giving its possessor nearly unlimited access to all computer records.

"One of the primary functions of the Central Intelligence Agency, by virtue of its long and very close history of relationships with Wall Street, has been a mandate to track and monitor all financial markets worldwide—and to look for anomalous trades, indicative of either economic warfare, or insider currency trading, or speculation—which might affect the US Treasury, or, as in the case of the September 11 attacks, to look for trades that indicated foreknowledge of attacks like we saw," Ruppert told *OnLine Journal* on October 12, 2001. "I am absolutely convinced that the Central Intelligence Agency had complete and perfect foreknowledge of the attacks, down to the date, time, place and location," he concluded.

Author Don Radlauer, who specializes in stock options and derivatives, noted the suspicious stock trading and stated, "Obviously, anyone who had detailed knowledge of the attacks before they happened was, at the very least, an accessory to their planning; and the overwhelming probability is that the trades could have been made only by the same people who masterminded the attacks themselves."

Now, just who might that be?

The US government itself was holding the majority of the international and domestic "short" positions, according to commodity trading advisor Walter Burien, a financial analyst and former tenant of the World Trade Center. According to Burien, government money managers are the primary players within the trillion-dollar international derivative market. "A derivative gives the ability for selling the market 'short' on paper even if you do not own the stock, commodity, currency, bonds, etc.," explained Burien. "The government investment managers over the last thirty years have become very familiar with using this tactic to reap hundreds of billions of dollars each year.

"The government—which controls the economic reports, media coverage and wealth—is in a position to manipulate the above and create an environment to secure substantial revenue while everyone else is lying on the shoulder of the road bleeding to death. For three months prior and going into 9/11, the government investment funds had increased their short positions to the largest diversified short positions ever held by them," noted Burien.

As documented previously, foreknowledge of 9/11 was widely distributed. It is not hard to image that this knowledge migrated to highly placed investors throughout the world who felt safe enough to capitalize on this insider information for a quick profit.

The suspicious stock market trading indicating foreknowledge of the 9/11 attacks only added to the ever-growing belief that people in high positions knew what was coming in September 2001.

SELLING STOCKS SHORT INDICATES FOREKNOWLEDGE

Speaking of all the warnings that poured into government agencies, Jerry Bremer, a former State Department terrorism expert, said, "We all predicted this. We had strategic warning. This is not something the analysts missed."

The evidence of foreknowledge contained within the stock issue and the desire to cover it up may explain the cursory glance given this subject by the 9/11 Commission, along with its rather questionable logic.

Commission authors dismissed the entire issue of insider trading in a buried footnote, stating, "Some unusual trading did in fact occur, but each such trade proved to have an innocuous explanation." In making this final conclusion, it refers to the "enormous resources" expended on the investigation of the issue by the FBI and the CIA and other agencies both domestic and foreign, but does not provide the reader any means to access to these references in order to independently check on the commission's conclusions.

Buried in the same footnote, the commission did manage to trace most of the United Airlines "puts" to one institutional US investor, but dismissed this case simply because this unnamed trader "had no conceivable ties to al Qaeda..."

But any hope that the truth of the foreknowledge behind the unusual put options might be forthcoming in some future honest investigation were dashed in 2010, when it was learned that the Security and Exchange Commission had destroyed all documents pertaining to the pre-9/11 put options purchases. According to the website *Washington's Blog*, David Callahan, the executive editor of *SmartCEO*, submitted a Freedom of Information Act request to the SEC regarding the pre-9/11 put options. In a letter to Callahan dated December 23, 2009, the SEC stated:

"This letter is in response to your request seeking access to and copies of the documentary evidence referred to in footnote 130 of Chapter 5 of *The September 11 [9/11] Commission Report*. Based on the information you provided in your letter, we conducted a thorough search of the commission's various systems of records and consulted with other commission staff. However, we have been advised that the potentially responsive records have been destroyed."

Such cavalier treatment of potentially explosive evidence of 9/11 foreknowledge prompted the author of *Washington's Blog* to comment: "If the SEC had responded by producing documents showing that the pre-9/11 put options had an innocent explanation (such as a hedge made by a smaller airline), that would be understandable. If the SEC had responded by saying that the documents were classified as somehow protecting proprietary financial information, I wouldn't like it, but I would at least understand the argument. But destroyed? Why?" Understandably, 9/11 researchers smelled a cover up.

## WHAT ABOUT ISRAELI FOREKNOWLEDGE?

Since the September 11, 2001, attacks, many commentators have noted that the chief beneficiaries of the terrorism were the Bush administration, the United Kingdom, and Israel. The tragedy spurred the public to rally around President Bush, offering him welcome relief from bad economic news and his own sagging popularity, while the Israel government suddenly found a new pretext for unleashing its forces against the Palestinians. Meanwhile, British Prime Minister Tony Blair was able to quickly discover common ground with Bush for aggressive actions in the Middle East.

At a deeper level, the dominant "neo-conservative" faction in the White House and the Pentagon now had a premise for two of its most cherished projects: a pre-emptive military attack on Iraq as part of a more expansionist US foreign policy, and increased American support for Israel's strategic Middle Eastern objectives.

In concert with that agenda, was there a covert role of Israeli intelligence in the attacks? There were many indications of Israeli foreknowledge of the attacks, and many instances establishing Israel's ability to penetrate deep inside both the al Qaeda network and even its own staunchest ally, the United States.

A major German newspaper, the *Frankfurter Allgemeine Zeitung*, reported on September 13, 2001, that German intelligence sources had stated that both the American and Israeli governments received warnings of the attacks via the Echelon monitoring network. The article said information concerning a plan to hijack commercial airliners to use as weapons against the West was received at least three months prior to the attacks.

Several accounts regarding the number of Israelis killed on 9/11 were disregarded by the corporate mass media as reflections of anti-Semitic bias. But, legitimate questions remain.

On September 12, 2001, a *Jerusalem Post* headline read "Thousands of Israelis Missing near WTC, Pentagon." The accompanying story stated, "The Foreign Ministry in Jerusalem has so far received the names of 4,000 Israelis believed to have been in the areas of the World Trade Center and the Pentagon at the time of the attacks. The list is made up of people who have not yet made contact with friends or family."

It should be noted that this 4,000 figure originated not with US news media or Arabic sources but in Israel. The Arab media, however, was quick to seize on it. A week later, a Beirut television station reported that 4,000 Israeli employees of the WTC were absent the day of the attack, suggesting foreknowledge of the attacks. This information spread across the Internet but was quickly branded a hoax.

On September 19, the *Washington Post* reported about 113 Israelis were missing at the WTC, and the next day, President Bush noted more than 130 Israelis were victims. Finally, on September 22, the *New York Times* stated that amazingly only one Israeli was killed when the WTC towers collapsed. "There were, in fact, only three Israelis who had been confirmed as dead: two on the planes and another who had been visiting the towers on business and who was identified and buried," reported the *Times*.

Undoubtedly, WTC victims included many Jews but given the large number of Israelis believed to be working in the towers, this minimal number of dead—along with other factors—would seem to indicate the possibility of Israeli foreknowledge.

There was also a little-noticed story regarding the New York instant messaging firm, Odigo. Officials of Odigo confirmed soon after the attacks that two of their employees in Herzliya, Israel had received text messages warning of the attacks two hours before planes crashed into the WTC. The pair received electronic instant messages declaring that some sort of attack was about to take place. The notes ended with an anti-Semitic slur. "The messages said something big was going to happen in a certain amount of time, and it did—almost to the minute," said Alex Diamandis, vice president of sales for the high-tech company, whose offices in Lower Manhattan are near the WTC. He said the employees did not know the person who sent the message, but they traced it to a computer address and have given tha information to the FBI.

Diamandis said employees in the company's research and development and international sales office in Israel received the warnings from another Odigo user unknown to them. They declined to state exactly what was in the messages or who sent them, saying the FBI was looking into the matter. Micha Macover, Odigo's CEO, later said that while the company usually zealously protects the privacy of registered users, in this case it provided the FBI with the originating Internet Protocol (IP) address of the message so the bureau could track down the Internet Service Provider and the originator of the message. There was no further word from the FBI. Diamandis explained that Odigo offers a "People Finder" program that allows users to seek out and contact others based on common interests. He said it was possible that other Odigo members got the warnings but that the company had not heard from other recipients.

Another small item that raised eyebrows concerned a broken lease at the World Trade Center just days before the 9/11 attacks by a company with close ties to Israel. The *American Free Press* reported that Zim American Israeli Shipping Co. broke its lease on two floors of the WTC's North Tower when it vacated the rented offices in early September 2001. The company's lease was good until the end of the year and the early pullout cost the company a reported $50,000.

The company is owned by Zim Israel Navigation Co., one of the world's largest container shipping firms. It is jointly owned by the state of Israel and Israel Corp. Inquiries on the early withdrawal by Zim were routed to the WTC lease owner Silverstein Properties, which in turn passed questions to its public relations firm, Howard J. Rubenstein, which also represents the nation of Israel. A spokesman for Rubenstein said they had no information on the lease issue.

But such stories raise the question: Would a staunch friend of the United States like Israel conduct activities detrimental to its ally?

Two academic observers of Middle Eastern politics, Professors John Mearsheimer of the University of Chicago and Stephen Walt of the John F. Kennedy School of Government at Harvard University, sought to answer this question in a controversial 83-page study entitled, "The Israel Lobby and US Foreign Policy." First published in digest form in the *London Review of Books* on March 10, 2006 and originally published in full as a working paper of the John F. Kennedy School of Government at Harvard University, the paper quickly prompted a raging controversy between pro and anti-Zionists.

"The US national interest should be the primary object of American foreign policy," the pair wrote. "For the past several decades, however, and especially since the Six Day War in 1967, the centerpiece of US Middle East policy has been its relationship with Israel. The combination of unwavering US support for Israel and the related effort to spread democracy throughout the region has inflamed Arab and Islamic opinion and jeopardized US security. "This situation has no equal in American political history. Why has the United States been willing to set aside its own security in order to advance the interests of another state? One might assume that the bond between the two countries is based on shared strategic interests or compelling moral imperatives...However, neither of those explanations can account for the remarkable level of material and diplomatic support that the United States provides to Israel."

The true explanation, say the professors, is that a pro-Israel lobby in the US has exercised pervasive influence in Washington and in the US through its intimidation of the press, and by the use of powerful think tanks and influential positions in academia. Some members of the neocon faction even carry duel citizenship with Israel.

The Israeli lobby keeps press scrutiny away from Israeli activities and this lack of attention may well serve as a cover for Israeli intelligence activities that may not be in our best interests, asserted Mearsheimer and Walt. This allegation found support by studying the number of shocking instances of US penetration by agents of the Israeli Mossad in the wake of the 9/11 attacks.

To begin with, it might be remembered that on the day of the attacks, five Israelis were arrested for "puzzling behavior," namely shouting and dancing just after shooting video of the destruction of the World Trade Center from the roof of the New Jersey building where they worked. The five, identified as Oded Ellner, Omer Marmari, Yaron Shmuel, and Sivan and Paul Kurzberg, were seen videotaping the WTC attack by neighbors, who interpreted their shouts as jubilation and agreement with the tragedy. Police were notified and later stopped their van bearing the company name Urban Moving Systems. In their van, police found $4,000 in cash and a box cutter. One investigator told the *Bergen Record* on September 12, "There were maps of the city in the car with certain places highlighted. It looked like they're hooked in on this. It looked like they knew what was going to happen." ABC News quoted one of the Israelis as saying, "Our purpose was to document the event."

After the names of two of the five turned up on a CIA-FBI database of foreign intelligence nationals, Marc Perelman of *Forward* reported that the FBI launched a Foreign Counterintelligence Investigation (FCI), which is undertaken quietly at the highest levels of the bureau. One of the men's attorneys, Steven Gordon, confirmed that "counterintelligence officials from the FBI" were involved in the case.

Dominick Suter, owner of the Weehawken, New Jersey, moving company, was questioned by the FBI agents, who took documents and computer hard drives but allowed Suter to go free. A few days later, Suter left the US for Israel. In late November, the five were quietly released and sent back to Israel, where they charged that American authorities tortured them by keeping them unclothed in solitary confinement, beating them, and depriving them of food.

Irit Stoffer, a spokesperson for the Israeli Foreign Ministry, denied the men were spies and said they were deported for "only visa violations." Chip Berlet, a senior analyst for Political Research Associates in Boston, explained, "[There] is a backdoor agreement between allies that says that if one of your spies gets caught and didn't do too much harm, he goes home. It goes on all the time. The official reason is always a visa violation."

But was there no real harm done? This case seemed to be just another odd anomaly lost in the cascading news of the 9/11 attacks and the subsequent attack of Afghanistan. But it turned out to be only the barest tip of an iceberg that was to become public in mid-2002. The story began to surface in early 2002 when a secret report by the Drug Enforcement Agency (DEA) was leaked to the European media. The report stated that most distribution of the drug Ecstasy was "controlled by organized crime figures in Western Europe, Russia and Israel." According to several reports, a DEA investigation into the Ecstasy supply uncovered a number of Israeli citizens operating in the United States.

"The report shows the clandestine network was engaged in several intelligence operations. It was a long-term project," said Guillaume Dasquie, editor of *Intelligence Online*, which broke the story in March 2002. The French website threatened to publish the entire DEA report if US and Israeli officials continued to deny its existence. The report mentioned investigations of the spy network in Florida, Texas, and California, with many of its participants posing as art students.

Beginning in early 2002, Fox News reporter Carl Cameron began to break the story that the US government was holding more than one hundred Israeli citizens with direct links to foreign military, criminal, and intelligence organizations. A bureau spokesperson would not talk about the case but did not deny it either. He referred reporters to the FBI's National Security Division.

Cameron too said he was hampered in trying to obtain information. "It's very explosive information, obviously, and there's a great deal of evidence that they say they have collected." He added that the biggest question—one regarding the 9/11 attacks—that investigators shared with him was "How could they [the Israelis] not have known?"

By summer 2002, the estimated number of Israeli nationals being held had climbed to nearly two hundred, yet still the story went largely unreported by America's corporate mass media. One can only imagine what the newspaper headlines and TV crawl tags would look like if a gigantic Iraqi spy ring had been uncovered.

Reportedly, several of the Israelis lived in close proximity to some of the 9/11 terrorists, increasing the speculation that Israel knew more about the attacks than officially admitted. More than one-third of 120 deported Israelis lived in Florida, home to at least 10 of the 19 identified hijackers. At least 5 lived in Hollywood, Florida, home to Mohamed Atta and three other hijackers. Two others lived near Delray Beach, where other hijackers temporarily stayed. Six of the Israelis used cell phones purchased by a former Israeli vice consul in the United States, reported *Le Monde*. Furthermore, several of the persons involved in this "art student scandal" were observed taking pictures and reconnoitering US military bases and the homes of government officials.

In March 2001, the National Counterintelligence Center (NCIC) issued a warning that "in the past six weeks, employees in federal office buildings have reported suspicious activities concerning individuals representing themselves as foreign students selling artwork."

Paul Rodriguez with *Insight* magazine reported, "Besides federal law enforcement incidents, DEA's I[nternal] S[ecurity] unit found that several military bases also had experienced unauthorized entries by some of the students including two bases from which Stealth aircraft and other super-secret military units operate. Unauthorized photographing of military sites and civilian industrial complexes, such as petroleum storage facilities, also was reported to the DEA, the documents show and interviews confirm."

Many of these young men and women had known connections to Israeli military, intelligence, or even criminal organizations. Some even worked in electronic signal intercept units in the Israeli army. Most claimed to be art students from Israel's Bezalel Academy or the University of Jerusalem. The Jerusalem university does not exist, and officials with Bezalel Academy said no names of the "art students" turned up in the school's data bank.

According to the prestigious French newspaper *Le Monde*, student art sales were merely a cover for a vast Israeli spy ring whose primary purpose was to track al Qaeda in the United States without informing American authorities. The paper said this was the biggest Israeli spy case in the United States since 1984, when naval intelligence officer Jonathan Pollard, an American Jew, was caught giving military secrets to Israel.

The German newspaper *Die Zeit* reported in late 2002 that the CIA was given a detailed report on the actions of terrorists within the United States by the Mossad but failed to act on the information. The paper also said that if the CIA had notified German authorities that Ramzi bin al-Shibh, a key logistician for the attacks, had attended the meeting of al Qaeda members in Malaysia more than eighteen months prior to 9/11, the Germans could have prevented him from entering Germany and making contact with the Hamburg cell that planned the 9/11 atrocities.

According to BBC News, "The paper [*Die Zeit*] has uncovered details of a major Israeli spy ring involving some 120 agents for the intelligence service Mossad operation across America and some masquerading as art students. The ring was reportedly hard on the heels of at least four members of the hijack gang, including its leader Mohamed Atta. But the Israeli agents were detected by their American counterparts and thrown out of the country. The US authorities said then that they were students whose visas had expired."

WHAT ABOUT ISRAELI FOREKNOWLEDGE?

The paper also said that if the CIA had notified German authorities that Ramzi bin al-Shibh, a key logistician for the attacks, had attended the meeting of al Qaeda members in Malaysia more than eighteen months prior to 9/11, the Germans could have prevented him from entering Germany and making contact with the Hamburg cell that planned the 9/11 atrocities.

Central to this tale of spies infiltrating the United States is the fact that the people taken by the FBI in connection with the spy ring included employees of two Israeli-owned high-tech companies that currently perform nearly all official wiretaps in the United States.

Such wiretaps are authorized by the Communications Assistance for Law Enforcement Act (CALEA), passed during the Clinton administration. Actually "wiretap" is a misnomer, because today's communications systems may be accessed by electronic signals rather than physical "taps," but the end result is the same—eavesdropping.

Two firms that handle most of this wiretapping are Amdocs, Ltd. and Comverse Infosys, both identified by Fox News as Israeli telecommunications companies. Amdocs reportedly keeps records of virtually every call made in the United States, although not the content of the calls. Comverse provided custom computers and software that allowed US investigators to intercept, record, store and receive data from the US phone system.

According to NewsMax.com reporter Charles R. Smith, "The spy ring enabled criminals to use reverse wiretaps against US intelligence and law enforcement operations. The [spy ring's] illegal monitoring may have resulted in the deaths of several informants and reportedly spoiled planned anti-drug raids on crime syndicates."

Officials at both Amdocs and Comverse denied any knowledge of the Israeli spy ring. Comverse spokesman Paul Baker stated, "In full compliance with the US Department of Defense regulations, this subsidiary's operations are completely segregated from all other Comverse businesses and are insulated from any foreign influence."

The official response to the allegations of widespread spying and even foreknowledge of the 9/11 attacks has prompted overly strenuous denials from US officials and even attacks in the major media.

Daniel Pipes in an article for *Jewish World Review*, which was then published as an op-ed piece in the *New York Post*, decried the spy ring story as "conspiracy theories" based on a "crazy-quilt of unsourced allegations, drive-by innuendoes, and incoherent obscurities, but no hard facts." Pipes, a member of the Council on Foreign Relations, is the director of the Middle East Forum and the author of *Conspiracy: How the Paranoid Style Flourishes and Where It Comes From*, is trotted out from time to time to dispel what he considers conspiracy theories. But Pipes himself holds some extreme political views for a Middle Eastern scholar. The only road to peace in Israel, he told a recent Zionist conference in Washington, D.C., is "an Israeli victory and a Palestinian defeat."

If the major news media are cowed about negative reporting on Israel, US government officials may be worse. *Insight* magazine reporter Paul Rodriguez said one Justice Department official told him, "We think there is something quite sinister here but are unable at this time to put our finger on it." Another official flatly stated, "The higher ups don't want to deal with this and neither does the FBI because it involves Israel." Fox News reported that, "investigators within the DEA, INS and FBI have all told Fox that to pursue or even suggest Israel is spying through Comverse is considered career suicide."

Critics have voiced opposition to the wiretapping system. "From the beginning, both the political right and left warned Congress and the FBI that they were making a huge mistake by implementing CALEA, that it would jeopardize the security of private communications, whether it's between a mother and her son or between government officials," said Lisa Dean, vice president for technology policy at the Free Congress Foundation. The foundation's Brad Jansen added, "The CALEA form of massive surveillance is a poor substitute for real law enforcement and intelligence work. Massive wiretapping does not equal security. Instead, we have elected to jeopardize our national security in exchange for poor law enforcement. The current mentality of law enforcement is what failed to protect the US from 9/11. CALEA wiretaps will not protect us from terror attacks in the future. The system does not provide better intelligence information. It actually leads to less security and more crime. We get the worst of both worlds."

Some observers of today's geopolitical scene, including the authors of the aforementioned study entitled "The Israel Lobby and US Foreign Policy," Professors Mearsheimer of the University of Chicago and Walt

WHAT ABOUT ISRAELI FOREKNOWLEDGE?

of the John F. Kennedy School of Government at Harvard University, believe that the 9/11 attacks provided a pretext to implement a plan to strengthen Israel, as articulated in a 1996 paper by an Israeli think tank that was influential in the Clinton administration.

The leader of the study group that produced this paper was Richard Perle. In 2002, Perle was chairman of Bush's Defense Policy Board, which reported to Deputy Defense Secretary Paul Wolfowitz. Perle is a ranking member of the Council on Foreign Relations and a key advocate of "neo-conservative" foreign policy. Perle's 1996 paper, entitled "A Clean Break: A New Strategy for Securing the Realm," was prepared for the Institute for Advanced Strategic and Political Studies (IASPS), a Jerusalem-based think tank with an affiliated office in Washington. The institute issues policy studies and trains Israeli graduates in economic and strategic studies, helping them become research aides in the Israeli Parliament (Knesset) and the US Congress.

The "Clean Break" paper, prepared by IASPS consultants—two of whom were also members of the CFR, stated in 1996 that Israel had an opportunity to make a "clean break" with past policies and formulate "a new strategy to seize the initiative." The paper urged Israeli leaders to "work closely with Turkey and Jordan to contain, destabilize, and roll back some of its most dangerous threats. This implies a clean break from the slogan 'comprehensive peace' to a traditional concept of strategy based on balance of power." This would mean, as the paper goes on to explain, that "Israel can shape its strategic environment, in cooperation with Turkey and Jordan, by weakening, containing, and even rolling back Syria. This effort can focus on removing Saddam Hussein from power in Iraq—an important Israeli strategic objective in its own right—as a means of foiling Syria's regional ambitions."

Perle's paper also calls for changing "the nature of [Israel's] relations with the Palestinians, including the right of hot pursuit for self-defense into all Palestinian areas and nurturing alternatives to Arafat's exclusive grip on Palestinian society."

On February 19, 1998, Richard Perle and former Congressman Stephen Solarz released an open letter to the president, demanding a full-scale US-led drive for "regime change" in Baghdad. Among the signers of the original Perle-Solarz letter were the following current or recent Bush administration officials: Elliot Abrams (National Security Council), Richard Armitage (State Department), John Bolton (State Department), Doug Feith (Defense Department), Fred Ikle (Defense Policy Board), Zalmay Khalilzad (White House), Peter Rodman (Defense Department), Donald Rumsfeld (Secretary of Defense), Paul Wolfowitz (Defense Department), David Wurmser (State Department), and Dov Zakheim (Defense Department).

Considering that seven of the eleven men listed above are members of the Council on Foreign Relations, this plan could also be viewed as advancing the policy of that globalist organization as well. Once the Bush II administration had brought these men back in power, these neo-conservatives—along with the Israeli government and the US Israeli lobby—were able to see their favored policies acted upon, virtually without restraint.

Shortly after the invasion of Iraq began in late March 2003, Perle resigned as chairman of the Bush administration's Defense Policy Board amid charges of conflict of interest. The *New Yorker* magazine's investigative writer Seymour Hersh reported that Perle had met in France with a Saudi arms dealer while soliciting investments for Trireme Partners, a firm he helped create and that planned to profit from homeland security activities. Perle threatened to sue Hersh and called him "the closest thing American journalism has to a terrorist" shortly before resigning.

According to Mearsheimer and Walt's study, the ongoing drive to induce President Bush to launch a war against Iraq was virtually foisted upon the president by the Israeli lobby, after years of efforts to implement the precepts of the "Clean Break" paper. The events of 9/11 finally gave them the pretext they needed for aggressively pursuing their objective.

And there are other intriguing sources filling in this picture. General Hameed Gul, former director general of the Pakistani intelligence services, or ISI, who worked closely with the CIA during the years of fighting against the Soviets in Afghanistan, made the incredible statement during an interview with UPI news service that it was his belief that the Israeli Mossad orchestrated the 9/11 attacks with the support of its own assets already within the United States.

While obviously anti-Israel, Gul nevertheless was in an insider's position. His views should be considered when he explained how there was little or no response from security forces on the morning of 9/11. "This was clearly an inside job," Gul said.

## WHAT ABOUT ISRAELI FOREKNOWLEDGE?

Gul went on to explain that Israel had grown to detest both President Bush and his father because they are considered "too close to oil interests and the [Arab] Gulf countries."

"Bush conveniently overlooks—or is not told—the fact that Islamic fundamentalists got their big boost in the modern age as CIA assets in the covert campaign to force the Soviets out of Afghanistan. All summer long [2001] we heard about America's shrinking surplus and that the Pentagon would not have sufficient funds to modernize for the 21st century. And now, all of a sudden, the Pentagon can get what it wants without any Democratic Party opposition. How very convenient.

"Even [America's] cherished civil liberties can now be abridged with impunity to protect the expansion of the hegemony of transnational capitalism. There is now a new excuse to crush anti-globalization protests. And now the Israelis have given the US the pretext for further expansion into an area that will be critical in the next 25 years—the Caspian basin," Gul stated.

The tight relationship between the Pakistani ISI and our CIA, which may include evidence of cooperative ties between the two agencies in providing covert funding to lead hijacker Mohamed Atta. Thus, by blaming Israel, Gul might well be attempting to deflect attention from the involvement of the ISI on behalf of the terror plot.

But lest one think that Gul had his own agenda for making such statements, similar ideas about Israel's role were expressed by two former German intelligence chiefs. Eckhardt Werthebach, former president of Germany's domestic intelligence service, *Verfassungsschutz*, and Andreas von Bülow, Germany's former defense minister who also served on a parliamentary commission with oversight over Germany's secret service, both said the 9/11 attacks gave every evidence of being a state-sponsored event. Recall that US Attorney General Ashcroft soon after 9/11 announced that at least three of the hijackers were traced to a terrorist cell that had operated out of Hamburg, Germany, since at least 1999.

Werthebach said a sophisticated operation such as displayed on 9/11 would require a state intelligence service behind it, totally unlike the "loose group" of terrorists reportedly led by Mohamed Atta.

Von Bülow said the 9/11 planners used mercenaries or "guns for hire," such as Palestinian terrorist leader Abu Nidal, whom von Bülow described as an "instrument of the Mossad." Such people as Nidal and other Arab mercenaries are the "working level," according to von Bülow, pointing out the problems with such low-level agents.

He said they were "like assailants who, in their preparations, leave tracks behind them like a herd of stampeding elephants. They made payments with credit cards with their own names; they reported to their flight instructors with their own names. They left behind rented cars with flight manuals in Arabic for jumbo jets. They took with them, on their suicide trip, bills and farewell letters, which fall into the hands of the FBI, because they were stored in the wrong place and wrongly addressed. Clues were left behind like in a child's game of hide-and-seek, which were to be followed!"

He said such an operation is carefully conducted with an eye toward deception that is widely propagated in the mainstream media, creating an accepted version of events. "Journalists don't even raise the simplest questions," he added. "Those who differ are labeled as crazy."

Von Bülow specified Israel as the most likely sponsor and said that the attacks were designed to turn public opinion against Arabs while boosting military and security spending.

Interestingly enough, the day before the 9/11 attacks, the *Washington Times* ran a story, quoting members of the US Army's School of Advanced Military Studies (SAMS). Speaking about the capability of Israel, the paper noted, "Of the Mossad, the Israeli intelligence service, the SAMS officers say: 'Wildcard. Ruthless and cunning. Has capability to target US forces and make it look like a Palestinian/Arab act.'"

While bearing in mind these remarkable and controversial statements and allegations, it must be remembered that—in the convoluted world of international covert operations—almost nothing is as it seems. The whole spectrum of Middle East politics is so full of agents, spies, counterspies, dupes, mercenaries and provocateurs that one needs an almost impossible degree of sophistication to be able to tell the players apart.

9/11 researchers have presented evidence of significant collusion by elements of the Pakistani government in the events of 9/11 and it is widely believed that Pakistani Intelligence is controlled by the CIA.

This story was first broken by Michel Chossudovsky, a professor of economics at the University of Ottawa and author of *War and Globalisa-*

WHAT ABOUT ISRAELI FOREKNOWLEDGE?

*tion: The Truth Behind 9/11.* He also serves as director of the Center for Research on Globalization which hosts globalresearch.ca, an important background source for 9/11 researchers.

In a little-noticed mainstream television news story cited by Chossudovsky, it was revealed that the FBI had told ABC News in late September 2001 that the 9/11 "ring leader," Mohamed Atta, had been financed by unnamed sources in Pakistan: The FBI had tracked more than $100,000 that had been wired from banks in Pakistan into accounts held by Atta in two Florida banks.

A short time later, according to Chossudovsky, "these findings of the FBI were confirmed by Agence France Presse (AFP) and the *Times of India*, which quoted an official Indian intelligence report dispatched to Washington. According to these two reports, the money used to finance the 9/11 attacks had allegedly been 'wired to WTC hijacker Mohamed Atta from Pakistan, by Ahmad Umar Sheikh, at the insistence of [ISI Chief] General Mahmoud [Ahmad].' And, according to the AFP [quoting the intelligence source]: 'The evidence we have supplied to the US is of a much wider range and depth than just one piece of paper linking a rogue general to some misplaced act of terrorism.'"

As if this were not enough, Chossudovsky discovered that none other than General Mahmoud Ahmad himself, the successor of Hameed Gul and the alleged "money-man behind 9/11," was in the US when the attacks occurred. The ISI chief arrived on September 4, 2001, one week before 9/11, on what was described as routine consultations with his US counterparts, including meetings at the Pentagon, the National Security Council, and with CIA Director George Tenet. And on the morning of September 11, Pakistan's chief spy was at a breakfast meeting on Capitol Hill hosted by Senator Bob Graham and Representative Porter Goss, the then-chairmen of the Senate and House Intelligence committees. Goss would later serve as director of the CIA from 2004–2006.

It should be recalled that in October 2001, although largely lost in the post-9/11 media frenzy, there were brief mainstream news reports of an attack on the Mexican parliament. Two terrorists, armed with guns, hand grenades and C-4 plastic explosives were apprehended in the Mexican Chamber of Deputies. Although carrying Pakistani passports, the pair were soon identified as Salvador Gerson Sunke, a Mexican Jew, and Sar ben Zui, a colonel in the Israeli special forces. Some conspiracy researchers suspected that Mexico had not been eager enough to join in President Bush's War on Terrorism and needed special incentive. Although the story made major headlines in the Mexican media, the story quickly disappeared in the US. The suspects, Sunke and Zui, were quietly released and deported to Israel.

As to which foreign government entity may be behind the events of 9/11 and in collusion with a rogue faction in the US—the Saudis, the Israeli Mossad, the Pakistani ISI, or some combination—it can only be said at this point that current evidence points to the likelihood that 9/11 marks the convergence of overlapping and surreptitious agendas of several hidden parties, both international and domestic. Further research will be needed to connect the many dots on the global landscape that have been revealed thus far.

## WERE THE HIJACKED PLANES REMOTELY CONTROLLED?

On October 7, 2001, the first operational deployment of "Global Hawk" spearheaded the American air and missile strikes on Afghanistan. Global Hawk is the name of the latest version of a high-altitude, long-endurance unmanned air vehicle (UAV); in other words, an unarmed pilotless drone plane that can take off, fire missiles, conduct missions such as photographing battlefields and land by remote electronic control. The jet aircraft, equivalent in wing size to a Boeing 737 commercial airliner, has a publicly announced range of 14,000 nautical miles (about halfway around the world) and can fly at altitudes of 65,000 feet for about forty hours.

"Working alongside other UAV reconnaissance assets, at least one Global Hawk was used to provide reconnaissance prior to the [Afghanistan] strikes and for successive post-strike battle damage assessment," reported *Jane's Aerospace* on October 8, 2001.

Such remote-control and on-board-computer-capture technology was largely unknown to the American public at the time of 9/11. However, such Buck Rogers equipment had been developed in the 1970s and, by several credible accounts, was operational in the 1980s. By the spring of 2001, this unmanned drone, designated the RQ-4A Global Hawk UAV, was capable of flying a mission to Australia.

"On 23 April 2001," according to Australia's Defence Science and Technology Organisation (DSTO), "Global Hawk flew non-stop from Edwards Air Force Base, California, to Edinburgh Air Force Base, South Australia, where it was based for nearly two months undergoing a series of demonstration flights. Global Hawk returned to the US on 7 June 2001."

Dr. Brendan Nelson, Australia's parliamentary secretary to the minister of defense, said Global Hawk made aviation history when it became the first unmanned aircraft to fly nonstop across the Pacific Ocean in twenty-three hours and twenty minutes. The previous record for crossing the Pacific had stood for twenty-six years.

During its six weeks of demonstrations in Australia, Global Hawk undertook eleven missions with crews from both the US Air Force and the Royal Australian Air Force. It was the first time the United States had operated Global Hawk with another nation.

According to the Defense Advanced Research Projects Agency (DARPA), a newly designed Global Hawk aircraft was first flown at Edwards AFB on February 28, 1998. A Defense Department news release said, "The entire mission, including take-off and landing, was performed autonomously by the aircraft based on its mission plan." The craft's ground controllers monitored the status of the flight.

The Global Hawk program is managed by DARPA for the Defense Airborne Reconnaissance Office. The primary contractor is Teledyne Ryan Aeronautical and the principal suppliers are Raytheon Systems, Allison Engine Co., Boeing North American, and L3 Com. So what does this unmanned flight system have to do with September 11?

Former German Defense Minister Andreas von Bülow, in a January 13, 2002, interview with the newspaper *Tagesspiegel*, in speaking about the 9/11 attacks, noted, "There is also the theory of one British flight engineer [and] according to this, the steering of the planes was perhaps taken out of the pilots' hands from outside. The Americans had developed a method in the 1970s whereby they could rescue hijacked planes by intervening into the computer piloting [the electronic flight system]. This theory says this technique was abused in this case." Von Bülow could well have knowledge of this technology as several researchers and websites have stated that Lufthansa, Germany's national airline, was aware of the possibility of electronic capture and had quietly stripped the flight control systems out of its American-built jetliners in the early 1990s.

The British flight engineer Von Bülow mentioned is Joe Vialls, a journalist, author, private investigator, and a former member of the Society of Licensed Aeronautical Engineers and Technologists based in London. In an article published on several websites, Vialls claimed, "[T]wo American multinationals collaborated with the Defense Advanced Research Projects Agency (DARPA) on a project designed to facilitate the remote recovery of hijacked American aircraft. Brilliant both in concept and operation, 'Home Run' [Vialls' designation, not its real code name] allowed specialist ground controllers to listen in to cockpit conversations on the target aircraft, then take absolute control of its computerized flight control system by remote means." wrote Vialls in late 2001.

"From that point onwards, regardless of the wishes of the hijackers or flight deck crew, the hijacked aircraft could be recovered and landed automatically at an airport of choice, with no more difficulty than flying a radio-controlled model airplane. The engineers had no idea that almost thirty years after its initial design, Home Run's top-secret computer codes would be broken [or passed to unauthorized personnel] and the system used to facilitate direct ground control of four aircraft used in the high-profile attacks in New York and Washington on 11 September 2001."

After news of Global Hawk and its remote-controlled capability was first released, there was speculation that UAV technology might be used to thwart airline hijackings. Once a hijacking took place, the Global Hawk flight technology would be triggered and the electronically captured plane flown to a landing at a safe location regardless of the actions of the flight crew or the hijackers.

The seemingly outlandish suggestion that remote-controlled planes were crashed into American targets is backed by several intriguing facts, beginning with a little-noticed item in the September 28, 2001, edition of the *New York Times* in which President Bush announced his plans to protect air passengers. Along with the usual proposals, such as strengthening cockpit doors and transponders that cannot be turned off, he mentioned "new technology, probably far in the future, allowing air traffic controllers to land distressed planes by remote control." Apparently, Bush was familiar with the Global Hawk technology but chose to present it as technology not yet available.

One aviation authority who did speak out on remote control was Robert Ayling, former CEO of British Airways who was quoted in *The Economist* in 2001 suggesting "aircraft could be commandeered from the ground and controlled remotely in the event of a hijack."

After the 2001 attacks, many websites speculated that perhaps Global Hawk's first true operational use might have been conducted on September 11. After all, as all experienced aviation and military persons well know, if a technology such as Global Hawk is publicly revealed, it most probably has been in secret use for many years previously.

According to aviation insiders, while it may indeed be years before air traffic controllers can take electronic control of flying airliners, such technology already exists in certain modern jumbo jets equipped with electronic flight control systems, such as the Boeing 757 and 767, both of which were involved in the 9/11 attacks. This assertion seemed to be confirmed by a technical and operational analysis white paper published shortly after the 9/11 attacks by two Arizona technology companies, KinetX, Inc. of Tempe and Cogitek Corp. of Chandler.

These firms were trying to market their version of Global Hawk as an anti-hijacker system. "The National Flight Emergency Response System (NFERS) was developed to prevent the terrorist incident of 9/11 from ever happening again," stated the companies' white paper. "This system will protect passenger and cargo aircraft from being used as terrorist weapons. NFERS is essentially the integration of *existing technology* [emphasis added] for the purpose of transferring cockpit operations to a secure ground station in case of an emergency. It is important to note that the essential technology exists now."

The two Arizona companies reported that they could have a prototype system ready for use in twelve months. If independent firms could manage a prototype that soon, it is clear that the government most probably has the same technology operational. Under such a system, a computer command ground station could electronically capture a plane equipped with such technology and direct it wherever the controllers wished it to go. Some experts contended that flying electronic command centers—

Airborne Warning and Control System (AWACS) aircraft—can perform the same function as a ground station.

Other news items that reinforce the idea that electronically captured planes were used on 9/11 include the tape of Osama bin Laden made public by the CIA in late 2001, in which he revealed that some, if not all, of the hijackers did not realize they were on a suicide mission. This could also explain the Boston reports that the hijackers spent their last night drinking heavily and looking for hookers.

More common-sense reasoning was advanced in an article by Carol A. Valentine, curator of the Waco Holocaust Electronic Museum. She wrote: "Put yourself in the shoes of the masterminds of Operation 911. The attacks had to be tightly coordinated. Four jets took off within 15 minutes of each other at Boston, Dulles, and Newark airports, and roughly two hours later, it was over. The masterminds couldn't afford to take needless chances. Years ago I saw a local TV news reporter interview a New York mugger about the occupational hazards of his trade...If a freelance New York mugger realized the unpredictable nature of human behavior, surely the pros who pulled this job off must have known the same truth. Yet we are asked to believe that the culprits took four jet airliners, with four sets of crew and four sets of passengers—armed with (depending on the news reports you read) 'knives,' 'plastic knives' and 'box cutters'. Given the crazy and unpredictable nature of humans, why would they try this bold plan when they were so poorly armed?

"A lady's handbag—given the weight of the contents most women insist on packing—is an awesome weapon. I know, I have used mine in self defense. Are we to believe that none of the women had the testosterone to knock those flimsy little weapons out of the hijackers' hands? And what of the briefcases most men carry? Thrown, those briefcases can be potent weapons. Your ordinary everyday New York mugger would never take the chances that our culprits took.

"Flight attendant Michelle Heidenberger was on board Flight 77. She had been 'trained to handle a hijacking.' She knew not to let anyone in the cockpit. She knew to tell the hijacker that she didn't have a key and would have to call the pilots. None of her training mattered." [This was reported in the article "On flight 77: 'Our Plane Is Being Hijacked'," *The Washington Post*, September 12, 2001]

## WERE THE HIJACKED PLANES REMOTELY CONTROLLED?

"That's right, the *Washington Post* for once is telling the whole truth. Heidenberger's training didn't matter, the pilots' training didn't matter, the ladies handbags didn't matter, the mens' briefcases didn't matter. The masterminds of Operation 911 knew that whatever happened aboard those flights, the control of the planes was in their hands. Even if the crew and passengers fought back, my hypothesis is that they could not have regained control of the planes, for the planes were being controlled by Global Hawk technology."

Another new piece of information raises serious questions concerning the official story of Muslim hijackers taking over Flight 77, which reportedly struck the Pentagon. According to Pilots for 9/11 Truth, a growing organization of several hundred aviation professionals from around the world who analyze data provided by the National Transportation Safety Board (NTSB) concerning the 9/11 attacks. These professionals state such data does not support the government story. Rob Balsamo, a commercial airline pilot and co-founder of the aviation organization, said, "When I started my research, I said to myself, I am going to do everything in my power to figure out and back up the official story, the government's story—the government fairy tale, I now call it—so I can have faith and believe in my government. We have gotten to the point where I haven't been able to find anything to confirm the government's story."

One of the most eyebrow-raising facts recently found by this group came from data decoded in late 2009 showing that the reported hijacking aboard American Airlines Flight 77 was impossible to have occurred as reported. A data parameter labeled "FLT DECK DOOR", confirmed by cross checks with previously decoded data obtained by Pilots For 9/11 Truth from the NTSB through a Freedom Of Information Act, indicated that the cockpit door was never opened during flight.

"On the morning of September 11, 2001, American Airlines Flight 77 departed Dulles International Airport bound for Los Angeles at 8:20 a.m. Eastern Time. According to reports and data, a hijacking took place between 08:50:54 and 08:54:11 in which the hijackers allegedly crashed the aircraft into the Pentagon at 09:37:45. Reported by CNN, according to Ted Olson, [his] wife Barbara Olson had called him from the reported flight stating, '...all passengers and flight personnel, including the pilots, were herded to the back of the plane by armed hijackers...'"

The group's website posed the question, "However, according to flight data provided by the NTSB, the Flight Deck Door was never opened in flight. How were the hijackers able to gain access to the cockpit, remove the pilots, and navigate the aircraft to the Pentagon if the Flight Deck Door remained closed?"

Also concerning Flight 77, the *Washington Post* noted, "Aviation sources said that the plane was flown with extraordinary skill, making it highly likely that a trained pilot was at the helm, possibly one of the hijackers. Someone even knew how to turn off the transponder, a move that is considerably less than obvious." This same story noted, "But just as the plane seemed to be on a suicide mission into the White House, the unidentified pilot executed a pivot so tight that it reminded observers of a fighter jet maneuver. The plane circled 270 degrees from the right to approach the Pentagon from the west, whereupon Flight 77 fell below radar level, vanishing from the controller's screens, the sources said."

As previously noted and as detailed in the Appendix, it is quite possible that the plane executing this amazing maneuver was not Flight 77, but actually a fighter jet ordered to buzz the Pentagon moments after the building was rocked by an explosion.

However, at least one Internet source said this was proof that the plane had been electronically captured because software with built-in safety programs would not have allowed such a maneuver. But the software could have been overridden if the craft was taken over electronically as the outside capture would have negated the airliner's safety software.

A news story has already been cited about the suspected pilot of Flight 77, Hani Hanjour, who reportedly had flown so poorly in a flight test just weeks before 9/11 that he was rejected for a small plane rental at a suburban airport. Another news article also pointed out that Hanjour had trained for a few months in Scottsdale, Arizona, but did not finish the course "because instructors felt he was not capable."

Mohamed Atta and Marwan-al-Shehhi, two other hijackers suspected of flying planes, also were reported to be mediocre-to-poor pilots. One flight instructor said neither man was able to pass a Stage 1 rating test. In addition, suspected hijackers Nawaf al-Hazmi and Khalid al-Midhar both were sent packing from Sorbi's Flying Club in San Diego. "Their English was horrible and their mechanical skills were even worse,"

WERE THE HIJACKED PLANES REMOTELY CONTROLLED?

commented one flight instructor. "It was like they had hardly even ever driven a car."

Could a capture by Global Hawk and NFERS technology explain why none of the recordings from either air traffic controllers or the cockpit recorders have been made available to the public? Some reports claimed the tapes were blank. It could also explain how the transponders in all four captured aircraft were switched off nearly simultaneously, a most unlikely event if the planes were truly taken by different persons at different times.

According to some, an electronic capture of the flight control systems would have prevented any normal recordings. Others argue that the recordings were sequestered to prevent the public from hearing how the crews were unable to control their planes.

Investigator Vialls offered this explanation of why the cockpit voice recorder did not send a warning of the hijacking via their transponders. "Technically, a transponder is a combined radio transmitter and receiver which operates automatically, in this case relaying data between the four aircraft and air traffic control on the ground. The signals sent provide a unique 'identity' for each aircraft, essential in crowded airspace to avoid mid-air collisions, and equally essential for Home Run controllers trying to lock onto the correct aircraft.

"Once it has located the correct aircraft, Home Run 'piggy backs' a data transmission onto the transponder channel and takes direct control from the ground. This explains why none of the aircraft sent a special 'I have been hijacked' transponder code. This was the first hard proof that the target aircraft had been hijacked electronically from the ground."

Journalist Joe Vialls said one big reason why electronic capture of jetliners cannot be admitted is the billions of dollars required to replace the flight control systems, an expense the already hard-pressed airlines cannot afford. "The most innovative anti-hijacking tool in the American arsenal has now become the biggest known threat to American national security," he lamented.

One bit of evidence which added strength to the electronic capture theory of the 9/11 aircraft concerned the very real Boeing E-4 Advanced Airborne Command Post, built for the US Air Force on a Boeing 747-200 frame. The four flying command centers—at least one is on alert at all times—were created for survivability in the event of a nuclear attack The first were produced in 1973 but the first upgraded version, the Boeing E-4B, did not become operational until 1979. According to promotional material, the Boeing E-4B is designed to survive a nuclear attack or an electromagnetic pulse with its systems intact. The craft is capable of operating with a crew of 48 to 112 people, the largest crew of any aircraft in US Air Force history. In a test flight for endurance, the aircraft remained airborne and fully operational for more than 35 hours.

"The $250-million-dollar aircraft has all of the advanced electronics needed for worldwide communication," explained Mark H. Gaffney, an author and environmentalist who was the principal organizer of the first Earth Day at Colorado State University in April 1970. "If Air Force One can be accurately described as a flying White House, then the E-4B is a substitute Pentagon. The plane's electronics cover the full radio spectrum, from extremely low frequency (ELF) to [ultra]high frequency (UHF), [which] enables the E-4B to communicate with all US military commands, worldwide, including tactical and strategic forces, naval ships, planes, nuclear-armed missiles, even submarines. In short, the E-4B is a fully equipped communications platform and can serve as an airborne command center for all US military forces in a national crisis. The plane carries its own electrical generating plant to power its electronic hardware, which is also shielded against the damaging electromagnetic pulse (EMP) effects generated by nuclear explosions. Even the plane's white color is a design feature not simply cosmetic. Its purpose is to help the E-4B survive in a nuclear battlefield by reflecting heat away from the plane."

What has the Boeing E-4B got to do with 9/11?

The morning of the 9/11 attacks, a large white four-engined aircraft, closely resembling an E-4B, was seen and photographed over both Manhattan and Washington. In his 2003 book *Black Ice*, author Dan Verton, a former Marine intelligence officer and senior writer for *Computerworld*, identified this aircraft as an E-4B taking part in the 2001 operational exercise "Global Guardian." Verton wrote that the E-4B took off from "an airfield outside of the nation's capital" carrying both civilian and military officials who were participating in the wargame exercise. He added the military exercise involved "the use and testing of the aircraft's various advanced technology and communications equipment."

WERE THE HIJACKED PLANES REMOTELY CONTROLLED?

According to Joe Dejka writing in the *Omaha World-Herald* in 2002, military briefers told him the "Global Guardian" exercise was "in full swing" at the time of the 9/11 attacks. He also wrote, after noting that three E-4Bs were based at Offutt AFB, that aboard one of the three planes was Brent Scowcroft, then chairman of the Federal Advisory Committee [the Foreign Intelligence Advisory Board (FIAB)], along with other committee members there to observe Global Guardian as well as attend the ninth annual Buffett Classic golf tournament. He said military authorities "canceled the exercise after the attacks on the World Trade Center towers and the Pentagon, but all three of the E-4Bs remained in the air."

Shortly after his 1:50 p.m. arrival at Offut AFB, President Bush convened a secured video-link national security meeting during which then-CIA Director George Tenet stated he was virtually certain that Osama bin Laden and his network were behind the attacks as only al Qaeda had the capability of conducting such a well-coordinated operation. Tenet also said that intelligence monitoring had overheard a number of known bin Laden operatives congratulating each other after the strikes.

Reportedly, the Global Guardian exercise was canceled at the time the second hijacked plane struck the South Tower of the WTC. But by Verton's account, it was only at the time of the Pentagon attack that the E-4B launched near Washington was ordered to stop the exercise. Why then this half hour discrepancy in times and was the white plane over the Pentagon the same E-4B?

Author Gaffney is convinced it was. Citing news reports from CNN's senior White House correspondent John King and correspondent Kate Snow mentioning the white plane, Gaffney also noted that ABC anchor Peter Jennings mentioned during the news coverage, "...the White House is certainly, certainly been very heavily defended. And this plane circling the White House adds to the trauma that people are feeling today, but we have no idea precisely what that means." NBC's Katie Couric reported, "And in the most surreal of this morning's scenes here at the White house, a white plane, a very big jet, was flying an unusual pattern near the White House, over Lafayette Park, very slowly. It made one circle, and then we have not seen it since. There was a lot of concern about what that plane might be. But, again, it's only speculation, but most people say that since flights have been cleared from US airspace, and it was a totally white plane, looked unusual to all of us, that it was a government plane of some kind."

Linda Brookhart, then vice president of the Taxpayer Federation of Illinois, was in Washington that morning for a conference in the Executive Office Building located next to the White House. She snapped a clear photograph of the large white plane with her Pentax camera.

After matching US news footage, plus film from the Discovery Channel's program "The Flight That Fought Back," a film clip from the Spanish Telemundo network and Brookhart's photo, Gaffney stated, "[I]n the video the plane makes a banking turn. The angle is fortunate, because it brought the plane's unique features and markings into plain view. There can be no doubt as to the plane's identity. The aircraft belonged to the US Air Force. Moreover, this was no ordinary plane. It was an E-4B, the US military's most advanced electronics platform. Even a casual comparison shows that the still-shot from the docudrama matches an official photo of the E-4B from a USAF website. There can be no mistake."

He added, "The clincher, however, is the 'bump' directly behind the bulging 747 cockpit. It is clearly discernible in both photos. No other plane has this piggy-backed appendage. It is unique to the E-4B, and is integral to the plane's military role as an airborne command center. The appendage contains a communication satellite dish and perhaps other advanced electronic hardware. In fact, this is the same plane that Linda Brookhart photographed outside the White House. Although her vantage point was not ideal—Linda was standing in the street looking almost straight up when she snapped the shot—nonetheless, a careful inspection shows that the plane in her photo is an E-4B...[T]he aircraft has four engines and all of the characteristics of a Boeing 747. In addition to the white color, which is also a match, there is another crucial detail that positively identifies the airplane...[T]he tiny blue spot near the rear of the aircraft. Several close-ups of an E-4B clearly show that this blue spot is simply the place where the blue stripes painted on the fuselage come together at the rear of the aircraft. This same blue spot can also be seen in the still-shot from the Telemundo network. No mistake. It's the same plane.

"This is the only place on the 747 fuselage where the E-4B's otherwise conspicuous blue stripes are visible, from beneath. No other airplane has this combination of features. Linda explained to me that at the time of the evacuation she believed the White House was the target of the attack.

WERE THE HIJACKED PLANES REMOTELY CONTROLLED?

She snapped the picture before the towering plume of smoke became visible at the Pentagon, which suggests that the E-4B was already circling at the time of the Pentagon strike. Linda later contacted the FBI about her photograph. After she developed the film an agent came by her office to pick up a copy. But she never heard back. Nor did the 9/11 Commission ask her to testify. In fact, they never even contacted her."

That a solitary large white aircraft, apparently a Boeing E-4B, was circling over prohibited Washington airspace at the time of the Pentagon strike and that a similar craft was seen over New York at the time of the WTC destruction led some researchers to suspect that this flying electronic command craft may have played some role in the events of 9/11, perhaps even remotely controlling the captured airliners. The fact that the Air Force, Secret Service and FAA all have denied any knowledge of this mysterious over flight in the face of the news accounts, videos and photographs, has only increased the suspicions of those searching for 9/11 truth. Gaffney voiced a sentiment echoed by thousands of Americans when he stated, "Without a genuine investigation, we will probably never learn the true role that the E-4B played on September 11."

The idea of the hijacked aircraft may have been remotely controlled was echoed by Donn de Grand Pre, a retired US Army colonel and author of *Barbarians Inside the Gates*. Shortly after the 9/11 attacks, Grand Pre, along with several commercial and military pilots, participated in a marathon discussion of the events. He acknowledged that the US, Russia, China, and Israel all possess Airborne Warning and Control System (AWACS) aircraft that "have the capability to utilize electromagnetic pulsing (EMP) to knock out on-board flight controls and communications of targeted aircraft, and then, fly them by remote control." "The 9/11 activity and horrific destruction of US property and lives was intentionally meant to trigger a psychological and patriotic reaction on the part of the US citizens, which is paving the way for 'combined UN activity' (using the fig leaf of NATO) for striking key targets in both the Middle East/South Asia and the Balkans. The goal continues to be the ultimate destruction of all national sovereignty and establishment of a global government," he added.

Responding to the accounts of eyewitnesses in Washington who said they clearly saw a large commercial airplane flying low over the city moments before the Pentagon was struck, some researchers, based on flight data, believe that an airliner did fly over the city drawing the attention of those on the ground, but did not hit the Pentagon.

According to Pilots for 9/11 Truth, data from Flight 77 showed an altitude of 180 feet. "This altitude has been determined to reflect pressure altitude as set by 29.92 inHg [inches of mercury used to determine barometric pressure] on the altimeter. The actual local pressure for DCA [Ronald Reagan Washington National Airport] at impact time was 30.22 inHg. The error for this discrepancy is 300 feet. Meaning, the actual aircraft altitude was 300 feet higher than indicated at that moment in time. Which means aircraft altitude was 480 feet above sea level (MSL [Mean Sea Level], 75-foot margin for error according to Federal Aviation Regulations)," stated the pilots' site. They added, "The aircraft is too high, even for the official released video of the five frames where you see something cross the Pentagon lawn at level attitude. The five frames of video captured by the parking gate cam are in direct conflict with the aircraft flight data recorder information released by the NTSB [National Transportation Safety Board]." Furthermore, the recently-released data shows Flight 77 on a different flight path than stated in the official narrative, one in which it could not have knocked down the street light poles so well depicted in that day's photos.

This discrepancy adds weight to the theory that a jumbo jet did fly over the Pentagon, as stated by several witnesses, but did not strike the building, an event apparently claimed to have been seen by only a few persons. But this event would have been recorded by approximately 82 security cameras trained on the structure. The videotapes from the cameras were confiscated by the FBI that day and have never been released to the public with the exception of a few frames which show an explosion at the Pentagon but do not show a large jet plane. One theory—keep in mind there has never been truthful in-depth investigation—is that a large airliner indeed was flown over Washington drawing attention to its low pass over the Pentagon. This craft then perhaps banked quickly and flew eastward along the Potomac River and until lost from sight. This over-flight was timed to coincide with bombs inside the Pentagon and/or a missile strike on the west wall.

WHAT ABOUT THE CELL PHONE CALLS?

## WHAT ABOUT THE CELL PHONE CALLS?

We all know that the crazed Muslim hijackers used small boxcutters to overpower both flight crews and passengers on four commercial airliners on the morning of 9/11. But do we? This scenario has caused problems right from the start as some of the flight crews of the hijacked airliners were former military combat pilots, men unlikely to have meekly turned over the control of their craft to hijackers armed only with boxcutters or small pen knives without a fight. For example, Captain Charles "Chic" Burlingame, pilot of Flight 77, was a graduate of the United States Naval Academy who flew F-4 Phantoms from the carrier USS *Saratoga* from 1976 to 1979. His brother Mark said, "I don't know what happened in that cockpit, but I'm sure that they would have had to incapacitate him or kill him because he would have done anything to prevent the kind of tragedy that befell that airplane." LeRoy Homer Jr., the flight officer of Flight 93, was a graduate of the Air Force Academy and a veteran of the Gulf War.

And there is the problem, as we have seen, that flight data showed that at least on Flight 77, the cockpit door was never opened during flight.

But a major problem with the official story concerns the cell phone calls. As the idea that cell phones could not have been successfully used on September 11 gained credence, the official story that passengers had used cell phones changed. It was argued that passengers such as Edward Felt, actually had used the airline $10-a-minute back-of-seat Airfones. This explanation crumbled after it was learned that Felt, along with newscaster Barbara Olson, reportedly called from inside locked lavatories, which carry no Airfones.

Additionally, according to American Airlines, their Boeing 757s carried no such phones. In response to a request verifying that American Flight 77 did not have radio telephones, Chad Kinder with American Airlines customer relations wrote, "That is correct we do not have phones on our Boeing 757. The passengers on Flight 77 used their own personal cellular phones to make out calls during the terrorist attack."

To explain the reported cell phone calls from passengers on the flights, Joe Vialls stated his belief that many of the calls were concocted after the fact. "There are no records of any such calls," he said. "We had the media's invisible 'contact' at an airline who 'said' a hostess called to report a hijacking and we had a priest who 'said' he received a call from a man asking him in turn to call his wife and tell her he loved her."

Lending support to Vialls' allegations was a news release in July 2004, detailing a joint effort between the San Diego-based electronics firm Qualcomm and American Airlines to develop a practical method for allowing airline passengers to make a cell phone call at altitude in midflight. Cell phones long have been banned from use in flight as a precaution against interference with flight and navigation systems.

New technology was announced in 2004 using a satellite system and a "Picocell," which acted as a cellular tower, to allow airline passengers to make an in-flight cell phone call. "Before this new 'Picocell,' it was nigh on impossible to make a call from a passenger aircraft in flight. Connections were impossible at altitudes over 8,000 feet or speeds in excess of 230 mph," noted Alan Cabal of the *New York Press*. All of the jets that suffered hijacking were initially above altitudes in excess of 30,000 feet and all were eventually traveling at speeds far in excess of 415 mph, the structural integrity redline past which pilots tend to lose control. According to an article in the July 16, 2004, edition of *USA Today*, reception during the initial test of the Picocell was "generally good, although some calls were dropped."

Additional arguments against the cell-phone story were the facts that airplane flights were generally too high for successful cell phone communication coupled with the fact that the chances of a cell phone tower being able to capture an airliner call at speeds in excess of 400 mph were almost nonexistent.

The case of Barbara Olson, a broadcaster for Fox News and CNN, only added more mystery to the issue. The wife of a Bush administration official, Solicitor General Theodore "Ted" Olson, she had repeatedly aligned herself with conservative causes and was a frequent critic of the Clinton administration. Olson reportedly called her husband at least twice on the morning of 9/11, according to her husband and the 9/11 Commission. At the time, Ted Olson advised CNN that his wife told him all passengers and flight personnel, including the pilots, were herded to the back of the plane by armed hijackers. The only weapons she mentioned were knives and box cutters.

WHAT ABOUT THE CELL PHONE CALLS?

It was only from the Olson call that the public learned of box cutters. Calls on other flights mentioned knives too but also guns and bombs. No explanation has been offered on if or how hijackers managed to slip guns and bombs on-board the aircraft.

But the main problem with the Olson calls is that they never happened, at least according to the FBI. During the 2006 trial of Zacarias Moussaoui, officials of the bureau presented FBI Prosecution Trial Exhibit Number P200054, a summary of their Flight 77 investigation which included phone calls. This document noted that only one phone call was attempted by Barbara Olson at 9:18:58 a.m. and that it was "unconnected."

In other words, Olson reached nobody. There was never a completed call. Ted Olson's report of his wife's call is critical to the official 9/11 theory. This was the only evidence that American Airlines Flight 77, was in the air after it had dropped from FAA radar screens about 9 a.m. Additionally, as his wife had been a well-known commentator on CNN, her reported death at the hands of Arab Muslims was instrumental in gaining support for the Bush administration's "War on Terrorism." Barbara Olson's words also were the only source for the widely accepted idea that the hijackers overcame resistance with mere box cutters.

Ted Olson's ever-changing story of the phone call(s) seems to indicate deception—that he was lying. And Olson previously had made a statement which could call into question his own words. While arguing a case before the Supreme Court, Olson declared, "It is easy to imagine an infinite number of situations...where government officials might quite legitimately have reasons to give false information out. It's an unfortunate reality that the issuance of incomplete information and even misinformation by government may sometimes be perceived as necessary to protect vital interests."

But there is an intriguing possibility which might explain the communication with his wife. A 1999 *Washington Post* article revealed the development of voice "morphing" technology at the Los Alamos National Laboratory in New Mexico. During a demonstration of this new technology, the former Commander-In-Chief, US Special Operations Command, Gen. Carl W. Steiner, was chagrined to hear his own voice say, "Gentlemen! We have called you together to inform you that we are going to overthrow the United States government." By taking a few minutes of digitally recorded samples of Steiner's voice, scientists had cloned his speech patterns and developed an accurate facsimile of his speech. Daniel T. Kuehl, chairman of the Information Operations department of the National Defense University in Washington, remarked, "Once you can take any kind of information and reduce it into ones and zeros, you can do some pretty interesting things." The Los Alamos team also cloned then-Secretary of State Colin Powell's voice using clips from public speeches. Powell's voice was heard to clearly state, "I am being treated well by my captors."

Persons in the Pentagon, following the 1991 Gulf War, even conceived of a plan to distribute a computer-faked videotape of Saddam Hussein crying or displaying other such manly weaknesses, as a psychological warfare weapon for use in the Middle East. William M. Arkin, commenting in the *Post*, stated, "Whereas early voice morphing required cutting and pasting speech to put letters or words together to make a composite, [the] software developed at Los Alamos can far more accurately replicate the way one actually speaks. Eliminated are the robotic intonations. Video and photo manipulation has already raised profound questions of authenticity for the journalistic world. With audio joining the mix, it is not only journalists but also privacy advocates and the conspiracy minded who will no doubt ponder the worrisome mischief that lurks in the not too distant future."

Could voice-morphing technology have been used on 9/11?

Such technology could explain the odd phone call—one of the few that actually reached a relative as most were relayed by third persons—to Alice Hoglan, the mother of Flight 93 victim Mark Bingham.

On the morning of 9/11, Bigham's aunt, Cathy Hoglan, took a call from Bingham and was told his plane had been taken over by hijackers. He then said, "I love you all very much in case I don't see you again." His mother then took the phone and told CNN soon after 9/11 she answered, "Mark?" and her son responded with, "'Hi, Mom, this is Mark Bingham. I'm in the air...I'm calling you on the Airfone of the airplane....I want to let you know that I love you very much. I'm calling you from the plane. We've been taken over. There are three men who say they have a bomb."

His mother then asked, "Who are they, Mark?" Hoglan said the caller then repeated that he loved her and seemed to become distracted, said something to the effect that "It's true," and then the call was discon-

WHAT ABOUT THE CELL PHONE CALLS?

nected. The question has been raised by researchers as to why Bingham would identify himself by his full name when he was talking to his own mother, who had taken the phone from his aunt, knew who was supposedly on the phone and had already addressed him by his name?

On July 15, 2005, 150 relatives of passengers and crew aboard the four airliners hijacked on September 11, 2001, were invited by the US Department of Justice to hear tapes of calls from the doomed 9/11 planes. They told the media they were moved by the the accounts of heroic efforts of the passengers. However, they were not allowed to divulge any details of what they heard as government officials told them the phone calls might be used as evidence in the trial of Zacarias Moussaoui. They were required to sign non-disclosure agreements prohibiting them from discussing the contents of the tapes or the briefings and they were not allowed to make recordings or take notes. Furthermore, calls from just two people—American Flight 11 attendants Betty Ong and Amy Sweeney—were played during the three-hour briefing. All other calls were summarized and related to the family members by Justice Department prosecutors, who then took questions.

"The one thing that the [Justice Department] made irrefutably clear to us was that to the extent we disclose any information, we are only aiding the terrorists," said Hamilton Peterson, whose father and stepmother were on United Flight 93.

But one person did speak out and that was the mother of Mark Bingham. By 2005, her account has changed slightly. She emotionally recalled the conversation, saying she was told, "'Mom, this is Mark Bingham. I just want to tell you that I love you. I am on a flight from Newark to San Francisco. There are three guys on board who have taken over the plane and they say they have a bomb. You believe me don't you, Mom? I'm calling you from the air phone.' And then we were disconnected...That's not information I got today. That's information I got at 6:44 a.m. Pacific Daylight Time [on September 11, 2001] from the lips of Mark Bingham." But ws it? Without an objective investigation, the truth may never be known.

Even later, Bingham's mother tried to explain the use of his full name, saying, "Once in a while he would say that. He would call up, and he was, he was a young businessman, and used to, used to introduce himself on phone as Mark Bingham, and he was trying to be, uh, strong, and level-headed, and, and strictly business. 'Mom, this is Mark Bingham.'"

But there were other oddities. For example, Flight 93 passenger Todd Beamer's famous and heroic last words, "Are you guys ready? Let's roll," were only heard by GTE Customer Service Center supervisor Lisa Jefferson in Oakbrook, IL, who then called Beamer's wife and repeated the message.

But even when the Moussaoui trial finally got underway in 2006, no one got to actually hear the reported tape recordings of the Flight 93 phone calls. According to the *Los Angeles Times*, Detective Sgt. Ray Guidetti of the New Jersey State Police, who had been assigned to a special FBI anti-terrorism task force in Newark, "methodically led the jury through what law enforcement has pieced together of the last minutes of the flight."

Theologian and author David Ray Griffin questioned the phone calls from Tom Burnett, another Flight 93 passenger. "[E]xcept for uttering [his wife] Deena's name a few times, 'Tom' never mentioned a name. For example, when he, in his final call, asked about the children, he simply called them 'the kids.' That was not terribly surprising, but then, when Deena told him that the kids were asking to talk to him, he said, 'Tell them I'll talk to them later.' This was 20 minutes after he had purposefully realized that the hijackers were on a suicide mission…Given the reported fact that the hijackers had already killed one person, the real Tom Burnett would have known that there was a good chance that he would die in the next few minutes, one way or another. Is it believable that, rather than taking this perhaps last opportunity to speak to his children, he would instruct his wife to tell them that he would 'talk to them later'?"

The only message from Flight 93 passenger Lauren Grandcolas was a recording left on an answering machine. She apparently made the call from an Airfone.

Other than Barbara Olson, the most important of the 9/11 phone calls reportedly came from two flight attendants on American Flight 11—Madeline "Amy" Sweeney and Betty Ong—the ones who provided authorities, and hence the American public, with the information that there were hijackers aboard of "Middle Eastern descent" who had killed one passenger. They also are the ones who gave seat numbers out leading to the identification of three of the proclaimed perpetrators.

WHAT ABOUT THE CELL PHONE CALLS?

Yet, all the public information on these critical calls did not come from actual recordings but from reports from the FBI agents, who also warned all concerned not to discuss the calls with the media. FBI reports on the calls became suspect after they were changed from the use of cell phones to back-of-the seat Airfones following authoritative sources claiming that cell phone calls from high-flying jets—especially Sweeney's call which lasted 12 minutes according to American Flight Service manager Michael Woodward.

But again, questions arose over the use of the Airfones. Initially, it was said that most of the 9/11 calls were made from cell phones. But since it was only in 2004 that cell phone technology had advanced to the point where a call from an airliner at altitude was feasible, the official story changed. During the Moussaoui trial, it was stated that the calls from Flight 93 were made from the Airfones. Why then did Deena Burnett's caller ID show her husband's cell phone number? Why did FBI Agent James Lechner's report on Sweeney's phone call state she used a cell phone when *The 9/11 Commission Report* on page 453 stated she used an Airfone? And why was it only 2004 (the year that cell phone calls from jetliners became possible) that it was announced that a tape recording of Sweeney's call existed? Even Sweeney's husband, Mike Sweeney, was stunned when first informed of the tape by David Novak, an assistant US attorney involved in prosecuting the Moussaoui case, who admitted to Sweeney that the existence of the tape was news to him and offered him a private hearing. "I was shocked that I'm finding out, almost three years later, there was a tape with information given by my wife that was very crucial to the happenings of 9/11. Suddenly it miraculously appears and falls into the hands of FBI? Why and how and for what reason was it suppressed? Why did it surface now? Is there information on that tape that is of concern to other law-enforcement agencies?" asked Sweeney.

Even then, the tape played was not the voice of Amy Sweeney, but of American Airlines flight service manager and friend Michael Woodward. As there was no tape recorder in Woodward's office, he repeated Sweeney's account to a colleague, Nancy Wyatt, the supervisor of pursers at Logan. On yet another phone, Wyatt was simultaneously passing along Sweeney's words to the airline's Fort Worth headquarters. It was the relayed account that was played for the families.

Others did not even get a belated tape. When Peg Ogonowski, the wife of the American Flight 11 pilot, asked American Airlines to allow her listen to that tape, she never received a reply.

Many questions remain unanswered regarding the phone calls from the doomed 9/11 flights, although it was such calls which formed the basis for the entire "Muslim hijackers with boxcutters" theory of the attacks.

## WHAT REALLY HAPPENED TO FLIGHT 93?

One apparently legitimate account of a call from one of the doomed airplanes involved Jeremy Glick, an Internet company salesman. Left unguarded with the rest of the passengers in the rear of Flight 93, Glick called his family using an Airfone, not his cell phone. "These three Iranian guys took over the plane," Glick told his wife, Lyz. "They put on these red headbands. They said they had a bomb. I mean, they looked Iranian....A passenger said they're crashing planes into the World Trade Center, is that true?" Told that the World Trade Center buildings were on fire and that the Pentagon had just been struck, Glick cursed and said, "Okay, I'm going to take a vote. There's three other guys as big as me and we're thinking of attacking the guy with the bomb." Three big guys and Glick, being a national collegiate judo champion and student at the University of Rochester, could not overcome three slender hijackers armed only with small knives?

Bombs? Small men with pocket knives? The questions kept piling up. According to Pilots For 9/11Truth, air traffic control (ATC) transcripts even revealed United Flight 93 was still airborne after it's reported crash time. According to the National Transportation Safety Board (NTSB) Flight Path Study, United 93 allegedly impacted the ground at 10:03 a.m., September 11, 2001. But transcript excerpts of the conversations between Air Traffic Control System Command Center (ATCSCC) East, management officers and other various facilities provided by the Federal Aviation Administration revealed these words:

10:05 a.m. Ok, United Ninety-Three we're now receiving a transponder on and he is at eighty-two hundred feet...now transponder and he's eighty-two hundred...southeast-bound still...eighty-two hundred feet and now getting a transponder on him…correct.

10:10 a.m. Ya, thirty-nine fifty-one north, zero seven eighty four-six west…that's the last known position of United Ninety-Three.

So, seven minutes after Flight 93 reportedly crashed into the Pennsylvania countryside, air traffic controllers were still receiving a transponder signal and had a fix on the plane. Furthermore, seismic records from four seismology stations in the area, originally pegged the impact time at 10:06 a.m. It was only later that the Pentagon and the 9/11 Commission decreed that the correct impact time to have been at 10:03 am.

In addition to official dissembling, it is indeed difficult for many people to believe that four jetliners with crews, some military veterans, trained in detecting and deflecting a hijacking attempt could all be taken at the same time by a handful of men armed only with knives—some reports said plastic knives—and "box cutters" and then flown with great precision from high altitudes into targets while evading the defenses of the American military on its home turf—and to do all this with rudimentary flying skills at best. It is more believable to think that the four craft were captured by electronic technology such as that used on Global Hawk.

After learning of the WTC and Pentagon attacks and the news that a fourth jetliner was in the air and that fighter jets had been scrambled, many people's first thought upon learning of the Flight 93 crash was that it had been shot down.

The government quickly denied this and, instead, built up the legend of the courageous passengers deciding to attack their captors. This, of course, provided a foundation for the story that the jet crashed during a ferocious battle on board. It would appear, however, that this story was constructed to give the American people an inspiring drama of struggle around which to rally in the grim aftermath of the attacks rather than a truthful account of the facts concerning the fate of Flight 93.

For example, the last cell phone call received from the doomed flight came from an unidentified male passenger who called the 911 emergency number about eight minutes before the plane crashed. Operator Glen Cramer told the Associated Press on September 11 that the man said he had locked himself in a toilet. "We're being hijacked! We're being hijacked!" the man screamed into his phone.

"We confirmed that with him several times," said Cramer, "and we

## PART I – THE EVENTS OF SEPTEMBER 11, 2001

asked him to repeat what he had said. He was very distraught. He said he believed the plane was going down. He did hear some sort of an explosion and saw white smoke coming from the wing, but he didn't know where. And then we lost contact with him." The FBI confiscated Cramer's tape and ordered him not to discuss the matter further. No explanation of this cell phone conversation has been offered.

Supporting the original theory of a shoot-down was a statement by top government officials that President Bush had authorized the use of military force early on the morning of September 11.

Speaking on NBC's *Meet the Press* less than a week after the attacks, Vice President Cheney said Bush "made the decision that if the plane [Flight 77, which reportedly struck the Pentagon] would not divert, if they wouldn't pay any attention to instructions to move away from the city, as a last resort, our pilots were authorized to take them out."

Deputy Defense Secretary Paul Wolfowitz acknowledged that the military was closing in on Flight 93. "We responded awfully quickly, I might say, on Tuesday," he said in a PBS interview. "And in fact, we were already tracking in on that plane that crashed in Pennsylvania. I think it was the heroism of the passengers on board that brought it down, but the air force was in a position to do so if we had had to."

General Richard Myers, chairman of the Joint Chiefs of Staff, also confirmed that fighters approached Flight 93, but denied that they fired on the craft.

Adding to this confusion was the small furor created in late 2004 by an off-the-cuff remark from Donald Rumsfeld during a surprise Christmas Eve visit to troops in Iraq. Recalling past terrorist events, Rumsfeld included, "…the people who did the bombing in Spain or the people who attacked the United States in New York, shot down the plane over Pennsylvania and attacked the Pentagon…" The Pentagon later said this was simply a misstatement, not some sort of Freudian slip of the tongue.

More difficult to explain was the well publicized story of Andrews, AFB F-16 pilot Billy Hutchinson. After refueling, Hutchinson learns of the attack on the World Trade Center is vectored by the FAA to the area where Flight 93 was last picked up on radar. Locating the errant airliner, Hutchinson realized he only had 105 rounds of training ammunition, as he had been participating in the wargame exercise of that morning. This

WHAT REALLY HAPPENED TO FLIGHT 93?

ammo was not lethal enough to stop a jumbo jet. Actually contemplating ramming the airliner with his fighter, Hutchinson was relieved when he saw the plane go down.

"This is a thrilling, inspiring tale of fighter jock heroism," wrote 9/11 Commission senior counsel John Farmer. "There is only one problem with it: it never happened. It is flat-out not true."

The 9/11 Commission presented radar records of the day which indicated Hutchison did not take off until more than a half-hour after United 93 had crashed near Shanksville and some 20 minutes after the wreckage had been located. He could not have seen United 93 on his scope, and could not have intercepted it. According to Farmer, when Hutchinson was question by commission staffers regarding the discrepancies between his media accounts and the radar and radio transmission, "...he stormed out of the room. 'You know what happened,' he said. 'Why are you asking me?'"

In a 2008 op-ed article in the *New York Times*, 9/11 Commission staff members John Azzarello and Miles Kara joined Farmer in noting that Major Hutchison's false account was "part of a larger and totally discredited story."

"After 9/11, military and government officials undertook an aggressive public relations effort," they wrote. "In testimony before Congress and the 9/11 Commission, in numerous interviews, and in an official Air Force history, these officials told the country that by the time United 93 turned toward Washington, President Bush had issued the shoot-down authorization, Vice President Dick Cheney had passed it on, fighters were standing by over Washington and, as the military's commander at the Northeastern Air Defense Sector (NEADS) headquarters in Rome, NY, told ABC News of the authorization to shoot down the planes: 'We of course passed it on to the pilots. United Airlines Flight 93 will not be allowed to reach Washington.'

"Yet the commission established that none of this happened. Once we subpoenaed the relevant tapes and other records, the story fell apart. Contrary to the testimony of retired Gen. Larry Arnold, who on 9/11 was the commander of continental defense for the North American Aerospace Defense Command [NORAD], fighters were not scrambled that morning to meet the threat posed by United 93. In fact, the fighters were sent up in response to an unrelated and mistaken report that General Arnold and others had not disclosed to the commission. Flight 93 hadn't even been hijacked when the planes were ordered scrambled, and General Arnold's command found out the plane was hijacked only after it had crashed. The authorization to shoot it down came after it had crashed, and was never passed on to the pilots."

Many ground witnesses reported sighting a small aircraft—some described it as a military jet—circling the area before and after Flight 93 crashed. Many thought this plane in the area supported the idea of a shoot down. Later, the FBI explained that it was a Fairchild Falcon 20 business jet that was asked to descend to 5,000 feet some minutes after the crash to locate and give co-ordinates to the site.

The FBI's explanation is wanting for a number of reasons. First of all, by the time of the crash of Flight 93—at 10:06 a.m. and not 10:03 a.m. (according to this book's independent timeline)—all air traffic nationwide had been grounded for about a half hour. In addition, the plume of smoke from the wreckage, plus numerous calls to 911, would have provided a sufficient location bearing. Furthermore, FBI has failed to provide any information concerning this aircraft or its passengers, none of whom has come forward to give their account.

One craft that was in the area was a single-engine Piper piloted by Bill Wright. Wright said he was within sight of Flight 93, in fact so close he could see its United markings. He said he suddenly received orders to get away from the airliner and land immediately. "That's one of the first things that went through my mind when they told us to get as far away from it as fast as we could, that either they were expecting it to blow up or they were going to shoot it down," Wright told newsmen.

There is also a serious factual question concerning the wreckage. According to the official story, Flight 93 barreled into the ground at close to five hundred miles per hour. Yet, wreckage was strewn for up to eight miles, including paper mail, personal belongings and even magazines and newspapers the plane was carrying. One engine, which weighs in excess of one thousand pounds, was found more than two thousand yards from the crash scene, indicating it came loose prior to ground impact. One piece of fuselage the size of a dining room table was recovered from a marina in Indian Lake, a couple of miles away from the crash site.

On the day of 9/11, TV audiences were shown aerial views of a hole

WHAT REALLY HAPPENED TO FLIGHT 93?

with horizontal scars stretching out from both sides, indicative of an airplane body and wings hitting the ground. This was depicted as the crime scene at Shanksville. However, a 1994 US Geological Survey photo of the area showed the same lengthy scar or gouge in the earth. So, the only new addition on 9/11 was the crater, which, according to local officials only measured about six to eight feet deep and no more than 20 feet in diameter prompting the question of how could the 100 tons of a Boeing 757 fit into such a small space? Then there was an additional question of the bodies.

Rick King of the Shanksville Volunteer Fire Department told newsmen when he arrived at the scene, he found small brush fires, some insulation and debris but no human remains. "I looked around and I'm thinking, 'Where are the people?'" wondered King.

Shanksville coroner Wallace E. Miller was among the first to arrive at the scene. He said it looked "like someone took a scrap truck, dug a 10-foot ditch and dumped all this trash into it." He added, "I stopped being coroner after about 20 minutes, because there were no bodies there." Miller was required by law to establish the cause of death of the victims. "I put down 'murdered' for the 40 passengers and crew, 'suicide' for the four terrorists," Miller told a reporter, adding significantly that he could not prove what actually happened.

Subsequent actions by government authorities did little to dissuade conspiracy theorists. For example, as mentioned previously, the FBI didn't make public the flight data recordings until April 18, 2002, and then only played edited excerpts to the victims' family members, who were ordered not to discuss what they heard. It was played once again in closed chambers for the jury at the Zacarias Moussaoui trial on April 12, 2006. A transcript that included English translations of Arabic statements that were alleged to have been made by the hijackers was made available to the public at that time. However, this translation could not be compared to the recording itself.

Bureau agents also muzzled Cleveland air traffic controllers involved in the last moments of the flight, ordering them not to speak about what they saw on their radar screens.

Amidst near-hysterical cries of national security, the public was once again asked to blindly accept official pronouncements backed by little, no, or even contradictory evidence. With all hard evidence locked away by the government, speculation has run rampant on the true cause of Flight 93's demise. Countering the official story of the crash occurring during a heroic battle with the hijackers are other equally credible theories. One plausible theory holds that, since one air traffic controller tape available on the Internet speaks of a bomb on board and considering the Airfone calls, including the one from Jeremy Glick, one of the hijackers may have been carrying a bomb, which was detonated in the air either by one of the hijackers or by remote control. But the most prevalent theory is that a US aircraft downed the craft with missile and/or cannon fire, a suspicion supported by all the available evidence.

Furthermore, the shoot-down theory takes on great strength when one analyzes the obvious distortions of known facts about Flight 93 in *The 9/11 Commission Report*, which appear to be an attempt to cover-up the truth about the real fate of that flight. We've noted earlier that the report falsely claims that the military was not even notified that Flight 93 had been hijacked until after it had crashed at 10:06 a.m. But even the aforementioned statements attributed to Cheney and Wolfowitz themselves flatly contradict that assertion, with Wolfowitz saying for example that "the air force was in a position" to shoot the plane down if need be. The Commission's assertion also conflicts with statements of Norman Mineta, Richard Clarke and Barbara Honegger as well. Furthermore, numerous reports in the *New York Times*, the *Washington Post*, and other major newspapers made it clear a few days after 9/11 that the final shoot-down order had been issued at least by 9:56 a.m., in time to engage Flight 93 before it was supposedly brought down by the on-board struggle. Author David Ray Griffin convincingly shows that, while offering no supporting evidence for its revisionist position, the 9/11 Commission ignores the well-established fact that the shoot-down order had been issued earlier and simply asserts that this order was not given until 10:25 a.m. It is not hard to see that this falsehood was promulgated in a "desperate attempt," as Griffin puts it, to rule out the possibility that an American president could actually shoot down a civilian plane.

In this connection, a variety of theorists have suggested that the shoot-down was ordered and then covered up when it was realized that—if the plane had been successfully taken over and landed by the passengers—the real truth about the plot might have been more easily learned through interviews with the surviving hijackers or that the flight crew would tell how they had lost control of the craft. Others have even suggested that Flight 93 was headed toward WTC Building 7, with the mission of obliterating the evidence of the plot contained in its OEM center. Its failure to arrive necessitated the "plan B" demolition of Building 7 later in the day.

A more fanciful theory, though not backed by solid science, was offered by researchers citing Harvard academic Elaine Scarry. In a series of articles and books, Scarry postulated that some recent airline crashes were caused by high-tech military "electronic warfare" weaponry akin to Global Hawk remote-control technology and capable of disrupting an aircraft's control system, the FBI did confirm that a C-130 military plane was within twenty-five miles of Flight 93, and since 1995 the air force has installed "electronic suites" in twenty-eight of its C-130 aircraft.

Numerous and credible witness accounts of a mysterious white jet seen in the air just after Flight 93 went down support the idea of another craft in the area. Jim Brant, owner of the Indian Lake marina where a large piece of debris was found, reported the roar of jet engines overhead. He said he then saw a fireball rise into the air. He looked up and noticed a white plane circling the wreckage that "reminded me of a fighter jet."

Witness Tom Spinelli, said, "I saw the white plane. It was flying around all over the place like it was looking for something. I saw it before and after the crash." Spinellii described the craft as having high tail wings and no markings on it. John Feegle, another witness, said, "It didn't look like a commercial plane. It had a real goofy tail on it, like a high tail. It circled around, and it was gone." Dennis Decker and a friend, Rick Chaney, were close to the impact site. They too noticed "a mid-sized jet flying low and fast." They too said it was white with no markings. "It appeared to make a loop or part of a circle, and then it turned fast and headed out," they said. Together, there were at least 12 eyewitnesses to the white jet. Witness Susan McElwain complained that the FBI did not make a record of her comments after telling her there was no such plane.

Based on this eyewitness testimony and descriptions that seem to match that of a Global Hawk craft capable of firing missiles such as used in Afghanistan, the Scarry scenario does not seem so fanciful. This scenario also leads to yet another possibility positing that the plane's passengers were successful in their attempt to regain control of the craft but then found they could not control the plane due to electronic seizure. Under the theory that all the aircraft were captured and flown remotely using Global Hawk technology, the masterminds behind such a scheme could not possibly allow Flight 93 to land safely and give away the game. Since both the shoot-down orders and the fighters were in place, it would be simply a matter of giving the go-ahead and then sweeping it all under the rug of "national security."

If the questionable phone calls, the missing engines and scattered debris and lack of bodies mean that it was not Flight 93 that crashed in Shanksville, what became of that flight? The answer to this question may be found in the strange mix-up that took place at Cleveland Hopkins International Airport. There is intriguing information that a United Airlines plane, initially identified as Flight 93, landed there on the morning of September 11, 2001.

An Associated Press news bulletin was published on the ABC affiliate station WCPO-TV website stating that about 11 a.m. that day, Cleveland Mayor Michael R. White announced that "a Boeing 767 out of Boston made an emergency landing Tuesday at Cleveland Hopkins International Airport due to concerns that it may have a bomb aboard." He said an unconfirmed report was that the plane might have been hijacked or was carrying a bomb and that the craft had been moved to a secure area of the airport and the passengers evacuated. The story also stated United Airlines had identified the craft as its Flight 93 and also was concerned about another plane, Flight 175.

In a brief news conference, White stated, "Let me walk through the most current situation that we are grappling with. At this moment, we have a Boeing 767 in a secure area of Cleveland Hopkins International Airport. The initial reports were that this plane was hijacked and that there was a bomb on board. There was, before this, an additional plane in our airspace. I am told through unconfirmed reports that we could hear screaming in the control tower. This plane has been diverted from Cleveland and at last report was in the Toledo airspace."

However, in the middle of the news conference, he suddenly said the plane had not been hijacked, and later in the day, he said no bomb had been found and White later failed to mention the screaming.

The station also quoted from a United bulletin issued at 11:17 a.m. on

9/11, in which United Airlines CEO James Goodwin said, "The thoughts of everyone at United are with the passengers and crew of these flights. Our prayers are also with everyone on the ground who may have been involved. United is working with all the relevant authorities, including the FBI, to obtain further information on these flights."

Some time later, WCPO's Liz Foreman, who had posted the original AP news report, said the whole thing was just a mix-up on a very confusing day. She said the AP quickly changed the story and that, while she pulled the link from the station's website, she simply failed to remove the story itself. Sources at the airport were saying the FBI evacuated the plane and searched it with bomb-sniffing dogs after the passengers had deplaned but no bomb was found.

Oddly enough, the story of White's news conference was removed from WCPO's website in June 2004, during the time of the 9/11 Commission hearings. Later, the story shifted and it was claimed the entire incident was a case of mistaken identity as the grounded plane actually was Delta Air Lines Flight 1989, a regularly scheduled Boeing 767 nonstop flight from Boston to Los Angeles. On September 11, 2001, Delta Flight 1989 was one of several flights initially thought to be hijacked. Adding to this apprehension was the fact that a Cleveland air traffic controller overheard a male voice state, "Please sit down. Keep remaining seating. We have a bomb on board." Cleveland controllers "realized" a hijacking was taking place but confused Flight 1989 for Flight 93. The Cleveland operators then notified the FAA's Herndon Command Center and asked for jet fighter assistance but were told "personnel well above them in the chain of command were responsible for making that decision and were working on it."

Once it was established that the hijacked plane was actually Flight 93, the FAA's attention continued to be fixed on Delta 1989 as, like American Flight 175 and Flight 11, it too had originated from Boston and was due to fly to Los Angeles. By 9:57 a.m., about the time of the reported passenger counter-attack on Flight 93, officers at the Northeast Air Defense Sector (NEADS) were still tracking Delta 1989, not Flight 93. According to 9/11 Commission counsel John Farmer, "The essential 'flaws by design' that separated the top policy-making officials within virtually every department of government from operational employees, and that left individual agencies largely isolated from one another and alienated from the national command structure, were now playing out in the frenzied and compressed final moments of United 93."

Flight 1989, after finally notifying the FAA that it was not hijacked, agreed to land at Cleveland, which it did about about 10 a.m. But confusion continued to reign at the Cleveland airport. There were conflicting statements about Delta 1989 concerning the moment of landing, the number of the passengers, and even the ultimate location of the grounded plane. The Associated Press, the *Akron Beacon Journal* and the *Cleveland Plain Dealer* all reported that a plane landed at 10:45 a.m., which must have been Flight 1989 as United 93 had crashed at 10:03 a.m., according to the 9/11 Commission which based this time on analysis by commission staffers of ATC transmissions, infrared satellite data, the flight data recorder and the NTSB. Yet, Delta Air Lines recorded that a plane landed at 10:10 a.m. and firemen at Cleveland Hopkins confirmed that a landing took place before 10:30 a.m. *The 9/11 Commission Report* merely gave a time of 9:42 am and stated Delta 1989 "reversed course over Toledo, headed east, and landed safely in Cleveland."

One Delta 1989 passenger related her experience on in a letter posted on the Internet but with her name and other personal details obscured for privacy. She said, "Many of you knew that [my spouse] and I and many [fellow] employees were on an 8 a.m. flight from Boston to LA on Tuesday morning. I am happy to be alive and to be able to tell you of the events of our harrowing journey. Even though it has been only 48 hours since we departed Logan, it feels as though a lifetime has passed.

"[My spouse] and I and six other fellow [company] employees were on the 8 a.m. flight from Boston to Los Angeles on Tuesday, but we were on the Delta Flight [1989], the one out of three 8 a.m. flights departing Logan that did not get hijacked. Instead, we were forced to make an emergency landing in Cleveland because there were reports that a bomb or hijacking was taking place on our plane. The pilot had radioed that there was suspicious activity in the cabin since one of the passengers was speaking urgently on his cell phone and ignored repeated flight attendant requests to stop using his cell phone while in flight. Also, there was an irregularity in the passenger manifest because there were two people [with the same Middle Eastern name] who were listed but only one aboard.

WHAT REALLY HAPPENED TO FLIGHT 93?

"After our emergency landing, our plane was directed to go to an isolated area of the airport, and we waited for over two hours in quarantine before FBI agents and bomb-sniffing dogs came out to the plane. Just after we landed, the pilot gave us permission to make one very brief telephone call before we were banned from any further telephone use. The sixty or so passengers were thus able to gather some alarming details of the unbelievable fates of the other two LA-bound planes and the collapse of the World Trade Center towers, the suicide bombing of the Pentagon as well as reports of other plane crashes in PA and LA (LA proved unfounded) before we were cut off from any further communication. Unfortunately, all this information only added to the alarm and confusion we felt as we waited for over two hours far away from the gates of the airport.

"Finally, a caravan of cars bearing FBI and Treasury agents and bomb-sniffing dogs approached our airplane. About twenty or so armed FBI agents and police officers boarded the plane and said there were concerns about our flight and that they were taking precautions to rule out any further danger. We finally were allowed off the plane, told to take all of our personal items and leave everything at the edge of the tarmac. While our personal effects were examined we were taken to a secure building at the airport where for three hours we were interrogated at length about any unusual or suspicious activities we observed at Logan that morning or during our flight. We were all alarmed and distraught about the dribs and drabs of information we were slowly getting from our telephone calls (none of us was able to see a TV or listen to a radio) and feeling unbelievably lucky to be alive."

Both airport visitors and employees mentioned that some 200 passengers were removed from a grounded airplane and moved to a NASA facility at one end of the airport. But rumors persisted that a second plane, the earlier arrival, had been moved to a separate area of the airport. Jason Bermas, one of the producers of the popular video *Loose Change* said an airport employee told him, "Well, that one Delta flight was grounded here and another was grounded at NASA Glenn [Research Center]." The employee denied the second plane was Flight 93, but could not explain its presence or what happened to it. Bermas recalls. "We told her we had heard the plane at NASA was United 93. "But there was another plane at NASA Glenn that day and no one has ever explained that. I'm hoping a news agency will go ove and follow up on that," added Bermas.

One possible explanation for a second plane at Cleveland might be a flight of NASA scientists dressed as civilians, who deplaned from a military craft during this same time period. Vernon "Bill" Wessel, director of safety and mission assurance at NASA Glenn Research Center, said he and other workers watched the horror taking place at the World Trade Center, then called an emergency meeting of directors. It was decided to evacuate the NASA facility. Wessel said when he learned that Delta Flight 1989 was on the tarmac and that it might have a bomb on-board, he decided to evacuate the 3,500 NASA Glenn employees out a back gate of the airport. "It took about an hour and a half to evacuate everybody," Wessel recalls. He said a scientific team was on hand from Houston's Johnson Space Center, conducting gravity experiments. The plane which was to return them to Houston, a large KC-135 transport, had returned before taking off to the hanger after all planes were grounded. The scientists, "dressed as civilians" according to Wessel, were taken to a nearby hotel on shuttle buses.

Of course, a group of scientists stuck in Cleveland did not account for the mayor's news conference nor reports of a bomb and screaming on an aircraft. It should also be noted that the KC-135 could not have seated the 200 passengers reported on Delta Flight 1989 and that, according to FAA data, this plane landed at 10:08 a.m., some time after the 10:45 a.m. landing of Flight 1989 as reported by the news media and the 9/11 Commission. It is also problematic to believe that anyone might mistake a military transport plane for a commercial airliner. Plus the NASA evacuation and the landing of Delta Flight 1989 did not really explain the draconian measures taken at Cleveland Hopkins—the facility was sealed with not even bus drivers or taxis allowed to enter of leave and departing passengers had to leave their cars parked and walk out.

Delta Flight 1989, with a reported 69 passengers landed at 10:10 a.m., according to news reports, and was quarantined near the I-X Center, a convention facility created in 1985 from a former air defense hangar located on 188 acres adjacent to the Cleveland airport. Other media reports as well as airport visitors reported a plane landing about 10:45 a.m. with some 200 passengers evacuated after 11 a.m. near the NASA Glenn Research Center.

But yet even another plane was added to this confused mix. Lt. Col.

Alan Scott, a retired officer who analyzed the air responses for the Air Force, told the 9/11 Commission, "[At] 9:27 [a.m.] Boston FAA reports a fifth aircraft missing, Delta Flight 89—and many people have never heard of Delta Flight 89. We call that the first 'red herring' of the day, because there were a number of reported possible hijackings that unfolded over the hours immediately following the actual attacks. Delta 89 was not hijacked, enters the system, increases the fog and friction if you will, as we begin to look for that....He is kind of a red herring for us....9:47 is when Delta 89 clears the system by landing in Cleveland. So he is not a hijack."

What does all this mean? Keep in mind, that it is a simple matter to repaint aircraft and copy or substitute tail identification numbers. In fact, two of the 9/11 airliners—the aircraft reported as United Flights 175 and 93—remained on the "active" flight list until September 28, 2005. This designation was only changed a month after inquisitive researchers made repeated calls to the FAA inquiring about this anomaly. "[W]hy it took United more than four years to 'de-register' the airplanes and fill out the official FAA paperwork remains a mystery and never has been fully explained by the FAA, United or the government," noted journalist Greg Szymanski. "In fact, in stark contrast, a check of FAA records shows the two other American Airlines flights, Flight 11 and 77, both were 'deregistered' and classified as 'destroyed' only months after 9/11 on January 14, 2002." According to FAA records, United Airlines Flight 93, identified as N591UA, and United Airlines Flight 175, identified as as N612UA, were both officially taken out of service in 2005 with the reason given as "canceled," unlike the American Airlines craft which were listed as "destroyed."

There were even further questions regarding American Airlines Flights 11 and 77, neither of which apparently existed on 9/11, according to Bureau of Traffic Safety (BTS) records. Szymanski reported that according to BTS statistics, both American Flights 11 and 77 officially never took off. "The meticulous data kept on every airliner taking off at every airport in the country also showed no elapsed run-way time, wheels-off time and taxi-out time, not to mention several other categories left blank on 9/11 concerning the two flights. Although Flights 11 and 77 have the above data meticulously logged on September 10, it was suspiciously absent on 9/11, even when every other plane that took of that day had been recorded and logged by the BTS."

Such confusion within both the US military and the American airline industry, which has an exemplary safety record, has lead many researchers to suspect that an insidious plot was devised and carried out within the wargame exercises being conducted on 9/11.

A commentator on Alex Jones' website *PrisonPlanet.com* wrote, "There is an elegant possibility to clean up this mess: Delta 1989 had a dark doppelganger, not only when it landed at Cleveland Airport, but when it was flying, too. [Delta Flight 89?] This doppelganger started probably in Boston, too. It was part of the wargames which were taking place on this day...The transponder of the doppelganger was off from start...Its radar blip was hidden behind the blip of Delta 1989 from now on. The screams at 9:28 were not coming from Delta 1989, but from the doppelganger flight. That's why the Cleveland controller was so confused: he determined the origin of the screams by radio direction finding, a standard technique, and they were coming from Delta 1989's position.

"The controller was not involved in the wargames, so he didn't know that there was a plane hiding behind Delta 1989. On board of the doppelganger flight, a simulated hijacking took place. Boston Center—or a department of Boston Center—was apparently in charge of the wargame, this explains why Boston Center was still involved at 9:27...Note that Boston Center reported directly to the military. At 9:41, the doppelganger left its cover, so its radar blip was visible. This was the moment when it was reported hijacked, falsely labeled as Delta 1989. The doppelganger was reported in the broadcast news as the 'fifth' plane. So what happened to the passengers of Delta 1989's doppelganger? [Delta Flight 89?]"

War games. Doppleganger aircraft. Changed tail numbers. It all sounds like a Hollywood movie script until one considers the "Northwoods" documents of 1962. This story came to light when, incredibly, 40-year-old government documents thought to have been destroyed long ago were made public in the early 1990s. They show that the US military in the early 1960s proposed staging terrorist attacks in the United States and blaming them on Fidel Castro. Between the failure of the CIA-backed Bay of Pigs Invasion of Cuba in April 1961, and the Cuban Missile Crisis of 1962, there was a time when the Pentagon was given authority over the ongoing, and mostly secret, war against Fidel Castro's Cuba. The entire project was known as "Operation Mongoose" and was headed by Gen.

Edward Lansdale, then deputy director of the Pentagon's Office of Special Operations. Mongoose was a gathering point for CIA agents, virulent anti-Castro Cubans, gung-ho military operatives and even organized crime figures, all of whom detested President Kennedy and thought him "soft" on communism and a threat to their own preserves.

From this volatile fusion of violent elements came "Operation Northwoods," which was to end up with then-Defense Secretary Robert McNamara. In recent years, McNamara said, "I never heard of it." However, the then chairman of the Joint Chiefs had heard of it, for it was Chairman Gen. Lyman Lemnitzer who recommended that the Joint Chiefs approve and administer this plan to turn world opinion against Castro. The Joint Chiefs of Staff were going along with this pernicious program but President Kennedy rejected Operation Northwoods. Senior military officers ordered the documents destroyed. But someone slipped up and ironically the papers were discovered in the early 1990s by the Assassination Records Review Board, created to look into Kennedy's assassination in the wake of the Oliver Stone film *JFK*.

The Northwoods plans called for hijacking American airliners and ships, setting off bombs in American cities and even assassinations—all to be done in such a manner as to lay the blame on Castro's Cuba. One proposed operation detailed in the Northwoods documents may have provided a prototype of the tactics used on September 11, 2001. On page 10 of the Northwoods plan it states: "An aircraft at Eglin, AFB would be painted and numbered as an exact duplicate for a civil registered aircraft...At a designated time the duplicate would be substituted for the actual civil aircraft and would be boarded with the selected passengers, all boarded under carefully prepared aliases. The actual registered aircraft would be converted to a drone [remotely-controlled aircraft]...[From a] rendezvous point the passenger-carrying aircraft will descend to minimum altitude and go directly into an auxiliary field at Eglin, AFB where arrangements will have been made to evacuate the passengers and return the aircraft to its original status. The drone aircraft meanwhile will continue to fly the filed flight plan. When over Cuba the drone will be[gin] transmitting on the international distress frequency a 'May Day' message stating he is under attack by Cuban MIG aircraft. The transmission will be interrupted by destruction of the aircraft which will be triggered by radio signal." Could some slight variation of this Northwoods plan have been put into effect on September 11, 2001?

Phil Jaylan, administrator for *LetsRollForums.com*, voiced the suspicions of many conspiracy-minded researchers by outlining this hypothetical scenario: "The planes which picked up the passengers [in Boston, Washington and Newark] were drones previously fitted for the war games of 9/11; They were in all actuality the respective airplanes the people should have been boarding; Only difference is this; They are boarding planes with all the equipment pre-installed to fly remotely, turn off the oxygen and radio communication directly after take-off, and then be flown remotely to the spot in the Atlantic where the planes would be ditched, most likely...the Milwaukee Deep in the Puerto Rico Trench. So, in this scenario, Flights 11 and 175 are combined into one flight to make things easier for the planners. [A] Saab military drone which takes off just prior to Flight 11, and is the plane which transponds after take-off that it is Flight 11. Flights 11 and 175 are now combined into one flight, on one plane, yet unknown to them, they are on a military drone, recently retrieved from the sand desert junkyard, and refurbished for this last mission. This also explains why on the one-year anniversary of 9/11, some passengers' family members from Flight 11, showed up at the wrong terminal for the memorial. Is [this] what happened when the single plane with the passengers from Flight 11 were done boarding, the plane pulled up to another tarmac and now became Flight 175?"

According to this scenario, this combined flight rendezvoused with a phony aircraft 18 minutes into its flight, which then became the official Flight 175. Oxygen and communication were cut-off on the combined flight which was then flown out to sea and ditched or shot down as part of the Vigilant Guardian wargame exercise by a distant controller who never knew his "drone" was full of unconscious passengers.

Jaylan's theorized the switch was made on the ground prior to the flights because it would have been the easiest way to dispose of both planes and passengers. He added, "The same scenario was done with Flight 77 and Flight 93, except they were individual flights. Thus, three planes were shot down over the Atlantic that day as part of Operation V[igilant]G[uardian]. Occam's Razor. This accounts for all of the aircraft. It accounts for why the plane which hit the first WTC [tower] was so

WHAT REALLY HAPPENED TO FLIGHT 93?

small, because it was [a] Saab military drone. It accounts for the missing aircraft, Flight 175, which we know wasn't the plane at the 2nd WTC. It accounts also for the now missing plane in Pennsylvania, as well as the missing Boeing at the Pentagon. It also helps avoid any messy [mid-air] plane swapping [by radar] and the nightmare it might have been to do the logistics neccessary to get all the people onto one plane...

"I also now believe...that the entire days events, from start to finish was a four-part, multi-stage computer program completely out of the hands of men...[T]he actual take-off of the aircraft started each additional stage of the operations pre-programmed plan, with all the variants included. This is the only way in which they could so precisely time the... events...That is also the reason why Dick Cheney, even *after* [emphasis in the original] he was told we were under attack, commanded the [war] games go forward, and needed to be completed no matter what. This is odd behavior..."

Jaylan also noted,"[I]f Flight 93 really did land in Cleveland on 9/11, it was more than likely the Part B hypothesis of this scenario. Simple and short—Flights 93 and 77 are combined at Cleveland, and then the plane with the people, a drone, takes off, oxygen is then turned off, the plane taken over by remote, and shot down over the Yukon in Canada. At my old website...a Canadian girl came in the week after 9/11 and left this message, paraphrased on my old message boards: 'My brother who is a ham radio freak, picked up a transmisson in the afternoon of 9/11 that the Canadian Air Force was shooting down a 'commercial heavy' over the Yukon in Canada.' This would more than likely have been done under the cover of Operation V[igilant] G[uardian]; In this Part B scenario, the Canadian Air Force, which was participating in Operation VG, was scripted to have shot down a drone for the war games. In this case, the drone they shot down, more than likely over a large lake, was the combined passengers from [Flights] 77 and 93."

While many people would consider Jaylan's theory—as well as any of all those who express doubt about the official government 9/11 theory— outlandish and not worthy of consideration, it might be pointed out that the official version, as expressed by the 9/11 Commission, has been demonstrated to be incomplete at best and untrue at worst. It is even doubted by some of its own staff members. As journalist Greg Szymanski remarked, "[The] state sponsored US media ignores the story, leaving 'Internet hounds' to smell out the truth behind what really happened to the passengers on the doomed flights."

Considering the Northwoods plan to hijack commercial airliners and substitute unmanned drones slated for destruction; the war game exercises which were not known—even denied—for almost a year after 9/11; and the grim fact, as will be documented later in this work, that national leaders will allow deadly attacks on Americans if it is thought to further their purposes, it is not such a stretch of the imagination to think that an attack on the magnitude of 9/11 could be a false-flag operation—an inside job.

## REMOTE VIEWERS LOOK AT 9/11

For several decades, the US intelligence community and the Army secretly developed and utilized a technology they called "remote viewing" as a means of obtaining critical national security data on the activities of our enemies normally outside the normal means of detection.

Thus it is not far-fetched to use this tool in an effort to look at 9/11 from an entirely different point of view. Several experienced remote viewers were commissioned by this author to make a remote viewing study of the people and circumstances surrounding the 9/11 attacks.

One of the viewers who agreed to participate in this study was Lyn Buchanan, formerly the trainer of the US Army's then-Top Secret "Grill Flame" and "Stargate" remote-viewing programs. This technique for viewing persons, places and things by means other than the normal five senses has been known in the past as clairvoyance. The term "remote viewing" was substituted to avoid the ongoing arguments over psychic phenomena and is used to describe the controlled use of psychic abilities.

Remote viewing was extensively studied in the 1960s, '70s and '80s first by the CIA, then by the US Army, Defense Intelligence Agency and National Security Agency. Many believe this approach to be a valid means for getting at the truth as this once-secret program was funded through six administrations, both Republican and Democrat, for more than a quarter of a century.

The use of this faculty of the mind has been pervasive in all of the world's religions, from the Bible to the Koran to Oriental mysticism. Most spiritual traditions contain a wealth of stories involving prophecy, visions, shamanic "journeying," and spiritual instruction. And all seem to involve visual input. The biblical book of Isaiah, for example, opens with the statement, "These are the messages that came to Isaiah, son of Amoz, in the visions he saw during the reigns of King Uzziah, King Jotham, King Ahaz and King Hezekiah—all kings of Judah."

Biblical prophecy was not limited to men. In the Old Testament book of Judges, we find that a "prophetess" named Deborah provided the Israelite leader Barak with information about the military disposition of Sisera, the commander of the forces of Jabin, the King of Canaan. Sisera's forces were routed and thus Deborah, using psychic intelligence, played a pivotal role in the conquest of the Promised Land. She might rightly be called the world's first military remote viewer.

Even in the New Testament, prophesy and visions played an important role as the messianic plan unfolded. St. Paul offered some advice on remote viewing that modern people might well take to heart. "Do not scoff at those who prophesy, but test everything that is said to be sure if it is true, and if it is, then accept it," he wrote to church members in Thessalonica.

Throughout the ages, men and women have practiced "spiritualism," to include versions of remote viewing but it was never accepted by the mainstream public because modern science, while able to demonstrate that some phenomenon was occurring in laboratory experiments, could never quite get a handle on the how and why of it.

But after reports leaked out from behind the Iron Curtain in the early 1970s that Soviet Russia and its Eastern European allies were experimenting with psychics, the American intelligence establishment felt the need to join in the pursuit of psychic spies. Beginning in 1972, the CIA began funding scientific studies into psychic phenomena at California's Stanford Research Institute (SRI). According to former investigator Jack Anderson and author Ron McRae, it was "the most severely monitored scientific experiment in history." And it got results. By 1976, the remote viewing program had left the CIA and by 1977 was under the US Army's newly-formed Intelligence and Security Command (INSCOM). Soon a full-time operational unit, code named "Grill Flame," was underway and producing remarkable results from about a dozen remote viewers. In 1985, the unit was placed within the secretive Defense Intelligence Agency (DIA).

Some people have argued that the use of psychic spies by both sides may have ended the Cold War, which was based primarily on secrecy. Once this secrecy was penetrated by remote viewers, the impasse between the USA and Russia fell apart. In 1995, the story of remote viewing broke in the *Washington Post* and the *New York Times* after the CIA issued a press release acknowledging the psychic program. The story never really reached the American heartland and many people are still unaware of this most significant issue.

According to several sources, remote viewing continues to be used within both the military and intelligence communities. Most recently, according to some sources, military-trained remote viewers have been used in the search for Osama bin Laden. Viewers were also used to help identify and locate the sniper around Washington in October 2002, according to several news reports. In 2003, several experienced remote viewers were commissioned by this author to make a remote-viewing study of the people and circumstances surrounding the 9/11 attacks.

In this specially commissioned study, eleven remote viewers with extensive track records took a psychic look at the events of September 11, 2001. Several of the viewers involved asked not to be identified. Among those who agreed to be identified were Lyn Buchanan, formerly the trainer of the US Army's then-Top Secret "Grill Flame" and "Stargate" remote viewing programs, who now heads up Problems Solutions Innovations of Alamogordo, NM, and Gail Ferguson, author of *Cracking the Intuition Code*.

These eleven viewers gave yes-or-no answers to questions. The answers below reflect the majority of the viewers' responses:

1. Did President George Bush have foreknowledge of the 9/11 attacks? *No.*
2. Did George Bush, Sr. have foreknowledge of the 9/11 attacks? *Yes.*
3. Did Dick Cheney have foreknowledge of the 9/11 attacks? *Yes.*
4. Did the Israeli Mossad have foreknowledge of the 9/11 attacks? *Possibly.*
5. Did Osama bin Laden have foreknowledge of the 9/11

attacks? *Yes.*
6. Were the planes that crashed into the WTC controlled from the planes' cockpits? *No.*
7. Was the collapse of the WTC towers caused only by the planes striking the buildings? *Equally divided.*
8. Was any US intelligence agency involved in the 9/11 attacks? *Yes.*
9. Were any members of The Trilateral Commission, Council on Foreign Relations or Bilderberger group responsible of the 9/11 attacks? *Yes.*
10. Was United Airlines Flight 93 shot down? *Yes.*

Since the answers to most of these questions would seem provocative to many people, it should be pointed out that remote viewing, despite extensive and careful laboratory experiments, is more of an art than a science. It also should be noted that none of the remote viewers knew the questions before their session.

They were simply given a 10-digit set of numbers that represented each question. It was discovered in the research of remote viewing that these numbers somehow directed the viewer's mental attention to the object of the query on a subconscious level. The viewer picked up the question of the tasker.

For example, the question concerning President Bush was "48965-74123." Those numerals were the extent of information given to the viewers, yet there was a certain consistency in their answers with the exception of one question that was nearly a tie. Some of the answers were obvious. For example, the question of whether or not the WTC planes were controlled from the cockpits of the craft resulted in seven "no's," only three "yes's" and one "no answer." "No answer" responses resulted from either no data returned or no answer given due to an inconclusive session.

Other answers were much closer. The question concerning the involvement of the Israeli Mossad prompted an almost even split, with six "yes's" compared to five "no's." The question regarding President Bush's foreknowledge yielded seven "no's" to four "yes's" while the same question regarding his father resulted in the opposite, seven "yes's" to three "no's" with one "no answer."

Another near tie was the question that asked if the planes alone were responsible for the collapse of the WTC towers. This query brought five "yes" responses to four "no's" with two "no answer's." The question regarding the involvement of secret society members also was a near tie, with five answering "yes," four "no" and two "no answer."

While this one small remote viewing study cannot be taken by anyone as ground truth, based on the remarkable track record of the US government's operational use of this mental technology, it certainly should be the cause for sober reflection and further investigation.

Interestingly enough, in May 2008, one of the best of the Army's remote viewers offered to do an remote-viewing session for this author. The number he was given represented the question "Who was at the controls of the planes that struck the World Trade Center towers?" The surprising answer came back, "No one." This was further clarified when the viewer indicated that the planes that hit the towers were under the control of yet another airplane, which naturally prompted thoughts the Boeing E-4B Advanced Airborne Command Post.

While one small remote-viewing study cannot be taken by anyone as ground truth, based on the remarkable track record of the US government's operational use of this mental technology, it certainly should be the cause for sober reflection and further investigation. If even half of the information outlined in this remote-viewing section as well as the preceding sections is proven in error, the balance remains a damning indictment of official malfeasance. It's much worse than what *Newsweek* termed "a whole summer of missed clues."

The totality of the information available today can only lead to two inescapable conclusions: either the highest leadership of the United States is composed of imbeciles and incompetent blunderers or they are criminally negligent accessories to the crimes, if not worse.

Researchers who believe the latter thesis will want to test their evidence and arguments against the chief bulwark of the official "incompetence" theory, *The 9/11 Commission Report*, the product of the only major investigation of the 9/11 attacks, as well as the long-awaited commission that produced it.

# THE OFFICIAL 9/11 INQUIRY:

THE OFFICIAL 9/11 INQUIRY: ANOTHER WARREN COMMISSION?

## ANOTHER WARREN COMMISSION?

By 2011, the only people who did not know at least some of the truth about 9/11 were those who chose not to look at the evidence and, instead, chose to place full faith and confidence in the government's investigation.

And that investigation was meagerly funded and filled, not with academics, scientists or engineers, but instead veterans of the FBI, CIA and other national security agencies under the direction of Philip Zelikow, a longstanding operative for the Bush administration.

According to Eric Margolis, a longtime print journalist who has appeared frequently on CNN, the 9/11 investigation was a "whitewash, as are all such government commissions. They are designed to obscure, not reveal, the truth."

As previously mentioned, the commission's chief attorney, John Farmer, has stated that their official version of the events of 9/11 are "almost entirely, and inexplicably, untrue."

Even 9/11 Commission Co-Chairman Lee Hamiliton has admitted many flaws in the commission's work. "I don't believe for a minute we got everything right. We wrote a first draft of history," said Hamilton in an interview. "People will be investigating 9/11 for the next 100 years in this country and they're going to find some things that we missed."

Hamilton also admitted that he believed the official 9/11 Commission investigation was "set up to fail." "[W]e got started late. We had a very short time frame. Indeed, we had to get it extended. We did not have enough money. They [the Bush White House] were afraid we were going to hang somebody, that we would point the finger [of guilt]. A lot of people had things to hide."

The National Commission on Terrorist Attacks upon the United States, popularly known as the 9/11 Commission, released its final report to the public in mid-summer 2004, nearly three full years after the horrifying attacks of September 11, 2001. The voluminous 567-page report answered virtually none of the vital questions that have been raised by independent researchers and the 9/11 families.

It also quickly became clear that when it came to the two prominent views of history—conspiracy or accidental—the commissioners were solid supporters of both schools. According to them, the attacks of 9/11 resulted from a malignant conspiracy of freedom-hating Muslim fanatics who successfully carried out a complex terrorist plot for less than $1 million. However, they were aided and abetted by a systematic series of miscues, mistakes and malfeasance on the part of a variety of US government officials and agencies that lacked "imagination" due to hardened Cold War mindsets. Yet, to date, not one single government employee has been fired, re-assigned or even disciplined due to the failures of that day. In fact, many of those who should have been called on the carpet for incompetence instead were promoted and their budgets increased.

Immediately, many commentators likened the report to that of the infamous Warren Commission Report issued less than one year after the assassination of President John F. Kennedy. And the similarities are indeed striking. Like the Warren Commission before it, the 9/11 Commission's sins were more of of omission rather than commission. For example, there was no mention of the collapse of WTC Building 7 or of FBI Special Agent Coleen Rowley, the Minneapolis division counsel, who accused higher FBI officials of blocking investigations into al Qaeda prior to 9/11 or of the numerous examples of foreknowledge of the attacks.

And like the Warren Commission's 26 volumes, *The 9/11 Commission Report* has no index, making it difficult for any serious researcher to move through it and connect both personages and events. And like that earlier report, this latest government account has met unqualified acceptance by the corporate-controlled mass media as well as those members of the public who blindly accept the views presented on television and the major print publications. As occurred with the Warren Report, will it also take 40 years for the general public to learn of the many revelations that undo the official 9/11 account?

Both the Warren volumes and *The 9/11 Commission Report* inundates the readers with pages of superfluous and tedious historical and operational data on government agencies and policies. Yet, it fails to adequately address some of the more serious issues raised in this book and elsewhere.

Numerous factual distortions have already been pointed out, but there are just as many large omissions, the most egregious being no mention of WTC Building 7. In other examples, the report fails to mention Operation Northwoods, the early 1960s plan approved by the Joint Chiefs of Staff to encourage public support for another attack upon Castro's Cuba by false-flag attacks on America designed to incriminate Castro. Nor is there any mention of the Project for a New American Century, the neoconservative think tank filled with current Bush Administration officials that long before the events of 9/11 laid out a plan to invade Afghanistan and Iraq based on a "new Pearl Harbor."

Retired Lt. Col. Karen U. Kwiatkowski, a graduate of both the Air Command and Staff College (ACSC) and the US Naval War College who was in the Pentagon when it was struck on 9/11, remarked how swiftly the military moved to prepare for the invasions of Afghanistan and Iraq. "The invasion plan for Afghanistan was moving rapidly," she noted. "At the time I wondered how we could do the planning and the work as quickly as we did. But I found out later that their plans to topple the Taliban had been in place months before 9/11 and that Iraq was discussed openly as a target within days of 9/11."

The Warren Report rested on the shaky premise of Arlen Specter's single bullet theory—the idea that one rifle slug passed through both President Kennedy and Texas Governor John Connally—causing seven separate wounds to both men including hitting at least two bones—yet emerged to be found unscathed in a hospital hallway. Similarly, the 9/11 Commission's verdict that 9/11 was simply the result of miscues, miscommunication and a system badly in need of centralization is based on the equally implausible premise that at least 19 fanatical Arab Muslims—some with expired visas or questionable passports and some on security watch lists—traveled to various countries where plans were hatched, came in and out of the USA and trained at US flight schools directly under the nose of US authorities without arousing any notice or suspicion, but were then easily identified to a man within hours of the attacks.

Likewise, the 9/11 Commission failed to report the historic fact that Osama bin Laden's al Qaeda network grew directly out of the force of Islamic fundamentalists recruited to fight the Soviets in Afghanistan under the auspices of the CIA. It even omits mention of the fact that Osama himself, under the name "Tim Osman," had received aid and training from US military and intelligence assets.

Even if there was no intent to cover up the truth, the commission was not funded at a level sufficient to do its work. Incredibly, more than three times as much money was spent on George W. Bush's 2005 inauguration than was originally allocated to investigate the attacks on September 11, 2001. While a total of $112.6 million was spent to investigate the 2003 space shuttle *Columbia* disaster and $50 million was once spent to look into Las Vegas gambling casinos, the 9/11 tragedy received a mere $13 million to probe the greatest attack on America since 1812. The Presidential Inaugural Committee estimated Bush's 2005 inauguration events cost about $40 million, with the federal government and District of Columbia bearing an additional $20 million as the cost of providing security.

From the outset, President Bush made clear that he wanted no independent investigation into the attacks. Bowing to the entreaties of 9/11 families, the Bush administration initially promised only $3 million to investigate 9/11; it later relented after additional public pressure, plus complaints from the commission itself that this amount was inadequate, and released another $10 million. It should be noted that even the inadequate first official inquiry into 9/11—the Joint Intelligence Congressional inquiry in 2002 which probed activities of the intelligence community in connection with the attacks—also was resisted by the Bush administration.

In 2002, many of the 9/11 families embittered by the omissions and limitations of the congressional inquiry into 9/11, these bereaved Americans found themselves back in Washington lobbying for a truly independent commission, while submitting a lengthy list of unanswered questions.

President Bush staunchly resisted further efforts to investigate the 9/11 attacks until November 2002, when, under intense pressure from victims' families and the public alike, he signed into law a bill creating the National Commission on Terrorist Attacks Upon the United States—usually referred to as simply the 9/11 Commission. The new commission, whose charter was to conduct an independent and nonpartisan investigation, was intended to pick up where the congressional inquiry left off. It held its first hearings in late March 2003.

Curiously, as if historical amnesia had settled over it, the commission's final report never mentioned the delays and the obstructions perpetrated by the Bush administration, including numerous instances of administration stonewalling during the entire life of the commission.

Nor was the American public told of the iron-handed leadership of the commission as applied by Executive Director Philip Zelikow.

Hardly "independent" or "nonpartisan," Zelikow was, for starters, a Republican and a member of President Bush's own Foreign Intelligence Advisory Board. He had previously served as a national security adviser in the Ford and Bush I administrations, and was director of the Aspen Strategy Group, a policy program of the Aspen Institute, considered by many as a key globalist think tank. Zelikow, along with National Security Advisor Condoleezza Rice, both prominent members of the Council on Foreign Relations, co-authored a book entitled *Germany Unified and Europe Transformed*. In yet another example of blatant conflict of interest, Zelikow was also a member of the Bush-Cheney transition team, which helped form the current National Security Council, which oversees national security policy.

Zelikow was widely considered by many as Bush's "gatekeeper" on the 9/11 Commission. Zelikow tightly controlled the scope and reach of the investigation. As executive director, he guided the staff, which did virtually all the work of the commission, and decided which topics were to be investigated and which witnesses would be interviewed. In concluding his comprehensive study of the commission's report, Professor David Ray Griffin declared that, given the direct ties of Zelikow to the White House and his ability to shape the investigation, his presence as the executive director was the equivalent of its work being "conducted by Condoleezza Rice, Dick Cheney, or George Bush."

A White House insider with longstanding connections to foreign policy decisions, Zelikow was the principal author of the administration's 2002 Statement on National Security Strategy, in which the controversial new neo-conservative doctrine of pre-emptive warfare was first articulated and adopted as a foundation of US foreign policy.

This document was to provide crucial doctrinal support for the pre-emptive wars in Afghanistan and Iraq soon to follow. "We can understand, therefore," says Griffin, "why the commission, under Zelikow's leadership, would have ignored all evidence that would point to the truth: that 9/11 was a false-flag operation intended to authorize the doctrines and funds needed for a new level of imperial mobilization."

Zelikow is a member of the Council on Foreign Relations, that secretive body at the heart of American foreign policy. Contrary to his pledge of no contact with the Bush administration, Zelikow held surreptitious telephone conversations with Bush's Deputy Chief of Staff Karl Rove during the time of his 9/11 Commission leadership.

And he was no stranger to the idea of terrorism against America. In 1998, he co-authored an article along with former CIA Director John Deutch and former Assistant Secretary of Defense Ashton B. Carter that was published in the Council on Foreign Relations publication *Foreign Affairs* under the title "Catastrophic Terrorism: Tackling the New Danger." Under a section oddly entitled "Imagining the Transforming Event," they foresaw, "[a] successful attack with weapons of mass destruction [that] could certainly take thousands, or tens of thousands, of lives. If the device that exploded in 1993 under the World Trade Center had been nuclear, or had effectively dispersed a deadly pathogen, the resulting horror and chaos would have exceeded our ability to describe it.

"Such an act of catastrophic terrorism would be a watershed event in American history. It could involve loss of life and property unprecedented in peacetime and undermine America's fundamental sense of security, as did the Soviet atomic bomb test in 1949. Like Pearl Harbor, this event would divide our past and future into a before and after. The United States might respond with draconian measures, scaling back civil liberties, allowing wider surveillance of citizens, detention of suspects, and use of deadly force. More violence could follow, either further terrorist attacks or US counter-attacks."

Such prophetic foresight prompted journalist Christopher Bollyn to comment, "This article is clearly an architectural-level document. It is meant to explain what should be done in the event of the catastrophic terror attack its authors are 'imagining.' For this reason, the authors deserve to be investigated to see what kind of relationship they might have to those who carried out the false-flag terror attacks of 9/11."

In an incident filled with incredible irony, Bush's first choice to head the 9/11 Commission was Henry Kissinger, a prominent Council on Foreign Relations member and perhaps the man most responsible for producing the past thirty years of United States foreign policy. It is this deeply flawed foreign policy, mostly thinly disguised neocolonialism and nation looting, that has resulted in worldwide antipathy for America's role in the world in recent years. Many observers believe that events like 9/11 represent revenge, or "blowback," for such neo-imperial policies.

Though pictured in the corporate mass media as a prominent statesman, there is a darker side to Kissinger, as evidenced by several warrants outstanding in two European countries for war crimes and complicity in murder. In May 2001, for example, during a stay at the Ritz Hotel in Paris, he was visited by the criminal brigade of the French police, and served with a summons. Kissinger made a hasty exit, never to return to France.

Christopher Hitchens, a regular contributor to *Vanity Fair* and author of several noted books, including *The Trial of Henry Kissinger*, presents a wealth of documentation showing that Kissinger was the responsible party behind a number of acts that can be considered war crimes, including atrocities during the war in Indochina—notably in Vietnam and Cambodia—and planned assassinations in Santiago, Chile; Nicosia, Cyprus; and Washington, D.C., and even genocide in East Timor. For example, in 1970, Kissinger ordered the removal of Chilean army commander in chief Rene Schneider. Schneider was a supporter of Chile's constitution who opposed what later became a right-wing coup against Socialist President Salvadore Allende, and was murdered in 1970 by right-wing plotters within the Chilean military. Former US ambassador to Chile Edward Korry confirmed Kissinger's direct role in these events. Strong evidence ties Kissinger to the actual CIA-sponsored coup itself on September 11, 1973, which resulted in the deaths of Allende and thousands of his left-wing supporters, and the imposition of a military dictatorship in that country for almost two decades.

Following a public outcry over Bush's choice to head the 9/11 Commission, Kissinger quickly withdrew, claiming he did not want to make known the client list of Kissinger Associates, which reportedly included the name bin Laden. It was known in Washington that Kissinger's firm was receiving consulting fees from corporations with large investments in Saudi Arabia, and from the oil giant Unocal, whose desire to build a pipeline through Afghanistan is discussed later in this book. Kissinger also has long been a prominent member of secretive societies such as the Council on Foreign Relations and the Bilderbergers.

Bush continued to look to the secret societies for appointments, finally settling on former New Jersey Governor Thomas H. Kean and former

Indiana Representative Lee Hamilton to co-chair the commission. Both Kean and Hamilton are members of the secretive Council on Foreign Relations as were Allen Dulles and John J. McCloy of Warren Commission fame. Conflicts of interests abound with both Kean and Hamilton.

Kean's connections to the oil industry go deep. He was an official of Amerada Hess, one of the giant oil companies involved in planning the oil pipeline through Afghanistan. One Hess oil project involves a partnership with Saudi oil executive Khalid bin Mahfouz, whose name has been linked to President George W. Bush in both Texas oil deals and the BCCI banking scandal. Kean also has had exceptional input into our nation's security reformation through his co-chairmanship of this Homeland Security project.

From the Bush administration's point of view, Hamilton was ideal for the job of vice chair. Former Congressman Hamilton chaired a House committee looking into the October Surprise, a reported plan in which Reagan-Bush campaign officials made a deal with Iranian authorities not to release US hostages held in Tehran so as to insure the election of Ronald Reagan in 1980. But Hamilton could find no wrongdoing despite testimony from the pilot who claimed to have flown both CIA Director William Casey and Vice President-Elect George H. W. Bush to Paris for talks with the Iranians and the fact that the hostages were released within hours of Ronald Reagan being sworn in as president on January 20, 1981. As co-chair of the House Select Committee investigating the Iran-Contra Affair, Hamilton again could find no wrongdoing in the Reagan administration's decision to secretly and illegally sell arms to Iran, as part of a national scandal that included the administration's usurpation of Congress by secretly using profits from such illegal arms sales to covertly fund a civil war in Nicaragua—plus the systematic cover-up by the Reagan administration that followed these events. Hamilton told PBS's *Frontline* in the late 1980s he felt it would not have been "good for the country" to put the public through the impeachment process. Hamilton likewise turned his head from the massive documentation concerning drug smuggling by the CIA to fund the Iran-Contra operations. In the late 1990s, a CIA inspector general's report confirmed direct CIA involvement in the importation of cocaine.

It should be recalled that many of the names involved in the Iran-

Contra Affair, described by journalist Bill Moyers as an attempted *coup d'etat*, are currently members of the Bush administration, including John Poindexter who was convicted of lying to Congress and by extension the American public.

Hamilton is a member of the Homeland Security Advisory Council and also on the board of the National Endowment for Democracy, a congressionally supported non-profit organization notorious for funneling money in support of candidates for office in foreign countries who support the rights of US corporations to invest in those countries.

Despite his government background and co-chairmanship, in later years Hamilton joined with chorus of criticism for the 9/11 Commission. "It was a huge amount of data to sort through," said Hamilton in an interview. "We put a tremendous weight on the facts. But doing something this complex in the amount of time we were given was difficult. Oh, there were loose ends....But I don't believe we have written the final draft. There's bound to be some information that comes out which we didn't have then."

"We were misled by the FAA and NORAD," he said. "When we went to NORAD command center in New York, we found tapes that had not been furnished to the commission. By listening to those tapes, we discovered that their official story didn't add up. So we issued subpoenas and started from scratch." Admitting that there were unexplained gaps in the accounts of both the president and the vice president, Hamilton said, "When you have that, you obviously leave an opening for the conspiracy questions. But sometimes you cannot answer every question that is raised. We made a lot of judgments. I don't know if we made all the judgments correctly."

Without explanation why the destruction of WTC Building 7 was not addressed by his commission, Hamilton merely said, "We consulted with expert architects. You simply cannot answer every question about why Building 7 collapsed."

Other commission members also were former senior government officials and Washington insiders, such as Fred Fielding, former White House counsel to Nixon; Jamie Gorelick, deputy attorney general under Clinton; and John Lehman, Reagan's secretary of the navy.

Gorelick, yet another CFR member on the 9/11 Commission as well as a sitting board member of the oil drilling giant Schlumberger, also co-chaired the Intelligence Community Law Enforcement Policy Board along with CIA Director George Tenet at the time that Philippine authorities were reporting "Project Bojinka," a terrorist plot to hijack commercial airliners and fly them into prominent structures. The Pentagon and the World Trade Center towers were specifically named. Gorelick was one of only two 9/11 commissioners allowed access to Bush administration classified materials.

Without belaboring the point, it becomes clear that the 9/11 Commission was loaded with persons who most probably should have been called as witnesses rather than sitting in judgment. Other commission members were striking in their lack of knowledge or experience in criminal investigations, aerodynamics or engineering, including:

John Lehman, an investment banker, was a secretary of the Navy under President Reagan; former Nebraska Senator and Governor Bob Kerrey, was trained as a pharmacist and had founded a chain of restaurants and health clubs; former Senator Slade Gorton was a lawyer a with military service background; former Rep. Timothy J. Roemer, an original sponsor of the legislation to create the Department of Homeland Security, moved from his service to the 9/11 Commission to become president of the Center for National Policy, a national security think tank, before being named US Ambassador to India by President Obama in 2009; former Illinois Governor James R. "Big Jim" Thompson held a law degree and was a former federal prosecutor whose law firm once legally represented American and United Airlines.

One commission member with an extensive background in probing government conspiracies was attorney Richard Ben-Veniste, who had been a leading prosecutor in the Watergate scandal and a chief counsel to the Senate Whitewater Committee investigating President Clinton's real estate business dealings.

As with the Warren Commission, the 9/11 Commission's final report is notable not so much for what it says but for what it does not say. Presenting time lines that contradict sworn testimony, the report nevertheless offers to the unwary a compelling and detailed narrative of the hijacking horrors of that morning.

Yet even the accommodating commission soon found itself stymied by the Bush administration, which continued to drag its feet in supplying White House key internal documents and intelligence briefings to the commission, in addition to various forms of procedural delay.

The stonewalling reached its highest point when President Bush himself was asked to testify. After a long period of declining its invitations, in February 2004 the president finally agreed to meet with the commission. This meeting took place on April 29, but not until White House counsel had negotiated restrictive terms: Vice President Cheney had to be present also, the two men were not to testify under oath, and the meeting had to take place in the Oval Office. In addition, no recording was to be made of the session, nor was a stenographer permitted to be in the room. Bush and Cheney also declined to permit notes of the three-hour session to be shared with the 9/11 families.

Through the spring of 2004, commissioners continued to complain that their work was delayed repeatedly because of disputes with the administration over access to documents and other witnesses.

"It's obvious that the White House wants to run out the clock here…" commented former Senator Max Cleland during his stint on the commission. "As each day goes by, we learn that this government knew a whole lot more about these terrorists before September 11 than it has ever admitted." In November 2003, following a Bush White House dictate setting conditions for the examination of documents by the commission, Cleland said, "If this decision stands, I, as a member of the commission, cannot look any American in the eye, especially family members of victims, and say the commission had full access. This investigation is now compromised."

Cleland, a Democrat who was widely regarded to be the commission's most vociferous and outspoken critic of the Bush administration. Such activity by Cleland came to a halt in December 2003 when he resigned to accept a position on the board of directors of the Export-Import Bank of the United States after being nominated by President Bush on November 21, 2003. Many observers saw Cleland's new job as nothing less than a blatant buy-off by the Bush administration. In early 2004, Cleland groused, "One of these days we will have to get the full story because the 9/11 issue is so important to America. But this White House wants to cover it up."

John Farmer, the commission's chief counsel, added this comment, "I was shocked at how different the truth was from the way it was described.

The tapes told a radically different story from what had been told to us and the public for two years....This is not spin. This is not true."

In a *New York Times* article published in January 2008 and co-authored by 9/11 Commission Co-Chairmen Hamilton and Kean, they flatly stated their investigation was stonewalled by the CIA, an arm of the executive branch. "The commission's mandate was sweeping and it explicitly included the intelligence agencies. But the recent revelations that the CIA destroyed videotaped interrogations of al Qaeda operatives leads us to conclude that the agency failed to respond to our lawful requests for information about the 9/11 plot. Those who knew about those videotapes—and did not tell us about them—obstructed our investigation," wrote Kean and Hamilton.

It is quite apparent today that the 9/11 Commission which declined to ask any hardball questions of President Bush or his staff, was as compromised and controlled as the Warren Commission of 1964. The hardball questions, according to some, were instead reserved for 9/11 witnesses. New York firefighter Louie Cacchioli appeared before commission staffers in 2004 but quickly left. "I felt like I was being put on trial in a court room," said Cacchioli, "They were trying to twist my words and make the story fit only what they wanted to hear. All I wanted to do was tell the truth and when they wouldn't let me do that, I walked out."

"I met with the 9/11 Commission behind closed doors and they essentially discounted everything I said regarding the use of explosives to bring down the North Tower," said William Rodriguez, who previously had been invited to the White House for his heroism on 9/11. In fact, neither the names of Cacchioli, Rodriguez nor the names of any other witness who reported multiple explosions at the World Trade Center can be found in the 567-page *9/11 Commission Report*.

Another wrinkle in the progress of the 9/11 Commission came about due to the actual interpretation of its charter by the commissioners. This interpretation was voiced by Co-Chairman Hamilton who explained, "The focus of the commission will be on the future. We're not interested in trying to assess blame; we do not consider that part of the commission's responsibility."

So, it was now openly acknowledged that the commission would not hold key officials accountable for their actions; instead, it would focus on ways to prevent a recurrence in the future. And indeed, the commission has lived up to this charter. This was especially revealed in its forgiving and friendly treatment of government officials offering conflicting testimony under oath. For starters, the commission's account of its interview with President Bush, with Dick Cheney present—though not under oath—was marked by the extremity of its deferential treatment of the president. In fact, according to one exhaustive review that appeared in *Harper's Magazine*, the commissioners permitted the president to lie repeatedly about crucial questions of fact, without challenge—according to the commission's own account of these facts.

This time on national television and for all to see, Attorney General John Ashcroft's appearance before the commission provided one of the best examples of the kid-glove treatment afforded to high administration officials who should have been directly in the line of fire for the greatest crime ever committed on American soil. According to the mainstream Democratic think tank, the Center for American Progress, Ashcroft's testimony was a "deceptive, disingenuous, and dishonest account of his record prior to 9/11 and a Pollyanna-type view of his actions following the attack. Worse, the commissioners largely accepted Ashcroft's testimony at face value and passed on opportunities to aggressively question the attorney general on inconsistencies and inaccuracies in his statements."

The acting FBI director for the three months before 9/11, Thomas Pickard, had just testified to the commission that Ashcroft had waved off an update on the terrorist threat, telling Pickard that he didn't want to hear about the subject anymore. It fell to former Illinois Governor Jim Thompson—usually the fiercest Republican defender on the commission—to ask the only critical question about this statement. When asked by Thompson about Pickard's claim, Ashcroft replied, "I never said I didn't want to hear about counterterrorism."

But the exchange ended there, with no follow-up question. Obviously, either Ashcroft or Pickard was lying—but the commissioners didn't seem to notice this obvious contradiction. Later in his testimony, Ashcroft insisted that he had added more money to the Justice Department's budget for counterterrorism than for any other function. But according to *Slate* magazine, this claim is patently untrue. "It has been disputed by the commission's staff, several previous witnesses, and public budget documents. Yet none of the commissioners called him on it." The fact is that in August 2001, Attorney General Ashcroft, had turned down a bureau request for $50 million to beef up its counterterrorism efforts.

Even Commissioner Richard Ben-Veniste, the Democratic former Watergate prosecutor, went easy on the attorney general. He asked why Ashcroft's top five priorities listed in a policy document of May 10, 2001, did not include fighting terrorism. Ashcroft answered that at the May 9 hearings before the Senate Appropriations Committee he had cited terrorism as his No. 1 priority. Ben-Veniste let Ashcroft go unchallenged, even though the commission staff report released just prior to Ashcroft's testimony revealed that a May 10, 2001, budget guidance paper he released made no mention of counterterrorism. Many had predicted before the Ashcroft appearances that the attorney general was so vulnerable on the issue of 9/11 that he might have to be sacrificed as an administration fall guy. But Ashcroft was left unscathed by the commission.

Perhaps the chief embarrassment to the Bush administration during this period of testimony before the commission was the revelations of Richard A. Clarke, the Reagan appointee who was the government's top counterterrorism expert under President Clinton and President George W. Bush. On the CBS television program *60 Minutes*, and in dramatic testimony before the 9/11 Commission that electrified the country, Clarke charged that the Bush administration "failed to act prior to September 11 on the threat from al Qaeda despite repeated warnings." Clarke alleged that the Bush administration received repeated warnings that an al Qaeda attack was imminent, yet it under-funded and subordinated counterterrorism in the months leading up to 9/11—and even after.

Among the casualties of this downgrade was "a highly classified program to monitor al Qaeda suspects in the United States," which the White House suspended in the months leading up to 9/11, according to Clarke. Clarke went on to claim that the president was improperly attempting to "harvest a political windfall" from 9/11, charging that the administration began making plans to attack Iraq on 9/11—despite its claim that that the terror attack had been engineered by al Qaeda.

Clarke's latter assertion was consistent with earlier reports. CBS News had reported on September 4, 2002, that five hours after the 9/11 attacks, "Defense Secretary Donald Rumsfeld was telling his aides to come up with plans for striking Iraq—even though there was no evidence linking Saddam Hussein to the attacks." Similarly, then-Secretary of Treasury Paul O'Neill said the administration "was planning to invade Iraq long before the September 11 attacks and used questionable intelligence to justify the war." Noted earlier in this book is the fact that the commission's official timeline grossly contradicts Clarke's own hands-on, eyewitness account of the government's response to the events of the morning of the attacks, despite the preponderance of evidence for Clarke's version.

National Security Adviser Condoleezza Rice emerged as the administration's point person in its efforts to refute Clarke's accusations. In an opinion piece in the *Washington Post* on March 22, Rice wrote: "Despite what some have suggested, we received no intelligence that terrorists were preparing to attack the homeland using airplanes as missiles, though some analysts speculated that terrorists might hijack planes to try and free US-held terrorists." This claim was restated on numerous TV talk shows, and Rice elaborated on these assertions in her reluctant testimony before the 9/11 Commission; the National Security Adviser of the United States had agreed to testify under oath about the greatest security breach in modern history only after extreme public pressure.

To its credit, pressure from the commission in connection with the testimony of Rice forced the rather embarrassing release of the President's Daily Briefing (PDB) for August 6, 2001 a document that clearly outlined al Qaeda plans to strike within the United States. The PDB was declassified on Saturday, April 10, 2004. Below is the entire text of the intelligence briefing that was released by the White House. Most remarkable are the chilling revelations in its final two paragraphs:

### Bin Ladin Determined To Strike in US

*Clandestine, foreign government, and media reports indicate bin Ladin since 1997 has wanted to conduct terrorist attacks in the US. Bin Ladin implied in US television interviews in 1997 and 1998 that his followers would follow the example of World Trade Center bomber Ramzi Yousef and "bring the fighting to America."*

*After US missile strikes on his base in Afghanistan in 1998, Bin Ladin told followers he wanted to retaliate in Washington, according to a...(redacted portion)...service. An Egyptian Islamic Jihad*

(EIJ) operative told an...(redacted portion)...service at the same time that Bin Ladin was planning to exploit the operative's access to the US to mount a terrorist strike.

The millennium plotting in Canada in 1999 may have been part of Bin Ladin's first serious attempt to implement a terrorist strike in the US.

Convicted plotter Ahmed Ressam has told the FBI that he conceived the idea to attack Los Angeles International Airport himself, but that Bin Ladin lieutenant Abu Zubaydah encouraged him and helped facilitate the operation. Ressam also said that in 1998 Abu Zubaydah was planning his own US attack.

Ressam says Bin Ladin was aware of the Los Angeles operation. Although Bin Ladin has not succeeded, his attacks against the US Embassies in Kenya and Tanzania in 1998 demonstrate that he prepares operations years in advance and is not deterred by setbacks. Bin Ladin associates surveilled our Embassies in Nairobi and Dar es Salaam as early as 1993, and some members of the Nairobi cell planning the bombings were arrested and deported in 1997.

Al Qaeida members—including some who are US citizens—have resided in or traveled to the US for years, and the group apparently maintains a support structure that could aid attacks. Two al-Qa'ida members found guilty in the conspiracy to bomb our Embassies in East Africa were US citizens, and a senior EIJ member lived in California in the mid-1990s.

A clandestine source said in 1998 that a Bin Ladin cell in New York was recruiting Muslim-American youth for attacks.

We have not been able to corroborate some of the more sensational threat reporting, such as that from a...(redacted portion)... service in 1998 saying that Bin Ladin wanted to hijack a US aircraft to gain the release of "Blind Shaykh" Umar Abd al-Rahman and other US-held extremists.

Nevertheless, FBI information since that time indicates patterns of suspicious activity in this country consistent with preparations for hijackings or other types of attacks, including recent surveillance of federal buildings in New York.

> *The FBI is conducting approximately 70 full field investigations throughout the US that it considers Bin Ladin-related. CIA and the FBI are investigating a call to our Embassy in the UAE in May saying that a group of Bin Ladin supporters was in the US planning attacks with explosives.*

A few days after her testimony, a damning response to Rice swiftly came from a major new whistleblower, reviewed in an earlier section. In public statements intended to directly contradict Condoleezza Rice's testimony before the commission, Sibel Edmonds revealed that she had previously provided information to the panel investigating the September 11 attacks, which she believes proved that senior officials knew of al Qaeda's plans to attack the US with aircraft months before the strikes happened. In three hours during a closed session with the commission, she reiterated that information was circulating within the FBI in the spring and summer of 2001 that strongly suggested that an attack using aircraft was just months away and the terrorists were in place.

True to form, the Bush administration immediately sought to silence Edmonds, obtaining a gag order from a court as earlier noted. On March 24, 2004, in front of about fifty reporters and a dozen news cameras, Edmonds said "Attorney General John Ashcroft told me 'he was invoking State Secret Privilege and National Security' when I told the FBI I wanted to go public with what I had translated from the pre-9/11 intercepts."

In an effort to place a popular stamp of approval on the shoddy 9/11 Commission work, *Popular Mechanics* (*PM*) in March 2005, published an issue largely devoted to an article entitled "9/11—Debunking the Myths." The magazine's cover uses the word "lies" instead of "myths" and stated: "Conspiracy Theories Can't Stand Up To The Hard Facts." But did we get the hard facts? Not according to many 9/11 researchers who studiously combed through the popular magazine's report.

The "senior researcher" for this piece was Benjamin Chertoff. When contacted by reporter Christopher Bollyn and asked if he was any relation to Homeland Security chief Michael Chertoff, Benjamin replied, "I don't know." Yet, when Bollyn contacted Benjamin Chertoff's mother and ask the same question, she promptly replied, "Yes, of course, he is a cousin."

This is just one small example of the deceit which riddles the entire 9/11 case. "This means that Hearst [Corporation] paid Benjamin Chertoff to write an article supporting the seriously flawed explanation that is based on a practically non-existent investigation of the terror event that directly led to the creation of the massive national security department his 'cousin' now heads," Bollyn noted dryly.

Longtime conspiracy writer Joel Skousen said the authors of articles attempting to debunk 9/11 theories use four primary tactics:

- They refuse to mention, much less attempt to disprove, the most irrefutable and damaging evidence.
- They take great delight in debunking only those conspiracy theories that are the weakest or that are planted by other government sympathizers to try and discredit the more credible conspiracy facts.
- They select only those "experts" who agree with the official conclusions.
- They snicker at or mock anyone who suggests that the government might engage in criminal behavior or would cover up crimes in collusion with judges, investigators, prosecutors, media heads and hand-picked commissions.

Skousen noted that these tactics were used extensively in the *Popular Mechanics* story. "In the March 2005, *PM* magazine singled out 16 issues or claims of the 9/11 skeptics that point to government collusion and systematically attempted to debunk each one," he wrote. "Of the 16, most missed the mark and almost half were 'straw men' arguments—either ridiculous arguments that few conspiracists believed or restatements of arguments that were highly distorted so as to make them look weaker than they really were. *PM* took a lot of pot shots at conspiracy buffs, saying that those "who peddle fantasies that this country encouraged, permitted or actually carried out the attacks are libeling the truth—disgracing the memories of the thousands who died that day.'"

Researcher and journalist Jeremy Baker, after pointing out that the *PM* authors were guilty of "inventing nonsense and distorting data" as well as only challenging "the poorest 9/11 researchers" while ignoring more credible work, characterized the *PM* article as "a train wreck of disinformation and as conspicuous a propaganda ploy as one could imagine."

THE OFFICIAL 9/11 INQUIRY: ANOTHER WARREN COMMISSION?

Other serious researchers were just as quick to attack the work of the official 9/11 Commission itself. Nafeez Mosaddeq Ahmed is executive director of the Institute for Policy Research & Development in Brighton, England, and author of the award-winning book *The War on Freedom: How & Why America was Attacked: September 11, 2001*. After a detailed study of the 9/11 Commission's work, he concluded, "...the National Commission on Terror Attacks Upon the United States has failed dismally to investigate the 9/11 terror attacks in an appropriately credible and critical manner. Huge amounts of relevant historical and contemporary data have been ignored; irrelevant data and narratives have been used to construct an inaccurate chronology of 9/11 and its historical context; the embarrassing and damaging implications of ample evidence, including testimony presented to the commission, have been overlooked; blatantly dishonest testimony contradicting well-documented facts has been uncritically accepted."

After closely studying the final *9/11 Commission Report*, author David Ray Griffin concluded that far from refuting the evidence of government complicity in the attacks, the commission "simply ignored most of it and distorted the rest." He added, "I suggested that the commission's attempt to defend the US military in particular against [public] suspicion is at best seriously flawed, at worst a set of audacious lies." Throughout the text of his scholarly study, Griffin repeatedly points out that the commission took great pains to give an account of only those facts that were consistent with the Bush administration's official story.

In a later essay entitled *"The 9/11 Commission Report*: A 571-Page Lie," Griffin analyzed the pattern of lying in the report's pages, and provided a long list of 115 omissions and distortions that could be justifiably be portrayed as lies. For reasons of space, these few items should suffice to demonstrate the omissions of the 9/11 Commission:

1. No mention of that fact that several credible sources stated that at least six of the alleged hijackers are still alive—including Waleed al-Shehri, accused of stabbing a flight attendant on Flight 11 before it crashed into the WTC North Tower.
2. The omission of reports concerning Mohamed Atta's fondness for alcohol, pork, and lap dances at odds with the commission's claim that he had become a religious fanatic.

# PART I – THE EVENTS OF SEPTEMBER 11, 2001

3. No mention of the role of Pakistani Intelligence (ISI), a pivotal element with reported ties to both the 9/11 hijackers and the CIA.
4. No reporting on the blocking of meaningful terrorist investigations by the FBI during both the Clinton and Bush administrations.
5. The total lack of reporting on the 200 Israelis expelled from the US in 2002 as part of a massive spy ring, including five arrested after filming the destruction of the WTC from a New Jersey rooftop.
6. No mention of that fact that the CIA created al Qaeda in the 1980s when former CIA Director and then-Vice President George Bush, Sr., controlled the government following the shooting of President Reagan.
7. Not one word about the close business and social ties between the Bush family and the bin Ladens nor of the fact that about 140 Saudis, including about 40 bin Laden family members, were allowed to congregate by air during the "no fly" period beginning the morning of 9/11.
8. The obfuscation of the evidence that Hani Hanjour was too poor a pilot to have flown an airliner into the Pentagon.
9. The omission of the fact that the publicly released flight manifests contain no Arab names.
10. No explanation of how, within hours of the attacks, FBI agents turned up in hotels, restaurants and flight schools used by the hijackers, and knew where to look.
11. The omission of the fact that fire has never, before or after 9/11, caused steel-frame buildings to collapse.
12. No mention of how it was possible that the South Tower collapsed first even though it had been burning a much shorter time the North Tower and also had less fire.
13. Omission of the collapse of WTC 7—which was not hit by an airplane and which had only small, localized fires—an occurrence that FEMA admitted it could not explain.
14. The omission of the fact that the collapse of the Twin Towers—like that of Building 7—demonstrated at least 10 fea-

THE OFFICIAL 9/11 INQUIRY: ANOTHER WARREN COMMISSION?

tures suggestive of controlled demolition.
15. No explanation for the claim that the core of the Twin Towers was "a hollow steel shaft," even though even a cursory examination of the WTC plans showed 47 massive steel columns constituting the core of each tower which should have prevented the "pancake theory" of the collapses.
16. The omission of WTC lease-holder Larry Silverstein's statement that he and the fire department commander decided to "pull" Building 7.
17. No mention of the fact that the steel from "ground zero" was quickly removed from the crime scene and shipped overseas before it could be analyzed for evidence of explosives.
18. Omission of Mayor Giuliani's statement that he had evacuated his temporary command center because he had received word that the World Trade Center towers were about to collapse.
19. No presentation of the fact that President Bush's brother Marvin and his cousin Wirt Walker III were both principals in the company in charge of security for the WTC.
20. Omission of the fact that there have been no photos released of the reconstructed debris of Flight 77 although this has been standard procedure in past airline disasters.
21. No discussion on how the damage done to the Pentagon was inconsistent with the impact of a Boeing 757 going several hundred miles per hour.
22. Omission of the fact that photos of the Pentagon's west wing's facade prior to its collapse 30 minutes after the strike revealed a hole too small to accommodate a Boeing 757.
23. No mention of all the various testimony that has been used to cast doubt on whether remains of a Boeing 757 were visible either inside or outside the Pentagon.
24. The omission of any discussion of whether the Pentagon had an anti-missile defense system that would have brought down a commercial airliner— even though the commission suggested that the al Qaeda terrorists did not attack a nuclear power plant because they assumed that it would be thus defended.

JIM MARRS

25. Absolutely no mention of fatal anthrax attacks in the days following 9/11, which involved weapons-grade pathogens obtainable only through the US military and were directed against leading Democrats who might have balked at the anti-terrorist measures within the Patriot Act.
26. Only one small footnote mentioned the "Vigilant Guardian" war games exercises which many feel were responsible for the confusion within the FAA and NORAD on 9/11.

It has been noted here that the 9/11 Commission unilaterally altered the time frame of 9/11 events, ignoring or brushing aside contradicting evidence presented under oath.

Such manipulation may have even reached into some US agencies. Democratic Senator Mark Dayton of Minnesota, noted such inconsistencies during the first congressional hearing on the 9/11 Commission's report. "For almost three years now, NORAD officials and FAA officials have been able to hide their critical failures that left this country defenseless during two of the worst hours in our history," Dayton declared during a Senate Governmental Affairs Committee hearing. He angrily stated NORAD, "lied to the American people, they lied to Congress and they lied to your 9/11 Commission to create a false impression of competence, communication and protection of the American people."

He added, "We can set up all the organizations we want, but they won't be worth an Enron [the failed energy corporation] pension if the people responsible lie to us."

Considering the secret societies' goal of concentrating power through "globalization," it was no surprise that the commission's report called for a number of sweeping changes in government structure and policies—all without exception aimed at gathering more power to a centralized authority armed with vastly increased budgets.

Their call for revamping the intelligence community reflected further inconsistency. After detailing the problems the Director of Central Intelligence (DCI) has in coordinating various government agencies, the commission commented, "No one person can do all these things." Their solution? Place all such intelligence operations under the control of one person, a new cabinet-level "National Intelligence Director."

The final *9/11 Commission Report* is chock full of inconsequential and distracting details and backgrounding, filled with gaps and inconsistencies and, over all, merely a clarion call for a more centralized federal government presented as our best protector against further terrorism. No wonder that even some commissioners and even their chief counsel have publicly questioned their own work.

Even if there was no intent to cover up the truth, the commission was never funded at a level sufficient to do its work. Incredibly, more than three times as much money was spent on President George W. Bush's 2005 inauguration than was originally allocated to investigate the attacks on September 11, 2001. Consider that a total of $112.6 million was spent to investigate the 2003 space shuttle *Columbia* disaster and $50 million was once spent to look into Las Vegas gambling casinos. The investigation of the 9/11 tragedy received a total of $13 million.

The Presidential Inaugural Committee estimated Bush's 2005 inauguration events cost about $40 million, with the federal government and District of Columbia bearing an additional $20 million as the cost of providing security. So the total cost of Bush's 2005 inauguration festivities costs $60 million while a paltry $13 million went to probe the greatest attack on America since 1812.

As in the Kennedy assassination, it is apparent that the federal government cannot be trusted to police itself. Uncovering answers to the many 9/11 mysteries will be left to a grassroots army of private researchers.

Perhaps author David Ray Griffin asked the most pertinent question: "[F]ar from lessening my suspicions about official complicity, [the 9/11 Commission's report] has served to confirm them. Why would the minds in charge of this final report engage in such deception if they were not trying to cover up very high crimes?

Why indeed? What agenda or criminal activity might high-level officials in the US government desire to cover up? To discern a possible answer to this question, attention should be directed to the Middle East.

## PART II – WAR FOR OIL AND DRUGS

*"We haven't heard from [Osama bin Laden] in a long time. I truly am not that concerned about him."*

—President George W. Bush,
in a news conference on March 13, 2002

Oil and drugs are among the most profitable commodities in the world, coming in close behind the top moneymaker—armaments. Therefore, it should be no surprise that foreign policy, political maneuvering and open warfare have resulted from the struggle to control oil and drugs. This struggle can be clearly seen in the US military action in Afghanistan.

Its genesis began on the high plateau of Iran, which curves along the southern shore of the Caspian Sea. In ancient times, this area was known as Persia and was the spawning ground of several great civilizations. It was also the home of the "eternal pillars of fire" worshiped by the followers of Zoroaster, a sixth-century BCE sage who added monotheism to an even older Aryan creed. Today, most believe that the pillars of fire were flaming petroleum gas escaping through holes in the local limestone. Marco Polo wrote of springs in the area that produced water that was undrinkable but burned well and removed mange from camels. It was not until the modern era that man found a practical use for liquid petroleum—fuel for transportation and the machines of war.

In 1873, Robert and Ludwig Nobel, sons of the famed inventor of dynamite, Alfred Nobel, came to the Baku area on the western shore of the Caspian Sea and soon were supplying half of the world's petroleum supply. The Swedish Nobel brothers were soon in competition with the French branch of the powerful Rothschild banking family. At the same time, John D. Rockefeller's Standard Oil was becoming a major force in the burgeoning oil industry and also coveted the Caspian Sea oil. With the help of their respective governments, these powerful families competed for control over the Caspian Sea oil for decades. This struggle has been called "the Great Game."

Today, with the controversial claim that the world is rapidly running out of oil, public attention has been focused on the issue of "Peak Oil." But the quest for oil is nothing new.

Petroleum has been behind all recent wars, beginning in the early 1940s, when a mostly rural and isolationist America was suddenly thrown into a world war as a reaction to the Japanese attack on Pearl Harbor. Americans mourned the loss of some three thousand soldiers and civilians in Hawaii and, in righteous indignation, allowed their country to be turned into a giant military camp. The federal government, which had consolidated so much power unto itself under the Depression-busting policies of President Franklin Delano Roosevelt, would now grow even stronger and more centralized under the aegis of "national security." It all seemed quite natural and necessary at the time.

But serious students of history now know that even that "good war" was the result of machinations by a handful of wealthy and powerful men. By closing off Japan's oil supplies in the summer of 1941, Roosevelt, closely connected to Wall Street power, ensured an eventual attack on the United States. It has now been well established that Roosevelt and a few close advisers knew full well that Pearl Harbor would be attacked on December 7, 1941, but chose to allow it to happen to further their agenda for dragging the isolationist American population into war.

In an odd addendum, the 9/11 attacks apparently blocked an effort to bring the truth concerning foreknowledge of the Pearl Harbor attack to the American public.

Ever since the war, efforts have been mounted to exonerate the two military commanders who were initially blamed as being unprepared for the attack on Pearl Harbor. The latest attempt, aided by Delaware Representative Michael Castle, was stopped when White House Chief of Staff Andrew Card refused to pass along a plea for exoneration to President Bush despite the admission that Rear Admiral Husband Kimmel and Major General Walter Short "were, without question, honorable and patriotic Americans who served our country with bravery and dedication." Furthermore, *White House Weekly*, in reporting this effort, declared, "Subsequent investigations by those inside and outside the military proved that Washington knew the Japanese were on the move but never told Hawaii."

According to reporter James P. Tucker, Jr. the rationale for not forwarding the plea from the officers' families to Bush was that the White House considered the issue too explosive in light of the questions being raised regarding the Bush administration's foreknowledge of the 9/11 attacks.

During World War II, Hitler's Army Group South rampaged through the Ukraine in Russia and moved inexorably toward Baku and the rich Caucasian oil fields. With these oil reserves in hand, Hitler planned to turn south and capture the oil of the Middle East in a combined operation with Field Marshal Erwin Rommel's famed Afrika Korps' assault from North Africa. This scheme was thwarted by Rommel's defeat at El Alamein and the eventual destruction of the German Sixth Army at Stalingrad.

The Vietnam War was about the oil and mineral wealth of Southeast Asia and was prosecuted by men who had been close to Roosevelt and the secretive Council on Foreign Relations (CFR). CFR position papers had long voiced a desire for the United States to gain control over Indochina's oil, magnesium and rubber assets. There also has been incessant speculation that drugs played a major role in US activities in the region, as some have argued that the war was a cover for allowing covert protection for the "Golden Triangle" of opium production and to insure the clandestine importation of drugs to the United States.

In order to move into position in Southeast Asia, a provocation was again created. In August 1964, President Lyndon Johnson whipped Congress into a frenzy claiming that North Vietnamese gunboats had attacked the US Sixth Fleet in the Gulf of Tonkin off the coast of Vietnam.

"Our boys are floating in the water," he cried. Congress responded by passing the Gulf of Tonkin Resolution, which bypassed the Constitution and gave Johnson the power to wage war to stop attacks on Americans. Soon after this, ground combat troops augmented American military advisers there. It was the beginning of the real shooting war in Vietnam.

But the attack was all a lie. No evidence has ever been brought forward that such an attack ever took place. In fact, editors for *US News & World Report* (July 23, 1984) called it "The 'Phantom Battle' That Led to War."

While America was waging war against North Vietnam, which we were told was merely a puppet of communist Russia and China, Johnson was encouraged by his CFR advisers to grant the Soviet Union loans at higher levels than offered during World War II, when they were our ally. US-backed loans provided Russia with funds to build facilities that turned out war materials that were then sent to North Vietnam for use against American troops. This support for the opposing sides was a prime example of the duplicity of the financiers behind our modern wars.

Everyone understood that the Persian Gulf War of 1991, as with most Middle-East conflicts, was a war for oil that ended with its cause celebre, Saddam Hussein, the "new Hitler," still in power. This conflict also began with a fabricated provocation.

The well-publicized testimony of a young girl named Nayirah telling Congress how babies were dumped onto the floor from their incubators in a Kuwaiti hospital stirred angry support for war with Iraq. Months later, it was learned that "Nayirah" was actually the daughter of Kuwait's ambassador to the United States and that she had not actually seen the reported atrocities.

It was also learned that the American public relations firm of Hill & Knowlton had been paid $10.7 million by the Kuwaiti government to orchestrate a campaign to win American support for the war. Hill & Knowlton president Craig Fuller had been then-President George Bush's chief of staff when the senior Bush served as vice president under Ronald Reagan.

Interestingly, no one in Congress or the US news media bothered to substantiate the atrocity story. Similar unsubstantiated stories were presented to the UN a few weeks later by "witnesses," who were never placed under oath and were also coached by Hill & Knowlton.

Fabricated atrocity stories, stock purchases, oil and grain deals, arms sales, loans and guarantees, the weakening of the Arabs to benefit Israel, the movement toward a global army and government controlled by a global elite created a mind-numbing entanglement during this struggle. "It is doubtful whether the 'real' reasons why the United States went to war in the Persian Gulf will ever emerge," wrote authors Jonathan Vankin and John Whalen. "Unlike in Vietnam, where the ambiguous outcome elicited natural suspicions, in the Gulf the decisiveness of victory has buried the reality deeper than any Iraqi or American soldier who went to a sandy grave."

But at least one American leader understood the futility of attempting to occupy Iraq to further objectives of the West. In a 1998 book entitled *A World Transformed*, former President George H. W. Bush explained his decision to call a halt to the Gulf War.

"Trying to eliminate Saddam, extending the ground war into the occupation of Iraq, would have violated our guideline about not changing objectives in midstream, engaging in 'mission creep,' and would have incurred incalculable human and political costs. Apprehending him was probably impossible...We would have been forced to occupy Baghdad and, in effect, rule Iraq. The coalition would instantly have collapsed, the Arabs deserting it in anger and other allies pulling out as well. Under the circumstances, there was no visible 'exit strategy' we could see, violating another of our principles. Furthermore, we had been self-consciously trying to set a pattern for handling aggression in the post-Cold War world. Going in and occupying Iraq, thus unilaterally exceeding the United Nations' mandate, would have destroyed the precedent of international response to aggression that we hoped to establish. Had we gone the invasion route, the United States could conceivably still be an occupying power in a bitterly hostile land. It [the Gulf War] would have been a dramatically different—and perhaps barren—outcome."

Apparently, Bush's reasoned argument against any occupation of Iraq was lost on his son. Even the arrival of Democratic President Barack Hussein Obama did little to stop the violence in that strife-torn nation.

Although by 2010 the Obama administration announced that under an agreement with the Iraqui government—which after all was kept in power by the US military presence—all US combat troops would be withdrawn by Dec. 31, 2011. Some duplicity seemed to be taking place.

Some combat troops remained in Iraq but received a name change. According to the *Army Times*, the 2nd Stryker Brigade combat team of the 25th Infantry Division remained but its name was changed to the "Advise and Assist" Brigade. Apparently at least two other combat brigades would remain under this policy. So, almost 50,000 US troops would remain, though not officially designated combat troops, despite the fact that they were the same personnel with the same weapons and equipment that operated there a year earlier. According to Army spokesman Lt. Col. Craig Ratcliff, seven "Advise and Assist" Brigades as well as two National Guard infantry brigades for "security" purposes will continue operations in Iraq. This number does not include the more than 150,000 private contractors such as Blackwater (now Xe).

To bastardize Shakespeare, a combat brigade by any other name is still a combat brigade. But such duplicity seems only appropriate in an occupation begun in lies and dissembling.

## THE CENTRAL ASIAN GAS PIPELINE

Oil also came to drive the politics of Central Asia when, in the late 1970s, the Soviet Union discovered further untapped oil in the southern republic of Chechnya. This discovery, along with the oil deposits throughout the Caspian Sea region, upped the ante for the lands north of Persian Gulf nations. The region was ripe for exploitation but control over Afghanistan was needed to ensure the safety of a pipeline to bring the oil to world markets.

With beginning of the collapse of communism accompanied by the the withdrawal of the Soviets from Afghanistan in 1989, international bankers and oilmen gained a foothold in cash-strapped Russia and the estimated $3 trillion in Caspian Sea oil was once again attracting serious attention. In 1997, six international companies and the government of Turkmenistan formed Central Asian Gas Pipeline, Ltd. (CentGas) to build a 790-mile-long pipeline to link Turkmenistan's natural gas reserves with Pakistan and perhaps on to the New Delhi area of India.

Leading this consortium was America's Unocal Corporation, whose president, John F. Imle, Jr., said the project would be "the foundation for a new commerce corridor for the region often referred to as the Silk Road for the 21st century."

Also involved were these companies: Delta Oil Company Limited of Saudi Arabia, Indonesia Petroleum Ltd. of Japan, ITOCHU Oil Exploration Co. Ltd. of Japan, Hyundai Engineering & Construction Co., Ltd. of Korea, and the Crescent Group of Pakistan. RAO Gazprom of Russia also was interested in joining the consortium.

But problems developed with the fundamentalist Muslim government in Afghanistan, not the least of which was the Taliban government's treatment of women, which prompted feminist-led demonstrations in America against firms seeking to do business there. Additionally, the Taliban regime was creating chaotic conditions by pitting the various Islamic sects against each other in order to maintain control. In early December 1998, Unocal withdrew from the pipeline consortium, citing the hazardous political situation, and the project languished.

Some event, some provocation, was required to propel the normally disinterested American public into supporting some sort of US military action in Afghanistan.

Many people have noticed that in President Bush's declaration of war on terrorism, he never mentioned terrorists in Northern Ireland or the Palestinian suicide bombers. Attention was only focused on Afghanistan, the one nation necessary to complete the lucrative pipeline and the leading supplier of opium. It should also be noted that Vice President Dick Cheney had been heavily involved in the oil industry. He headed the giant oil industry service company Halliburton and was generally thought to wield more power than the president. Halliburton had a major stake in the central Asian pipeline project as it would gain lucrative service contracts.

Despite Unocal's public announcement that it was withdrawing from the CentGas project, industry insiders said the firm never completely abandoned hopes for the project. The Texas-based Unocal never actually dropped plans for a trans-Afghanistan oil pipeline, which it considered a separate venture, and even held discussions on worker safety with the Taliban regime in March 2000.

With the coalition forces fully involved in Afghanistan by mid-2002, the gas pipeline project was back on a front burner. BBC News reported on May 13 of that year that interim leader Hamid Karzai was to hold talks with Pakistan and Turkmenistan officials to revive the $2 billion pipeline. Karzai, according to European news reports, formerly worked for Unocal, as did US envoy John J. Maresca. "The work on the project will start after an agreement is expected to be struck at the coming summit," said Mohammad Alim Razim, minister for Mines and Industries.

Mr. Razim stated Unocal was the "lead company" among those that would build the pipeline. He added that the pipeline is expected to be built with funds from donor countries earmarked for the reconstruction of Afghanistan.

A mere nine days after the new interim government of Hamid Karzai took power in Afghanistan, President Bush appointed National Security Council official Zalmay Khalilzad his special envoy. Unsurprisingly, Khalilzad, an American born in Afghanistan, had been employed by the oil giant Unocal. He also had taught political science at Columbia where he worked with former national security adviser Zbigniew Brzezinski, a co-founder of the Trilateral Commission. Khalilzad had been a longtime supporter of the Taliban. Khalilzad was also a member of the Project for the New American Century (PNAC), the neo-con think tank which in a 2000 paper declared that it would require a "catastrophic and catalyzing event—like a new Pearl Harbor" to gain the support of the American public for their Middle East agenda.

When George W. Bush was appointed president, Khalilzad was selected by Cheney to head the Bush transition team in the area of defense. In the spring of 2002, he was named by Bush as the chief National Security Council official working under National Security Adviser Condoleezza Rice, dealing with issues pertaining to the Persian Gulf and Central Asia. According to BBC reporter Mike Fox, Khalilzad "played an important part in developing the defense strategy of the Bush administration, both before and after the September the eleventh attacks."

The need for more and more petroleum impacted on America's security in other odd ways. Former FBI counterterrorism chief John O'Neill said in an interview with French authors Jean Charles Brisard and Guillaume Dasquie, "(T)he main obstacles to investigate Islamic terrorism were US oil corporate interests and the role played by Saudi Arabia in it." Early in 2002, the former oil minister of Saudi Arabia, Ahmad Zaki al-Yamani, put it bluntly when he stated, "[The] US has a strategic objective, which is to control the oil of the Caspian Sea and [thereby] to end dependence on the oil of the [Persian] Gulf."

Of course, to challenge the oil and gas monopoly is to challenge the inner core leadership of Wall Street, the Council on Foreign Relations and other powerful interests, who have owned or controlled the federal government since before World War II. Until the American people gather the will to wean politicians off the oil spigot, this nation will continue to pursue a petroleum-based energy policy.

## AFGHAN ACTION WAS PLANNED LONG AGO

With $3 trillion in Caspian Sea oil as the prize, it can now be demonstrated that military action against Afghanistan had been in the works long before the September 11 attacks.

Shortly after Bush was selected for the presidency in late 2000, S. Frederick Starr, head of the Central Asia Institute at Johns Hopkins University, stated in the *Washington Post*, "The US has quietly begun to align itself with those in the Russian government calling for military action against Afghanistan and has toyed with the idea of a new raid to wipe out bin Laden." Others in that area were gearing up for an armed attempt to oust the Taliban.

Officials in India said their nation and Iran would only play the role of "facilitator" while the US and Russia would combat the Taliban from the front with the help of two Central Asian countries, Tajikistan and Uzbekistan, to push the Taliban lines back to the 1998 position.

Thus began the build up of American-led military operations against Afghanistan as reported by the Indian News Agency on June 26, 2001, more than two months prior to the attacks on the World Trade Center and the Pentagon.

As reported by BBC's George Arney, former Pakistani foreign secretary Niaz Naik was alerted by American officials in mid-July that military action against Afghanistan would be launched by mid-October. At a UN-sponsored meeting in Berlin concerning Afghanistan, Naik was informed that unless bin Laden was handed over, America would take military action either to kill or capture both him and Taliban leader Mullah Omar as the initial step in installing a new government there.

In other words, contrary to the words of America's leadership, who proclaimed that "everything has changed" because of the 9/11 attacks, US foreign policy stayed right on track, right down to the October date given out in the summer for military action in Afghanistan.

This was confirmed in early 2004 in a preliminary report by the 9/11 Commission. The report said the decision to overthrow the Taliban government of Afghanistan was made by senior Bush administration officials the day before the September 11, 2001, attacks. The panel stated that despite diplomatic efforts of both the Clinton and early Bush administrations coupled with a pledge to Saudi Arabia, the Taliban still had not made any effort to expel Osama bin Laden by September 2001. No mention was made of the oil/gas pipeline deals.

However, it should be noted that American intervention in Afghanistan had actually begun years ago, even prior to the Soviet occupation.

In a 1998 interview with former national security adviser Zbigniew Brzezinski in the French publication *Le Nouvel Observateur*, he admitted that American activities in Afghanistan actually began six months prior to the 1979 Soviet invasion.

Brzezinski, Jimmy Carter's national security adviser, said the Carter administration began secretly funding anti-Soviet rebels in July 1979 with the full knowledge such action might provoke a Soviet invasion. Soviet leaders at the time argued the invasion was necessary to thwart American aggression in Afghanistan.

Brzezinski told French interviewers, "According to the official version of history, CIA aid to the Mujahideen began during 1980, that is to say, after the Soviet army invaded Afghanistan, 24 December 1979. But the reality, secretly guarded until now, is completely otherwise. Indeed, it was July 3, 1979, that President Carter signed the first directive for secret aid to the opponents of the pro-Soviet regime in Kabul."

Based upon this admission, it would appear that the Soviets were speaking the truth when they told the world they were forced to move Russian troops into that nation to prevent a secret American takeover.

Brzezinski expressed no regret at this hidden provocation, stating, "That secret operation was an excellent idea. It brought about the demoralization and finally the breakup of the Soviet empire." It also led to the creation of the Taliban regime as well as empowering Osama bin Laden.

But after almost ten years of brutal, no-quarter fighting against Afghans and Arab mercenaries backed by the United States, including Osama bin Laden, the Soviets were forced to withdraw from Afghanistan, a pertinent fact to remember as the US-led fighting there reaches its 10th year. The economic stress of this Russo-Afghan War was enough to help topple communism in the early 1990s and Brzezinski was happy enough to take full credit for this even though it resulted in introducing militant Muslim theology into that volatile region.

Asked if he regretted such activities, Brzezinski replied, "What is most important to the history of the world? The Taliban or the collapse of the Soviet Empire? Some stirred up Moslems or the liberation of Central Europe and the end of the cold war?"

It is pertinent to note three things about the Brzezinski interview: one is that he is a leading luminary of the Council on Foreign Relations as well as a founder and today a member of the Trilateral Commission's executive committee; second, that with the apparent exception of a copy in the Library of Congress, his interview was not included in a truncated version of the article circulated in the United States; and third, no one in 1979 could have foreseen the collapse of communism, with or without the Afghan incursion.

In a 1997 Council on Foreign Relations study entitled *The Grand Chessboard: American Primacy and its Geostatic Imperatives*, Brzezinski clearly showed why he and his fellow CFR members believed it necessary for the United States to maintain a military presence in the Near East. "[A]s America becomes an increasingly multicultural society, it may find it more difficult to fashion a consensus on foreign policy issues," he wrote, "except in the circumstance of a truly massive and widely perceived direct external threat." He was explicit that such a threat would need to be on the order of the one that involved America in the last world war. "The attitude of the American public toward the external projection of American power has been much more ambivalent. The public supported America's engagement in World War II largely because of the shock effect of the Japanese attack on Pearl Harbor," Brzezinski wrote.

Shortly after 9/11, the *Guardian*, a British newspaper, conducted its

AFGHAN ACTION WAS PLANNED LONG AGO

own investigation and concluded that both Osama bin Laden and the Taliban received threats of possible American military attacks on them two months before 9/11. According to "senior diplomatic sources," the threats were passed along by the Pakistani government.

The newspaper elaborated on BBC reporter Arney's report of the pre-attack warnings by stating that the warning to the Taliban originated at a four-day meeting of senior Americans, Russians, Iranians and Pakistanis at a hotel in Berlin in mid-July 2001. The conference, the third in a series dubbed "brainstorming on Afghanistan," was part of a classic diplomatic device known as "track two," a method whereby governments can pass messages to each other. "The Americans indicated to us that in case the Taliban does not behave and in case Pakistan also doesn't help us to influence the Taliban, then the United States would be left with no option but to take an overt action against Afghanistan," said Niaz Naik, former foreign minister of Pakistan, who attended the Berlin meeting.

Many Internet sources have quoted from an interview with French authors Jean Charles Brisard and Guillaume Dasquie who told of US representatives threatening, "Either you accept our offer of a carpet of gold, or we bury you under a carpet of bombs." However, no other source, including Naik, has confirmed this quote.

But the implication of the talks was much the same. Naik did say he was told that unless bin Laden was handed over quickly, America would take military action to kill or capture, not only bin Laden, but also Taliban leader Mullah Omar. He added that he was informed that the broader objective was to end the Taliban regime and install a transitional government in Afghanistan, presumably one less intransigent on the oil pipeline negotiations.

The former Pakistani diplomat was further informed that if such military action were to commence, it would happen before the first snows in Afghanistan, no later than the middle of October. Naik's prophetic words were reported on September 18, 2001, almost three weeks before the start of the US bombing campaign.

According to the *Guardian* article, the American representatives at the Berlin meeting were Tom Simons, a former US ambassador to Pakistan, Karl "Rick" Inderfurth, a former assistant secretary of state for South Asian affairs, and Lee Coldren, who headed the office of Pakistan, Afghan and Bangladesh affairs in the State Department until 1997.

Naik was quoted as saying that he specifically asked Simons why such an attack would be any more successful than President Clinton's missile strikes against Afghanistan in 1998. That attack killed twenty persons but missed bin Laden. "He said this time they were very sure. They had all the intelligence and would not miss him this time. It would be aerial action, maybe helicopter gunships," Naik said, adding, "What the Americans indicated to us was perhaps based on official instructions. They were very senior people. Even in 'track two' people are very careful about what they say and don't say." No representative from the Taliban was present but Naik, representing one of only three governments that recognized the Taliban, said he passed the warning along to the Afghan authorities.

Coldren told the British paper, "I think there was some discussion of the fact that the United States was so disgusted with the Taliban that they might be considering some military action." But he added that it was not an agenda item at the meeting.

According to the article, Nikolai Kozyrev, Moscow's former special envoy on Afghanistan and one of the Russians in Berlin, would not confirm the contents of the US conversations, but said: "Maybe they had some discussions in the corridor. I don't exclude such a possibility."

Naik's recollection is that "we had the impression Russians were trying to tell the Americans that the threat of the use of force is sometimes more effective than force itself."

Simons denied having said anything about detailed operations and Inderfurth told the *Guardian*, "There was no suggestion for military force to be used. What we discussed was the need for a comprehensive political settlement to bring an end to the war in Afghanistan that has been going on for two decades and has been doing so much damage."

Told the American participants were denying the pre-attack warnings, Mr. Naik was quoted as saying, "I'm a little surprised but maybe they feel they shouldn't have told us anything in advance now we have had these tragic events."

Perhaps the reason that no one in the American delegation wanted to admit the pre-attack threats was given by the *Guardian* writers who speculated, "The Taliban refused to comply but the serious nature of what they were told raises the possibility that bin Laden, far from launching the attacks on the World Trade Center in New York and the Pentagon out of the blue ten days ago, was launching a pre-emptive strike in response to what he saw as US threats."

A pre-emptive strike? Could Osama bin Laden have been acting in self-defense? No one has mentioned that in the major corporate media.

The destruction of the Taliban actually was the object of several diplomatic discussions months before the events of 9/11, including a May 2001 meeting between the State Department and officials from Iran, Germany and Italy. The talks centered around replacing the Taliban with a "broad-based government." This same topic was raised at the Group of Eight (G-8) talks in Genoa, Italy, in July 2001.

Many people have questioned why we bombed Afghanistan when apparently none of the listed hijackers was an Afghan, but instead all but four were Arabs from Saudi Arabia. Since Iraq was implicated in the 1993 WTC attack, why did we not bomb that "rogue" nation in 2001? Better yet, since Attorney General John Ashcroft announced soon after 9/11 that the "masterminds" of the attacks were operating out of Hamburg, Germany, why not bomb Germany, an activity with which America has had considerable experience in the past?

Such questions grew as American troops moved into Afghanistan, especially when it was found that the oil reserves might not be as productive as first believed.

Sources in the oil industry have reported that with the American military incursion into Afghanistan came the troubling news that the country might prove to be a dry hole. Once old seismic data was compared with actual drilling, it was learned that the Caspian Sea oil was concentrated in small pools rather than in large deep reserves. Another source of plentiful oil was needed. That source may have become known to the public in late 2002, when the Bush administration appeared hell-bent on attacking Iraq despite howls of protest from other Middle East nations, many Americans and other NATO countries.

Despite the questions over Afghanistan's oil supply, American military action there was swift and deadly effective and not always aimed at strictly military targets. Only three days after the US bombing began in early 2003, American firepower appeared to violate international conventions. In Afghanistan's capital, Radio Kabul was knocked off the air by US bombs, silencing the voice of the Taliban. Farhad Azad of Afghanmagazine.com reported that the station's stored musical library was lost. "The Taliban made music illegal, but it was US bombs that physically destroyed the hidden archive," he said. But more suspiciously, a month later the Kabul offices of satellite television station Al-Jazeera, which sat in the middle of a residential neighborhood, were struck by two five hundred-pound bombs.

Colonel Brian Hoey, a spokesman for the US Central Command, confirmed that the United States had bombed the building but stated, "[T]he indications we had was that this was not an Al-Jazeera office."

Al-Jazeera had already come under figurative fire from US authorities for broadcasting interviews with Osama bin Laden. The station also had aired interviews with Donald Rumsfeld and National Security Adviser Condoleezza Rice.

The military action against a civilian TV station "could prove to be a public relations fiasco for the US government," noted the *Washington Post* at the time. But this could only occur if the American people were told about it. In fact, little or no reporting on this incident reached the public.

The evidence that operations against Afghanistan were planned long before the 9/11 attacks prompted author Gore Vidal to remark, "With that background, it now becomes explicable why the first thing Bush did after we were hit was to get Senator Daschle and beg him not to hold an investigation of the sort any normal country would have done. When Pearl Harbor was struck, within twenty minutes the Senate and the House had a joint committee ready. Roosevelt beat them to it, because he knew why we had been hit, so he set up his own committee. But none of this was to come out and it hasn't come out."

Since it is now plain that military operations against Afghanistan were in the planning stages months before 9/11, the question must be asked why there was no buildup of propaganda in the American media. Before every military action, the reasons and rationales must be placed before the public to accustom them to the idea and gain their support. Yet, while both diplomatic and military preparations were being made for war against Afghanistan, the American public remained ignorant and contented. Some researchers contend this is an indication that national leaders knew such a propaganda campaign would be unnecessary because a surprise attack would do the job.

AFGHAN ACTION WAS PLANNED LONG AGO

## WAG THE DOG IN IRAQ?

Just such a propaganda campaign was in progress prior to the invasion of Iraq in March 2003, President Bush told Americans that Saddam Hussein was preparing weapons of mass destruction that demanded a preemptive strike. There was little mention of other nations who also have weapons of mass destruction, such as India, Pakistan, France, Israel, Russia and China. At the time, India and Pakistan seem frighteningly determined to use theirs. Nor was there any mention of traditional terrorist groups like the Irish Republican Army, the Shining Path, Hamas, Islamic Jihad or others.

In fact, it was later announced that the Bush administration had been informed as early as October 3, 2002, that North Korea, a military power more than twice the size of Iraq, had developed nuclear capability as well as even "more powerful" chemical or biological weapons. Yet no mention of this "Axis of Evil" nation was made during the remainder of the month when Bush sought and won a congressional resolution approving an attack on Iraq. Democrats, especially in the Senate, fumed because Bush officials kept them in the dark about North Korea's plans just as they were deliberating the Iraqi resolution. Ordinary Americans snickered that, of course, North Korea has no oil to covet.

Also missing amongst the press coverage of North Korean's nuclear development plans was the fact that the funds needed to produce weapons-grade plutonium in their nuclear reactors came from US taxpayers, approved by President Bush in the spring of 2002.

In early April, Bush released about $94 million to North Korea as part of the 1994 Agreed Framework agreement to replace older nuclear reactors despite suspicions that their nuclear project was being used to produce weapons (North Korea had refused to allow UN inspections). According to BBC News, Bush argued that his decision was "vital to the national security interests of the United States." About that same time, Bush argued that it was equally vital to attack Iraq.

Prominently missing from the crescendo of corporate mass media pieces on the need to move into Iraq were the names and arguments of many prominent persons who counseled caution. Eighteen former high-ranking US military leaders, intelligence analysts, diplomats and academics in early 2002 sent President Bush a letter urging him to "resist military actions against Iraq and focus on capturing the terrorists responsible for the September 11 attacks."

Among those who signed the letter were retired navy admiral Eugene Carroll, former CIA national intelligence officer William Christison, former chief of mission to Iraq Ed Peck, former ambassador to Saudi Arabia James Atkins, and former senator George McGovern.

The story of this letter was featured in China's official news agency Xinhau but received little attention at home.

Democratic Senator Robert Byrd of West Virginia claimed Bush's effort to start a war with Iraq was nothing more than a conscious effort to distract public attention from domestic problems. "This administration, all of a sudden, wants to go to war with Iraq," Byrd said. "The polls are dropping, the domestic situation has problems. All of a sudden we have this war talk, war fervor, the bugles of war, drums of war, clouds of war. Don't tell me that things suddenly went wrong." Byrd said his allegiance to the Constitution prevented him from voting for Bush's war resolution. "But I am finding that the Constitution is irrelevant to people of this administration."

According to former counterterrorism chief, Richard A. Clarke, Bush wanted to connect Iraq and 9/11. "Invading Iraq for 9/11 is like China attacking us and we invade Mexico," said Clarke. In a 2004 online *Newshour* interview with Margaret Warner, Clarke stated, "It would have been irresponsible for the president not to come in and say, 'Dick, I don't want you to assume it was al Qaeda. I'd like you to look at every possibility, and I'd like you to look at every possibility to see if maybe it was al Qaeda with somebody else,' in a very calm way, with all possibilities open. That's not what happened. What happened was the president, with his finger in my face, saying, 'Iraq, a memo on Iraq and al Qaeda, a memo on Iraq and the attacks.' Very vigorous, very intimidating, and in a way that left all of us with the same impression, that he wanted that answer. Well, we couldn't give him that answer because it wasn't true."

It was soon discovered that the decision for war against Iraq also had come prior to the 9/11 attacks, with which there was no evidence indicating Iraqi involvement.

According to the August 30, 2002 edition of *WorldTribune.com*, Israeli military sources reported that a visiting American general, whose name was not disclosed, had told them in mid-August that Washington authorities intended to strike Iraq and remove Saddam Hussein, perhaps as early as November 2002. Yuval Steinetz, chairman of the Israeli Knesset's subcommittee on military doctrine, spoke of talks with American officials in mid-June 2002 concerning a new order in a post-Saddam Middle East.

Once the 9/11 attacks occurred, such pre-planning moved rapidly. According to CBS Correspondent David Martin, notes taken by aides just five hours after the attacks show Secretary of Defense Rumsfeld ordered up plans for a strike against Iraq. According to notes made at the time, Rumsfeld ordered, "Go massive; sweep it all up; destroy it all. Things related and not, it doesn't matter."

By mid-2002, the push for war against Iraq continued to increase within the Bush administration despite lack of any real proof that Saddam represented a threat to the United States. In fact, much of the proof that was presented later proved dubious at best.

For example, on September 7, 2002, President Bush was trying to summon support for an attack on Iraq. In a news conference with British Prime Minister Tony Blair, Bush announced, "I would remind you that when the inspectors first went into Iraq and were denied access, a report came out of the IAEA [International Atomic Energy Agency] that they were six months away from developing a weapon; I don't know what more evidence we need."

However, Mark Gwozdecky, chief spokesman for the IAEA, stated days later, "There's never been a report like that issued from this agency. We have never put a time frame on how long it might take Iraq to construct a nuclear weapon." Bush and Blair also cited an IAEA report claiming satellite photography had revealed that the Iraqis were starting construction at several nuclear-related sites. Again, the IAEA, the agency charged with assessing Iraq's nuclear capability for the UN, denied any such report.

When asked about the contradictions White House Deputy Press Secretary Scott McClellan said, "He's [Bush] referring to 1991 there. In '91, there was a report saying that after the war they found out they were about six months away." 1991? Much more time than six months had passed between 1991 and late 2002.

Gwozdecky, speaking from IAEA headquarters in Vienna, said there was no such report issued in 1991 either. In fact, in an October 1998 report to the UN secretary-general, IAEA director-general Mohamed Elbaradei stated, "There are no indications that there remain in Iraq any physical capability for the production of weapon-usable nuclear material of any practical significance."

Gwozdecky told one reporter, "There is no evidence in our view that can be substantiated on Iraq's nuclear weapons program. If anybody tells you they know the nuclear situation in Iraq right now, in the absence of four years of inspections, I would say they're misleading you because there isn't solid evidence out there."

The chief UN weapons inspector confirmed Hans Blix in April 2003 that plans to attack Iraq were longstanding and had little to do with weapons of mass destruction. "There is evidence that this war was planned well in advance," Blix stated in an interview with the Spanish daily *El Pais*. Blix said that despite assurances from President Bush in late 2002 that he supported the UN's efforts to determine if Iraq had any biological, chemical or nuclear weapons, "I now believe that finding weapons of mass destruction has been relegated, I would say, to fourth place...Today, the main aim is to change the dictatorial regime of Saddam Hussein."

America's own weapons inspector, Scott Ritter, a member of the United Nations Special Commission (UNSCOM) created just after the Gulf War to locate and eliminate Saddam Hussein's secret weapons caches, resigned in August of 1998 and accused the US government of using the commission to justify an attack on Iraq. Ritter said before his resignation that he had initially disbelieved Baghdad's minister of defense when he told him the UNSCOM team was being used to "provoke a crisis." But now, though slowly, he had come to agree with the charge. Ritter's superiors scoffed at the allegation, claiming Ritter's knowledge of the situation was "limited."

However, in early 1999 it was reported that Washington had used UNSCOM to plant electronic bugs in the Iraq's Ministry of Defense. Other US officials confirmed many of Ritter's accusations.

"The relationship between the United States and the inspection commission ... has long been a subject of debate," wrote *U.S. News & World Report*'s Bruce B. Auster. "The issue is sensitive because UNSCOM is an arm of the UN Security Council, not an agency of the United States, although it does rely on the United States for intelligence and personnel."

On February 5, 2003, Secretary of State Colin Powell stood before the

United Nations and presented a scathing indictment of Iraq's transgressions and called for a coalition to oust the regime of Saddam Hussein. "My colleagues, every statement I make today is backed up by sources, solid sources. These are not assertions. What we're giving you are facts and conclusions based on solid intelligence," Powell told his audience.

It was later learned and widely reported in Europe that Powell's presentation was based on a British government dossier which had plagiarized the work of a California graduate student named Ibrahim al-Marashi. Large portions of al-Marashi's essay had been taken by British intelligence and, in some cases, altered in a manner damaging to Iraq. The essay had been published in September 2002 in a small journal entitled the *Middle East Review of International Affairs*.

If this wasn't problem enough to the hawks pushing for war in Iraq, Powell also produced for the UN a satellite photo of a northern Iraqi installation said to be producing chemical weapons for both Saddam Hussein and the al Qaeda network. Some days later when news reporters actually toured the camp they found nothing but a bunch of dilapidated huts with no indoor plumbing or the electrical capability to produce such weapons.

But the most amazing evidence of official duplicity came with media reports concerning a meeting in the Waldorf Astoria between Powell and British Foreign Secretary Jack Straw just prior to his rousing speech at the UN. Powell complained that the claims coming out of the Pentagon—particularly those made by Deputy Secretary Wolfowitz—could not be substantiated. Faced with the possibility that the evidence for WMD in Iraq might "explode in their faces," Powell reportedly tossed briefing documents into the air and cried, "I'm not reading this. This is bullshit!"

Despite all this, Powell went ahead with his speech and the corporate-controlled mass media did their job of dutifully supporting his assertions. Even his own staff was apparently taken in by the "evidence" put before them. US Army Colonel (Retired) Lawrence B. Wilkerson served as the Department of State's chief of staff from August 2002 to January 2005. He also served as special assistant to General Colin Powell when Powell was chairman of the US Joint Chiefs of Staff.

In a February 2006, interview with PBS host David Brancaccio, Wilkerson said that despite the fact that both the Intelligence Bureau and the State Department concluded there was no active nuclear program in Iraq,

"...neither of those dissents in any fashion or form were registered with me [or others]...In fact it was presented in the firmest language possible that the mobile biological labs and the sketches we had drawn of them for the secretary's presentation were based on the iron clad evidence of multiple sources...

"My participation in that presentation at the UN constitutes the lowest point in my professional life. I participated in a hoax on the American people, the international community and the United Nations Security Council. How do you think that makes me feel?"

Host Brancaccio suggested that senior government officials also might not have known the truth. "I have to believe that. Otherwise I have to believe some rather nefarious things about some fairly highly placed people in the intelligence community and perhaps elsewhere," responded Wilkerson.

Unaware of Powell's doubts and concerns, the American public only heard comments such as these from corporate media commentators and pundits: "an accumulation of painstakingly gathered and analyzed evidence," so that "only the most gullible and wishful thinking souls can now deny that Iraq is harboring and hiding weapons of mass destruction," "a massive array of evidence," "a detailed and persuasive case," "a powerful case," "an overwhelming case," "a compelling case," "the strong, credible and persuasive case," "a persuasive, detailed accumulation of information," "a smoking fusillade...a persuasive case for anyone who is still persuadable," "The skeptics asked for proof; they now have it," "Powell's evidence overwhelming," "ironclad...incontrovertible," "succinct and damning...the case is closed," "If there was any doubt that Hussein...needs to be...stripped of his chemical and biological capabilities, Powell put it to rest."

Such problems with the rationales given for war prompted one Democratic Congressman to state that President Bush would lie to provoke war with Iraq. Jim McDermott of Washington State in an ABC interview pointed out that in fall 2002, the Iraqis had pledged to allow unrestricted inspections within their country. "They should be given a chance," said McDermott, who voted against war with Iraq in 1991, "otherwise we're trying to provoke them into war." Following a visit to Iraq, McDermott said he believed Bush "would mislead the American people" to go to war with Iraq.

## WAG THE DOG IN IRAQ?

Another congressman on the visit to Baghdad, Michigan Democrat David Bonior, said a renewed war with Iraq would bring further suffering to the Iraqi people, especially children suffering from cancers caused by the US use of depleted uranium shells, which he described as "horrific and barbaric."

Apparently lacking the spirit of American freedom of speech, Republican Senate Minority Leader Trent Lott referred to McDermott saying, "He needs to come home and keep his mouth shut."

Even former president Clinton weighed in by urging the Bush administration to finish the job with Osama bin Laden before taking on Iraq. Speaking at a Democratic Party fund-raiser in early September 2002, Clinton undoubtedly spoke for millions of Americans when he said, "Saddam Hussein didn't kill 3,100 people on September 11. Bin Laden did, and as far as we know he's still alive. I also believe we might do more good for American security in the short run at far less cost by beefing up our efforts in Afghanistan, Pakistan and elsewhere to flush out the entire network."

One pivotal Democrat who spoke out against war with Iraq was Minnesota Senator Paul Wellstone, who also was one of the few congressmen calling for an independent investigation of the 9/11 attacks. Wellstone, who according to supporters worked for the benefit of all his constituents including workers, unionists and the needy, in late October 2002 was in a tough political fight against a Republican challenger backed by both GOP money and the Bush White House. Wellstone's seat could have tipped the entire Senate into the Republican camp, giving Bush a majority in Congress.

But the question of whether Wellstone might have won his battle will never be answered. He, his wife and daughter, three staffers and two pilots were killed in a private plane crash on October 25, 2002. It was reminiscent of the many plane crashes that have taken so many members of Congress, especially during the Reagan administration. In fact, well into 2010, disturbing questions were still being raised about the cause of Wellstone's fatal crash.

Texas Representative Ron Paul even noted that his challenge to the constitutionality of a war with Iraq was blocked on live TV and prompted the chairman of one congressional committee to openly declare that the US Constitution is no longer relevant. In a late 2002 newsletter to his constituents, Paul wrote that during hearings on the Iraqi war resolution before the International Relations Committee being televised live by C-SPAN, he tried to bring up the issue that declaring war was a power granted only to Congress by the Constitution, but the ranking minority member called his attempt to add an amendment declaring war "frivolous and mischievous." "The proposed resolution on the use of force mentioned the United Nations twenty-five times. That was considered safe. Not once did it mention the Constitution. I do not look to the UN to find the authority for this sovereign nation to defend herself," stated Paul. "It was almost noon on October 3, the second day of the hearings, when my turn came [after offering his war amendment] I reminded the committee of the words of James Madison, who in 1798 said, 'The Constitution supposes what the history of all governments demonstrates, that the Executive is the branch of power most interested in war and most prone to it. It has accordingly, with studied care, vested the question of war in the legislature.' The Chair[man, Illinois Republican Henry J. Hyde] went on to say that the Constitution has been 'overtaken by events, time' and is 'no longer relevant.' At least it was out in the open. Now surely the display of such disdain for their oath to 'support and defend the Constitution' would light up Capitol Hill switchboards with angry callers!

"Little did I know that no one watching the hearings over C-SPAN not one single person of what statistically is an audience of several million Americans even heard those inflammatory comments. When my staff called C-SPAN to get a copy of the video record to document these outrageous statements, we were told 'technical difficulties' prevented that portion of the proceedings from being recorded and that same portion of the proceedings was also the only part missing on the internal record the House makes of such official hearings. It was as though it never happened."

One Democrat who dared to simply raise questions about the War on Terrorism lost her seat in Congress. Representative Cynthia McKinney represented the 4th District of Georgia, which includes Decatur, just outside Atlanta. This was the district that sent Newt Gingrich to Washington. McKinney had three strikes against her in this Dixie district: she was a woman, black and a Democrat. The forty-seven-year-old former college professor was also quite outspoken.

At a peace rally in Washington on April 20, 2002, Rep. McKinney told the crowd, "despite our differences, we are here today as one community with one thing in common: a desire to see the restoration of the true ideals of America. America—where the fundamental rights to vote, speak and practice religion mean something. But America today is still a far cry from the noble republic founded upon these words: All men are created equal." She then declared, "Sadly, nor is ours a democratic society. In November 2000, the Republicans stole from America our most precious right of all: the right to free and fair elections.

"Florida Governor Jeb Bush and his secretary of state, Katherine Harris, created a phony list of convicted felons, 57,700 to be exact, to 'scrub' thousands of innocent people from the state's voter rolls. Of the thousands who ultimately lost their vote through this scrub of voters, 80 percent were African-Americans, mostly Democratic Party voters. Had they voted, the course of history would have changed. Instead, however, Harris declared Bush the victor by only 537 votes. It might be noteworthy that within two months of the 2000 election, according to *U.S. News & World Report*, Harris was inducted into the Council on Foreign Relations.

"Now President Bush occupies the White House, but with questionable legitimacy. But, however he got there, his administration is now free to spend one to four billion dollars a month on the wars in Afghanistan and Iraq; free to cut the high deployment overtime pay of our young service men and women fighting in that war; free to propose drilling in the Arctic National Wildlife Reserve National Park; free to stonewall on the Enron and Energy Task Force investigations; free to revoke the rules that keep our drinking water free of arsenic; free to get caught in Venezuela and free to propose laws that deny our citizens sacred freedoms cherished under the Constitution.

McKinney concluded her remarks with this admonition, "We must dare to remember all of this. We must dare to debate and challenge all of this." Some time later, McKinney drew the ire of Washington insiders when she dared to suggest that Bush administration officials may have ignored warnings of the terrorist attack to further their political agenda and that they and their cronies were profiting from the War on Terrorism. The war-for-profit argument has much objective data to support it, as will be seen later. McKinney certainly spoke for many when she said that the Bush administration has created a climate in which elected officials must censor themselves or be branded as less than patriotic.

McKinney also suggested that the War on Terrorism has benefited the Washington based Carlyle Group investment firm, which employs a number of former high-ranking government officials, including former President George H. W. Bush.

A Carlyle Group spokesman, while not addressing McKinney's facts, nevertheless asked, "Did she say these things while standing on a grassy knoll in Roswell, New Mexico?" It was truly ironic that such dismissive tactics should come at a time when a growing number of persons believe there is compelling evidence that there was a conspiracy to kill President Kennedy, and have a willingness to consider that there may be substance to the claims of a UFO crash near Roswell in 1947.

Typical of the attacks against McKinney to be found in the mainstream corporate media were the remarks of *Orlando Sentinel* columnist Kathleen Parker, who described the congresswoman as "a delusional paranoiac" and called for an investigation of the woman "as passionately as she demands we investigate Bush's 'involvement' in the 9/11 terror attacks." Parker added, "We no longer can afford to tolerate people like McKinney, who should never be taken seriously."

In the face of such mass media diatribes, not to mention that Georgia allows cross-over voting, McKinney was defeated in the 2002 Democratic Primary but rallied by regaining her congressional seat in the 2004 election.

In May 2002, McKinney retorted, "Several weeks ago, I called for a congressional investigation into what warnings the Bush administration received before the terrorist attacks of September 11, 2001. I was derided by the White House, right-wing talk radio, and spokespersons for the military-industrial complex, as a conspiracy theorist.

Even my patriotism was questioned because I dared to suggest that Congress should conduct a full and complete investigation into the most disastrous intelligence failure in American history...Today's revelations that the administration, and President Bush, were given months of notice that a terrorist attack was a distinct possibility, points out the critical need for a full and complete congressional investigation. It now becomes clear why the Bush administration has been vigorously opposing congressional hearings. The Bush administration has been engaged in a conspiracy of silence."

## WAG THE DOG IN IRAQ?

She went on to conduct crucial congressional hearings concerning the possibility of administration complicity in 9/11 in the summer of 2005 and early 2006.

Columnist Parker's attack was echoed throughout the mass media, which called attention to the fact that McKinney had accepted, long before 9/11, campaign contributions from Abdurrahman Alamoudi, founder of the American Muslim Council, and a man who has voiced support for terrorist organizations such as Hamas and Hezbollah.

Naturally, no one in the mainstream media called attention to the fact that the Bush administration blocked a number of investigations into their connections with terrorist groups or that the Bush family has been longtime friends with the Saudi royalty.

For example, about a week after McKinney's primary defeat, President Bush telephoned Saudi crown prince Abdullah and praised "eternal friendship" between the United States and Saudi Arabia. The president then retired to his Crawford, Texas, ranch for some private time with Saudi ambassador Prince Bandar bin Sultan and his family. The visit was styled as a family trip and a casual get-together. No cameras were allowed and neither Bush nor his royal guest would agree to be interviewed.

Also the media failed to mention that, according to British publications, the Republican Party had been receiving sizeable contributions from the Arabic Safa trust, which at the same time was funneling money to terrorist groups.

All of this came about shortly after a Rand Corporation analyst briefed a Pentagon advisory panel, stating, "The Saudis are active at every level of the terror chain, from planners to financiers, from cadre to foot soldier, from ideologist to cheerleader. Saudi Arabia supports our enemies and attacks our allies."

It must be noted that no one disputes the fact that fifteen of the nineteen 9/11 hijackers named by the FBI were Saudis and that six hundred families of 9/11 victims of the attacks filed a trillion-dollar lawsuit against Saudi officials, including members of the royal family, contending complicity in the terror attacks.

It is also interesting to note that some media lose enthusiasm for polling when the outcome deviated from the desired results. For example, in 2002 the *Atlanta Journal-Constitution* placed a poll on its Web site asking,

"Are you satisfied the Bush administration had no warning of the September 11 attacks?"

Visitors could vote "Yes," "No, I think officials knew it was coming" or "Not sure." The vote seesawed back and forth for one day. When the final count of 23,145 voters showed 52 percent for "Yes," 46 percent "No" and only 1 percent "Not sure," the poll was suddenly pulled with no real explanation.

Even more odd was the lack of mass media attention given to a Zogby International poll conducted between August 24 and 26, 2004, on the eve of the Republican National Convention.

The poll showed that one half of New York City residents (49.3 percent) and 41 percent of New York state residents believed that some national leaders "knew in advance that attacks were planned on or around September 11, 2001, and that they consciously failed to act."

Despite the political implications of such an accusation, nearly 30 percent of registered Republicans and more than 38% of those who described themselves as "very conservative" supported this proposition.

The Bush administration continued its push for war with Iraq despite such polls and massive, though under-reported, anti-war demonstrations in American cities.

What were considered controversial concerns over the pretext for war against Iraq in 2002 became solidified in May 2005, with the public release of a "secret" memo in the United Kingdom.

What came to be known as the "Downing Street Memo" was a report written by British National Security Aide Matthew Rycroft of a July 2002, meeting between British Prime Minister Tony Blair and advisers, including Richard Dearlove, head of the MI6 intelligence service, who had just returned to England from Washington after a briefing on Iraq by Bush administration officials.

The contents of the memo caused a considerable stir in Europe but were largely unreported by the US mass media.

The memo fully supported accusations that Bush—contrary to his public statements—had not taken seriously any course of action but military. Further, it revealed that the intelligence on Weapons of Mass Destruction (WMD) was known to be flimsy and that Bush and Blair had no clear exit strategy. It stated, "...There was a perceptible shift in [the administration's] attitude [toward Iraq]. Military action is now seen as inevitable. Bush wanted to remove Saddam, through military action, justified by the conjunction of terrorism and WMD. But the intelligence and facts were being fixed around the policy. The NSC [National Security Council] had no patience with the UN route and no enthusiasm for publishing material on the Iraqi regime's record. There was little discussion in Washington of the aftermath after military action."

Farther down in the document, it added, "It seemed clear that Bush had made up his mind to take military action, even if the timing was not yet decided. But the case was thin. Saddam was not threatening his neighbors, and his WMD capability was less than that of Libya, North Korea or Iran."

The crucial passage in this memo, of course, was that Bush had "fixed" the intelligence around his policy. Yet, this admission by America's strongest ally did not seem to faze either the US corporate mass media or the ill-informed American public.

Hearst newspaper columnist Helen Thomas lamented the lack of public response, writing, "I am not surprised at the duplicity. But I am astonished at the acceptance of this deception by voters in the United States and the United Kingdom. I've seen two US presidents go down the drain—Lyndon B. Johnson on Vietnam and Richard Nixon in the Watergate scandal—because they were no longer believed. But times change—and I guess our values do, too."

Other commentators politicized the implication of the memo by blaming Bush's enemies and by tossing its contents off as unworthy of serious debate. *Christian Science Monitor* columnist Bud Beck wrote, "This is not the Watergate burglary and it is not a fabricated Gulf of Tonkin incident. It is nothing new, just a new version of something that is old—so old it has become all but too boring."

But by 2006, the deceitful ramp-up to the Iraqi invasion gained further confirmation, again from a once-secret British document.

Philippe Sands, a professor of international law at University College in London, made public a memo regarding a January 31, 2003 meeting between Bush and Blair in which Blair gave assurance he was "solidly" behind plans to attack Iraq. This was despite any second UN resolution and before Blair sought advice on the invasion's legality.

In this memo, there was even the mention of the bizarre possibility that Bush was contemplating a provocation to tempt Saddam into firing on United Nations' aircraft. According to the memo, Bush was so concerned about the failure to find any hard evidence against Saddam, he considered "flying U2 reconnaissance aircraft planes with fighter cover over Iraq, painted in UN colors" hoping that "[i]f Saddam fired on them, he would be in breach [of UN resolutions]."

It should be noted that the two British memos have been acknowledged as genuine by the British government, but White House spokesman Scott McClellan, true to form, denied the interpretation of the Downing Street Memo brandished by Bush critics.

Despite such ongoing controversy over the deceptive plan to go to war with Iraq—including peace demonstrations rivaling those during the Vietnam era—a cowed and compliant Congress had long before opted out. In the wake of the wave of fear generated by 9/11, it had voted overwhelmingly in October 2002 to authorize Bush to launch his war whenever he desired. Once again the ugliest side of politics revealed itself: The politicians in Congress knew that if Bush's action in Iraq proved successful, they could share the credit and glory come the next elections; but if it proved to be an unwise decision, they could shift the blame to the president. So, an affirmative vote was much safer than to stand among the courageous few for the sake of honesty and integrity.

The irony of Bush urging war with Iraq because of Saddam Hussein's actions was not lost on commentators in other parts of the world. "There is something almost comical about the prospect of George Bush waging war on another nation because that nation has defied international law," wrote George Monbiot of London's *Guardian*. "Since Bush came to office, the United States government has torn up more international treaties and disregarded more UN conventions than the rest of the world has in twenty years."

The deceit, dissembling and outright lies in regards to Iraq continued well into the Obama administration. On April 19, 2010, Vice President Joseph Biden announced the deaths at the hands of American and Iraqi security forces of two reported top al Qaeda leaders, Abu Ayyub al-Masri and Abu Omar al-Baghdadi. "Their deaths are potentially devastating blows to Al Qaeda Iraq," Biden told the media, adding, "But equally important in my view is this action demonstrates the improved security strength and capacity of Iraqi security forces." According to General Ray Odierno, top commander of US troops in Iraq, "The deaths of these terrorists is potentially the most significant blow to al-Qaeda in Iraq since the beginning of the insurgency." Annoucnement of the deaths came from Iraqi Prime Minister Nouri al-Maliki, who according to the *Washington Post* gained "additional political leverage at a crucial time."

The only problem with this seemingly good news from the frontlines of the War on Terrorism was that both Abu Ayyub al-Masri and Abu Omar al-Baghdadi had been reported killed several times in the past. Furthermore, in 2007, US Brigadier General Kevin Bergner told the media that Abu Omar al-Baghdadi, proclaimed as the leader of the al Qaeda arm called the Islamic State of Iraq, did not exit. Bergner said Baghdadi was a fictitious person according to Khalid al-Mashadani, who claimed to be an intermediary to Osama bin Laden. Mashadani was captured in July 2007. US military officials in Iraq continued to have problems in trying to explain the link between al Qaeda in Iraq and bin Laden's reported global network. Interestingly enough, the man who reportedly created the character of Baghdadi was none other than Abu Ayub al Masri, one of those reported killed in 2010. However, Iraqi police officials had previously reported that Masri was killed in 2007 when his explosives belt detonated during fighting with security forces.

A year earlier, in April 2009, Baghdad's security spokesman, Major Genernal Qasim Atta had announced that Abu Omar al-Baghdadi had been arrested and jailed. In 2007 the capture of Baghdadi, followed by a retraction, was provided to the media three times. According to James Hider of the UK *Times*, "Iraqi security forces have reported al-Baghdadi's death and capture on several different occasions in the past, as well as claiming to have captured the man believed to be al-Qaeda's overall leader in the country, Abu Ayyub al-Masri. Some intelligence sources have denied that either man even exists, claiming that they are fronts either to throw the security forces off the scent or, in the case of al-Baghdadi, to give the terrorist network an Iraqi face."

This ever-changing scenario hopefully came to an end with Baghdadi's most recent announced death, as US authorities said DNA tests confirmed the kill. But skeptics weren't so sure. Steve Watson, writing on *PrisonPlanet.com*, wrote, "Presumably the ridiculous loose ends of this soap opera will now be tied off and memory holed—although we cannot put it past al Masri and his imaginary friend to rise from the grave one more time a year down the line, particularly given that the Baghdadi character keeps being resurrected and acknowledged by the Iraqi government, the US military and the mainstream media. This saga is another example of how a manufactured smoke and mirrors propaganda veils reality. The 'War on Terror' mantra continues to be propagated as justification to wage permanent occupation and control over the Middle East by the global elite."

As such confusion amid the continuing occupation of Iraq added to mounting losses proved a drain on public morale. A worldwide poll showed most respondents did not believe themselves any safer from terrorism. The BBC World Service in early 2006 reported that the majority of those polled believed the war in Iraq has increased rather than diminished the chances of terrorist attacks.

This survey of 41,856 people in 35 countries found about 60 percent of those polled shared this view. Only 12 percent thought the war had reduced the chances of an attack, with 15 percent saying it had no effect either way. In Britain, 77 percent of those questioned thought the terrorist threat had risen since the 2003 invasion.

"Though the Bush administration has framed the intervention in Iraq as a means of fighting terrorism, all around the world most people view it as having increased the likelihood of terrorist attacks." said Steven Kull, director of the Program on International Policy Attitudes at the University of Maryland, which helped conduct the survey between October 2005 and January 2006.

Even more disconcerting were the results of a poll of US troops in Iraq in early 2006. This poll, conducted by Zogby International and Le Moyne College, showed 72 percent of respondents said they should withdraw from Iraq within 12 months. A surprising 29 percent said there should be an immediate pull-out. Only 23 percent said US troops should remain in Iraq "as long as they are needed."

The president of Zogby International, John Zogby, said US commanders in Iraq unofficially approved the poll of 944 respondents, which was conducted before the escalation in violence in February 2006.

WAG THE DOG IN IRAQ?

Showing that military personnel are not immune to misconceptions, the poll of service personnel indicated 85 percent of the troops agreed that the US mission in Iraq was "to retaliate for Saddam's role in the 9/11 attacks," even though President Bush has publicly acknowledged that Iraq played no role in the attacks. John Zogby described this notion as "bewildering."

The disillusionment of American service personnel was reflected in a CBS News poll conducted in late February 2006, which show less than 30 percent of respondents approved of Bush's handling of the war.

Despite such negative public opinions and the questionable intelligence leading to the US invasion, there were still large profits to be made in Iraq. Vice President Dick Cheney, already under attack for his involvement in profiting from doing business in Iraq despite US sanctions in place since the Gulf War, was pinpointed as one whose business interests profited from the 9/11 attacks. For example, approximately $20 billion for supplying the US military with food, fuel and housing has been paid to KBR, a division of Haliburton where Cheney served as CEO from 1995 to 2000.

But the cost of doing such business is high. As of February 2010—despite the fact that most other nations had already withdrawn their troops from Iraq—more than 65,000 US soldiers remained. These troops were outnumbered by US private contractors, which numbered more than 180,000. Total US military casualties had reached 4,416 dead and 31,897 wounded. This number did not include the psychologically damaged.

Then there is the estimated $9 billion of US taxpayer money that has gone missing in Iraq not to mention some $550 million in spare parts and equipment shipped to US contractors there.

By 2010, the cost of occupying Iraq was estimated at more than $12 billion a month or, about $5,000 every second. Nobel Prize-winning economist Professor Joseph Stiglitz estimated that the total costs, including the long-term costs, will amount to about $25 billion a month. *New York Times* editorialist Nicholas D. Kristof explained, "Granted, the cost estimates are squishy and controversial, partly because the $12.5 billion a month that we're now paying for Iraq is only a down payment. We'll still be making disability payments to Iraq war veterans 50 years from now."

"A congressional study by the Joint Economic Committee found that the sums spent on the Iraq War each day could enroll an additional

58,000 children in Head Start or give Pell Grants to 153,000 students to attend college. Or if we're certain we want to invest in national security, then a day's Iraq spending would finance another 11,000 border patrol agents or 9,000 police officers. Imagine the possibilities," opined Kristof. "We could hire more police and border patrol agents, expand Head Start and rehabilitate America's image in the world by underwriting a global drive to slash maternal mortality, eradicate malaria and deworm every child in Africa. All that would consume less than one month's spending on the Iraq War."

## CHENEY'S DEALINGS IN IRAQ

"Under the guidance of Richard Cheney, a get-the-government-out-of-my-face conservative, Halliburton Company over the past five years [1995 to 2000] emerged as a corporate welfare hog, benefiting from at least $3.8 billion in federal contracts and taxpayer-insured loans," stated a 2000 report by the Washington-based Center for Public Integrity.

And it was Cheney who led the effort to wage war on Iraq and Afghanistan. "But Cheney isn't just selling the policy. He is on the inside making it," noted Kenneth T. Walsh of *U.S. News & World Report*. "In fact, to understand the Bush presidency, it is necessary to understand how central Cheney's role actually is and how his innate conservatism is an anchor for administration policy not just on Iraq but across the board."

In 1991, the elder President Bush awarded Cheney the Presidential Medal of Freedom. Cheney, age sixty-one in 2002, was an important choice for Bush Jr. in the election year of 2000. Ironically, it was Cheney who had promised the nation "light at the end of the tunnel" in Vietnam during his stint with the Nixon administration. He was a crucial part of the defense policy team around Rumsfeld, Wolfowitz, and other up-and-coming neo-conservatives who succeeded in exaggerating the Soviet threat of WMDs during the Ford and Reagan administrations; these efforts led to the greatest peace-time military buildup in American history, and to a nuclear confrontation with USSR in the mid-1980s. Cheney had also staunchly supported such questionable covert operations as the Contra war in Nicaragua and the CIA-led war in Afghanistan during his congressional service under the Reagan administration. And he had overseen the 1989 invasion of Panama, with its egregious loss of civilian life, and the massive destruction of Saddam Hussein's war machine while serving as secretary of defense during the Gulf War under the previous Bush administration. He then helped push through onerous trade sanctions against Iraq through the United Nations that impoverished the country.

Following the defeat of Bush Sr. in 1992 Cheney entered the world of corporate business and by 1995 became president and chief executive officer of the Halliburton Company of Dallas. Halliburton is the world's largest oil service firm and, according to *Oil & Gas Journal*, the company ranks twenty-fourth in the top energy corporations in the world, with a market value of $18.2 billion. The company employs about 100,000 people in 120 countries.

Cheney's firm soon began to lay down a record of questionable ethics—and through a subsidiary, gained a lion's share of the $30 billion emergency funds appropriated in 2001 by Congress in the War on Terrorism. "From building cells for detainees at Guantanamo Bay in Cuba to feeding American troops in Uzbekistan, the Pentagon is increasingly relying on a unit of Halliburton called KBR, sometimes referred to as Kellogg, Brown & Root," reported Jeff Gerth and Don Van Natta Jr. of the *New York Times*. "Although the unit has been building projects all over the world for the federal government for decades, the attacks of September 11 have led to significant additional business. KBR is the exclusive logistics supplier for both the Navy and the Army, providing services like cooking, construction, power generation and fuel transportation. The contract recently won from the Army is for 10 years and has no lid on costs, the only logistical arrangement by the Army without an estimated cost."

As detailed in *Crossfire: The Plot That Killed Kennedy*, George and Herman Brown, who created the construction firm back in the late 1930s, are credited with putting Lyndon B. Johnson in Congress and have benefited from prime government contracts ever since, beginning with a large naval base in Corpus Christi, Texas, and later in South Vietnam. After merging with Halliburton, the company provided logistical support for the Pentagon in Haiti, Somalia, the Balkans and more recently, in Afghanistan and Iraq.

Halliburton officials denied that Cheney played any role in assisting KBR in obtaining government contracts but did admit that the senior vice president responsible for the lucrative KBR contracts, former four-star navy admiral Joe Lopez, was hired in 1999 on the recommendation of Cheney.

There have been a number of other accusations made against Halliburton during Cheney's stint as CEO. According to the Environmental Rights Action (ERA) group, Halliburton ordered Nigerian Mobile Police officers to shoot youthful demonstrators protesting what they perceived as environmental damage caused by Chevron Oil, which had contracted for Halliburton's services. One youth, Gidikumo Sule, was killed, and others claimed to have been beaten. The oil companies countered this charge by claiming the youth was killed during an attempt to rescue officers who had been detained and disarmed by the youths.

It should come as no surprise that environmental groups have long been upset with Halliburton in general and Cheney in particular. Among other actions in his career unfriendly to environmental concerns, Cheney has co-sponsored legislation to open the Arctic Wildlife Refuge in Alaska to oil drilling and supported it while in the White House. He had even voted against the Clean Water Act while serving as a representative from Wyoming. And Halliburton's environmental record was deplorable under Cheney's tenure. Its Duncan, Oklahoma, facility was identified by the Environmental Protection Agency in 1997 as one of the top 20 percent of polluting companies in the nation.

Aspersions have also made about the fact that Halliburton joined Bush's now-defunct Harken Energy in maintaining offshore subsidiaries in the Cayman Islands, the favorite site for tax dodgers, such as Enron, which had 692 subsidiaries of its own there.

Under Cheney's leadership, Halliburton's subsidiaries in tax havens grew from nine in 1995 to forty-four in 1999. This coincided with a drop in Halliburton's federal taxes from $302 million in 1998 to an $85 million tax refund in 1999. But the deepest criticism of Cheney came from his company's dealings in Iraq and his role in the Enron scandal.

In 1998, the UN passed a resolution permitting Iraq to purchase material to repair and maintain its oil industry, which had become dilapidated following the country's defeat in the Gulf War. Immediately, US companies, including Halliburton, Baker Hughes, Schlumberger, Flowserve, Fisher-Rosemount and others, moved surreptitiously to get a part of this lucrative business.

These firms used European subsidies to front for multimillion-dollar business deals. "It is a wonderful example of how ludicrous sanctions have become," noted Raad Alkadiri, an analyst for Petroleum Finance Company, a Washington consulting firm.

Furthermore, Halliburton brought in substantial business in other markets by hiding behind other business entities. Reporter Carola Hoyos noted, "From September 1998, until it sold its stake last February [2000], Halliburton owned fifty-one percent of Dresser-Rand. It also owned forty-nine percent of Ingersoll-Dresser Pump, until its sale in December 1999. During the time of the joint ventures, Dresser-Rand and Ingersoll-Dresser Pump submitted more than $23.8 million worth of contracts for the sale of oil industry parts and equipment to Iraq. Their combined total amounted to more than any other US company; the vast majority was approved by the sanctions committee."

Cheney also came under fire for Enron-like accounting practices. According to Judicial Watch, which in 2002 filed a lawsuit in Dallas, Texas, against Cheney on behalf of Halliburton shareholders, he artificially boosted the share price of Halliburton stock while he was CEO. The suit charges that Cheney overstated profits by $445 million between 1999 and 2001, resulting in "huge losses" for some investors.

In early 2002, Cheney was considered as the object of an unprecedented lawsuit by the General Accounting Office for his failure to give congressional investigators documents relating to the formulation of energy plans by the energy task force he once headed. Cheney claimed the GAO did not have the authority to demand the information, despite the fact that the Bush administration task force was funded by public money. The task force's energy proposals carried many provisions sought at the time by the energy giant Enron, a major contributor to the Bush/Cheney campaign, but Cheney never disclosed which energy corporations and lobbyists had met with his task force. In early 2003, the GAO, under pressure from Republicans who threatened to cut its budget, quietly dropped the matter. A private lawsuit asking for full disclosure, launched soon thereafter by the Sierra Club and the conservative Judicial Watch, made its way to the US Supreme Court. The Justices upheld Cheney's claim to complete secrecy.

During the 2000 campaign, Cheney told audiences that since leaving government under the original Bush administration, he had been "out in the private sector creating jobs." He did not mention that just after Halliburton absorbed Dresser, Cheney laid off 10,000 workers.

Meanwhile, Halliburton announced in May 2002 that the Securities and Exchange Commission was investigating the company for accounting practices related to how it reported cost overruns on construction projects, but no charges were immediately filed.

Many researchers and more knowledgeable members of the public have questioned the hypocrisy and ethics of Cheney, the man who prosecuted a war against Iraq in the early 1990s, and then oversaw $23.8 million in business to Iraq during a time of UN sanctions against that nation. Next, as vice president, he led the effort to put an end to the "murderous dictator" that was marked by fear-mongering and deception, and whose firm had now became embroiled in profiting from a second war in that country.

Such talk only gained strength as reports of no-bid contracts and overcharges continued to plague Halliburton.

In early 2003, Bunnatine Greenhouse, the top contracting officer for the Army Corps of Engineers, objected to Halliburton's $7 billion no-bid contract for services in Iraq. Describing one contract as "the most blatant and improper contract abuse I have witnessed during the course of my professional career," she said the Halliburton deal should have been the standard one-year contract and that an official of the company should not have been present during contract discussions.

Halliburton was forced to bid for half the contract and Greenhouse was forced into protection under whistleblower legislation. Listed as a public speaker by the National Whistleblowers Center in 2010, she was still fighting Halliburton misconduct while making appearances on CNN and PBS.

Meanwhile, the FBI apparently is still investigating Halliburton after a December 2003 audit revealed that the company overcharged the government $61 million for fuel in Iraq. Halliburton subsidiary KBR had hired a Kuwaiti firm, Altanmia Commercial Marketing Company, to supply fuel at twice the current price while adding a markup.

Following in the steps of Bunnatine Greenhouse, Mary Robertson, a senior contracting officer at the Army Corps of Engineers, protested that Altanmia's cost estimates were too high. "Since the US government is paying for these services, I will not succumb to the political pressures from the [government of Kuwait] or the US embassy to go against my integrity and pay a higher price for fuel than necessary," she wrote in an internal memo made public by Corpwatch.org.

The internal documents also revealed that due to the Altanmia deal, US taxpayers were paying an average of $2.64 a gallon and as much as $3.06 for fuel. By comparison, the Defense Department's Energy Support Center (ESC) had been doing a similar job supplying fuel at $1.32 a gallon, and SOMO, the local oil company, was doing the same provision for only $0.96 a gallon. The total bill to the taxpayer for 61 million gallons of fuel from Kuwait and about 179 million gallons from Turkey was $383 million, more than $100 million more than local providers would have charged.

In mid-2004, the Pentagon's Defense Contract Audit Agency "strongly" urged the Army to withhold about $60 million a month from Halliburton payments until full documentation was provided for $1.8 billion of charges made by the company. In late 2004, several sub-contractors working for Halliburton in Iraq filed suit to recover what they said were unpaid bills. One firm, La Nouvelle, filed a lawsuit against Halliburton subsidiary KBR in the US District Court of Eastern Virginia demanding $224 million.

A separate lawsuit charged that KBR refused to pay $20.4 million for food services and other work near the city of Tikrit provided in 2003 by the Kuwait Company for Process Plant Construction & Contracting (KCPC) and the Morris Corporation of Australia for several months after the invasion of Iraq.

Allegations of demands for a $3 million kickback during the original 2003 contract negotiations from individuals associated with KBR first surfaced after KBR fired KCPC and Morris because the two companies had fallen behind schedule. "They wanted kickbacks of 3 percent to 4 percent, which pushed up the prices because then the subcontractors would add the price of the kickbacks to their costs," an unnamed source told the *Sydney Morning Herald*.

Laszlo Tibold, a former KBR official, told journalist David Phinney that if anyone is to blame for KBR's poor contracting process in Iraq, it is

KBR's senior management and planners at the US Defense Department who were woefully unprepared for establishing an immediate presence for occupying the war-torn country. Tibold said when he first arrived at Anaconda base in Iraq, KBR failed to provide even the most basic of office supplies such as computers, reliable telephones, contract forms or a list of pre-approved contractors to work with.

"Everyone was in pure reactionary mode," he said, adding that KBR's staff at Camp Anaconda began with six employees who were burdened with work "by industry standards" that only a staff of 185 could effectively handle. After a month, KBR's staff at Camp Anaconda was increased to 30, he said, yet was responsible for writing contracts totaling a value in the hundreds of millions of dollars. "KBR had no clue," he said. "They didn't know what they were getting into."

And there is even more: In mid-2005, even as the Bush administration tried to work up national passion against Iran's nuclear program, Halliburton sources leaked to the press the fact that the scandal-plagued oil services company had sold Iran key components for a nuclear reactor.

Company sources said Halliburton officials worked with Cyrus Nasseri, vice chairman of the board of directors of Oriental Oil Kish, one of Iran's largest private oil companies, on oil development projects. Nasseri has been identified as a key member of Iran's nuclear development program. According to Iranian officials, Nasseri was questioned in mid-2005 regarding his providing Halliburton with Iran's nuclear secrets and accepting as much as a $1 million bribe from the company.

This connection became public in January 2005, when Halliburton announced it had subcontracted an Iranian natural gas drilling project to Halliburton Products and Services, a subsidiary of Dallas-based Halliburton registered in the Cayman Islands.

Some conspiracy researchers thought it meaningful that in 2006 Halliburton subsidiary KBR announced that it had been awarded a $385 million contract by the Department of Homeland Security to build "temporary detention and processing facilities," in other words, internment camps in America, thought to be modeled on KBR's Guatanamo Bay facility in Cuba.

It should also be mentioned that in its September 10, 2010, "Deepwater Horizon Accident Report," British Petroleum (BP) cited poor practices by Halliburton employees as contributing to the disaster in the Gulf of Mexico earlier that year. Investigators were hampered by the fact that Halliburton refused to release either cement samples from the destroyed oil rig or equivalent material. They also noted discrepancies in lab test results provided by Halliburton. Not surprisingly, the US government had absolved Halliburton of any fault in the calamity.

## IRAQIS AND THE MURRAH FEDERAL BUILDING BOMBING

Many researchers consider the April 19, 1995, bombing of the Alfred P. Murrah Federal Building in Oklahoma City to be yet another case of an inside job—one that foreshadows the covert machinations that led to 9/11 six years later. The connection of the Oklahoma bombing to the growing scandal around 9/11 and the Iraq war becomes evident in the account below. Despite a loud silence in the corporate-controlled mass media, many alternative articles as well as researchers have pointed to the involvement of Iraqis in the event.

So much evidence became available pointing to Iraqi complicity in that terrorist act that in March of 2002, *Judicial Watch* filed suit against the Republic of Iraq on behalf of seventeen survivors of the bombing. The complaint, filed in the US District Court for the District of Columbia, was brought against Iraq, as a State Department-designated terrorism sponsor, under the provisions of the Antiterrorism and Effective Death Penalty Act of 1996. This suit was still being pursued in the mid-2000s but seemed destined for oblivion following the US invasion of Iraq.

According to court papers, the bombing of the Murrah Federal Building "was not as simple as has been portrayed by the United States government. The entire plot was, in whole or in part, orchestrated, assisted technically and/or financially and directly aided by agents of the Republic of Iraq." However, researchers looking into recent developments in the investigation are encountering confusion and obstructions in confirming such a connection.

The suit also charges that Iraq knew in advance of the 9/11 attacks and that there was wrongdoing in both the Clinton and Bush administrations.

A portion of the evidence concerning foreknowledge of 9/11 involves an Iraqi newspaper column published on July 21, 2001, in which it stated that Osama bin Laden was thinking "seriously, with the seriousness of the Bedouin of the desert, about the way he will try to bomb the Pentagon after he destroys the White House." The column also mentioned that bin Laden was "insisting very convincingly that he will strike America on the arm that is already hurting," an apparent reference to the 1993 World Trade Center bombing.

Jim Kreindler, one of the lawyers pursuing the suit, said the columnist, Naeem Abd Muhalhal, had advance knowledge of bin Laden's plans and that "Iraqi officials were aware of plans to attack American landmarks." He added, "Further, we have evidence that Iraq provided support for bin Laden and his al Qaeda terror organization for nearly a decade."

This charge was supported by Craig Roberts, a former Oklahoma policeman and National Guard officer, who said, "At the end of the Gulf War, over 5,000 former Iraqi soldiers (mainly consisting of officers) were transported (illegally) to this country by the administration for 'humanitarian purposes' and resettled at taxpayer expense. This created a massive stir in the veterans organizations, who remembered how many American POWs had been abandoned by our government in past wars, but was only publicized in their magazines."

Roberts, a decorated Vietnam veteran and author who participated in the official Oklahoma City investigation of the Murrah Building bombing, said these Iraqi officers had worked with the CIA during the eight-year war between Iraq and Iran. They feared Saddam's wrath after losing the Gulf War. Within this group were many men who joined various Muslim extremist groups, such as Hamas and the Islamic Jihad, after arriving in the US. Some of these soldiers, along with a considerable amount of Semtex and other military explosives, were transported to Fort Sill, Oklahoma.

"This [transfer of Iraqi soldiers] was well publicized. One of the largest groupings of resettled former Iraqi soldiers, coincidentally, became Oklahoma City. This places the Iraqis who were experts in demolition (re: Kuwaiti oil field destruction) only 60 miles from the stored Semtex, cratering charges and other military explosives stored at Fort Sill," stated Craig.

Initial reports from witnesses placed two "Middle Eastern males" wearing blue jumpsuits or jogging suits in the vicinity of the Murrah building at the time of the explosions. The FBI put out "John Doe" sketch bulletins on at least three men, all of whom resembled Middle Eastern males. In fact, one such man, a Jordanian living in Oklahoma City, was arrested at London's Heathrow Airport only to be released shortly thereafter. FBI and media attention then shifted to right-wing extremists. Interestingly, the British media reported that this man had photos of weapons and missiles in his possessions as well as a blue jogging suit.

Yet despite the compelling evidence of Iraqi involvement in what to that time had been the worst bombing in US history, there was no federal-level investigation. Despite the rush to judgment by the federal authorities that only one man, Timothy McVeigh, bombed the Murrah Federal Building, controversy continues today over the facts of the tragedy. Oklahoma City has been added to the list of controversial and never properly investigated American tragedies beginning with the assassinations of President John F. Kennedy, Martin Luther King, Jr., Robert Kennedy, and the killings at Ruby Ridge, Idaho, and Waco, Texas. Sadly, public interest in the Oklahoma City bombing waned following the attacks of 9/11.

Oklahoma State Representative Charles Key in 1997 tried to bring facts concerning the Middle East connection in the Oklahoma City bombing to the public and finally produced a five hundred-page report released in 2001. As far back as 1997, Key and many others had raised questions about McVeigh's contacts prior to the bombing that killed 161 men, women and children.

Many still recall the FBI "John Doe" bulletins issued immediately after the bombing seeking several Middle Eastern men reportedly driving a brown pickup truck. This was in addition to the reports of the alleged Arab men seen in the vicinity of the federal building shortly before the explosions.

As in the case of District Attorney Jim Garrison attempting to question the official verdict of the Kennedy assassination, Key was raked over the coals by the mainstream media and accused of "howling at the moon" by Oklahoma governor Frank Keating, a former FBI agent. "Why was there such extreme opposition?" Key wrote in a letter to constituents. "I believe the answer is because some in our federal law enforcement agencies (i.e., ATF and FBI) had prior knowledge that certain individuals were planning to bomb the Murrah Federal Building! I believe that because of at least four reasons:

1. "Six different individuals have come forward and reported seeing the bomb squad in the immediate vicinity of the Murrah Building early on the morning of the bombing.
2. "The Oklahoma City Fire Department received a call from the FBI the Friday before the bombing and was told to be on the alert for a possible terrorist attack on a government building.
3. "Bruce Shaw, who had frantically come to look for his wife inside the smoldering building, was told by an ATF agent, 'You won't find any ATF agents in the building because they were warned on their pagers not to come in this morning and they're now in debriefing.' This conversation was corroborated by his boss, who accompanied Bruce to help him find his wife.
4. "Carol Howe, a paid informant for the ATF, has recently come forward to confirm that she informed the ATF that two individuals, Dennis Mahon and Andreas Strassmier, were planning to bomb the federal building in Oklahoma City. She also said that the likely date for the bombing was April 19!"

In addition to the suppressed information concerning the Middle East connection to the federal building bombing, at least one Oklahoma City investigative reporter claimed to have gathered evidence that Osama bin Laden was involved. Jayna Davis, former news reporter for the NBC affiliate in Oklahoma City, KFOR-TV, tried to make public this information several months prior to 9/11.

Davis said she developed information that a Middle Eastern terrorist cell was operating only blocks from the Murrah Building and that Timothy McVeigh on the day of the bombing was in contact with an Iraqi who had served in Saddam Hussein's Republican Guard. This man was the object of an "all-points" bulletin immediately after the bombing that was later inexplicably withdrawn.

Davis said her evidence led her to believe that McVeigh, along with Terry Nichols (now serving a life sentence without possibility of parole as an accomplice in the bombing) and at least seven men of Middle Eastern ethnic backgrounds were involved in a conspiracy masterminded by bin Laden. The reporter said she took her evidence, composed of hundreds of court records, twenty sworn witness affidavits and reports from law enforcement, intelligence and terrorist experts, to the FBI but bureau officials refused even to accept the material.

Further clouding the issue of why the FBI refused to even look at the evidence that refuted the Clinton administration's assurance that the bombing was the work of one lone man, McVeigh, plus a friend, was evidence showing that the FBI's top counterterrorism expert checked into an Oklahoma City hotel just after midnight on the morning the federal building was destroyed.

Danny Coulson, then director of the FBI's Terrorist Task Force, checked into the Embassy Suites Hotel at 12:20 a.m., about nine hours prior to the bombing, according to a hotel receipt obtained by *WorldNetDaily*. The hotel receipt showed Coulson checked out of the hotel on April 27. Coulson, in a book published in 1999, claimed he was in Fort Worth, Texas, when he received a call from John O'Neill, the FBI counterterrorism expert, informing him of the Murrah Building bombing. The discrepancy of these stories adds support to those who claim the FBI was involved in the case well before the explosion.

One lawsuit alleged that Ramzi Yousef, convicted in the 1993 World Trade Center bombing, was an Iraqi government agent who, prior to his arrest, went to the Philippines, where he recruited Terry Nichols, McVeigh's accomplice in Oklahoma, to join in the "Bojinka" plot to blow up several US-bound airliners.

It is a matter of fact that Terry Nichols made more than a dozen trips to the Philippines right up until 1995 but the Yousef connection has not been fully substantiated. Yousef, of course, was the al Qaeda operative with the plans for "Operation Bojinka," the plan to crash planes into prominent structures including the World Trade Center towers.

Author David Hoffman, writing in 1998, stated that FBI reports as well as research by McVeigh's defense attorneys established that in the early 1990s, terrorist leaders met on the Philippine island of Mindanao. "It was there [according to one informant] that Ramzi Yousef, Abdul Hakim Murad, Wali Khan Amin Shah and several others discussed the

Oklahoma City bombing plot," wrote Hoffman.

Further evidence of a connection between McVeigh and the bin Laden network, over and beyond the Philippine meeting, which may have involved Nichols, is the testimony of witnesses at the Sands Motel just outside Oklahoma City.

A co-owner of the motel, who asked for anonymity, told reporter Jim Crogan of *LA Weekly* that he distinctly recalled terrorist leader Mohamed Atta at his motel with Zacarias Moussaoui, the infamous "twentieth hijacker," about August 1, 2001, just six weeks prior to the 9/11 attacks. He identified a third man as Marwan al-Shehhi, reportedly one of the terrorists aboard Flight 175.

He said the men asked for a weekly rate on some rooms at the motel but they were told the rooms were all occupied. He said all three men were friendly but that Atta did most of the talking. "I asked him what they were doing here in the area," the owner said. "And Atta told me they were going to flight school. I thought he meant training in Oklahoma City. But Atta told me no, they were taking flight training in Norman. "I said I didn't understand why they would want to rent one of my rooms, since we were about twenty-eight miles from Norman and there are a lot of reasonably priced motels a lot closer. But he said they had heard good things about my place and wanted to stay there."

The man explained that there were no weekly rooms available and the trio left. Later, following the 9/11 attacks, the motel owner saw their pictures on the news and called the FBI. But there was never any significant follow-up to his report. One law enforcement source said he considered the motel owner's story credible and took the information to the FBI but was told, "it probably wouldn't go nowhere." "They were afraid the whole Oklahoma City bombing can of worms would be opened up and the FBI would have to explain why they didn't investigate this material before," the officer told a reporter.

"One reason for the FBI's apparent lack of interest might be this motel's alleged connection to Timothy McVeigh and a group of Iraqis who worked in Oklahoma City," noted reporter Crogan. "According to the motel owner and other witnesses and investigators interviewed by the *Weekly*, McVeigh and several of these Iraqis were motel guests in the months preceding the 1995 bombing. Witnesses also claimed they saw

IRAQIS AND THE MURRAH FEDERAL BUILDING BOMBING

several of the Iraqis moving barrels of material around on the bed of a truck. The motel owner said the material smelled of diesel fuel and he had to clean up a spill. Diesel fuel was a key component of the truck bomb that blew up the Federal Building."

The motel owner was interviewed by the FBI on several occasions but there was no indication that prosecutors in the case of Moussaoui were even notified of the Moussaoui-Atta connection, who was arrested prior to 9/11, and has been characterized as a marginal figure in the plot. But if he was connected to Atta, it makes him much more of a participant than previously thought. Reporter Crogan wrote, "If this recollection is correct, the entire incident, and its absence from the public record, raises new questions about the FBI investigation of Moussaoui and the 1995 destruction of the Federal Building in Oklahoma City."

There were so many leads and bits of information about the cover-up in the Oklahoma City bombing that it occasionally slipped into the mainstream media. According to a report in *U.S. News & World Report* in late 2001, McVeigh possessed several Iraqi telephone numbers, which prompted Pentagon officials to suspect that he was some sort of Iraqi agent. Writer Paul Bedard wrote, "Why haven't we heard this before about the case of the executed McVeigh? Conspiracy theorists in the Pentagon think it's part of a coverup."

Since there is such compelling evidence of Iraqi involvement in the Oklahoma City bombing, one might well ask why this was not brought out by the Bush administration to rally support for their invasion of that nation. The only answer would seem to be that to admit that FBI- and CIA-supported Iraqis were involved in that terrorist event might prompt speculation about the true culprits behind the 9/11 attacks.

## ANCIENT TECHNOLOGY IN BAGHDAD?

The record shows that plagiarized papers, secret pre-planning, a lack of post-war planning, distortion of evidence, fear-mongering, and outright lies permeated the Bush administration's effort to win support for the invasion of Iraq. No wonder so many other US allies declined to back the US effort before and after the war.

Support among the American public consistently spiraled downward, from the first couple of years following the invasion of Iraq when a distinct majority of Americans supported the war. Of particular interest is an October 2002, poll done by Pew Research Center in collaboration with the Council on Foreign Relations which indicated "a solid majority" of 62 percent supported a war to oust Saddam Hussein.

By early 2006 that showed less than 30 percent support. By February 2008, a Pew Research Center national polling showed a 54 percent majority said the US made the wrong decision in using military force in Iraq. Only 38 percent said it was the right decision. Last March, 49 percent said the decision to go to war was wrong, while 43 percent said it was right. During the third and fourth years of the conflict public opinion on this question was divided, while in the war's first two years clear majorities backed the decision to use force in Iraq.

In the run up to the invasion, there was scant coverage of dissenting voices, such as the march by 100,000 to 150,000 people in Washington on Sunday, October 27, 2002. Led by celebrities such as musician Patti Smith and actress Susan Sarandon, the protests were hailed as some of the largest in the nation since the Vietnam War. Jesse Jackson told a crowd gathered by the Vietnam Veterans Memorial, "If we launch a pre-emptive strike, we will lose all moral authority. We must have a higher order than a one-bullet diplomacy." The protest marches came following a poll conducted for the *New York Times* and CNN that showed half of those queried were uneasy at the prospect of war with Iraq.

As war approached in early 2003, there were large demonstrations in both America and other nations, and the day of March 15, 2003 witnessed what some called the largest day of anti-war protest ever witnessed on the planet. Protest rallies involving an estimated 30 million people took place in England, Germany, Spain, Belgium, France, Turkey, South Korea, Taiwan, Thailand, and Australia, and other countries—including thousands of arrests. But none of this seemed to sway President Bush, who declared, "If the UN won't act, if Saddam won't disarm, we will lead a coalition to disarm him."

On March 20, 2003, Bush made good on these words by launching US forces across Iraq's borders. By the time of the actual invasion, the cause celebre had been pared down to the search for weapons of mass de-

ANCIENT TECHNOLOGY IN BAGHDAD?

struction (WMD). One intriguing premise is that just such weaponry was indeed recovered but not any of the conventional technology thought to be in the possession of Saddam Hussein.

US troops promptly made a bee-line for Baghdad, failing to follow normal military tactics, which call for a period of consolidating forces in a captured area, after seizing a series of initial objectives. This failure to subdue the countryside brought deadly repercussions long after the initial fighting had ceased.

The search for weapons of mass destruction that precipitated such a hurried rush into Baghdad may have concerned the many rare antiquities, to include perhaps ancient technologies, that comprise the heritage of Iraq.

According to ABC News, nearly four hundred ancient Sumerian artifacts were discovered in Iraq in 1999 in the southern Iraqi town of Basmyiah, about one hundred miles south of Baghdad. The Iraqi News Agency said the objects ranged from animal and human-shaped "toys" to cuneiform tablets and even "ancient weapons." At least one cylinder seal depicted a tall person thought to represent the ancient king, Gilgamesh. The antiquities were dated to about 2500 BCE, said excavation team leader Riyadh al-Douri.

Further discoveries in Iraq were made in 2002 and early 2003 by archaeologists from the Bavarian department of Historical Monuments in Munich, Germany using digital mapping technology. According to spokesman Jorg Fassbinder, a magnetometer was utilized to locate buried walls, gardens, palaces and a surprising network of canals that would have made Uruk a "Venice in the desert."

This equipment also located a structure in the middle of the Euphrates River which Fassbinder's team believed to be the tomb of Gilgamesh, the ancient Mesopotamian king who claimed to be two-thirds god and only one-third human. An epic poem describing Gilgamesh's search for the secret of immortality was inscribed on clay tablets more than 2,000 years ago and is thought to be one of the oldest books in history.

Reportedly, other astonishing finds were being made during this time by both German and French archaeological teams given permission to excavate by Saddam Hussein. It may be worth noting that Germany and France were the two nations most opposed to the US invasion.

The new discoveries were added to those stored in the Iraqi National Museum in Baghdad, which had been closed to the public since the first Gulf War in 1991.

McGuire Gibson, of the Oriental Institute of the University of Chicago and president of the American Association for Research in Baghdad, had previously lamented the loss of ancient artifacts and writings due to the 1991 Gulf War and subsequent embargo of Iraq.

"The aftermath of the war witnessed the looting and sometimes the burning of nine regional museums and the loss of more than 3,000 artifacts, only a few of which have been recovered," wrote Gibson. "The loss of the objects, although grave, was not as destructive as the change that the attacks on the museums will have on the future relationship of museums to the people of Iraq. It is unlikely that there will ever again be an effort at public education about archaeology on the scale that was represented by those regional museums."

In addition to the destruction of historical artifacts, such as the American bombing of the giant ziggurat at Ur and the losses due to construction by US troops at Tell al-Lahm, economic conditions caused by the American embargo have caused an increase in the illegal trading of Iraqi artifacts. Gibson added that almost all archaeological research in Iraq came to a halt because of the war and embargo.

The problems with Iraq's antiquities were greatly exacerbated in late April 2003, when more than 50,000 priceless artifacts and tablets were taken from the Baghdad museum by what appeared to be an organized band of looters who targeted the museum's basement. This deliberate thievery was masked from the Western media by chaotic scenes of common looters thought by some to have been hired for this purpose.

Despite prior attempts to alert American military officers of the danger of losing artifacts dating back 7,000 years—especially precious antiquities stored in the museum's lower floor—American authorities failed to prevent the wholesale looting of humankind's most ancient treasures.

"It was my impression that the Department of Defense had made provisions for the safeguarding of monuments and museums," lamented Maxwell Anderson, president of the Association of Art Museum Directors. Anderson was among a group that in January 2003 alerted Pentagon and State Department officials to the importance of these antiquities.

ANCIENT TECHNOLOGY IN BAGHDAD?

Although promised protection for the antiquities, this alert apparently fell on deaf ears.

According to an Associated Press report, the thieves had keys to the museum and its vaults. Gibson said what appeared to be random looting actually was a carefully planned theft. "It looks as if part of the theft was a very, very deliberate, planned action," he said. "They were able to obtain keys from somewhere for the vaults and were able to take out the very important, the very best material. I have a suspicion it was organized outside the country. In fact, I'm pretty sure it was."

"Glass cutters not available in Iraq were found in the museum and a huge bronze bust weighing hundreds of pounds…[that] would have required a fork lift to remove it indicate that well organized professional cultural thieves were mixed in with the mob," noted Christopher Bollyn of the *American Free Press*.

The fact that some display cases were empty without being broken indicated that some of the precious materials may have been taken out prior to the arrival of the looters. "It was almost as if the perpetrators were waiting for Baghdad to fall to make their move," commented a writer for *Business Week*.

When the looting began on April 17, 2003, one Iraqi archaeologist summoned US troops to protect the national museum. Five Marines accompanied the man to the museum and chased out the thieves by firing shots over their heads. However, after about 30 minutes, the soldiers were ordered to withdraw and the looters soon returned. Apparently, the only building in Baghdad to receive full American protection was the Ministry of Oil.

"Not since the Taliban embarked on their orgy of destruction against the Buddhas of Bamiyan and the statutes in the museum of Kabul—perhaps not since World War II—have so many archaeological treasures been wantonly and systematically smashed to pieces," reported British newsman Robert Fisk, who toured the museum shortly after the incident.

The preventable looting prompted three members of the White House Cultural Property Advisory Committee to resign, disgusted that the alerted American military had failed to protect the Mesopotamian treasures. "This tragedy was not prevented, due to our nation's inaction," wrote committee chairman Martin E. Sullivan in his resignation letter.

The theft of ancient artifacts of undetermined value, particularly in the basement where uncatalogued new arrivals would have been stored, was confirmed by Colonel Matthew Bogdanos in early 2004. Bogdanos headed an investigation of the looting as deputy director for the Joint Interagency Coordination Group originally assigned to seek out weapons of mass destruction in Iraq. After gaining permission from General Tommy Franks, the group probed the museum looting.

In an interview published in the January/February issue of *Archeology*, Col. Bogdanos was asked what is still missing from the Iraqi National Museum. He replied, "You have the public gallery from which originally 40 exhibits were taken. We've recovered 11. Turning to the storage rooms, there were about 3,150 pieces taken from those, and that's almost certainly by random and indiscriminate looters. Of those, we've recovered 2,700. About 400 of these pieces remain missing.

"The final group is from the basement. The basement is what we've been calling the inside job. And I will say it forever like a mantra: it is inconceivable to me that the basement was breached and the items stolen without an intimate insider's knowledge of the museum. From there about 10,000 pieces were taken. We've only recovered 650, approximately."

It has been widely reported that Saddam Hussein believed himself to be the reincarnation of the King Nebuchadnezzar, the biblical figure who performed wondrous achievements in construction—including the Hanging Gardens of Babylon—in an attempt to communicate with ancient Mesopotamian gods from the heavens. Could the rush to war with Iraq, the hurried rush to Baghdad, and the "inside job" at the Baghdad Museum have something to do with gaining control over recently-discovered knowledge, and perhaps even technology, which might undo modern monopolies in science and even disrupt cherished beliefs in religion?

Recent scientific studies into heretofore unknown monatomic (single atom) elements have linked such discoveries to ancient writings from Mesopotamia and Egypt. It has been suggested that these discoveries may link modern experiments with scalar and Tesla technology, weather modification and even the notorious HAARP [High-Frequency Active Auroral Research Program] system with the ancient technologies many believe were utilized by King Nebuchadnezzar's "fiery furnace," the true builders of the Great Pyramid and even prehistorical "stargates." [See *Rule by Secrecy* for further information concerning the significance of these ancient Mesopotamian artifacts.]

After a lop-sided fight, victorious Americans celebrated the "liberation" of Iraq, never realizing for the remainder of the decade almost two American soldiers a day would still be dying there. By 2010, US military deaths in the Iraqi occupation topped 4,400, the majority of these counted after the invasion was complete. Meanwhile, the US Treasury was paying out more each month to sustain the war in Iraq than it did during the Vietnam War.

An odd sidelight to this was the comment of evangelist Pat Robertson in October 2004. Robertson, a longtime Bush supporter, told CNN that he urged the president to prepare the American people for the prospect of casualties before launching the war in March 2003. Robertson said Bush told him, "Oh, no, we're not going to have any casualties."

White House Press Secretary Scott McClellan was quick to state, "The president never made such a comment." Americans were left to wonder who was telling the truth—the president or the evangelist?

It is interesting to note that in 2010, when the corporate mass media was assuring the American public that the number of US combat troops was being reduced, more than 180,000 private contractors were still deployed to Iraq. The number of contractors had outnumbered combat troops almost from the beginning of the fighting.

On September 8, 2003, long after the official fighting in Iraq had ended with conventional no weapons of mass destruction in hand, President Bush finally conceded another article of faith concerning that nation's leader. To newsmen who gathered as he met with congressional members on energy matters, Bush confessed, "We have no evidence that Saddam Hussein was involved with the 11 September attacks."

Yet only the week before Bush's concession, Cheney still refused to rule out such a connection. "We don't know," he said, adding, "[In invading Iraq] we will have struck a major blow right at the heart of the base, if you will, the geographic base of the terrorists who've had us under assault now for many years, but most especially on 9/11."

Washington appeared to be playing a duplicitous game—ignoring the obvious Iraqi ties to the Oklahoma City bombing while placing unwarranted suspicion on Iraq for the 9/11 tragedies—and harboring weapons of mass destruction. In 2003, President Bush hailed "Mission Accomplished" in Iraq. Considering the covert recovery of artifacts from the Baghdad Museum, perhaps American troops did recover weapons of mass destruction, even though they may have come from ancient technologies long thought lost to the modern world.

# US COMPLICITY IN THE WORLD DRUG TRADE

Eric S. Margolis, an awardwinning columnist whose articles have appeared in the *New York Times*, the *International Herald Tribune* and the *Los Angeles Times*, has written, "I've said ever since 9/11 that the danger and size of al Qaeda has been vastly exaggerated—as an explosive report this week [September 10, 2010] by the London's esteemed International Institute for Strategic Studies has just confirmed. Al-Qaeda, dedicated to fighting the Afghan communists, never had more than 300 members at its peak. Today, according to [former] CIA Chief Leon Panetta, there are no more than 50 al Qaeda men in Afghanistan. Yet President Barack Obama has tripled the number of US troops in Afghanistan to 120,000 because of what to calls the al Qaeda threat. What is going on?"

What's going on in Afghanistan may well have to do with the drug trade. The current War on Drugs has been going on for so long that most people have forgotten when it began. Most authorities trace this failed but ongoing war to President Richard Nixon who, in 1970, established the National Commission on Marijuana and Drug Abuse as a response to concerns over "hippies" smoking weed.

According to the commission's report, *Marijuana, A Signal of Misunderstanding*, "Soon after funds became available on March 22, 1971, we commissioned more than fifty projects, ranging from a study of the effects of marijuana on man to a field survey of enforcement of the marijuana laws in six metropolitan jurisdictions. Of particular importance in our fact-finding effort were the opinions and attitudes of all groups in our society."

In other words, this was a genuine, objective report. Its conclusions?

After dismissing public approval of recreational drug use as counter to the benefit of society, the commission likewise opposed the option of using criminal penalties to eliminate drug use, stating, "Marijuana's relative potential for harm to the vast majority of individual users and its actual impact on society does not justify a social policy designed to seek out and firmly punish those who use it."

Commission members pointed out that "even during Prohibition, when many people were concerned about the evils associated with excessive use of alcohol, possession for personal use was never outlawed federally and was made illegal in only five States." The commission concluded that criminal sanctions on marijuana was counterproductive, stating, "We recommend to the public and its policy-makers a social control policy seeking to discourage marijuana use, while concentrating primarily on the prevention of heavy and very heavy use."

But Nixon, who has been connected to men with organized crime connections, disagreed with this finding, thereupon launching what then came to be an ineffective and indeed counterproductive drug war.

By 2010, the number of US prison inmates held on drug charges is about half a million, greater than the entire jail population of Western Europe. And most of these are persons of color who lived below the poverty line.

Another possible explanation for the never-ending War on Drugs came when Senator Carl Levin, a Michigan Democrat, documented in 2001 how more than $300 billion in drug money moves yearly through the US banking system. Levin's estimate, based on a staff investigation lasting more than a year, was augmented by the Brookings Institution in 2001. Brookings spokesman Raymond Baker reported that despite the strictest money-laundering laws in the world, US banks still held an estimated $500 billion a year in money from drug dealers and terrorists.

In one sting operation by US Customs, $7.7 million was deposited in the Citibank account of a Cayman Islands bank. When the money was transferred to a firm called M. A. Bank, it turned out to be a shell company without any physical office.

In December 2009, the UN's Office on Drugs and Crime chief, Antonio Maria Costa, credited billions of dollars in drug money with keeping the global financial system afloat at the height of the financial crisis. Costa said illegal drug profits were the "only liquid investment capital" available to some banks on the brink of collapse in 2008–9 and that a majority of this estimated $352 billion was absorbed into the economic system.

In the more naive times of the early 1970s, no one foresaw the advent of synthetic cocaine, adulterated hash, rock cocaine, PCP and the recent designer drugs such as Ecstasy. Then, the greatest drug bugaboo was heroin, the drug that placed a "monkey on your back." Interestingly enough, heroin use in the 1970s was reported at about 2 percent of the drug-taking population, a percentage that has remained remarkably stable up to this day. But the heroin business accounts for a higher percentage of the profits in the world's illicit drug trade.

Everyone knowledgeable of the world drug trade knows that the two primary sources of poppies, the flower from which heroin is made, are the Golden Triangle in Southeast Asia and Afghanistan.

The modern Afghan drug trade began with US involvement in Afghanistan in 1979, a provocation that led to the Soviet invasion, as recounted by Alfred McCoy, author of the respected *The Politics of Heroin in Southeast Asia*: "CIA assets again controlled this heroin trade. As the Mujahedeen guerrillas seized territory inside Afghanistan, they ordered peasants to plant opium as a revolutionary tax. Across the border in Pakistan, Afghan leaders and local syndicates under the protection of Pakistani Intelligence operated hundreds of heroin laboratories. During this decade of wide-open drug-dealing, the US Drug Enforcement Agency in Islamabad failed to instigate major seizures or arrests. US officials had refused to investigate charges of heroin dealing by its Afghan allies 'because US narcotics policy in Afghanistan has been subordinated to the war against Soviet influence there.'

"In 1995, the former CIA director of the Afghan operation Charles Cogan, admitted the CIA had indeed sacrificed the drug war to fight the Cold War. 'Our main mission was to do as much damage as possible to the Soviets. We didn't really have the resources or the time to devote to an investigation of the drug trade, I don't think that we need to apologize for this. Every situation has its fallout.... There was fallout in terms of drugs, yes. But the main objective was accomplished. The Soviets left Afghanistan.'" The Taliban were not so lenient on the opium trade.

It was reliably reported that zealous Muslims within the Taliban government had banned the growth of poppies and had succeeded in destroying nearly 95 percent of the crop by the spring of 2001. Britain's *Financial Times* reported in 2002, "The Taliban's ban on opium poppy two years ago was 'enormously effective' in reducing poppy crops almost entirely in areas under the regime's control. The US estimates that Afghanistan produced 74 tons of opium last year, compared to 3,656 tons the previous year." Anti-Taliban hard-liners in the United States believed this reduction of the poppy crop was merely a "business decision" designed to drive prices up and ensure higher profits to the Taliban. More knowledgeable drug experts have pointed out that the Taliban are not peddling heroin on the streets of LA or New York and that powerful drug distributors must have viewed the poppy loss as a business disaster.

After the US invasion of Afghanistan in 2001, despite spending $5 million of taxpayer money on drug eradication programs there, opium production began to soar. Under the Taliban no more than 185 tons of opium was produced annually. By the end of 2002, that figure had risen to an estimated 3,400 tons, according to BBC's Central Asian analyst Pam O'Toole. By 2005, *U.S. News & World Report* noted that almost 500,000 acres of poppies were under cultivation.

In fact, following the American occupation of Afghanistan, opium production grew so vast that a government study in 2004 stated that nation was "on the verge of becoming a narcotics state." This White House report was sent to Congress by Secretary of State Condoleezza Rice on behalf of President Bush.

In 2005, despite being occupied by thousands of US and allied troops, Afghanistan earned $2.7 billion from opium exports, amounting to 52 percent of the country's $5.2 billion gross domestic product. In 2007, US Ambassador William Wood announced that Afghan farmers harvested 457,135 acres of poppies that year, setting a new poppy-growing record. In 2006, Afghan farmers cultivated 407,715 acres.

Although the War on Drugs continued unabated, in 2010, with officials of US Office of National Drug Control Policy (ONDCP) claiming total Afghan acreage in poppy cultivation had dropped to slightly under 400,000 acres, there appeared little help from the military occupation authorities. Western military commanders have resisted local pleas to intervene in the Afghan drug trafficking, arguing that they don't have the resources to broaden their mission. "Our primary mission is a combat mission," said Col. Jim Yonts, a spokesman for the US forces in Afghanistan. "We stay focused on our role of defeating the Taliban and al Qaeda."

This hands-off-drugs policy continued into 2009 with Anne Gearan of the Associated Press writing, "Convinced that razing the cash crop grown by dirt-poor Afghan farmers is costing badly needed friends along the front lines of the fight against Taliban-led insurgents, US authorities say they are all but abandoning the Bush-era policy of destroying drug crops." It is unclear on where these officials got the idea that Bush-era policies were to decimate drug crops as credible statistics show poppy cultivation reach new heights following the Bush-ordered invasion of Afghanistan. This announcement of backing off the anti-drug war came following the completion of the 2009 harvest.

Just in case the Afghan farmers need help with their crops, according to Gearan, the Obama administration plans to send "dozens of agronomists and irrigation specialists to Afghanistan…as part of what it says is the new, less militarized look of the Afghan mission."

The drug issue continued into well into 2010, when the *New York Times* reported that NATO troops in Afghanistan were under orders not to eradicate some poppy crops. The decision not to destroy the drug crops was based on concern for the hearts and minds of the farmers. "We don't trample the livelihood of those we're trying to win over," said Comdr. Jeffrey Eggers, a member of Gen. Stanley A. McChrystal's chief advisory group.

Such leniency went against the grain with some Afghan authorities. Zulmai Afzali, spokesman for the Afghan Ministry of Counternarcotics, complained, "How can we allow the world to see lawful forces in charge of Marja [in Afghanistan's Helmand Province] next to fields full of opium, which one way or another will be harvested and turned into a poison that kills people all over the world? The Taliban are the ones who profit from opium, so you are letting your enemy get financed by this so he can turn around and kill you back."

The post-invasion growth of poppies means that Afghanistan has reverted back to late-1990s levels, when the country produced 70 percent of the world's illicit opium. To fully explain the politics of drugs would require a separate book, but it must be understood that drugs—particularly opium-based drugs such as heroin—have been the basis for both social control and wealth for centuries. In more recent times, Samuel Russell, second cousin of General William Huntington Russell, founder of the Skull and Bones Order at Yale, founded Russell and Company in 1823 with the intent of smuggling opium to China. He later acquired Perkins and Company, another opium smuggling operation controlled by some of Boston's finest blue-blood families. These families were enriched first by the slave trade, and then by opium smuggling in the nineteenth century. Other Boston families integrated Russell's firm into an opium syndicate that include the Cabots, Lowells, Higginsons, Forbeses, Cushings, and Sturgises. An early investor was Joseph Coolidge whose grandson, Archibald, was a founder of the Council on Foreign Relations.

Thus, it may come as less than a surprise to learn that—ever since the Vietnam War—it has been charged that the CIA, initially founded as a "good old boy" network of Eastern preppies, has imported drugs to support its clandestine operations. Mounds of court papers and news stories attest to this criminal activity yet no one in high authority seems capable of doing anything about it. One former British commando who operated in Afghanistan during the Soviet occupation has stated that both American and British military officers tolerated opium smuggling by the Mujahideen as the profits were used to support their actions against the Russians. Tom Carew said after debriefing sessions in both London and Washington, he quickly became aware that both British and American authorities turned a blind eye to the Mujahideen drug smuggling.

What becomes clear in all this is that anyone desiring to profit from the drug trade and its billions that circulate through the banking system, would be opposed to the destruction of the poppy crop. The facts also call into question the sincerity of US government officials and their dedication to the War on Drugs. More recent allegations of US involvement with the illicit drug trade reach all the way to the top. Indeed, at least five books and many websites have connected both President George W. Bush and his father with the drug trade.

Perhaps the most revealing—and shocking—episode involves the celebrity NFL football hero Pat Tillman, who made national headlines when he quit professional football to serve in the Army in Afghanistan. In April 2004, it was announced by the Pentagon that Tillman had died bravely in battle with the Taliban. However, after more facts came to light, his death was changed due to "friendly fire." The truth may have been even worse than that. According to Tillman's military autopsy report, "no evidence at all of enemy fire was found at the scene. No one was hit by enemy fire, nor was any government equipment struck." Instead, three bullet holes were described within a half-dollar diameter in Tillman's forehead raising the possibility that the football star was murdered to keep him quiet. But quiet about what?

Anthony Orlando, a close friend to Tillman, told mourners at his funeral, "For those who do not know, Tillman was questioning why he should guard opium fields while there [Afghanistan] to make America safe. He wrote letters about this and sent them home." According to journalist and author Pat Shannan, Tillman was shot "execution style" from only 10 yards away while yelling out his name. His uniform and body armor were burned, destroying essential evidence, and journals he kept detailing his experiences in Afghanistan were never found.

*OpEdNews* reporter Richard Clark posed the questions, "Was Pat Tillman assassinated to prevent him from coming home to expose the fact that our troops have been ordered to guard, and even help produce and store the opium of Afghan warlords? Was it also because he had been corresponding with Noam Chomsky and was planning on returning to the US to help reinvigorate the anti-war movement?"

After reviewing the questionable circumstances of Tillman's death, Clark concluded, "I think Tillman had been asking too many questions and wanted to know why we were doing nothing (except protecting) the many vast fields planted with opium poppies in Afghanistan. And he got murdered for it. The US Army and other organizations continue to cover up the real story behind Ranger Pat Tillman's murder."

Another prominent anecdote closer to home involves a colorful assassinated drug dealer and DEA informant named Barry Seal. Daniel Hopsicker, formerly executive producer of a business news television show aired on NBC, published a book on Seal in 2001 entitled *Barry & 'the boys': The CIA, The Mob and America's Secret History*.

In this book, Hopsicker details how Seal, who was at the same time one of America's most successful drug smugglers and a CIA agent, became angry at George H. W. Bush when he was Reagan's vice president. Seal felt Bush had betrayed him by not getting him out of legal problems concerning drugs. Seal had been implicated in the CIA drug smuggling connected to the airport at Mena, Arkansas. These covert operations were in turn linked to Bill Clinton during his tenure as that state's governor, when at least one Arkansas lawman publicly stated that it was then-Governor Clinton who squashed a state investigation into the drug smuggling activities at Mena.

In retaliation for the apparent betrayal by Bush, Seal reportedly arranged for a DEA "sting" at a Florida airport in 1985. But instead of nabbing ordinary drug dealers, the operation caught Bush's sons, Jeb and George W., accepting a shipment of cocaine. Both were already prominent political leaders at that time. According to Hopsicker, "Seal then stepped in and 'took care' of things. The Bushes were now supposedly in his debt. Plus he hung on to the videotape shot of the sting for insurance."

This same story was echoed in a book by former air force intelligence officer and CIA asset Terry Reed, along with former *Newsday* prize-winning investigative reporter John Cummings. In *Compromised*, Reed asserts that Seal told him, "It seems some of George Bush's kids just can't say no ta drugs, ha, ha, ha, ha. Well, ya can imagine how valuable information like that would be, can't ya? That could get you out of almost any jam, it's like a get-out-of-jail-free card. I even got surveillance videos catchin' the Bush boys red handed. I consider this stuff my insurance policy."

Seal's "insurance policy" lapsed quickly. He was machine-gunned in Baton Rouge, Louisiana, on February 19, 1986, less than a year later and whatever tapes he may have had disappeared.

His death inspired a lengthy letter to then-Attorney General Ed Meese from the Louisiana attorney general, William J. Guste Jr., stating, "I, for one, was shocked when I learned of his death. In October, as chairman of the Subcommittee on Narcotics and Drug Interdiction of the President's Commission on Organized Crime, I had presided over a seminar at which Barry Seal had testified. His purpose there was to inform the commission and top United States officials of the methods and equipment used by drug smugglers."

According to investigator Hopsicker, three boxes of documents, including audio/videotapes, which Seal had kept with him at all times, were taken from the scene of his murder by an FBI special agent from the Baton Rouge office. The agent arrived at the crime scene less than ten minutes after the shooting.

Was Barry Seal's murder just another drug-related street shooting or did someone not want him to reveal what he knew? Hopsicker did discover that the very plane Seal claimed was used to fly cocaine to the 1985 sting ended up as the property of George W. Bush sometime after Seal's death. The writer also found in tracing the ownership of the turboprop King Air 200 that the trail led to several persons connected to either the Iran-Contra or the savings and loan scandals of the 1980s. Hopsicker also found FAA records that showed that Seal had flown aircraft connected through a Phoenix firm to Southern Air Transport, a known CIA proprietary company.

Voters might recall that the younger Bush never actually denied using cocaine when the issue came up in his 2000 campaign for president. He simply brushed the allegation aside with a claim of youthful foolishness. Some of the thousands still serving prison sentences for possession of cocaine must wish their convictions could be overturned and excused as the foolishness of youth.

Cheney also has had questions raised about drug running through Halliburton's subsidiary KBR as well as the firm's connection to a suspect Russian oil company. At least one of the fat loans given by the US Export-Import Bank in 2000 after being lobbied by Halliburton was to the Tyumen Oil Co., controlled by the Alfa Group conglomerate. The loan was approved in April 2002. A Center for Public Integrity investigative report stated, "It guaranteed $489 million in credits to a Russian oil company whose roots are embedded in a legacy of KGB and Communist Party corruption, as well as drug trafficking and organized crime funds, according to Russian and US sources and documents."

In 1997, the Russian equivalent of our FBI presented Russia's lower House of Parliament a report alleging both organized crime and drug running involving Tyumen's parent company, the Alfa Group. The report stated that two Alfa entities, Alfa Bank and the trading company Alfa Eko, in the early 1990s were deeply involved in laundering both Russian and Colombian drug money and in importing drugs from the Far East into Europe. A former KGB officer said Alfa Bank was founded with Communist Party and KGB funds and utilized former government agents who had served in anti-organized crime units under the communist regime. He said heroin was often disguised as flour and sugar shipments bound for Germany.

Russian reports showed that in 1995 a Siberian railroad worker stole a sack of sugar from a rail car leased to Alfa Eko and that shortly afterward many people in his town became "poisoned" after eating the heroin-laced sugar. This incident prompted official raids on Alfa Eko that turned up "drugs and other compromising documentation." Even Alfa Group's 1998 takeover of Tyumen Oil prompted allegations of impropriety and connections to Moscow's Solntsevo crime family. Despite all this evidence of drug smuggling, Cheney's Halliburton prevailed and US taxpayers supported the loans.

More heavy political pressure may have come from Tyumen's lead attorney, James C. Langdon Jr., a managing partner of the worldwide law firm of Akin Gump Strauss Hauer & Feld. Langdon was one of George W. Bush's "Pioneers," a group of fund-raisers that gathered at least $100,000 each for the 2000 campaign. Another helpful person was Halliburton's top lobbyist, Dave Gribbin, who served as Cheney's chief of staff when he headed the Pentagon under the elder Bush.

Drugs, oil, politics, intelligence agencies, and shady and complicated business dealings all found a focal point in 2001. It was in the form of a wayward son from a prominent Saudi family named Osama bin Laden.

## BIN LADEN, THE MADE-TO-ORDER ENEMY

As in the JFK assassination, on the day of the 9/11 attacks authorities had a suspect even before anyone knew for certain what had happened. He was identified as Osama bin Laden, the son of a wealthy Saudi Arabian family and a man who during the Russo-Afghan War of the 1980s received arms and financing from the US government.

Despite the fact that bin Laden repeatedly denied knowledge of the attacks, he was presumed guilty by both the government and the press. No other interpretation of the attack was allowed in the corporate mass media. Bin Laden was a made-to-order enemy. He is the man blamed for the 1993 WTC attack, and the bombing of American embassies in Africa in 1998, and had been a fugitive from US justice for more than a decade. No one might ever have heard of Osama bin Laden if President Bill Clinton had not fired missiles indiscriminately into Afghanistan in an attempt to kill him in 1998.

Bin Laden's history is relatively nondescript yet fascinating as an example of a piously religious man being drawn into a world of geopolitics and murder. A lengthy biography of bin Laden was presented by PBS's *Frontline* that relied in part on a document that the show's editors said came from an anonymous source close to bin Laden. They added that while some of the information could not be independently verified and even ran contrary to other sources, the document nevertheless was "a very useful source of information." The document seemed to be a fairly accurate and somewhat sympathetic biography of bin Laden.

According to this document, bin Laden was born in 1957 to a Syrian mother. He was the seventh son of more than fifty brothers and sisters. His father, Mohammed Awad bin Laden, had immigrated to Saudi Arabia in about 1930, where he worked as a laborer in the port city of Jeddah on the Red Sea. During the post-World War II reign of King Ibn Saud, the founder of modern Saudi Arabia, the elder bin Laden gained a fortune by constructing the king's palaces. He impressed the king and began to build good relations with the royal family, especially Faisal, who took the throne when his brother, King Saud IV, was forced to abdicate in 1964. The elder bin Laden reportedly played a role in convincing Saud IV to step down in favor of Faisal. For his support, Faisal issued a decree that all construction projects would go to bin Laden. This included contracts to restore the holy mosques in Mecca and Medina, the most venerated of Muslim shrines.

According to the PBS document, the elder bin Laden was a stern disciplinarian who kept his children in one location and instilled in them strict business and religious mores. To his credit, the father reportedly showed no difference in the treatment of his vast brood. During the Haji holy season, the elder bin Laden spent his construction company wealth on funding the travels of many Islamic leaders and scholars. Through the father's generosity, the son made many long-lasting friendships.

Mohammed Awad bin Laden died in a 1968 plane crash when Osama bin Laden was still a teenager. By age seventeen, bin Laden had married a young Syrian relative and had completed his early education. In 1981, he received a degree in public administration from the King Abdul-Aziz University in Jeddah. During this time, bin Laden followed many other educated Arabs in joining the Muslim Brotherhood. As early as the first two weeks of the Soviet invasion of Afghanistan in December 1979, bin Laden was taken to Pakistan to meet leaders of the anti-Soviet forces and to witness the pitiful columns of refugees. Returning to Saudi Arabia, he began collecting for the Afghan cause. He made several short trips to Pakistan during the next couple of years, taking with him an immense amount of money and materials.

In 1982, bin Laden finally entered Afghanistan to meet with the Mujahideen fighters, taking along construction machinery and even a few of the bin Laden construction workers. He also reportedly established a "guesthouse" in Peshawar on the Afghan-Pakistan border that became a way station for Arab fighters, sent by him to various Afghan factions fighting the Soviets. By 1988, he had established more than six camps of his own in Afghanistan and his own force, the Maktab al-Khidimat (MAK), which soon was engaging the Soviets. Composed primarily of devout Muslims, these fighters came from Egypt, Lebanon, Syria, Turkey, Saudi Arabia and other Middle Eastern nations.

From 1984 through 1989, he spent more than eight months out of each year in Afghanistan, where he participated in several major battles and numerous smaller skirmishes. His relations with the Taliban were warm because they both saw themselves as devout practitioners of Islam. Theirs was a bonding of religion, not of politics.

Returning to Saudi Arabia in late 1989 as the Soviets were withdrawing from Afghanistan, bin Laden found himself trapped by a royal ban on his travels. He had angered the Saudi royals by announcing his intention of spreading his holy war into South Yemen and warned of invasion by Saddam Hussein, who then had warm relations with the Saudis. When Saddam Hussein invaded Kuwait in 1991, he saw it as a sign of his prophecy come true and proposed to the Saudis that he bring in his Arab Mujahideen to protect the kingdom. Before a decision was made on his suggestion, bin Laden was shocked to learn that American troops had arrived in Saudi Arabia.

It was a transforming moment, as the presence of any foreign troops on Saudi soil was considered intolerable by many Muslims. He had much earlier stated that the next great battle would be against America. His virtual house arrest in Jeddah and an armed raid on his suburban farm by the National Guard caused his relations with the Saudis to sour. Bin Laden convinced a brother to arrange for him to visit Pakistan on business, but once he arrived there in the spring of 1991 he sent back a letter stating he would not return and apologized for his perfidy.

Heading immediately for Afghanistan, he tried unsuccessfully to mediate between the various factions there. His devout demeanor endeared bin Laden to fellow Muslims. He was considered a truthful person, a simple person with good manners and a humble and generous personality. Despite his frail appearance and bland speeches, his followers saw him as an inspirational leader and showed him great respect. He also evinced a cunning caution, to the point of avoiding electronic devices, including wristwatches, which he believed might be used to track him.

During his stay and later in Sudan, the Saudis with the aid of Pakistani intelligence and perhaps their close associates, the CIA, reportedly tried to kill him but his many friends within the Pakistani establishment tipped him off each time. Apparently, the forces of the status quo desired to eliminate this religious fanatic who heeded neither bribes nor Western reasoning. By 1994, the Saudis publicly renounced bin Laden, withdrawing his citizenship and freezing his assets, estimated at between $200 million and $300 million. But this was only money traceable to him through the bin Laden Group. Millions more are tied up in bin Laden family money and their complex joint ventures with the royal Saudi family, including the late King Fahd.

During a stay in Sudan, there were anti-American incidents in Somalia and South Yemen, followed in 1995 by a car bombing in the Saudi capital of Riyadh. Although bin Laden was blamed in each of these incidents, the PBS document claimed he had no direct knowledge of them. They reportedly were carried out by Arabs who had trained with bin Laden in Afghanistan and had been imbued with anti-American feelings. There was no indication of who truly was behind them and the perpetrators may not have known themselves.

Sought by both the Americans and the Saudis, bin Laden returned to Afghanistan, where he was granted sanctuary by the ruling Taliban. Shortly after arriving back there in mid-1996, the Khobar Towers on an American base in Saudi Arabia was bombed, killing nineteen American soldiers. Although no one claimed responsibility for the attack, once again Arab Afghan fighters who had been connected to bin Laden were blamed.

But no one was paying much attention to the diminutive "freedom fighter," so bin Laden issued what may have been his first public anti-American message, a twelve-page declaration of war against America. At that time his only demands were that American troops leave Saudi Arabia.

Reportedly, American special forces planned to attack his residence in 1997 but canceled the plan when an Arab newspaper in London published a report on the operation, again apparently provided by leaks from the sympathetic Pakistani military and intelligence personnel. By now, bin Laden was completely caught up in his own war against what he considered "infidels." He utilized every resource at his command, including the media. He even allowed an ABC television interview in April 1998, warning at that time that attacks would come within weeks.

An attack was expected inside Saudi Arabia. Instead American embassies in Kenya and Tanzania were bombed on August 7, 1998, provoking outrage all around the world. President Clinton responded by ordering missiles fired at bin Laden's Afghan camp in Khost. About 250 Arabs were killed but bin Laden was not there. A plant in the Sudan, suspected of producing chemical weapons, also was targeted by sixteen cruise missiles. Later it was found that the plant, owned by Saudi businessman Saleh Idris, actually was producing medicine, not chemical weapons.

The Taliban government of Afghanistan offered to put bin Laden on trial on condition that the US government supply sufficient evidence of his guilt in the bombings. Nothing came of this offer. By then, some members of the US intelligence establishment were saying that bin Laden was training Islamic fighters for action in Chechnya and other areas of Russia, through an organization called al Qaeda.

In fact, the al Qaeda network is quite different from World War II "fifth columnists" and traditional insurgent movements in that its far-flung groups of operatives are not closely connected and do not have a clear command structure. It is a loose conglomeration of dedicated fighters operating across continents. Such an organization would be susceptible to penetration by any number of national security forces, in fact, almost anyone.

At least one intelligence insider has suggested that al Qaeda—translated as "the base"—does not mean a central headquarters but rather a CIA database of Arab mercenaries available for missions at a price. If this is the case, al Qaeda could well be following orders from someone other than bin Laden or his god.

However, the PBS document stated that bin Laden's followers are not true mercenaries but religious zealots who do not require much money.

"Explosives and weapons are very cheap in some parts of the world," it stated. "In Somalia, TNT, for example, is cheaper than sugar. In Yemen, you can buy an RPG [Rocket Propelled Grenade] for less than a TV set. The role of money here is over-exaggerated by many writers."

According to this document, bin Laden was nearly forgotten by his Arab followers until the African bombings that killed twelve Americans, about three hundred Kenyans and Tanzanians and wounded five thousand. President Clinton, after briefings by US intelligence officials, told the public, "Our target was terror. There is convincing evidence from our intelligence community that the bin Laden terrorist network was responsible for these bombings. Based on this information, we have high confidence that these bombings were planned, financed and carried out by the organization bin Laden leads."

With bin Laden's name bantered about by the news media, his notoriety rose once again. The PBS document stated, "People's reaction, however, was mixed. While many Muslims felt triumph for scaring the Americans, many others felt upset by the picture of hundreds of civilians killed and injured in the attack. They felt this can never be justified.

"After the American [missile] attack on Sudan and Afghanistan, it became almost shameful to criticize bin Laden. The American strike with associated remarks by Clinton and American officials proved that bin Laden is a big challenge to America. In the minds of the average Arab and Muslim, bin Laden appeared as the man who was able to drive Americans so crazy that it started shooting haphazardly at unjustified targets. Their view was that while bin Laden or others can make 'executive' mistakes because of their difficult circumstances, logistics and communication, America is not supposed to [make] mistakes unless it is done on purpose."

## BIN LADEN REPLIES

What did the primary suspect have to say about the 9/11 attacks? A great deal—but one had to know where to look. Early on, the Bush administration asked the major news media not to report on what bin Laden had to say, arguing that he might use the opportunity to pass secret messages along to his al Qaeda network. Next, White House spokesman Ari Fleischer instructed the press to censor any future tape-recorded messages from bin Laden, although he didn't actually use the word "censor." Fleischer spent some time arguing with the media representatives, saying only, "we have the power but this is only a request." In the end, the sycophantic corporate media agreed to self-censor any word from bin Laden. However, the European media and alternative outlets in America, especially on the Internet, made no such agreement.

In an interview on September 28, according to the Pakistani newspaper *Ummat*, bin Laden stated, "I have already said that I am not involved in the 11 September attacks in the United States. As a Muslim, I try my best to avoid telling a lie. I had no knowledge of these attacks, nor do I consider the killing of innocent women, children and other humans as an appreciable act. Islam strictly forbids causing harm to innocent women, children and other people. Such a practice is forbidden even in the course of battle. It is the United States, which is perpetrating every maltreatment on women, children and common people."

In this interview, largely unreported in the United States, bin Laden unsurprisingly blamed the attacks on Israel, claiming, "All that is going on in Palestine for the last eleven months is sufficient to call the wrath of God upon the United States and Israel, (and) what had earlier been done to the innocent people of Iraq, Chechnya and Bosnia." Bin Laden went on to state, "we are not hostile to the United States. We are against the [US government] system which makes other nations slaves to the United States or forces them to mortgage their political and economic freedom."

In one of the few truly authenticated communications from bin Laden, he told the Arabic satellite channel Al Jazeera in mid-September 2001, "The U.S. government has consistently blamed me for being behind every occasion its enemies attack it. I would like to assure the world that I did not plan the recent attacks, which seems to have been planned by people for personal reasons." One cannot, of course, take bin Laden at face value, but then the same could be said for the US government, which in the past has been caught in so many lies and misstatements that it is surprising that anyone pays serious attention to official pronouncements. Asked if he believed bin Laden's denial, President Bush responded, "No question he is the prime suspect. No question about that."

Later in the fall of 2001, a videotape of Osama bin Laden was offered to the public by the CIA and proclaimed by President Bush as a smoking gun, "a devastating declaration of guilt" in the 9/11 tragedies. Immediately, voices rose criticizing the tape. Bin Laden's mother, Alia Ghanem, told a British newspaper, "There are too many gaps and the statements are very unlike him. Osama is too good a Muslim and too good a person to say or do what the script of the video suggests." Ghanem, who still lives in Saudi Arabia, said the tape was "doctored." Ghanem also denied reports that her son had called her prior to September 11 and told her he would be out of touch for some time because something big was about to happen. Some days later, his mother's claim was supported by Arabic language experts, who claimed that the Pentagon's translation of the tape was incorrect, taken out of context and that incriminating words had been put in bin Laden's mouth.

Two independent translators and an expert on Arabic culture reported their findings on the German state television program *Monitor*, which broadcast on December 20, 2001, over Germany's Channel One, *Das Erst*, often compared to NBC or the BBC. Dr. Abdel El M. Husseini stated, "I have carefully examined the Pentagon's translation. This translation is very problematic. At the most important places which have been presented as proof of bin Laden's guilt, it is not identical with the Arabic."

In the Pentagon translation given great publicity by the United States corporate media, bin Laden was quoted as saying, "We calculated in advance the number of casualties from the enemy." But, according to Dr. Murad Alami, "The words 'in advance' are not even heard on the tapes. This translation is wrong. When we take the original Arabic from the tape there are no misunderstandings which would allow for us to read this into the original."

At another point in the Pentagon translation, bin Laden was reported saying, "We had notification since the previous Thursday that the event would take place that day." But Alami stated, "'Previous' is never said. The following sentence that the event would take place on that day is not heard in the original Arabic." Alami said the sentence "We ordered each of them to go to America" was in the active voice while the original Arabic was in the passive voice, "they were ordered to go to America." He added the translation with the word "we" was simply wrong. The expert said the sentence translated by the Pentagon as "they didn't know anything about the operation" is not understandable on the original tape.

Another of the experts interviewed, Gernot Rotter, a professor of Islamic and Arabic studies at the University of Hamburg, after studying the Pentagon's translations, stated, "The American translators who listened and transcribed the tapes have apparently written a lot of things into the text that they wanted to hear, which are actually not heard on the tape no matter how many times you listen to it."

This was somewhat supported by a December 20, 2001 *USA Today* article that described how the tape was hurriedly translated in twelve hours by a Lebanese and an Egyptian who "had difficulties with the Saudi dialect that bin Laden and his guest used in the tape. Regardless of whether bin Laden or his organization was involved in the attacks or not, this tape is of such bad quality, in some places it cannot be understood at all, and those parts which can be understood are torn out of context so that the tape cannot be used as evidence to prove anything."

After a hiatus of three years, a bin Laden tape was suddenly produced in January 2006. Parts of an audiotape purportedly of bin Laden were played on Al-Jazeera television and later a full version was published on its website. CBS News styled the tape as "chilling" and reported that bin Laden threatened more attacks on the United States. The news agency also reported that the CIA had verified the authenticity of the tape and that it proved bin Laden was still alive.

As in 2001, independent researchers once again questioned the authenticity of the latest bin Laden tape. Syndicated columnist Eric Margolis wrote, "Tapes that appeared to confirm bin Laden's guilt were clumsy fakes. They were supposedly 'found' in Afghanistan by the anti-Taliban Afghan Northern Alliance, which was created and funded by Russian intelligence. I had met Osama bin Laden in Afghanistan and told CNN viewers that he was not the man in the tapes."

Internet columnist and Washington insider Wayne Madsen noted, "What's not right about the Osama bin Laden audio tape? One thing that the Bush administration does well is manage perceptions of the public. Amid protests over the NSA wiretapping, the extension of the Patriot Act, and the nomination of neo-Fascist Samuel Alito to the Supreme Court, an audio tape on Osama bin Laden is sent to Al Jazeera. On the tape, bin Laden suddenly veers from being a traditional right-wing Wahhabi fanatic to the right of the House of Saud to a leftist progressive. The tape by bin Laden was quickly verified as 'authentic' by a CIA that is now firmly in the grasp of neo-cons under Porter Goss. However, the tape is an obvious fake being used by the Bush administration to scare Americans into believing 'al Qaeda' is making plans for another attack and an attempt to link bin Laden to Democrats.

"The reason the tape is as phony as Niger yellowcake documents and Saddam's weapons of mass destruction is as plain as day. 'Bin Laden' allegedly quotes from the introduction of a book written by long-time Washington, D.C. progressive author and journalist and a friend of mine, Bill Blum. Bill was once an editor and contributor to *Covert Action Quarterly*, a magazine devoted to exposing CIA operations like the arming, funding, and training of bin Laden and his Mujaheddin guerrillas during the Afghan-Soviet war. The Bush perception managers are either incredibly stupid or are trying to ensnare liberal journalists as aiders and abettors of al Qaeda, something that is certainly within their scope.

"Bin Laden allegedly quotes the following passage from Blum's book, *Rogue State*: 'If you [Americans] are sincere in your desire for peace and security, we have answered you. And if Bush decides to carry on with his lies and oppression, then it would be useful for you to read the book *Rogue State*, which states in its introduction: 'If I were president, I would stop the attacks on the United States: First I would give an apology to all the widows and orphans and those who were tortured. Then I would announce that American interference in the nations of the world has ended once and for all.'

"However, this quote is not from *Rogue State*, again, pointing to a very bad forgery of the bin Laden audiotape....Bin Laden might not be so eager to quote Blum if he was aware of his other work, *Killing Hope*, an expose of the CIA's covert wars. In it, Blum defends the Soviet occupation of Afghanistan as self-defense against the CIA-backed Islamist guerrillas, including bin Laden's forces that were backed by the CIA. Now, why would bin Laden plug an author like Blum who backed bin Laden's hated enemies, the Soviet Communists and their Afghan allies? Because the bin Laden tape and his purported oratory are frauds."

Even the staid BBC saw the obvious connection between President Bush's troubles and the release of the bin Laden tape by stating, "The commander-in-chief has been under intense pressure in recent weeks, accused of trampling on civil liberties in pursuit of terror suspects. His defence has been that America is a nation at war. So bin Laden's latest threats to launch new attacks on the US will only serve to underline this argument."

But the true revelation came in May 2010, when two CIA officials admitted that people within the agency had recorded fake Osama bin Laden tapes. While this did not prove beyond doubt that the agency had faked the 2001 and 2006 tapes, it proved that it certainly had the capability.

According to Jeff Stein's Spy Talk column in the *Washington Post*, "The agency actually did make a video purporting to show Osama bin Laden and his cronies sitting around a campfire swigging bottles of liquor and savoring their conquests with boys, one of the former CIA officers recalled, chuckling at the memory. The actors were drawn from 'some of us darker-skinned employees,' he said."

Other CIA officials would neither confirm nor deny the production of such faked bin Laden tapes but argued that such plans never moved to completion because the agency did not have enough money or expertise to carry out such projects, an excuse which was not believable to those with knowledge of CIA operations and history. One CIA official, according to Stein, said projects such as the fabrication of bin Laden tapes has been turned over to military for "psy-war" development at Fort Bragg.

Paul R. Pillar, who until his retirement in 2005 was the CIA's National Intelligence Officer for the Near East and South Asia, offered the rationale for any bin Laden tape, saying, "Any statement from bin Laden serves at least the modest purpose, for him and his group, of showing that he is alive and kicking and sufficiently engaged to make new threats that play off recent issues or events."

Many persons, both researchers and others, came to the belief that bin Laden has been dead for years. Some military sources claimed he was killed in the fighting at Tora Bora following the invasion of Afghanistan in late 2001. Others said he died from natural causes. On December 26, 2001, Fox News reported the *Pakistani Observer* as stating "...bin Laden has died a peaceful death due to an untreated lung complication." This information, according to the Pakistani publication, came from a Taliban leader who attended bin Laden's funeral.

But despite the argument over how he died, a number of people claimed bin Laden was dead before the beginning of the year 2002. As far back as 2003, the possibility that bin Laden had been long dead was voiced by none other than former Secretary of State Madeleine Albright when she mentioned to Fox News commentator Morton Kondracke the possibility that the Bush administration had Osama bin Laden's corpse hidden away somewhere and might bring him out before the 2004 election. Kondrake said Albright was not smiling and did not seem to offer this as a joke.

In October 2008, CIA case officer Robert Baer old Terry Gross, host of the National Public Radio show *Fresh Air*, that bin Laden was dead. "He hasn't shown up," noted Baer. "I've taken in the last month a poll of CIA officers who have been on his trail, and what astounded me was not a single one was sure he was alive or dead. They have no idea, I mean this man disappeared off the side of the earth. That has never happened before in all my years with the CIA. And while we're at it, when in history has a country fought another country or another entity when the leader may be dead?" Bear warned that the so called "War on Terrorism" could be an eternal war if the goal continued to be the capture of bin Laden.

Other prominent persons who have indicated that Osama bin Laden died long before 2011 include Pakistani President Asif Ali Zardari; former Pakistani President Pervez Musharraf; Dale Watson, former head of FBI counterterrorism; Afghan President Hamid Karzai; US Senator Harry Reid; Professor Bruce Lawrence, head of Duke University's Religious Studies; and Angelo Codevilla, former US foreign intelligence officer and professor of international relations at Boston University. One of the most prominent people to speak publicly about bin Laden's death was Benazir Bhutto, the former Pakistani prime minister who was assassinated by gunmen on December 27, 2007, while campaigning in preparation for the 2008 general election.

The month before her assassination, during an interview with David Frost, Bhutto suddenly blurted out that Osama bin Laden was murdered by Ahmed Umar Saeed Sheikh in 2006. Umar Sheikh was one of the men convicted of kidnapping and killing *Wall Street Journal* reporter Daniel Pearl and the man who wired $100,000 to 9/11 ringleader Mohamed Atta for distribution to his men in Florida just prior to the 9/11 attacks. Pakistani President Pervez Musharraf has claimed that Umar Sheikh was recruited by British intelligence agency, MI6, while studying at the London School of Economics.

BIN LADEN REPLIES

Despite her bombshell statement about bin Laden's death, there was no follow-up question to Bhutto from Frost and later her comment was edited out when distributed by the BBC. A BBC website later apologized stating, "...editing out her comment was clearly a mistake, for which we apologize, and it should not have happened. There was no intention on our part to distort the meaning of the interview." Yet to date there has been no investigation to determine if Bhutto's statement was true or not. If true, of course, the entire meaning of the official 9/11 conspiracy story has been badly distorted.

Another top-level American official who cannot be ignored is Dr. Steve R. Pieczenik, who served under the Nixon, Ford and Carter administrations. Recruited as an assistant secretary of state, the former Navy captain served as a senior policy planner under Henry Kissinger, Cyrus Vance, George Schultz and James Baker. He also worked on George W. Bush's election campaign against Al Gore. In an April 24, 2002 interview with radio talk show host Alex Jones, Pieczenik shocked the audience by stating bin Laden had been "dead for months," and that the government was waiting for the most politically expedient time to roll out his corpse. He also said certain officials within the US government knew bin Laden was dead before they invaded Afghanistan.

Pieczenik, who had personally met bin Laden and worked with him during the proxy war against the Soviets in Afghanistan back in the early '80s, said bin Laden died from natural causes. "I found out through my sources that he had had kidney disease. And as a physician, I knew that he had to have two dialysis machines and he was dying. And you could see those in those films [the videotapes released by the government in the fall of 2001], those made-up photos that they were sending us out of nowhere. I mean, suddenly, we would see a video of bin Laden today and then out of nowhere, they said, 'Oh it was sent to us anonymously,' meaning that someone in the government, our government, was trying to keep up the morale on our side and say, 'Oh, we still have to chase this guy,' when, in fact, he's been dead for months." He added that the government was only awaiting the most politically expedient time to roll out his corpse.

Some researchers surmised that such revelations by Albright and Pieczenik may have prevented the announcement of bin Laden's death during the Bush administration as such an act following these predictions would have caused serious suspicion in the public mind. According to Pieczenik, Osama bin Laden "was used in the same way that 9/11 was used to mobilize the emotions and feelings of the American people in order to go to a war that had to be justified through a narrative that Bush Junior created and Cheney created about the world of terrorism."

If Bhutto, Albright, Pieczenik and others are correct and bin Laden has been dead these past years, then the rationale for the invasion and occupation of Afghanistan has lost all credence.

But such speculation ended on May 1, 2011, when President Obama made the latest—and most probably the final—report of Osama bin Laden's death. This time the story was that a super-secret Navy SEAL (Sea, Air and Land) team had finally located the elusive fugitive in a multi-million-dollar mansion in Abbottabad, Pakistan. Utilizing the increasingly used police tactic of a "no knock" entrance, the heavily armed team killed bin Laden in what was initially described as a fierce firefight, destroyed one of their damaged helicopters, and then flew off to a waiting aircraft carrier where, to honor Muslim customs, they gave his corpse a burial at sea.

However, as the days passed, large holes began to appear in the official story. Initially, the attacked abode, formerly a safe house of Pakistani intelligence, was called a million-dollar mansion. *Time* magazine toned this down by merely stating it was located in the "prosperous neighborhood of Bilal Town." Soon this description changed to a normal home in a middle class area. This then evolved into a white-washed, trash-strewn dump. It should be noted that the home, rented by Afghan nationals, is located just a little more than 2,600 feet away from the Pakistan Military Academy and several former senior military officials live in this security-sensitive area.

Bin Laden's wife initially was reported as killed when the fugitive used her as a shield. This quickly proved untrue as she was merely wounded in the leg and was not used as a shield. Then the public learned that bin Laden was not even armed. One tabloid claimed he was "crying like a baby and begging for his life." The statement that Muslim tradition required a burial at sea proved specious.

Even a photograph purportedly of the dead bin Laden proved to be a faked composite fabrication. This photo, never actually presented to the public, nevertheless found its way onto the Internet and, worse yet, into the hands of selected congressmen. Republican Senator Scott Brown of Massachusetts, a member of the Armed Services Committee, told the media he was shown the photo among others as part of an official briefing but was told they were too graphic to release to the public. At least two other committee members, New Hampshire's Kelly Auotte and Georgia's Saxby Chambliss, said they too had seen the photo. Brown later said in an interview, "Listen, I've seen the picture. He's definitely dead. And if there's any conspiracy theories out there, you should put them to rest." He later admitted that the photos were a hoax. "The photo that I saw and that a lot of other people saw is not authentic," Brown acknowledged in a prepared statement.

Even the now-famous photo of President Obama and Secretary of State Hillary Clinton "watching intently" as the attack on the Abbottabad mansion took place has been established as a fake. The media reported, "President Obama was watching on a TV screen as a commando gunned down Osama bin Laden. Via a video camera fixed to the helmet of a US Navy SEAL, the leader of the free world saw the terror chief shot in the left eye. However, according to CIA director Leon Panetta, there was a blackout of the live feed which was cut off for security purposes before the SEAL team even entered the building. "Once those teams went into the compound I can tell you that there was a time period of almost 20 or 25 minutes where we really didn't know just exactly what was going on. And there were some very tense moments as we were waiting for information," Panetta said in a PBS interview. Panetta's account is likely true as it is otherwise hard to explain the contradictory and confusing statements made by the White House if indeed top officials were watching the drama unfold live as claimed.

Even the widely-circulated photograph of President Obama addressing the nation about the bin Laden operation was staged. According to Reuters photographer Jason Reed, "As President Obama continued his nine-minute address in front of just one main network camera, the photographers were held outside the room by staff and asked to remain completely silent. Once Obama was off the air, we were escorted in front of that teleprompter and the president then re-enacted the walk-out and first 30 seconds of the statement for us."

In a move some saw as an effort to prevent Americans from investigating the truth of the bin Laden death reports, a few days after the attack, the Internet Crime Complaint Center of the FBI warned Internet users that emails and websites purporting to show photos or videos of bin Laden's "recent death" might contain computer damaging viruses. The center urged users not to open unsolicited emails even if the sender was familiar to them.

While many Americans cheered bin Laden's reported death as a victory in the "War on Terrorism," many others voiced concerns. Many wondered that since bin Laden—if it was indeed bin Laden—was admittedly unarmed, why wasn't he taken captive, flown out of Pakistan along with the large amount of computers and other property taken from the mansion, and flown to the US to stand trial for his crimes to prove that America is a land of law and justice? If he was indeed dead, why wasn't his body available for inspection like so many past criminals such as Mussolini, Lenin, Stalin and Mao Zedong?

Others noted that in its broadest implications, US soldiers attacked a private residence in a neutral nation and committed murder since several people were killed and Osama bin Laden had never been formally charged with the attacks of 9/11. Murder is a crime under both national and international law (even prosecuted within the military) and civilized people never condone murder, let alone celebrate it. Even our worst criminals are entitled to a fair trial.

Considering the numerous inconsistencies, prevarications and missteps surrounding the report of his 2011 death, coupled with the hard evidence being sequestered by the US government, the controversy over his true end may never be resolved.

## THE BIN LADEN FAMILY AND FRIENDS

Osama bin Laden as well as many of his al Qaeda operatives, not to mention the majority of the named 9/11 hijackers, are Saudis. And this makes for a very troublesome aspect to the War on Terrorism.

To understand the problem, one must understand that the United States, and perhaps most of the industrialized world, is immeasurably dependent on the eight major oil fields of Saudi Arabia. Loss of even a significant portion of this petroleum could mean unthinkable consequences to the economy of both America and the world.

Control over this much-needed energy source is concentrated in one ruling family, a family with longstanding and well-documented ties to major oil players including the Bush family.

Media reports to the contrary, Osama bin Laden continued to receive financial support from his family even if they did not agree with his views and actions. According to the PBS biography, most of the bin Ladens are faithful Muslims, who are taught that it is a sin to keep something that is not rightfully yours. Whether they agree with their sibling or not, they sincerely believe that bin Laden's share of the family fortune rightfully belongs to him and they see that he receives his due.

So, while the bin Laden assets are held by other family members, who can rightfully argue that bin Laden owns none of it, his share of the family profits continued to go to him. Some family members supported bin Laden because they feel it is their religious duty. Others are more circumspect, not wishing to offend the Saudi royals, while others still make no effort to hide the fact that they send bin Laden money.

Of all the nations that are the most probable sponsors of bin Laden, first place must go to Saudi Arabia, home of bin Laden, the fundamentalist Wahhabi sect, and the Saudi royal family, primary business partners of the Bush family. This may go far in explaining the dearth of reporting on the Saudis in the mainstream media.

In fact, Defense Secretary Donald Rumsfeld tried to suppress a mid-2002 special report by the Defense Department naming Saudi Arabia as the "kernel of evil" and stating that Saudi funds support most of the Middle East's terrorist groups because the Saudis have a vested interest in perpetuating tension in the region. According to federal whistle-blower Al Martin, "It has always been a guideline of Republican administrations, starting with Richard Nixon, to suppress the truth about Saudi Arabia."

Likewise, as reported previously, by mid-2004, the Bush administration continued to drag its feet in supplying White House intelligence briefing documents to the 9/11 Commission. In July 2003, the Bush administration asked Congress to withhold 28 pages of its official 9/11 report. It was reported that the pages claimed there were ties between the

Saudi government and the hijackers. The connection was through Saudi financiers Omar al Bayoumi and Osama Brassman, both of whom conducted business with Saudi government officials.

Individual Saudis also became the defendants of a $1 trillion lawsuit filed on behalf of more than six hundred families of 9/11 victims in 2002. Since then, many more families have joined the suit raising the total number of persons involved to about 4,000. Yet to date this story has received scant mention in the mainstream media. The suit was filed by attorney Ron Motley of Charleston, South Carolina, best known for his landmark $350 billion settlement from the tobacco industry in the late 1990s.

"This has become a true mission for me," said Motley. "The individuals that we've sued facilitated the events of September 11." Liz Alderman of Armonk, New York, whose son Peter died in the WTC attack, said she joined the suit because "there is no other way for the truth to come out. I've learned and I believe that an awful lot of the funding that enabled the terrorists to attack America was provided by Saudi Arabia," she said.

Two of the most prominent Saudis named in the suit were Prince Sultan bin Abdul Aziz al-Saud, Saudi Arabia's defense minister, and Prince Turki bin Faisal, a former intelligence chief and ambassador to Britain. The Saudi embassy in Washington had no comment on the suit, but, according to the *New York Times*, a State Department source said, "The Saudis have made their concerns known at a senior level [of the US government]."

The *Times* also reported that the Bush administration might well move to dismiss or delay the suit because it might damage the already strained relationship between the two countries. The paper made no mention of the close business relationships between the Saudis and the Bush family nor the fact that victims' families have implored Bush not to block the suit.

In August 2003, Motley cleared his first major legal hurdle when a federal judge in Washington, D.C., refused to dismiss a Saudi bank, two large Muslim charities and two other defendants from the suit. The suit continued. Lawyers for the Saudi defendants had argued that the charges against their clients was "guilt by association" but Motley countered by pointing out that under the new US anti-terrorism laws there is no demand to show a direct link to a crime. He pointed out that under new anti-terrorist legislation, if a person or organization knowingly gives money to a terrorist group, that person or organization can be sued. Motley presented evidence that the chairman of the Al Rajhi bank had connections to Osama bin Laden's former personal secretary.

The US Court of Appeals for the Second Circuit in 2009 supported the Saudis by ruling that the US Foreign Sovereign Immunities Act (FSIA) applies to foreign government officials acting in their official capacities. This meant the Saudi princes were immune from claims in the United States arising from the events of 9/11 based on their status as agents of the Saudi state. The court also held that a Saudi charitable organization was immune from US jurisdiction because it was an organ of the Saudi state under the FSIA, and that allegations about the activities of the Saudi princes relating to al Qaeda otherwise were "too attenuated to support the jurisdiction of a US court."

The court ruled that none of the FSIA exceptions to immunity noted by the plaintiffs applied and thus set an important precedence for foreign nations. The court noted that while the FSIA had been amended to allow for terrorism-related claims, such exceptions only apply to states on a list maintained by the US government. Saudi Arabia is not on that list.

The stonewalling and obfuscation of the Bush administration toward 9/11 in general and the 9/11 Commission's emphasis on the Saudi funding of al Qaeda in particular proved too much for one victim's relative.

On November 26, 2003, Ellen Mariani, the whose husband, Louis Neil Mariani, was killed when Flight 175 struck the South Tower of the WTC, filed a $911 million plus damages class action civil suit in the United States District Court of the Eastern District of Pennsylvania. Defendants included President Bush, Vice President Cheney, Attorney General Ashcroft, Secretary of Defense Rumsfeld, CIA Director George Tenet, Transportation Secretary Mineta, National Security Adviser Rice and former President George Herbert Walker Bush. The suit was brought under the Racketeer Influenced and Corrupt Organizations Act (RICO), usually reserved for organized crime figures.

Interestingly, another defendant in the suit was Peter G. Peterson, chairman of the Council on Foreign Relations (CFR). The suit claims CFR members "are believed to have provided Defendant [Bush], et. al., while acting under color of federal law with critical national security advice not believed to be in the best interests of the Plaintiff [Mariani] and the American public." In the conclusion to the suit, Mariani's attorney, Philip J. Berg wrote, "Defendants must be held to account for their actions prior to and after 9/11 for the good of our nation and our security. Anything less will render the United States Constitution and out leaders' ritual vows 'to preserve and protect our Constitution against all enemies, foreign and domestic' meaningless."

By 2005, personal conflicts had caused Mariani to withdraw from the suit which was then resubmitted by Berg, this time naming World Trade Center worker and rescue hero William Rodriguez as the plaintiff. (Rodriguez's eyewitness account of bombings in the basement levels of one of the towers is covered in Part I of this book.)

In yet another 9/11 legal development, on November 28, 2004 a group of New York City citizens including 9/11 family members and survivors formally submitted a Citizens Complaint and Petition to New York State Attorney General Eliot Spitzer. The complaint demanded that Spitzer's office open a criminal inquiry and/or grand jury investigation into "the many still unsolved crimes of 9/11, over which he has jurisdiction," urging him to address "previously suppressed or ignored areas of inquiry identified by the 9/11 Family Steering Committee, 9/11 CitizensWatch and many independent researchers." Spearheading the effort were activists from within the grassroots 9/11 truth movement, led by a national organization noted earlier called 911truth.org.

The lead complainants included Bob McIlvaine, who lost his son Robert in the World Trade Center collapse; Patricia Perry, who lost her son John, a New York City Police officer; William Rodriguez, the WTC maintenance worker and rescue effort hero mentioned previously; numerous other 9/11 family members and survivors; and a variety of activist organizations.

Despite this demand for a grand jury plus proving a wealth of documented evidence, Spitzer failed to move, instead devoting himself to winning the governorship of New York in 2006. By early 2008, he became increasingly public in his blaming the Bush administration for the ongoing financial and economic crisis. In a February nationwide TV interview, he laid responsibility for the economic collapse directly on the Bush Administration and on February 14, the *Washington Post* published an article by Spitzer entitled, "Predatory Lenders' Partner in Crime: How the Bush Administration Stopped the States From Stepping In to Help Consumers."

Few conspiracy researchers were surprised on March 17, 2008 – only one month after his article appeared – when Spitzer resigned his governorship in the wake of the exposure of his involvement as a client in a high-priced prostitution ring. "With that article, some Washington insiders believe, Spitzer signed his own political death warrant," wrote F. William Engdahl in an article entitled "Why Bush Watergated Eliot Spitzer."

It might be noted that the prostitution ring leader, Deborah Jeane Palfrey, better known as the "Mayflower Madame," reportedly committed suicide after appearing on Alex Jones' nationally syndicated radio program claiming to have inside information about the 9/11 attacks. She also voiced concern for her safety, vowed she would never commit suicide and added if she was found dead "They will make look like suicide."

In the wake of such suits and complaints, plus considering the quarrels between the 9/11 Commission and the Bush administration, it now seems probable that any state sponsorship of the 9/11 terrorists, outside or the US, must have come from either Saudi Arabia or perhaps Israel or both.

Concerning the suppressed 28 pages of the congressional investigation, *U.S. News & World Report* quoted an unnamed government official who had read the report as saying, "There is so much more stuff about Saudi government involvement, it would blow people's minds."

This statement was clarified in that same issue by Florida Senator Bob Graham, co-chairman of the report committee. "The reality is that the [Saudi] foreign government was much more directly involved in not only the financing but the provision of support— transportation, housing and introduction to a network which gave support to the terrorists." He added, "They were not rogue agents, [but] were being directed by persons of significant responsibility within the government."

The *9/11 Commission Report* supported Graham's conclusion by stating, "Al Qaeda appears to have relied on a core group of financial facilitators who raised money from a variety of donors and other fund-raisers, primarily in the Gulf countries and particularly in Saudi Arabia." The report added that although the commission could find no evidence that the Saudi government as an institution or senior Saudi officials individually funded al Qaeda, "This conclusion does not exclude the likelihood that charities with significant Saudi government sponsorship diverted funds to al Qaeda."

According to author Craig Unger, who investigated the elder Bush's role in both the Iran-Contra and Iraqgate scandals, the estranged sister-in-law of Osama bin Laden, Carmen bin Laden, said she thought family members might have provided funds for Osama.

Saudi Arabia has long profited from its cozy relationship with American leaders. That nation profited most from the 1991 Gulf War. According to London's *Financial Times*, "Saudi Arabia oil revenues have tripled since mid-1990 because of the closure of production in Iraq and Kuwait."

Interestingly enough, it was the elder Bush's own secret society—the Council on Foreign Relations (CFR)—that blew the whistle on his business partners and friends in Saudi Arabia. In a report issued in October 2002, a CFR task force reported that Saudi Arabian officials for years have ignored countrymen and Muslim charities that provided major funding for the al Qaeda network and that US officials had systematically refused to acknowledge this connection.

"Saudi nationals have always constituted a disproportionate percentage of al Qaeda's own membership; and al Qaeda's political message has long focused on issues of particular interest to Saudi nationals, especially those who are disenchanted with their own government," stated the CFR report. Such connections are so numerous and documented that by late 2002 even the mass media began to question the Saudi role.

In his widely noted book *House of Bush, House of Saud: The Secret Relationship Between the World's Two Most Powerful Dynasties*, Craig Unger argues that the seeds for 9/11 were planted nearly thirty years ago in a series of savvy business transactions that subsequently translated into a long-term political union between the Saudi royal family and the extended family of George H. W. Bush.

Unger's book begins with a single question: "How is it that two days after September 11, 2001, even as American air traffic was tightly restricted, a Saudi billionaire socialized in the White House with President George W. Bush as 140 Saudi citizens, many immediate kin to Osama bin Laden, were permitted to return to their country?"

According to Unger's account, a potential treasure trove of intelligence was allowed to flee the country—including an alleged al Qaeda intermediary who was said to have foreknowledge of the 9/11 attacks. Unger asks: "Why did the FBI facilitate this evacuation without questioning these people? Why did Saudi Arabia, the birthplace of most of the hijackers, receive exclusive and preferential treatment from the White House even as the World Trade Center continued to burn?"

Saudi Arabia is not only in conflict over the politics but there are serious schisms within its religious community too. There is a serious division in the Muslim faith between the followers of the prophet Mohammed and its most extreme sect, the Wahhabi. The Wahhabis are taught that Jews are sub-humans who should be killed, while Muslims who have studied the *Hadith*, or Traditions, know that Mohammed married a Jewish woman and stated that faithful Jews would join Muslims in Paradise.

The most vicious opponents of Israel are the Wahhabis and there is one very good reason for their fear and anger. Statistics tell the tale. Literacy in the Arab world is below 50 percent. "Wahhabis are functionally illiterate, they cannot read about this conflict on their own. Typically, they memorize a few passages of the Koran taken out of context, and never read the accompanying *Hadith* for explanation," noted author John Loftus. Loftus said Muslim scholars and leaders do not speak out against the "primitive Wahhabi apostasy" because most Muslim mosques are impoverished and depend on Saudi subsidies. To the Saudi royalty, literacy and knowledge would mean an end to their domination, so for years they have funded anyone who might aid their cause.

Why? Israel's literacy rate is 97 percent and it is the only nation in the Middle East that allows Arab women to vote. "To the Saudis, a democratic Palestinian nation would be a cancer in the Arab world, a destabilizing example of freedom that would threaten Arab dictators everywhere," explained Loftus, an attorney who has represented a number of federal whistle-blowers within the US intelligence community.

As information slowly leaked to the public, more and more attention was drawn to the role of the Saudis in supporting terrorism. In early October, the congressional committee investigating the 9/11 attacks was shocked to hear testimony from FBI special agent Steven Butler concerning the bureau's knowledge of Saudi money going directly to two of the accused hijackers.

Butler said one of his confidential informants, Abdussattar Shaikh, rented rooms in San Diego to Khalid al-Midhar and Nawaf al-Hazmi, both accused of hijacking American Airlines Flight 77. Two other Saudi nationals, Osama Basnan and Omar al-Bayoumi, also aided the hijackers by paying their rent, helping to open a bank account and arranging flight training, despite the fact that both had been charged with visa fraud.

Agent Butler also said he alerted his superiors in the FBI about this money flow but it went nowhere. Perhaps this inaction was due to evidence that at least some of the funding of the two terrorists came from the Saudi embassy. It was reported that Princess Haifa bint Faisal, wife of the Saudi ambassador, wrote cashier checks to Bayoumi, which were believed to have been passed along to the hijackers al-Midhar and al-Hazmi.

The worldwide banking connections of the Saudis—including banks controlled by globalist financiers—make untangling their funds difficult. For example, The National Commerce Bank in Saudi Arabia maintains a correspondent bank relationship with JP Morgan Chase as well as the Bank of America, according to the worldwide bank database, bankersalmanac.com. Correspondent banks act like branch banks, offering a variety of services including payments, wire transfers and stock trades. US officials charged that National Commerce Bank was used by wealthy Saudi businessman Yasin al-Qadi to funnel money to the al Qaeda network through a charity called the Muwafaq Foundation.

Jeff Hershberger, a spokesman for Bank of America, declined to say if the bank had a relationship with the Saudi bank, but Kristin Lemkau, speaking on behalf of JP Morgan, confirmed that her bank had a correspondent relationship with the Saudi bank.

The business circles involving the Saudis grew to include the Bush family in Texas. "The famous Saudi family [bin Laden] and the Bushes of Texas moved in similar financial circles down in Houston," noted the *Austin American-Statesman* in late 2001. In 1973, the oldest son of the bin Laden clan, Salem bin Laden—though at the time he spelled it Binladen or Binladin—came to Texas to recruit his father's former pilot to fly the family's corporate jet. Soon, Salem became involved in a number of Texas businesses, including ownership of a small Houston airport, a San Antonio aviation services company and a home in a San Antonio suburb called Enchanted Valley.

Under a policy of primogeniture [the first born gains the inheritance], only the oldest bin Laden son has control of the family fortune. This is the same method with which the European Rothschilds have managed to maintain their immense wealth over the centuries. Salem bin Laden then represented his family's fortune.

When Salem found that his father's old pilot, Gerald Auerbach of San Antonio, did not want to leave Texas, he established Binladen Aviation at San Antonio International Airport and put Auerbach in charge. Salem also purchased a lot from Auerbach in Kingsland, Texas, and built a house there. "I had owned [the lot] for several years, but I couldn't afford to build a house myself," Auerbach told a news reporter. "I really think he did it for me. He let us use it when he wasn't there." He added that Salem would jet into Texas for brief stays two or three times a year.

After 9/11, just up the road from the house once used by Salem bin Laden, there were clumps of American flags with a sign reading, "Bomb bin Laden!" According to a Texas news article, "Had it not been played out in the Middle East, the bin Laden family story could have been pure Texas—a business dynasty linked to power, politics and big money. Besides its business ties to the Lone Star State, the family acquired holdings that range from waterfront condos in Boston to property in California to holdings in medical research firms and a US private investment firm to which former President Bush serves as an adviser [the Carlyle Group].

"The family's high-level connections were longstanding and well-known: The former president visited the bin Laden family in Saudi Arabia in 1998 and 2000." Incredibly, the evidence also indicates that George W. Bush was put into the oil business by bin Laden money.

According to several published reports, Bush family friend James R. Bath used money from Osama bin Laden's brother to open a partnership with George W. Bush in Arbusto Energy, a West Texas drilling company.

Bath and the younger Bush had served together in the Texas Air National Guard. Later, according to *The Houston Chronicle*, Salem bin Laden named Bath his business representative in Texas shortly after the senior Bush was named CIA director by appointed President Gerald Ford in 1975. According to Texas court and financial records, Bath, a Houston entrepreneur, represented Salem bin Laden in such business deals as the $92 million customization of a Boeing 747 jet for use by the Saudi royal family and the purchase of the single-runway Houston Gulf Airport.

In 1992, Bath came under investigation by federal authorities for lobbying illegally for Saudi interests but nothing came of the inquiry. But, in sworn depositions, Bath acknowledged he represented four prominent Saudis, including Salem, as a trustee and used his name on their investments in return for a 5 percent commission on each deal. Bath, whose resume stated he handled all North American investments and operations for Sheikh Salem bin Laden, has consistently declined to discuss his business dealings for the record.

"Throughout Salem bin Laden's dealings in Texas, he cloaked himself in third parties and offshore companies that gave few clues to his identity," wrote Mike Ward of the *Austin American-Statesman*. "Other Texas investments were listed in the names of trustees, not Salem." Documents that are normally public, such as aviation, registration and other records that might provide more detail about the bin Laden family connections in Texas, have been denied to the public on the orders of Attorney General John Ashcroft in the wake of 9/11.

Salem bin Laden had a keen interest in aviation and it proved his undoing. On May 29, 1988, the forty-two-year-old flying enthusiast went up in an ultra-light craft that suddenly and inexplicably veered into power lines. He was pronounced dead after being rushed to San Antonio's Brooke Army Medical Center.

Another prominent Saudi represented by Bath was Sheikh Khalid bin Mahfouz, former CEO of National Commerce Bank, Saudi Arabia's largest bank and the one most closely associated with the royal family. It has already been noted that this bank is one that US authorities have identified as a conduit to the al Qaeda terrorist network. Sheikh Khalid bin Mahfouz was one of several Saudi defendants named in the one trillion dollar lawsuit filed in 2002 by attorney Motley, representing more than six hundred families of 9/11 victims.

Mahfouz was described by author J. H. Hatfield as a "deal broker whose alleged associations run from the CIA to a major shareholder and director of the Bank of Credit & Commerce International (BCCI). BCCI was closed down in July 1991, amid charges of multibillion-dollar fraud and worldwide news reports that the institution had been involved in covert intelligence work, drug money laundering, arms brokering, bribery of government officials and aid to terrorists."

The wealthy Saudi also reportedly paid $200 million for Dallas's Texas Commerce Bank Tower in 1985, which had cost only $140 million to build. This deal not only helped cash-strapped Texas oilmen at the time but also benefited the founders of Texas Commerce Bank, the family of James Baker, former secretary of state under President George H. W. Bush. Mahfouz, Bath and former Texas Governor John Connally were also partners in Houston's Main Bank, according to *Time* magazine reporter Jonathan Beaty.

In the early 1980s, Bath was listed as a $50,000, 5 percent investor in two limited oil exploration partnerships controlled by George W. Bush. This venture, Arbusto Energy, evolved into Harken Energy. The Bush White House has consistently argued that the money invested in Arbusto Energy belonged to Bath, not bin Laden. However, several researchers have maintained that Bath at the time could not have had this kind of money to invest. This was supported by Bath's former business partner, Charles W. White of Houston.

White said, based on his knowledge of Bath's finances at the time coupled with Bath's financial records filed during a divorce, that Bath had no substantial money of his own at the time the investment was made. In an interview with Beaty, White described a variety of backroom business deals with Bath, rich Arabs, Texas wheeler-dealers and the now defunct Bank of Credit & Commerce International (BCCI).

"You have to understand that they thought I was one of them," White explained. "Bath told me he was in the CIA. He told me he had been recruited by George Bush [Sr.] himself in 1976, when Bush was director of the agency. This made sense to me, especially in light of what I had seen once we went into business together. Bath and George, Jr., were pals and flew together in the same Air National Guard unit, and Bath lived just down the street from the Bush family when George, Sr., was living in Houston. He said Bush wanted him involved with the Arabs, and to get into the aviation business.

"That's how Bath, who didn't know anything about the aviation business, became one of the biggest jet aviation dealers in the country within a couple of years. Look, here's a Boeing he's leasing to the Abu Dhabi National Oil Company. That's a multimillion-dollar jet. That's how he became a representative for Sheikh Khalid bin Mahfouz, whose family controls the National Commerce Bank of Saudi Arabia."

White also said Bath was investigated by the DEA in the 1970s. He was suspected of flying currency to the Cayman Islands. Nothing came of the investigation when no evidence of drug involvement was found. It was at this same time that Main Bank, according to Beaty, "made the news when a bank examiner discovered that it was purchasing $100 million in hundred-dollar bills each month from the Federal Reserve, an amount that dwarfed its minuscule asset base."

While representing Mahfouz's business interests in Texas, Bath had racked up more than $12 million in contract overruns by overcharging for aviation fuel at his Southwest Aviation Services company at Houston's Ellington Field.

According to an October 28, 1991, report in *Time* magazine, Southwest Aviation in 1990 was charging government military aircraft—including then-President Bush's *Air Force One*—anywhere from twenty-two to more than forty cents per gallon more than the Air National Guard base at Ellington was paying for jet fuel. The article pointed out that each time Bush's government-owned jet landed at Ellington, it was serviced by Bath's company rather than the lower-priced government facility. *Houston Post* reporter John Mecklin estimated that between 1985 and 1989, the Department of Defense paid Mahfouz's agent Bath more than $16.2 million for fuel under government contracts that should have cost $3.6 million.

In 1990, the same year Southwest Aviation was overcharging the government and Bush for fuel, the president drew a "line in the sand" to block Iraqi intrusion into Saudi Arabia. It is interesting to note that this line was located between the Iraqi forces and the Harken oil interests owned by his son, then-soon-to-be Texas Governor George W. Bush.

The president's eldest son was a $50,000-a-year "consultant" to and a board member of Harken Energy Corp. of Grand Prairie, Texas, near the home of the Texas Rangers baseball team of which Bush was a managing general partner.

It should be noted that while connected to Harken in the late 1980s, the younger Bush received low-interest loans from the company while he served as a director and most certainly benefited from insider transactions. Ironically, Bush denounced similar shenanigans in mid-2002 following the scandals of Enron and WorldCom. One Bush official explained, "Corporate officers should not be able to treat a public company like their own personal bank."

According to filings with the Securities and Exchange Commission, the low-interest Harken loans totaled more than $180,000 and allowed Bush to purchase 105,000 shares of stock through a stock option program for senior company officials.

In January 1991, just days before Desert Storm was launched, Harken shocked the oil industry by announcing an oil-production agreement with the small island nation of Bahrain, a former British protectorate and a haven for international bankers just off the coast of Saudi Arabia in the Persian Gulf. Harken Energy, of which President Bush was a director from 1986 to 1993, formed an offshore subsidiary in September 1989 in the Cayman Islands. The subsidiary, Harken Bahrain Energy Company, was set up in anticipation of the company's venture drilling for oil off the coast of Bahrain.

Veteran oilmen wondered aloud how unknown Harken, with no previous drilling experience, obtained such a potentially lucrative deal. Furthermore, it was reported that "Harken's investments in the area will be protected by a 1990 agreement Bahrain signed with the US allowing American and 'multi-national' forces to set up permanent bases in that country."

Through a tangled web of Texas oilmen, wealthy Saudi sheiks and unscrupulous bankers connected to the BCCI criminal bank, the younger Bush eventually gained a sizable interest in Harken Energy. Two months before Saddam Hussein sent Iraqi troops into Kuwait, Bush sold two-thirds of his Harken stock, netting himself nearly a one-million-dollar profit. The stock dropped when the Iraqi invasion began.

In October 1990, the younger Bush told *Houston Post* reporter Peter Brewton that accusations that his father ordered troops to the area to protect Harken drilling rights was "a little far-fetched." He further claimed he sold his Harken stock before the Iraqi invasion but Brewton could find no record of the sale in the files of the Securities and Exchange Commission (SEC).

Records of Bush's Harken stock sale finally turned up in March 1991, eight months after the July 10, 1990, SEC deadline for filing such disclosures. One week after Saddam's troops entered Kuwait, Harken stock had dropped to $3.03 a share. The tardy SEC records revealed that by some good fortune, Bush had sold 66 percent of his Harken stock on June 22, 1990—just before the Iraqi invasion of Kuwait on August 2—for the top-dollar price of $4 a share, netting him $848,560.

Common business interests brought the Bush and bin Laden families a special closeness. An *Austin American-Statesman* article detailed both the financial and social connections between the two families, stating "bin Ladens traveled in the same financial circles as Bush." It should be remembered that from 1989 to 1993, it was the Bush family, particularly Jeb and Neil, who were involved in the savings and loan debacle that cost taxpayers more than $500 billion.

It also should be noted that during the Persian Gulf War, it was Binladen Brothers Construction [now the Binladen Group] that helped build airfields for US aircraft. The bin Laden brothers were then described as "a good friend of the US government."

Later the bin Laden firm continued to construct an American air base in Saudi Arabia despite the fact that Osama bin Laden had already been blamed for terrorist acts such as the truck bombing of the Khobar Towers at the Dhahran base that killed nineteen Americans. A *WorldNetDaily* writer commented, "So let's get this straight. Bin Laden blows up our facilities, and his family gets the contract for rebuilding them. Do you get the feeling there is more going on than meets the eye?"

The Bank of Credit & Commerce International (BCCI)—another joint business endeavor of the Bushes and bin Ladens—was closed by federal investigators in 1991 after suffering some $10 billion in losses. BCCI was a Pakistani-run institution with front companies in the Cayman Islands that used secret accounts for global money laundering and was used by US intelligence to funnel money to bin Laden and the Mujahideen in Afghanistan fighting against the Soviet-backed government. During this struggle in Afghanistan, the Binladen Group joined other wealthy Saudis in an effort that came to be known as "the Golden Chain," which helped create the al Qaeda network.

Kahlid bin Mahfouz, mentioned earlier as a major player with well-to-do Texas oilmen, owned a controlling interest in BCCI. It has been called the most corrupt financial institution in history. The interconnections between BCCI and Bush's Harken Energy prompted a *Wall Street*

*Journal* writer in 1991 to comment, "The number of BCCI-connected people who had dealings with Harken—all since George W. Bush came on board—likewise raises the question of whether they mask an effort to cozy up to a president's son."

Another close connection between bin Laden and the Bush family is a private international investment firm known as the Carlyle Group, which in 2006 boasted the management of more than $34 billion. Although it has renovated its website since the September 11 attacks, it is known that Carlyle directors include former Reagan Secretary of Defense Frank Carlucci, former Bush Secretary of State James Baker and former Reagan aide and GOP operative Richard Darman. The *New York Times* reported that former President Bush was allowed to buy into Carlyle's investments, which involve at least 164 companies around the world.

In fact, two years after Bush Sr. left public office in 1993, he signed on as a senior counselor with the Carlyle Group. He was later joined by former British Prime Minister John Major and soon the pair was jetting off to Saudi Arabia to meet with the royal family, the bin Ladens and the Mahfouzes. Mahfouz's two sons soon became investors in the Carlyle Group although one, Abdulrahman bin Mahfouz, was a director of the Muwafaq Foundation, designated by the US Treasury Department as "an al Qaeda front."

According to the September 28, 2001 *Wall Street Journal*, "George H. W. Bush, the father of President Bush, works for the bin Laden family business in Saudi Arabia through the Carlyle Group, an international consulting firm." It has been confirmed by the senior Bush's chief of staff that Bush sent a thank-you note to the bin Laden family after a social visit in early 2001. But it has been reported that after the attacks of 9/11, the Carlyle Group distanced itself from the family by buying out substantial bin Laden holdings in the firm.

Perhaps the closest Saudi friend to the Bush family was Saudi Arabian Ambassador to the United States Prince Bandar bin Sultan, the man who arranged the secretive flight of the bin Ladens in the days following 9/11.

The $1 trillion dollar lawsuit filed against the Saudis alleges that Prince Bandar's father, who serves as the Saudi defense minister, contributed at least $6 million to four charities known to finance Osama bin Laden and al Qaeda.

Prince Bandar's relationship with the Bush family goes back to the days of the Reagan administration when Bush Sr. and Bandar would lunch regularly. "After Bush became president in 1989," wrote journalist Craig Unger, "Bandar acted as an envoy between him and Saddam Hussein, assuring Bush that the US could count on Saddam to provide a bulwark against extremist Islamic fundamentalism." Unger further stated that after the 2000 election, Bandar joined Bush Sr., former National Security Advisor Brent Scowcroft and General Norman Schwarzkopf for a hunting trip in Spain.

With such connections and his son as a sitting president of the United States, the senior Bush's Carlyle involvement was questioned by Larry Klayman, chairman and general counsel of Judicial Watch, who said, "Any foreign government or foreign investor trying to curry favor with the current Bush administration is sure to throw business to the Carlyle Group. And with the former President Bush promoting the firm's investments abroad, foreign nationals could understandably confuse the Carlyle Group's interests with the interests of the United States government."

After detailing some of the Carlyle/bin Laden investments in several businesses, including aerospace industries as well as the tremendous defense buildup since 9/11, writer Michael C. Ruppert commented, "In other words, bin Laden's attacks on the WTC and Pentagon, with the resulting massive increase in the US defense budget, have just made his family a great big pile of money."

There is evidence that President Bush and his father tried to block past efforts to find and prosecute Osama bin Laden despite documentation linking terrorism to both the bin Ladens and the CIA. According to a special BBC investigation reported in the November 10, 2001, issue of the *Times of India*, a "secret FBI document, numbered 1991 WF213589" emanating from the FBI's Washington field office, blamed the recent terrorist attacks on "connections between the CIA and Saudi Arabia and the Bush men and bin Ladens."

The British newspaper, the *Guardian* wrote apparently of another document, marked "Secret" and coded "199 (national security)," concerning two of bin Laden's relatives. These two documents allege that the FBI had been told to "back off" an investigation of his brother, Abdullah bin Laden, who along with another brother, Omar, lived in Falls Church, Virginia just outside Washington. Abdullah was the United States director of the World Assembly of Muslim Youth (WAMY) until 2000. Although listed in FBI files as a "suspected terrorist organization," WAMY was not placed on the Bush administration's terrorist list, which would have frozen its assets. Despite several grand jury probes, no charges have been brought against the organization, which claims to be dedicated to guarding Muslim youth against "destructive ideologies."

Yet according to journalist Greg Palast, in mid-2002 Pakistan expelled several WAMY operatives, and officials in both India and the Philippines have accused WAMY of funding militant Muslim groups. Furthermore, in 2003, an unnamed security official who served under George W. Bush told journalist Craig Unger, "WAMY was involved in terrorist-support activity. There's no doubt about it."

Documents disclosed that the FBI file on the two bin Laden brothers was closed in 1996. According to Palast, "High-placed intelligence sources in Washington told the *Guardian*: 'There were always constraints on investigating the Saudis.'" The source said restrictions became worse after Bush took office and added, "There were particular investigations that were effectively killed."

The Saudis' attempts to lobby in Washington brought several Muslim organizations into the far-flung web of post 9/11 investigations. According to the *Washington Post*, federal agents since the mid-1990s had sought to track an estimated $1.7 billion that moved between these organizations. Investigators said the groups were created in the 1970s by the al-Rajhi family, one of Saudi Arabia's primary banking dynasties. Collectively, the organizations own or control a number of businesses worldwide. A spokesman for the al-Rajhis denied any wrongdoing on their part.

In late March 2002, federal agents raided sixteen homes and offices in northern Virginia believed to be involved in a nexus of Saudi-backed organizations with connections to terrorist groups. The after-the-fact and sweeping raids infuriated Muslims and non-Muslims alike.

Grover Norquist, a Republican Party activist who shared offices with the one of the raided organizations and was a board member of the Islamic Institute, said the groups existed "to promote democracy and free markets. Any effort to imply guilt by association is incompetent McCarthyism." Norquist, along with Islamic Institute chairman Khaled Saffuri, helped arrange meetings between Islamic leaders and senior Bush administration officials.

Then there is the case of a former employee at the US Consulate in Saudi Arabia who took bribes to provide fake visas. Abdullah Noman, fifty-four, a citizen of Yemen, worked at the consulate from September 1996 until November 2001. He admitted to taking bribes of both money and gifts worth thousands of dollars in exchange for visas for entry into the United States, making it appear that the bearers were members of legitimate trade delegations. "They would come in with everybody else and then disappear," noted Assistant US Attorney Lee Vilker.

Vilker said there was no known connection between Noman and al Qaeda terrorists but he admitted that authorities had not been able to locate all those who obtained visas from Noman, who was arrested in Las Vegas in late 2001 while accompanying a Middle Eastern trade delegation. He faced a prison term of fifteen years and a $250,000 fine plus deportation after serving time.

But even more ominous revelations came in 2002 from Michael Springman, a twenty-year veteran of the US Foreign Service and former chief of the American visa bureau in Jeddah, Saudi Arabia, who told of suspicious behavior there many years ago.

In a BBC News interview, Springman said, "In Saudi Arabia, I was repeatedly ordered by high level State Department officials to issue visas to unqualified applicants. These were, essentially, people who had no ties either to Saudi Arabia or to their own country. I complained bitterly at the time there. I returned to the US, I complained to the State Department here, to the General Accounting Office, the Bureau of Diplomatic Security and to the Inspector General's office. I was met with silence.

"What I was protesting was, in reality, an effort to bring recruits, rounded up by Osama bin Laden, to the US for terrorist training for the CIA. They would then be returned to Afghanistan to fight against the then-Soviets.

"The attack on the World Trade Center in 1993 did not shake the State Department's faith in the Saudis, nor did the attack on the American barracks at Khobar Towers in Saudi Arabia three years later, in which nineteen Americans died. FBI agents began to feel their investigation was being obstructed."

THE BIN LADEN FAMILY AND FRIENDS

With the information above in hand, it is now clear that if there was a state sponsor behind the 9/11 attacks, as argued by the Bush administration to justify the invasions of Afghanistan and Iraq, that state would have to be Saudi Arabia. And considering the close business and social connections between the Saudi royals and bin Ladens with the Bush family, much closer scrutiny of this connection is fully justified.

Either the Bushes were too stupid to see what is happening right under their very noses or their resistance in revealing evidence about the Saudis' role is guided by something more sinister. Few people have ever accused the Bushes of being merely stupid.

## PART III – THE 9/11 BACKLASH

*"In order to make sure that we're able to conduct a winning victory, we've got to have the best intelligence we can possibly have. And my report to the nation is we've got the best intelligence we can possibly have."*

—President George W. Bush
in a September 26, 2001 speech to the CIA.

Fear mongering has always been a favored tool of despots and tyrants. After all, why would a free and prosperous population willingly give up their rights and liberties? Ever since 9/11, both the Bush and Obama administrations have has gained increasing social control by holding the threat of terrorism over the heads of the American people.

Under the control of its corporate masters, the "watchdog" media have turned into lapdogs for their owners, which, in turn, have allowed the government to manipulate the public through national fear mongering.

A classic example of the use of this age-old device came in early 2006, when President Bush—under fire for the unresolved wars in Iraq and Afghanistan, the torture of terrorist suspects, and unconstitutional spying on Americans—played the fear card yet again, declaring: "We cannot let the fact that America hasn't been attacked in four and a half years since September 11 lull us into the illusion that the threats to our nation have disappeared." He then went on to detail what he described as a thwarted terrorist attack on Los Angeles in 2002. Bush revealed that the California strike was planned by a man named Hambali, reportedly a key lieutenant of Khalid Sheikh Mohammed, the alleged mastermind of the 9/11 attacks. Both Hambali and Mohammed were reported captured in 2003.

Bush said these al Qaeda leaders recruited Asian men who were to use shoe bombs to blow open the cockpit door of a commercial airliner, which then would be crashed into the US Bank Tower in Los Angeles. Bush mistakenly referred to this building as "Liberty Tower," but was quickly corrected that its original name had been "Library Tower." Bush said the plot was foiled when a key Asian al Qaeda member was arrested but declined to name the suspect or his nationality.

Soon, this story filled the mass media airwaves with some stations airing scenes from the Hollywood alien invasion film *Independence Day* as graphic representation of the destruction of the US Bank Tower.

But even before Americans could heave a collective sign of relief at being spared this carnage, serious questions arose over Bush's statement. Many thoughtful persons wondered why Bush had not called attention to the saving of Los Angeles early in 2003 when such news might have blunted the large and numerous anti-war demonstrations conducted prior to the invasion of Iraq.

Concern increased when Los Angeles Mayor Antonio Villaraigosa told newsmen he knew nothing of such an attempt and felt "blindsided" by Bush's announcement of the 2002 attack. He said communication regarding such an attack with the White House had been "nonexistent" despite at least two requests by him to meet with Bush regarding security issues. "I'm amazed that the president would make this [announcement] on national TV and not inform us of these details through the appropriate channels," Villaraigosa told newsmen. "I don't expect a call from the president, but somebody."

Others were even less considerate in their characterization of Bush's sudden story of the 2002 Los Angeles attack. Doug Thompson, a writer for *Capitol Hill Blue*, the oldest political news site on the Internet, said he was contacted by members of the US intelligence community, who disputed

Bush's claim. Thompson said he was able to confirm the intelligence credentials of at least four of the persons who contacted him. All asked not to be identified for fear of reprisals. "The president has cheapened the entire intelligence community by dragging us into his fantasy world," Thompson quoted a longtime CIA operative as saying. "He is basing this absurd claim on the same discredited informant who told us al Qaeda would attack selected financial institutions in New York and Washington."

Indeed, in August 2004, during the heat of the presidential election, the Bush White House had sought to increase the terror alert level by claiming attacks were imminent on major financial institutions. This alert was later withdrawn after officials admitted it was based on old information from a discredited source.

The Obama administration has been no better. Shortly after the 2008 election, White House Chief of Staff Rahm Emanuel uttered these words, "Rule 1: Never allow a crisis to go to waste. They are opportunities to do big things." Secretary of State Hillary Rodham Clinton has said, "Never waste a good crisis," and in 2009, President Barack Obama told a radio audience, there is "great opportunity in the midst of" the "great crisis" befalling America.

"[N]ow we have the president, along with his chief aides, admitting—boasting!—that they want to exploit a national emergency for their preexisting agenda, and there's no scandal. No one even calls it a gaffe. No, they call it leadership. It's not leadership. It's fear-mongering," proclaimed Jonah Goldberg in the *Los Angeles Times*. Yet, that same Barack Obama, speaking during the 2008 presidential campaign in South Dakota, had accused George W. Bush and John McCain, of "hypocrisy, fear-peddling and fear mongering."

And Obama's spate of stimulus bills and government takeovers prompted Steve Verdon, writing on the *Outside the Beltway* website to note, "The more Obama fear mongers over the economic situation the more wary I become of these stimulus packages. I've noted before that this is the standard tactic used by politicians to increase the size and scope of government."

On Christmas Day 2009, as Congress was deliberating rescinding some of the more odious sections of the Patriot Act, a 23-year-old Nigerian, Umar Farouk Abdulmutallab, tried to set off explosive powder in hidden in his undergarments aboard Northwest Flight 253. Dubbed the "underwear bomber," this was big news at the time, but the whole episode had a bad smell about it. As facts slowly emerged, it appeared to be more—or perhaps less—than the mass media allowed.

According to other passengers Abdulmutallab was escorted by a well-dressed man who talked his way past airline employees despite the fact that Abdulmutallab had only carry-on bags and has paid cash for the trans-Atlantic flight to Detroit. Additionally, Abdulmutallab's father, Alhaji Umaru Mutallab, former chairman of First Bank Nigeria and a former Nigerian minister, had reported his son's militant activities to the US Embassy and Nigerian security agencies six months before the incident. Adding to the suspicion that the Abdulmutallab incident was contrived, it was found that US intelligence agencies had prevented the State Department from revoking Abdulmutallab's US visa, a move that would have prevented him from boarding the plane. In January 2010, before the House Committee on Homeland Security, State Department Undersecretary Patrick F. Kennedy said intelligence officials asked his agency not to deny a visa to the suspected terrorist because they felt it might have hampered an investigation into al Qaeda. Others saw the action as evidence that elements with intelligence agencies have paved the way for Abdulmutallab.

Another problem regarding this story were reports that claimed Abdulmutallab had attempted to ignite pentaerythritol tetranitrate (PETN), an explosive used by the US military. Persons familiar with PETN said a blasting cap, not simple fire from a match or lighter, is required to detonate PETN. No blasting caps or primers were found on Abdulmutallab and the chemicals he carried were inadequate to generate an explosion. This information led conspiracy researchers to suspect that the whole episode was another false-flag attack, one engineered to cast blame on others rather than the real culprits. But to what purpose?

The answer may be that a new terrorist scare was needed to dissuade Congress from rescinding of some Patriot Act measures, particularly warrantless searches. The measures were continued. Also, existing plans to equip major airports with full-body scanning devices went into high gear. Leading this public relations blitz was former Homeland Security Chief Michael Chertoff, co-founder of the Chertoff Group, a security and risk-management firm whose clients include Rapiscan Systems, a manufacturer of the body-imaging screening machines, 150 of which were purchased by the TSA for $25 million in early 2010.

Kate Hanni, a founder of *FlyersRights.org*, an airport passengers' rights group opposed to the use of the full-body scanners, complained, "Mr. Chertoff should not be allowed to abuse the trust the public has placed in him as a former public servant to privately gain from the sale of full-body scanners under the pretense that the scanners would have detected this particular type of explosive [PETN]." By January 2010, about 40 body scanners were in use at 19 US airports. This number was expected to climb by more than 300 machines by the end of that year, mostly due to the publicity over the Christmas Day incident.

Despite Chertoff's claim that scanners could have detected PETN, British Member of Parliament Ben Wallace, who formerly had worked on developing such scanners, told newsmen that trials had shown low-density materials such as PETN went undetected. Wallace said scanners picked up shrapnel, heavy wax and metal, but plastic, chemicals and liquids were missed.

Other concerns over the fully-body scanners involved health and privacy. The terahertz radiation waves used in body scanner penetrate non-conducting material like clothing, but also deposit energy in the human body. Boian Alexandrov, heading a team of researchers at Los Alamos National Laboratory in New Mexico, announced they found the teraherz radiation used in the full-body scanners damages human DNA. "Based on our results, we argue that a specific terahertz radiation exposure may significantly affect the natural dynamics of DNA, and thereby influence intricate molecular processes involved in gene expression and DNA replication," reported Alexandrov's team. The team said that while the radiation from body scanners produces only subtle changes, it nevertheless is able to unzip double-stranded DNA, creating bubbles in the double strand that may significantly interfere with normal processes such as gene expression and DNA replication.

Added to these health concerns are privacy advocates who claim the TSA was not being truthful about the body scans being able to depict the whole human body including details of the sex organs. TSA officials have said that the scanning machines cannot clearly show an individual's genitalia and, certainly in all media stories on these scanners, one can only see blurry outlines of the body. However, alternative media, such as *PrisonPlanet.com* exposed the TSA statement as untrue by quoting Melbourne Airport's Office of Transport Security manager Cheryl Johnson, who admitted, "It is possible to see genitals and breasts while they're going through the machine…It will show the private parts of people, but what we've decided is that we're not going to blur those out, because it severely limits the detection capabilities."

In England, where full-body scanning has been declared mandatory although it violates UK child pornography laws against the depiction of the genitals of underage children, opponents have declared the images so graphic as to amount to "virtual strip searching." They called for more safeguards to protect passengers' privacy.

Others also criticize the TSA for failure to be truthful in their public statements regarding the full-body scanners. While TSA officials tried to assure the public that flyers' naked images will not be saved, printed or transmitted, government documents obtained by the Washington-based Electronic Privacy Information Center (EPIC) told a different story. The documents showed the TSA specifies that body scanners must have the ability to store and send images when in "test mode." EPIC executive director Marc Rotenberg said such a requirement makes it possible for the machines to be abused by TSA insiders and even hacked by outsiders. Rotenberg said he did not believe the TSA had been truthful about the true capability of such devices. "They've done a bunch of very slick promotions where they show people—including journalists—going through the devices. And then they reassure people, based on the images that have been produced, that there's not any privacy concerns. But if you look at the actual technical specifications and you read the vendor contracts, you come to understand that these machines are capable of doing far more than the TSA has let on," he said.

It appeared that not only do the full-body scanners take full-color nude photos of air travelers but, contrary to public assurances, such photos are being stored by the government. Government spokespersons have assured the public that full-body scanner photos would not be saved but discarded after an airport review. However, in August 2010 the US Marshals Service admitted it had surreptitiously saved tens of thousands of images in a single Florida courthouse. Marshals Service associate general counsel William Bordley acknowledged that "approximately 35,314 images [were] stored" in the Orlando federal courthouse. "TSA is not being straightforward with the public..." stated EPIC's Rotenberg, who claimed such scanning is a violation of the Fourth Amendment prohibiting "unreasonable" searches. "This is the Department of Homeland Security subjecting every US traveler to an intrusive search that can be recorded without any suspicion—I think it's outrageous."

Despite the concerns over health hazards and privacy violations, in late July 2010, Homeland Security Secretary Janet Napolitano announced that the full-body scanners would be be operating in virtually all major US airports. Prior to 9/11, the siege mentality of some American leaders was not so prevalent. In testimony before joint hearings of the Senate Armed Services Appropriations and Intelligence committees in the spring of 2001, Secretary of State Colin Powell explained why Americans should not give up their freedoms for the hope of security. "If we adopted this hunkered-down attitude, behind our concrete and our barbed wire, the terrorists would have achieved a kind of victory," he declared.

But such reasoned rhetoric was to change completely as new and constitutionally questionable laws and regulations were put into effect later that year. Within days of the 9/11 attacks, President Bush declared a "War on Terrorism." He initially called it a "crusade," but that term was quickly dropped when it was pointed out that Muslims, both within and without the Middle East, still remember the bloody history of that word and would take offense. To initiate a war, there first must be a perceived enemy. That one grand enemy was now claimed to be Osama bin Laden and his al Qaeda network. As previously noted, the FBI announced a list of suspected hijackers with unbelievable speed, while at the same time acknowledging that the men used false identity papers. But this list was questioned in many quarters, including government agents.

"There are people within the US intelligence community who doubt that the hijacker list from 9/11 has much truth in it," said one unnamed intelligence source as quoted by author Jon Rappoport. "They see it as a more-or-less invented list. They know that if you start with men showing false passports (or no passports) to get on four planes on 9/11, you can't assemble a correct list of nineteen suspects within a few days—especially since all those men are presumed dead and missing, untraceable.

"Al Qaeda is being used as a term to convince people that these terrorists are all connected in a vast, very well-organized network that is global in reach, that has a very sophisticated and far-flung communication setup, that issues orders from the top down to cells all over the world," stated the intelligence source. "There are a number of people inside the US intelligence agencies who know this is a false picture. They know that false intelligence is being assembled in order to paint a picture which is distorted, so that the American people will have a single focus on one grand evil enemy."

As mentioned previously, in October 2004, the BBC broadcast a documentary entitled *The Power of Nightmares: The Rise of the Politics of Fear*, which challenged the Bush administration's concept of al Qaeda as a multi-faceted globe-spanning octopus of terrorism. The documentary also noted this was not the first time that American political figures had hyped a foreign enemy to achieve their own goals—in fact, many of these same neoconservatives are responsible for today's fear mongering.

Their goal in the early 1970s was to cut short President Richard Nixon's efforts at "détente" with the Soviet Union, and the leaders of this faction were none other than Secretary of Defense Donald Rumsfeld and Chief of Staff Dick Cheney in the Ford administration. Both Rumsfeld and Cheney claimed that reconciliation with the Soviets was impossible because they were hiding weapons of mass destruction (WMDs), a new generation of nuclear submarines that were undetectable by current technology. This claim was firmly denied by the CIA at the time, which called it "complete fiction." The charge ultimately proved false, but not before trillions were spent on the biggest peace-time military build up in American history during the subsequent Reagan administration.

Also mentioned in Part I, in Britain it has been suggested that al Qaeda is not a real organization but rather a computer list of Arab mercenaries—freedom fighters/terrorists for hire. "Bin Laden...was armed by the CIA and funded by the Saudis to wage jihad against the Russian occupation of Afghanistan. Al Qaeda, literally 'the database,' was originally the computer file of the thousands of Mujahideen who were recruited and trained with help from the CIA to defeat the Russians," noted British commentator Robin Cook, a former leader of the House of Commons.

Often supposed enemies prove to be mirror images of each other. Noted author Thom Hartmann pointed out that both Bush's neocons and

Muslim terrorists operate from the same ideology—both believe the end justifies the means and that people must be frightened into accepting religion and nationalism for the greater good of morality and a stable state.

## A HISTORY OF UNCONSTITUTIONAL ACTIONS

If the idea of strong federal protection during times of terrorist threats seems comforting, picture this: A pimple-faced 18-year-old dressed in camouflage and armed with a fully loaded M-16 arrives at your door and informs you that you must leave your home and come with him because the authorities fear a biological attack in your city. If you protest and say you'll stay and take your chances, you are in violation of the law and subject to arrest, fine and imprisonment. After seeing his armed companions, you decide to join your neighbors in a military truck destined for a "relocation camp" situated many miles from your home. At the camp, you are instructed to stand in line for a vaccination against smallpox, anthrax or whatever the latest threat might be. If you refuse the inoculation, recalling that in past years so many such vaccines were proven to be tainted, you are again subject to fine and jail.

If this sounds like some paranoid's view of an Orwellian nightmare, you should know that laws authorizing such action had already been passed in 16 states and the District of Columbia by the end of 2002. Maine, New Hampshire, Maryland, Virginia, South Carolina, Georgia, Tennessee, Florida, Missouri, Oklahoma, Minnesota, South Dakota, Utah, Arizona and New Mexico had passed all or parts of the model law. The other states had either rejected or stalled the legislation.

And don't take comfort if your state is not among these as most of this overreaching law was incorporated into the Homeland Security legislation. Many states modified or outright rejected this legislation, which was drawn up as a model law for the federal Centers for Disease Control and Prevention following the anthrax attacks that occurred in the Capitol on the heels of 9/11. One might have noticed that not much has been mentioned in recent years about these anthrax attacks. Perhaps this is because investigation showed that the anthrax pathogens involved were military grade and unavailable outside the United States. The one suspect, whose life was wrecked after being identified as a suspect by federal authorities, was exonerated after several years and the next man named in those attacks conveniently died while in federal custody. To date, no one has been charged with those attacks.

The Model State Emergency Health Powers Act was sent to each state legislature with a federal endorsement for its passage. Federal officials claimed the laws were needed to provide local authorities the legal right to make quick decisions in an emergency involving contagious or deadly pathogens. One advocate, attorney Gene Matthews with the Department of Health and Human Services argued, "We have not used emergency powers in probably 50 years. This is something we need to attend to."

Under this act, authorities would be able to federalize all medical personnel, from EMTs to physicians, and enforce quarantines. They would have the right to vaccinate the public, with or without their consent, seize and destroy private property without compensation and ration medical supplies, food, fuel and water in a declared emergency. "[This act] goes far beyond bioterrorism," said Andrew Schlafly of the Association of American Physicians and Surgeons. "Unelected state officials can force treatment or vaccination of citizens against the advice of their doctors."

The Federal Emergency Management Agency (FEMA), designated as the lead agency under the Department of Homeland Security, also has plans in its files for the evacuation of cities and the use of sprawling temporary camps to house their residents.

Under the pretext of planning for the War on Terrorism, FEMA has dusted off and augmented contingency plans to counter the effects of nuclear, biological and chemical attacks.

By mid-2002, FEMA was notifying its vendors, contractors and consultants to envision the logistics of millions of displaced Americans forced to leave cities that come under attack. The firms were given a deadline of January 2003, to be ready to establish such displaced person camps. FEMA made it known that it already had ordered significant numbers of tents and trailers to be used for housing. As already mentioned, Halliburton was given a contract to construct camps to contain unspecified occupants.

History has provided proof that traditional American openness and fairness will not necessarily be supported by the nation's highest authorities. During the War Between the States, President Abraham Lincoln suspended the writ of habeas corpus, that mainstay of American justice, which demands that the accused has the right to face his accusers and evidence. This action was later overturned by the US Supreme Court, but only because Lincoln had not sought approval from Congress.

During World War I, that same court upheld the right of the president to seize the property of enemy aliens without a hearing, stating, "National security might not be able to afford the luxuries of litigation and the long delays which preliminary hearings traditionally have entailed." And, of course, the Supreme Court upheld the rounding up, incarceration and property seizure of Japanese Americans following the attack on Pearl Harbor. Many Americans, from leading academics to the man on the street, wondered aloud what would become of traditional American liberties in the War on Terrorism.

Frank Serpico, the former New York policeman who turned in corrupt officers in the 1960s and was the subject of a popular film of that same name, spoke at a July 4, 2002, reading of the Declaration of Independence in Chatham, NY: "It is my opinion that never before have we, as a nation, stood in greater danger of losing our individual liberties as we are today," he told the audience. "We, the people of this great nation, are being punished for the transgressions of our leaders and their consorts... When I still have the freedom to speak, I'll always use it." Ironically, several in the audience there to hear Serpico read the Declaration of Independence booed his remarks.

Even former Attorney General Janet Reno, under whose leadership the tragedies at Ruby Ridge and Waco unfolded, expressed concern. "I have trouble with a war that has no endgame and I have trouble with a war that generates so many concerns about individual liberties," she told an audience at Old Dominion University in Norfolk, VA, in 2002.

Reno asked Americans to remember the lessons learned from the unjust imprisonment of Japanese-Americans during World War II, adding that she believed the government would be hard pressed to find a legal basis to prosecute many of the Taliban and al Qaeda prisoners detained at Guantanamo Bay Naval Base in Cuba.

Indeed, horror stories had begun to leak out about the degrading treatment of prisoners who had been captured "on the battlefield" in the War on Terrorism, and held thereafter at Abu Ghraib, the Guantanamo prison or other points of rendition as "enemy combatants." The Bush administration's response was that since such prisons were not on American soil, the legal protections provided by the US Constitution did not apply, and that secret military tribunals would be convened.

But for months and then years, hundreds of men languished in the naval prison without trial, in apparently cruel conditions. By 2005, a wide variety of human rights organizations—including Amnesty International, Physicians for Human Rights, and even the United Nations—had charged that the conditions in Guantanamo were in violation of international conventions to which the US is a party.

Regardless, in early 2006, at least 556 persons still remained indefinitely detained at Guantanamo. A FOIA request brought by the Associated Press revealed their names for the first time only on April 20, 2006. The roster indicated that the prisoners came from 41 countries, with the largest groups from Saudi Arabia, Afghanistan, and Yemen. Over 200 had been transferred to other facilities and a few released, but many had been held for over four years; only a handful had ever faced formal charges.

Also at that time, Congress, at the urging of the Bush administration, passed the Military Commissions Act of 2006. This law, controversial even at the time it was passed, allows the president to designate certain people – including US citizens—as "unlawful enemy combatants" subject to trial military commissions, which are conducted with fewer civil rights for the defendant than regular trials.

It was not until June 12, 2008, that the Supreme Court finally ruled that at least some Guantanamo prisoners were entitled to the protection of the US Constitution. In December 2009, it was announced that since 2002, the Guantanamo prisoner population had dwindled with more than 550 detainees being sent to other destinations, including the nations of Albania, Algeria, Afghanistan, Australia, Bangladesh, Bahrain, Belgium, Bermuda, Chad, Denmark, Egypt, France, Hungary, Iran, Iraq, Ireland, Italy, Jordan, Kuwait, Libya, Maldives, Mauritania, Morocco, Pakistan, Palau, Portugal, Russia, Saudi Arabia, Spain, Sweden, Sudan, Tajikistan, Turkey, Uganda, United Kingdom and Yemen.

But even as some Guantanamo prisoners were being shuffled quietly off to other locations, officials of the International Committee of the Red Cross was sending confidential reports to the US Government accusing the American military of intentionally practicing psychological and even physical coercion "tantamount to torture" on prisoners at the Guantanamo Bay facility. The Red Cross inspectors also accused some doctors and medical personnel at Guantanamo with "flagrant violation of medical ethics." This was the first time the Red Cross had asserted strongly that the treatment of detainees, both physical and psychological, amounted to torture. Unsurprisingly, the Red Cross allegations were rejected by the Bush administration.

From the outset, such unconstitutional activities prompted cries of outrage from civil libertarians and even some congressmen. Senator Patrick Leahy of Vermont said the use of military tribunals could send "a message to the world that it is acceptable to hold secret trials and summary executions without the possibility of judicial review, at least when the defendant is a foreign national."

Initially, most Americans gave little thought to the jailing of terrorism suspects in Cuba. It was only after the prosecutions that followed the revelations of the horrors at Abu Ghraib Prison in Iraq beginning in 2004 that the average American began to question the American military's methods.

Democratic Senator Richard Durbin, a member of the Senate Judiciary Committee, tried for more than two years to conduct hearings on the treatment of the Guantanamo prisoners—Durbin had himself spent six-and-a-half years as a prisoner in North Vietnam. "This is not a new question," he said. "We are not writing on a blank slate. We have entered into treaties over the years, saying this is how we will treat wartime detainees. The United States has ratified these treaties. They are the law of the land as much as any statute we passed. They have served our country well in past wars. We have held ourselves to be a civilized country, willing to play by the rules, even in time of war.

"Unfortunately, without even consulting Congress, the Bush administration unilaterally decided to set aside these treaties and create their own rules about the treatment of prisoners."

Durbin pointed out that President Bush and his appointees had unilaterally created a new detention policy claiming that prisoners in the War on Terrorism have no legal rights—no right to a lawyer, no right to see the evidence against them, no right to challenge their detention. In fact, the government has claimed detainees have no right to challenge their detention, even if they claim they were being tortured or executed.

"For example," he explained, "they have even argued in court they have the right to indefinitely detain an elderly lady from Switzerland who writes checks to what she thinks is a charity that helps orphans but actually is a front that finances terrorism."

Senator Durbin shocked his colleagues and angered Bush supporters in June 2005, when he cited an FBI account of how Guantanamo prisoners had been chained to cells in extreme temperatures and deprived of food and water and stated, "If I read this to you and did not tell you that it was an FBI agent describing what Americans had done to prisoners in their control, you would most certainly believe this must have been done by Nazis, Soviets in their gulags, or some mad regime—Pol Pot or others—that had no concern for human beings. Sadly, that is not the case. This was the action of Americans in the treatment of their prisoners."

The Democratic whip in the Senate some days later was forced to issue an apology. A tearful Durbin told his fellows, "Some may believe that my remarks crossed the line. To them, I extend my heartfelt apologies."

It was a clear example of the pitfalls of speaking one's true feelings in the midst of patriotic hysteria.

## POSSE COMITATUS IGNORED

Less than a month after the 9/11 attacks, Tom Ridge, a former governor of Pennsylvania, arrived in his new office only steps away from the Oval Office of President Bush, the man who created his job. Ridge's new job was chief of the Department of Homeland Security. Here was the man who was to coordinate 46 different federal government agencies in an effort to protect the American people from terrorists, a position designed from its inception to become a permanent government department.

It was announced that Ridge would work in conjunction with Bush's deputy national security advisor, Army General Wayne Downing, indicating that the military would play a prominent role in counterterrorism activities. Few thought to ask if this was a violation of the Posse Comitatus Act (PCA), the law prohibiting the US military from conducting law enforcement duties against the American public.

The PCA has never really been challenged in this nation's history because it addresses a concern dating back to one of the grievances that caused the American Revolution. The act embodies the traditional principle of separation of military and civilian authority, one of the fundamental precepts of our form of government and a cornerstone of American liberty.

The early colonists were distressed at being placed at the mercy of King George's troops plus being forced to feed and quarter them. But Posse Comitatus, Latin for a support group of citizens for law enforcement, i.e. a posse, was passed in 1878 as a direct result of the outrage over Reconstruction in the South following the War Between the States. Following that war, the Southern states were at the mercy of military authorities, many of whom proved inept or corrupt.

Yet, in recent years this act has been slowly shredded, beginning at least in 1981 when Congress allowed an exception to be made for the War on Drugs. The military was allowed to be used for drug interdiction along the nation's borders. This small and what appeared to be sensible action at the time soon grew out of proportion. Congress, still unable to come to grips with the true social causes of drug abuse, in 1989 designated the Department of Defense as the lead agency in drug interdiction.

In the tragedy at Waco on April 19, 1993, military snipers were on hand and tanks were used to bulldoze the burning Branch Davidian church. The use of the Fort Hood tanks under the command of General Wesley Clark was authorized because federal officials used the pretext that the Davidians were involved with drugs. But no evidence of drugs was ever found.

On April 19, 1995, when the Murrah Federal Building in Oklahoma City was bombed, President Clinton proposed yet another exception to the PCA, this time to allow the military to aid civilian investigators looking into weapons of mass destruction. About this same time Congress considered but did not pass legislation to allow troops to enforce customs and immigration laws at the borders.

During the 1996 presidential campaign, Bob Dole promised to heighten the military's role in the War on Drugs while another primary contender, Lamar Alexander, suggested that a new branch of the military be formed and substituted for the INS and Border Patrol.

In 2005, President Bush announced that he would use military troops in the event of a national pandemic. "The need for reaffirmation of the PCA's principle is increasing," wrote legal scholar Matthew Hammond in the *Washington University Law Quarterly*, "because in recent years, Congress and the public have seen the military as a panacea for domestic problems."

He added, "Major and minor exceptions to the PCA, which allow the use of the military in law enforcement roles, blur the line between military and civilian roles, undermine civilian control of the military, damage military readiness, and inefficiently solve the problems they supposedly address. Additionally, increasing the role of the military would strengthen the federal law enforcement apparatus that is currently under close scrutiny for overreaching its authority."

Yet in the wake of 9/11 and prior to the creation of the Transportation Security Administration (TSA), military troops were seen patrolling airports and the streets of Washington and New York with no outcry from a citizenry apparently appreciative of perceived new security. Such scenes were a brief glimpse of life under martial law.

Even after the creation of the TSA, problems persisted.

Eighty-year-old Fred Hubbell, a retired engineer from Texas visiting in Connecticut, was arrested and handcuffed at Bradley International Airport in August 2002, for mentioning one word. Cranky after enduring repeated searches at the airport, the World War II veteran observed a security guard poking through his wallet, "What do you expect to find in there, a rifle?" Hubbell asked sarcastically. "Do you think that was an appropriate remark?" responded the guard. "I do," replied Hubbell, who was promptly arrested.

Judy Powell, a 55-year-old tourist from Britain, bought a GI Joe toy soldier in Las Vegas and packed it in her bag for her return flight home. But she was refused boarding privileges when an airport security officer spotted GI Joe's tiny plastic rifle. "I was simply stunned when I realized they were serious," said Mrs. Powell. "I was really angry to start with because of the absurdity of the situation. But then I saw the funny side of it and thought this was simple lunacy." A spokesman for Los Angeles International Airport defended the action, saying, "We have instructions to confiscate anything that looks like a weapon or a replica. If GI Joe was carrying a replica then it had to be taken from him." This excuse, of course, carried echoes of Sgt. Schultz from TV's *Hogan's Heroes* explaining, "I vas chust following orders." It is such unthinking responses to orders based on hastily passed laws that so trouble civil libertarians.

If there was any doubt that planning for martial law did not start with the terrorist attacks on 9/11, just ask the residents of Kingsville, TX.

Beginning on the night of February 8, 1999, a series of mock battles using live ammunition erupted around the 25,000 inhabitants of the town, located near Corpus Christi. In a military operation named "Operation Last Dance," eight black helicopters roared over the town. One nearly crashed when it hit the top of a telephone pole and started a fire near a home. Soldiers of the elite 160th Special Operations Aviation Regiment, known as the "Night Stalkers," ferried by the choppers, staged an attack on two empty buildings using real explosives and live ammunition. During the action, an abandoned police station was accidentally set on fire and a gas station was badly damaged when one or more helicopters landed on its roof.

Citizens of Kingsville were terrified during the drill as only the Police Chief Felipe Garza and Mayor Phil Esquivel were notified of the attack in advance. Both men refused to give any details of the operation, insisting they had been sworn to secrecy by the military. Only Arthur Rogers, the assistant police chief, would admit to what happened. "The United States Army Special Operations Command was conducting a training exercise in our area," he said but refused to provide any details.

Local emergency management coordinator for FEMA, Tomas Sanchez, was not happy with the frightening attack and the lack of information and warning. Sanchez, a decorated Vietnam veteran with 30 years service in Naval Intelligence, was asked what the attack was all about. He replied that based on his background and knowledge, the attack was an operational exercise based on a scenario where "Martial law has been declared through the Presidential Powers and War Powers Act, and some citizens have refused to give up their weapons. They have taken over two of the buildings in Kingsville. The police cannot handle it. So you call these guys in. They show up and they zap everybody, take all the weapons and let the local PD clean it up."

One resident told a reporter, "This is total BS. If we don't stop it now it's going to get worse." Asked for comment, then-Texas Governor George W. Bush said he was not his job to get involved in the concerns over the Night Stalkers using live ammunition in a civilian area of his state.

POSSE COMITATUS IGNORED

Sanchez and other military experts told *World Net Daily* that the night attack indicated the use of Presidential Decision Directive (PDD) 25, a Top Secret document that apparently authorizes military participation in domestic police situations. Some speculated that PDD 25 may have surreptitiously superseded the 1878 Posse Comitatus Act.

The events in Kingsville may date as far back as 1971 when plans were drawn up to merge the military with police and the National Guard. (State Guards were gradually eliminated during the past two decades.) In that year, Senator Sam Ervin's Subcommittee on Constitutional Rights discovered that military intelligence has established an intricate surveillance system to spy on hundreds of thousands of American citizens, mostly anti-war protesters. This plan was code named "Garden Plot." Britt Snider, who worked for the subcommittee, said the plans seemed too vague to get excited about. "We could never find any kind of unifying purpose behind it all," he told a reporter. "It looked like an aimless kind of thing."

Four years later Garden Plot began to come into sharper focus. "[C]ode named Cable Splicer [and] covering California, Oregon, Washington and Arizona, under the command of the Sixth Army, [it] is a plan that outlines extraordinary military procedures to stamp out unrest in this country," reported Ron Ridenhour and Arthur Lubow in *New Times* magazine. "Developed in a series of California meetings from 1968 to 1972, Cable Splicer is a war plan that was adapted for domestic use procedures used by the US Army in Vietnam. Although many facts still remain behind Pentagon smoke screens, Cable Splicer [documents] reveal the shape of the monster that the Ervin committee was tracking down."

During the time of Cable Splicer, several full-scale war games were conducted with local officials and police working side by side with military officers in civilian clothing. Many policemen were taught military urban pacification techniques. They returned to their departments and helped create the early SWAT (Special Weapons and Tactics) teams.

For more than two weeks in June 2008, it was planned for some 2,300 Marines to be deployed throughout Indianapolis and its civilian population as a "simulated urban combat zone" under the direction of FBI and the Department of Homeland Security. In an apparent violation of the Posse Comitatus Act, Mayor Greg Ballard offered up 26 sites around Indianapolis for "pre-deployment training in a realistic urban environment."

"I think it's very good training for them...actually, city fighting, urban fighting is really the most dangerous type of fighting there is," explained Ballard. The question was who exactly were these Marines practicing to combat? After all, Camp Lejeune, a major Marine Corps training facility located in North Carolina, is home of Military Operations in Urban Terrain (MOUT), an urban combat training center modeled after an Iraqi town. Another highly realistic urban MOUT training facility covering 30 acres and costing taxpayers 15 million to build is located in Kuwait.

For those who might view the events in Kingsville and Indianapolis as some aberration from the past, a similar military exercise took place in 2009. Soldiers from Fort Campbell, including the 101st Airborne Division (Air Assault) and other infantry brigades, performed a training air assault in Troy, Tennessee on September 29-30. It was called "Operation Diomedes," after the ancient Greek warrior who wounded Aphrodite, the goddess of love.

After being helicoptered from Fort Campbell, soldiers were dropped into multiple locations throughout the town. Once on the ground, the troops were to clear predetermined buildings in four different objective areas based on a combat scenario. Military spokesmen said this air assault was the first time that soldiers from the 101st Airborne had conducted such training in the area. The purpose of the exercise was to provide the troops with "pertinent realistic training in unfamiliar terrain to prepare them for possible contingency operations around the world." Some saw this exercise as practice for the military capture of small towns in the US.

Rep. Clair Burgener of California, a staunch Reagan Republican who had attended the Cable Splicer II kickoff conference, was flabbergasted when shown Cable Splicer documents. "I've read *Seven Days in May* and all those scary books...and they're scary!...This is what I call subversive."

Subcommittee chief counsel Doug Lee read through the documents and blurted, "Unbelievable. These guys are crazy! We're the enemy! This is civil war they're talking about here. Half the country has been designated as the enemy." Snider agreed, stating, "If there ever was a model for a takeover, this is it."

The War on Terrorism following 9/11 has provided the pretext for the activation of plans such as Cable Splicer, a clear violation of the Posse Comitatus Act. In June 2002, despite promises by the Bush administration that it would not initiate any new intelligence reforms until after the joint congressional committees had completed their inquiry into the 9/11 attacks, the Pentagon quietly requested permission to create a powerful new position—Under Secretary of Defense for Intelligence. This request for yet another layer of authority was inserted into a Senate defense bill slated for congressional approval. Stephen A. Cambone was confirmed by the US Senate as the under secretary of defense for intelligence on March 7, 2003, and sworn in four days later.

"The Pentagon's gambit has been such a brilliant stealth attack that many members of Congress aren't even aware it is happening, let alone what it means," noted reporter Linda Robinson. "No hearings have been held, and Pentagon officials portray it as merely an internal managerial matter with few broader implications. But intelligence officials and experts say that could not be further from the truth. The new under secretary position is a bureaucratic coup that accomplishes many Pentagon goals in one fell swoop."

Insiders thought this slippery move served to circumvent the Posse Comitatus Act and deliver even more power into the hands of top Bush administration officials Dick Cheney and Donald Rumsfeld. Initially, the new under secretary for intelligence was to have been Richard Haver. Haver had been Rumsfeld's special assistant for intelligence and was Cheney's very first assistant secretary of defense for intelligence in the elder Bush's administration. The new job eventually went to Cambone, himself a neocon who had served under Rumsfeld and one of the participants in the 2000 PNAC report which foresaw the need for a catastrophic attack to gain support for an increased US military presence in the Middle East.

Cambone resigned at the beginning of 2007. His replacement, James R. Clapper Jr., had headed the Defense Intelligence Agency (DIA) as well as the National Geospacial-Intelligence Agency (NGA), formerly known as the Pentagon's National Imagery and Mapping Agency (NIMA), which is headquartered in Bethesda, MD, and charged with charged with gathering and analyzing geo-spacial intelligence for national security purposes.

Fears of secretive, overreaching agencies with military connections that might violate the Posse Comitatus Act appeared to find substantiation in January 2005, when news outlets reported that, since 2002, the Pentagon's Defense Intelligence Agency had operated an intelligence-gathering and support unit called the Strategic Support Branch (SSB) with authority to operate clandestinely anywhere in the world where it is ordered to go in support of antiterrorism and counterterrorism missions. The SSB previously had been operating under an undisclosed name.

The defense official confirmed that the SSB reports to Vice Admiral Lowell Jacoby, director of the DIA, but that policies were set by Undersecretary of Defense Cambone, one of Rumsfeld's most senior aides.

According to Barton Gellman writing in the *Washington Post*, "The Strategic Support Branch was created to provide Rumsfeld with independent tools for the 'full spectrum of humint [human intelligence] operations,' according to an internal account of its origin and mission. Human intelligence operations, a term used in counterpoint to technical means such as satellite photography, range from interrogation of prisoners and scouting of targets in wartime to the peacetime recruitment of foreign spies. A recent Pentagon memo states that recruited agents may include 'notorious figures' whose links to the US government would be embarrassing if disclosed."

Pentagon officials told Gellman the Strategic Support Branch was created covertly using "reprogrammed" funds that lacked explicit congressional authority or appropriation. SSB missions were not subject to the same stringent congressional oversight conditions imposed on the CIA. In fact, two veteran members of the House Intelligence Committee, one a Democrat and the other a Republican, told reporter Gellman they knew no details about the SSB before being interviewed for his article.

Gellman found "Rumsfeld's ambitious plans [for the SSB] rely principally on the Tampa-based US Special Operations Command, or SOCOM, and on its clandestine component, the Joint Special Operations Command. Rumsfeld has designated SOCOM's leader, Army General Bryan D. Brown, as the military commander in chief in the war on terrorism."

"The Strategic Support Branch is intended to add missing capabilities—such as the skill to establish local spy networks and the technology for direct access to national intelligence databases—to the military's much larger special operations squadrons. Some Pentagon officials refer to the combined units as the 'secret army of Northern Virginia.' Known as 'special mission units,' Brown's elite forces are not acknowledged publicly. They include two squadrons of an Army unit popularly known as Delta Force, another Army squadron—formerly code-named Gray Fox—

POSSE COMITATUS IGNORED

that specializes in close-in electronic surveillance, an Air Force human intelligence unit and the Navy unit popularly known as SEAL Team Six. The Defense Department is planning for further growth. Among the proposals circulating are the establishment of a Pentagon-controlled espionage school, largely duplicating the CIA's Field Tradecraft Course at Camp Perry, Va., and of intelligence operations commands for every region overseas," reported Gellman.

With such secret units operating within the government and military, with little or no oversight or public knowledge, is it any wonder that conspiracy-minded researchers suspect insider manipulation in the 9/11 attacks?

## A QUESTIONABLE MILITARY RECORD

If the Posse Comitatus Act is rewritten or eliminated, the recent history of the Defense Department has done little to inspire confidence that traditional American liberties will be respected.

For example, following the 9/11 attacks, the Pentagon announced the creation of an Office of Strategic Influence (OSI) designed to present a more favorable view of the US military to foreign news media. The new unit provoked an immediate controversy when it was learned that it planned to influence international opinion by planting false stories in the foreign media. Critics felt such phony stories might find their way back to the domestic media. This, of course, was nothing new. The CIA had done the same thing for decades but this was too blatant. Even the major media, including the *New York Times*, were stirred to action.

In a rare step backward, the government announced in early 2002 the office would be closed. Rumsfeld, while arguing that criticism of the office was "off the mark," nevertheless admitted that, "the office has been so damaged that…it's pretty clear to me that it cannot function."

However, the defense secretary refused to let the matter lie. At a November 18, 2002, press briefing, Rumsfeld brought up the controversial office, defiantly stating, "And then there was the Office of Strategic Influence. You may recall that. And 'oh my goodness gracious isn't that terrible, Henny Penny, the sky is going to fall.' I went down that next day and said fine, if you want to savage this thing fine I'll give you the corpse.

There's the name. You can have the name, but I'm gonna keep doing every single thing that needs to be done and I have."

Rumsfeld's vow to continue the program of disinformation was not repeated in the corporate mass media yet apparently the functions of the OSI have continued within the Office of Global Communications, established by President Bush in 2002, and the Information Awareness Office (IAO), a creation also in 2002 of the Defense Advanced Research Projects Agency (DARPA) for the purpose of using surveillance and information-gathering technology to track suspected terrorists.

Causing further anxiety among knowledgeable persons was a plan revealed in late 2002 for the US Army to use computers to investigate hundreds of thousands of law-abiding Americans on the chance one might be a terrorist. The plan called for the Army's Intelligence and Security Command (INSCOM) headquartered at Fort Belvoir, VA, to use high-powered computers to secretly search email messages, credit card purchases, telephone records and bank statements on the chance that one might be associated, or sympathetic to, terrorists. Known as the Pentagon's new Information Awareness Office (IAO), this organization was to create a "vast centralized database" filled with information on the most minute details of citizens' private lives.

To add insult to injury in the minds of opponents of this plan was the appointment of former National Security Adviser Vice Admiral John Poindexter to head this new office. Poindexter lost his national security adviser job in 1990 after being convicted of lying to Congress, defrauding the government and destroying evidence in the Iran-Contra scandal during the Reagan administration. That scandal involved the illegal sale of weapons to Iran and the profits being sent illegally to the CIA-backed "Contra" army fighting in Nicaragua, all done in defiance of Congress. But as vice president of Syntek Technologies, Poindexter had worked with the Defense Advanced Research Projects Agency (DARPA) to develop "Genoa," a powerful search engine and information harvesting program. Poindexter's convictions were later reversed because Congress had promised him immunity for his testimony. "And he has been given a $200 million budget to create computer dossiers on 300 million Americans," warned William Safire in the *New York Times*.

Critics, already suspicious over such an overreaching program so susceptible to abuse, were not assuaged by the DARPA logo, which depicts the occult "all-seeing eye" of knowledge perched on an incomplete pyramid overlooking an image of the Earth.

Christopher H. Pyle, a teacher of constitutional law and civil liberties at Mount Holyoke College, wrote, "That law enforcement agencies would search for terrorists makes sense. Terrorists are criminals. But why the Army? It is a criminal offense for Army personnel to become directly involved in civilian law enforcement [the Posse Comitatus Act]. Are they seeking to identify anti-war demonstrators whom they harassed in the 1960s? Are they getting ready to round up more civilians for detention without trial, as they did to Japanese Americans during World War II? Is counterterrorism becoming the sort of investigative obsession that anti-Communism was in the 1950s and 1960s, with all the bureaucratic excesses and abuses that entailed? This isn't the first time that the military has slipped the bounds of law to spy on civilians. In the late 1960s, it secretly gathered personal information on more than a million law-abiding Americans in a misguided effort to quell anti-war demonstrations, predict riots and discredit protesters. I know because in 1970, as a former captain in Army intelligence, I disclosed the existence of that program."

Pyle, in writing two book-length reports on the Army's spying for Senator Sam Ervin's Subcommittee on Constitutional Rights, was struck by the harm that could be done if the government ever gained untraceable access to the financial records and private communications of its critics. "Army intelligence was nowhere near as bad as the FBI [with its infamous COINTEL program], but it responded to my criticisms by putting me on Nixon's enemies list, which meant a punitive tax audit. It also tried to monitor my mail and prevent me from testifying before Congress by spreading false stories that I had fathered illegitimate children. I often wondered what the intelligence community could do to people like me if it really became efficient."

Today the national security apparatus is gaining that efficiency, thanks to the computer, yet the public awareness of the danger is not nearly as great as it was in the pre-computer 1970s.

Many people fear any control over the civilian population by the military, even in times of "national emergency," will lead to draconian measures such as the establishment of large concentration camps.

FEMA's call for contractors to build such camps did little to ease the anxiety of the more extreme conspiracy minded. The Internet is alive with sites detailing a string of concentration camps across America, just primed and waiting for the lines of detainees or dissidents to be herded inside.

For the uninitiated, this undoubtedly sounds like paranoia and most people pay little attention to what they perceive as delusional statements; however the record clearly shows that such camps do exist. Many such camps are in actuality military bases, either reported closed or maintained by skeleton crews. Others are operated by FEMA and some facilities began as World War II camps for Axis prisoners.

Author and retired USAR Lt. Col. Craig Roberts stated, "In actuality, there are two true sets of camps. First is the military, which can use any base at will to house detainees...Fort Chaffee, for instance, has in the past had warehouses full of mattresses, bunks, barbed wire rolls, fence posts, etc. All of these were to be used around empty barracks to provide for a detention facility if needed...Some of the 'closed' military bases have been designated as 'emergency holding facilities' and already have barracks, mess halls, compounds and latrines in place. All they need are guards, administrators, logistics people and they're in business. All this can be accomplished in 72 hours...Operational plans are in existence for the 'handling' of civilian prisoners and laborers on military installations, both male and female.

"The second category is FEMA. We know they have let a contract for 1,000 'emergency relocation camps' in case of widespread terrorism, biological or chemical attacks on the cities. Again, this can be speedy. The President can declare a national emergency, evoke [Executive Order] 11490, and take over the country without deferring to Congress or the Constitution. Bingo! New World Order in a couple of days." Roberts said the most ominous of these potential concentration camps is located at Elmendorf AFB in Alaska. "Millions of acres adjoining this base have been deeded to the federal government by the State of Alaska. Its designated use is for a 'mental health facility.' It is our version of Siberia and the gulag," he added.

The creation and maintenance—even the very existence—of such camps is lost in a bewildering maze of Executive Orders (EO) dating back to World War II. Many EOs can be traced to the Kennedy presidency and were issued under the duress of the Cold War and the Cuban Missile

Crisis. Many of the EOs detailed on the Internet are outdated, canceled, revoked or superseded by others. Even a careful search of the Federal Register fails to clarify this issue.

But it is clear from the FEMA website that that agency has many plans—including tornadoes, hurricanes, flooding in addition to a nuclear or biological strike—that include evacuation of major cities. Where are those people to go? Who will feed them? How will they live? The answers to these questions remain elusive. And in the meantime, dozens of large military installations sit, mutely awaiting future inhabitants.

As the Department of Homeland Security moved closer to reality in 2002, the US military was also reshuffling its command structure to include a new United Command Plan which would include a new combatant command responsible for homeland security called US Northern Command (USNORTHCOM). Headed by at least a four-star general or Flag Officer, USNORTHCOM would control all military efforts in North America, to include Alaska, Canada, the United States and Mexico and out to 500 nautical miles offshore. Conceived as part of the response to the War on Terrorism, an "appropriate" role also was under consideration for USNORTHCOM in the flagging War on Drugs.

Even though the Posse Comitatus Act seems to have been largely ignored in recent years, there were ongoing calls to alter or even abolish the law. In an October 2001, letter to Rumsfeld, Senator John Warner, a Republican from Virginia and a member of the Council on Foreign Relations, wrote, "Should this law [PCA] now be changed to enable our active-duty military to more fully join other domestic assets in this war against terrorism?"

This cry continued into late 2002 when Rep. Tom Trancredo along with members of the Immigration Reform Caucus and families of victims slain in the course of immigration troubles presented Congress with a petition demanding that military troops patrol the US borders. Jumping on the anti-terrorist bandwagon, Trancredo stated, "As long as our borders remain undefended, we cannot claim that we are doing everything possible to protect the nation from terrorism...It's time to authorize the deployment of military assets on our borders."

Also in 2002, a FEMA official named John Brinkerhoff wrote a paper stating, "President Bush and Congress should initiate action to enact a new law that would set forth in clear terms a statement of the rules for using military forces for homeland security and for enforcing the laws of the United States. Things have changed a lot since 1878, and the Posse Comitatus Act is not only irrelevant but also downright dangerous to the proper and effective use of military forces for domestic duties."

This paper remained on the Homeland Security website in 2010.

## CREATING HOMELAND SECURITY

Since 9/11, incremental but significant changes began being made to the American system of government. This movement culminated in hurried passage of the Homeland Security bill in late November. This act, which authorized an entirely new cabinet-level department, was the greatest restructuring of the federal government since the National Security Act of 1947, yet with none of that act's deliberation and review.

In early June 2002, Bush began urging the creation of a permanent and cabinet-level position for Tom Ridge and his Homeland Security staff, hurriedly created in the wake of the 9/11 attacks. Ridge was calling for bringing myriad government agencies under one central control. And it all needed to be done rapidly, Bush argued, because "we face an urgent need, and we must move quickly, this year, before the end of the congressional session." Thus began the push to create the Department of Homeland Security with Ridge holding a cabinet-level position controlling more than 170,000 federal employees and 22 federal agencies.

But Bush would not allow Ridge to confront Congress directly, claiming his was simply an adviser role, not a policy maker. Congress fumed but, as usual, rolled over and played dead.

"The real losers are the American people..." groused Senator Robert Byrd, a Democrat from West Virginia. "The Congress and the American people are forced to learn about the administration's homeland security efforts in piecemeal, patchwork fashion."

On July 15, 2002, Ridge finally submitted a written statement to the House Select Committee on Homeland Security. In it, Ridge wrote, "We are today a nation at risk to terrorist attacks and will remain so for the foreseeable future. The terrorist threat to America takes many forms, has many places to hide, and is often invisible. Yet the need for improved homeland security is not tied solely to today's terrorist threat. It is tied to our enduring vulnerability."

Ridge indicated that in studying how best to implement homeland security, it became clear that the federal government would need reorganization, and that "the structure of the federal government must be adapted to meet the challenges before us." He admitted that this new reorganization would result in the most significant transformation of the US government in over a half-century.

"It would transform and largely realign the government's confusing patchwork of homeland security activities into a single department whose primary mission is to protect our homeland," he wrote, adding that the new department must have the "right set of tools to work with" and that undue oversight would be "damaging to the new department's ability to carry out its mission successfully."

He stated that FEMA would be a leading component of the new Homeland Security Department. "The new department would build on FEMA to consolidate the federal government's emergency response assets to better prepare all those pieces for all emergencies—both natural and man-made, stated Ridge.

Without mentioning that this consolidation would bring concentrated and unparalleled powers to the presidency, Ridge added that in a national emergency, Homeland Security would "provide a line of authority from the president through the secretary of homeland security to one on-site federal coordinator. The single federal coordinator would be responsible to the president for coordinating the entire federal response to incidents of national significance." In vague generalities, Ridge indicated he sought changes deep within the American infrastructure. "We must therefore promote the efficient and reliable flow of people, goods, and services across borders, while preventing terrorists from using transportation conveyances or systems to deliver implements of destruction," he stated.

How to accomplish this? In writing, Ridge explained that, "the principal border and transportation security agencies—the US Customs Service, the US Coast Guard, the Immigration and Naturalization Service (INS), the Animal and Plant Health Inspection Service, and the Transportation Security Administration—would be unified within a single, powerful division of the new Department of Homeland Security. The new department also would control the issuance of visas to foreigners through the Department of State and would coordinate the border-control activities of all federal agencies that are not incorporated within the new department. As a result, the department would have sole responsibility for managing entry of people and goods into the United States and protecting our transportation infrastructure."

He added that the federal budget for 2003 provided $7.1 billion to the US Coast Guard, and admitted it was "both the largest increase and the highest level of funding in Coast Guard history."

While Ridge paid some homage to the "longstanding principles" of the United States and said he believed that government intrusion into the daily lives of citizens should be strictly limited, he nevertheless noted that the president would serve as the ultimate authority over the control of sensitive intelligence information. "The president, as commander-in-chief, must have the ability to make decisions about how the nation's most sensitive intelligence information is handled in order to carry out his sworn duties. The President will be able to exercise his authority in regard to intelligence distribution through such tools as presidential decision directives and executive orders." Ridge explained.

"Therefore the new Homeland Security Department would incorporate the Secret Service and would have its director report directly to the secretary of homeland security. It would also assume all authority for controlling the nation's borders."

"Terrorists are determined, opportunistic, and agile, and the secretary [of Homeland Security] must build a department that can continually adapt to meet this rapidly changing threat," explained Ridge. "Moreover, even if our adversary were not so devious and nimble, the sheer organizational and management challenge confronting the new secretary of homeland security is enormous. The creation of this new department is larger and more complex than most corporate mega-mergers. History shows that a governmental reorganization of this magnitude is never easy. Providing the secretary with the freedom to manage the department is, therefore, profoundly important to achieving our goal of securing the homeland. Without this authority, an already challenging task will be far more difficult. If the new department is to be greater than the sum of its parts—if it were not, it would obviously not be worth creating—its leadership must have the flexibility to organize it in the optimal way, create a new institutional culture, motivate and reward an outstanding workforce, and respond quickly to changing circumstances, emerging threats, and emergency situations.

In other words, give me the power and I will protect you.

Just four months after the 9/11 attacks, such power was approved by Congress through the Department of Homeland Security Act of 2002.

By 2006, Homeland Security encompassed more than 87,000 government jurisdictions at both the state and local level. Its directorates included Preparedness, Science & Technology, and Management and Policy. By 2010, DHS listed nearly 400,000 employees and, like the armed forces in Iraq, private contractors outnumbered federal employees 200,000 to 188,000. In a letter to DHS chief Janet Napolitano, Senators Joseph Lieberman and Susan Collins wrote,"The sheer number of DHS contractors currently on board again raises the question of whether DHS itself is in charge of its programs and policies, or whether it inappropriately has ceded core decisions to contractors."

As requested by Ridge, Homeland Security included FEMA, the TSA, Customs, Border Patrol, the INS, the Federal Law Enforcement Training Center, US Coast Guard and the Secret Service. By 2010, Homeland Security had spent federal money to intrude into all of the more than 18,000 police and sheriff's offices in the US. If Congress, the media or the public wanted to know what exactly was going on with Homeland Security, their queries were doomed to failure as all DHS employees, both federal employees and contractors, were required to sign nondisclosure agreements prohibiting them from disclosing any information, whether classified or not. Watchdog organizations such as the Federation of American Scientists [FAS] described this policy as a potentially precedent-setting expansion of official secrecy whose provisions are overly broad and unworkable, if not unconstitutional. Steven Aftergood, editor of the FAS newsletter said the DHS was sweeping whole categories of government information under restrictions previously used only for classified data. "Employees will naturally fear that even the most trivial conversation could mean a violation of this draconian agreement, and so the result will be a new wall between the government and the public," predicted Aftergood.

Even workers within DHS apparently disdained their own department. A 2007 government poll showed out of 36 agencies surveyed, Homeland

Security employees rated theirs as last: 36th in job satisfaction, 35th on leadership and 36th on results-oriented performance. A former inspector general of DHS, Clark Kent Ervin, warned, "Dysfunction equals danger. The less good people feel about their jobs, the less likely they are to be attentive and alert."

Critics also have questioned how such a massive restructuring of the US government has helped protect the nation, especially in light of the dangerously open national borders both north and south. To many thoughtful Americans it would seem to be a common-sense first step in the War on Terrorism to tighten security on the United States borders but this does not appear to have happened. On the southern border, despite an increasing clamor for tighter security, a flood of illegal immigrants continues unabated.

Border security also came into question in the case of Gregory Despres, who on April 25, 2005, arrived at the US-Canadian border at Calais, Maine, carrying a homemade sword, a hatchet, knife, brass knuckles and a chainsaw stained with what appeared to be blood. Customs agents confiscated Despres' weapons, but then allowed him to enter the United States.

The next day, the decapitated body of 74-year-old Frederick Fulton along with his wife, who had been stabbed to death, was discovered in Despres' hometown of Minto, New Brunswick. Despres, who had a history of violence, was immediately suspected of the crimes and eventually arrested in Massachusetts and deported.

Bill Anthony, a spokesman for US Customs and Border Protection, said the Canada-born Despres could not be detained because he is a naturalized US citizen and was not wanted on any criminal charges on the day in question. "Being bizarre is not a reason to keep somebody out of this country or lock them up. We are governed by laws and regulations, and he did not violate any regulations," explained Anthony.

Almost a decade after its creation, elements of Homeland Security were still under attack by civil libertarians. For example, in mid-September 2010 the American Civil Liberties Union (ACLU) filed a lawsuit against the Department of Homeland Security over its policy allowing customs agents to seize and view the contents of laptops and other electronic devices without reasonable suspicion of wrongdoing. In its complaint, the ACLU stated that between Oct. 1, 2008, and June 2, 2010, more than

6,500 travelers, including 3,000 Americans had their electronic devices searched as they crossed US borders under policies originating from US Customs and Border Protection, and Immigration and Customs Enforcement, both Homeland Security agencies.

The ACLU represented, among others, Pascal Abidor, a US-French dual citizen and doctoral student at McGill University in Montreal. Abidor was returning by train in May 2010 when a customs agent confiscated his laptop after finding images related to Islamic studies, Abidor's academic specialty. He was handcuffed and detained. The laptop was finally returned 11 days later, after agents viewed several personal files, including the transcript of a chat with his girlfriend. The ACLU argued that such searches violate both the Fourth Amendment prohibition of unreasonable searches and seizures and the First Amendment's protection of free expression.

"We agree," stated an editorial in the *Los Angeles Times*. "Searching a computer, which can contain a wealth of personal information, is much more intrusive than inspecting baggage for drugs, weapons or other contraband. Possession of child pornography is a vile offense, as is terrorism, but in combating those and other crimes, law enforcement agents aren't free to randomly search homes. Neither should they be allowed to engage in electronic fishing expeditions at the border."

The editorial sought support for two bills introduced in the Congress, one by Democratic Representative Zoe Lofgren which would clarify that US sovereignty rights do not include the power to search laptops or similar devices, and another by former Democratic Senator Russ Feingold, which would largely exempt American citizens and make searches and seizures permissible only with probable cause. "The [ACLU] lawsuit is a worthy attempt to close a gaping loophole in the protection of personal privacy. But courts so far have been inhospitable to such claims, which is why Congress must act," argued the editorial.

According to the Bill of Rights, the states have more control than the federal government. Many people suspect that the creation of Homeland Security was nothing less than a plan to stealthily take control over state governments and hence, the population.

Many libertarians look to the county sheriff for relief. After all, the local sheriff is the highest elected law enforcement agent in the land, answerable to his constituents. Yet today, sheriff's offices across the country are coming under the sway of Homeland Security. For example, in Denton County, Texas, which includes the regional headquarters of FEMA, the commissioners court in 2007 began to turn all accounts receivable over to the state through Homeland Security. Everyday, a gun-toting member of Homeland Security in an unmarked car would come to pick up the days receipts. This process supposedly saved the county money on bounced checks and charge backs on credit cards, but the trade off was the loss of power through loss of fiduciary control not to mention requirements that extensive reporting procedures on citizens be provided.

Such reporting seems innocuous enough, but the reports requested by Homeland Security include all vaccination records kept by the local health departments and information regarding who is getting aid from the Special Supplemental Nutrition Program for Women, Infants and Children, better known as the WIC program. Certain counties also offer data from the various county and city-wide wellness programs, which keep extensive records on an individual's health, medications, doctors, blood tests and daily exercise plans.

Homeland Security has gained control over state departments of transportation and the police departments by supplying them with grossly expensive equipment in return for report uploading—information sharing—with Homeland Security databases. Also Homeland Security through state transportation agencies supply city governments with expensive $100,000 computerized street lights which come equipped with closed-circuit surveillance cameras and high technology RFID readers to record the exact location of individuals. This system is tied into all insurance databases so if a driver is caught without car insurance, they can easily be ticketed or arrested.

Adding to this ever-growing maze of regulations and policies from Homeland Security is the fact that since the creation of the department, police officers and sheriff's deputies have been exposed to monthly and bi-monthly newsletters coming from Homeland Security fed to it by the Southern Law Poverty Center (SPLC) as well as the Anti-Defamation League (ADL). Critics contend that these reports have tagged everyday citizens as possible terrorists, and worse, that these reports have slowly changed the worldview of law enforcement officers to one that perceives all citizens as potentially dangerous suspects.

In 2009, for example, DHS distributed a "Reference Aid" from its Homeland Environment Threat Analysis Division entitled "Domestic Extremism Lexicon." This paper claimed to "provide operational and intelligence advice and assistance to other elements of DHS, as well as state, local and regional fusion centers." Among the topics of concern listed by this DHS arm are alternative media; animal rights, anti-abortion, anti-immigration, environmental and anti-technology extremism; black nationalism; Christian identity; hate groups, defined as white supremacist groups; Jewish extremism; Mexican separatism; neo-Nazis; the patriot, sovereign citizen and tax resistance movements; and even "leaderless resistance." Such loosely-defined criteria could conceivably be applied to more than half the US population.

A pamphlet issued by the Texas Department of Public Safety's Counterterrorism Intelligence Unit in the mid-2000s described these among "characteristics of terrorists:
- Will employ a variety of vehicles and communicate predominately by cell phone, email, or text messaging services.
- Well prepared to spend years in a "sleeper" mode until it is time to attack.
- In many cases, will try to fit in and not draw attention to themselves.
- May appear "normal" in their appearance and behavior while portraying themselves as a tourist, student, or businessperson.
- May be found traveling in a mixed group of men, women and children of varying ages, who are unaware of their purpose.
- Trained to avoid confrontations with law enforcement and therefore can be expected to project a "nice-guy" image.
- Known to use disguises or undergo plastic surgery, especially when featured on police wanted posters.

Since such nebulous "characteristics" could be applied to a majority of US citizens, is it any wonder that law enforcement officers today increasingly view the public as adversaries, if not potential enemies? Critics have attacked such questionable definitions. Americans for Legal Immigration Political Action Committee (ALIPAC) issued a national advisory warning all local, state, and federal law enforcement agencies and officers against any reliance upon "faulty and politicized research" issued by the Southern Poverty Law Center (SPLC) and Anti Defamation League (ADL).

This advisory came on the heels of criticism leveled against the Missouri Information Analysis Center (MIAC) for issuing an eight-page report which, according ALIPAC, "attempted to politicize police and cast suspicion on millions of Americans." By mid-2009 there were at least 75 such fusion centers designed to gather anti-terrorist information from both government and, most significantly, private sector sources. The centers are a joint project of Homeland Security and the Justice Department begun during the Bush administration. They were designed to facilitate information sharing between government agencies such as the FBI, CIA, and the military in the fight against terrorism.

The "Missouri Documents" as the report came to be known during a brief national scandal, listed more than 32 characteristics that police should be alert to as signs of domestic terrorists. Such suspected terrorists included persons who might like gun shows, short wave radios, combat movies, movies with white male heroes, Tom Clancy novels, and presidential candidates Ron Paul, Bob Barr, and Chuck Baldwin.

William Gheen of ALIPAC complained, "When many of us read these 'Missouri Documents' we felt that the false connections, pseudo-research, and political attacks found in these documents could have been penned by the SPLC and ADL. We were shocked to see credible law enforcement agencies disseminating the same kind of over-the-top political propaganda distributed by these groups." Gheen said ALIPAC was advising all media sources, law enforcement officers and agencies, that the SPLC and the ADL are political organizations, with "stated political goals and agendas which are contrary to the candidates, political parties, and millions of Americans besmirched by the MIAC documents."

The SPLC was widely suspected of being the source of the MIAC information. This prompted ALIPAC to send a letter of inquiry to Missouri Governor Jay Nixon on March 20, 2009 asking for more specific sourcing information. Such action may have led to Lt. Governor Peter Kinder placing Missouri Public Safety Director John Britt on administrative leave. Kinder also issued a public apology to presidential candidates Ron Paul, Bob Barr, and Chuck Baldwin.

Superintendent of the Missouri State Highway Patrol, Col. James F.

Keathley later sent a response to ALIPAC and others, stating the Missouri Documents were being withdrawn as they did not meet the standards expected from the MIAC, and that "certain subsets of Missourians will not be singled out inappropriately in these reports for particular associations." He said closer oversight will be applied to future releases from the fusion center.

The SPLC has come under its share of criticism, despite well-funded self promotion—in 2005 the SPLC reported an endowment fund of more than $152 million—and close ties to Democratic machine politics. Founded in 1971 by Morris Dees, himself a controversial figure impugned regularly on the internet, and Joseph J. Levin Jr., the nonprofit center has led the effort to enact laws against "hate crimes," which range from hate-inspired murder to simple outbursts of speech. Despite its ongoing efforts for further "hate crime" legislation, the SPLC's own website, quoting crime experts, admitted that the whole hate crime reporting system is plagued with errors and its hate crime statistics "worthless."

It did nothing to lessen concerns over spurious and prying information being push onto law enforcement when Pennsylvania Homeland Security Director James F. Powers Jr., resigned under a cloud in early October 2010. He had drawn criticism for releasing terror bulletins that listed law-abiding protest groups.

The bulletins, distributed to law enforcement agencies, local governments and private security officials, warned of protests by environmental activists, anti-war demonstrators and anti-tax groups. They were based on information provided by something called the Institute of Terrorism Research and Response, a for-profit company that had won a $103,000 contract from Powers. Pennsylvania Governor Ed Rendell said the contract would be renewed.

Powers, decline to comment to the media, but released a statement saying that after "a thorough examination, detailed consideration, and reflection on emerging events," he had decided to resign to protect the state Homeland Security office from further distraction.

State Senator Lisa Baker, who chaired a Pennsylvania Senate committee hearing on the matter, commented, "Given the troubling revelations about the security contract and his continuing defense of it, his position was untenable. So his decision to resign is the right one. His departure opens the door to some badly needed changes, but restoring credibility to the operation now looks to be a monumental task." Others were not satisfied that the problem was fixed. State Representative Daryl Metcalfe, whose anti-tax and Second Amendment rallies were among those groups listed in the bulletins, said Gov. Rendell should have fired Powers.

In Texas, State Rep. Lon Burnam voiced concern over the expansion of fusion centers there, which had grown to include 170 agencies in more than a dozen counties. Civil libertarians feared such police collusion could lead to racial profiling, the targeting of perfectly legal groups, and even harassment of individuals. "I am tremendously concerned about the potential violation of privacy [in such fusion centers]," said Burnam. "I have been trying through the Open Records Act to discover what they have gathered on me."

According to journalist Peter Gorman with *Fort Worth Weekly*, the first fusion center in Texas was opened in 2004 by the Department of Public Safety's Intelligence and Counterterrorism Division. "Since then several others have been created...All the participating agencies supply data to [a data] 'bank'...The result thus far has been the creation of overlapping data centers with different missions, each run independently—and some taking the kind of actions that civil libertarians have feared all along."

One example of abuse involved the fusion center in Collin County, which in February 2009 distributed a "prevention awareness bulletin" ordering law enforcement authorities to report on all civil rights meetings involving Muslims and to gather and pass along information on any antiwar groups in the 16-county jurisdiction. "It turned out that the bulletin was not authorized by the Collin County head of Homeland Security, but was sent out by a computer worker in the center. In the months that followed, everyone from the ACLU to religious groups objected to it," wrote Gorman. "This memo is not a plea for legitimate intelligence, and seems to endorse discrimination against Muslims," noted Caroline Fredrickson, director of the ACLU's Washington Legislative Office. "The idea that the tolerance advocated by the groups being targeted would be treated as a menace to American security demonstrates a disregard for civil liberties and a disdain for democracy itself."

Abuses range from the sublime to the ridiculous. Dallas Police Lt. Todd Thomasson, who headed that city's fusion center, stated that other centers have "passed out documents that suggest that if a person has a certain bumper sticker they might be a terrorist and other misleading things."

Of particular concern was the Texas Fusion Center run by the state's Department of Public Safety (DPS) in Austin, which shares information with the Texas prison system, Homeland Security, the US Treasury Department, immigration agencies, the Air and Army National Guard, and many other police and non-police agencies. *D Magazine* blogger Bill Baumbach noted that the DPS center also collects personal information every time a police officer talks with someone, including drivers who are pulled over and issued nothing beyond a warning. "That is gathering information on people who were not only not convicted of a crime—they weren't even charged with one. That's very frightening to me," said Baumbach. Decrying the lack of oversight on the fusion centers, he added, "But these fusion databases have escaped scrutiny because they wave the flag of national security. They're all mavericks. You can have a good one in Dallas but one that overreaches in Collin County and affects millions of people."

State Rep. Burnam saw the fusion centers as "a direct result of 9/11 and all of the phobias that have ensued since that day. People think that if they sacrifice enough of their own liberty they will be safe, but that just isn't the case. There is a huge potential for abuse of people's right to privacy in this dragnet approach to gathering data."

## WAS GEORGE ORWELL RIGHT ABOUT 1984?

None of this is really new. Plans to change America from a constitutional republic to an imperial state ironically date back to 1984 when the Reagan National Security Council (NSC) drafted a plan to impose martial law in the United States through FEMA. Helping author this plan was Marine Lt. Col. Oliver North, who later admitted that he lied to Congress about a number of matters but was later rewarded by being hired as a highly-paid talk show host. But in 1987, when the plan leaked to the media, his work inspired a sharp protest from then-Attorney General William French Smith.

Arthur Liman, then chief counsel of the Senate Iran-Contra committee, declared in a memo that North was at the center of what amounted to a "secret government-within-a-government," a term similar to Bush's "shadow government." Officials at the time said North's involvement in the proposed plan to radically alter the American government by executive order was proof that he was involved in a wide range of secret activities, foreign and domestic, that went far beyond the Iran-Contra scandal.

North's shadow-government plan called for suspension of the Constitution, turning control of the government over to the then-largely unknown Federal Emergency Management Agency (FEMA), appointment of military commanders to run state and local governments and the declaration of martial law in the event of a crisis such as "nuclear war, violent and widespread internal dissent or national opposition to a US military invasion abroad." At the time he drafted these plans, North was the NSC's liaison to FEMA.

It is the last two scenarios that bother many people when they view the national events of today, especially since so many members of the Reagan administration were back in power during the administration of President George W. Bush. Some, such as Bush's secretary of defense, Robert Gates, were retained by the Obama administration.

North's contingency plan was to be part of an executive order or legislative package that Reagan would sign but hold secretly within the NSC until such a time as a crisis arose. It was never revealed whether Reagan had signed the plan.

Could the consolidation of power within Homeland Security be a continuation of this plan? No one knows for certain as President Bush, immediately upon taking office, ordered all records of former presidents, including Reagan, sealed from the public. President Obama apparently maintained this control of presidential documents by signing Exectuive Order 13489 within hours of taking office in January 2009. This order stipulates that upon any question concerning the release of such documents, the "[National] Archivist shall abide by any instructions given him by the incumbent President or his designee unless otherwise directed by a final court order."

Ironically, one of those voicing concern over this loss of access was former Nixon counselor John Dean, who warned that America was sliding into a "constitutional dictatorship" and martial law.

Further concerns were voiced by Timothy H. Edgar, legislative counsel for the American Civil Liberties Union. In testimony to various congressional committees, Edgar noted that the Homeland Security Department would have substantial powers as well as more armed federal agents with arrest authority than any other government agency. He questioned whether the new department would have structural and legal safeguards to keep it open and accountable to the public.

"Unfortunately, [this] legislation not only fails to provide such safeguards, it eviscerates many of the safeguards that are available throughout the government and have worked well to safeguard the public interest," stated Edgar. He went on to enumerate some problems areas within the proposed Homeland Security Department saying it:

- Hobbles the Freedom of Information Act (FOIA) by creating broad new exemptions to the act such as "any information voluntarily submitted to the department about threats to the nation's infrastructure." Edgar pointed out that exceptions to FOIA already include information concerning national security and sensitive law enforcement and confidential business information. "This is a deeply misguided proposal, and it should be rejected," he added.
- Limits citizen input by exempting advisory committees to Homeland Security from the Federal Advisory Act (FACA) passed in 1972 to ensure openness, accountability and the balance of viewpoints in government advisory groups. "By exempting from FACA requirements *any* [emphasis in the original] advisory committees established by the secretary of the Department of Homeland Security, [this act] severely undermines the openness and public-access goals of FACA," argued Edgar.
- Muzzles whistleblowers protected under the federal Whistleblower Protection Act (WPA) by allowing the Homeland Security secretary to make his own personnel rules. "Title 5 [under the new department] does not guarantee employees of the Department of Homeland Security the protections of the WPA," stated Edgar. "Without such protection, employees who are in the best position to spot problems, violations of the law or dangers to the public are effectively silenced."

- Lacks strong oversight by allowing the Homeland Security secretary to override Inspector General investigations in many areas including intelligence, criminal investigations, undercover operations, identity of confidential sources, protective matters of the Secret Service and any matter considered a threat to national security. "Given the mission of the Homeland Security Agency, it is conceivable that many of the functions performed by this new agency could be said to fall under one of these exempted categories," noted Edgar. "We are concerned that transferring these agencies [FEMA, INS, Animal and Plant Inspection Service of the Agriculture Department, Coast Guard] into a department whose primary function is to protect the United States against terrorism could erroneously be perceived as elevating their regular duties to those of national security, thereby making such currently non-exempt activities exempt from Inspector General oversight."
- Threatens personal privacy and constitutional freedoms because the vagueness of the wording in the Homeland Security Act does not provide sufficient guarantees.

One huge concern voiced by the ACLU counsel concerned plans to combine the CIA and the FBI under Homeland Security, a plan still under consideration in 2010.

"The CIA and other agencies that gather foreign intelligence abroad operate in the largely lawless environment," noted Edgar. "To bring these agencies into the same organization as the FBI risks further damage to Americans' civil liberties." Edgar urged Congress to resist this move, instead placing clear limits on Homeland Security's ability to retain files on Americans that have no connection to criminal activity but relate to First Amendment freedoms. Congress did not. He said combining domestic and foreign intelligence gathering under Homeland Security could have "a severe impact on civil liberties potentially leading to widespread spying on Americans constitutionally-protected political and religious activity."

"There is already a danger under the relaxed FBI guidelines for domestic investigations recently announced by Attorney General Ashcroft," Edgar added. "No one wants a repeat of the J. Edgar Hoover era, when the FBI [under the infamous Cointelpro program] was used to collect information about and disrupt the activities of civil rights leaders and others whose ideas Hoover disdained. Moreover, during the Clinton administration, the 'Filegate' matter involving the improper transfer of sensitive information from FBI background checks of prominent Republicans to the White House generated enormous public concern that private security-related information was being used for political purposes. Congress should not provide a future administration with the temptation to use information available in Homeland Security Department files to the detriment of its political enemies."

Interestingly enough, President Bush himself had some conflict with Congress over Homeland Security legislation, but it had nothing to do with constitutional issues. Congress wanted the department's employees covered by civil service protections and Bush did not. Many observers believed this objection by Bush was a cover to exempt Homeland Security workers from the whistleblower and Freedom of Information protections. If an employee did not go along with the Bush-Ridge program, they could be summarily fired and replaced with someone who would.

Some Democrats welcomed the new department, such as Senator Joseph Lieberman of Connecticut, an early advocate of the administration change, who said, "In fact, I think it will help us immediately." Others of his party objected to many provisions of the Homeland Security bill, charging that many had nothing to do with security, such as liability protection for vaccine manufacturers and exemptions to the Freedom of Information Act.

Despite misgivings, the Homeland Security Act passed speedily through Congress with little or no revision. In the US Senate, the proposal passed on a 90–9 vote. Apparently Senators were so confident that they were about to do a genuine service for America that on November 13 they voted themselves a pay raise for the fourth consecutive year. This vote was tighter, with 36 senators voting to reject a measure that would have denied them the raise. President Bush signed the Homeland Security bill into law on November 25, 2002. Noting that the agencies responsible for border, coastline and transportation security were now under the same command structure, Bush remarked, "The continuing threat of terrorism, the threat of mass murder on our own soil, will be met with a unified, effective response." But this "unity" quickly was questioned as troubles arose within this new labyrinthine system.

One notorious item that came into existence with the creation of Homeland Security was the listing of names of persons known or just suspected of international terrorist connections. By early 2010, this list had grown to 420,000 names, compiled by the FBI's Terrorist Screening Center from more than 26 terrorism-related databases from the intelligence and law enforcement communities. By 2010, the TSA's Terrorist Identities Datamart Environment (TIDE), the intelligence community's central repository of information on known and suspected international terrorists, had grown to more than a half million persons.

"We have lists that are having baby lists at this point," commented Timothy Sparapani, legislative counsel for privacy rights at the American Civil Liberties Union. "If we have over 300,000 known terrorists who want to do this country harm, we've got a bigger problem than deciding which names go on which list. But I highly doubt this is the case."

Sparapani and many others voiced concern over such an ever-growing list. Georgetown University Law Professor David D. Cole said, "If being placed on a list means in practice that you will be denied a visa, barred entry, put on the no-fly list, targeted for pretextual prosecutions, etc., then the sweep of the list and the apparent absence of any way to clear oneself certainly raises problems.

Former Attorney General Alberto R. Gonzales tried to assure members of the Senate Judiciary Committee that "information is collected, information is retained and information is disseminated in a way to protect the privacy interests of all Americans."

But Attorney General Gonzales likely had a hard time convincing one former committee member, the late Senator Edward "Ted" Kennedy, who was prevented from flying five times in March 2004 because a "T. Kennedy" appeared on the secret no-fly list.

In terminals in Washington, Boston and other locations, airline employees refused to issue a boarding pass because his name was on the no-fly list. Kennedy was delayed until supervisors were called and approved his travel. Even after supposedly clearing up the mistake in names, Kennedy was stopped yet again from flying, prompting a personal telephone apology from Homeland Security Secretary Tom Ridge.

"That a clerical error could lend one of the most powerful people in

Washington to the list—it makes one wonder just how many others who are not terrorists are on the list," commented senior ACLU counsel Reginald T. Shuford. "Someone of Senator Kennedy's stature can simply call a friend to have his name removed but a regular American citizen does not have that ability. He had to call three times himself."

Another ACLU attorney, David C. Fathi, said he was stopped more than seven times at airports, but not on every flight. Once he was led from the counter by armed police and questioned extensively.

Fathi, who is of Iranian ancestry, said it is possible to contact the Transportation Security Administration and obtain a letter of clearance. But his letter didn't help. "By the time I show the letter, it's already too late," he lamented, adding, "There is no rhyme or reason... It illustrates the ridiculousness of the system. If it stops [suspects] because they're on the list they should stop them every time. Not every third time."

And lest anyone think that abuse of such power as wielded by Homeland Security would be tempered by time and experience, consider what happened in Bethesda, MD, in February 2006.

Two uniformed men wearing baseball caps with the words "Homeland Security" emblazoned on them walked into the Little Falls Library and loudly announced that the viewing of pornography was forbidden. They then proceeded to ask that one library Internet viewer step outside.

After complaints were lodged against the two "security" officers, Montgomery County chief administrative officer, Bruce Romer, issued a statement calling the incident "unfortunate" and "regrettable." Romer said the two officers were members of the security division of Montgomery County's Homeland Security Department, an unarmed unit charged with patrolling about 300 county buildings. He added this group was not tasked with seeking out pornography and that the two officers had "overstepped their authority" and had been reassigned.

At least in one incidence, the no-fly listing of an American may have had political overtones. Dr. Robert Johnson, a heart surgeon in upstate New York, was a retired Lt. Colonel in the US Army Reserve who had served during the time of the first Gulf War. But when he arrived at a Syracuse airport for a flight, he was barred and told he was on the federal no-fly list as a possible terror suspect.

"Why would a former lieutenant colonel who swore an oath to defend and protect our country pose a threat of terrorism?" Johnson rhetorically asked a local newspaper. Johnson answered himself by speculating that he was placed on the list because in 2004 he, as a Democrat, had challenged Republican Representative John McHugh. Johnson said he planned to run against McHugh again for his 23rd District congressional seat. The colonel also had been an outspoken critic of the invasion and occupation of Iraq.

Like the growing number of citizens who are finding themselves on the no-fly list, Johnson is demanding answers as to who decides which name goes on the list and what is the mechanism for getting off.

By 2010, even many small suburban and rural counties had their own Homeland Security departments, all answerable to the national department. Some civil libertarians began to view Homeland Security as a renewed version of the Nazi Gestapo, Germany's *Geheime Staatspolizei* or Secret State Police, which encompassed all of that nation's police agencies.

To concentrate so much power in one new government department head requires a thorough examination of the man who initially wielded such power. And in the case of Tom Ridge, there were worrisome aspects.

## TOM RIDGE AND THE PHOENIX PROGRAM

In the conventional biographies, Ridge is reported to have been a Catholic alter boy who won a scholarship to Harvard and went on to earn a BA in 1967. He was drafted into the Army while attending Dickinson Law School in Carlisle, PA. In Vietnam, he was awarded a Bronze Star for leading an action that cleared a small Viet Cong force from an area. This war hero won six consecutive terms in the House before becoming the governor of Pennsylvania. Under that state's term limits, he was due to leave office in 2003.

But there is a disquieting side to this all-American-boy-makes-good story. According to investigative reporters Jeffrey St. Clair and Alexander Cockburn, "He passed up officer training school because it would have meant an extra year of service. Ridge arrived in Vietnam [where he was given the nickname T-Bone] in November 1969, and joined Bravo Company, First Battalion, 20th Infantry Brigade, American Division."

One man who served with Ridge wrote to a veteran's webpage stating, "The last several months I participated in the Pacification program along the Red Ball. My squad consisted of four other US soldiers and up to ten ARVN [Army of the Republic of Viet Nam] What a waste. I was not impressed with Ridge either. He was the squad leader of my squad before I became sergeant. The pathetic SOB would have caused all of us to get killed if we hadn't taken care of him. I was glad when he no longer led us."

But Ridge's leadership ability is not what concerned researchers the most. The "Pacification program" referred to by the Vietnam vet was the infamous "Phoenix Program," in which more than 45,000 Vietnamese were assassinated and many thousands more tortured and abused.

Douglas Valentine, author of *The Phoenix Program*, explained, "During the Vietnam War, under the CIA's Phoenix program—which is the model for the Homeland Security Office—a terrorist suspect was anyone accused by one anonymous source. Just one. The suspect was then arrested, indefinitely detained in a CIA interrogation center, tortured until he or she (in some cases children as young as twelve) confessed, informed on others, died, or was brought before a military tribunal (such as Bush is proposing) for disposition.

"In thousands of cases, innocent people were imprisoned and tortured based on the word of an anonymous informer who had a personal grudge or was actually a Viet Cong double agent feeding the names of loyal citizens into the Phoenix blacklist. At no point in the process did suspects have access to due process or lawyers, and thus, in 1971, four US Congresspersons stated their belief that the Phoenix Program violated that part of the Geneva Conventions guaranteeing protection to civilians in time of war."

Ridge received a medal for a small action during his stint in Vietnam. His Bronze Star citation states, "Sgt. Ridge moved forward and began placing accurate bursts of rifle fire on the insurgents, eliminating one and forcing the remainder of the hostile elements to take evasive action."

Vietnam veterans noticed that the citation did not mention enemy troops but instead "insurgents," a term given to any Vietnamese under suspicion by the US authorities.

So, Tom Ridge, a man who participated in a CIA-sponsored terror program in Vietnam that included arrest without due process, torture and assassination, was brought in to be the first head of our newest federal agency, one that is drawing power from more than 200 existing agencies.

Another man who participated in the CIA Phoenix program was Bruce Lawlor, who after serving in Vietnam went on to became a major general. Author Valentine said Lawlor admitted to his participation in Phoenix during an interview for Valentine's book.

"What Lawlor told me basically confirmed everything," said Valentine. "Except there were some additional, startling details. To begin with, Lawlor told me that he joined the CIA in 1967, while he was getting his BA at George Washington University. The CIA hired him to work the night shift, and after he graduated, he was given the chance to become a regular CIA staff officer. He took the paramilitary course, which included instruction in weapons and military tactics, but he was also trained as a foreign intelligence officer, the kind who manages secret agents. After that he was assigned to the Vietnam Desk at Langley headquarters, where he received specialized training in agent operations in Vietnam, and took a language course in Vietnamese. During this time, Lawlor formed a rapport with the Vietnam Desk officer, Al Seal, and when Seal was assigned as the base chief in Danang, he asked that Lawlor accompany him."

In 1984, after leaving the military, Lawlor was the Democratic Party nominee for attorney general of Vermont. He listed the Phoenix Program on his political resume that was handed out to the press.

One journalist with a small weekly, *Vermont Vanguard*, published the first critical article about Lawlor and Phoenix. By the time of the state Democratic convention, activist groups in the state had organized and produced signs for convention delegates reading "No Assassins for Attorney General." Lawlor lost the Fall primary despite a visit from former CIA Director William Colby, the CIA official who headed the Phoenix Program.

"Imagine my surprise to learn that the Bruce Lawlor is serving as the Office of Homeland Security's senior director for protection and prevention!" remarked Valentine. "To get right to the point, I have a sneaking suspicion that Lawlor...is still working for the CIA, and thus poses a major threat to democracy in America. He's someone who has access to Ashcroft's political blacklist, and he has control over the covert action teams that can be used to neutralize...dissidents. One of the reasons I have this crazy feeling, is that nowhere in any of Lawlor's official looking, on-line biographies is there any mention of his CIA service. It's like his biographers are deliberately trying to hide his CIA connection from us."

Yet another ranking first Bush administration senior official with a checkered background is Richard Armitage, best friend of Colin Powell and unanimously endorsed by the Senate Foreign Relations Committee for the position of deputy secretary of state in 2001. He too was a major Phoenix Program operative, according to Valentine and others.

Valentine noted, "HR 19, just introduced [in January 2001] by Georgia Congressman Bob Barr, would repeal the Executive Orders of Presidents Reagan and Carter prohibiting federal employees, including the military, from carrying out assassinations. This implies that the Bush administration plans to deal harshly with terrorists and other inconvenient persons. Richard Armitage, who was involved in the Iran-Contra deal as well as CIA covert operations in Vietnam, will reportedly head up what's called 'The Terrorist Elimination Act of 2001.' That's our new deputy secretary of state." Armitage, a neocon and Council on Foreign Relations member, also became a key figure in the federal grand jury investigation over who outed CIA spy Valerie Plame in 2003.

It should be noted that this was not the first time that Armitage's name has come up in connection with criminal behavior. Once again, the issue of illegal drugs cropped up.

In 1987, Col. James "Bo" Gritz, a much-decorated Vietnam veteran, met with Burmese General Kuhn Sa, the head of the Golden Triangle drug trade, in an effort to locate American POWs. Gritz, in his 1988 book, *A Nation Betrayed*, wrote that General Sa detailed for him the heroin trade and named then-Assistant Secretary of Defense for International Security Affairs Armitage as the person who handled the financial end of the US narcotics trade through banks in Australia. Armitage reportedly was involved in a shadowy group of US government officials and mobsters conspiring to import heroin into the United States.

Shocked at this revelation, Gritz asked himself, "How could men sworn before God to defend the Constitution so befoul their office? What form of stand-up sewage would facilitate the movement of deadly addictive narcotics into their own homeland? It took several long moments for the full impact to be realized. Then it was as if someone had turned on a light in my mind. Until that moment my mental and emotional conditioning from a career of military service refused to allow such a contemplation. It was so un-American and alien as to be incomprehensible. But, if true, it explained a train of unexplained events. If Richard Armitage was, as Kuhn Sa avowed, a major participant in parallel government drug trafficking, than it explained why our efforts to rescue POWs had been inexplicably foiled."

But if illegal drugs continued to pour into the United States, more conventional products did not in mid-2002. A labor dispute between the International Longshore and Warehouse Union (ILWU) and the Pacific Maritime Association (PMA) caused a stack up of cargo ships along the West Coast from San Diego to Seattle that threatened to cut deeply into the 2002–03 holiday season profits. The strike was broken in October when President Bush invoked the Taft-Hartley Act, a controversial 1947 union busting law that was passed over President Truman's veto. Under this law, an 80-day "cooling off" period can be ordered during a "national emergency."

Although Bush's action received scant attention in a media focused on the proposed invasion of Iraq, one official of ILWU, Jack Heyman, termed Bush's intervention "a historic juncture in the labor movement." Heyman added, "By invoking Taft-Hartley against the longshore workers, Bush is effectively declaring war on the working class here and the Iraqi people simultaneously."

## HOMELAND SECURITY AT WORK

It was not just labor unionists that were feeling the chill in the wake of the hot patriotism caused by 9/11. Two members of a Chicago group opposed to the sanctions against Iraq were confronted by police when they went to buy some postage stamps.

Daniel Muller, a coordinator for Voices in the Wilderness, along with Andrew Mandell, went to a Chicago post office to purchase a quantity of stamps. They were paying in cash. "We needed 4,000 stamps for a mailing we were doing," explained Muller, "and I asked for one not with the American flag on them." When the clerk asked if Statue of Liberty stamps were acceptable, Mandell replied, "Yes, we love liberty." "She asked us to step aside from the counter and she went to the back, out of view," recalled Muller. "I knew something was up because this was a bit out of the ordinary. And Andrew said, 'She's calling the cops,' but I didn't believe him."

However, about 20 minutes later two policemen entered and asked for the pair's identification. "They asked if we had any outstanding warrants. They ran a check on us. They asked why we had asked for stamps without American flags on them. I said we're very rooted in nonviolent activities and we would rather have the Statue of Liberty than the American flag."

The pair was finally released but had to return to the post office the next day to obtain their stamps and then, only after a further half-hour interview with a postal inspector.

"The fact that they did ask for anything but flag stamps did raise a question for the clerk," explained Silvia Carrier, a public relations officer for the Chicago Postal Inspector's office. "Right now, since September 11, clerks have been told to be cautious, to be looking out for anything suspicious.

The experience of Muller and Mandell shows that it matters little that in mid-July 2002 the US Postal Service stated that it would not participate in a snitch program called Operation TIPS.

TIPS or Terrorism Information and Prevention System was trotted out in mid-summer 2002, and was hailed on its website as "a national system for concerned workers to report suspicious activity." The program was part of the Citizen Corps, a program announced by President Bush in his State of the Union address. It was originally scheduled to be launched by early fall 2002 but eventually was officially dropped following public outrage.

In a statement, the Postal Service stated it had "been approached by Homeland Security regarding Operation TIPS; however, it was decided that the Postal Service and its letter carriers would not be participating in the program at this time." Nothing was said about individual carriers deciding to join and the "at this time" left the final word unsaid.

And the experience of the men and the stamps indicated that some persons within the Postal Service still were reporting anything they viewed as suspicious behavior.

In published material, TIPS advocates said the program was to be administered by the Justice Department and coordinated with FEMA, which would bring it under the Homeland Security Department. It would involve "millions of American workers who, in the daily course of their work, are in a unique position to see potentially unusual or suspicious activity in public places." This, of course, referred to postmen, meter readers, repairmen or anyone who might have an axe to grind against their neighbors.

The TIPS plan was immediately compared to the Nazi Gestapo, the former East German secret police service and to Fidel Castro's Committees for the Defense of the Revolution (CDR) in which Cubans are encouraged to spy on and report any "counterrevolutionary" behavior by their neighbors. An estimated eight million Cubans belong to more than 121,000 committees in the CDR, established by Castro on September 28, 1960.

In October 2000, the CDR held parties across the island nation to celebrate their 40 years of existence. "If we see some sort of attack on society or the government, then that is counterrevolution and you have to root it out," voiced one jubilant CDR member while toasting with a glass of rum at a Havana street party.

The CDR's keep detailed records of all neighborhood inhabitants, not only listing each inhabitant but also keeping files on schooling and work history, spending habits, any potentially suspicious behavior, any contact with foreigners and attendance at pro-Castro meetings. The system has evolved into one that routinely provides an individual's information to prospective employers, medical authorities or any law enforcement official.

Needless to say, the American Civil Liberties Union (ACLU) and other public watchdog organizations reacted negatively to Operation TIPS, saying it would create an atmosphere in which Americans would be spying on each other. "The administration apparently wants to implement a program that will turn local cable or gas or electrical technicians into government-sanctioned Peeping Toms," declared ACLU legislative counsel Rachel King.

John Whitehead, executive director of the Rutherford Institute, said, "This is George Orwell's '1984.' It is an absolutely horrible and very dangerous idea. It's making Americans into government snoops. President Bush wants the average American to do what the FBI should be doing. In the end, though, nothing is going to prevent terrorists from crashing airplanes into buildings."

A review of the Citizen Corps website showed a marked softening of both language and details after the program began to make a national stir.

In July 2002, the website stated Operation TIPS "will be a nationwide program giving millions of American truckers, letter carriers, train conductors, ship captains, utility employees and others a formal way to report suspicious terrorist activity. Operation TIPS, a project of the US Department of Justice, will begin as a pilot program in 10 cities...Operation TIPS, involving 1 million workers in the pilot stage, will be a national reporting system that allows workers, whose routines make them well-positioned to recognize unusual events, to report suspicious activity... Everywhere in America, a concerned worker can call a toll-free number and be connected directly to a hotline routing calls to the proper law enforcement agency or other responder organizations when appropriate."

By early August, the list of occupations had been dropped and "suspicious terrorist activity" and "unusual events... suspicious activity" had changed to "suspicious and potentially terrorist-related activity" and "Potentially unusual or suspicious activity in public places."

The TIPS program was merely an official extension of snooping in America, already so pervasive that author Jim Redden called modern life a "snitch culture." Neighborhood Watch groups already in existence were being brought into Homeland Security. In the spring of 2002, Ashcroft had earmarked almost $2 million in an effort to double the number of Neighborhood Watch groups to about 15,000. He claimed this would "weave a seamless web of prevention of terrorism" across the country.

TV personality Ed McMahon went from pitching for Publishers Clearinghouse Sweepstakes to pitching the War on Terrorism. The National Neighborhood Watch Institute already had been shipping out rectangular street signs reading, "We Support Homeland Security."

From the school kid Drug Abuse Resistance Education (DARE) program to professional finger pointers such as the Southern Poverty Law Center, more and more Americans were being encouraged to spy and report on one another.

Although most Americans believe that neighborhood snooping went out with Bush-era fear mongering, it has continued through the Obama administration. The Major Cities Chiefs Police Association, which includes police chiefs from 63 of the largest departments in the US and Canada, endorsed a program called iWATCH during an annual conference in Denver on October, 3, 2009. Los Angeles Police Chief William Bratton, whose department developed the iWATCH program, called it "the 21st century version of Neighborhood Watch." The program's watchword is "If you see something, say something."

As a policy counsel for the American Civil Liberties Union and a former FBI agent who worked terrorism cases, Mike German criticized iWATCH despite assurances that the program would not infringe on individual liberties. German told the Associated Press he suspects people will fall back on personal biases and stereotypes of what they think a terrorist should look like when deciding to report someone to the police. He said "That just plays into the negative elements of society and doesn't really help the situation."

In 1997, informing on fellow citizens was codified, at least for the federal government, when the Supreme Court in *US vs. Singleton* exempted federal prosecutors from a statute prohibiting the bribery of witnesses to testify favorably for the government.

There have been many cases, usually not played up in the media, in which innocent people have had their lives unsettled, ruined or even lost due to egregious snitching. The purchase of "snitch" information continues to be a mainstay of federal law enforcement. In 1994, the DEA spent $31.7 million while Customs spent $16.5 million on thousands of informants. Such practices have prompted protests from civil libertarians and attorneys but in today's fearful society, no one seems too concerned.

Although accurate numbers are hard to come by, a book entitled *Informants and Undercover Investigations* reported that a 2005 Inspector General's report revealed the DEA has about 4,000 "confidential sources" at hand on any given day. They may be paid up to $100,000 a year for their information, although their paycheck must be approved by DEA headquarters. The book's author, Dennis G. Fitzgerald, is a former police supervisor with the Miami Police Department and was a special agent with the DEA. He was the co-founder and director of the National Institute for Drug Enforcement Training and a visiting faculty member at the FBI's International Law Enforcement Training Academy.

The FBI can pay up to $25,000 to informants for information on serious crimes. Under a program called "Rewards for Justice," both US State and Treasury Department, can offer money to informants for information leading to the arrest and conviction of any terrorist or terrorist group. By September 2005, more than $50 million had been paid out from this fund. One can only imagine how the lure of $100,000 to a million dollars simply to find some sort of terrorist activity could highly induce an average person to make false claims.

If opposition to the TIPS network and the growing "snitch culture" in America seems a bit paranoid, consider the plight of A. J. Brown, a freshman at Durham Tech in North Carolina who received some unwelcome visitors on October 26, 2001. Answering a knock on her apartment door, Brown found herself face to face with two men in suits. "Hi, we're from the Raleigh branch of the Secret Service," said one of the men flipping out an ID folder. "I was like, 'What?'" recalled Brown. "And they say, 'We're here because we have a report that you have un-American material in your apartment.' And I was like, 'What? No, I don't have anything like that.' 'Are you sure? Because we got a report that you've got a poster that's anti-American.' And I said no." The agents wanted to enter Brown's apartment but she asked if they had a warrant. "And they said no, they didn't have a warrant but they wanted to just come in and look around. And I said, 'Sorry, you're not coming in.'"

Standing in her doorway, the agents said they knew she had a poster in her apartment of President Bush hanging himself. Brown denied this and after long minutes opened the door wide enough for the agents to see her poster. It was a picture of Bush holding a rope with the caption, "We Hang on Your Every Word. George Bush Wanted: 152 Dead." The poster also contained drawings of people being hanged. It was a political poster referring to the number of persons subjected to the death penalty in Texas while Bush was governor.

The agents finally left after about 40 minutes but called Brown back two days later to confirm her name, address, phone number and nicknames. "Obviously, I'm on some list somewhere," she commented.

Dwight Scarbrough is a Navy veteran who served as a machinist on submarines from 1975 to 1980. He was a good American until February 7, 2006 when he showed up for his work at a federal natural resource agency at Boise, Idaho. That's when he was ordered to the parking lot by armed officers of Homeland Security and told he was in violation of the Code of Federal Regulations. His violation? His pickup truck had bumper stickers reading "Honor Vets, Wage Peace," and "Another Veteran Against War with Iraq." Even though Scarbrough noted the stickers were not on federal property but on his own private property, he was told to remove them or be cited for a violation.

The quick-thinking vet brought a tape recorder and taped the following conversation: "Sir, you've got signs posted on your vehicle. I'm informing you that you're in violation," said one officer.

Scarbrough replied, "That's not illegal. That's not illegal."

The Homeland Security men continued to demand that he remove the signs or be cited for a violation.

"You know this is BS," Scarbrough exclaimed. "So any vehicle that comes on with, like a police sign, or with delivery or FedEx or something, that's not a sign?"

One officer replied: "All signs are prohibited."

Once this story broke in the local media, no further action was taken and no official of Homeland Security would comment on the incident.

And it's not all about college students or Navy veterans. A New York comedian, reported only as "Joe" on National Public Radio in September 2010, for reasons which will become obvious, became irked when he could not get an iPhone to work after spending $600 and getting the runaround at the store where he made the purchase. After picking some aggressive lines from the cult movie *Fight Club*, Joe posted them on his "personal" profile on Facebook. He intended them only for some of his friends, so Joe was shocked when less than an hour after his posting he answered his door to find four plainclothes government agents with drawn guns. They pushed their way into his home and began ransacking the place, all the time telling Joe, "Homeland Security wants to talk to you, so we're taking you downtown."

After the agents quoted lines back to him from his Facebook post, Joe realized they had monitored his private Facebook profile. Joe was told by the agents he would get into even more trouble if he gave speeches about the Constitution or suggested that surrendering our rights to a police state would mean the "terrorists have won." Joe was charged with two counts of "terroristic threatening," but after he kept demanding a jury trial and refusing government plea bargains, the charges were dropped.

Even school kids are not immune to Homeland Security. Katie Sierra, a 15-year-old sophomore at Sissonville High School in West Virginia, wanted to form an Anarchist Club at her school and handed out fliers, stating, "Anarchism preaches to love all humans, not just of one country..." She also wore a tee shirt which read, "Racism, Sexism, Homophobia, I'm So Proud of People in the Land of the So-Called Free."

Sierra was suspended and her fellow students shoved her and posted pictures of the girl with bullet holes in her head. After losing a court battle for reinstatement in the State Supreme Court by a 3-to-2 vote, Sierra said, "I'm really disgusted with the courts right now and with the school. I'm being punished for being myself."

Children were especially susceptible to recruitment through the various programs being dreamed up today. And the US military played it own role. The principal of Mount Anthony Union High School in Bennington, VT, was shocked in the spring of 2002 to receive a letter from military recruiters demanding a list of all students, including names, addresses and telephone numbers. As the school's privacy policy prevented the disclosure of such individual information, the principal told the recruiters no. She was doubly shocked to learn that buried deep within President Bush's new education law passed earlier in 2002, the No Child Left Behind Act, public schools must provide such information to military recruiters or face a cutoff of federal funds.

Republican Rep. David Vitter of Louisiana, who sponsored the recruitment requirement in the education bill, noted that in 1999, more than 19,000 US schools denied military recruiters access to their records. Vitter said such schools "demonstrated an anti-military attitude that I thought was offensive."

"I think the privacy implications of this law are profound," commented Jill Wynns, president of the San Francisco Board of Education. "For the federal government to ignore or discount the concerns of the privacy rights of millions of high school students is not a good thing, and it's something we should be concerned about."

Even journalists and academics have come under fire for not acceding to the mob mentality. Robert Jensen is an associate professor of journalism at the University of Texas at Austin. He published a column in the *Houston Chronicle* on September 14, 2001, pointing out that while the 9/11 attacks were "reprehensible and indefensible," the acts were "no more despicable [than] the massive acts of terrorism, the deliberate killing of civilians for political purposes, that the US government has committed during my lifetime."

Jensen's column was rebutted by the university president, Larry R. Faulkner, who labeled Jensen as "not only misguided but [he] has become a fountain of undiluted foolishness on issues of public policy." "I've been marginalized on this campus," lamented Jensen.

Newspaper writers Dan Guthrie of Oregon's *Grants Pass Daily Courier* and Tom Gutting of the *Texas City Sun* both wrote caustically of President Bush's irregular flight across American on 9/11. "What we are stuck with is a crippled President who continues to be controlled by his advisers. He's not a leader. He's a puppet," wrote Gutting, who said that the day his piece ran his publisher assured him he would not be fired for expressing his opinion. But the publisher printed a front-page apology for Gutting's column and a few days later changed his mind about firing him.

Guthrie, who had won several awards, including best columnist in Oregon, wrote that Bush "skedaddled" on September 11. "The picture of Bush hiding in a Nebraska hole [was] an embarrassment," he wrote. Even though the paper's editor and his city editor had signed off on his piece, Guthrie soon joined Gutting in the ranks of the unemployed.

Still, the reporters got off lighter than Richard Allen Humphreys, who described himself as a religious prophet. He was found guilty in late October 2002, by a Sioux Falls jury of threatening President Bush and faced as much as five years in prison and a $250,000 fine. A bartender at a truck stop overheard Humphreys mention "burning bush" and called police. A search of Humphreys' hotel room yielded a card with President Bush's name on it and the words, "Intimidation in the First Degree." In a transcript of a Internet Chat room conversation, Humphreys had written, "now going to ask Bush for justice, and if I don't get it don't be surprised to see a Burning Bush." Humphreys, who represented himself in court, said he was on a "discipleship journey" and was not threatening the president but merely exercising his right to religious expression.

Apparently not even traditional American activities such as taking pictures around town are exempt from the scrutiny of Homeland Security enforcers. Amateur photographer Mike Maginnis was intrigued by all the activity around Denver's Adams Mark Hotel in early December 2002, which included Denver police, Army rangers and rooftop snipers. Maginnis, who works in information technology and frequently shoots photos of corporate buildings and communications equipment, took a few snapshots. He was then confronted by a Denver policeman who demanded his camera. When he refused to hand over his expensive Nikon F2, he was pushed to the ground and arrested.

After being held in a Denver police station, Maginnis was interrogated by a Secret Service agent. He learned that Vice President Cheney was staying in the area and that he was to be charged as a terrorist under the USA PATRIOT Act. According to Maginnis, the agent tried to make him confess to being a terrorist and called him a "raghead collaborator" and "dirty pinko faggot."

After being held for several hours, Maginnis was released without explanation. When his attorney contacted the Denver police for an explanation, they denied ever arresting Maginnis.

Yet another case involved a kindergarten student who only wanted to play. In May 2002 Scott and Cassandra Garrick of New Jersey, sued the Sayreville School District after their 6-year-old kindergarten student and three classmates were disciplined for playing cops and robbers. It seems other students saw the youngsters playing on the school-yard while pretending their fingers were guns. They told a teacher and the kindergartners were suspended from school.

US District Judge Katherine S. Hayden dismissed a civil suit filed by the parents, claiming school authorities have the right to restrict violent or disruptive games. The parents' attorney, Steven H. Aden, commented, "They have the right to be children. The school and the courts shouldn't censor their play [even if] it's politically incorrect."

Such incidents are rarely covered in the corporate mass media and never distributed to a large audience but they worry thoughtful people.

"I'm terrified," said Ellen Schrecker, author of *Many Are the Crimes: McCarthyism in America*. "What concerns me is we're not seeing an enormous outcry against this whole structure of repression that's being rushed into place by the Bush administration." Former ACLU President Nadine Strossen also voiced concern. "I've been talking a lot about the parallels between what we're going through now and McCarthyism. The term 'terrorism' is taking on the same kind of characteristics as the term 'communism' did in the 1950s. It stops people in their tracks and they're willing to give up their freedoms. People are too quickly panicked. They are too willing to give up their rights and to scapegoat people, especially immigrants and people who criticize the war."

"Besides being unconstitutional and un-American, snooping on innocent people in a free society is cowardly, divisive and just plan evil," argued Internet columnist Paul Proctor. "Regardless of whether or not President Bush's motives are honorable, the fact remains that in tattle tailing for the federal government, anyone with a personal grievance against another individual or group could literally wreck havoc on them with such powers. Needless to say, the potential for tragedy and abuse is huge.

"How secure do you think you are going to feel in this escalating 'War on Terrorism' burdened with the grim knowledge that you're always going to be watched by someone somewhere reporting your personal activities, conversations and correspondence to an unaccountable hierarchy that, in the interest of 'Homeland Security,' has the legal authority to take from you whatever they want, anytime they want, without so much as a warrant or a knock on the door."

Such concerns came to full fruition in September 2010, when, under President Obama's administration of "change," government agents launched raids against anti-war activists in Illinois, Minneapolis, Michigan, and North Carolina. One of the homes raided by FBI and BATF agents was that of Minneapolis activist Mick Kelly, who viewed the government's action as nothing more than harassment to intimidate those who organize war protests. Some saw this action as a natural follow up to the words of Homeland Security Secretary Janet Napolitano, who claimed such efforts were "to counter violent extremism right here at home." Former Reagan administration official Paul Craig Roberts said such words "clearly indicate that the federal police agency and the judges who signed the warrants do not regard anti-war protesters as Americans exercising their constitutional rights, but as unpatriotic elements offering material support to terrorism."

Explaining the tactics in play, Roberts explained, "As this initial FBI foray is a softening up move to get the public accustomed to the idea that the real terrorists are their fellow citizens here at home, Kelly will get off this time. But next time the FBI will find emails on his computer from a 'terrorist group' set up by the CIA that will incriminate him. Under the practices put in place by the Bush and Obama regimes, and approved by corrupt federal judges, protesters who have been compromised by fake terrorist groups can be declared 'enemy combatants' and sent off to

Egypt, Poland, or some other corrupt American puppet state—Canada perhaps—to be tortured until confession is forthcoming that anti-war protesters and, indeed, every critic of the US government, are on Osama bin Laden's payroll.

"Almost every Republican and conservative and, indeed, the majority of Americans will fall for this, only to find, later, that it is subversive to complain that their Social Security was cut in the interest of the war against Iran or some other demonized entity, or that they couldn't have a Medicare operation because the wars in Central Asia and South America required the money."

Even under the Obama administration, the erosion of civil liberties continued unabated. In September 2010, Obama's Justice Department urged a federal appeals court to allow the government to place GPS tracking devices on suspects' vehicles without a court warrant, arguing that Americans should not expect privacy in public places. This argument came after Justice Department attorneys sought to rehear a case in which a three-judge panel had reversed the conviction of a drug dealer whose vehicle was tracked for a month without a court-issued warrant. Assistant US Attorney Peter Smith argued, "The panel's conclusion that [the defendant] had a reasonable expectation of privacy in the public movements of his Jeep rested on the premise that an individual has a reasonable expectation of privacy in the totality of his or her movements in public places." Smith noted three other circuit courts had already ruled that authorities do not need a warrant for GPS vehicle tracking.

Noting President Bush's claim that terrorism threatens our freedom, columnist Paul Proctor added, "But, you see—terrorists don't want your freedom—they want your life. It is tyrants and dictators that want your freedom."

## ENTER THE PATRIOT ACT

The first advice any good lawyer gives his or her client is to not sign anything without first reading and understanding it. Yet, a panicky House of Representatives, still in shock over 9/11 and the subsequent anthrax attacks, rushed the Patriot Act into law by a vote of 339–79.

The Act was 342 pages long and made changes, both great and small, to more than 15 different US statutes, most of them enacted in the wake of previous misuse of surveillance powers by the FBI and CIA.

It was hurriedly and enthusiastically signed into law by President Bush on October 26, 2001. The speed with which this legislation was presented to Congress left little doubt in many minds that it had long been prepared and simply needed some provocation as an impetus for action.

According to some congressmen, many lawmakers had not even read the entire document when it was passed. The ACLU reported that some members of Congress had less than one hour to read the extensive changes of law contained within the act. Many civil libertarians felt those two facts alone should be cause for wholesale dismissals at the Capitol.

Rep. Dennis Kucinich, a Democrat from Ohio, described the atmosphere in which the Patriot Act was passed: "[T]here was great fear in our great Capitol...The great fear began when we had to evacuate the Capitol on September 11. It continued when we had to leave the Capitol again when a bomb scare occurred as members were pressing the CIA during a secret briefing. It continued when we abandoned Washington when anthrax, possibly from a government lab, arrived in the mail...It is present in the camouflaged armed National Guardsmen who greet members of Congress each day we enter the Capitol campus. It is present in the labyrinth of concrete barriers through which we must pass each time we go to vote."

Rep. Ron Paul, one of only three Republicans to vote against the House bill, said he objected to how opponents were stigmatized by the name alone. "The insult is to call this a 'patriot bill' and suggest I'm not patriotic because I insisted upon finding out what was in it and voting no. I thought it was undermining the Constitution, so I didn't vote for it—therefore I'm somehow not a patriot. That's insulting."

Paul confirmed rumors that the bill was not read by most members of the House prior to their vote. "It's my understanding the bill wasn't printed before the vote—at least I couldn't get it," he told *Insight Magazine*. "They played all kinds of games, kept the House in session all night, and it was a very complicated bill. Maybe a handful of staffers actually read it, but the bill definitely was not available to members before the vote."

Paul's view of the Patriot bill was echoed by the only independent in the House, Rep. Bernie Sanders of Vermont, who said, "I took an oath to support and defend the Constitution of the United States, and I'm concerned that voting for this legislation fundamentally violates that oath. And the contents of the legislation have not been subjected to serious hearings or searching examination."

The Electronic Frontier Foundation (EFF) of San Francisco, a donor-supported membership group dedicated to protecting freedom when "law and technology collide," published an overview of the Patriot Act. They concluded that, "it seems clear that the vast majority of the sections included have not been carefully studied by Congress, nor was sufficient time taken to debate it or to hear testimony from experts outside of law enforcement in the fields where it makes major changes.

"This concern is amplified because several of the key procedural processes applicable to any other proposed laws, including inter-agency review, the normal committee and hearing processes and thorough voting, were suspended for this bill. The civil liberties of ordinary Americans have taken a tremendous blow with this law, especially the right to privacy in our online communications and activities. Yet there is no evidence that our precious civil liberties posed a barrier to effective tracking or prosecution of terrorists."

In a move to assert some control over the new legislation, Congress tacked on a sunset provision requiring that portions of the act must come under review by Congress or expire by December 31, 2005, unless President Bush decided to extend them in the "national interest." But it was Congress, which extended the "sunset" provisions into 2006 to allow for negotiations with the Bush administration.

In early 2005, Republican supporters of the act attempted to have the legislation reauthorized in accordance with the Bush administration's desire to make all powers permanent, but a series of hearings in both House and Senate were held instead. Various reforms to the act were submitted in both chambers, but were blocked by the partisan leadership.

Still, efforts to make the Patriot Act permanent met with strong opposition from across the political spectrum and included such groups as the American Conservative Union and Americans for Tax Reform. It appeared that congressional leaders feared the proposed reforms would pass if brought to a full and fair vote.

According to the ACLU, "The House and Senate passed different versions of legislation to reauthorize the Patriot Act. Since they were not the same bill, the differences were resolved in a 'conference committee' with representatives from both chambers, but critical compromises were made while excluding Democrats from negotiations. The ensuing conference report failed to include the most important civil liberties protections included in the Senate version of the bill. A final bill and a small amendments package have now passed both houses of Congress.

"The amended Patriot Act continues to fail to adequately protect the privacy rights of innocent, ordinary people in this country." The debate over the Patriot Act continued into 2010 with a number of organizations vowing to seek further reforms in the legislation.

The official title of the bill originally was the "Uniting and Strengthening America by Providing Appropriate Tools Required to Intercept and Obstruct Terrorism Act"—USA PATRIOT Act. The name was reminiscent of Hitler's 1933 legislation passed hurriedly following the burning of the *Reichstag* in 1933, which evolved into the Third Reich. It was called "The Law To Remove the Distress of the People and State."

This act, which clearly abridges many rights of Americans, was built upon the little-known Foreign Intelligence Surveillance Act of 1978 (FISA) which cracked the door open to secret government searches. FISA was passed in the contingencies of the Cold War and in the wake of revelations of misused surveillance by the FBI and CIA.

The FISA law created the secret federal Foreign Intelligence Surveillance Court (FISC), which meets in total secrecy to routinely approve covert surveillances on non-Americans by intelligence agencies. The attorney general must approve all applications to the court. Either federal prosecutors are extremely efficient and effective in their work or the seven federal judges who make up this secret court are not picky about the Constitution because out of the some 12,000 requests for secret surveillances and physical searches made during the first 23 years of the FISC, not one application was denied until four in 2003.

"Then came the USA PATRIOT Act," wrote journalist Walter Brasch, "drafted by the Bush administration and fine-tuned in secret by the House and Senate leadership following the September 11 terrorist attacks. The Patriot Act, which incorporates and significantly expands FISA to include

American citizens, was overwhelmingly approved by the Congress, most of whom admit they read only a few paragraphs, if any at all..."

"The intent behind the passage of the FISA legislation was to impose limits and a review process upon warrantless surveillance and searches conducted for 'national security' purposes in light of the numerous abuses by federal agencies against US citizens," wrote Patrick S. Poole in a treatise on both the FISA and the FISC. "But the politicization and present use of the FISA process [now expanded through the Patriot Act and its revisions] has resulted in the erosion of numerous constitutional rights and basic legal procedures that have their roots in free societies dating back to the Magna Carta."

The act also greatly expanded law enforcement power into areas that have little to do with terrorism. One provision provides for the collection of DNA from terrorists, then expands this to include anyone suspected of "any crime of violence." Both the scope and penalties under the Computer Fraud and Abuse Act were increased along with the use of wiretaps. In fact, the act was so broad and subject to abuse that the Foreign Intelligence Surveillance Court took the unprecedented move of forcing then-Attorney General Ashcroft to modify Justice Department guidelines concerning FBI terrorism searches and wiretaps. The FISC, for the first time in nearly two decades, rejected some of Ashcroft's guidelines as "not reasonably designed" to safeguard Americans' privacy.

Ashcroft's instructions came in March 2002, and were addressed to FBI Director Robert Mueller and senior Justice Dept. officials. They were intended to make it easier for investigators in espionage and terrorism cases to share information from searches or wiretaps. The FISC ruled that his guidelines could cause misuse of information in criminal cases, which traditionally required higher legal standards to procure searches and wiretaps.

Ashcroft had cited the USA PATRIOT Act as the justification for expanded guidelines used in wiretaps and searches. "The attorney general seized authority that has not been granted to him by the Constitution or the Congress," noted Marc Rotenberg, head of the Washington-based Electronic Privacy Information Center.

The Electronic Frontier Foundation said Internet users particularly should be concerned about provisions of the act which expand government surveillance while reducing checks and balances, the forced handing over of records by Internet Service Providers (ISP), new and vague definitions of "terrorism," and surveillance without a court order. Provisions of the original Patriot Act that most concerned civil libertarians were that:

- The federal government may now monitor religious and political institutions without suspecting criminal activity to assist terrorism investigations (a violation of the First Amendment right of association).
- The feds now can close to the public once-open immigration hearings and secretly detain hundreds of people without charge while encouraging bureaucrats to resist Freedom of Information requests (a violation of the 5th and 6th Amendments guaranteeing due process, speedy trials and freedom of information).
- The government may prosecute librarians or other keepers of records if they tell anyone that the government subpoenaed information related to a terrorism investigation (a violation of the First Amendment right of free speech).
- The government now may monitor conversations between federal prisoners and their attorneys and may even deny access to lawyers to Americans accused of crimes (a violation of the 6th Amendment right to have legal representation).
- The government now may search and seize individual and business papers and effects without probable cause to assist an antiterrorism investigation (a violation of the 4th Amendment right against unreasonable searches and seizures).
- The government now may jail Americans indefinitely without a trial or charges (a violation of the 6th Amendment right to a speedy trial and to be informed of the charges against them).

Despite some slight reforms passed in 2006, these same provisions continue to concern civil libertarians. And lest anyone think that the government will hold in abeyance any power given to it, many worrisome incidents of application of the draconian law were quickly reported.

In March 2002 John Ashcroft's Justice Department, announced that it planned to use secret evidence to justify financial sanctions against a Chicago-area Muslim charity as part of its effort to stop the funding of terrorists.

Attorneys for the Global Relief Foundation filed a lawsuit claiming the government violated the Constitution when it froze the charity's assets in December 2001. The government said it would share its evidence with the judge but not with the charity or its attorneys. Legal experts said that this may be the first time the government has tried to use secret evidence in a trial, citing the Patriot Act as its authority.

Global Relief, along with two other charities—Benevolence International and the Texas-based Holy Land Foundation for Relief and Development—had their assets frozen by the government pending an investigation of their links to terrorism.

Innocent until proven guilty? "It's completely contrary to anything that's ever happened in this country. This country was founded on the idea of confronting your accuser. If they submit secret evidence or present it to the judge in such a way that we can never see it, we can't cross examine and we can never rebut," said Global Relief attorney Roger Simmons, adding that such government action set "a very dangerous legal precedent."

## THE PATRIOT ACT AT WORK

Although when the Patriot Act was passed, the American public was assured it would never be used against normal American citizens, the FBI raids of anti-war activists in 2010 demonstrated otherwise. And such concern takes on even more substance when viewed against the government's track record in such cases long before the 9/11 attacks. Following the WTC bombing in 1993, a Palestinian named Hany Kiareldeen living in New Jersey was held after being secretly accused of meeting with one of the men convicted in the bombing. Kiareldeen suspected the information came from someone with a personal axe to grind.

A federal judge, after reviewing the case, questioned not only the evidence against Kiareldeen but the manner in which it was presented. He wrote, "The [Immigration and Naturalization Service's] reliance on secret evidence raised serious issues about the integrity of the adversarial process, the impossibility of self-defense against undisclosed charges, and the reliability of government processes initiated and prosecuted in darkness."

Niels Frenzen, a University of Southern California law professor, agreed with the judge, stating, "Without exception, when the government uses this one-sided evidence, it's gotten it wrong. Why should anyone think they are going to get it right now?"

Another example of what to expect under the new expanded powers of the federal government, already under fire for its questionable actions in the 1990s at Ruby Ridge and Waco, came at 5 a.m. in San Antonio, Texas, the day after 9/11 when heavily-armed federal agents raided the home of Dr. Al-Badr Al-Hazmi. Al-Hazmi was a 34-year-old radiology resident at the University of Texas Health Science Center who had been working in Lackland Air Force Base's military hospital in the days before September 11.

According to news reports, Al-Hazmi's home was ransacked by agents without a search warrant, his wife and young children held at gunpoint and later the doctor was thrown naked into a cold FBI holding cell without being charged with any crime. He was then flown to a New York prison where Al-Hazmi said he was beaten repeatedly during FBI interrogations. After a week, he was finally allowed to speak to his attorney and discovered the cause of his problems was that his name, a common name in the Middle East, was similar to that of two of the suspected 9/11 hijackers. Another week passed before Al-Hazmi was released and allowed to return home, still without having been charged with any crime.

And don't think that arrests such as those above could only happen to someone with a Middle Eastern name. Robert Lee "Bob on the Job" Lewis is a fervent Christian who has spent decades researching government scandals. He worked with airline lawyers during the investigation of the bombing of Pan Am Flight 103 over Lockerbie, Scotland.

In April 1998, Lewis was in a restaurant in Houston, Texas, regaling waiters with his knowledge of government skullduggery, including little-reported information on former President George H. W. Bush. Lewis admitted he made a remark about Bush along the lines of, "I'll have his ass."

Sitting in the restaurant was Secret Service Agent Tim Reilly who promptly placed Lewis under arrest for threatening the former president. The next day, in a short hearing, federal Magistrate Marcia Crone avoided any First Amendment issue and instead accepted the hearsay testimony of Agent Reilly. The impecunious Lewis was held for nearly a year in federal custody. His ordeal included being sent to the Fort Worth Federal Correctional Institution where he was placed in the same cell where Whitewater scandal figure James McDougal reportedly committed suicide. Lewis knew full well who McDougal had been and felt his placement there was a form of intimidation. Some months later, Lewis was transferred to a federal hospital in Springfield, MO, where he was involuntarily drugged until letters from some journalists and academic contacts protesting his drugging gained him a release. There was never a court trial or even an adversarial hearing in the case.

Secret evidence, closed trials, false imprisonment, warrant-less searches, involuntary drugging, the seizing of private property all seem like something out of the Nazi era, but fear has pushed many Americans into a passive and accepting mode.

Congressman Paul when asked what was wrong with the Patriot Act, replied, "The worst part of this so-called antiterrorism bill is the increased ability of the federal government to commit surveillance on all of us without proper search warrants." Paul was referring to Section 213 of the Act entitled, "Authority for Delaying Notice of the Execution of a Warrant," also called the "sneak-and-peek" provision that allows authorities to search personal property without warning.

*Insight Magazine* reporter Kelly Patricia O'Meara wrote that, "With one vote by Congress and the sweep of the president's pen, say critics, the right of every American fully to be protected under the Fourth Amendment against unreasonable searches and seizures was abrogated."

Paul pointed out the obvious flaw in the idea that the government would act in a restrained and responsible manner when given this authority. "I don't like the sneak-and-peek provision because you have to ask yourself what happens if the person is home, doesn't know that law enforcement is coming to search his home, hasn't a clue as to who's coming in unannounced...and he shoots them. This law clearly authorizes illegal search and seizure, and anyone who thinks of this as antiterrorism needs to consider its application to every American citizen."

By early 2006, the controversy over surveillance and privacy reached new heights when it was reported that President Bush had instructed the secretive National Security Agency (NSA) to electronically monitor Americans for signs of terrorism.

The potential for "Big Brother" surveillance had been there all along. As far back as 1975, Senator Frank Church, who performed a study of the NSA, warned, "That [the NSA] capability at any time could be turned around on the American people and no American would have any privacy left, such is the capability to monitor everything: telephone conversations, telegrams, it doesn't matter. There would be no place to hide."

Church's warning proved true 30 years later when the news media reported an outcry over Bush's order to turn the NSA against Americans without seeking warrants from the special intelligence court (FISA) or any other court. It was also revealed in 2006 that the NSA had been secretly collecting phone call records of tens of millions of Americans using data from AT&T, Verizon and BellSouth, the three largest phone companies in the US. Moreover, the program was overseen by the new director of the CIA, General Michael Hayden, during his tenure heading the NSA.

Attorney General Gonzales publicly argued that such spying was within the legal rights of a wartime president, again demonstrating that the 9/11 attacks and subsequent War on Terrorism continue to be the foundation for the events of today. When members of the Senate Judiciary Committee asked to see how the Bush administration arrived at this argument, the White House denied requests for classified legal documents that were behind Gonzales' defense.

Opponents to NSA warrantless spying—including some Republicans—claimed it not only was intrusive and a violation of constitutional safeguards on privacy but ineffective by overloading law enforcement agencies with bad leads. They also saw the surveillance program as a serious step to consolidating power in the executive branch. "The history of power teaches us one thing," said former Reagan administration attorney Bruce Fein, "if it's unchecked, it will be abused."

It was seen as ironic by knowledgeable persons that the 1978 Foreign Intelligence Surveillance Act, bypassed by Bush's orders, was passed in the wake of revelations of how President Nixon used the NSA to spy domestically on political enemies.

Even some of the 2006 revisions of the Patriot Act failed to correct portions that concerned both libertarians and congressmen. Rep. C. L. "Butch" Otter of Idaho was one of the three Republicans who found the entire act potentially unconstitutional from the onset. "Section 215 authorizes the FBI to acquire any business records whatsoever by order of a secret US Court. The recipient of such a search order is forbidden from telling any person that he has received such a request. This is a violation of the First Amendment right to free speech and the Fourth Amendment protection of private property," commented Otter, adding, "[S]ome of these provisions place more power in the hands of law enforcement than our Founding Fathers could have dreamt and severely compromises the civil liberties of law-abiding Americans. This bill, while crafted with good intentions, is rife with constitutional infringements I could not support."

The issue of penalties against persons who simply reveal that government intrusion is taking place was a cornerstone of controversy over renewal of the Patriot Act in late 2005.

Section 215's "gag order" was retained by Congress after a compromise on the wording so that it remained effective only for a year after a secret search was conducted. One year, obviously, is too long for any American to wait to learn that their government is spying on them.

According to a *New York Times* editorialist, "The compromise also fails to address another problem with Section 215: it lets the government go on fishing expeditions, spying on Americans with no connection to terrorism or foreign powers. The act should require the government, in order to get a subpoena, to show that there is a connection between the information it is seeking and a terrorist or a spy."

One feature of the Act as approved in 2001 had actually been introduced much earlier, in 1998, only to be struck down after a public outcry.

In this case during the Clinton administration, there was a brief furor over proposed new federal banking regulations that would require all banks to report to the government any large deposits or withdrawals or unusual activity on the part of the banking public. Euphemistically called the "Know Your Customer" program, it heralded a new era wherein law-abiding citizens might have to defend their financial matters before government agents. Under this program, banks would be required to create a profile of each customer and report any deviation from the profile to the feds. For example, consider a citizen who sold an unneeded car and deposited the cash in his bank account. Under this program, the bank computer would flag the transaction because this was an unusually large deposit based on the person's previous deposit record. Federal authorities would be notified and soon agents would be sent to interrogate the customer on the chance he or she might be a drug dealer or terrorist.

Rep. Ron Paul in 1998 had planned to introduce legislation to stop this intrusive program but an irate citizenry saved him the trouble. The schemers behind the proposal, the Federal Deposit Insurance Corp; the IRS and other agencies quickly backed off. Paul said quite prophetically, "Somehow, though, I imagine such action will not stop them, only slow them down." Ron Paul was right. Almost all of the provisions of the "Know Your Customer" program can be found in the Patriot Act.

A clear example of the danger of such intrusive legislation came in early 2006 when Rhode Island retired schoolteacher Walter Soehnge and his wife tried to pay down an excessive credit card bill with a JC Penney MasterCard. They sent in a check for $6,500 to pay down their debt.

When the Soehnges found the money had not been credited to their account, they began to make inquires. They were told that when a payment is much larger than usual, Homeland Security must be notified and that the money is held until a threat assessment is made. The couple's money was eventually freed although they never found out how making a large credit card payment posed a threat to national security.

"If it can happen to me, it can happen to others," Soehnge noted dryly.

Another of those who actually read the Patriot Act and were appalled at its unconstitutional provisions was Nadine Strossen, a professor of law at New York Law School and president of the American Civil Liberties Union from 1991 to 2008. Her main complaint was that the sweeping changes codified by the act have little or nothing to do with fighting terrorism

"There is no connection between the September 11 attacks and what is in this legislation," Strossen argued. "Most of the provisions related not just to terrorist crimes but to criminal activity generally. This happened too, with the 1996 antiterrorism legislation where most of the surveillance laws have been used for drug enforcement, gambling and prostitution." By 2005, the Patriot Act provisions had been expanded into cases far beyond terrorism.

According to Pittsburgh *Star-Ledger* writer Mark Mueller, "While the Justice Department says it does not uniformly track the Patriot Act's use in such cases, a reading of government reports and congressional testimony shows it has been used hundreds of times against the likes of drug dealers, computer hackers, child pornographers, armed robbers and kidnappers. In Washington State, investigators invoked the law to surreptitiously bug a tunnel that had been bored beneath the US-Canadian border by drug runners. In Las Vegas, prosecutors used it to seize the financial records of a strip-club owner suspected of bribing local government officials.

Reporter O'Meara noted that a similar antiterrorist act in England allows government investigators to obtain information from Internet Service Providers (ISPs) about their subscribers without a warrant. The British law is now being applied to minor crimes, tax collection and public health measures.

The ACLU has already filed a number of lawsuits trying to make the government accountable for its law enforcement activities under the Patriot Act. An ACLU press release stated the organization believed "it is critically important that the public learn how [the Justice Department] is using the vast new surveillance powers granted the government." In their suits under the Freedom of Information Act, the ACLU wanted to know among other things:

- The number of times the FBI used pen registers [the numbers that a person has called is kept in a register] or trap and trace devices against US citizens or permanent residents as provided in Section 214 of the Patriot Act.
- The number of times the FBI has ordered libraries, bookstores or newspapers to divulge records or other tangible things as provided in Section 215 of the act.
- The number of United States citizens or permanent residents who have been subjected to new surveillance orders since the enactment of the Patriot Act.

The ACLU stated that it did not believe that the release of such aggregate, statistical information would jeopardize national security or any other legitimate government interest. Former ACLU President Strossen said her overriding concern with the Patriot act is the power that is being concentrated in the presidency. "The concern here is about the third branch of government," she explained. "One of the overreaching problems that pervades so many provisions is reduction of the role of judicial oversight. The executive branch is running roughshod over both of the other branches of government. I find it very bothersome that the government is going to have more widespread access to email and websites and that information can be shared with other law enforcement and even intelligence agencies. So again, we're going to have the CIA in the business of spying on Americans..."

Strossen, Paul, Otter and others were pointed but polite in their criticisms of the Patriot Act. Others were not so courteous. "In light of the egregious evisceration of the Bill of Rights that this law undertakes, those who blindly supported and signed this blatantly unconstitutional act into law should be collectively condemned and charged with high treason to the Constitution and the people of the United States," wrote columnist Doreen Miller for *YellowTimes*, an online publication of alternative news. "The USA PATRIOT Act creates and allows for a virtual police state with little to no judicial oversight. We, as a nation, are literally treading the razor's edge when it comes to flirting with the grave dangers inherent in giving up our rights for the empty promises of 'safety' and 'national security' masquerading under the guise of a 'patriotic' Patriot Act. Once we fall off that edge, reclaiming and reinstating our rights, authority and power as 'We The People' of this great nation might prove very difficult."

Public concerns over the Patriot Act prompted renewed interest in civil rights and brought membership in the Americal Civil Liberties Union (ACLU) from about 200,000 to more than 500,000 by 2010.

In October 2004, the ACLU rejected $1.5 million from both the Ford and Rockefeller Foundations due to language in the donation agreements sounded like wording of the Patriot Act. ACLU officials said a donation stipulation denying funds for "underwriting terrorism or other unacceptable activities" was overly broad and ambiguous and a threat to civil liberties.

Karen G. Schneider, writing for the American Library Association website, wrote, "First of all, I'm a hawk. I believe we should be in Afghanistan, I'd like to see bin Laden oh, say, six feet under, and behind my bifocals, this middle-aged veteran cheers her colleagues in the armed forces defending our nation. However, the USA PATRIOT Act is treason pure and simple, and you need to know how and why, because it presents particularly pernicious issues for the users who rely on your Internet services. The Patriot Act is not antiterrorism legislation; it's anti-speech legislation, and is no more a direct response to the September 11 attacks than the Children's Internet Protection Act is a direct result of sincere concern by members of Congress about the safety of minors. The cold, cynical reality is that the Patriot Act is a bloated hodgepodge of speech-chilling law that lurked in congressional corridors not only before September 11 but in large part before the Bush administration. It was hustled into reality in the post 9/11 environment so quickly, secretively, and undemocratically that our Bill of Rights had been clocked with a one-two punch well before any of us realized it was under attack."

Schneider's concern was clearly illustrated in an incident in which FBI agents showed up some time back at a Bloomsburg, PA, bookstore owned by Arline Johnson. The agents weren't tracking criminals, they were asking which customers bought copies of the Tom Clancy book, *The Hunt for Red October*. Johnson, who has been challenged for selling books on everything from Karl Marx to gay rights to dinosaurs, said she tells the "book police" that "it's important that people learn and read about everything, whether they believe it or not…It's not the government's job to tell me or anyone what they can read…I once lived and taught in Bulgaria and I don't like totalitarian regimes."

Booksellers do indeed seem most vulnerable to the Patriot Act. In November 2001, the American Booksellers Foundation for Free Expression (ABFFE) sent a letter to its members stating, "Dear Bookseller, it begins. Last week, President Bush signed into law an antiterrorism bill that gives the federal government expanded authority to search your business records, including the titles of the books purchased by your customers… There is no opportunity for you or your lawyer to object in court. You cannot object publicly either. The new law includes a gag order that prevents you from disclosing 'to any person' the fact that you have received an order to produce documents…because of the gag order…you should not tell ABFFE that you have received a court order…you can simply tell us that you need to contact ABFFE's legal counsel."

Marsha Rummel of the Rainbow Bookstore Cooperative in Madison, WI, commented, "[T]he danger to booksellers is just one small part of this new landscape. We must collectively take a stand to defend our democratic rights, including the right to protest our government and oppose the war, and the right to read whatever we like."

According to *Newsweek*, the ACLU had been searching for "Conan the Librarian," some librarian who would be willing to serve as a test case against the Patriot Act, with little success. The act was being used by the FBI as an excuse for broad new powers to check library records, Internet use, business records and anything else that they claim might lead them to terrorists. "This statute trumps protections in place in 49 of 50 states," observed Gregory T. Nogeim of the ACLU. The aforementioned "Conan the Librarian" may have come in the form of George Christian, executive director of the Library Connection in Hartford, CT, a small nonprofit concern that oversaw the computer systems of 27 area libraries.

In 2006, two special agents of the FBI Hartford office appeared in Christian's office with a National Security Letter (NSL) issued under Section 2709 of the Patriot Act which demanded that the Library Connection hand over to the agents all identifying personal information on all users of the 27 libraries for a particular day a few months earlier. The letter went on to state that Christian was ordered to comply with this demand and that he was not to inform anyone of the investigation. Shocked, Christian replied, "I believe this is unconstitutional and I am not going to give you anything." One agent proceeded to point to a section of the letter which warned of fine and/or jail time for noncompliance and told Christian he had better think about what he was doing and get back to them immediately.

Calling a hasty meeting of the Library Connection's board, it was decided to fight. Joining with the ACLU, they filed suit against the attorney general of the US. Since their names could not be used under provisions of the Patriot Act, the suit originally was titled *John Doe v. John D. Ashcroft*, which later changed to *John Doe v. Alberto R. Gonzales*. Christian and his fellow board members and co-plaintiffs were branded by the Bush administration as "threats to national security" and were not allowed to attend their own court trial. They were forced to view the proceedings via close-circuit television. Fearful they had taken on the entire national security establishment of the US, they were apprehensive until they saw a "sea of librarians" sitting in the audience in support. They also got a view of Connecticut US Attorney Kevin J. O'Connor, who had been touring the state assuring the public that the Patriot Act would never be used against honest American citizens. O'Connor later would be appointed chief of staff to Attorney General Gonzales.

At the time of the trial in early 2006 the Patriot Act was up for reauthorization by Congress, so several legal maneuvers were thrown in the path of the librarians' suit until the act was indeed continued in effect, after which in 2007 the National Security Letter provision of the act was struck down as unconstitutional by the Second Circuit Court of Appeals.

The government appealed this ruling and arguments continued for the next several years. David Goodman, an investigative journalist for *Mother Jones* termed the librarians involved in this case the most "tenacious and courageous freedom fighters in this country."

Since mid-2003, other librarians have flexed their freedom muscles by daily shredding library records to prevent federal agents from obtaining records of what books were being checked out. In a 2002 survey sent to libraries across the nation by the Library Research Center at the University of Illinois, the staffs of 219 libraries said they would cooperate with requests for information about patrons. But 225 said they would not.

"The effect of the USA PATRIOT Act upon businesses that loan, rent or sell books, videos, magazines and music CDs, is not to find and incarcerate terrorists—there are far more ways to investigate threats to the nation than to check on a terrorist's reading and listening habits—but to put a sweeping chilling effect upon constitutional freedoms," wrote *Online Journal* writer Walter Brasch.

James R. Elwood, executive vice president of the International Society for Individual Liberty, an umbrella organization representing individuals and groups in more than 80 countries, stated that the "rule of law—enshrined in the Bill of Rights—which protects the innocent—must be strictly upheld and that the new 'antiterrorist' laws be repealed."

By 2008, the continuing abuses of the Patriot Act were becoming more public. An investigation by the Justice Department's Inspector General Glenn Fine found that FBI headquarters officials sought to cover their informal and possibly illegal acquisition of phone records on thousands of Americans from 2003 to 2005 by issuing 11 improper, retroactive "blanket" administrative subpoenas in 2006 to three phone companies that are under contract to the FBI. According to this audit, officials at the FBI's Counterterrorism Division signed the blanket subpoenas "retroactively to justify the FBI's acquisition of data through the exigent letters or or other informal requests."

This investigation followed up on a 2007 report that the FBI abused a key Patriot Act power, the National Security Letter. The investigation showed that FBI agents were routinely sending out flawed follow-up letters in which the Counterterrorism Division attempted to provide retroactive legal justification for telephone data the division had gotten on

3,860 phone numbers, obtained through verbal requests to the companies or false emergency requests.

According to Ryan Singel writing in *Wired* magazine, "The letters are related to still-secret contracts the FBI's Communication Analysis Unit has with AT&T, Verizon and MCI. The contracts pay the companies to store subscribers' phone records for longer periods of time and to provide faster service for FBI subpoenas. Those contracts began in May 2003, but the FBI refuses to release them. At least one of the letters was signed by an assistant director and none were cleared with the FBI's general counsel."

The inspector general's report also indicated that the FBI was increasingly targeting the American public and green card holders for scrutiny and eavesdropping, with more than 11,517 requests in 2006 targeting US persons, while non-citizens were targeted with 8,605 requests.

Under Section 112 of the Patriot Act as well as the 2006 Military Commissions Act, a "suspected terrorist" may be determined solely by certification by the attorney general on "reasonable ground" that he "believes" someone to be such. "Section 236A gives the attorney general unprecedented powers untouchable by any court, whereby he may detain a suspect in increments of up to six months at a time if he believes the suspect's release would threaten national security or the safety of the community or any person," wrote columnist Doreen Miller, noting that the act states, "At the attorney general's discretion, no court shall have jurisdiction to review, by habeas corpus, petition, or otherwise, any such action or decision." One might think that by the end of the first decade of the 21st century the problems and abuses of the Patriot Act, rushed into law in the panic immediately following the attacks of 9/11, would be smoothed out. But this was not to be.

For example, at 10 p.m. March 5, 2009, 12 armed FBI agents along with three local law enforcement officers stormed the Granville County, NC, home of Annette Lundeby looking for her son. After presenting a search warrant, they handcuffed 16-year-old Ashton Lundeby and led him away from his room which was festooned with American flags. Young Lundeby was held on a criminal complaint that he had made a bomb threat from his home on the night of Feb. 15. His mother told newsmen the family was at a church function that night and that the agents were acting on false information. "I was terrified," recalled Lundeby's mother. "There were guns, and I don't allow guns around my children. I don't believe in guns." She said she tried to tell the agents that someone had hacked into her son's IP address and was using this address to make crank calls connected through the Internet, making it look like the calls had originated from her home but her explanation was ignored. The raiders seized a computer, a cell phone, gaming console, routers, bank statements and school records, based on a federal search warrant. "There were no bomb-making materials, not even a blasting cap, not even a wire," said Lundeby.

The teenager was taken to a juvenile facility in South Bend, ID. His mother, who could not afford to travel to Indiana, said she has had little access to him since his arrest. She said the Patriot Act stripped her son of his due process rights. "We have no rights under the Patriot Act to even defend them, because the Patriot Act basically supersedes the Constitution. It wasn't intended to drag your barely 16-year-old, 120-pound son out in the middle of the night on a charge that we can't even defend."

Dan Boyce, a defense attorney and former US attorney not connected to the Lundeby case, told the media, "They're saying that 'We feel this individual is a terrorist or an enemy combatant against the United States, and we're going to suspend all of those due process rights because this person is an enemy of the United States.' There's nothing a matter of public record. All those normal rights are just suspended in the air."

Amanda Lamb of WRAL-TV reported, "Because a federal judge issued a gag order in the case, the US attorney in Indiana cannot comment on the case, nor can the FBI. The North Carolina Highway Patrol did confirm that officers assisted with the FBI operation at the Lundeby home on March 5."

"Never in my worst nightmare did I ever think that it would be my own government that I would have to protect my children from. This is the United States, and I feel like I live in a third world country now," bemoaned Lundeby.

Apparently the trickle-down theory also works for the insanity of abuses of "national security" in public schools. On April 3, 2010, 12-year-old Alexa Gonzalez was arrested, led from her junior high school in Queens, NY, and detained at a local police precinct for hours. Her offense? Alexa was caught doodling on her school desk. The girl had used a water-soluble, erasable marker to send this message to some pals, "I love my friends Abby and Faith." She added, "Lex was here. 2/1/10" and a smiley face. She admitted to making a mistake and expected detention or perhaps an afternoon cleaning desks.

In June, Alexa and her mother, Maraima Comacho, sued the New York City Education Department and the New York Police Department for $1 million in damages, citing excessive use of force and violation of the Alexa's rights in what Comacho described as a "nightmare." Family attorney Joseph Rosenthal explained, "We want to stop this from happening to other young children in the future." Legal papers filed by Rosenthal said the mother was not permitted to accompany her daughter to the precinct, where Alexa was detained in "an enclosed room" and handcuffed to a pole for more than two hours.

New York school officials later acknowledged that Alexa's treatment had been a mistake while police spokesman Paul Browne admitted "Even when we're asked to make an arrest, common sense should prevail, and discretion used in deciding whether an arrest or handcuffs are really necessary." Such advice might be taken to heart by law officers across the nation.

## INTERNMENT CAMPS IN PLACE

For such power as encompassed in the Patriot Act to be concentrated in the hands of the US attorney general prompts questions concerning the person in that position. The public should closely scrutinize attorney general's integrity, ambition and philosophical outlook.

A brief look at former Attorney General John Ashcroft, who first supervised this new act, reveals some disturbing facts. These facts were conveniently ignored or downplayed by a mass media cowed in the patriotic furor following the 9/11 attacks.

In 2000, the Democratic governor of Missouri, Mel Carnahan, was battling Ashcroft for a US Senate seat. Carnahan died in a small plane crash. His wife, Jean, was not with him. Jean agreed to fill the seat for her late husband should he win it and Missouri voters delivered a blow to Ashcroft by casting their votes for a dead man, a clear indication of the respect held for Ashcroft in his home state.

A distinct warning about Ashcroft and what was to come came long before the 2001 terror attacks. In testimony opposing the nomination of

John Ashcroft as attorney general given on January 16, 2001, Dr. Debra H. Freeman, a contributing editor of *Executive Intelligence Review*, warned the Senate Judiciary Committee that Ashcroft would bring under the guise of "crisis management" a "form of brutal bureaucratic fascism on the United States that bears striking similarities to the conditions under which Adolf Hitler seized power in Germany in 1933."

Until the 9/11 attacks, Ashcroft who had been most noticeable to the American public when he ordered an exposed breast covered on the statue called The Spirit of Justice that stands in the Justice Department's Hall of Justice, rapidly patched together a spate of antiterrorism laws, most of which would never have made it through Congress under normal circumstances. He was already warping US laws beyond recognition by detaining without trial as many as 1,200 persons, most in violation of immigration laws. Many were later released without charges being filed against them.

But at least one vision of Ashcroft was absolutely outrageous. In a little publicized announcement in August 2002, Ashcroft said he wanted the power to strip American citizens of their constitutional rights, including access to the court system, and indefinitely imprisoned them in interment camps on his word that they were "enemy combatants."

"The proposed camp plan should trigger immediate congressional hearings and reconsideration of Ashcroft's fitness for this important office," declared Jonathan Turley, a professor of constitutional law at George Washington University Law School who actively supported Ashcroft during his contentious nomination hearing. "Whereas al Qaeda is a threat to the lives of our citizens, Ashcroft has become a clear and present threat to our liberties."

An example of the unevenness of Ashcroft justice was seen in the treatment of two Americans captured while fighting for the Taliban in Afghanistan—John Walker Lindh and Yaser Esam Hamdi. Lindh was given a lawyer and a trial where he plea bargained for a reduced prison sentence. Hamdi, a Louisiana-born prisoner captured in Afghanistan and held in the US detention camp at the Guantanamo Bay naval base in Cuba, was transferred to a Navy brig floating off the Virginia coast where he remained indefinitely.

When a federal judge ordered that the Justice Department present evidence justifying Hamdi's treatment, the government simply refused to comply, insisting that the judge could not interfere with the president's "absolute authority in a time of war." Then when Hamdi's father filed a habeas corpus petition in the United States District Court for Norfolk, VA, the court, though never denying outright that Hamdi had no right to habeas corpus, nevertheless claimed only Hamdi himself could bring the habeas petition. Such action while being held incommunicado is obviously impossible.

It appeared that the Bush administration attempted intimidation as prosecution motions warned that any judge who opposed the government's action risked "a conflict of military and judicial opinion highly comforting to the enemies of the United States." This wording was most interesting as the US Constitution defines treason as giving "aid and comfort" to the enemy.

On top of all this, Hamdi was denied access to legal representation prompting a lower-court judge, Reagan appointee Robert Doumar, to state, "I tried valiantly to find a case of any kind, in any court, where a lawyer couldn't meet with a client....This case sets the most interesting precedent in relation to that which has ever existed in Anglo-American jurisprudence since the days of the Star Chamber."

Hamdi was released and deported to Saudi Arabia in October 2004 after agreeing to renounce his US citizenship accepting restrictions on his travel to several Middle East nations such as Israel, Syria, Iraq, Afghanistan, and Pakistan. He also was required to promise not to sue the US government over his captivity.

Then there's the case of another American citizen Jose Padilla, the "dirty" bomber. Padilla was arrested after federal authorities claimed they learned he was planning to construct a radioactive bomb. However, the Bush administration some time later quietly admitted they had no evidence that Padilla actually was planning anything like that. "What is clear [in this case] is that Padilla is an American citizen and was arrested in the United States—two facts that should trigger the full application of constitutional rights," said law professor Jonathan Turley.

"If you think this law applies only to foreign nationals, think again," admonished columnist Doreen Miller. "Jose Padilla, although by no means a model US-born citizen, had his civil rights stripped from him [in May 2002] just by Ashcroft's uttering the magic words, 'enemy combatant' and 'suspected terrorist.' To this day, no solid evidence has been produced to substantiate Ashcroft's claims—neither bomb parts, nor bomb assembly instructions, nor any plans or maps of intended strike areas."

Padilla was shunted about by the federal government for nearly four years until early in 2005, when a federal judge ruled that Padilla had to be charged with a crime or released. It was only then that Padilla was transferred from military authority to the criminal justice system.

After ongoing argument over his legal status by both prosecutors and defense attorneys, on August 16, 2007 Padilla was found guilty by a federal jury of conspiring to kill people in overseas battle while funding and supporting terrorism. The so-called "dirty bomber," however, was neither charged nor convicted of this crime. His 17-year prison sentence was on appeal in 2010.

According to Internet commentator Mike Whitney, "Padilla became the test case for shattering the Bill of Rights with one withering blow. It has succeeded beyond anyone's wildest expectation. There's no chance that the Supreme Court will retry the case and draw more attention to the shocking details of this judicial coup; they already punted once before preferring to pass it along to the lower court. Rather, the meaning of the case will be ignored until the president needs to exercise the newly bestowed powers of supreme leader. That authority is now firmly rooted in the legal precedent established by the Padilla ruling."

"Okay, now let's play a game," wrote columnist Carl Worden. "Replace the name Jose Padilla with Carl Worden. I get picked up and thrown into a military brig where I don't get my call or a visit with my attorney. I am being held without charges as an 'enemy combatant' and the government does not have to appear in open court to present evidence at my arraignment, and they don't have to release me until hostilities have ended—which in the case of the War on Terrorism, that would translate into a life sentence. In the meantime, they can say anything about me they want—but they don't have to prove it. They will probably allege a conspiracy of some sort, which means they don't have to produce hard evidence like illegal weapons or explosives. They will throw in a couple of verifiable facts for credibility purposes, such as my membership in the Southern Oregon Militia and my outspoken 'anti-government,' 'Right Wing Extremist' rhetoric. They will display the weapons I own...they will claim I had bomb-making supplies and equipment in my garage when they searched my premises [common household materials can be construed as bomb-making supplies]. That's right. They found my diabolical [ammunition] reloading bench...Now replace my name with yours and play the same game."

Worden's scenario gets to the heart of cases like Padilla. Such persons may be of dark complexion, absolute creeps or religious freaks. But if the American people allow their individual rights to be trampled, then no one is safe. Libertarians clearly see that the only way to guarantee freedom and liberty is to see that laws are applied equally without exceptions, even in deplorable cases.

"We are only now getting a full vision of Ashcroft's America," mused Professor Turley after a study of the attorney general's activities. "Ashcroft [was] a catalyst for constitutional devolution, encouraging citizens to accept autocratic rule as their only way of avoiding massive terrorist attacks. His greatest problem has been preserving a level of panic and fear necessary to induce a free people to surrender rights so dearly won by their ancestors," he added. "Every generation has had Ashcrofts who view our laws and traditions as mere obstructions rather than protections in times of peril. But before we allow Ashcroft to denude our own constitutional landscape, we must take a stand and have the courage to say, 'Enough.' Every generation has its test of principle in which people of good faith can no longer remain silent in the face of authoritarian ambition. If we cannot join together to fight the abomination of American camps, we have already lost what we're defending."

Even the *New York Times* editorialized, "The Bush administration seems to believe, on no good legal authority, that if it calls citizens combatants in the war on terrorism, it can imprison them indefinitely and deprive them of lawyers. This defiance of the courts repudiates two centuries of constitutional law and undermines the very freedoms that President Bush says he is defending in the struggle against terrorism."

Writer Nat Hentoff grumbled, "It bothers me that the executive branch is taking the amazing position that just on the president's say-so, any American citizen can be picked up, not just in Afghanistan, but at O'Hare Airport or on the streets of any city in this country, and locked up without access to a lawyer or court just because the government says he's connected somehow with the Taliban or al Qaeda. That's not the American way. It's not the constitutional way...and no court can even figure out whether we've got the wrong guy."

When asked what the Founding Fathers might say about the Bush-Ashcroft vision for the Patriot Act, Congressman Paul laughed and said, "Our forefathers would think it's time for a revolution. This is why they revolted in the first place. They revolted against much more mild oppression."

Troublesome questions also followed Alberto R. Gonzales, who was sworn in as the nation's 80th attorney general on February 3, 2005. Gonzales, a former White House counsel to President George W. Bush, immediately played the terror card in his initial remarks to Justice Department employees. He noted they have "a special obligation to protect America against future acts of terrorism. We will continue to make that our top priority while remaining consistent with our values and legal obligations. That will be the lodestar that guides us in our efforts at the department."

Prior to serving in the White House, he served as a justice of the Supreme Court of Texas. Before his appointment to the Texas Supreme Court in 1999, he served as Texas' 100th secretary of state from December 2, 1997 to January 10, 1999. Among his many duties as secretary of state, Gonzales was a senior advisor to then-Governor Bush, chief elections officer, and the governor's lead liaison on Mexico and border issues.

Upon taking up his new office, Gonzales was immediately assailed for a series of questionable decisions as White House counsel. In August 2002, following meetings between Gonzales and other Bush administration officials, a Justice Department memo was issued explaining that laws prohibiting torture of prisoners do "not apply to the president's detention and interrogation of enemy combatants." The memo added that only "injury such as death, organ failure or serious impairment of body functions...constitute torture."

Earlier that year, Gonzales had written a memo arguing that al Qaeda and Taliban prisoners were not subject to the provisions of the Geneva Convention because "the war against terrorism is a new kind of war" which "renders obsolete Geneva's strict limitations on questioning of enemy prisoners and renders quaint some of its provisions." Many members of the military, including Secretary of State Colin Powell, warned that ignoring the Geneva Convention might well prove dangerous to future US soldiers captured by the enemy. In fact, a federal judge ruled, "President

Bush had both overstepped his constitutional bounds and improperly brushed aside the Geneva Conventions."

Gonzales' lack of concern over the rights of prisoners may have begun in the days when he served as chief legal counsel for then-Texas Governor George W. Bush. In his official capacity, it was Gonzales who sent Bush memos concerning the facts of all death penalty cases. Bush would then decide who lived and who died. Note that it was during this time that Texas gained national notoriety for the number of death penalties. According to a study of Gonzales' memos, *Atlantic Monthly* concluded, "Gonzales repeatedly failed to apprise the governor of crucial issues in the cases at hand: ineffective counsel, conflict of interest, mitigating evidence, even actual evidence of innocence." According to this study, Gonzales' memos "seemed attuned to a radically different posture, assumed by Bush from the earliest days of his administration—one in which he sought to minimize his sense of legal and moral responsibility for executions."

Gonzales also caused controversy in 1996 when as counsel to Texas Governor Bush he helped keep Bush from jury duty, a service which would have required Bush to disclose his then-secret 1976 conviction for drunken driving in Maine. Gonzales suggested to the judge and defense lawyer that if Bush served, then as governor, he would not be able to pardon the defendant in the future.

Like others in the Bush administration, Gonzales came under fire for his close relationships with energy corporations, including the failed giant, Enron. According to The Center for American Progress, a nonpartisan research and educational institute, Gonzales accrued about $100,000 from the energy industry in 2002, the same year that he authored a Texas Supreme Court opinion, which "handed the energy industry one of its biggest Texas legal victories in recent history." After entering the White House with Bush, it was Gonzales who worked hard to keep secret the meetings held by Cheney's energy task force.

Succeeding Gonzales, who resigned in August 2007 amid controversies over government-sanctioned torture, illegal eavesdropping and even allegations of perjury before Congress, was US District Court Judge Michael Bernard Mukasey, the jurist who presided over the court case of Jose Padilla as well as the insurance claims of Larry Silverstein for the loss of the World Trade Center towers.

INTERNMENT CAMPS IN PLACE

Although constitutionally guaranteed the position for life, Mukasey resigned his judgeship in August 2006, to return to private law practice. Yet one year later accepted President Bush's offer to become attorney general replacing Gonzales. In 2009, ethics complaints were filed against Mukasey and others for their support of Bush administration policies on torture.

President Obama's attorney general, Eric Holder, is the first African-American to hold that position. Holder voiced opposition to the Patriot Act saying its abuses are "bad ultimately for law enforcement and will cost us the support of the American people." He also criticized the euphemistically named "enhanced interrogation techniques," torture to most citizens, and the NSA's warrantless surveillance program, stating, "This disrespect for the rule of law is not only wrong, it is destructive in our struggle against terrorism."

Persons with a secretive and conspiring mindset, when they are allowed in positions such as US attorney general, are especially worrisome when considered within the rapid growth of eavesdropping and surveillance technology available today.

## BIG BROTHER'S TECHNOLOGY

In light of recent legislation, the only factor required today to turn the United States into the type of dictatorship described in the novel *1984* is the technology to do so. Such technology was largely unavailable in 1984 but it is today. Consider the gradual encroachment made by the government in assigning each and every member of the United States a computer or identity number:

- 1935—Social Security initiated.
- 1936—The current Social Security numbering system began.
- 1962—The IRS started requiring Social Security numbers on tax returns even though Social Security cards plainly stated the number was "Not For Identification."
- 1970—All banks were required to have your Social Security number.
- 1971—Military ID numbers were changed to Social Security numbers.

- 1982—Anyone receiving any sort of government largess was required to obtain a Social Security number.
- 1984—Any person being declared a dependent for IRS tax purposes required a Social Security number. Within two years, even new-born babies were required to have a Social Security number under penalty of fine.

A national identification card has been talked about for years but civil libertarians have consistently cooled the public's receptivity to such a concept—until now.

In mid-2002, even as the initial fear over 9/11 began to subside, Rep. Jim Moran of Virginia, citing increased concerns over terrorism, introduced legislation in Congress called the Driver's License Modernization Act of 2002 (H.R. 4633). This bill was styled as a law, which would set uniform standards for drivers' licenses in all 50 states and the District of Columbia. But it also included provisions to establish a national database and identification system. This bill codified a plan previously sent by Congress to the Department of Transportation urging the development of electronic "smart" drivers' licenses that contain embedded programmable computer chips that could be checked by law enforcement authorities across the nation.

"So it's more of a national ID *system* [emphasis in the original], a linking of Department of Motor Vehicles—and the records they keep on you—across state lines, with some extra on-card security measures thrown in," wrote Frank Pellegrini of *Time.com*. "The plan, Congress hopes, will be cheaper and easier to implement, and less likely to incur the talk-show ire of civil libertarians and states' rights purists (the same type who squawked in 1908 when the FBI was born). But the approach is mere stealth—50 different state ID cards all linked together is pretty much the same as one national ID card, just as all those new quarters are still worth 25 cents each, no matter which state is on the back."

The House bill also states the new ID card must "conform to any other standards issued by the secretary [of Transportation]," an open invitation for bureaucrat tinkering.

Such fears were realized when the Rearing and Empowering America for Longevity against acts of International Destruction (REAL ID) Act of 2005 was passed in an effort to set standards for all driver's licenses making them acceptable for "official purposes" as defined by the secretary of Homeland Security. These purposes included entering any federal building and boarding any commercial airliner. But the states balked at the plan, not due to privacy and control concerns but because of the cost of implementing it, and by 2008, an extension was given to all states. As concerns over REAL ID grew, by October 2009, at least 25 states had passed resolutions or legislation withdrawing from REAL ID. Many civil libertarians saw this resistance as a worthy step in breaking free from overreaching federal authority.

In April 2009, without acknowledging the rebellion of the states over the Real ID Act, Homeland Security Secretary Janet Napolitano announced she was working with governors to repeal the Real ID Act, which was passed in 2005 and was to go into effect in 2008. Many governors scorned the responsibility and cost of ensuring that holders of driver's licenses are citizens or legal residents of the United States. Napolitano, a former governor of Arizona, said she wanted to substitute the federal law with "something else that pivots off of the driver's license but accomplishes some of the same goals." She added, "And we hope to be able to announce something on that fairly soon."

Other governmental entities were also moving to tag every citizen. New York City became one of the first major cities to announce plans to try out micro-chipped identification cards for the city's 250,000 employees. Some 50,000 officers and workers for the NYPD were scheduled to receive ID cards.

The state-of-the-art plastic cards contain microchips, holograms and other security devices to prevent theft and to track employee work hours. On the front of this picture ID is the Statue of Liberty and two chips, one containing fingerprints and handprints and the other filled with personal information, including blood type and emergency telephone numbers. Police officials said eventually the ID cards will be used in conjunction with "biometric" hand scanners to ensure the person bearing the card is the correct one. They also hoped to save money in computing paychecks by using the cards to keep track of employee hours.

Pellegrini and others have warned that the real fight will come over when and where citizens will have to show such IDs. "The average American's driver's license gets a pretty good workout these days. He said, "certainly far more than traffic laws themselves would seem to warrant—but you can only get arrested for *driving* without one. If the US domestic response starts to resemble Zimbabwe's, which passed a law in November [2001] making it compulsory to carry ID on pain of fine or imprisonment, well, that's something to worry about."

According to author Steven Yates, a teaching fellow at the Ludwig von Mises Institute, "The long and the short of it is, the Driver's License Modernization Act of 2002 would bring us closer than ever before to establishing a comprehensive national ID system. The present excuse is that extreme measures are necessary to 'protect us against terrorism.'

"It is a testimony to how much this country has changed since 9/11 that no one has visibly challenged H.R. 4633 as unconstitutional and incompatible with the principles of a free society. The 1990s gave us the obviously corrupt Clinton Regime and a significant opposition to federal power grabs. Now it's Bush the Younger, beloved of neocons [neo-conservatives] who see him as one of their own and believe he can do no wrong…Clearly, the slow encirclement of law-abiding US citizens with national ID technology would advance such a cause [globalism or The New World Order] while doing little if anything to safeguard us against terrorism."

Yates also offered up a vision of the near future that disturbs many thinking people. He noted that if the feds really wanted to stifle dissent, they could 'freeze' the dissident's assets by reprogramming his database information. Scanners would not recognize him and he would become officially invisible, unable to drive or work legally, have a bank account, buy anything on credit, or even see a doctor. "Do we want to trust *anyone* [emphasis in the original] with that kind of power?" he asked.

It is just such a prospect that concerns many Christians, who see government control through computers and identification computer chips as the fulfillment of biblical prophecy warning that no one will be able to conduct business without the "Mark of the Beast." This theme also was the premise of the popular Sandra Bullock film, *The Net*, and the *Left Behind* book series which have sold more than 50 million copies.

Lest anyone think this is naïve or even paranoid nonsense, consider that in late October 2002, Applied Digital Solutions, Inc., a high-tech development company headquartered in Palm Beach, FL, announced the launching of a national promotion for its new subdermal personal verification microchip. Entitled "Get Chipped," the promotion is hyping a device that can be implanted under a person's skin to transmit data to various locations. Describing the "VeriChip," company literature states it is "an implantable, 12mm by 2.1mm radio frequency device...about the size of the point of a typical ballpoint pen. It contains a unique verification number. Utilizing an external scanner, radio frequency energy passes through the skin energizing the dormant VeriChip, which then emits a radio frequency signal containing the verification number. The number is displayed by the scanner and transmitted to a secure data storage site by authorized personnel via telephone or Internet."

In addition to "VeriChip Centers" in Arizona, Texas and Florida, the firm also fields the "ChipMobile," a motorized marketing and "chipping" vehicle. The new "Get Chipped" campaign was launched just days after the Food and Drug Administration ruled that the chip is not a regulated medical device.

Uses for the chip include controlling access to non-public facilities such as government buildings and installations, nuclear power plants, national research laboratories, correctional institutions and transportation hubs, either by itself or in conjunction with exiting security technologies such as retina scanners, thumbprint scanners or face recognition devices. Company officials envision the chip will come to be used in a wide range of consumer products including PC and laptop computers, personal vehicles, cell phones, homes and apartments. They said the implanted chip will help stop identity theft and aid in the war against terrorists.

By early 2006, fears of the chip became reality when a Cincinnati video surveillance firm, CityWatcher.com, began to require its employees to implant the VeriChip device in their arm when working in certain areas.

Several members of Congress seemed quite at home with the idea of a national ID card or chip. Rep. Jane Harman of California said, "I think this issue must be looked at. We don't automatically have to call it a national ID card, that's a radioactive term, but we can certainly think about smart cards for essential functions, but we need the database to support that."

This need for a national database was addressed in the USA PATRIOT Act, Which authorized $150 million in tax money for the "expansion of the Regional Information Sharing System [to] facilitate federal-state-local law enforcement response related to terrorist acts."

Asked if she thought the public was ready for such measures, Harman replied, "I think most people are really there. Keep in mind that if we have a second wave of attacks. The folks who are raising objections will probably lose, totally."

Others agree, such as former District of Columbia Mayor Anthony A. Williams, who only added to the fear factor when he warned, "[I]ncreased government surveillance is a reality of the post-September 11 world. "We are in a new...really dangerous world now, and we have to maintain a higher level of security." Williams' plan for increased security was to emulate such cities as London and Sydney by installing hundreds of video cameras throughout the city of Washington, all linked to a central command office. Williams predicted that Washington eventually will have such a surveillance system as England which boasts more than two million cameras in airports, train stations, streets and neighborhoods.

Asked if such a scheme would seriously impact individual civil rights, Williams admitted, "There will be trade-offs."

The Nevada Supreme Court in spring 2002 ruled it was okay for police to hide electronic monitoring devices on people's vehicles without a warrant for as long as they want. The court ruled that there is "no reasonable expectation of privacy" on the outside of one's vehicle and that attaching an electronic device to a man's car bumper did not constitute unreasonable search or seizure. In early 2004, a Louisiana court ruled it was permissible for police there to make warrantless searches of homes and business even without probable cause.

Civil libertarians breathed a little easier after at least three state supreme courts—Massachusetts, New York and Washington—struck down warrantless GPS tracking by police. But efforts toward this end were continuing in 2010. Then there must be some consideration of eavesdropping technology, which includes the two greatest electronic threats to privacy and individual freedom: "Echelon" and "Tempest."

"The secret is out," wrote Jim Wilson in *Popular Mechanics*. "Two powerful intelligence gathering tools that the United States created to eavesdrop on Soviet leaders and to track KGB spies are now being used to monitor Americans." Echelon, the previously discussed global eavesdropping satellite network and massive super computer system, is operated from the Maryland headquarters of the National Security Agency. It intercepts and analyzes phone calls, faxes and email sent to and from the United States, both, with or without encryption. Encrypted messages are first decrypted and then joined with clear messages. The total is then checked by software known as "dictionary" for "trigger words." Such terms as nuclear bomb, al Qaeda, Hamas, anthrax, etc. are then shuttled to appropriate agencies for analysis.

Although speculation and warnings about Echelon were circulating on the Internet for a number of years, it was not until 2001 that the US government finally admitted to its existence. This came about because of high-profile investigations in Europe where it was discovered that Echelon had been used to spy on Airbus Industries and Thomson-CSF, two European companies. In actuality, the government had been using an early version of Echelon even as it was evolving into the futuristic tool of today. In the late 1960s and 1970s, Presidents Lyndon Johnson and Richard Nixon used National Security Agency (NSA) technology to gather files on thousands of American citizens and more than 1,000 organizations, mostly those opposed to the Vietnam War. In a program called "Operation Shamrock," the NSA collected and monitored nearly every international telegram sent from New York.

Although paid for primarily by US taxpayers, Echelon is now multinational, involving overseas clients such as the United Kingdom, Canada, Australia, New Zealand and even Italy and Turkey. Information gleaned from Echelon flows mostly to the CIA. According to investigator Jim Wilson, "Based on what is known about the location of Echelon bases and satellites, it is estimated that there is a ninety percent chance that NSA is listening when you pick up the phone to place or answer an overseas call. In theory, but obviously not in practice, Echelon's supercomputers are so fast, they could identify Saddam Hussein by the sound of his voice the moment he begins speaking on the phone."

Amazing as all this may sound to those unfamiliar with Echelon, the sheer fact that the government now acknowledges it may indicate that it already has become obsolete, largely due to burgeoning Internet traffic. Researchers now believe that Echelon may be phased out in favor of a ground-based technology known as "Tempest," which secretly reads the displays on personal computers, cash registers, television sets and automated teller machines (ATMs).

Jim Wilson said documents now available from foreign governments and older sources clearly show how these systems are used to invade our right to privacy. "We think you will agree it also creates a real and present threat to our freedom," he added.

In September 2002, the Associated Press obtained US government documents showing that the Bush administration was considering the creation of a fund that would combine tax dollars with funds from the technology industry to pay for "Internet security enhancements." The documents, one under the title "Executive Summary for the National Strategy to Secure Cyberspace," discussed "sweeping new obligations on companies, universities, federal agencies and home users" to make the Internet more secure, presumably from terrorists.

This new Internet strategy was being headed up by Richard Clarke, formerly a top counterterrorism expert in both the Bush and Clinton administrations, and Howard Schmidt, a former senior executive at Microsoft Corp. The plan, when released in 2003, offered up more than 80 recommendations to tighten Internet security.

Such efforts to shut down the free flow of information came to fruition in 2009 with the introduction of Senate Bills No. 773 and 778, by Democratic Sen. Jay Rockefeller of West Virginia. This legislation continued to put the power to curtail free speech into the hands of the Executive branch. These bills are part of what is called the Cybersecurity Act of 2009, and they essentially give the president of the United States the power to shut down Internet sites he feels might compromise national security. This has been referred to by critics as an Internet "kill switch."

This law, if passed, would create a new office of the national cybersecurity advisor to protect the nation from cybercrime, espionage and attack. The new cybersecurity advisor would report directly to the president. In the event of cyber attack, which is being ill-defined in the proposed laws, the president, through this national cybersecurity advisor, would have the authority to disconnect "critical infrastructure" from the Internet, which would include citizens' banking and health records. According to an early draft of the bill, the secretary of commerce would have access to all privately owned information networks deemed critical to the nation "without regard to any provision of law, regulation, rule or policy restricting such access."

In talks to Congress, Senator Rockefeller warned that "...we must protect our critical infrastructure at all costs." and the bills' co-sponsor, Republican Maine Senator Olympia Snowe said that failure to pass this law would risk a "cyber-Katrina." However, privacy advocates immediately attacked the legislation. Leslie Harris, president of the Center for Democracy and Technology, stated, "The cybersecurity threat is real, but such a drastic federal intervention in private communications technology and networks could harm both security and privacy."

Larry Selzer, a technology writer for the Internet news source *eWeek*, agreed with Harris. "The whole thing smells bad to me. I don't like the chances of the government improving this situation by taking it over generally, and I definitely don't like the idea of politicizing this authority by putting it in the direct control of the president."

Jennifer Granick, civil liberties director at the Electronic Frontier Foundation, said that by concentrating Internet control in one individual, the Internet could actually become less safe. When one person can access all information on a network, "it makes it more vulnerable to intruders," argued Granick. "You've basically established a path for the bad guys to skip down." Granick added that the nonspecific scope of this legislation is "contrary to what the Constitution promises us." Should the Commerce Department decide to use information gained while accessing "critical infrastructure" on the net against the user, privacy would be lost. According to Granick, this is a clear violation of the US Constitution's Article IV, which states the "right of the people to be secure in their persons, houses, papers, and effects, against unreasonable searches and seizures, shall not be violated..."

"Who's interested in this [legislation]?" asked Granick. "Law enforcement and people in the security industry who want to ensure more government dollars go to them." In March 2010, the Cybersecurity Act of 2009 was recommended for consideration by the Senate by the Senate Commerce, Science, and Transportation Committee even as opposition, especially on Internet sites, gained strength.

The Associated Press also wrote about a "key-logger" device, which, during the new "sneak and peek" incursions by federal agents, can be secreted inside a computer using a virus-like program. The device, coded named "Magic Lantern," records every key stroke on the computer, allowing authorities to capture passwords and use them to access encrypted data files. The FBI has acknowledged using such a device in a recent gambling investigation.

William Newman, director of the ACLU in Western Massachusetts, said the use of such technology could easily spread to all Americans. He pointed out that federal law enforcement agencies now are permitted "the same access to your Internet use and to your email use that they had to your telephone records." He said this could lead to agencies overstepping their authority. "The history of the FBI is that they will do exactly that."

Other high-tech items to be employed in the War on Terrorism include a program being developed by the CIA called "Fluent," which searches foreign websites and displays an English translation back to Langley. This may be used in conjunction with "Oasis," a technology, which transcribes worldwide radio and TV broadcasts.

The FBI and some police departments are now using a software program called "dTective" to trace financial transactions by dramatically improving the grainy video of surveillance cameras at banks and ATMs.

The feds are even working on techniques for restoring videotapes and computer disks that have been destroyed, cut up or tossed in water. One software program entitled "Encase" can recover deleted computer files and search for incriminating documents on any computer. This was used by the FBI to examine computers seized in the wake of the 9/11 attacks.

The numbering of individual humans is already in place. A tracking system will be next. And don't count on government watchdog organizations to maintain your privacy rights.

In late 2002, the American Civil Liberties Union gave its stamp of approval to an electronic tracking system utilizing Global Positioning System (GPS) satellites to track suspects and criminals. This "VeriTracks" system is offered by the Veridan company of Arlington, VA. Such GPS tracking not only keeps tabs on convicted criminals but also suspects and can even correlate their position with high-crime areas or crime scenes. Law enforcement agencies can create "electronic fences" around areas they deem off-limits to wearers of a cell-phone-size GPS receiver. The module that records its exact position is carried on the waist while an electronic bracelet worn on the ankle acts as an electronic tether to the GPS receiver. The module is placed in a docking system at night to recharge batteries and upload its data to a central headquarters which checks to see if the wearer has been at any crime scenes.

How do you get someone to agree to this monitoring system? Sheriff Don Eslinger of Seminole County, FL, answered, "It's either wear the GPS device or go to jail. Most of them find this much more advantageous than sitting in a cold jail cell, and it also saves us between $45 and $55 a day." Eslinger said his county had equipped 10 pre-trial suspects with the GPS device as a condition of making bond and that county officials hoped to expand the program to include non-violent probationers and parolees.

And such surveillance technology is not being limited to felons and probationers. In Texas, some 1,000 drivers allowed an insurance company to place a transponder in their vehicles to keep track of teenaged drivers and their speed.

The firm Digital Angel was developing a wrist band that allows parents to log on to the Internet and instantly locate their children while another company, eWorldtrack, is working on a child-tracking device that will fit inside athletic shoes. The German firm Siemens has tested a seven-ounce tracking device that allows constant communication between parents and their children. Author Joe Queenan quipped, "Fusing digital mobile phone technology, a satellite-based global positioning system and good old-fashion insanity, the device can pinpoint a child within several yards in a matter of seconds."

Such GPS devices reminded civil libertarians of the 1987 film *The Running Man*, in which Arnold Schwarzenegger is equipped with a collar, which will blow his head off if he leaves a prescribed area. They also note that the difference between a suspect and an innocent man is often unclear.

But some concern over GPS may be misplaced since it appears that the average cell phone is essentially a tracking device.

"The average citizen is not aware that they are carrying a location-tracking device in their pocket," said Kevin Bankston, an attorney for a San Francisco-based group that works to preserve privacy rights called the Electronic Frontier Foundation. According to Bankston, cell phones constantly emit locator signals called pings so their companies know to which towers to route phone calls. Government agents and police can obtain logs from wireless companies containing such data to track people's movements, he said, explaining that in places with many towers, a location can be narrowed down to within blocks.

Bankston added that most new phones contain Global Positioning System chips that communicate with satellites, allowing authorities to pinpoint a precise location of the handset. The chips are one way companies can comply with federal rules designed to give emergency dispatchers more information on the location of cell phone callers, he said.

All this technology leads to scary scenarios such as this one envisioned by *Village Voice* writer Russ Kick: "You just got a call that your sister is in critical condition in the hospital. So you jump in your car and hit the gas. Trouble is, the speed limit is 30 miles per hour and your car won't let you drive any faster. Or maybe you're lucky enough to have a vehicle that still lets you drive at the speed you choose. A cop pulls you over and demands a saliva sample, so he can instantly match your DNA to a data bank of criminals' genes. You refuse and are arrested. After booking you, the authorities force you to submit to 'brain fingerprinting,' a technology that can tell if memories of illegal events are in your mind.

"By this point, you're thinking this is a worst-case scenario, a science-fiction dysphoria. Well, wake up and smell the police state, because all this technology—and more—is already being implemented."

## GOVERNING BY SECRECY AND DECREE

While waging its War on Terrorism, the Bush administration expanded government secrecy in ways hardly imaginable only a few years before. Information has been sequestered away from the public and the Congress while law enforcement agencies were allowed to operate in the shadows.

And this was not all in response to the 9/11 attacks. Well before September 11, Bush kept secret some 4,000 pages related to presidential pardons granted by President Clinton as he was leaving office. The administration shielded Vice President Cheney by keeping secret the members and minutes of an energy policy task force headed by Cheney.

Shortly after 9/11, as previously noted, Bush held up the release of presidential papers from the Reagan administration in which his father played such a big role.

Unfortunately, such machinations continued through the "change" of the Obama administration. An editorial in the *Baltimore Sun* questioned Obama's campaign promises, stating, "Let's see. Is Guantanamo Bay closed? No. Any action on disclosures on lobbying or restricting role of lobbyists? No—all the happy talk about closing the revolving door was just that, talk. Transparency for government agencies, posting bills on-line before signing? Nope. Increased protection for whistleblowers? No, actually he's acted against whistleblowers. Overhaul of immigration? Nothing there. Increased oversight on surveillance? No, in fact the opposite. And does anyone buy that the war in Iraq is over? Tell that to the widows of the men killed in action within days of that premature celebration.

"Meanwhile, the Obama administration has been extending executive privilege and increasing the culture of secrecy at a pace that puts his predecessor's efforts to shame. Oh, and we got to see him hand pots and pots of money to the financial services industry—notice how many ex-employees of Goldman Sachs work for him—then watch while these companies had banner years and paid out humongous bonuses."

However, secrecy decreased somewhat in the first months of the Obama administration, according to the *Federal Times*. The Washington publication reported that the government's backlog of Freedom of Information Act requests dropped more than 40 percent from 133,295 in fiscal 2008 to 77,377 in fiscal 2009 and that government classification of document decisions decreased to 183,224, the lowest number since fiscal 1999.

But this lessening of secrecy remained sporadic in Obama's Washington with some 73 percent of federal advisory committee meetings closed to the public, an increase of about 5.5 percent from fiscal 2008. *Federal Times* reported that 16 percent—or $35.2 billion—of the Defense Department's fiscal 2009 weapons acquisition budget remained classified in "black" budgets, up from 14 percent in fiscal 2008. This report covers the last months of the Bush administration and the first months of the Obama administration.

Among Obama's predecessor, George W. Bush's many secrets included the fact that he has gathered around him one of the most wealthy circle of government officials in the history of the United States, earning mention in the *Guinness Book of World Records, 2000*.

According to *Guinness*, "George W. Bush (inaugurated as the 43rd US president on January 20, 2001) has assembled the wealthiest cabinet in

American history by appointing more multimillionaires to the top rank of his government than any of his predecessors. Of the 16 full government members at the heart of the Bush administration, 13 are multimillionaires, seven of them own assets more than $10 million. His cabinet has acquired the nickname 'tycoon's club.' Defense Secretary Donald Rumsfeld and [then] Treasury Secretary Paul O' Neill each have declared assets of at least $61 million, while [then] Secretary of State Colin Powell has at least $18 million."

Information such as this seeped into the public's consciousness during 2001 despite the distraction of the terrorist attacks and the subsequent bombing of Afghanistan and the war talk against Iraq. A mid-2002 poll by the *New York Times* and CBS News found that out of 1,000 adults polled by telephone, 58 percent—a clear majority—thought that big business had too much influence on government and Bush himself. The poll also showed that a majority of respondents felt Bush was hiding some things about his own corporate past and that the national economy was in its worst shape since 1994. By more than two to one, respondents said the Bush administration was more interested in protecting the interests of large companies than those of ordinary Americans.

And Bush was only slightly ahead of Cheney when it came to belief in their word that they had not done anything wrong while in the business sector. Of those surveyed, only seventeen percent thought Bush was telling the truth about his dealings at Harken Energy, while only eleven percent thought Cheney was truthful about the accounting practices of Halliburton while under his control.

Of course, this means that the majority in both cases thought the two top national leaders were hiding something or outright lying about their business dealings. And no one was asked about Halliburton's under the table dealings with Iraq despite US sanctions.

This public distrust in the presidency was reflected in a 2010 CBS News poll showing President Obama's job approval rating has dropped to its lowest point since taking office in 2009. The poll showed a 44 percent approval rating compared to 41 percent who voiced disapproval, with 15 percent undecided. That compared to a 49 percent to 41 percent approval rating in March 2010, 50 percent to 40 percent in January, and 68 percent to 23 percent in early 2009. The numbers dropped further on the issue of health care. The poll showed 55 percent disapproved of Obama's plans compared to 34 percent who approved. Many felt that lobbyists from Big Pharma and the giant insurance companies had unduly influenced the health care issue.

Such public concern over big business exerting undue influence over the government is fully supported by a brief survey of recent administrations and their connection to multinational corporations, especially oil companies, not to mention secret societies. Consider that through the past four administrations cabinet-level posts have largely been held by members of the Trilateral Commission and its predecessor the Council on Foreign Relations (CFR).

From 1989–1993 during the administration of George H. W. Bush, all cabinet members were members of the CFR, except for Vice President Dan Quayle, Secretary of State James Baker and Health and Human Services Secretary Louis W. Sullivan.

In the Clinton administration, from 1993–2001, all cabinet members were CFR except for Secretary of Defense William Perry.

In the George W. Bush administration, CFR members included Vice President Dick Cheney, Secretary of State Colin Powell, later Secretary of State Condoleeza Rice, Secretary of Defense Donald Rumsfeld, later Secretary of Defense Robert Gates, Secretary of Labor Elaine Chao and EPA Administrator Christine Todd Whitman.

President Barack Obama, elected in 2008 largely due to public indignation over the excesses of the Bush II administration, offered "Hope" and "Change." Such hope dwindled as more Americans became aware that little had changed. The Obama cabinet read like a roster of the CFR, including Bush holdover Secretary of Defense Robert Gates, Secretary of Homeland Security Janet Napolitano, Secretary of Commerce Bill Richardson, UN Ambassador Susan Rice, National Security Advisor James L. Jones, Secretary of Treasury Timothy Geithner, Director of National Economic Council Larry Summers, and Economic Advisor Paul Volcker. Secretary of State Hillary Clinton, though not a registered CFR member, nevertheless was an attendee of the secretive Bilderberg meetings.

To view the never-changing reach of the globalists, consider that Obama's national security advisor, Gen. James L. Jones, told attendees at the 2009 Munich Security Conference, "As the most recent national security advisor of the United States, I take my daily orders from Dr. [Henry] Kissinger, filtered down through General Brent Scowcroft and Sandy Berger, who is also here. We have a chain of command in the National Security Council that exists today." Kissinger, who served under the Republican Presidents Nixon and the elder Bush, is one man widely viewed as the architect of a US foreign policy that has turned foreign extremists into implacable enemies. In October 2010, Jones resigned and was replaced by former Fannie Mae lobbyist Thomas E. Donilon.

The evidence is clear. The idea that America today is run by corporate executives for corporate executives is no conspiracy theory; it is a fact. And they are doing their best to see that it all operates in secrecy. In Nazi Germany, the state took over the corporations. In modern America, the corporations have taken over the state. The end result is the same.

And while Bush has claimed meager experience with the corporate world, his 2000 campaign contributions list tells a different story. According to *Sierra Magazine*, the president received almost $1.9 million from the gas and oil industry, $203,000 from the mining industry and $300,000 from the timber and forest-products industry. The Republican Party got more than $20 million from the gas and oil industry, $4.7 million from the mining industry and $5.4 million from the timber and forest-products industry.

Enron's former CEO, Kenneth Lay, along with another officer, Jeffrey Skilling, was convicted on May 25, 2006, of conspiracy, securities fraud and wire fraud. Lay, a "Bush Pioneer," personally raising more than $550,000 for the Bush 2000 campaign. Lay was also convicted in a separate non-jury trial of bank fraud and making false statements to banks—charges related to his personal finances.

On July 5, 2006, a little more than a month after Lay's conviction, at a time when he must have been pondering whether to serve his time or implicate others in the Enron scandal, he suddenly died of a massive heart attack. Some researchers claimed that the unaccounted for millions missing from Enron were used to pay operatives to manipulate the 2000 presidential election in favor of Bush.

More than 30 former energy executives, lobbyists and lawyers served in high-level jobs for the Bush administration. "The people running the United States government are from the energy industry," acknowledged

Peabody Energy executive Fredrick Palmer. If the close corporate connections aren't enough to raise questions about conflict of interest, some have even raised the specter of nepotism, a word apparently forgotten by today's "watchdog" media. Although apparently a non-issue to the corporate mass media, George W. Bush's first administration was filled with family and relatives.

Another troublesome aspect of both Bush terms is president's contention that he must defend his office from the loss of power. This is blatantly untrue. The American president today carries far more power than ever imagined by our Founding Fathers or even more modern chief executives like Franklin D. Roosevelt.

Bush's secretive manner of drawing ever more power unto himself by issuing "signing statements" drew criticism from credible legal sources. Jennifer Van Bergen, a journalist with a law degree, explained that "signing statements" are statements by the president issued upon signing a bill into law. Van Bergen noted that from 1817 until the end of the Carter administration in 1981, only 75 "signing statements" were issued. From the Reagan administration until the end of the Clinton administration, this number had grown to 322. But in the first term alone, Bush issued at least 435 "signing statements, many noting his concept of a "unitary executive." Such "signing statements" convey a President's view toward the law and his own power. Bush's use of the term "unitary executive," according to Van Bergen, is merely a code word for a doctrine "that favors nearly unlimited executive power."

"In his [Bush's] view, and the view of his administration, that doctrine gives him license to overrule and bypass Congress or the courts, based on his own interpretations of the Constitution—even where that violates long-established laws and treaties, counters recent legislation that he has himself signed, or (as shown by recent developments in the Padilla case) involves offering a federal court contradictory justifications for a detention," Van Bergen wrote on an Internet legal site.

She took particular note of Bush's "signing statement" while signing into law legislation curtailing torture on prisoners. "When President Bush signed the new law, sponsored by Senator [John] McCain, restricting the use of torture when interrogating detainees, he also issued a presidential signing statement," said Van Bergen. "That statement asserted that his power as Commander-in-Chief gives him the authority to bypass the very law he had just signed."

The use of signing statements did not end when Bush left office. By mid-2010, President Obama had signed 10 such documents.

Civil libertarians historically have heeded the statement of patriot Thomas Paine, who wrote in *Common Sense*, "In America, the law is king. For as in absolute governments the King is law, so in free countries the law ought to be king; and there ought to be no other."

Yet, Bush argued that such actions, allowing him to ride roughshod over the Congress, the courts and the Constitution are somehow necessary to preserve the presidency. "I have an obligation to make sure that the presidency remains robust and that the legislative branch doesn't end up running the executive branch," Bush argued in mid-2002. He either ignored or didn't realize that by preparing an attack on Iraq, he was preempting the power of Congress. When he and his appointees rammed the USA PATRIOT Act through a Congress, which had had little or no input, he likewise took powers from the representatives of the people.

Bush's first press secretary, Ari Fleischer, also failed to study recent history when he stated that presidential powers have been diminished "in multiple ways" as part of a "long-standing, gradual process."

Perhaps this effort to take power away from legislators was the reason that Bush announced his legal advisers had told him he did not need to consult Congress before ordering a strike on Iraq, despite the fact that war-making powers are explicitly granted to the Congress by the US Constitution.

"What the president is claiming is legally and historically absurd and politically stupid," stated Bruce Fein, a former Justice Department official who worked for several past Republican administrations. "[The US] has never had a more imperial presidency, at least since Roosevelt during his conduct of World War II."

Bush argued that he must work in secrecy to regain open dialog with his advisers and various experts. Bush-appointed chairman of the Republican National Committee, Mark Racicot, explained that, "the ability of the president to carry on communications and get unvarnished advice has eroded over a period of time."

Many Washington insiders, including Fein, scoffed at this argument.

"I've been around this town a long time, almost 30 years, and I've never encountered one individual who told me he's not going to the Oval Office unless he's promised confidentiality. It's the biggest hoax in the world. Why he's making up all this stuff is utterly and completely baffling." President Bush wrapped the Oval Office in more secrecy than any previous president. President Bill Clinton's White House looked absolutely transparent compared to Bush's.

But in the matter of executive privilege, Bush was two faced: documents which placed President Clinton in a bad light were released with impunity, while documents which might have put Clinton in a more favorable light were withheld using executive privilege. For example, in summer 2001, congressional investigators requested transcripts of three discussions between Clinton and Israeli Prime Minister Ehud Barak concerning a Clinton pardon for Marc Rich, the financial wizard who stiffed the IRS for $48 million and claimed citizenship in the US, Israel and Spain. The Bush White House promptly turned them over with the explanation that they were not classified.

"Given the secrecy that the Bush-Cheney administration has pursued, it's inconceivable that they would turn this information over if it affected President Bush," commented Democratic staff director for the House Government Reform Committee Phil Schiliro.

On November 1, 2001, with the nation still in turmoil following the 9/11 attacks, Bush signed an executive order "reinterpreting" the 1978 Presidential Records Act, which provided for the public release of former presidents' documents after they left office. Bush claimed the executive privilege to veto the release of any such documents and thereby establish a "process that I think will enable historians to do their job and at the same time protect state secrets."

Historians were so unimpressed with Bush's logic that before the month was out a group had filed a lawsuit to stop his executive order. Parties to the suit included the American Historical Association, the National Security Archive at George Washington University, the Organization of American Historians, Public Citizen, the Reporter's Committee for Freedom of the Press and history professors Hugh Graham and Stanley Kutler.

"The Presidential Records Act of 1978, which specified that after January 20, 1981, all official presidential and vice presidential records became the property of the federal government, was meant to shift power over White House documents from former presidents to professional government archivists, and ultimately, to the public," said Thomas Blanton, director of the National Security Archives. "But the Bush order attempts to overturn the law, take power back, and let presidents past and present delay public access indefinitely."

Joan Claybrook, president of Public Citizen, charged that Bush's decree "violates not only the spirit but the letter of the law." "We will not stand by while the administration tramples on the people's right to find out about their own government," she added.

The group's attorney Scott Nelson summed up the feeling of many people when he said, "It's interesting that the first beneficiary of this new doctrine would be the father of the man who announced it." He referred, of course, to Bush's father who served as vice president and virtually ran the government for some time after Ronald Reagan was seriously wounded in March 1981.

"This administration is the most secretive of our lifetime, even more secretive than the Nixon administration," said Larry Klayman, chairman of Judicial Watch, the conservative group that sued the government for release of the names of Cheney's energy task force. "They don't believe the American people or Congress have any right to information."

Just after the 9/11 attacks, Attorney General Ashcroft sent a memo to all government agencies urging them to turn down more Freedom of Information requests in favor of "institutional, commercial and personal privacy interests."

This represented a dramatic reversal of decades of open government. "We are moving from a right to know to a need to know society," observed Gary Bass of OMB Watch, a private group that monitors government spending and legislation.

Since 9/11, thousands of pages of documents have vanished from the Internet. Some that might have a direct impact on security measures are understandable, others less so. But the new heightened security has proven a boon to corporate despoilers who would like their sordid track records on safety and environmental pollution kept from the public. Activists and newsmen can no longer gain information on polluting chemical plants or locate hazardous waste dumps.

GOVERNING BY SECRECY AND DECREE

"There is a pattern of secrecy that is a defining characteristic of the Bush administration," noted Steven Aftergood, who heads government secrecy research for the Federation of American Scientists. "It resists even the most mundane requests for information."

By 2006, with the wars in Iraq and Afghanistan still raging with no end in sight, the economy slumping and multiple charges of domestic spying, President Bush saw his approval rating dip as low as 35 percent, one of the lowest in recent history.

In February 2006, Vice President Cheney shot a companion while hunting for birds in Texas. Hunting accidents are not that unusual. What was unusual was the day and a half lag time between the shooting and Cheney's appearance before authorities. Even though the local sheriff ruled the shooting an accident, rumors began to fly. According to Doug Thompson of *Capitol Hill Blue*, a written report from Secret Service agents guarding the vice president stated that Cheney was "clearly inebriated" when he shot Texas lawyer Harry Whittington on the hunting outing. The report stated that agents observed several members of the hunting party, including the Vice President, consuming alcohol before and during the hunting expedition and that Cheney exhibited "visible signs" of impairment, including slurred speech and erratic actions. Thompson concluded that the time lag offered all members of the hunting party time to sober up.

Even the conservative *U.S. News & World Report* voiced concern over this time lag and the secrecy surrounding the incident. Addressing the time lag between the shooting and Cheney's appearance, editors asked, "Would the average Joe have gotten such a pass?"

One editorial noted, "Cheney has constructed something very unusual for a vice president: a world that is almost beyond public and media scrutiny, with little accountability. He hasn't held a full-fledged news conference for nearly four years. He doesn't talk about his advice to the president, even though his influence is by all reports extraordinary. He travels without letting people outside his orbit know what he's up to. He doesn't even disclose his travel expenses, arguing that the law applies to heads of agencies, and he isn't one…He has done an amazing thing—creating a 'zone of privacy' unique in the modern era. President Bush has adopted many of his ideas, presiding over one of the most secretive White Houses in recent history. It sure makes things easier that way. And since the public doesn't seem to care, future leaders are likely to follow Cheney's example."

Taking a cue from President Clinton, Bush turned to executive orders, many activated without fanfare or publicity, to strengthen his rule.

## THE SHADOW GOVERNMENT KNOWS

Then there is the issue of the "shadow government." On March 1, 2002, well after the 9/11 attacks, President Bush announced that the American public needn't worry about the survival of vital federal government functions because a "shadow government" made up of unelected bureaucrats were working in underground bunkers stocked with supplies of food, water and electric generators to preserve the government. Many people found little consolation in the idea that while their cities might be devastated by biological, chemical or nuclear terrorism, the Agriculture Dept. and the IRS would still be there for them. Plans for COG, or Continuity of Government, have been in place since the beginning of the Cold War but were only revved up by the Bush administration in the wake of the 9/11 attacks.

Actually, authors and commentators have spoken out about a shadow government that runs the country in secret for many years. Col. L. Fletcher Prouty called it the "Secret Team," while Bill Moyers called it the "Secret Government." This scheme to concentrate all power within the federal government was continued through the Obama administration.

The shadow government made public by President Bush was only about the bureaucrats that would try to continue government services in the event of a massive attack or emergency. There was no mention of the shadow or parallel government that has operated since the signing of the National Security Act of 1947 and, according to a growing number of researchers, was behind the assassination of President Kennedy in 1963.

The federal shadow government could well have been named the "Secret Government." The Republican Speaker of the House Dennis Hastert said he only had a vague idea of this sub-rosa government and he is third in line to assume the presidency.

Although, in the event of a crisis, reportedly some 100 senior government managers would escape to one of two secret East Coast underground destinations, according to the *Washington Post*, "only the executive branch is represented in the full-time shadow government."

Following any designated national emergency, these shadow bureaucrats would try to contain national disruption of food, water, transportation, energy and telecommunications, then move on to reconstitute the federal government. But this is all hush-hush. Participants cannot reveal the whereabouts of these underground retreats even to their own families, who are not allowed to join them.

And the shadow government has now been tied to the Homeland Security apparatus, which refused to reveal any details on its cost or budget.

This prompted a threat from former Senate Majority Leader Tom Daschle that he might issue a subpoena to former Homeland Security Secretary Tom Ridge in order to find out what all these secret preparations are costing the American taxpayer. Bush had even refused to allow Ridge to testify to Congress about his plans and their costs. Ridge finally was allowed to send a written statement to a joint meeting of several committees.

Daschle said secrecy about the shadow government was so tight he had not learned about it until he read about it in the *Washington Post*. "We have not been informed at all about the role of the shadow government or its whereabouts or what particular responsibilities they have or when they would kick in," groused Daschle.

The executive director of Judicial Watch, the group that criticized President Clinton so doggedly, stated, "This is a case of where left and right agree...True conservatives don't act this way."

"We see an unprecedented secrecy in this White House that...we find very disturbing," said Larry Klayman of Judicial Watch.

Michael Ventura of the *Austin Chronicle* wrote, "Without an active free press (especially the *New York Times*, the *Washington Post* and the *Los Angeles Times*) our elected representatives in Congress would know virtually nothing of most of the major steps the Bush administration has taken... If America means to you a republic governed according to a Constitution that carefully stipulates checks and balances among the White House, Congress, and the judiciary—a system in which none can overwhelm the others, and in which each is responsible to the others—then you no longer live in America.

"This is not some dire warning about the future. This has happened and is happening. A free press is noting the process step by step: braver members of Congress, Republican and Democrat, have voiced alarm and are attempting legal measures to exercise their constitutional duties (so far to no avail); watchdogs on the right and left agree on the urgency of the situation...while most citizens say and do nothing, giving tacit approval to a new (yes, new!) de facto system of government that recognizes no obligation to obey or enforce the letter or spirit of the Constitution."

The Bush administration is packed with men and women who claim to be conservatives. But what is it they wish to conserve? It would appear not to be the conservation of a constitutional republic.

"[Conservative] does not describe the Bush administration at all," added Ventura. "They ignore Congress almost completely on crucial issues; they feel no obligation to inform American citizens of the White House's deliberations or even its policies, whether or not national security is at stake; they concentrate tremendous power among the very few. That is not conservatism. There is only one word that adequately describes the bent and preference of George W. Bush's White House: Totalitarianism."

In September 2009, President Barack Obama, at an AFL-CIO Labor Day picnic in Cincinnati, appointed Ron Bloom as senior counselor for manufacturing policy. Bloom will make the 33rd Obama "czar", counting Van Jones, who had just resigned as special advisor for green jobs after being criticized for reportedly signing a 2004 petition on *911Truth.org* accusing the Bush administration of complicity in the attacks.

Other special advisers, dubbed "czars" by the media, include:

1. Richard Holbrooke—Afghanistan Czar
2. Jeffrey Crowley—AIDS Czar*
3. Ed Montgomery—Auto Recovery Czar
4. Alan Bersin—Border Czar*
5. David J. Hayes—California Water Czar
6. Ron Bloom—Car Czar (moved to Manufacturing Czar today)
7. Dennis Ross—Central Region Czar
8. Todd Stern—Climate Czar
9. Lynn Rosenthal—Domestic Violence Czar
10. Gil Kerlikowske—Drug Czar*

11. Paul Volcker—Economic Czar*
12. Carol Browner—Energy and Environment Czar
13. Joshua DuBois—Faith Based Czar*
14. Jeffrey Zients—Government Performance Czar
15. Cameron Davis—Great Lakes Czar
16. Van Jones—Green Jobs Czar (resigned in 2009)
17. Daniel Fried—Guantanamo Closure Czar
18. Nancy-Ann DeParle—Health Czar*
19. Vivek Kundra—Information Czar
20. Dennis Blair—Intelligence Czar*
21. Ron Bloom—Manufacturing Czar
22. George Mitchell—Mideast Peace Czar
23. Kenneth R. Feinberg—Pay Czar
24. Cass R. Sunstein—Regulatory Czar*
25. John Holdren—Science Czar
26. Earl Devaney—Stimulus Accountability Czar
27. J. Scott Gration—Sudan Czar
28. Herb Allison—TARP Czar
29. Aneesh Chopra—Technology Czar
30. John Brennan—Terrorism Czar
31. Adolfo Carrion Jr.—Urban Affairs Czar
32. Ashton Carter—Weapons Czar
33. Gary Samore—WMD Policy Czar

*These "czars" were specifically created by President Obama.

These czars replace functions normally carried out by secretaries and directors subject to Senate confirmation and thereby accountable to Congress and the voters. "A less charitable observer might conclude that *President Obama is systematically creating a shadow government of special commissars* [emphasis in the original], which will allow Obama to bypass congressional oversight and the checks and balances of 'independent'" (in a sense) agencies to rule the United States directly by decree," noted author David Friedman, who often uses the pseudonym Dafydd Ab Hugh. "Shifting more and more governmental power into the hands of a single man on a white horse, who will personally speak for and on behalf of 'the people,' is a classical sign of incipient fascism."

# PART IV – HISTORICAL PRECEDENTS

*"But as the result of evil, there's some amazing things that are taking place in America."*
—President George W. Bush,
Daytona Beach, FL, January 30, 2002

Historical precedents that may provide insight into the events of 9/11 are so numerous that there is not enough space to present them all. But for the close student of history, there is a clear pattern governing such events. It is based on a Machiavellian manipulation of the often-used dialectic of the German philosopher Georg Wilhelm Friedrich Hegel.

In theory, the doctrine of the Hegelian dialectic—or the study of opposing forces over time—maintains that thesis encountering antithesis results in synthesis, sometimes described as problem plus reaction equals resolution. But some of the early students of Hegel, which included the Bavarian Illuminati and other secret societies, realized that they need not wait for a problem to present itself through the natural course of the dialectic. They could secretly create the problem or a provocation, build upon the reaction and then offer their own solution. In other words, in the world of ruthless power politics, one can apply the Hegelian dialectic in a perverse manner. Simply offer a draconian solution to a problem you have engineered, which, after compromises, still advances the secret agenda of those who created the problem in the first place.

The attacks of 9/11 certainly fit this mold. If they were not simply the result of a handful of Muslim fanatics armed only with small blades who miraculously hijacked four separate airliners simultaneously, then they were deliberate provocations instigated for the purpose of advancing a hidden agenda.

Consider a few cases of such provocations and responses from the last century.

## THE REICHSTAG FIRE

In January 1933, Germany was a free republic with one of the most educated and cultured populations in the world at that time. Germany was at peace and enjoying a blossoming of democratic freedom under a coalition government of the Weimar Republic. But on February 27, 1933, the German *Reichstag* or Parliament building was destroyed by fire. In those slower, gentler times, this act was as great a shock to the German people as the destruction of the World Trade Center in 2001 was to Americans.

German Chancellor Adolf Hitler and his Nazis blamed the destruction on communist terrorists. They even caught one, a retarded Dutch youth named Marinus van der Lubbe who carried a Communist Party card. After some time in custody, the youth confessed to being the arsonist. However, later investigation found that one person could not have started the mammoth blaze and that incendiaries had been carried into the building through a tunnel which led to the offices of Hitler's closest partner, Hermann Goering, head of the German Air Force, the *Luftwaffe*.

Despite misgivings in many quarters about the official explanation of the fire, it was announced, "the government is of the opinion that the situation is such that a danger to the state and nation existed and still exists." Law enforcement agencies quickly moved against, not only the communists, but also pacifists, liberals and democrats.

Less than a month later, on March 24, 1933, at Hitler's urging, a panicky German Parliament voted 441 to 94 to pass an "Enabling Act" which was the starting point for Hitler's dictatorship. As noted earlier, this sequence of events may sound eerily familiar to Americans living today under the Patriot Act.

As a result of this act, Germans soon saw national identity cards, racial profiling, the equivalent of a national homeland security chief (SS Commander Heinrich Himmler), gun confiscation and later, mass murders and incarcerations in concentration camps. In fact, according to Jews for the Preservation of Firearms Ownership (JPFO), a close examination of the US Gun Control Act of 1968 (Public Law 90-618) revealed it to be nearly word for word the gun legislation passed in Germany under Hitler.

"When Germany awoke," wrote British reporter Douglas Reed, "a man's home was no longer his castle. He could be seized by private individuals, could claim no protection from the police, could be indefinitely detained without preferment of charge; his property could be seized, his verbal and written communications overheard and perused; he no longer had the right to foregather with his fellow countrymen, and his newspapers might no longer freely express their opinions."

With the German population firmly under control due to massive propaganda and fear of government retaliation, Hitler was free to launch pre-emptive strikes in former German territories, as well as Poland. World War II ensued.

Although the German military surrendered unconditionally on May 7, 1945 at Rheims, France, no one representing the Nazi Party was present. The Nazis were not defeated but simply forced to move—many of them coming to the United States under various secret programs such as Project Paperclip, Project 63 and National Interest.

It is also interesting to note that throughout the war, many prominent American businesses continued to deal with Nazi Germany. IBM computing machines facilitated the shipment of prisoners to the concentration camps while General Motors produced vehicles for the German war effort. Chase Bank maintained its financial connections with the Nazis through its Paris branch and I. G. Farben chief Hermann Schmitz served as Chase president for seven years prior to the war. He eventually held as much stock in Standard Oil of New Jersey as the Rockefellers. "Schmitz's wealth—largely I. G. Farben bearer bonds converted to the Big Three successor firms, shares in Standard Oil of New Jersey...General Motors, and other US blue chip industrial stocks, and the 700 secret companies controlled in his time by I. G., as well as shares in the 750 corporations he helped [Hitler's Deputy Fuehrer Martin] Bormann establish during the last years of World War II—has increased in all segments of the modern industrial world. The Bormann organization in South America utilizes the voting power of the Schmitz trust along with their own assets to guide the multinationals they control, as they keep steady the economic course of the Fatherland," wrote journalist Paul Manning, who added, "The Bormann organization is not merely a group of ex-Nazis. It is a great economic power whose interests today supersede their ideology."

Such long-standing banking and business connections coupled with the Schmitz business network allowed Bormann to forge a formidable Nazi-controlled organization for postwar activities.

Jim Keith, author of numerous conspiracy books, wrote, "...in researching the shape of totalitarian control during this century, I saw that the plans of the Nazis manifestly did not die with the German loss of World War II. The ideology and many of the principal players survived and flourished after the war, and have had a profound impact on postwar history, and on events taking place today."

It was this blending of corporate and state power that is the very dictionary definition of fascism. It also serves as an ominous warning of what is taking place in America today.

Hitler's method for gaining unwarranted power was to fabricate a crisis, call for sweeping powers to protect the population and take totalitarian control. *Luftwaffe* Commander-in-Chief Goering verbalized this method clearly when he spoke at the Nuremberg Trials following the war: "Naturally, the common people don't want war; Neither in Russia, not in England, nor for that matter in Germany. That is understood. But, after all, it is the leaders of the country who determine the policy and it is always a simple matter to drag the people along, whether it is a democracy, or a fascist dictatorship, or a parliament, or a communist dictatorship. Voice or no voice, the people can always be brought to the bidding of the leaders. That is easy. All you have to do is tell them they are being attacked, and denounce the peacemakers for lack of patriotism and exposing the country to danger. It works the same in any country."

In the wake of the 9/11 attacks, both the Bush and Obama administrations along with their associates in the Council on Foreign Relations, Trilateral Commission and Bilderbergers have often mimicked Nazi tactics. Public notice of such methods is now becoming widespread, particularly in modern Germany. In Russia, two years prior to the 9/11 attacks, a series of mysterious apartment building bombings killed more than 200 people. Russian leaders blamed "Islamic terrorists" from Chechnya. The ensuing mediaspurred panic helped bring former KGB agent Vladimir Putin to power even though agents of the Russian Security Service (FSB) were caught red-handed planting explosives in another building. This story was kept from the public by a controlled media and when Alexander Litvinenko, a former FSB agent, tried to tell what happened, he was killed in London by radioactive polonium.

Such activities prompted German Justice Minister Herta Däubler-Gmelin in 2002 to comment on President Bush's threats against Iraq, by noting "Bush wants to distract attention from his domestic problems. That's a popular method. Even Hitler did that." She was quickly forced to resign for calling attention to this aging but effective ploy.

## PEARL HARBOR

In its immediate aftermath, the 9/11 attacks were compared to the attack on Pearl Harbor that launched America into World War II. This comparison was quite appropriate—but not for the reason most people believed.

Controversy has raged for years over the question of Franklin Roosevelt's foreknowledge of the December 7, 1941, attack on Pearl Harbor and it is now clear that certain elements in Washington, D.C. knew of the Japanese attack in advance.

While few journalists and some Republicans accused the Roosevelt administration of foreknowledge, government spokesmen and establishment historians blamed the attack on the failure of US intelligence and incompetence within the naval high command.

Today, the accumulation of available information has now caused wide acceptance of the idea that the devastating attack on Pearl Harbor was tolerated, even encouraged, in an effort to galvanize public support for America's participation in the war.

Roosevelt was quite open in his allegiance to England. While proclaiming neutrality, he had sent war ships and ammunition to Britain just as proposed by the Century Group, a foreign policy think-tank composed of CFR members. He ordered the occupation of Iceland, closing it off to the Germans, and authorized attacks on U-boats. He openly approved loans to Japan's enemy, nationalist China, and quietly approved the recruitment of well-paid American "volunteers" for Chiang Kai-shek's famous "Flying Tigers." Much of this was in violation of international war rules and was guaranteed to provoke the Axis powers.

"Roosevelt was himself a prototypic Wall Streeter," wrote CFR researcher James Perloff. "His family had been involved in New York banking since the eighteenth century. His uncle, Frederic Delano, was on the original Federal Reserve Board." Roosevelt's son-in-law, Curtis B. Dall, wrote, "Most of his [Roosevelt's] thoughts, his political 'ammunition,' as it were, were carefully manufactured for him in advance by the CFR-One World Money group." Dall, of course, was referring to the New World Order long before George Herbert Walker Bush popularized the term.

Those who accept the idea that Roosevelt and a few other insiders knew that Pearl Harbor was to be attacked point to these facts:

- During Pacific naval exercises in 1932 and 1938, and with Japanese military attachés closely observing, US Navy officers theoretically destroyed the Pacific Fleet at Pearl Harbor both times by using the same tactics used in 1941 by the Japanese.
- Roosevelt ordered the Pacific fleet moved to the exposed position at Pearl Harbor over the vigorous objections of Admiral James O. Richardson, who was replaced for refusing to issue the order.
- Roosevelt, Secretary of State Cordell Hull and other high-level officials knew that war was inevitable and that negotiations with Japan's Kichisaburo Nomura were hopeless because the broken Japanese code revealed Nomura was instructed not to yield to Hull's harsh demands.
- They also knew that a large Japanese task force, including six aircraft carriers, had dropped from sight after moving to-

wards America.
- This prompted US Army Chief of Staff George C. Marshall, a close associate to many CFR members, to send an oddly-worded message to Pearl Harbor commanders on November 27, 1941, "Hostile action possible at any moment. If hostilities cannot, repeat CANNOT, be avoided, the United States desires that Japan commit the first overt act. This policy should not, repeat NOT, be construed as restricting you to a course of action that might jeopardize your defense." Despite this clear warning, with its accompanying suggestion not to attack any attackers, Pacific Fleet ships remained at anchor and aircraft were bunched into clusters of "sitting ducks" as "security" against saboteurs.
- During the first week of December, Americans intercepted the Japanese diplomatic "Purple" code ordering the Washington embassy to destroy all secret papers and prepare to evacuate.
- On December 4, Australian intelligence reported sighting the missing Japanese task force moving toward Pearl Harbor but Roosevelt dismissed it as a rumor begun by pro-war Republicans.
- A Dutch submarine tracked the Japanese fleet to Pearl Harbor and radioed this news to headquarters, prompting a warning from Col. F. G. L. Weijerman, the Dutch military attaché in Washington.
- A British agent named Dusko Popov learned of Japan's plans from German sources but his warnings to Washington were ignored.
- According to John Toland, author of *Adolf Hitler*, separate warnings regarding a pending attack on Pearl Harbor, though varying as to a specific time, came from US Ambassador to Japan Joseph Grew; FBI Director J. Edgar Hoover; Senator Guy Gillette; Rep. Martin Dies; and Brig. Gen. Elliot Thorpe in Java.
- Dutch naval officer, Capt. Johan Ranneft, said sources in US Intelligence told him on December 6 that the Japanese carri-

ers were only 400 miles northwest of Hawaii.
- During investigations after the attack, Marshall and Navy Secretary Frank Knox both testified they could not recall their whereabouts the night of December 6. It was later revealed that they were both in the White House with Roosevelt.
- Then there is the issue of the aircraft carriers. In 1941, the American public, as well as a few hidebound military officers, still believed that the battleship was the ultimate weapon. But anyone who had been paying attention knew that Gen. Billy Mitchell had proven in the mid-1920s that a single bomb-laden airplane could destroy a battleship. Battleships were obsolete. Victory in any Pacific war would go to the side with the strongest air power and that meant aircraft carriers. Not one aircraft carrier was present when Pearl Harbor was attacked.

On November 25, 1941, Secretary of War Henry Stimson had a conversation with Roosevelt, after which he wrote in his diary, "The question was how we should maneuver them into the position of firing the first shot without too much danger to ourselves...It was desirable to make sure the Japanese be the ones to do this so that there should remain no doubt in anyone's mind as to who were the aggressors." The answer to this dilemma came on December 7.

The most damning evidence yet of Roosevelt's foreknowledge of an attack came from the 1948 interrogation of Germany's Gestapo chief Heinrich Mueller. In a 1995 book by Gregory Douglas, based on previously secret files, Mueller stated that on November 26, 1941, the Germans in Holland had intercepted a private trans-Atlantic telephone conversation between Roosevelt and British Prime Minister Churchill.

Churchill informed Roosevelt of the movements of the missing Japanese fleet and stated, "I can assure you that their goal is the (conversation broken) fleet in Hawaii, at Pearl Harbor." "This is monstrous," exclaimed Roosevelt, "Can you tell me...indicate...the nature of your intelligence?" "Reliable," answered Churchill, who mentioned agents within the Japanese military and foreign service as well as their broken code.

"The obvious implication is that the Japs are going to do a Port Arthur on us at Pearl Harbor. Do you concur?" asked Roosevelt. Churchill replied, "I do indeed unless they add an attack on the Panama Canal to this vile business." Port Arthur, today called Pinyun Lu-shun, was a strategic Russian port on China's Liaotung Peninsula. The Japanese launched a surprise torpedo attack against the port, which began the 1904–5 Russo-Japanese War.

Roosevelt then said, "...I will have to consider the entire problem...A Japanese attack on us, which would result in war between—and certainly you as well—would certainly fulfill two of the most important requirements of our policy." Roosevelt speaks about absenting himself from the White House on some pretext, adding, "What I don't know, can't hurt me and I cannot understand messages at a distance."

Addressing the unlikely proposition that US military officers would have knowingly allowed American units to be attacked, author Douglas explained, "[T]he warning did not come to Roosevelt from below but on a parallel level and from a foreign intelligence source which was far better equipped to decode and translate the Japanese transmissions."

## THE GULF WAR

Most people accept the idea that the Gulf War was all about oil—from the accusation that Kuwait was slant-drilling into Iraq's southern Rumaila reserves, to the destruction of the oil fields at its finish. Here we found a new enemy in Saddam Hussein, a former ally who had been armed and financed by the CIA, an agency whose top officials have long been connected to oil men and Council on Foreign Relations globalists.

The allied victory in the Persian Gulf War of 1991 was loudly trumpeted by the American mass media, but the actions leading to this conflict were sparsely reported throughout the coverage. These machinations involved elites in secret societies and indicated a very different rationale for the war than the one presented to the public.

No one can argue that the United States military, with some assistance from British, French and Arab forces, did not perform magnificently during this brief conflict. It only took between January 17 and February 28, 1991, for the coalition of Operation Desert Storm to soundly defeat the

Saddam Hussein's well-armed Iraqi forces, then representing the fifth largest army in the world. This astounding military success was due primarily to the allied forces' superiority in both weaponry and training as opposed to Saddam's conscripts who, though veterans of combat against Iran, had limited training and low morale.

This created a lop-sided war, which resulted in more than 300,000 Iraqi casualties, (both military and civilian) and 65,000 prisoners, compared to the extraordinary low allied losses of 234 killed, 470 wounded and 57 missing.

Of course, the prime mover of that war was President Bush's father, George Herbert Walker Bush, an oilman, former CFR member, and former CIA director, as well as a Trilateralist and Skull & Bonesman.

Both Bush and then-Secretary of State James Baker had been deeply involved in the oil business. Any Bush policy that increased the price of oil meant more profit to his companies, those of his oil-men supporters and, of course, to the Rockefeller-dominated oil cartel.

An added bonus was that any conflict which divided the Arab world would only strengthen the hand of the US, Britain and Israel in the region, while the act of creating a coalition of countries fighting for the United Nations could only advance the globalists' plan for a one-world military force. This "battle of the New World Order was some kind of manufactured crisis with a hidden agenda," concluded researchers Jonathan Vankin and John Whalen after careful study of the events leading to this conflict.

The war was a drastic reversal of fortune for Saddam Hussein, who previously had enjoyed a close relationship to the senior Bush. In his role as CIA director, and then as vice president, the elder Bush along with the Agency, had supported Hussein through his eight-year war against Iran, following the surprise ouster of the Shah in 1979. This included looking the other way when Hussein gassed Iraq's uncooperative Kurds. The US had supplied Iraq with the crop-dusting helicopters used in Hussein's 1988 gassing attacks as well as chemical and biological weapons.

But by 1990, Hussein's Iraq had become a primary threat to the balance of power between Israel and its Arab neighbors and Hussein was now strapped for cash due to the Iraq-Iran War and couldn't pay his bills. Under pressure from the international bankers for slow repayment of loans and from the Organization of Petroleum Exporting Countries (OPEC), which refused to allow him to raise oil prices, Saddam needed a quick source of cash. He therefore turned his eyes to Kuwait—the third largest producer of oil next to Iraq and Saudi Arabia.

Few Americans know that Kuwait was once a part of Iraq, having long since been carved out of Iraq by Britain. In 1899 the British took control of Kuwait's foreign policy under an agreement with the dictatorial Sabah family; the Sabahs had produced a series of ruling Sheikhs since assuming control of the area's nomad tribes in 1756. Kuwait then became a British Protectorate in 1914 when German interest suddenly gave the area strategic importance. British dominance was solidified by sending British troops to the area in 1961 after Iraq sought to reclaim it.

The Pentagon had known that Iraqi troops were massing along the Kuwait border since mid-July 1990. On July 25, Saddam sought advice from the United States on his intentions to reclaim Kuwait. He met with US Ambassador April Glaspie, who told him, "I have direct instructions from President Bush to improve our relations with Iraq. We have considerable sympathy for your quest for higher oil prices, the immediate cause of your confrontation with Kuwait....

"I have received an instruction to ask you, in the spirit of friendship not confrontation, regarding your intentions: Why are your troops massed so very close to Kuwait's borders?"

According to transcripts released long after the war, Hussein explained that, while he was ready to negotiate his border dispute with Kuwait, his design was to "keep the whole of Iraq in the shape we wish it to be." This shape, of course, included Kuwait, which Hussein considered still a part of Iraq. "What is the United States' opinion on this?" he asked.

"We have no opinion on your Arab-Arab conflicts, like your dispute with Kuwait," replied Glaspie. "Secretary Baker has directed me to emphasize the instruction, first given to Iraq in the 1960s, that the Kuwaiti issue is not associated with America."

In other words, the USA had no particular interest in Saddam's intention to reclaim Kuwait.

"Shortly after this, April Glaspie left Kuwait to take her summer vacation, another signal of elaborate American disinterest in the Kuwait-Iraq crisis," noted authors Webster Griffin Tarpley and Anton Chaitkin in

*George Bush: The Unauthorized Biography*. On July 31, Bush met with GOP congressional leaders but said nothing about the Gulf situation.

The crisis escalated on August 2, when Iraqi troops moved into Kuwait. Bush froze all Iraqi assets in the United States, adding to Saddam's money woes, which had worsened in 1990 after international bankers refused him further loans. Glaspie was prohibited from speaking out by the State Department, so the American public could not learn of Bush's duplicity.

In later testimony before the Senate Foreign Relations Committee, Glaspie pointed out that the July 25 conference was her first and only meeting with Hussein, who had not met with any foreign ambassador since 1984, the mid-point of his war with Iran.

But if Hussein had not met with US diplomats, the same could not be said of American businessmen. Economist Paul Adler noted, "…it was known that David Rockefeller met with the Iraqi leader on at least three known occasions after the Chase Manhattan consortium became the lead banker in a number of major Iraqi credit syndications." It was also reported that Alan Stoga, a vice president of [Henry] Kissinger Associates met with Iraqi leaders during the two-year period preceding the Gulf conflict.

"Saddam began to realize that he could not get what he wanted from the striped-pants set. He began doing business with the people who mattered to him—foreign businessmen, defense contractors, technologists and scientists, occasionally even visiting newsmen," reported the Washington newspaper, the *Spotlight*, now the *American Free Press*.

Following the money trail of such non-diplomatic contacts that led to the Gulf War, Rep. Henry Gonzalez, then chairman of the House Committee on Banking, Finance and Urban Affairs, discovered that almost $5 billion in loans had been passed to Saddam Hussein in the 1980s through the Atlanta, GA, branch of Italy's government-owned bank, Banca Nazional del Lavoro (BNL). The branch manager, Christopher Drogoul, was finally brought into federal court where he pled guilty to approving this huge cash transfer without the approval of BNL's head office in Italy. However, the whole investigation was put on hold during the Gulf War.

Most observers disbelieved that Drogoul could have conducted such a massive transaction without the knowledge of his superiors. Bobby Lee Cook, one of Drogoul's several defense attorneys, argued that his client had been made the patsy in "a scheme orchestrated at the highest levels of the US government."

In court, BNL official Franz Von Wedel testified that his boss Drogoul had acted on the advice of the bank's consultants, Kissinger Associates.

In both 1989 and 1990, the Bush Justice Department had quashed indictments against BNL by the Atlanta Attorney General's office following an FBI raid on the bank on August 4, 1989. Action against the bank managers was held up for more than a year. Indictments were finally handed down one day after Bush declared a cease-fire in the Gulf War. This scandal—dubbed "Iraqgate"—prompted Gonzalez to prepare a House resolution calling for the impeachment of Bush Attorney General William Barr for "obstruction of justice in the BNL scandal." House Judiciary Committee Chairman Rep. Jack Brooks called on Barr to appoint a special prosecutor in the case.

In a classic case of who-will-watch-the-watchers, Barr said he could find no evidence of wrongdoing on his part and refused to appoint a special prosecutor. It was one of the only times that an attorney general had failed to appoint a special prosecutor when asked to do so by Congress.

The clincher of this sordid story of financial scheming and official malfeasance was that not only had most of the $5 billion been used by Hussein to buy weaponry to be used against American servicemen, but that US taxpayers picked up the tab.

Gonzalez said $500 million of the loans to Hussein came through the government-backed Commodity Credit Corporation (CCC) and had been intended to purchase grain from US farmers. However, grain shipped through the port of Houston had gone to then-Soviet bloc nations in exchange for weapons, while the remainder of the grain purchase had freed Hussein's limited cash reserves to buy more military materials. The Bush administration had pledged taxpayer guarantees should Hussein default on the loans, which he did after sending troops to Kuwait. According to at least one public source, more than $360 million in American tax money was paid to the Gulf International Bank in Bahrain, which was owned by seven Gulf nations including Iraq. This amount was only the first of an estimated $1 billion to be paid to ten banks by the CCC to cover the $5 billion of Hussein's defaulted loans.

"The $1 billion commitment, in the form of loan guarantees for the purchase of US farm commodities, enabled Saddam to buy needed food on credit and to spend his scarce hard currency on the arms buildup that brought war to the Persian Gulf," wrote Russell S. Bowen, author of *The Immaculate Deception*.

Even after the Iraqi invasion began on August 2, Bush publicly appeared strangely non-committal. Asked by reporters if he intended any intervention in the Gulf crisis, Bush said, "I'm not contemplating such action…"

His attitude apparently changed drastically that same day after meeting with British Prime Minister Margaret Thatcher, a regular attendee of Bilderberg meetings who had been implicated with Bush in both the Iran-Contra and October Surprise scandals. After meeting with Thatcher, Bush began to describe Hussein as a "new Hitler" and said, "the status quo is unacceptable and further expansion [by Iraq] would be even more unacceptable." Despite assurances from Hussein that Kuwait was his only objective and with no concrete evidence to the contrary, Bush nevertheless personally telephoned the leaders of Saudi Arabia and warned that they would be the next target of this "new Hitler."

Panicked, the Saudis handed over as much as $4 billion to Bush and other world leaders as secret payoffs to protect their kingdom, according to Sabah family member Sheik Fahd Mohammed al-Sabah, chairman of the Kuwait Investment Office.

Long after the Persian Gulf War, when audits found this money had been diverted into a London slush fund, anti-Sabah elements in Saudi Arabia criticized the payoff. They were told by al-Sabah, "That money was used to buy Kuwait's liberation. It paid for political support in the West and among Arab leaders—support for Desert Storm, the international force we urgently needed."

Whether this money played any role or not, Bush soon drew a "line in the sand" to block further Iraqi intrusion, then launched Desert Storm, an offensive that drove Iraqi troops from Kuwait.

Yet, even as America's patriotic soldiers closed in on Hussein, the whole war was suddenly called off. George H. W. Bush's old business partner remained in power and the "Great Game," the continuing maneuvering for control of the oil as mentioned in Part III, continued.

Even through the ensuing years of the Clinton administration, periodic air forays into Iraq continued, ostensibly to punish Hussein for preventing UN inspection of his development centers for biological and nuclear weaponry. However, this time there was a big difference—probing questions were raised by both a suspicious public and a few less timid members of the news media.

In late 1998, a letter writer to a national news magazine asked, "By using weapons of mass destruction to deter Iraq from manufacturing weapons of mass destruction, would America not be doing the very thing we're warning Iraq not to do?" Others raised the question of why we attacked Iraq for refusing UN inspection of its sensitive military installations when President Clinton also had refused to allow such inspections in the United States—a refusal greeted with general approval by the American public.

Nearly a decade later, it was clear that no such weapons had been found unless one counted the possible acquisition of ancient energy-manipulation technology reportedly gained in the looting of the Iraqi National Museum following the American occupation of Baghdad as described previously.

## WOULD AMERICANS ALLOW ATTACKS ON AMERICANS?

The WTC/Pentagon attacks certainly provided a convenient excuse to launch the pre-laid plans for military action against Afghanistan and Iraq. But were they simply allowed to happen or were they contrived provocations such as the *Reichstag* fire and Pearl Harbor? Again the question arises: Would any American allow an attack on fellow Americans just to further his own business or political agenda?

Unfortunately, the answer is "Yes." A case in point is "Operation Northwoods." Following the ill-fated Bay of Pigs invasion of Cuba, President Kennedy, angered by the inept actions of the CIA, had shifted responsibility for Cuba from that agency to the Department of Defense. Here, military strategists considered plans to create terrorist actions that would alarm the American population and stampede them into supporting a military attack on Cuba.

Under consideration in Operation Northwoods were plans to create "a series of well-coordinated incidents" in or around the US Naval Base at Guantanamo Bay, Cuba, to include inciting riots, blowing up ammunition stores, aircraft and ships.

They also planned to "develop a Communist Cuba terror campaign in the Miami area, in other Florida cities and even in Washington" or to "...sink a boatload of Cubans en route to Florida (real or simulated)...foster attempts on the lives of Cuban refugees in the United States..."

Other highlights of Operation Northwoods included the tactics of exploding bombs in carefully chosen locations along with the release of "prepared documents" pointing to Cuban complicity, the use of fake Russian aircraft to harass civilian airliners and "Hijacking attempts against civil air and surface craft," even simulating the shooting down of a civilian airliner.

It seems clear in the aftermath of 9/11 that Operation Northwoods was not forgotten. In fact, it seemed like covert and "black operations" programs might be making a comeback. Further, it appeared that the success of 9/11 as an inside job had opened a Pandora's box of follow-on covert and "black ops" programs.

In addition to the tremendous military buildup following the 9/11 attacks, the military affairs analyst for the *Los Angeles Times* reported "what may well be the largest expansion of covert action by the armed forces since the Vietnam Era."

"The Defense Department is building up an elite secret army with resources stretching across the full spectrum of covert capabilities," wrote William M. Arkin. "New organizations are being created. The missions of existing units are being revised. Spy planes and ships are being assigned new missions in anti-terror and monitoring the 'axis of evil.'"

In summer 2002, Defense Secretary Rumsfeld's Defense Science Board (DSB) conducted a "Summer Study on Special Operations and Joint Forces in Support of Countering Terrorism." The panel recommended "new strategies, postures and organization."

One such new organization would be a super intelligence support activity called the Proactive, Preemptive Operations Group (P2OG), a unit combining the CIA, military covert action, information warfare, intelligence, and cover and deception. One line of the classified study, which was leaked to the public by the Federation of American Scientists called for "preemption/proaction/interdiction/disruption/quick-response capabilities," in other words, dirty fighting.

According to Arkin, the group would, among other things, "launch secret operations aimed at 'stimulating reactions' among terrorists and states possessing weapons of mass destruction—that is, for instance, prodding terrorist cells into action and exposing themselves to 'quick-response' attacks by US forces. Such tactics would hold 'states/sub-state actors accountable' and 'signal to harboring states that their sovereignty will be at risk.'"

Under the reorganized military, responsibility and accountability for the P2OG group would be held by a "Special Operations Executive" within the National Security Council (NSC). According to *Asia Times* writer David Isenberg, "The NSC would plan operations but not oversee their execution in order to avoid comparisons to past abuses, such as Iran-Contra operations runs out of the NSC by Oliver North during the Reagan administration. Under the board's proposal, NSC plans would be executed by the Pentagon or the CIA."

Several commentators could not help but recall the CIA's Phoenix Program in Vietnam and the Operation Northwoods plan of the Pentagon, which followed the disastrous Bay of Pigs Invasion of Cuba, a joint military-CIA activity.

The thought of such past abuses prompted one writer, Chris Floyd, in 2002 to rail against "...Bush and his cohorts [who] are plunging the world into an abyss, an endless night of black ops, retribution, blowback, deceit, or murder and terror..."

Pulitzer Prize-winning journalist Seymour Hersh, citing sources in both the Pentagon and CIA, in 2005 agreed with previous writers that the Bush-dominated military would continue to expand its operations both at home and abroad.

"George W. Bush's reelection was not his only victory [in 2004]. The President and his national-security advisers have consolidated control over the military and intelligence communities' strategic analyses and covert operations to a degree unmatched since the rise of the post-Second World War national-security state," Hersh wrote. "Bush has an aggressive and ambitious agenda for using that control—against the mullahs in Iran and against targets in the ongoing war on terrorism—during his second term. The CIA will continue to be downgraded, and the agency will increasingly serve, as one government consultant with close ties to the Pentagon put it, as 'facilitators' of policy emanating from President Bush and Vice President Dick Cheney. This process is well under way."

Such are the chilling plans for expanded covert ops, but false flag operations, the use of agents provocateur, misdirecting public opinion—we now see that fabricating crises to further political goals is a methodology well understood and utilized right up to today. Was this the game on 9/11? Was Osama bin Laden merely substituted for Fidel Castro, Saddam Hussein or some other enemy of the moment? And why has President Barack Hussein Obama continued this game?

## WAR AS AN ECONOMIC STIMULUS

The answer to why such policies continue may have more to do with economics than politics. Even the most cursory examination of past military actions shows a distinct correlation between such warfare and the national economy. Marine Major General Smedley D. Butler, writing in the 1930s, stated, "War is a racket...War is largely a matter of money. Bankers lend money to foreign countries and when they cannot pay, the president sends Marines to get it."

In the same vein, many historians and economists have argued that America's emergence from the Great Depression was made only possible because of World War II.

The controversial *Report From Iron Mountain* is prophetic on this point. This secret 1963 policy paper, leaked to the press and later published as a book in 1967, makes clear that war is not only necessary to maintain societal control but to prop up a sagging financial system. The study that led to this famous white paper reportedly began in 1961 with Kennedy administration officials such as McGeorge Bundy (CFR, Bilderberger and Skull and Bones), Robert McNamara (Trilateralist, CFR and Bilderberger) and Dean Rusk (CFR and Bilderberger). Knowing of Kennedy's goal of ending the Cold War, these men were concerned that there had been no serious planning for long-term peace.

Although denounced as a literary hoax in some circles, *Report From Iron Mountain* is an amazing document, written at the onset of our national experience in Vietnam. It most certainly reflects the elitist views of those who are said to have solicited the study. According to the report, "War itself is the basic social system, within which other secondary modes of social organization conflict or conspire. It is the system which has governed most human societies of record, as it is today." The report's authors saw war as both necessary and desirable as "the principal organizing force" as well as "the essential economic stabilizer of modern societies."

The report writers concluded, "...we must first reply, as strongly as we can, that the war system cannot responsibly be allowed to disappear until (1) we know exactly what (forms of social control) we plan to put in its place and (2) we are certain, beyond reasonable doubt, that these substitute institutions will serve their purposes..."

Most significantly, the report states, "The elimination of war implies the inevitable elimination of national sovereignty and the traditional nation-state," and added, "The possibility of war provides the sense of external necessity without which no government can long remain in power...The basic authority of a modern state over its people resides in its war powers."

The report goes on to say that war "has served as the last great safeguard against the elimination of necessary social classes"... and war functions serve to control "essential class relationships."

A former high-ranking Pentagon officer, Col. Donn de Grand Pre, has stated, "I'm talking about what happened to my boss, [then] Secretary of Defense Robert McNamara. He commissioned a study to be done. It was later generally known as the 'Report From Iron Mountain.'" He added, stated in a 2001 interview, "One of the policy makers that I was associated with at the time—for good or for ill—was Henry Kissinger. At that time Henry was an untenured professor at Harvard University and he was also working for the Operations Research Office at the Pentagon, which was paying him a stipend for that work. Simultaneously, Henry was also working for the Council on Foreign Relations under Nelson Rockefeller... Henry would come to the Pentagon and since my boss, General [Robert] York was his contact there, I became Henry's contact [while Gen.

York was off on a lengthy study in Vietnam]. It evolved into informal luncheons where Henry would come down from the Hudson Institute, which is close to Iron Mountain, where he and 14 others were working on this study. Henry was a little bit reluctant to talk about this study, but he gave us enough information to enable us to realize that there was such a study going on. It lasted anywhere from eight to 10 months....The Iron Mountain study was not fiction by any means.

"Here was the overall purpose of the study: to analyze different ways a government can perpetuate itself in power, control its citizens and prevent them from rebelling. Their major conclusion was that, in the past, war was the only reliable means to achieve that goal. Remember, this study was in the process of being formulated in early 1963. Kissinger's intellectual buddies from Harvard and also from Yale were already formulating this no-win war in Vietnam."

A document authenticity expert, who asked for anonymity expressing fear of government reprisals against his consulting business, told this author that after comparing the report to the 1967 book *The New Industrial State* and other works by John Kenneth Galbraith, he became convinced that the *Report From Iron Mountain* was written by Galbraith based on "idiosyncrasies and stylistic comparisons." This expert said the two books almost certainly could not have been authored by two different educated and highly perceptive writers. He concluded that the *Report From Iron Mountain* "is pretty much the sole and exclusive work of John Kenneth Galbraith..." He added that the term "special studies" has been a "preferred open rubric or code for military cover and deception planning and operations, indeed, historically, not limited to the US armed forces but also including the NSC, Department of State, CIA and others."

Interestingly, Galbraith, while denying he participated in the *Iron Mountain* study itself, nevertheless admitted in 1976 that he had acted in the capacity of a consultant and vouched for the report's authenticity.

Regardless of its origin or author, the tone of the *Report* is certainly conspiratorial and it most certainly reflects the mindset and class-conscious views of men connected to the secret societies. These same men were responsible for the involvement of America in Vietnam in the 1960s and 1970s and their mindset was behind the attempt to foment war in Central America in the 1980s as well as the conflicts of the 1990s in the

Middle East and Balkans. Is what we are seeing in Iraq and Afganistan today merely a continuation of the policies of such men?

We've noted that Georgia Democratic Rep. Cynthia McKinney was figuratively eviscerated in the mass media for charging that friends of George W. Bush and other corporate big wigs were profiting from the War on Terrorism.

Yet on December 20, 2001, when war hero Senator John McCain chided his fellow senators about pork and profits accumulated since 9/11, there was no comparable media reaction. McCain was particularly miffed at a proposal to lease 100 Boeing 767s as refueling tankers for 10 years and then spend $30 million to reconfigure the planes as commercial airliners and return them to Boeing. "This is the wrong thing to do," groused McCain. "We're going to spend $20 billion plus over a 10-year period and 10 years from now are going to have nothing to show for it."

"This kind of behavior cannot go on," he later told the Senate. "You will lose the confidence of the American people. This is called war profiteering." Only a few conspiracy researchers thought to ask is this huge pay-off to Boeing might have less to do with national defense and more to do with hushing Boeing executives expressing doubt about the explanation for the demise of TWA Flight 800 off Long Island.

Only on several Internet sites and in some alternative media were there snickers of understanding. For some time, rumors had flown that Boeing was being offered a sweetheart money package as a bribe to keep quiet about the fatal crash of TWA 800.

Controversy has continued to swirl around the crash, which involved a Boeing 747 passenger jetliner that crashed off Long Island on July 17, 1996. Although hundreds of witnesses reported seeing a streak in the sky prior to the plane exploding and the fact that military exercises were being conducted in the area at the time, the government concluded that a spark had somehow gotten into a central fuel tank and caused the explosion which killed 230 passengers and crew.

Books, magazine articles and the Internet have been filled with speculation that TWA 800 was accidentally shot down when its late departure took it into a weapons testing zone. Boeing officials initially objected to the conclusion that somehow their craft were defective, yet later became strangely silent giving birth to rumors that the aircraft company was being paid off for its silence.

The last minute and little publicized add-on to a defense spending bill which caused McCain such concern only added to such speculation. Apparently McCain and other senators had not heard this speculation. Junior Senator Rick Santorum of Pennsylvania naively asked a colleague why the Air Force could not simply keep the Boeing 767s after they were paid for. He was told, "We can't do that. It will queer the deal."

In the wake of the 9/11 attacks, Americans were asked to give up many things including some constitutional rights in the War on Terrorism. However, government contractors, especially those delivering military goods, gave up nothing. If fact, they gained plenty, even those companies that had been caught in past scandals.

Take the Lockheed Aircraft Company, for example. In the mid-1970s, Prince Bernhard of the Netherlands was forced to resign from the secretive and exclusive Bilderbergers, which represented the inner core elite of more than one secret society. In London, just after World War II, Lord Rothschild and Dr. Joseph Hieronim Retinger encouraged Prince Bernhard to create the Bilderberger group. The prince personally chaired the group until 1976 when he resigned following revelations that he had accepted large payoffs from Lockheed to promote the sale of its aircraft in Holland. Today, Texaco Inc. has sold its US gas stations to Dutch Shell, drawing yet another American firm into even closer ties with the global economy.

Despite the bribery scandal involving the Dutch prince and other public officials worldwide, Lockheed continued to enjoy the largess of the US government. Despite pledges to institute ethical reforms, Lockheed officials again came under fire in the mid-1990s. The company pled guilty to making payoffs to an Egyptian official to win approval for a deal involving C-130 cargo planes. Since 1995, Lockheed, which has since changed its name to Lockheed Martin, has been named in 33 more court cases involving charges of overcharging on government contracts, improper technology transfers to China, falsifying the results of nuclear safety tests, job discrimination, environmental pollution and more.

This dismal public record did not deter the US government, from awarding Lockheed Martin a contract in October 2001 to build the nation's newest military jet, the F-35 Joint Strike Fighter. The contract was expected to exceed $200 billion during its decades-long life. It was called "the richest military contract in history."

Lockheed Martin and the previously discussed Halliburton are not alone in repeatedly violating both laws and regulations while continuing to collect vast amounts of public money. According to *U.S. News & World Report*, "In the past dozen years, 30 of the 43 largest federal contractors have racked up more than 400 enforcement cases, resulting in at least 28 criminal convictions, 286 civil settlements, mostly involving their government contracts...Allegations included price fixing, bogus testing, polluting, overcharging, hiding product defects, violating export laws and withholding financial data from the government. They also represent more than accounting quibbles: Company workers have been killed and seriously injured and national security potentially put at risk."

Yet four out of every ten federal procurement dollars go to these same companies. "If it was a food-stamp recipient, they'd go to jail," complained Oregon Democrat Rep. Peter DeFazio. "It's an extraordinary double standard."

In research conducted by *U.S. News & World Report*, it was determined that only one of the government's 30 largest contractors—General Electric Co.—has ever been denied new contracts and that punishment only lasted a few days.

Due to the cost, bureaucratic paperwork and apparent indifference—not to mention undiscovered bribes—no government agency keeps tabs on which company has broken the law. So the fat contracts just keep coming.

Following the trend of the big corporations getting bigger, many defense contractors have merged into huge multinational entities, making it even more difficult for government watchdogs to detect unlawful activities and make cases. No one—either in the major news media or the government—seems capable of determining exactly which individuals are in control of these corporate behemoths.

With the sudden and burgeoning national defense buildup following the 9/11 attacks, no one expects these corporate zebras to change their stripes any time soon. But perhaps a better way to increase cash flow these days is just to— steal it.

Soon after the events of 9/11, as the dot.com bubble was bursting, and as Americans watched the unfolding of the greatest wave of corporate accounting scandals in the history of the country that were epitomized by the fall of President Bush's friends at Enron, an even larger accounting scandal was somehow lost in the shuffle of egregious corruption in Washington. According to reliable estimates from within the government itself, the Department of Defense (DoD) and other departments of the federal government were unable to account for trillions—yes trillions—in missing funds.

One can only imagine that, if there were any problems with defense appropriations in Congress over the missing money on September 10, the events of 9/11 put a quick end to any Congressman's hesitation to authorize fresh new funds for defense contractors.

One of those most responsible for bringing this and other government accounting scandals to light was Catherine Austin Fitts, former managing director of Wall Street investment bank Dillon, Read and former Housing and Urban Development (HUD) assistant secretary in the first Bush administration. Fitts is now a well-known federal whistleblower and economic reformer whose website, whereisthemoney.org, details the missing-money scandal at both the DoD and HUD, including quotes like this from David K. Steensma of the DoD's Inspector General office: "We reported that DoD processed $1.1 trillion in unsupported accounting entries to...DoD financial statements for FY 2000."

Fitts said the figure actually tops $3 trillion: "Total undocumented accounting adjustments for reported periods for the Department of Defense [and HUD for fiscal 1998–2000] amount to a whopping $3.3 trillion, or $11,700 for every American. The Department of Defense has failed to produce independent audited financial statements since the requirement went into effect in 1995."

At least $59 billion was also missing at HUD, said Fitts, as its Inspector General had refused—for starters—to certify HUD's fiscal 1999 financial statements. Characterizing the depths of the scandal, Fitts said that Americans are "at the mercy of a group of creditors who are our creditors because they are financing us with the money they stole from our public and private pension funds."

At her website solari.com, and in other writings and lectures, Fitts has explained that, beginning with the savings and loan scandal in the 1980's which involved the stripping of nearly $500 billion from banks and government, criminalized insider elites began a rise to power that is now epitomized by their perpetration of 9/11. Now in a greater position of power in the 1990's, "these same syndicates then stripped an estimated $6 trillion of investors' value in pump and dump stock market and mortgage market schemes and an estimated $4 trillion of taxpayer money." Where has the $10 trillion gone? Most likely, says Fitts, into offshore accounts that will be used to buy up assets back on shore once these elites have engineered the destruction of the dollar.

Meanwhile, the grand plan of globalization and centralization of the world's economy as envisioned by the globalists within the Bilderbergers, the Trilateral Commission and Council on Foreign Relations continued.

Following in the footsteps of their successful effort to combine the once sovereign nations of Europe into one union, the globalists today are putting into place a "North American Union," all without any authorization, oversight or funding by the US Congress.

Under a CFR-sponsored unilateral agreement called the Security and Prosperity Partnership, signed by President Bush, Mexican President Vincente Fox and then-Prime Minister of Canada Paul Martin at Waco, Texas, in March 2005, the United States, Mexico and Canada are being merged into one economic bloc.

Concurrently, public hearings were underway in Texas and other affected states for the construction of a CanaMex or NAFTA [North American Free Trade Area] superhighway stretching from southern Mexico up through the Midwest and into Canada. All this under the supervison of the North American Superhighway Coalition composed of representatives from Texas, Oklahoma, Kansas, Iowa, Missouri, the Ambassador Bridge, various federal agencies and private firms. Two attempts to pass legislation authorizing this unilateral partnership in Congress failed and there has been precious little accounts of this effort in the corporate mass media.

Randy Ghent, one of a growing number of opponents to the CanaMex Superhighway, stated, "I couldn't think of a more disastrous project if I had to think all year."

Critics say the NAFTA Superhighway scheme would add to air pollution, traffic congestion, oil dependence, global warming, roadkill and human death. Local economics and quality of life would suffer, as development moves from town centers to narrow strips along the highway while noting that NAFTA activities already have caused corporate exodus to the south, robbing the United States of more than 600,000 jobs. There is already talk of creating a "North American Parliament" to deal with the new economic union.

NAFTA and the WTO agreements have encouraged companies to move out of the country and social services continued to lag behind demand. Additionally, tremendous amounts of money including criminalized cash flows were flowing through the military-industrial complex and primarily into large corporate accounts, or into the private hands of the cronies and accomplices of the criminalized elites.

Detectives long have used the question of *qui bono*, who benefits, as the beginning of their investigation. Journalists also use this method, often couching it in the old adage, "Follow the money."

## THE MASS MEDIA

But don't look to the corporate mass media to seek truth about the War on Terrorism or the missing money. Corporate behemoths—be they media or energy or military contractors—share the same status-quo interests as the government, and for the corporate media to broadcast anything that might depart too far from the official government story about 9/11 and its aftermath is simply not in their interest.

But by 2006, as egregious problems caused by the Bush regime became all too obvious. Certain elements within the mass media were willing to question Bush's policies, particularly issues such as his unconstitutional spying and support for turning management of important sea ports over to a nation with known terrorist ties. But early on, the mainstream media stood firmly with the government.

For example, Fairness & Accuracy in Reporting (FAIR) noted that on October 10, 2001, network executives representing ABC, NBC, CBS, Fox and CNN were involved in a conference call with then-National Security Adviser and Council on Foreign Relations heavyweight Condoleezza Rice. The executives apparently agreed to limit how and what they would broadcast regarding bin Laden or his al Qaeda group. Bush people even tried unsuccessfully to have al Jazeera, described as the "CNN of the Mideast," tone down its coverage of bin Laden. When this effort failed, al Jazeera was "accidentally" bombed off the air by US warplanes.

The Bush administration's effort to block any far-reaching inquiry was even more successful with members of Congress. Free speech was curtailed when they threatened to cut off intelligence reports to legislators who spoke offhandedly to the media. Then-White House Press Secretary Ari Fleischer, already on the record saying Americans "need to watch what they say," extended this constraint by contacting major newspapers asking that they not print full transcripts of bin Laden's interviews.

According to a FAIR news release, "The point is not that bin Laden or al Qaeda deserve 'equal time' on US news broadcasts, but that it is troubling for the government to shape or influence news content. Withholding information from the public is hardly patriotic. When the White House insists that it's dangerous to report a news event 'in its entirety,' alarm bells should go off for journalists and the American public alike."

Another small, but insightful, example of the media glossing over 9/11 issues and questions came on April 18, 2002, when Associated Press writer Sheila Hotchkin reported on the relatives of the victims of Flight 93 who were allowed by the government to listen to cockpit audio tapes from the doomed plane. No reporters were allowed in and the relatives were encouraged not to speak to the media.

But a few did, such as Hamilton Peterson, whose father, Donald A. Peterson, had perished in the crash. In an initial version of the story, Hotchkin quoted Peterson as saying "he learned things from the tape he did not know before, but declined to elaborate." By the next day, Peterson's observation regarding things he had not known was deleted from news accounts. What did Peterson learn that the rest of us are forbidden to know? Who is behind this mass media control? As noted earlier, the tape was played once again for the jury at the Zacarias Moussaoui trial in April of 2006. A transcript that included English translations of Arabic statements that were alleged to have been made by the hijackers was made available to the public at that time, but the recording itself was withheld.

Particular attention should be paid to the five major corporations, which dominate the American mass media—Vivendi Universal, The Walt Disney Co., Viacom, News Corporation and Time Warner. This represents a concentration of media power unthinkable prior to the Clinton years.

One of the few members of Congress to address this monopoly of the news media by an increasingly small number of giant corporations was Rep. Bernie Sanders, an independent from Vermont.

"[O]ne of the best-kept secrets is the degree to which a handful of huge corporations control the flow of information in the United States. Whether it is television, radio, newspapers, magazines, books or the Internet, a few giant conglomerates are determining what we see, hear and read," he said.

During the 1990s, "Telecommunication firms were engaged in the most visible and dramatic drive for corporate alliance and consolidation," wrote author William Greider in *One World, Ready or Not*. "AT&T, Time Warner, TCI, MCI, Ameritech and Nynex, CBS, ABC, Disney and many others—the overlapping deals were stunning as US firms rushed to unite market power and technological assets in cable and telephone systems, broadcasting, film-making, publishing and other media, while simultaneously forging telecom partnerships abroad. US consumers would provide the capital for these huge new conglomerates through the deregulated rates they paid to cable and telephone companies. The winners, it was clear, would be a handful of broad and powerful media combines, as dominant as the railroad and oil trusts were in the 1890s."

In 2005, a Project Censored team researched the board members of 10 major media organizations from newspaper to television to radio. Of these ten organizations, they found there are a mere 118 people sitting on 288 different American and international corporate boards. This study proved the close interlocking of big media and corporate America.

"We found media directors who also were former Senators or Representatives in the House such as Sam Nunn (Disney) and William Cohen (Viacom). Board members served at the FCC such as William Kennard (*New York Times*) and Dennis FitzSimmons (Tribune Company) showing revolving door relationships with big media and US government officials," stated the report, adding, "These ten big media organizations are the main source of news for most Americans. Their corporate ties require us to continually scrutinize the quality of their news for bias. Disney owns ABC so we wonder how the board of Disney reacts to negative news about their board of directors' friends such as Halliburton or Boeing. We see board members with connections to Ford, Kraft, and Kimberly-Clark who employ tens of thousands of Americans. Is it possible that the US workforce receives only the corporate news private companies want them to hear? Do we collectively realize that working people in the US have longer hours, lower pay and fewer benefits than their foreign counterparts? If these companies control the media, they control the dissemination of news turning the First Amendment on its head by protecting corporate interests over people."

The national news media is not only linked by directorships to corporate business but also to higher education. The team found media board members associated with USC (the *Washington Post*), Columbia (Gannett), Georgetown (Disney), NYU (the *Washington Post*), and Wharton (Knight-Ridder) among others. Thornton, Walters, and Rouse wrote, "With the decreasing state and federal funding to universities, will we see our higher learning institutions tie themselves more to corporations than the government for their funding?...Will the universities eventually focus education around the production of workers or thinkers?"

In their report, Thornton, Walters, and Rouse noted how history was repeating itself with media corporations. "As the Roman Empire declined, feudalism took the place of the government. The feudal lord was one of the few sources of jobs in the fourth and fifth centuries. These lords owned most of the land and resources. Today, we replace feudalism with corporatism. The mass population has few choices for their news, information and education. As corporate media applauds an ownership society, we must realize who gets to own. In corporate-dominated capitalism, wealth concentration is the goal and the corporate media are the cheerleaders."

Apart from the corporate concentration of media ownership there is a corporate bureaucracy that rewards mediocrity and conformity while stifling initiative and hardhitting investigative journalism.

"Much of what is reported as 'news' is little more than the uncritical transmission of official opinions to an unsuspecting public," wrote media critic Michael Parenti.

"What [reporters] pass off as objectivity is just a mindless kind of neutrality," said journalist Britt Hume, who added reporters "shouldn't try to be objective, they should try to be honest."

The power of this combined media behemoth is overwhelming.

According to recent studies, the average American spends nearly half of his/her waking hours with some form of the major consumer media—TV, radio, Internet, newspapers, magazines, recorded music, DVDs/VHS tapes, video games and books. It is projected that by the end of 2007 this time spent on media will only increase, mostly on the Net.

Studies in 2006 posted at medialiteracy.com revealed that the typical American spends more than four hours a day watching TV, two and a half hours listening to radio, more than 30 minutes on the Internet, about one hour listening to recorded music and reading newspapers, 20 minutes reading magazines and 17 minutes reading books.

Over and above this increasing consumer usage and ownership consolidation, there is a corresponding decrease in the number of distribution companies, critical to the widespread dissemination of information. *Standard & Poor's* editors noted that for years distribution problems caused by the consolidation of formerly independent distributors "disrupted deliveries and relationships with retail clients...canceled, missed and late deliveries were common occurrences." Authors have complained for years that books on controversial subjects always seem to encounter distribution or publicity problems. With an estimated 800 new magazines added each year to the existing 18,000 or so (most fail within the first year), it is easy to understand the importance of distribution.

Major banks, most controlled by secret society members, own significant amounts of stock in the ever-decreasing number of media corporations. "Through elite policy-shaping groups like the Council on Foreign Relations and the Business Roundtable, they steer the ship of state in what they deem to be a financially advantageous direction," noted authors Martin A. Lee and Norman Solomon in 1990. "GE, CapCities, CBS, the *New York Times* and the *Washington Post* all have board members who sit on the Council on Foreign Relations."

Little has changed today. A cursory glance at the *Standard & Poor's Corporation Records* shows CFR and Trilateral members sit on the boards of the major media corporations.

Corporate ownership intermingled with secret society members, many of whom are employed in the media, may explain why Bilderberg, Trilateral and CFR meetings are not reported by America's "watchdog" media. In fact, the membership lists of these societies read like a "Who's

Who" of the mass media.

These members include many past and present media corporate leaders such as Laurence A. Tisch and William Paley of CBS; John F. Welch, Jr., of GE/NBC; Thomas S. Murphy of ABC; Robert McNeil, Jim Lehrer, Hodding Carter III and Daniel Schorr of Public Broadcast Service; Harold Anderson and Stanley Swinton of the Associated Press; Michael Posner of Reuters; Joan Ganz Cooney of Children's TV Workshop (Sesame Street); W. Thomas Johnson of CNN; David Gergen of *U.S. News & World Report*; Richard Gelb, William Scranton, Cyrus Vance, A. M. Rosenthal and Harrison Salisbury of the *New York Times*; Ralph Davidson, Henry Grunwald, Sol Linowitz and Strobe Talbott of *Time*; Robert Christopher and Phillip Geyelin of *Newsweek*; Katherine Graham, Leonard Downie Jr. and Stephen S. Rosenfeld of the *Washington Post*; Arnaud de Borchgrave of the *Washington Times*; Richard Wood, Robert Bartley and Karen House of the *Wall Street Journal*; William F. Buckley Jr. of *National Review* and George V. Grune and William G. Bowen of *Reader's Digest*. Furthermore, sitting on the boards of directors of the corporations, which own the media are multiple secret society members.

Some of the well-known reporters, anchors and columnists who are members of the CFR and/or the Trilateral Commission include Dan Rather, C. C. Collinwood, Diane Sawyer, David Brinkley, Ted Koppel, Barbara Walters, John Chancellor, Marvin Kalb, Daniel Schorr, Joseph Kraft, James Reston, Max Frankel, David Halberstam, Harrison Salisbury, A. Ochs Sulzberger, Sol Linowitz, Nicholas Katzenbach, George Will, Tom Brokaw, Robert McNeil, David Gergen, Mortimer Zuckerman, Georgie Ann Geyer and many others. Small wonder so many researchers see a conspiracy of silence among these media peers.

Then there are "media watchdog" organizations such as Accuracy in Media (AIM). Many persons assume such groups are watching out for the public's interests. Not according to writer Michael Collins Piper, who in 1990 made public that AIM founder Reed Irvine was paid $37,000 a year as an "adviser for the division of international finance" of the Federal Reserve System. Noting that many Fed members also belong to the secret societies, Piper wrote, "To this day, Irvine and AIM never touch on any subject which is sensitive to the interests of the international Establishment: whether it be the Bilderberger group, the Trilateral Commission, the Council on Foreign Relations or the truth about the privately owned Federal Reserve."

There are also choke points within the flow of information, such as the international desk at Associated Press headquarters in New York where one person decides what news from outside the United States makes it onto the wire service. It is important to understand that the real control over the mass media is not direct control over the thousands of hard-working editors, reporters and news directors throughout the nation, but rather the control over the distribution of the information. If one doesn't see or hear about a story, to them it didn't happen.

Then there is the tremendous pressure created by fear of job security and loss of sources. Many national columnists must rely on insider sources to provide juicy information. Much of this information comes from government sources, which would dry up if they published the wrong story. Even the more hard-hitting national reporters still must pull their punches if they want to maintain their insider sources.

The ever-concentrated corporate ownership of the media has meant objective news, long viewed as a public service, flies out the window in favor of bottom-line profits based on ratings. At the time of the JFK assassination, the three major TV networks—ABC, CBS and NBC—supported their news departments with public service funds. Today, these same news departments are funded as programming with a resultant concern over ratings. News today is "a kind of commodity in the marketplace, no longer a holy profession," commented former CBS correspondent Daniel Schorr, "Today, it doesn't matter anymore. You just make your money and to hell with public service."

Veteran newsman Walter Cronkite agreed. Quoted in a professional journal, he said the current state of television journalism is "disastrous and dangerous" and decried "unreasonable profits...to satisfy shareholders." "[I]n demanding a profit similar to that of the entertainment area, they're dragging us all down."

"I challenge any viewer to make the distinction between [TV talk show host] Jerry Springer and the three evening newses and CNN," commented *60 Minutes* correspondent Morley Safer.

Anyone reading the news today will know that journalism has not been as profitable as it once was. While many point their finger at the Internet and the 2008–2009 economic crisis, Professor Robert McChesney with the Department of Communication at the University of Illinois at Urbana-Champaign, said journalism got itself into trouble decades ago. "The crisis began before news advertising revenue was lost to craigslist," he wrote. "The real problem is the corporate consolidation and monopoly control over journalism, which began in the late 1960s and unfolded throughout the '70s. In highly profitable monopolistic news entities (newspaper firms and network broadcasters), media owners, seeking to make more money, began to cut newsroom staff and commercialize news values. By the 1980s there was already a huge crisis in US news journalism. Journalists became despondent about the commercial pressures shaping their work. The Internet and the world economic crisis have only intensified this deeper crisis in journalism."

As corporate takeovers of news outlets grew, older editors, trained in true journalism, were squeezed out, either by attrition, corporate shuffling, downsizing or early retirement. Quality news suffered, as these mentors were no longer available to bring their experience and wisdom to young incoming reporters. Even journalism publications such as *The Quill*, a newsletter produced by the Society of Professional Journalists, today seems more concerned about cultural diversity in the newsroom or how to research on the computer than if any truth is being presented in the news columns.

McChesney said professional journalists have always been comfortable with corporate ownership, the dependency on advertising, and the status quo. "The idea of professional journalism has been a very conservative force. It gives working journalists the illusion that they are being fair, balanced, and neutral when reporting. In fact, the code of professionalism they abide by has built into it certain values that push them, almost unconsciously, in certain directions. This was as true in the 1960s as it is today. But the situation has become worse today because newsrooms have been gutted. There are fewer and fewer professional journalists trying to cover more and more news stories."

And, more often than not, these "news" stories concern celebrities, sports figures or sometimes, the downtrodden. "We used to call these 'sob stories'. They are human interest pieces that glorify celebrities so that later they can be sniped at," said Michael H. Price, a Texas print editor with a long history in newspaper work. "And editors today want stories written with attitude. But since almost any personal attitude will result in the charge of advocacy, attitude means no attitude. Reporters today are often sent out on stories and told to be 'snarky,' a British term meaning arrogant or sarcastic.

Price said the news media today is little more than a ventriloquist dummy for corporate interests and the ruling class "pandering with shallow and flippant writing to a mass audience who have never read newspaper anyway and, in this process, they are losing the literary, discerning readership. The media has allowed itself to be dumbed down and the reading public won't follow which is why they are losing subscribers."

The Obama administration, realizing a frontal attack on the First Amendment would meet stiff resistance, apparently was making an end run around it. On October 2, 2009, American diplomats for the first time attended a Geneva meeting of the United Nations' Human Rights Council as full council members. In a dramatic departure from past policy, they supported a resolution to limit freedom of expression.

Despite the fact that nations and groups accused of human rights abuse, including the Organization of the Islamic Conference, China, Cuba and Saudi Arabia, hold sway within the council, President Obama chose to send American representatives. According to Anne Bayefsky, a senior fellow at the Hudson Institute and a professor at Touro College in New York City, Islamic states saw Obama's participation in the council as "meaning fundamental rights were now up for grabs."

After the 2008 publication of images of Mohammed in a Danish newspaper, Cuba and various Islamic countries pushed an amendment limiting any speech they claimed was an "abuse...[that] constitutes an act of racial or religious discrimination." America ended up by co-sponsoring a resolution which sustained this idea along with Egypt, a nation not known for its freedom of expression.

Speaking on behalf of the Organization of the Islamic Conference, Pakistan Ambassador Zamir Akram said the resolution and its protection against religious stereotyping would allow the curtailment of individual free speech by anything that defames or negatively stereotypes religion. "The idea of protecting the human rights 'of religions' instead of individuals is a favorite of those countries that do not protect free speech and which use religion—as defined by government—to curtail it," said Bayefsky. "The Obama administration's debut at the Human Rights Council laid bare its very different priorities. Threatening freedom of expression is a price for engagement with the Islamic world that it is evidently prepared to pay."

The watch-dog media in America, as they like to portray themselves, appear to be more like lap-dogs to their corporate owners. This can be seen in a quick glance at *Project Censored*, a yearly posting of stories judged to be of importance to the public but which are ignored, downplayed or "spiked" by the major mass media corporations.

The sins committed by the mass media are more sins of omission than commission. In 2009 and 2010, the majority of news stories underplayed or ignored by mass media news involved corporate and government malfeasance. Project Censored is a media research program at Sonoma State University that for more than 30 years has worked in cooperation with numerous independent media groups in the US to protect freedom of the press. Here are Project Censored 2009/2010's top 25 stories of "news that didn't make the news":

1. US Congress Sells Out to Wall Street
2. US Schools are More Segregated Today than in the 1950s
3. Toxic Waste Behind Somali Pirates
4. Nuclear Waste Pools in North Carolina
5. Europe Blocks US Toxic Products
6. Lobbyists Buy Congress
7. Obama's Military Appointments Have Corrupt Past
8. Bailed out Banks and America's Wealthiest Cheat IRS Out of Billions
9. US Arms Used for War Crimes in Gaza
10. Ecuador Declares Foreign Debt Illegitimate
11. Private Corporations Profit from the Occupation of Palestine
12. Mysterious Death of Mike Connell—Karl Rove's Election Thief
13. Katrina's Hidden Race War
14. Congress Invested in Defense Contracts
15. World Bank's Carbon Trade Fiasco
16. US Repression of Haiti Continues
17. The ICC Facilitates US Covert War in Sudan
18. Ecuador's Constitutional Rights of Nature
19. Bank Bailout Recipients Spent to Defeat Labor

20. Secret Control of the Presidential Debates
21. Recession Causes States to Cut Welfare
22. Obama's Trilateral Commission Team
23. Activists Slam World Water Forum as a Corporate-Driven Fraud
24. Dollar Glut Finances US Military Expansion
25. Fast Track Oil Exploitation in Western Amazon

One reason these stories are missed by the public is that, if they are reported at all, they get lost in the bewildering barrage of continuous but extraneous media content. For example, in the January 29, 2010, edition of the *Dallas Morning News* carried news stories such as "winter weather advisory," the death of novelist J. D. Salinger, the normal murders and a Department of Commerce announcement that the "worst recession since the 1930s ended last year." Yet these stories were overshadowed by blogs, a dog story, copious sports coverage, travel and lifestyle articles, and an entertainment guide. One business story in this edition concerned homebuilders who hoped that baby boomers would beat a path to their door again. Perhaps the point to be made here is that, according to the newspaper's website, the most read story in the entire edition concerned Dallas Cowboys quarterback Tony Romo.

And one-sided stories along with claims of censorship are now reaching onto the Internet. An investigation posted on *Alternet.org* in August 2010 revealed that a conservative group had coordinated such methods as vote padding, using multiple accounts and outright censorship in an effort to stifle liberal or progressive discourse on the social media site *Digg.com*. One posting mentioned in the investigation stated, "The more liberal stories that were buried the better chance conservative stories have to get to the front page. I'll continue to bury their submissions until they change their ways and become conservatives."

*Digg.com*, one of the world's most popular websites—it was ranked 50th among US websites by Alexa—generates about 25 million page views per month, more than one third of that of the *New York Times*. Practicing what has been termed "democracy in the Internet," webpages submitted to *Digg* can be voted up (digging) or down (burying) by users. A collective effort can result in stories being prominently featured or buried.

According to the *Alternet* article, one group dedicated to "burying" stories they disagreed with is known as the Digg "Patriots," a conservation bunch that has become "so organized and influential that they are able to bury over 90 percent of the articles by certain users and websites submitted within 1-3 hours, regardless of subject material. Literally thousands of stories have already been artificially removed from *Digg* due to this group. When a story is buried, it is removed from the upcoming section (where it is usually at for ~24 hours) and cannot reach the front page, so by doing this, this one group is removing the ability of the community as a whole to judge the merits or interest of these stories on their own (in essence: censoring content)."

Czech author Milan Kundera, writing about life under communist dictatorship in *The Book of Laughter and Forgetting*, noted, "The first step in liquidating a people is to erase its memory. Destroy its books, its culture, its history. Then have somebody write new books, manufacture a new culture, invent a new history. Before long the nation will begin to forget what it is and what it was."

## A DISMAL FOREIGN POLICY RECORD

In the aftermath of the 9/11 attacks, the Bush White House and corporate mass media were quick to blame Muslims who hated America's lifestyle and values. Thus began the concept of Islamic terrorism, the idea that Muslim religion was the cause of the attacks, not the foreign policy of the United States.

Such diversion has created Islamaphobia in America which expressed itself well into 2010 with the controversy over a Muslim community center in downtown New York and the Florida preacher who threated to burn Korans.

The reported 9/11 terrorists that attacked New York and Washington were said to be punishing America for backing Israel's repression of Palestinians and what they saw as the US "occupation" of Saudi Arabia. "Though they were all Muslims, religion was not the motivating factor," noted journalist Eric S. Margolis, adding, "As the CIA's former bin Laden expert Michael Scheuer rightly observed, the Muslim world was furious at the US for what it was doing in their region, not because of America's values, liberties or religion. These motives for the 9/11 attack have been largely obscured by the whipping up hysteria over 'Islamic terrorism.' The planting of anthrax in New York, Florida and Washington soon after 9/11 was clearly designed to promote further anti-Muslim furor. The perpetrators of this red herring remain unknown. But the anthrax attack hastened passage of the semi-totalitarian Patriot Act that sharply limited the personal freedoms of Americans and imposed draconian new laws."

Osama bin Laden himself alleged that US foreign policy attempts to enslave other nations prompted a violent backlash. It this an outrageous lie or could some truth be found in his statement?

A serious study of United States foreign policy since World War II indeed presents a picture that is contrary to the image that the US promotes peace, democracy, and prosperity overseas, as envisaged by the American public engendered largely through stories in the corporate mass media.

"I don't think we, the American people, deserved what happened [on 9/11]. Nor do we deserve the sort of governments we have had over the last 40 years," said Gore Vidal in a mid-2002 interview. "Our governments have brought this upon us by their actions all over the world... Unfortunately, we only get disinformation from the *New York Times* and other official places. Americans have no idea of the extent of their government's mischief. The number of military strikes we have made unprovoked, against other countries, since 1947–48 is more than 250. These are major strikes everywhere from Panama to Iran. And it isn't even a complete list. It doesn't include places like Chile, as that was a CIA operation. I was only listing military attacks."

As confirmed by the *New York Times* years ago, US foreign policy has been in the hands of the Council on Foreign Relations elite since at least 1939. In addition to the media corporate leaders, mainstream reporters and anchors listed above, this elite and its associates include present and former government officials such as Hillary Clinton, Robert Gates, Janet Napolitano, James. L. Jones, Timothy Geithner; former Presidents Bill Clinton, George H. W. Bush, Gerald Ford, Jimmy Carter and Richard Nixon; virtually every CIA director; as well as a considerable number of familiar past and present government officials such as Paul Volcker, Dick Cheney, Henry Kissinger, Wesley Clark, Strobe Talbott, Alexander Haig, Alan Greenspan, Bruce Babbitt, James A. Baker III, Sandy Berger, Colin Powell, Harold Brown, Zbigniew Brzezinski, Frank C. Carlucci, Richard

Darman, John Deutch, Lawrence Eagleburger, Robert McFarlane, Brent Scowcroft, Condoleezza Rice, Casper Weinberger, Bill Richardson, Susan Rice and Larry Summers.

Within three hours after the attacks of 9/11, Kissinger, Talbot, Clark and Haig, among others, were all prominently seen on both CNN and the broadcast networks. Their message was so similar that one would have thought they were reading from the same CFR script: The attacks were terrible, something must be done, terrorism transcends national boundaries and therefore all the nations must come together under the United Nations to successfully combat this new type of warfare.

This clarion call was seen by some as nothing more than an effort to use the 9/11 tragedy as another reason to perpetuate the disastrous status quo of foreign policy: support for America's ongoing policy of neo-colonialism; the use of the United Nations as a tool in that strategy; the political subjugation and control of other nations through military dictators or wealthy families supported by, and often placed in power, by the US military or intelligence services; and the wholesale stripping away of the native wealth of other nations, including the US itself, through the kind of economic globalization and financial centralization that has been promoted by CFR elites for decades.

But as the very phenomenon of 9/11 itself reveals, the result of this empire-building policy has been dismal at best and catastrophic at worst.

Never mind the historical aggression displayed by American foreign policy in the Mexican War of 1848 and the Spanish-American War of 1898. Consider this selection of our misguided foreign policy adventures just since World War II:

In 1953, a few years after Iran's Prime Minister Mohammed Mossadegh engaged in a gradual and lawful nationalization of the oil industry in that Mideast nation, he and his democratic government were deposed by a coup instigated by the CIA. This brought the Shah to power, with the monarchy assuming complete control in 1963, and turning Iran into a client state of the US. Thousands of Iranians, perhaps millions, died during the repressive rule of the Shah and his brutal SAVAK secret police. The Shah was finally forced out in 1979 by the Ayatollah Khomeini, who quickly became the US's latest foreign enemy despite the fact that he had been on the CIA payroll while living in Paris. The Shah was granted asylum in the

United States and a medieval version of Islam took control over Iran.

In Guatemala in 1954, the CIA toppled the popularly elected government of Jacobo Arbenz, which had nationalized United Fruit property. Prominent American government officials such as former CIA Director Walter Bedell Smith, then-CIA Director Allen Dulles, Secretary of State for Inter-American Affairs John Moors Cabot and Secretary of State John Foster Dulles were all closely connected to United Fruit. An estimated 120,000 Guatemalan peasants died in the resulting military dictatorships.

Fidel Castro, with covert aid from the CIA, overthrew the military dictatorship of Fulgencio Batista and instituted sweeping land, industrial and educational reforms as well as nationalizing American businesses. Swiftly labeled a communist, the CIA then organized anti-Castro Cubans resulting in numerous attacks on Cuba and the failed Bay of Pigs Invasion in 1961. The island nation has been the object of US economic sanctions since that time.

More than 3,000 persons died in the wake of an invasion of the Dominican Republic by US Marines in 1965. The troops ostensibly were sent to prevent a communist takeover, although later it was admitted that there had been no proof of such a takeover.

Also in 1965, the US began the bombing of North Vietnam after President Lyndon Johnson proclaimed the civil war there an "aggression" by the north. Two years later, American troop strength in Vietnam had grown to 380,000, and soon after climbed to more than 500,000. US dead by the end of that Asian war totaled some 58,000, with casualties to the Vietnamese, both north and south, running into the millions.

In 1968, General Sukarno, the unifier of Indonesia, was overthrown by General Suharto, again with aid from the CIA. Suharto proved more dictatorial and corrupt than his predecessor. A reported 800,000 people died during his regime. Another 250,000 persons died in 1975 during the brutal invasion of East Timor by the Suharto regime aided by the US government and Henry Kissinger.

In 1973, the elected government of Salvador Allende in Chile was overthrown by a military coup aided by the CIA. Allende was killed and some 30,000 persons died in subsequent violence and repression, including some Americans. Chile was brought back into the sphere of influence of the US and remained a military dictatorship for the next two decades.

In 1979, the powerful and corrupt Somoza family, which had ruled Nicaragua since 1937, was finally overthrown and Daniel Ortega was elected president. But CIA-backed Contra insurgents operating from Honduras fought a protracted war to oust the Ortega government in which an estimated 30,000 people died. The ensuing struggle came to include such shady dealing in arms and drugs that it created a scandal in the United States called Iran-Contra, which involved persons connected to the National Security Council selling arms to Iran, then using the profits to buy drugs in support of the Contras. All of those indicted or convicted of crimes in this scandal were pardoned by then-President George H. W. Bush.

US Marines landed in Lebanon in 1982 in an attempt to prevent further bloodshed between occupying Israeli troops and the Palestine Liberation Organization. Thousands died in the resulting civil war, including hundreds of Palestinians massacred in refugee camps by right-wing Christian forces while Ariel Sharon, then an Israeli general, looked on in apparent approval. Despite the battleship shelling of Beirut, and the destruction of that great Mediterranean city, American forces were withdrawn in 1984 after a series of bloody attacks on them. More than two decades later, the conflict between Israel and the Palestinians remains as intractable and deadly as ever, in large part due to the virtually unconditional support of Israel by the US, which has been institutionalized by the Israel lobby discussed in Part I of this book.

In 1983, US troops invaded the tiny Caribbean island nation of Grenada after a leftist government was installed. The official explanation was to rescue a handful of American students who initially said they didn't need rescuing. The only real damage inflicted in this tiny war was to a mental health hospital partly owned by a White House physician and widely reported to be a CIA facility.

During the 1970s and 1980s, the US government gave aid and arms to the right wing government of the Republic of El Salvador, which represented the financial interests of a tiny oligarchy, for use against its leftist enemies. By 1988, some 70,000 Salvadorans had died.

More than one million persons died in the 15-year battle in Angola between the Marxist government aided by Cuban troops and the National Union for the Total Independence of Angola, supported by South Africa and the US government.

When Muammur al-Qaddafi tried to socialize the oil-rich North African nation of Libya beginning with his takeover in 1969, he drew the wrath of the US government. In 1981, it was claimed that Qaddafi had sent hit teams to the United States to assassinate President Reagan and in 1986, following the withdrawal of US oil companies from Libya, an air attack was launched which missed Qaddafi but killed several people including his infant daughter.

In 1987, an Iraqi missile attack on the US frigate *Stark* resulted in 37 deaths. Shortly afterward, Iraqi officials apologized for the incident. In 1988, a US Navy ship shot down an Iranian airliner over the Persian Gulf resulting in 290 deaths. The Reagan administration simply called it a mistake.

Thousands of freedom-seeking Chinese were killed in Beijing's Tiananmen Square in 1989 after government hardliners there conferred with former President Richard Nixon on how to deal with the dissidents. Nixon, of course, was the only US president to resign under threat of criminal indictment and was in power during the shooting of students at Kent State University on May 4, 1970.

As many as 8,000 Panamanians died over Christmas 1989, when President George H. W. Bush sent US troops to invade that Central American nation to arrest his former business partner, Manuel Noriega. The excuse was that Noriega was involved in the importation of drugs to the United States. *U.S. News & World Report* noted that in 1990, the amount of drugs moving through Panama had doubled.

We noted previously that Iraqi casualties, both military and civilian, totaled more than 300,000 during the short Persian Gulf War of 1991. It has been estimated that more than one million Iraqis, including women and children, have died as a result of the continued missile and air attacks (not including those killed since the US invasion in 2003) as well as economic sanctions against that nation.

Also in 1991, the United States suspended assistance to Haiti after the election of a liberal priest sparked military action and disorder. Eventually, US troops were deployed. Once again in 2004, the US fomented and backed the toppling of the same democratically elected president and replaced him with an unelected gang of militarists, CIA operatives, and corporate predators.

Other nations that have felt the brunt of CIA and/or US military activity as a result of foreign policy include Somalia, Afghanistan, Serbia, Kosovo, Bosnia, Brazil, Chad, Sudan and many others. As Dr. Martin Luther King Jr. stated during the Vietnam War, "My government is the world's leading purveyor of violence." He did not say "my country" or "my people"—it is the government, or rather those who control it, that are responsible. Of course, we the distracted and unaware citizens who claim to live in a democracy must take our fair share of the blame as accessories after the fact.

One American hero, Robert Bowman, flew 101 combat missions in Vietnam and so knows the results of US foreign policy first hand. Bowman rose to a lieutenant colonel (USAF) and later became head of advanced space programs for the Department of Defense. After his retirement he became a bishop of the United Catholic Church in Melbourne Beach, FL. Bowman noted in 1998, "President Clinton [and later President Bush] did not tell the American people the truth about why we are the targets of terrorism when he explained why we bombed Afghanistan and Sudan. [They both] said that we are a target because we stand for democracy, freedom, and human rights in the world. Nonsense! We are the target of terrorists because, in much of the world, our government stands for dictatorship, bondage and human exploitation. We are the target of terrorists because we are hated. And we are hated because our government has done hateful things."

The solution, Bowman said, is to change our ways. "Getting rid of our nuclear weapons, unilaterally if necessary, will enhance our security. Drastically altering our foreign policy will ensure it...In short, we should do good instead of evil. Who would try to stop us? Who would hate us? Who would want to bomb us? That is the truth the American people need to hear." Bowman had seen through to the heart of darkness of American foreign policy, going public with the charge that the Bush administration was behind the 9/11 attacks. "9/11 is based on a pack of lies. It wasn't misjudgment; it was treason...", proclaimed Bowman to a New York rally in 2005.

If America's dismal and counterproductive foreign policy was simply the result of incautious and insipid blundering, one might expect that occasional mistakes would be made in favor of the American people. But a careful study of the United States' errant policies during the past century clearly indicate a persistent pattern of policies which only enrich the wealthy and further the goals of the globalist elite.

## MANUFACTURED ENEMIES

We've seen how so many of our worst enemies of the past were actually created by the US government. Again, the primary question is whether America simply has a penchant for creating Frankenstein monsters or if such creations part of a conscious agenda?

The history of the Vietnam War can be personified in Nguyen Tat Thanh, the son of a lowly Vietnamese rural educator. This man later changed his name to Ho Chi Minh [He Who Enlightens] and became the driving force behind Indochinese nationalism for three decades.

As a young man during World War I, Ho Chi Minh lived in France where he came into contact with French socialists and their Illuminati and Masonic philosophies. In 1919, he spoke before the attendees of the Versailles Peace Conference, calling for expanded rights in Indochina.

In 1930, Ho founded the Vietnamese Communist Party, which later was changed at the urging of Soviet leaders to the Indochinese Communist Party to avoid being perceived as simply a national movement. However, the nationalism of his party was reaffirmed in 1941, when he and others entered Vietnam and created the League for the Independence of Vietnam, or the Viet Minh. When the Japanese overran Indochina in 1945, Ho Chi Minh and General Vo Nguyen Giap began working with the American Office of Strategic Services (the predecessor of the CIA) to oust the occupation forces.

Ho continued to receive American aid after the Japanese withdrew from Vietnam following their surrender on August 14, 1945. "We had a trusted agent to whom we regularly supplied with weapons, radio equipment, operators and medicine. All of it served to reinforce his position and status," wrote journalist Lloyd Shearer. Ho, along with his able General Giap, was then able to force the withdrawal of French troops from French Indochina and soon he was facing the US Army in the south.

There exists a wealth of documentation indicating that the Russian

Revolution—indeed the very creation of communism—sprang from Western conspiracies beginning even before World War I. "One of the greatest myths of contemporary history is that the Bolshevik Revolution in Russia was a popular uprising of the downtrodden masses against the hated ruling class of the Czars," wrote author G. Edward Griffin, who said both planning and funding for the revolution came from financiers in Germany, Britain and the United States. Although the revolution began as an uprising, the preponderance of Western support went to the Bolsheviks, emanating largely from Wall Street, as detailed in *Rule by Secrecy*.

In January 1917, Leon Trotsky was living in New York City working as a reporter for the *New World*, a communist newspaper. Trotsky had escaped an earlier failed attempt at revolution in Russia and fled to France where he was expelled for his revolutionary behavior. "He soon discovered that there were wealthy Wall Street bankers who were willing to finance a revolution in Russia," wrote journalist William T. Still.

One of these bankers was Jacob Schiff, whose family had lived with the Rothschilds in Frankfurt. Another was Elihu Root, attorney for Paul Warburg's Kuhn, Loeb & Company. According to the *New York Journal-American*, "[I]t is estimated by Jacob's grandson, John Schiff, that the old man sank about $20 million for the final triumph of Bolshevism in Russia." Root, a CFR member, contributed yet another $20 million, according to the *Congressional Record* of September 2, 1919.

To illustrate the interconnectedness of America's wealthy and powerful elite, another grandson, Andrew Schiff, is married to Karenna Gore, the daughter of 2000 Democratic presidential contender Al Gore.

Author Gary Allen noted, "In the Bolshevik Revolution we have some of the world's richest and most powerful men financing a movement which claims its very existence is based on the concept of stripping of their wealth men like the Rothschilds, Rockefellers, Schiffs, Warburgs, Morgans, Harrimans and Milners. But obviously these men have no fear of international communism. It is only logical to assume that if they financed it and do not fear it, it must be because they control it. Can there be any other explanation that makes sense?"

If there can be identified one single motivating factor behind the horror and tragedy experienced in the 20th century, it is surely anti-communism. The animosity between the so-called democracies of the West and the communism of the East produced continuous turmoil from 1918 through the end of the century. This animosity culminated in the Cold War and massive arms race against the Soviet Union that evolved out of World War II. This conflict gave the globalists and their military-industrial complex the "perceived enemy" they needed to maintain their rule and their permanent war economy.

As mentioned previously, more recent manufactured enemies—though on a smaller scale—have included Ho Chi Minh, Saddam Hussein, the Shah of Iran, Manuel Noriega, Ferdinand Marcos and many others.

But then such enemies are necessary to convince an otherwise peaceful population on the need for wars and foreign expeditions. It's all part of a formula that has proved quite successful down through the centuries. Create a boogeyman enemy to keep the public distracted but focused, then play both ends against the middle to maintain profits and control.

Just consider the words of Hitler's *Luftwaffe* chief Hermann Goering, who during the Nuremberg Trials explained how to persuade the public to go to war. He told one of his interrogators, "Why of course the people don't want war...That is understood. But after all it is the leaders of the country who determine the policy, and it is always a simple matter to drag the people along, whether it is a democracy, or a fascist dictatorship, or a parliament, or a communist dictatorship...Voice or no voice, the people can always be brought to the bidding of the leaders. That is easy. All you have to do is to tell them they are being attacked, and denounce the pacifists for lack of patriotism and exposing the country to danger." Does this have a familiar ring to it?

## THE HEGELIAN DIALECTIC

Conspiracy researchers were mystified for years how such high-level capitalists as the Morgans, Warburgs, Schiffs and Rockefellers could condone, much less support, the communists who espoused an ideology which overtly threatened their position and wealth.

To understand this seeming dichotomy, indeed to understand how the secret society members operate, we have noted that one must study the philosopher who most greatly influenced these men—the founder of idealism, Georg Wilhelm Friedrich Hegel.

Coming on the heels of the Age of Reason—the intellectual revolt against the authority of the church—German philosophers Hegel, Johann Gottlieb Fichte and Immanuel Kant inspired future generations with the idea that modern man need not be chained by religious dogma and tradition.

Hegel's unique theoretical method, known as the "Hegelian dialectic," has unfortunately proven to be an exceptional tool for manipulating people and events—that is, when in the hands of ruthless people. Generally it can be said that Hegel identified the universal process by which opposites—which he termed "thesis" and "antithesis"—are always reconciled in a higher-level compromise or "synthesis."

Hegel's dialectic reduced world history and human interaction itself to a simple formula: When one person or group desires one thing (the thesis) around which they organize for power or control, this in turn always evokes a reaction (the antithesis) around which an opposing person or group organizes itself. The confrontation of these two forces moves history forward, as the thesis and antithesis struggle toward a resolution that amounts to a compromise at a new level (the synthesis). This may be achieved through negotiation or some sort of violent battle.

Hegel's dialectic was a mind-boggling effort and a philosophic problem that has not yet been fully completed—adherents and opponents of Hegel may well continue to philosophize into the next millennium. It is therefore easy to understand why such a broadly conceived system has been interpreted in so many ways by Hegel's followers, which have included such opposites as Karl Marx and Adolf Hitler.

The application relevant here is the idea that Western capitalists, along with the Marxist followers of Hegel, created communism on one side (thesis) as a perceived enemy of the democratic nations on the other side (antithesis). The ensuing conflict produced huge markets for finance and armaments and eventually a general blending of both sides (synthesis). Often during the past 50 years it was said that the USA was becoming more like Russia while they were becoming more like the USA.

The members of secret societies traceable to Cecil Rhodes' Round Tables and the Illuminati understood the Hegelian dialectic quite well. Indeed, their predecessors had already for centuries cunningly deployed a version of the dialectic with which to manage events in their selfish interests. These early-day Machiavellies found it was but a small step to the realization that one needn't wait for the crisis and turmoil that Hegel said would naturally unfold in the normal course of history. Instead, these conflicts could be covertly created and then artificially controlled to one's own benefit.

No wonder that in modern times we have witnessed the cycles of financial booms and busts, crises and revolutions, wars and threats of war, all of which were engineered behind the scenes to maintain a "balance of power" in the interests of global elites—the Machiavellians of today.

Social activists and policy-makers alike have learned this both-ends-against-the-middle stratagem well, whether by experience, intuition or study. Demand more than you really need (thesis) from your opposition or employer (antithesis), manipulate the process in your favor wherever possible, and, even after some compromises, you'll usually end up with far more than you would have achieved (i.e., the synthesis) than if you had allowed the natural process of the dialectic to unfold unmolested.

"This revolutionary method—the systematic working of thesis vs. antithesis = synthesis—is the key to understanding world history," declared conspiracy author Texe Marrs.

Russian revolutionaries such as Lenin and Trotsky were being used by the Western elite to get Russia out of World War I, to the benefit of Germany. But at the elite level, communism was being created to stimulate the division of fear and mistrust presented as communism vs. capitalism vs. fascism.

Even Lenin apparently came to understand that he was being manipulated by more powerful forces. "The state does not function as we desired," he once wrote. "A man is at the wheel and seems to lead it, but the car does not drive in the desired direction. It moves as another force wishes."

This other "force" were the members of the secret societies that were behind the birth of communism itself, "monopoly finance capitalists" as Lenin described them.

# WHAT DO WE KNOW NOW?

The question now becomes, was 9/11 truly an unprovoked and surprise attack by a handful of Muslim zealots or was it yet another case of the Hegelian method being used to promote a pre-existing secret agenda?

And in view of the massive amount of well-documented material now available, what can we conclude? Just for starters:

We now know that the government in the form of the official 9/11 Commission did not tell the truth about what happened. This admission comes from the mouths of more than one commission member not to mention a host of critical commentators.

Despite shills proclaiming infallible scientific evidence, the conclusions of the 9/11 Commission are not credible to a growing number of professionals, including architects, engineers, physicists, demolition workers, military officers, commercial and military pilots, aviation experts, doctors, healthcare workers, construction managers and even survivors of that day.

It is undeniable that the occupations in Iraq and Afghanistan have been justified primarily by the events on 9/11 despite the fact that no one has claimed any Iraqis or Afghans were involved. It is also clear that these attacks were planned well in advance of 9/11.

According to many, the events of 9/11 propelled pro-Israel Zionist neoconservatives—a euphemism for National Socialists—to national power with the unwitting help of constitutional conservatives. Formerly a fringe group, this Zionist political movement brought totalitarianism to America. By defeating Iraq, the US rid Israel of one of its two most powerful enemies. The other threat, Iran, appears next on the target list.

Most ominously, journalist Eric Margolis saw that 9/11 "put America in what may turn out to be a permanent state of war with the Muslim world—a key goal of the neoconservatives." Despite the unresolved questions, the malfeasance, the dissembling, outright lies and the snafus within the military and the FAA, mainstream journalist Margolis—like so many of his fellow Americans—still tried to convince himself that 9/11 may have been "just, perhaps, the Mother of All Coincidences."

Many others were less sympathetic to America's national leadership.

They saw the true conspirators behind 9/11 as: (1) those who perpetrated the actual attack upon the United States, i.e., directed the planning for the many details and contingencies involving the hijackings, worked to hand off essential "match" details to the hijackers, planted explosives within the WTC and Pentagon, and flew or controlled the planes; (2) those who must have acted from the inside to suppress or alter normal defense and security precautions at the moment of crisis, such as the confusion caused by multiple simultaneous war games; and (3) powerful insiders who acted to create and narrate a fraudulent official story, remove evidence through the premature and hasty cleanup of the 9/11 crime scenes, and thwart or slow official investigations, including the blocking of antiterrorism efforts within the FBI and CIA through separate administrations.

We've seen that the goal of powerful rogue interests within the US must have been to create this provocation, and then breed an atmosphere of fear behind which to push a predetermined foreign policy and domestic security agendas—including an agenda that amounts to both the theft of American civil liberties and the theft of trillions from the federal treasury—through a confused, cowed and panicky Congress. And we have also considered the evidence that covert entities within the governments of Israel, Pakistan, and Saudi Arabia must surely have had foreknowledge of the attacks and may even have had a hand in supporting the perpetrators.

If any of this is true, how have we reached this dark place in our history?

The record is clear that since the National Security Act of 1947, the United States has slowly been turned into a national security state with more and more power being concentrated in the federal government, particularly the executive branch. Laws are being enacted by presidential orders and signing papers rather than through reasoned debate and careful study by our elected representatives. And no one seems to notice, especially since the news media has now come under the total control of a mere handful of international corporations. Trained and dedicated newsmen, in the mold of a Walter Cronkite, have been replaced by on-air personalities who are more conscious of ratings and their hair styles than world and national events. Citizens therefore have no choice but to study and learn for themselves, drawing from a variety of non-traditional news sources.

## PART IV – HISTORICAL PRECEDENTS

What specifically have we learned from this close examination of the 9/11 attacks and their aftermath?

We know that mere incompetence cannot explain the systematic failure of the normal security protections codified in both the civilian aviation and military sectors and we know that not one single person has yet been reprimanded for this failure.

"It has hardly been noticed in the hysteria surrounding 9/11, but this was ultimately an attack that failed," concluded veteran airline captain and former covert operations pilot Philip Marshall. "Through its two key tactical failures, the delay of American 77 and the extended tragedy of United 93, it failed to achieve its real strategic goal. The element of surprise—complete surprise, across the board—was to have been the key to its success as a truly long-term, world-changing event. If the plan had been executed perfectly, the footprints of the tactical planners may have never been discovered. 'If' being the operative word…

"If they had all struck at once, the disposition of the fighter jets would never have come into play. There would be no conversation about the shoot-down orders that weren't given, the bizarre hiding and delaying inside the classroom, the NORAD responses, the E4-B orbiting the Capitol before the Pentagon was hit, Cheney making the 'horrible decision' that he didn't actually make, the odd testimony of Gen. Arnold, and on and on. They all could have said—and I believe they were supposed to be able to say—'Gee, it was over before we could do anything.' Over by 9:11 [a.m.] on 9/11."

But it was not over. Questions arose faster than answers. Why did it take a year or more to learn that Cheney's antiterrorism task force was alerted to the problem months in advance, that President Bush saw a briefing paper stating bin Laden was preparing to strike in August 2001, and that war game exercises involving the idea of planes crashing into buildings were scheduled for 9/11?

The evidence of foreknowledge of the attacks, particularly within the FBI and CIA, is overwhelming. This raises the question as to who precisely blocked any investigation of this information and why. Why was there no warning to the public or beefed up security? Who had the power to misdirect and block official investigations?

We also know that actions against the Taliban in general and Osama bin Laden in particular were well under way long before the attacks. Does anyone truly believe that the Mossad and the Pakistani ISI, and hence the CIA, had no clue as to bin Laden's whereabouts, especially at a time when every American can be tagged by computer, especially if they fail to pay their taxes?

It is now clear that the bombing of Afghanistan had more to do with oil and gas pipelines and restoring the poppy fields than with catching bin Laden. And the War on Terrorism shifted from finding those responsible for the attacks to enforcing a "Pax Americana" on the world, exactly as articulated by the neo-cons Cheney, Rumsfeld, Perle and Wolfowitz—even before Bill Clinton was elected. And unlike every past American administration, this group has actually proposed a first-strike use of nuclear weapons in this new war for world domination.

We know now that Bush spurned more international treaties than any other world leader and released funds for North Korea's nuclear program at a time when he was preparing to seek war with Iraq, claiming that Saddam Hussein *might* be capable of building a weapon of mass destruction. The Bush forces pushed hard for an attack while the United Nations worked hard behind the scenes to ensure compliance by Saddam Hussein of UN demands.

Subsequent statements by administration officials including Colin Powell coupled with the now-public Downing Street memo make it clear that the Bush White House knew well that its evidence of Iraq's weapons of mass destruction was weak at best and that the intelligence was "fixed" around a policy of invasion. This could easily fit the definition of a lie.

We now know that plans to circumvent the Constitution were laid as far back as the Nixon years and that the new Department of Homeland Security carries within it concepts and programs which would have been greeted with howls of protests just a few short years ago. And the new technology to identify and classify each individual citizen is now in place. Administration critics cannot be summarily dismissed for using terms like "dictatorship," "1984" and "totalitarianism."

Bush and Cheney consistently fought any truthful investigation into the tragedies of 9/11 and when popular opinion in this matter turned against them, they turned to one of the leading lights of the secret societies—Henry Kissinger, a luminary of the Council on Foreign Relations. Again, a groundswell of public opinion as well as the possibility of dredging up old war crime charges prompted Kissinger's resignation even before he began work. Nevertheless, the two men Bush selected to replace Kissinger—Thomas Kean and Lee Hamilton—are both members of the secretive Council on Foreign Relations and elite insiders. The executive director of the 9/11 Commission, Philip Zelikow, was a White House foreign policy insider, and also the principal author of the administration's *National Security Strategy* statement of 2002 that first articulated the concept of preemptive warfare based on the threats posed by 9/11. This was the pre-eminent doctrine that led to the attack on Iraq and the War on Terrorism.

It can also be seen that President Bush attempted to place persons sympathetic to his worldview on the Supreme Court, the place where his father's friends handed him his office. And shifting to the CFR-dominated Democratic administration of Barack Hussein Obama won't make things much better as most of the groundwork for the current "War on Freedom" was laid during the CFR-dominated Clinton administration.

We now know that Bush and most other members of his cabinet were too locked into the monopolies of energy, pharmaceuticals, telecommunications and military/aerospace to allow alternative views to be heard. Bush, Cheney and many others are guilty of the same corporate shenanigans they were forced to criticize in the summer of 2002 following the collapse of Enron, Tyco, WorldCom and other major corporations. And these were merely precursors of the economic meltdown of 2008–2009.

We now can see clearly that the privatization of US industry, energy and institutions to include health care and education does not fulfill the promise of better service at less cost.

If the game plan of the masterminds behind the 9/11 attacks was to curtail American freedom, centralize more power in the federal government and set back the social agenda of the United States in favor of an open-ended military and intelligence buildup, then they succeeded admirably. To many long-time researchers, it all has a familiar ring to it.

In many ways, the aftermath of the 9/11 attacks fit the same template as the assassination of President Kennedy in 1963:

- Within hours, despite a lack of real evidence, one man was blamed for the event along with hints that he was connected to foreign enemies.

WHAT DO WE KNOW NOW?

- Official pronouncements were widely publicized only to be quietly admitted as errors later on.
- Although within the jurisdiction of the local authorities, the entire case was usurped by the FBI and CIA, both agencies under the control of a president who benefited from the tragedy. In 2001, FEMA, also controlled by the president, was added to this list.
- A group of specialists (medical in the JFK's case and engineers in that of the WTC) was convened but limited in what they could view and study, blocked from conducting an objective probe by federal officials.
- Evidence in the case was hastily removed and destroyed, forever lost to an impartial and meaningful investigation.
- More evidence was locked away in government files under the excuse of "national security."
- Federal malfeasance was excused by claiming lack of manpower and resources and no one was disciplined or fired. Federal agency budgets were increased.
- Any alternative to the official version of events was decried as "conspiracy theory" and "unpatriotic."
- The federal government used the event to increase its own centralized power.
- A foreign war (Vietnam in JFK's case and Iraq and Afghanistan today), which otherwise would have been opposed, was supported by a grieving population.
- A top government leader (then LBJ and now Bush), formerly under suspicion for election fraud and corrupt business dealings, was suddenly propelled to new heights of popularity.
- Many citizens knew or suspected that the official version of events was incorrect but were afraid to speak out.
- A compliant and sycophantic mass media was content to parrot merely the official version of events and studiously avoided asking the hard questions that might have revealed the truth.

In yet another strange parallel to the Kennedy assassination, in the months and years following 9/11, an increasing number of potentially crucial witnesses began suffering untimely deaths.

JIM MARRS

## PART IV – HISTORICAL PRECEDENTS

Barry Jennings, the deputy director of the New York Housing Authority's Emergency Services Department who told of multiple explosions and bodies inside WTC Building 7, died Aug. 19, 2008, just days before the National Institute of Standards and Technology (NIST) report on Building 7 was released to the public. No cause of death was released.

Some researchers wondered if the 53-year-old Jennings had been murdered to keep him silent about his knowledge of explosions and bodies in Building 7. Radio talk show host Jack Blood reported, "It seems that there is a very good possibility that Jennings' death could have been due to foul play. Though the investigations are on going, initial findings are somewhat alarming....It seems that Dylan [Avery, one of the young producers of *Loose Change* who had taped an interview with Jennings] had hired a private investigator to look into Jennings death which remains shrouded in mystery. His motive was simply to bring some closure to the life of Barry Jennings, and in doing so to honor the memory of this brave American. The investigator ended up referring the case to law enforcement before refunding his pay, and told Dylan never to contact him again. Very unusual to say the least. Dylan also paid a visit to the Jennings home. He found it vacant and for sale."

Kenneth Johannemann, a part-time janitor at the WTC who reported a "massive explosion" in the basement of one tower as well as multiple explosions on the upper floors, helped save a life on 9/11 and received a letter of commendation from the Bush White House. He died in September 2008 from a gunshot wound. A hand-printed note near his body stated the reason he killed himself was that 9/11 ruined his life, made him depressed and led to drinking. The letter ended with "Goodbye!!!" A separate note asked that someone take care of his cat, Papa-Boy. The shooting was called a suicide, a ruling his friends and associates couldn't accept.

Shreveport, LA dentist David Graham said he was threatened by FBI agents after telling them he had met three of the Sept. 11 hijackers in a Shreveport home. He died in 2004 from apparent poisoning. In 2006, Shreveport TV station KTBS reported, "His family says he was poisoned more than two years ago. At the time, Graham was trying to publish a manuscript about meeting three middle easterners in Shreveport, men he feared were plotting to bomb Barksdale Air Force Base. Graham wrote that he warned the FBI. Then after 9/11, he saw their pictures among the hijackers. Before Graham was poisoned, he was supposed to testify at a deportation hearing against a Pakistani man, Jamal Khan, who hosted the men Graham believed to be the hijackers. Dr. Graham's brother, Edwin Jones, told us...the family believes someone slipped poison into his drink, plunging him into a deadly illness.

Michael Doran was a lawyer for several of the 9/11 victims and undoubtedly had gather inside information. He died in a private plane crash in Ohio on April 28, 2009.

Christopher Landis, operations manager for the Virginia Department of Transportation's Safety Service Patrol, reported committed suicide, only a week after witnesses at the Pentagon confirmed his story that on the morning of 9/11 he saw and photographed people in government vehicles arriving at the Pentagon much sooner than normally would have been expected. Landis had shared his photos with the producers of the film entitled *The PentaCon*.

Paul Smith, a 60-year-old helicopter pilot for WABC-Channel 7 in New York and one of the first to film the burning Twin Towers, killed Oct. 7, 2007, when a runaway taxicab jumped the curb and plowed into him and three relatives on a city sidewalk. His wife, Donna, suffered a broken leg and all Smith's relatives were taken to area hospitals. According to journalist Pat Shannan, the cab driver claimed he was run off the road by a black car, which has never been identified and that Smith's cameraman on 9/11, John Del Giorno, has since refused to talk to newsmen about his filming of Flight 175, which crashed into the second tower.

Deborah Palfrey, known as the "DC Madam," headed a Washington, D.C. prostitution ring that reportedly included former CIA director and co-chairman of the 9/11 Intelligence Inquiry, Porter Goss, and other officials involved in 9/11, even hinting they might include Dick Cheney. She had publicly stated, "I have information that would have been of great interest to the 9/11 Commission." She said she was withholding the information to present to any official investigation. She told talk show host Alex Jones that she had explosive information, adding, "I'm not planning to let anyone buy me off or make any kind of deal with me and no, I'm not planning to commit suicide." On April 15, 2008, her mother found Palfrey hanging in a nylon rope in a shed behind her Florida home. The official verdict was suicide.

Maj. Gen. David F. Wherley Jr., the National Guard officer who played a "major role" in sending scrambled fighter jets into the Washington, D.C. area the morning of 9/11, was killed along with his wife in the Washington Metrorail train crash of June 22, 2009. They were among nine fatalities in the crash between two trains.

Salvatore Princiotta was a "first responder" with FDNY's Ladder 9. The 43-year-old Princiotta was found dead in his Scottsdale, AZ, home on May 14, 2007. While his family at first thought he died from the respiratory problems that had plagued him since 9/11 and prompted his move to Arizona, his death was considered a homicide. The cause of death was not immediately released.

WTC widow Beverly Eckert, who refused the condition-filled government money, was among the 49 victims of Continental Flight 3407 which crashed February 11, 2009, in a Buffalo, NY suburb.

Other untimely deaths noted by 9/11 researchers, but not fully confirmed, include Prasanna Kalahasthi, the widow of a Flight 11 Passenger, reportedly committed suicide by hanging; another reported suicide was the un-named Boston Logan Airport ticket agent who checked in two of the named hijackers and Ezra Harel, who managed security at airports connected with 9/11. Harel, who died of as reported heart attack, with his partner Menachem Atzmon, who was convicted of campaign finance fraud in Israel in 1996, took over management of security at the Boston and Newark airports when their company, International Consultants on Targeted Security (ICTS), bought Huntleigh USA in 1999. United Flight 175 and American Flight 11 both originated in Boston. United 93, which reportedly crashed in Shanksville, PA, departed from the Newark. ICTS management was responsible for inspecting the validity of passports and visas, searching cargo, and screening passengers. According to journalist and Israeli authority Barry Chamish, "Without Atzmon [and Harel] in charge of Newark and Logan Airports, 9/11 could not have happened."

Some researchers even looked back at other deaths suspected of being arranged by someone attempting to cover the evidence trail to 9/11. One such would be the grisly and unsolved 1998 stabbing death of Suzanne Jovin, a 21-year-old Yale senior who had produced a thesis on Osama bin Laden under her adviser, a former Naval Intelligence officer suspected of CIA connections. According to an article in the December 6, 2002 edition of the *Yale Herald*, "Jovin's thesis was on international terrorism, with a specific focus on a Saudi citizen by the name of Osama bin Laden. Even then, some thought that the subject matter might have gotten her killed by sparking the interest of those who sought to protect the terrorist and his work."

Another death was that of the previously mentioned John P. O'Neill, the FBI Counterterrorism expert obsessed with Osama bin Laden, who died in the attacks on the WTC. Many believe he was given the security job to place him at Ground Zero so as to prevent a man with his knowledge and credentials from voicing his suspicions to the public. Then there was the drug overdose death of Bruce Ivins, a microbiologist in the US Army Medical Research Institute of Infectious Diseases at Fort Detrick, MD. Ivins was the second man accused by the government of being behind the post-9/11 anthrax attacks in Florida and Washington, the first being released after years of harassment. Authorities said Ivins died of an overdose of Tylenol yet no autopsy was performed with the claim that the government already had a sample of his blood.

Some researchers even count the shooting death of Clemson University graduate Michael Zebuhr as the possible elimination of a crucial 9/11 witness. Zebuhr, who studied engineering, was shot twice in the forehead the evening of March 18, 2006, after leaving a restaurant in a normally safe section of Minneapolis. Two men approached Zebuhr's party and demanded that his mother hand over her purse, which she did. One of them then shot Zebuhr at point-blank range in front of his family and fled. Police chased a car matching the description of the assailants and arrested two men and a woman. All three were later released. Zebuhr had been a student of Judy Wood at Clemson and had aided her in her study of possible directed-energy weapons being used at the WTC. He also had organized a student group to investigate and pursue the attacks of 9/11 as an inside job.

But perhaps the strangest of these strange deaths was that of Bertha Champagne. The 62-year-old woman was a live-in baby sitter for Marvin Bush, the younger brother of then-President George W. Bush and a director of Securacom, the company that provided security for the World Trade Center, United Airlines, and Dulles International Airport. She apparently kept tabs on Bush's 13-year-old son and 17-year-old daughter. On September 29, 2003, police found Champagne's crushed body lying in a driveway in front of the Bush family home in the Alexandria section of Fairfax County, apparently the victim of her own car which was found nearby in a wooded area after crossing two streets. Police investigators said the woman went to retrieve something from her car which had been left in gear and was crushed when it rolled over her. They gave no explanation for why the car did not roll until Champagne was in a position to be crushed. Conspiracy researchers naturally speculated on the true cause of the woman's death and what she might have overhead at the Bush home.

One major difference in the two cases is that following JFK's death, less than 10 days went by before President Lyndon Johnson appointed a special commission to investigate the crime. Well more than a year after the events of 9/11, there was still only talk of creating some sort of investigative body, the time lag due primarily to pressure from President Bush and Vice President Cheney not to convene such an inquiry. It was almost two years before an official 9/11 commission was selected and put to work and by then, most of the primary evidence, such as the steel from the World Trade Center, was long missing or otherwise unavailable.

In the case of the Pearl Harbor attack, the JFK assassination and 9/11, a common denominator was the failure of normal security precautions. This is the tip off.

As Col. L. Fletcher Prouty, former Pentagon-CIA liaison officer, stated in regards to the Kennedy assassination, "The active role is played secretly by permitting it to happen. That was why President Kennedy was killed. He was not murdered by some lone gunman or by some limited conspiracy, but by the breakdown of the protective system that should have made assassination impossible...This is the greatest single clue to the assassination—who had the power to call off or reduce the usual security precautions that are always in effect whenever a president travels? Castro did not kill Kennedy, nor did the CIA. The power source that arranged that murder was on the inside. It had the means to reduce normal security and permit the choice of a hazardous route. It also had the continuing power to cover that crime for...years."

The same question could be asked regarding the tragedies of September 11, 2001:

Who had the power to call off or reduce normal airline and NORAD security procedures and who had the power to deflect any meaningful investigation into the events? This kind of power can only be found at the highest levels of government and corporate control. Today's big time criminals no longer worry about what the government might do to them because they *are* the government. It therefore becomes essential to identify and connect the inner core elite of the world's secret societies, to demonstrate their ownership and interlocking control over the multi-national corporations that dominate our national life.

"Most people prefer to believe their leaders are just and fair even in the face of evidence to the contrary, because once a citizen acknowledges that the government under which they live is lying and corrupt, the citizen has to choose what he or she will do about it. To take action in the face of a corrupt government entails risks of harm to life and loved ones. To choose to do nothing is to surrender one's self-image of standing for principles. Most people do not have the courage to face that choice. Hence, most propaganda is not designed to fool the critical thinker but only to give moral cowards an excuse not to think at all," noted Internet commentator Michael Rivero.

But the time has come for persons of good heart and conscience to stand up and regain the country handed down to them by men and women who not only were discomforted by fighting for a free and democratic republic but risked their very lives and fortunes.

Look to local leaders as they are the ones more likely to care about the public welfare. Our democratic republic, with its Constitution and Bill of Rights, is without a doubt the greatest form of government ever initiated in the written history of this planet. Make it work as it was intended.

By the time you read this, there is every likelihood that other major terrorist attacks will have been reported and that some new war may have broken out in some far corner of the world, certainly the attacks on Libya count. Next will come Pakistan, Iran, Syria or some other enemy of Israel. There will be more "experts" brought forward to generate fear and instruct us on the need to curtail freedom to save democracy.

Do not be stampeded.

We all agree that the true perpetrators of 9/11, of this or any future tragedy, must be identified and punished. But we must make certain through an objective investigation and cool reasoning that we indeed have the true culprits. We must not be played for suckers as so many times in the past.

The corporate news media has bombarded the public with facts, statistics, personal opinion, official pronouncements and commentary to the point of distraction and confusion.

Viewed in its broadest perspective, however, the picture is both clear and appalling:

The United States during both Bush administrations was under the control of a dynastic family, blood relatives to virtually all European monarchs, whose patriarch can be shown to have been both in sympathy and in business with Hitler and his Nazis. The Bushes controlled three of the nation's most populous and powerful states—Florida, Colorado and Texas, as Gov. Rick Perry is considered little more than a surrogate Bush. Considering the close connections between Arnold Schwarzenegger, the Bushes, Karl Rove and other New World Order luminaries like Warren Buffet and Jacob Rothschild, one could argue that they controlled California.

And the Bushes also are blood relatives to the royal family of England, as were Al Gore and John Kerry as documented by the prestigious genealogical publication *Burke's Peerage*. The Windsors originated in Germany and trace their ancestry to many major European royals.

The Bush family has been involved with the CIA since before the time of the 1961 Bay of Pigs invasion, with all that implies regarding covert wars, drug smuggling and assassinations, not to mention the creation of Saddam Hussein as well as Osama bin Laden and his al Qaeda network. One would imagine that the public would finally catch on after realizing that the same family supported three major world evildoers—Hitler, Hussein and bin Laden.

And each generation belonged to a secret college society—Skull and Bones—linked to the Bavarian Illuminati as well as prominent members of other such societies whose avowed purpose is to end United States sovereignty in favor of globalism. The family has even been linked to accused assassins, John Hinckley and Lee Harvey Oswald. What are the odds?

At least two Bush sons were at the heart of the savings & loan debacle, which cost every man, woman and child in the United States thousands of dollars. The eldest son, not elected but selected by a Supreme Court packed by previous Republican presidents including his father, has been linked to Enron, Harken and other shady oil company dealings and has surrounded himself with men of questionable ethics and truthfulness.

WHAT DO WE KNOW NOW?

Collectively, this family and their corporate cronies during the George W. Bush administration sought what amounts to dictatorial powers to combat the proclaimed War on Terrorism, despite the growing evidence that the attacks which launched this war were known in advance and allowed to happen to bring about the erosion of individual rights and the centralization of even more power unto themselves. And that view is putting the very best possible light on the affair. Considering the long-standing connections between this family, its political supporters, the secret societies, the CIA, overseas intelligence agencies, war-profiteering corporations, the energy industry, the bin Laden family, Saddam Hussein and the al Qaeda network, a case can be made that the 9/11 attacks were orchestrated by persons other than Osama bin Laden.

Immense federal power, which began in earnest during the Reagan years, when George H. W. Bush stood in for a president recovering from a gunshot wound, gained strength during the elder Bush and Clinton administrations, and was codified into law during the Bush Junior years. By 2011, the Obama administration has displayed little eagerness to curtail or mitigate these unconstitutional laws and his first cabinet read like a roster of leading members of the globalist Council on Foreign Relations.

The nature of public life in the US today has begun to resemble the very despotic societies—Hitler's Third Reich, Stalinist Russia, Communist Eastern Europe and China—that America contested during the entire last century.

Such totalitarian regimes stemmed from centralized governments that serve themselves rather than the people, that respond more swiftly to policies of the central government than evidence of criminal activities or public need and use every means at their disposal to spy on and intimidate their citizens. Thoughtful observers see much that same trend in the United States today.

These are not conjectures or conspiracy theories. These are the facts.

"I don't believe that," is not a legitimate argument. If the facts and information in this book are wrong, any rebuttal must be come from contradicting facts or more persuasive evidence.

Even Adolf Hitler understood the psychological willingness of people to believe a big lie more readily than a small one. In his book *Mein Kampf* [*My Struggle*], Hitler wrote, "[T]he great masses of people...with the primitive simplicity of their minds they will more easily fall victims to a great lie than to a small one, since they themselves perhaps also lie sometimes in little things, but would certainly still be too much ashamed of too great lies. Thus such an untruth will not at all enter their heads, and therefore they will be unable to believe in the possibility of the enormous impudence of the most infamous distortion in others; indeed they may doubt and hesitate even when being enlightened [with truth and facts]..."

The questions regarding the 9/11 attacks and their aftermath raise only further questions. These questions concern what the American peple intend to do about all this.

Will they continue to be led by a corporate mass media that deceives by omission more than commission and distracts them from the real issues?

Will they continue to reelect politicians who have been in office while all the causes of current problems were put into place?

Will they continue to blindly follow the standards of the two major political parties that have demonstrated that precious little difference exists in their major policies?

Will they continue to support a foreign policy that angers and alienates peoples all across the globe with its thinly-disguised neo-colonialism?

Will they allow the US military to continue enforcing this foreign policy while gaining unwarranted control over their own nation and lives?

Will they continue to permit their nation to be the primary seller of arms to the world and then bemoan the fact that those same arms are used against them?

Will they finally take a look behind the green curtain of media spin to identify the globalists who own and control that media corporations as well as the government and, hence, the military?

Will they stand up and exercise their own individual power or stand idly by, frozen by fear, intimidation or confusion, while their remaining liberties are swept away?

Only you, the reader, can answer these questions.

# SOURCES

## INTRODUCTION

XIX  84 percent agreed with Charlie Sheen: www.prisonplanet.com/articles/march2006/240306supportsheen.htm

XX  Farmer and Thomas Kean on NORAD: Dan Eggen, "9/11 Panel Suspected Deception by Pentagon," *Washington Post* (Aug. 6, 2006)

XXIV  Scholars for 9/11 Truth: www.st911.org

XXIV  Paul Craig Roberts: www.prisonplanet.com/articles/february2006/080206towerscollapse.htm

XXV  Stanley Hilton case: Pat Shannan, "Former Bob Dole Staffer Says Bush Had 9-11 Foreknowledge," *American Free Press* (Oct. 4, 2004); www.suetheterrorists.net

## PART I – THE EVENTS OF SEPTEMBER 11, 2001

5  Bush pledges to hunt down perpetrators: www.salon.com/news/feature/2001/09/11/bombings

6  John Farmer on criminal investigation: www.washingtonpost.com/wpdyn/content/article/2006/08/01/AR2006080101300.html

7  Commission road map questions: Family Steering Committee: www.scoop.co.nz/stories/WO0507/S00369.htm

8  Failure of government itself: John Farmer, *The Ground Truth: The Untold Story of America Under Attack on 9/11* (New York: Riverhead Books/Penguin Group, 2009), p. 7

9  Fighters at one-fourth speed: 911research.wtc7.net/planes/analysis/norad/index.html#otis

9  67 intercepts: William Thomas, "Pentagon Says Interceptors Flew: Too Far, Too Slow, Too Late," www.thetruthseeker.co.uk/article.asp?ID=1325

9  FAA official destroyed controllers tape: summeroftruth.org/nyt_06may04.html

9  Stand-down suspicion not removed: David Ray Griffin, *The 9/11 Commission Re-*

*port: Omissions and Distortions* (Northampton, MA: Olive Branch Press, 2005)
10 Flights still being cancelled: www.economist.com/blogs/gulliver/2010/06/flight_cancelltions
11 Steganography: Editors, "Digital moles in the White House?" *WorldNetDaily.com* (2001); www.worldnetdaily.com/news/article.asp?ARTICLE_ID=24594
12 Bin Laden not charged with 9/11: www.indymedia.org.uk/en/2006/06/343007.html
12 Kleinberg's comments about "luck": www.9-11commission.gov/hearings/hearing1/witness_kleinberg.htm
13 Bush's quote on terrible pilot: David Ray Griffin, *The New Pearl Harbor* (Northampton, MA: Olive Branch Press, 2004)
14 Media will be judged on resistance to intolerance: Editors, "Free Speech in Wartime," *Washington Post* (Sept. 29, 2001)
15 Bush capitulated: Webster Griffin Tarpley, *9/11 Synthetic Terror* (Joshua Tree, CA: Progressive Press, 2006)
17 Gen. Richard Myers on Vigilant Warrior: Richard A. Clarke, *Against All Enemies* (New York: Free Press, 2004), p. 5
17 Lt. Col. Marr: Scott, op. cit.; Col. Deskins: Hart Seely, "Amid Crisis Simulation, 'We Were Suddenly No-Kidding Under Attack'" *Newhouse News Service* (Jan. 25, 2002)
17 Sgt. Lauro Chavez: Author's interview, Sept. 28, 2006
18 William B. Scott: 911research.wtc7.net/cache/planes/defense/aviation-now_jumpstart.htm
19 Amalgam Virgo as sinister cover: Tarpley, op. cit.
21 Timothy McNiven: Greg Szymanski, "Army Theorists Crafted Model of 9-11 Attack Back in 1976," *American Free Press* (March 21, 2005); www.codenamegrillfire.com/index.php?n=1&id=1
21 Robert M. Bowman: www.prisonplanet.com/articles/april2006/040406mainsuspect.htm
22 Cheney and Office of National Preparedness: www.washingtonpost.com/ac2/wp-dyn?pagename=article&contentId=A64420-2001May8&notFound=true
23 Cheney and energy task force: Michael C. Ruppert, *Crossing the Rubicon* (Gabriola Island, Canada: New Society Publishers, 2004)
23 Flying bin Ladens: Jane Mayer, "The House Of Bin Laden," *New Yorker* (Nov. 12, 2001)
24 Bin Ladens flown from US: Craig Unger, "Saving the Saudis," *Vanity Fair* (Oct. 2003)
24 Tom Kinton: Cited in Ibid.
24 Bob Graham on smoking gun letter: www.nytimes.com/2004/09/08/politics/08graham.html?_r=1
25 Craig Unger on White House handling of bin Ladens: Unger, op. cit.

26 Unnamed intelligence source: Jon Rappoport, "Briefing on Al Qaeda," *StratiaWire* (Sept. 5, 2002)

26 Accused 9/11 hijackers turned up alive: Editors, "Hijack suspects alive and well," BBC News (Sept. 23, 2001)

26 Saeed al-Ghamdi: Cited in Ibid.

27 Al Qaeda an illusion: articles.latimes.com/2005/jan/11/opinion/oe-scheer11

28 Al Qaeda as CIA database: www.guardian.co.uk/uk/2005/jul/08/july7.development

29 No credible threat to Sears Tower: foxnews.com/story/0,2933,200683,00.html

30 Enemies operate from same ideology: www.commondreams.org/cgibin/print.cgi?file=/views04/1207-26.htm

30 No stone unturned: Editors, "They Saw It Happen," *America at War*, (New York: Personality Profiles Presents, 2001)

31 Saudi Prince al-Faisal: 911review.org/Wiki/HijackersAliveAndWell.shtml

31 Arab names similar: Hanna Rosin, "Some Cry Foul As Authorities Cast a Wide Net," *Washington Post* (Sept. 28, 2001)

31 Kristin Breitweiser: Jim Miklaszewski, "US had 12 warnings of jet attacks," NBC, MSNBC, Associated Press and Reuters (Sept. 18, 2002)

32 Venice Airport, Florida: Daniel Hopsicker, *Welcome to Terrorland*, (Eugene, OR: Madcow Press, 2004)

32 C-130 takes evidence: Ibid.

32 No Arabs on Flight 77: Thomas R. Olsted, M.D., "Autopsy: No Arabs on Flight 77," *SierraTimes.com* (July 6, 2003); www.sierratimes.com/03/07/02/article_tro.htm

33 Hani Hanjour's flight capabilities: www.newsday.com/ny-usflight-232380680sep23.story

34 Pilot Nila Sagadevan on absurdity of official story: www.veteranstoday.com/2010/08/13/nila-sagadevan-911-the-impossibility-offlying-heavy-aircraft-without-training

34 Danielle O'Brien: Griffin, op. cit.

35 Passport found: www.cnn.com/2001/US/09/16/gen.america.under.attack/; "Terrorist Hunt," ABC News (Sept. 12, 2001)

35 Iskandar credit cards miraculously appear: forums.canadiancontent.net/news/41589-more-miraculous-9-11-evidence.html

36 Capt. Jim Ingledue and driver's license: Ibid.

36 Trail left deliberately: Griffin, op. cit.

37 Spc. Peterson's arrest: Noelle Phillips, "Fort Stewart soldier jailed in Florida on $5 million bond," *Savannah Morning News* (May 16, 2002)

37 Foreigners arrested near Georgia power plant: DeAnn Komanecky, "Effingham deputies call feds after arresting Russians with shovel, wire cutters

outside Georgia Power plant," *Savannah Morning News* (Sept. 9, 2010)
38 Emad Salem: Ralph Blumenthal, "Tapes Depict Proposal to Thwart Bomb Used in Trade Center Blast," *New York Times* (Oct. 28, 1993)
38 Sheep-dipped dupes: Webster Griffin Tarpley, *9/11 Synthetic Terror* (Joshua Tree, CA: Progressive Press, 2006)
38 El Sayyid Nosair: Tarpley, op. cit.
39 Flight Data Recorders found: Greg Szymanski, "Black Box Cover-Up," *American Free Press* (Dec. 12, 2004)
39 Terrorists looked for hookers: Editors, "Reports: Hijack Suspects Looked for Hookers in Boston," Reuters (Oct. 10, 2001)
40 Atta and cocaine and Chertoff quote: Hopsicker op. cit.
40 Ari Fleischer: www.foxnews.com/story/0,2933,49226,00.html
41 Abu Zubaydah: Gerald Posner, *Why America Slept*, (New York: Random House, 2003); Johanna McGeary, "Confessions of a Terrorist," *Time* (Sept. 8, 2003)
42 Posner quote: Ibid.
42 Sgt. Ali A. Mohamed: John Sullivan and Joseph Neff, "An Al Qaeda operative at Fort Bragg," *Raleigh News & Observer* (Nov. 13, 2001)
44 Nazi Muslim Brotherhood and al Qaeda: www.canadafreepress.com/2006/loftus101106.htm
46 Jamie McIntyre, Ed Olaugher and Maj. Gen. Albert Stubblebine: www.twf.org/News/Y2005/0307-Pentagon.html
46 Pentagon survivor's story: Author's interview with April Gallop, April 18, 2004
47 Gerald A. Sterns: www.rawstory.com/news/2008/Legal_minds_respond_to_landmark_911_1218.html
47 Judge Denny Chin dismisses Gallop's suit: www.11-septembre.com/docs/GallopJudgment.pdf
48 Liquor store hold-up indictment without mentioning gunman: www.globalresearch.ca/index.php?context=va&aid=24557
48 Bombs in Pentagon: 911review.com/attack/pentagon/witnesses.html
49 $2.3 trillion missing: "The War On Waste," CBS News (Jan. 29, 2002); www.cbsnews.com/stories/2002/01/29/eveningnews/main325985.shtml
49 Accountants, bookkeepers killed in Pentagon: archive.southcoasttoday.com/daily/12-01/12-20-01/a02wn018.htm
49 Navy Command Center destroyed: www.chips.navy.mil/archives/03_spring/webpages/shaeffer.htm
50 Steve Riskus: Thierry Meyssan, editor, *Pentagate*, (London: Carnot Publishing Ltd., 2002)
51 Chris Murray: Griffin, op. cit.
51 Francois Grangier: Meyssan, op. cit.
53 Samuel Danner: Recorded interview on RBNLive's Piper Report, July 10,

2006; www.lookingglassnews.org/viewstory.php?storyid=6836
53 Steve Paterson: www.washingtonpost.com/wp-srv/metro/daily/sep01/attack.html
53 Tom Siebert: www.guardian.co.uk/world/2001/sep/12/expertopinions.charlieporteronmensfashion
53 Mike Walter: willyloman.wordpress.com/2008/06/01/meet-mike-walter-watchhim-lie-about-911
53 Witness Danielle O'Brien: 911review.org/Sept11Wiki/OBrien,Danielle.shtml
54 Rumsfeld's missile quote: www.defense.gov/transcripts/transcript.aspx?TranscriptID=3845
55 Cheney's comments: Secretary Norman Mineta's testimony to the National Commission on the September 11 Terrorist Attacks; www.cooperativeresearch.org/timeline/2003/commissiontestimony052303.html
55 Patently false account of Cheney's whereabouts: David Ray Griffin, *The 9/11 Commission Report*, p. 254
56 NORAD procedural change: DDOD 3025.15, Feb. 18, 1997; CJCSI 3610.01A, June 1, 2001
56 Jerry Russell: www.rumormillnews.com/cgi-bin/forum.cgi?read=46729
57 Dov Zakheim and remote control technology: www.onlinejournal.com/artman/publish/article_1047.shtml
58 WTC steel sold for scrap: Bill Manning, "Selling Out the Investigation," *Fire Engineering* (Jan. 2002)
59 Evidence treated like garbage: Francis Brannigan, "WTC 'Investigation'?: A Call To Action," *Fire Engineering* (Jan. 2002)
59 Corley and Murrah Building: www.fas.org/irp/congress/1998_hr/h980604-corley.htm
60 W. Gene Corley and team complaints: Avery Comarow, "After the fall," *U.S. News & World Report* (May 13, 2002)
60 Only one shrunken filing cabinet: drjudywood.com/articles/DEW/StarWarsBeam3.html
61 National Construction Safety Team report: www.nist.gov/public_affairs/releases/ncst_first_report.htm
63 Critical mysteries: Jim Hoffman, 911research.wtc7.net
63 Jimmy Walter: www.reopen911.org
64 "Inside job": Greg Szymanski, "Bush Insider Claims WTC Collapse Bogus," *American Free Press* (June 27, 2005); www.lewrockwell.com/reynolds/reynolds12.html
64 Jesse Ventura on Building 7: www.prisonplanet.com/articles/april2008/040208_jesse_ventura.htm
65 Dan Rather and Jerome Hauer: winterpatriot.blogspot.com/2007/02/meet-

jeromehauer-911-suspect-awaiting.html
66 Controlled implosions: Olivier Uyttebrouck, "Explosives Planted In Towers, N. M. Tech Expert Says," *Albuquerque Journal* (Sept. 11, 2001)
66 Romero reverses himself: John Fleck, "Fire, Not Extra Explosives, Doomed Buildings, Expert Says," *Albuquerque Journal* (Sept. 21, 2001)
67 Louie Cacchioli: Editors, "New York City," *People.com* (Sept. 12, 2001); people.aol.com/people/special/0,11859,174592-3,00.html
67 Lt. Paul Isaac Jr.: Randy Lavello, "Bombs in the Building: World Trade Center 'Conspiracy Theory' is a Conspiracy Fact," www.prisonplanet.com/analysis_lavello_050503_bombs.html
69 NYFD taped comments on explosions: www.911truth.org/article.php?story=20060118104223192
69 Teresa Veliz and bombs: Dean E. Murphy, "Teresa Veliz: A Prayer to Die Quickly and Painlessly," *September 11: An Oral History* (New York: Doubleday, 2002)
69 Ross Milanytch: *America at War*, op. cit.
69 John Bussey: www.911truth.org/article.php?story=20060118104223192
70 Explosion at base of building: Col. Donn de Grand Pre, "Many Questions Still Remain About Trade Center Attack," *American Free Press* (Feb. 11, 2002)
70 Steve Evans of BBC: Christopher Bollyn, "New York Firefighters' Final Words Fuel Burning Questions about 9-11," *American Free Press* (Aug. 19, 2002)
71 Tom Elliott: Peter Grier, "A Changed World—Part 1: The Attack," *The Christian Science Monitor* (Sept. 17, 2001)
72 Mike Pecoraro: Editors, "We Will Not Forget," *The Chief Engineer* (Feb. 10, 2005)
74 William Rodriguez's account: bellaciao.org/en/article.php3?id_article=6625
74 Rodriguez lawsuit: Pat Shannan, "Trade Towers Hero Files 9-11 Rico Suit," *American Free Press* (Oct. 29, 2004)
75 José Sanchez: Greg Szymanski, "Second WTC Janitor Comes Forward With Eye-Witness Testimony Of 'Bomb-Like' Explosion in North Tower Basement," *ArcticBeacon.com* July 12, 2005.
75 Special Report: Terrorism in the US," *Guardian* (Sept. 12, 2001)
75 CNN videotapes smoke from WTC 6: Christopher Bollyn, "Unexplained 9-11 Explosion at WTC Complex," *American Free Press* (July 22, 2002)
76 Transcripts: www.prisonplanet.com/eye_witness_account_from_new_york.html
77 Firefighters Palmer and Bucca: Bollyn (Aug. 19, 2002), op. cit.
77 Stanley Praimnath. Donovan Cowen and Ling Young: globalresearch.ca.myforums.net/viewtopic.php?t=523
79 Kevin R. Ryan: John Dobberstein, "Area Man stirs debate on WTC collapse: South Bend firm's lab director fired after questioning federal probe," *South Bend Tribune* (Nov. 22, 2004)
79 Peter Tully: Christopher Bollyn, "Seismologists Have Questions About

'Spikes' At Twin Towers," *American Free Press* (Feb. 7, 2005)
79 Loizeaux's speculation: Cited in Ibid.
80 Seismic evidence of two shocks: Christopher Bollyn, "Seismic Data Refutes Official Explanation," *American Free Press* (Sept. 9, 2002)
80 Arthur Lerner-Lam and Eric Hufschmid: Ibid; also Eric Hufschmidt, *Painful Questions* (Goleta, CA: Endpoint Software, 2002)
82 FEMA Study: www.fema.gov/library/wtcstudy.shtm
83 Meridian Plaza fire: Hufschmid, op. cit.
83 Never before: Griffin, op. cit.
84 No collapse observed: FEMA Report (1988) Appendix A
85 Thomas Eager, "clips" and "unzippering": www.worldnewsstand.net/2001/towers/trusseseager.html
85 Hollow shaft: Editors of the National Commission on Terrorist Attacks Upon the United States, *The 9/11 Commission Report* (New York: W. W. Norton & Company, 2004), p. 541, note 1
85 Enormous lie about WTC steel: David Ray Griffin, *The 9/11 Commission Report: Omissions and Distortions* (Northampton, MA: Olive Branch Press, 2005), p. 28
86 Ben Fountain and drills: 911research.wtc7.net/cache/sept11/people_benfountain.html
86 Scott Forbes and strangers in WTC: vids.myspace.com/index.cfm?fuseaction=vids.individual&videoid=3434567
87 Securacom and Bush: www.utne.com/web_special/web_specials_2003-02/articles/10292-1.html
87 Characteristics of explosives: www.ae911truth.org
89 *The Open Chemical Physics Journal* paper: www.scribd.com/doc/27132177/The-Open-Chemical-Physics-Journal-2009-2
90 Marie-Paule Pileni's response: 911blogger.com/node/19963
90 Niels Harrit on unchanged conclusions: Ibid.
91 Jonathan Cole's eutectic experiement: www.ae911truth.org/news/41-articles/321-ae911truth-engineer-does-for-free-what-nist-couldnt-for-millions.html
92 Dr. Peter Leitner: www.house.gov/jec/hearings/dualuse/leitner.htm
93 Patricia Ondrovic: killtown.blogspot.com/2006/02/911-rescuer-saw-explosionsinside-wtc.html
94 Robert Ruiz: graphics8.nytimes.com/packages/pdf/nyregion/20050812_WTC_GRAPHIC/9110333.PDF
94 EM pulses: nomoregames.net/index.php?page=911&subpage1=trouble_with_jones#Overview
95 Retaining wall undamaged: www.nytimes.com/2001/10/09/science/physical/09WALL.html?ex=1160625600&en=050e6f1940a42699&ei=5070
95 A million tons of material: drjudywood.com/articles/DEW/StarWarsBeam1.html

96 Scorched and melted vehicles: drjudywood.com/articles/DEW/StarWars-Beam5.html
96 T. Mark Hightower on unknown technologies: Victor Thorn, "Were 'Mini-Nukes' Used to Bring Down WTC?" *American Free Press* (Sept. 20 & 27, 2010)
96 Charred parking meters: Joel Meyerowitz, *Aftermath* (New York: Phaidon Press Limited, 2006)
96 Robert Larocco: graphics8.nytimes.com/packages/pdf/nyregion/20050812_WTC_GRAPHIC/9110081.PDF
97 Shirley Hoofard: Author's interview Feb. 2005
98 James Gourley's critique: www.journalof911studies.com/letters/b/scientific-critique-of-judy-woods-paper-star-wars-beam-weapons-by-james-gourley.pdf
98 Cancers at the Pile: www.villagevoice.com/2006-11-21/news/death-by-dust
99 Christine Todd Whitman and Kristen Lombardi: Ibid.
99 Gary White and John Devlin: www.prisonplanet.com/9-years-later-nearly-900-911-responders-have-died-survivors-fight-for-compensation.html
99 Elevated levels of tritium at the WTC: escholarship.org/uc/item/4xq88667
100 Dr. Ed Ward and nukes: www.thepriceofliberty.org/06/09/25/ward.htm
100 Mayor Giuliani warned: www.prisonplanet.com/eye_witness_account_from_new_york.html; physics911.org/net/modules/wfsection/article.php?articleid=15
101 Zarrillo's account: World Trade Center Task Force interview with Richard Zarrillo, Oct. 25, 2001, File No. 9110161
102 A few tiny fires: Hufschmid, op. cit.
103 Craig Bartmer on 'booms' in Building 7: www.prisonplanet.com/articles/february2007/100207heardbombs.htm
103 Thomas Sullivan on controlled demolitions: www.ae911truth.org/news/41-articles/315-explosive-evidence-at-wtc-cited-by-former-cdi-employee.html
104 Barry Jennings and Building 7: www.prisonplanet.com/barry-jennings-uncut.html
104 Larry Silverstein; Editors, "America Rebuilds," PBS-TV (Sept. 2002)
105 Jeffrey Scott Shapiro: www.foxnews.com/opinion/2010/04/22/jeffrey-scott-shapirojesse-venture-book-lies-truthers-ground-zero-sept-shame
106 Kurt Sonnenfeld's harassment: www.voltairenet.org/article160636.html
109 Kurt Sonnenfeld's descriptions at Ground Zero: Ibid.
109 BBC's Jane Standley and still standing Building 7: www.wtc7.net/bbc.html
110 FEMA's 2002 conclusions on Building 7: www.fema.gov/pdf/library/fema403_ch8.pdf
110 NIST 2008 Report: wtc.nist.gov/media/NIST_NCSTAR_1A_for_public_comment.pdf
111 Thomas Sullivan on small waves of explosions: www.ae911truth.org/news/41-articles/315-explosive-evidence-at-wtc-cited-by-former-cdi-employee.html

111 Dwain Deets on outrageous reasoning: www.opednews.com/articles/Why-Progressives-Should-Pr-by-Dwain-Deets-100723-333.html
112 $30 billion: Editors, "The Road to Sept. 11," *Newsweek* (Oct. 1, 2001)
112 Kenneth Katzman: www.washingtonpost.com/wo-dyn/articles/A14120-2001Sep11.html
112 State Dept. Warning: Phillip Matier and Andrew Ross, "State Department Memo Warned of Terrorist Threat," *San Francisco Chronicle* (Sept. 14, 2001)
113 Snider resigns from joint committee: Tabassum Zakaria, "Head of Congressional Probe Into September 11 Quits," Reuters (April 29, 2002)
113 Sen. Richard Shelby: Miklaszewski, op. cit.
113 Sen. Bob Graham: Ibid.
113 McCain co-sponsors inquiry: Lisa Stein, "Private Eye," Top of the Week, *U.S. News & World Report* (Oct. 7, 2002)
114 Small teams of investigators: Greg Miller, "Tactics Impede Investigation," *Los Angeles Times* (May 4, 2002)
114 FBI investigates leaks: Christopher Newton, "FBI Asks Lawmakers to Take Lie Detector Test in September 11 Leak Investigation," Associated Press (Aug. 2, 2002)
115 Attack seen as inevitable: John Dougherty, "Panel: Attack on US 'Inevitable'," *WorldNetDaily* (Sept. 21, 2001)
115 Terrorists trained to crash airliners: Yossef Bodansky, *Target America: Terrorism in the US Today* (New York: Shapolsky Publishers, 1993)
116 Italian wiretaps: Sebastian Rotella and Josh Meyer, "Wiretaps May Have Foretold Terror Attacks," *Los Angeles Times* (May 29, 2002)
116 Spanish wiretaps: Ibid.
116 Prime Minister warned: Michael Evans, "Spy Chiefs Warned Ministers of al Qaeda Attacks," *Times* (June 14, 2002)
116 Cayman Islands warning: Chris Hansen, "Warning Signs," *MSNBC* (Sept. 23, 2001)
117 Taliban warning: Kate Clark, "Revealed: The Taliban minister, the US envoy and the warning of September 11 that was ignored," *Independent* (Sept. 7, 2002); news.independent.co.uk./world/politics/story.jsp?story=331115
117 Manila warning: Editors, "Flashback: Airliner terror plan was code-named 'Project Bojinka,'" *WorldTribune.com* (Sept. 25, 2001)
118 Air France Flight 8969: Matthew L. Wald, "Earlier Hijackings Offered Signals That Were Missed," *New York Times* (Oct. 3, 2001)
118 Philippine warnings: Dorian Zumel Sicat, "Abu's long-standing ties to global terrorism bared," *Manila Times* (Feb. 15, 2002)
118 Terry Nichols and terrorists: Dorian Zumel Sicat, "RP cops aware of long-term rightwing, Muslim connection," *Manila Times* (April 26, 2002); www.manilatimes.net/national/2002/apr/26/top_stories/20020426top6.html

118 Chinese manual: www.NewsMaxstore.com/nms/showdetl. cfm?&DID=6&Product_ID=886&CATID=9&GroupID=12
119 China enters WTO: www.cnn.com/2001/WORLD/asiapcf/central/11/10/china.WTO
119 US-China Trade disputes grow: www.economyincrisis.org/content/us-china-trade-disputes-continue-mount
120 Dr. Tatyana Koryagina: www.newsmax.com/archives/articles/201/10/3/212706.shtml
120 Egyptian warning: Patrick E. Tyler and Neil MacFarquhar, "Egypt Warned US of a Qaeda Plot, Mubarak Asserts," *New York Times* (June 4, 2002)
121 Atwan warning: Editors, "Expert: Bin Laden Warned of 'Unprecedented' US Attack," Reuters, (Sept. 11, 2001)
121 Arab MBC channel: Editors, "US Airlines May Be a Terror Risk Over Next Three Days," *Airjet Airline World News* (June 23, 2001)
122 Letter to *New York Times*: judiciary.senate.gov/oldsite/childers.htm
123 Internet domain names: Jeff Johnson, "Internet Domain Names May Have Warned of Attacks," *Cybercast News Service* (Sept.19, 2001); www.middleeastwire.com/atlarge/stories/20010919_3_meno.shtml
123 Editor Russ Kick and school kids: Russ Kick, "September 11, 2001: No Surprise," *Everything You Know Is Wrong* (New York: The Disinformation Company, 2002)
124 Willie Brown's warning: Phillip Matier and Andrew Ross, "Willie Brown got low-key early warning about air travel," *San Francisco Chronicle* (Sept. 12, 2001)
124 Pentagon officials won't fly: Evan Thomas and Mark Hosenball, "Bush: 'We're At War'," *Newsweek* (Sept. 24, 2001)
124 Ashcroft uses charter jets: Jim Stewart, "Ashcroft Flying High," CBS News (July 26, 2001)
125 David Welna report: www.thememoryhole.org/tenet-9-11.htm
125 Dean Haglung on writers of "Twin Towers": www.youtube.com/watch?v=rUFfkueTgoU&feature=related
125 Rumsfeld lays off blame: www.defenselink.mil/news/Nov2001/t11182001_t1012pm.html
127 Carnivore and FBI memos: Editors, "FBI 'Carnivore' glitch hurt al Qaeda probe," Reuters (May 29, 2002). www.cnn.com/2002/US/05/28/attack.carnivore.reut/index.html
127 John O'Neill as most committed tracker: Lawrence Wright, "The Counter Terrorist," *New Yorker* (Jan. 14, 2002)
127 Richard A. Clarke: Ibid.
129 A major attack coming: Ibid.
129 FBI negligence: Wes Vernon, "Agent: FBI Could Have Prevented 9-11,"

*NewsMax.com* (May 31, 2002)

130 Mission jeopardized: Vernon, op. cit.

130 Phoenix suspicions: Editors, "FBI Agent Warned of Suspicious Flight Students Last Summer," Fox News (May 3, 2002)

130 Agent Williams' memo: Richard Behar, "FBI's 'Phoenix' Memo Unmasked," *Fortune.com* (May 22, 2002)

131 Philip Marshall on desert training in Arizona: Marshall, op. cit., p. 36

131 Gary Aldrich: www.newsmax.com/archives/articles/2001/12/28/111159.shtml

131 FBI and Clinton White House: James Risen, "CIA's Inquiry on al Qaeda Aide Seen as Flawed," *New York Times* (Sept. 22, 2002)

131 FBI Agent Ivan C. Smith: Paul Sperry, "Why FBI missed Islamic threat. Agents: Clinton shifted counterterror efforts to fighting 'right-wing' groups," *WorldNetDaily* (July 25, 2002)

131 Commerce Dept. report sanitized: Ibid.

132 FBI Director Robert Mueller: Eric Lichtblau and Josh Meyer, "Terrorist Signs Were Missed, FBI Chief Says," *Los Angeles Times* (May 30, 2002)

133 Randy Glass: John Mintz, "US Reopens Arms Case In Probe of Taliban Role," *Washington Post* (Aug. 2, 2002); Wanda J. DeMaarzo, "Feds reopen probe of Florida arms deal," *Miami Herald* (Aug. 2, 2002)

134 Operation Diamondback: www.opednews.com/duncan_011205_NJ_Terrorism_Michael_Chertoff.htm

134 Indicated the World Trade Center: Mintz and DeMaarzo, op. cit.

135 David Schippers: www.infowars.com/transcript_schippers.html

135 Sibel Edmonds, Andrew Buncombe, "I saw papers that show US knew al Qaeda would attack cities with aeroplanes," *Independent* (April 2, 2004)

137 System in need of repair: www.911citizenswatch.org/print.php?sid=329

138 Sibel Edmonds comments: baltimorechronicle.com/050704SibelEdmonds.shtml; www.breakfornews.com/Sibel-Edmonds.htm

138 Letter to Kean: www.911citizenswatch.org/modules.php?op=modload&name=News&file=article&sid=373

138 Leahy, Grassley letter: www.justacitizen.com/articles_documents/Leahy_Grassley_letter_to_Ashcroft_7-9-04.pdf

139 Ramzi bin al-Shibh in custody: Lisa Stein, "Man of the hour," *U.S. News & World Report* (Sept. 23, 2002)

139 FBI docs in Moussaoui's cell: Lisa Stein, op. cit.

140 Harry Samit: Richard A. Serrano, "Agent Faults FBI on 9/11," *Los Angeles Times* (March 21, 2006)

141 Coleen Rowley: www.counterpunch.org/sperry0613.html; www.apfn.org/apfn/WTC_whistleblower1.htm

142 Rowley testimony defused: Steve Perry, "How All the President's Men Bur-

## SOURCES

ied Coleen Rowley," *CounterPunch* (June 13, 2002)

142 Echelon like vacuum cleaner: Ned Stafford: "Newspaper: Echelon Gave Authorities Warning of Attacks," *Newsbytes.com* (Sept. 13, 2001)

143 French probe Echelon: Warren P. Strobel, "A fine whine from France," *U.S. News & World Report* (July 17, 2000)

143 Osama's big news: Ben Fenton and John Steele, "Bin Laden Told Mother to Expect 'Big News', *Daily Telegraph* (Oct. 2, 2001)

144 Predator strikes: en.wikipedia.org/wiki/RQ-1_Predator

145 Osama as Tim Osman: Mike Blair, "Public Enemy No. 1 Was Guest of Central Intelligence Agency," *American Free Press* (Jan. 7 & 14, 2002)

145 Olberg in Durenberger's office: Ibid.

146 Kahlid al-Midhar and Nawaq Al-Hazni: Risen, op. cit.

147 Khalid Shaikh Mohammed: Ibid.

148 Double agents: Ruppert, op. cit.

148 Mohammed identified before 9/11: Risen, op. cit.

149 Able Danger: www.foxnews.com/story/0,2933,165414,00.html

149 Anthony Shaffer on stunned silence: www.foxnews.com/politics/2010/10/04/exclusive-witnesses-defense-departmentreport-suggest-cover-findings

150 Pentagon tried to buy all books: Scott Shane, "Pentagon Plan: Buying Books to Keep Secrets," *New York Times* (Sept. 9, 2010)

150 Lt. Col. Anthony Shaffer on retaliation: www.nydailynews.com/news/national/2010/09/26/2010-09-26_gi_memoir_gets_trashed_by_pentagon.html

150 FBI tracked Mohamed Atta in Germany: Audrey Gillan, Giles Tremlett, John Hooper, Kate Connolly and Jon Henley, "Dozens detained as net spreads from US to Europe," *Guardian* (Sept. 27, 2001)

151 Osama bin Laden in Dubai: Alexandra Richard, "The CIA met Bin Laden While undergoing treatment at an American Hospital last July in Dubai," *Le Figaro* (Oct. 11, 2001), translation by Tiphaine Dickson; www.globalresearch.ca/articles/RIC111B.html; www.guardian.co.uk/world/2001/nov/01/afghanistan.terrorism

152 CIA team in Afghanistan: Editors, "Newspaper: Afghans tracked bin Laden," In brief, *USA Today* (Dec. 24, 2001)

152 CIA's James Pavitt: www.cia.gov/cia/public_affairs/speeches/pavitt_04262002.html

153 CIA Inspector General's report: Douglas Jehl, "C.I.A. Report Finds Its Officials Failed in Pre-9/11 Efforts," *New York Times* (Jan. 7, 2005)

153 Senior officials warned: Risen, op. cit.

153 Bush warned at Crawford: Michael Hirsh and Michael Isikoff, "What Went Wrong," *Newsweek* (May 27, 2002)

153 President's Daily Brief: *Final Report of the National Commission on Terrorist Attacks Upon the United States*, W.W. Norton & Company Ltd., (New York: 2004)

154 Keen on different circumstances: Editors, "September 11 attacks might have been prevented, inquiry chairman says," *AFP Worldwide* (March 22, 2004): www.afp.com/english/home

154 FAA issued hijack warnings in early 2001: Eric Lichtblau, "9/11 Report Cites Many Warnings About Hijackings," *New York Times* (Feb. 10, 2005)

155 Bush's credibility gap: Hirsh and Isikoff, op. cit.

155 JFK short selling: Jim Marrs, *Crossfire: The Plot That Killed Kennedy* (New York: Carroll & Graf, 1989)

157 Short selling estimates: Kyle F. Hence, "Massive pre-attack 'insider trading' offer authorities hottest trail to accomplices," Centre for Research on Globalisation (April 21, 2002)

157 FBI agents indicted: Alex Berenson, "Five, Including FBI Agents, Are Named in a Conspiracy," *New York Times* (May 23, 2002)

157 Kenneth Breen and Elgindy: Dave Eberhart, "Egyptians Knew of Planned 9-11 Attack Last August," *NewsMax.com* (May 29, 2002)

157 Asst. US Atty. Kenneth Breen: Whitley Strieber, "Is the FBI Penetrated?" *UnknownCountry.com* (May 25, 2002); www.unknowncountry.com/journal/print.phtml?id=95

157 Dylan Ratigan: dissidentvoice.org/Articles7/Wokusch_9-11-Insider-Trade.htm

159 Richard Crossley: James Doran, "Millions of shares sold before disaster," *Times* (Sept. 18, 2001)

159 John Kinnucan on high put-call numbers: web.archive.org/web/20020215082158/http://cjonline.com/stories/091901/ter_tradingacts.shtml

159 Alex Popovic: Marcy Gordon, "SEC Investigating Trading in Shares of 38 Companies; Asks Brokerages to Review Records," Associated Press (Oct. 2, 2001)

159 Harvey Pitt: Ibid.

160 A.B. Brown purchased some put options: web.archive.org/web/20020215082158/http://cjonline.com/stories/091901/ter_tradingacts.shtml

161 Buzzy Krongard, CIA, headed firm buying 'put' options: www.independent.co.uk/news/business/news/mystery-of-terror-insider-dealers-631325.html

161 "Buzzy" Krongard: www.cia.gov/cia/information/krongard.htm

161 Frightening implications: Rupert (2001), op. cit.

161 Mike Ruppert on CIA foreknowledge: globalresearch.ca/articles/RUP111A.html

163 Don Radlauer: Christopher Bollyn, "Revealing 9-11 Stock Trades Could Expose The Terrorist Masterminds," *American Free Press* (May 13, 2002)

163 Walter Burien: www.serendipity.li/wot/burien01.htm

163 Jerry Bremer: Elizabeth Neuffer, "Officials Aware in 1998 of Training," *Boston Globe* (Sept. 15, 2001)

164 No conceivable ties: *The 9/11 Commission Report*, op. cit.

164 David Callahan and the SEC response: www.zerohedge.com/article/

secgovernment-destroyed-documents-regarding-pre-911-put-options
165 Germans say US and Israelis warned: Ned Stafford, "Newspaper: Echelon Gave Authorities Warning of Attacks," *Washington Post,* Newsbytes (Sept. 13, 2001)
166 4,000 Israelis reported missing: Editors, "Thousands of Israelis missing near WTC, Pentagon," *Jerusalem Post* (Sept. 12, 2001)
166 Odigo message warnings: David S. Fallis and Ariana Eunjung Cha, "Agents Following Suspects' Lengthy Electronic Trail Web of Connections Used to Plan Attack," *Washington Post* (Oct. 4, 2001)
167 CEO Micha Macover: Yuval Dror, "Odigo says workers were warned of attack," *Ha'aretz Daily* (Nov. 3, 2001)
167 Zim American Israeli Shipping Co.: Christopher Bollyn, "Who Knew? Israeli Company Mum About WTC Pullout," *American Free Press* (Dec. 10, 2001)
168 Israeli Lobby controversial study: ksgnotes1.harvard.edu/Research/wpaper.nsf/rwp/RWP06-011
168 Israelis film WTC: Editors, "The White Van: Were Israelis Detained on September 11 Spies?" ABC News (June 21, 2002)
168 Maps in car: Paulo Lima, "Five Men Detained As Suspected Conspirators," *Bergen* [New Jersey] *Record* (Sept. 12, 2001)
169 Foreign Counterintelligence Investigation: Marc Perelman, "Spy Rumors Fly on Gusts of Truth," *Forward* (March 15, 2002)
169 Stoffer and Berlet: Ibid.
169 DEA report leaked: Ben Fenton, "US arrests 200 young Israelis in spying investigation," *Telegraph* (July 3, 2002)
169 Guillaume Dasquie: Christopher Bollyn, "120 Spies Deported," *American Free Press* (March 25, 2002)
170 Carl Cameron quotes investigators: Michael Collins Piper, "Israel Knew: Israel Conducts Massive Spying Operation in US," *American Free Press* (Dec. 24, 2001)
170 *Le Monde* on cell phones from vice consul: John F. Sugg, "Israeli Spies Exposed," [Tampa] *Weekly Planet* (April 2, 2002)
170 National Counterintelligence Center warning: Ibid.
170 Military bases and petroleum facilities: Justin Raimondo, 'The 'Urban Myth' Gambit," *Antiwar.com* (March 13, 2002)
171 Served in intel or signal intercepts: Ibid.
171 German paper *Die Zeit*: Rob Broomby, "Report details US 'intelligence failures'" BBC News (Oct. 2, 2002)
171 Ring after Mohamed Atta: news.bbc.co.uk/2/hi/world/europe/2294487.stm
172 Reversed wiretaps: Charles R. Smith, "US Police and Intelligence Hit by Spy Network," *NewsMax.com* (Dec. 19, 2001); www.newsmax.com/archives/articles/2001/12/18/224826.shtml
173 Pipes and conspiracy theories: Daniel Pipes, "An Israeli spy network in the

United States?" *Jewish World Review* (March 11, 2002)
173 Career suicide: Raimondo, op. cit.
173 Lisa Dean and Brad Jansen: Smith (Dec. 19, 2001), op. cit.
174 IASPS "Clean Break" paper: www.israeleconomy.org/strat1.htm
175 Hersh called terrorist: transcripts.cnn.com/TRANSCRIPTS/0303/09/le.00.html
176 Gen. Hameed Gul: Michael Collins Piper, "Former Pakistani Intelligence Chief Alleges Rogue Spook Agencies Behind Terror Attacks," *American Free Press* (Dec. 5, 2001)
177 Werthebach and von Bülow: Christopher Bollyn, "European Spooks Say Mideast Terrorists Needed State Support," *American Free Press* (Dec. 24, 2001)
177 Mossad has capability: "US troops would enforce peace under Army study," *Washington Times* (Sept. 10, 2001)
178 Chossudovsky on Pakistani link to 9/11: www.globalresearch.ca/articles/CH0111A
179 Global Hawk in Afghanistan: Editors, "Operational debut for Global Hawk," *Jane's Aerospace* (Oct. 8, 2001); www.janes.com/serospace/military/news/misc/globalhawk_ppv.shtml
180 Global Hawk made history: www.dsto.defence.gov.au/globalhawk/releases/parlsec18801.html
180 First flight: News Release, "Global Hawk Completes First Flight," United States Department of Defense (March 2, 1998); www.defenselink.mil/news/Mar1998/b03021998_bt091-98.html
180 Andreas Von Bülow: Joe Vialls, "'Home Run' Electronically Hijacking the World Trade Center Attack Aircraft," www.sweetliberty.org/issues/war/homerun.htm
181 Joe Vialls: Ibid.
182 Robert Ayling on remote controlled aircraft: www.publicaction.com/911/economist-autopilot
182 NFERS white paper: www.kinetx.com
184 Carol A. Valentine: www.serendipity.li/wot/valentine.htm
184 Data showed cockpit door never opened: pilotsfor911truth.org/forum/index.php?showtopic=18405
185 Hijackers flying skills: "Hijackers Suspects Tried Many Flight Schools," *Washington Post* (Sept. 19, 2001)
185 Alhazmi and Al-Mahar: "San Diegans See Area as Likely Target," *Washington Post* (Sept. 24, 2001)
186 Transponder explanation: Vialls, op. cit.
186 The biggest known threat: Ibid.
187 Mark Gaffeny on flying Pentagon: www.rense.com/general76/missing.htm
188 E-4Bs and Global Guardian: Joe Dejka, "Inside StratCom on September 11 Offutt Exercise Took Real-life Twist," *Omaha World Herald* (Feb. 27, 2002)
188 George Tenet on al Qaeda: Ibid.

189 Linda Brookhart and Mark H. Gaffney: www.rense.com/general76/missing.htm
190 Objective is loss of national sovereignty: Col. Donn de Grand Pre, "The Enemy Is Inside The Gates," *American Free Press* (Feb. 11, 2002)
192 Capt. Charle's Burlingame's brother Mark: 911research.wtc7.net/cache/planes/analysis/chic_remembered.html
192 Chad Kinder stated no phones on Boeing 757s: pilotsfor911truth.org
193 Impossible cell calls: Alan Cabal, "Miracles and Wonders," *New York Press* (July 27, 2004)
193 Some calls were cropped: "Cell phones test positive on AA flight," *USA Today* (July 16, 2004)
193 Barbara Olson tells of boxcutters: archives.cnn.com/2001/US/09/11/pentagon.olson
194 Ted Olson defends prevarication: portland.indymedia.org/en/2004/12/305124.shtml
196 Justice Depart. Briefing and Hamilton Peterson: www.cnn.com/2004/US/Northeast/06/04/911.calls/index.htm
197 Police sergeant leads jury through 9/11 calls: Richard A. Serrano, "9/11 phone drama replayed at Moussaoui sentencing trial," *Los Angeles Times* (April 12, 2006)
197 Tom Burnett declines to speak to his children: David Ray Griffin, *The New Pearl Harbor Revisited* (Northhampton, MA: Oliver Branch Press, 2008)
198 Mike Sweeney learns of tape in 2004: www.observer.com/node/49415
199 Lyz Glick and Dan Zegart, "Flight 93: What I Never Knew," *Readers Digest* (Sept. 2004)
199 Flight 93 still airborne after crash time: pilotsfor911truth.org/united-93-stillairborne.html
200 Glen Cramer: John Carlin, "Unanswered Questions—The Mystery of Flight 93," *Independent* (Aug. 13, 2002)
201 Cheney acknowledges shoot-down order: Editors, "Cheney Says Military Was Ordered To Shoot Down Planes," *Online NewsHour*, PBS (Sept. 16, 2001)
201 Paul Wolfowitz: Ibid.
201 Rumsfeld's remark: worldnetdaily.com/news/article.asp?ARTICLE_ID=42130
202 Hutchinson story not true: Farmer, op. cit.
202 Aggressive public relations effort: www.nytimes.com/2008/09/14/opinion/14farmer.html?pagewanted=1&_r=1
203 Bill Wright: Carlin, op. cit.
204 John King on no people: www.youtube.com/watch?v=UaBOpA2zMh4&NR=1
204 Wally Miller: pilotsfor911truth.org/forum/index.php?showtopic=14096
205 Commission's "desperate attempt": David Ray Griffin, *The 9/11 Commission Report*, see chapter fifteen.
206 Elaine Scarry: Emily Eakin, "Professor Scarry Has a Theory," *New York*

*Times Magazine* (Nov. 19, 2000)
206 Witnesses tell of white jet: www.dailymail.co.uk/news/article-401315/
   Flight-93-shot-claims-book.html#ixzz0y81qRRua
207 Mayor Michael R. White on Flight 93 at Cleveland: web.archive.org/
   web/20040604001502/www.wcpo.com/specials/2001/americaattacked/
   news_local/story14.html
208 Liz Foremand the the AP story: James Renner, "Plan 9/11 From Cyberspace: The Body Snatchers of United 93 and Other Tales of Terror From
   Cleveland," *Cleveland Free Press* (Vol. 14, Issue 20, Sept. 6, 2006)
208 Personnel in FAA 'working on it': Farmer, op. cit.
208 Flaws by design: Ibid.
210 Delta 1989 passenger's account: 256.com/gray/thoughts/2001/20010912/
   delta_flight_1989_9_11/travel.shtml
210 Vernon "Bill" Wessel and NASA aircraft: Ibid.
212 Col. Alan Scott and Delta 89: www.9-11commission.gov/archive/
   hearing2/9-11Commission_Hearing_2003-05-23.htm
212 Why so long to deregister United aircraft: www.rense.com/general68/911h.htm
212 BTS data missing for Flights 11 and 77: Ibid.
213 Website tells of doppelganger: www.prisonplanet.com/articles/january200
   5/250105darkdoppelganger.htm
214 Northwoods documents: "Report by the Department of Defense and Joint
   Chiefs of Staff Representative on the Caribbean Survey Group to the Joint
   Chiefs of Staff on Cuba Project," (March 9, 1962)
216 Phil Jaylan's 9/11 computer program hypothesis: letsrollforums.com/911-
   alteredhypothesis-plane-t16607.html
216 Greg Szymanski: www.rense.com/general68/says.htm
218 St. Paul: *The Holy Bible*, 1 Thessalonians 5:20–21 (Living Bible edition)
218 Severely monitored scientific experiment: Ronald M. McRae, *Mind Wars:
   The True Story of Government Research into the Military Potential of Psychic
   Weapons*, (New York: St. Martin's Press, 1984)
222 Eric Margolis on 9/11 Commission as a whitewash: www.ericmargolis.
   com/political_commentaries/--the-mother-of-allcoincidences.aspx
222 Lee Hamilton on commission set to fail: www.youtube.com/
   watch?v=fEkMnbpXKQs
224 Karen U. Kwiatkowski and plan to invade Afghanistan: David Ray Griffin and Peter Dale Scott, editors, *9/11 and the American Empire: Intellectuals
   Speak Out* (Northhampton, MA: Olive Branch Press, 2007)
226 Zelikow equivalent to Cheney or Bush: David Ray Griffin, *The 9/11 Commission
   Report: Omissions and Distortions* (Northampton, MA: Olive Branch Press, 2005)
226 Zelikow wrote military strategy document: Excerpted from the transcript of Grif-

fin's public lecture delivered March 30, 2006 at Oakland's Grand Lake Theater. Zelikow's authorship of this document is reported in James Mann's *Rise of the Vulcans*

227 The Transforming Event: Ashton B. Carter, John Deutch, and Philip Zelikow, "Catastrophic Terrorism: Tackling the New Danger," *Foreign Affairs* 77, no. 6 (Nov./Dec. 1998)

227 Christopher Bollyn on architectural document: winterpatriot.blogspot.com/2008/02/inside-account-to-detail-zelikows.html

228 Kissinger's quote and involvement in Chile: Christopher Hitchens, "Regarding Henry Kissinger: A panel discussion on the making of a war criminal," National Press Club (Feb. 22, 2001)

228 Kissinger resigns: Editors, "Kissinger resigns as head of 9/11 commission," CNN (Dec. 15, 2002); cnn.com/2002/ALLPOLITICS/12/13/kissinger.resigns

230 Lee Hamilton on unexplained gaps: James Renner, "Plan 9/11 From Cyberspace: The Body Snatchers of United 93 and Other Tales of Terror From Cleveland," *Cleveland Free Press*, Vol. 14, Issue 20 (Sept. 6, 2006)

232 Bush and complaining commission: Editors, "Chairman says commission needs more time," NBC, MSNBC and news services, (Feb. 13, 2004)

232 Max Cleland on compromised commission: www.democracynow.org/2004/3/23/the_white_house_has_played_cover

232 Max Cleland: Greg Pierce, Inside Politics, "9-11 Former Sen. Max Cleland Now Export-Import Bank," *Washington Times* (Nov. 25, 2003)

232 John Farmer on being shocked at untruths: www.washingtonpost.com/wp-dyn/content/article/2006/08/01/AR2006080101300.html

233 Kean and Hamilton on CIA obstruction: www.nytimes.com/2008/01/02/opinion/02kean.html?_r=1&ref=opinion

233 Cacchioli before staffers: Greg Szymanski, "NY Fireman Lou Cacchioli Upset that 9/11 Commission 'Tried to Twist My Words'" *ArcticBeacon.com*, (July 19, 2005)

233 Rodriguez discounted: Greg Szymanski, "WTC Basement Blast and Injured Burn Victim Blows 'Official 9/11 Story' Sky High," *ArcticBeacon.com* (June 24, 2005)

234 Permitted president to lie: *Benjamin DeMott*, "Whitewash as Public Service: How *The 9/11 Commission Report* defrauds the nation, *Harper's Magazine* (Oct. 2004)

234 Ashcroft's testimony was deceptive: Center for American Progress daily report, April 12, 2003; www.americanprogress.org

234 Ashcroft erroneously claims funds for counterterrorism: slate.msn.com/id/2098783

235 Ben-Veniste easy on Ashcroft: www.911commission.gov/hearings/hearing10/staff_statement_9.pdf

235 Clarke's claims Bush administration failed to act: www.irregulartimes.com/clarke.html

235 Highly classified program to monitor al Qaeda dropped: Editors, "In the Months Before 9/11, Justice Department Curtailed Highly Classified Pro-

gram to Monitor Al Qaeda Suspects in the US," *Newsweek* (March 21, 2004)
238 Rice's lies according to Sibel Edmonds: Andrew Buncombe, "I Saw Papers that Show US Knew al-Qa'ida Would Attack Cities With Airplanes," *Independent* (April 2, 2004)
238 Chertoff cousins: Christopher Bollyn, "Chertoff's Cousin Crafted Smear of 9-11 Researchers," *American Free Press* (March 7–14, 2005)
239 Four tactics: Joel Skousen, "Debunking the Debunkers," *World Affairs Brief* (Feb. 14, 2005); www.worldaffairsbrief.com
239 Skousen: Ibid.
239 *PM* train wreck of disinformation: Jeremy Baker, "Contrary to Popular (Mechanics') Belief," *Global Outlook*, Issue 10, p. 14 (Spring–Summer 2005)
240 Commission failed dismally: Nafeez Mosaddeq Ahmed, "The War on Truth," (Northampton, MA: Olive Branch Press, 2005)
240 Griffin's conclusions: Griffin, 2005, op. cit.
243 Sen. Mark Dayton on NORAD lies: www.911truth.org/article.php?story=20040731213239607
244 Cover up of high crimes: 911review.com/articles/griffin/commissionlies.html

## PART II – WAR FOR OIL AND DRUGS

247 Weekly report: James P. Tucker, Jr., "White House Whitewash: No Justice for Pearl Brass," *American Free Press* (July 8, 2002)
247 Tucker's statement: Ibid.
248 Loans to Russia: G. Edward Griffin, *The Creature from Jekyll Island* (Westlake Village, CA: American Media, 1994)
248 Kuwait "atrocities": Tom Regan, "When contemplating war, beware of babies in incubators," *Christian Science Monitor* (Sept. 6, 2002)
249 Real reason for Gulf War never known: Jonathan Vankin and John Whalen, *Fifty Greatest Conspiracies of All Time* (New York: Citadel Press, 1995)
249 Occupy a hostile land: George Bush and Brent Scowcroft, *A World Transformed*, (New York: Alfred A. Knopf, 1998)
250 Combat troops change names: Kate Brannen, "Combat brigades in Iraq under different name," *Army Times* (Aug. 21, 2010)
251 CENTGAS: Editors, BBC News, (May 13, 2002); news.bbc.co.uk/1/hi/business/1984459.stm
252 Khalilzad supports Taliban: Joe Stephens and David B. Ottaway, "Afghan Roots Keep Adviser Firmly in the Inner Circle," *Washington Post* (Nov. 23, 2001)
252 Khalilzad played important part: Mike Fox, "Bush Appoints Afghan Envoy," BBC News (Jan. 1, 2002)

253 French authors quote O'Neill: www.rense.com/general17/deal.htm.
253 US aligns with Russians: S. Frederick Starr, "Afghanistan Land Mine," *Washington Post* (Dec. 19, 2000)
254 Pakistani Naik warned: news.bbc.co.uk/1/hi/business/1984459.stm (May 13, 2002)
255 Brzezinski's admission: Bill Blum, translator; Zbigniew Brzezinski interview, *Le Nouvel Observateur*, (Jan. 15–21, 1998)
255 External threat needed for consensus: Zbigniew Brzezinski, *The Grand Chessboard: American Primacy and its Geostatic Imperatives* (New York: Basic Books, 1997); www.foreignaffairs.org/19971101fabook3692/zbigniew-brzezinski/the-grand-chessboard-american-primacy-and-its-geostrategic-imperatives.html
256 Pre-attack meeting: Jonathan Steele, Ewen MacAskill, Richard Norton-Taylor and Ed Harriman, "Threats of US strikes passed to Taliban weeks before NY attack," *Guardian*, Sept. 22, 2001
257 Naik and American representatives: Ibid.
259 Bombs destroy music cache: Laura Flanders, "'Arab CNN' First Berated, then Bombed by US," *WorkingForChange.com* (Nov. 14, 2001)
259 Colonel Brian Hoey: Jay Tolson, "World Disorder?" *U.S. News & World Report* (Oct. 21, 2002)
259 Bombing a PR fiasco: www.zmag.org/flandersarabcnn.htm
259 Gore Vidal's statement on Bush's plea for no investigation: Marc Cooper, "The Last Defender of the American Republic?" *LA Weekly* (July 5–11, 2002)
261 North Korean nuke news withheld: Paul Bedard, "Going Nuclear," Washington Whispers, *U.S. News & World Report* (Oct. 28, 2002)
261 Sen. Robert Byrd: Paul J. Nyden, "Bush's War Plans are a Cover-Up, Byrd Says," *West Virginia Gazette* (Sept. 21, 2002)
261 Richard Clarke on Bush wanting Iraqi connection: www.pbs.org/newshour/bb/terrorism/jan-june04/clarke_03-22.html
262 Rumsfeld notes: Editors, "Rumsfeld Wanted to Hit Iraq Hours After 9-11!" *NewsMax* (Sept. 8, 2002); www.newsmax.com/archive
262 Bush on IAEA report: Joseph Curl, "Agency disavows report on Iraq arms," *Washington Times* (Oct. 1, 2002)
262 IAEA denies reports: Ibid.
262 1998 IAEA report: Ibid.
263 Scott Ritter and Bruce Auster quotes: Bruce B. Auster, "Inspecting the Inspectors," *U.S. News & World Report* (Jan. 18, 1999)
264 Powell's UN report: Williams Rivers Pitt, "Blair-Powell UN Report Written by Student," *Truthout* (Feb. 7, 2003); truthout.org/docs_02/020803A.htm
264 Powell's cry: www.thenation.com/doc/20030922/alterman
265 Lawrence Wilkerson: www.pbs.org/now/politics/wilkerson.html
266 Two Democrats argue against war: Editors, "Democrat Congressman Accus-

es Bush of Lying to Provoke War!" *NewsMax.com* and UPI (Sept. 30, 2002)
266 Lott remark: www.cnn.com/2002/ALLPOLITICS/09/29/iraq.debate
266 Clinton's remarks: Editors, "Clinton: Get Bin Laden Before Pursuing Saddam," Associated Press (Sept. 5, 2002)
267 Constitution no longer relevant: www.rense.com/general32/longer.htm
268 McKinney's remarks: Rep. Cynthia McKinney, "We Come For Peace," *Truthout* (April 20, 2002); www.truthout.org/docs_02/04.24A.McKinney.Peace.htm
269 Grassy knoll in Roswell: Editors, "McKinney implied Bush knew of September 11 plot," *Atlanta Journal-Constitution* (April 12, 2002)
269 Irate columnist: Kathleen Parker, "McKinney's minions march to a different drummer indeed," *Orlando Sentinel* (April 21, 2002)
269 Cynthia McKinney's retort: www.globalresearch.ca/articles/WOO207A.html
270 Bush and the Saudi prince: Patricia Wilson, "Bush Celebrates Saudi Ties Before Meeting Envoy," Reuters (Aug. 27, 2002)
270 Rand analyst: Ibid.
271 Newspaper poll showed 47 percent believed officials knew of attacks: Michael Davidson, "Kill the Messenger," *From The Wilderness* (May 6, 2002)
271 Zogby International poll: www.911truth.org/article.php?story=20040830120349841
272 Downing Street Memo: www.timesonline.co.uk/printFriendly/0,,1-523-1593607-523,00.html
272 Thomas and Beck comments: www.csmonitor.com/2005/0517/dailyUpdate.html
273 Philippe Sands and memo: politics.guardian.co.uk/print/0,,5390333-111381,00.html
274 Joseph Biden and Gen. Ray Odierno on blows to al Qaeda: www.washingtonpost.com/wpdyn/content/article/2010/04/19/AR2010041901693.html?hpid%3Dtopnews&sub=AR
274 Brig. Gen. Kevin Bergner on ficticious Abu Omar al-Baghdadi: www.reuters.com/article/idUSL1820065720070718?rpc=92
274 Abu Ayub al Masri killed in 2007: www.foxnews.com/story/0,2933,269556,00.html
274 James Hider on several death reports: James Hider, "Iraq Al-Qaeda boss Abu Omar al-Baghdadi 'is captured'" *Times* (April 24, 2009)
275 Steve Watson on smoke and mirrors: www.prisonplanet.com/al-qaeda-chief-iniraq-captured-killed-never-actually-existed-re-captured-now-killed-again.html
275 Worldwide poll: Ewen MacAskill, "Worldwide Poll Shows 60% Fear Terror Threat Is Worse after War," *Guardian* (Feb. 28, 2006)
276 Zogby and CBS polls: Demetri Sevastopulo and Edward Alden, "Most Troops Want Swift US Pull-Out from Iraq," *Financial Times* (Feb. 28, 2006)
276 Iraqi statistics: See detailed numbers at www.brookings.edu/saban/iraqindex.aspx
277 $5,000 a second and Nicholas D. Kristof: www.nytimes.com/2008/03/23/opinion/23kristof.html?_r=2&th=&adxnnl=1&oref=slogin&emc=th&adx

nnlx=1281898841-Cw9UWdiu1VjHkd2FMh3XZg

277 $3.8 billion welfare hog: Knut Royce and Nathanial Heller, "Cheney Led Halliburton To Feast at Federal Trough," Investigative Report, *Center for Public Integrity* (Aug. 2, 2000)

278 Cheney making policy: Kenneth T. Walsh, "Cheney: Out of the bunker," *U.S. News & World Report* (March 25, 2002)

278 Kellogg Brown & Root: Jeff Gerth and Don Van Natta Jr., "In Tough Times, a Company Finds Profits in Terror War," *New York Times* (July 13, 2002)

279 Halliburton misdeeds: Editors, "Cheney accused of corporate fraud," BBC News (July 10, 2002); news.bbc.co.uk/1/hi/world/americas/2119981.stm

280 Raad Alkadiri: Carola Hoyos, "A discreet way of doing business with Iraq," *Financial Times* (Nov. 3, 2000)

280 Carola Hoyos: Ibid; www.truthout.org/docs_01/02.23D.Cheney.Circumvented.htm

280 Judicial Watch suit against Cheney, Halliburton: Editors, "Cheney, Halliburton face suit," *CNN Money* (July 10, 2002); money.cnn.com/2002/07/10/news/cheney_lawsuit

281 GAO pressured: Peter brand and Alexander Bolton, "GOP threats halted GAO Cheney suit," *The Hill* (Feb. 19, 2003)

281 SEC probes Halliburton: Editors, "Suit accuses Cheney, firm of fraudulent accounting," *CNN.com* (July 11, 2002); www.cnn.com/2002/LAW/07/10/cheney.suit

281 Bunnatine Greenhouse: www.truthout.org/docs_05/011905D.shtml

282 Altanmia fuel deal: www.corpwatch.org/article.php?id=11664

283 Kickbacks and Laszlo Tibold: www.corpwatch.org/article.php?id=11664

283 Halliburton and Iran: Jason Leopold, "Halliburton Secretly Doing Business With Key Member of Iran's Nuclear Team," *CommonDreams.org* (Aug. 6, 2005); www.commondreams.org/cgi-bin/print.cgi?file=/views05/0806-21.htm

283 Halliburton gains contract to build American camps: houston.bizjournals.com/houston/stories/2006/01/23/daily27.html

284 Halliburton would not release cement samples: www.bp.com/liveassets/bp_internet/globalbp/globalbp_uk_english/incident_response/STAGING/local_assets/downloads_pdfs/Deepwater_Horizon_Accident_Investigation_Report.pdf

285 Iraqi column showed foreknowledge: Larry Neumeister, "Lawsuit: Iraq Knew of 9/11 Attacks," Associated Press (Sept. 4, 2002)

285 Iraqis brought to US: Craig Roberts, *The Medusa File*, (Tulsa, OK: Consolidated Press International, 1997); Craig Roberts, "The Bombing of the Alfred P. Murrah Federal Building," Tulsa Police Department report (Sept. 4, 1996)

287 Four reasons for foreknowledge: Rep. Charles Key, "Rep. Charles Key on the Facts of the Oklahoma Bombing," mailed letter, (March 12, 1997)

288 Jayna Davis had evidence rejected: Editors, "Oklahoma City blast linked to bin Laden," *WorldNetDaily.com* (March 21, 2001)

289 Philippine plot: David Hoffman, *The Oklahoma City Bombing and the Politics of Terror* (Los Angeles, CA: Feral House, 1998)
289 Motel witnesses: Jim Crogan, "The Terrorist Motel: The I-40 connection between Zacarias Moussaoui and Mohamed Atta," *LA Weekly* (July 29, 2002)
290 Crogan's comments: Ibid.
290 McVeigh had Iraqi phone numbers: Paul Bedard, "Washington Whispers," *U.S. News & World Report* (Oct. 29, 2001)
291 Pew Poll with Council on Foreign Relations: www.cfr.org/publication/5051/most_americans_support_war_with_iraq_shows_new_pew-cfr_poll_commentary_by_lee_feinstein.html
291 Pew Research poll in 2008: pewresearch.org/pubs/770/iraq-war-five-year-anniversary
292 Artifacts in Iraq: Editors, "Artifacts Uncovered in Iraq," ABC News (Dec. 28, 1999)
293 Loss of antiquities: McGuire Gibson, "The loss of archeological context and the illegal trade in Mesopotamian antiquities," *Culture without Context* (Issue 1, Autumn 1997)
294 Pentagon alerted to museum importance: Andrew Curry, "History's Loss," *U.S. News & World Report* (April 28, 2003)
294 Looters had keys to vaults: Jocelyn Gecker, "Experts: Looters Had Keys to Iraq Museum," Associated Press (April 17, 2003)
294 Glass cutters: Christopher Bollyn, "Iraqis Robbed," *American Free Press* (April 21, 2003)
294 Robert Fisk: Ibid.
294 Martin E. Sullivan: Gecker, op. cit.
296 Robertson quotes Bush: www.cnn.com/2004/ALLPOLITICS/10/19/robertson.bush.iraq
296 Combat units renamed: www.armytimes.com/news/2010/08/dn-brigades-stayunder-different-name-081910
297 Eric Margolis on exaggerated al Qaeda threat: Margolis, op. cit.
298 Drug money absorbed into economy: www.guardian.co.uk/global/2009/dec/13/drug-money-banks-saved-un-cfief-claims
300 Taliban destroyed poppy crop: www.whitehousedrugpolicy.gov/publications/international/factsht/heroin.html
300 White House report: www.msnbc.msn.com/id/7090585
300 US Ambassador William Wood on poppy growth: Editors, "Afghanistan to break poppy growing record," *Jerusalem Post* (July 17, 2007)
300 Primary mission is combat: Philip Shishkin and David Crawford, "In Afghanistan, heroin trade soars despite US aid," *Wall Street Journal* (Jan. 18, 2006)
301 US abandoning drug crop destruction and sending agronomists: www.navytimes.com/news/2009/07/ap_afghanistan_poppies_071009

301 NATO troops stopped from eradicating crops: www.nytimes. com/2010/03/21/world/asia/21marja.html?_r=1
302 Opium trading by Boston families: Steven Sora, *Secret Societies of America's Elite* (Destiny Books: 2003)
302 Tom Carew: www.sabawoon.com/articles.asp?id=132&view=detail
303 Pat Tillman shot execution style: Pat Shannan, "September 11, Pat Tillman And the Afghanistan Debacle," *American Free Press* (Sept. 20 & 27, 2010)
303 Richard Clark on Pat Tillman asking too many questions: www.opednews. com/articles/Was-Pat-Tillman-murdered-b-by-Richard-Clark-100625-47.html
304 DEA "sting": Daniel Hopsicker, *Barry & 'the boys': The CIA, The Mob and America's Secret History* (Noti, OR: Mad Cow Press, 2001)
306 Halliburton and Russian drug smuggling: www.apfn.org/enron/halliburton.htm
309 Osama bin Laden background: Anonymous source, translated document provided to *Frontline*, PBS; www.angelfire.com/home/pearly/hjtmis1/osama-bio.html
311 President Clinton's address: Transcript of President Clinton's Oval Office remarks on anti-terrorist attacks, US Information Agency (Aug. 20, 1998)
311 Osama bin Laden background: Anonymous source, translated document provided to *Frontline*, op. cit.
312 *Ummat* interview with bin Laden: www.americanfreepress.net/10_22_01/al Qaeda_Not_Involved__Says_bi/al Qaeda_not_involved__says_bi.html
312 Bin Laden blames US Government for blame: articles.cnn.com/2001-09-16/us/inv.binladen.denial_1_bin-laden-taliban-supreme-leader-mullah-mohammedomar?_s=PM:US
312 Bush disregards bin Laden denial: Ibid.
313 Mother claims tape doctored: Editors, "Bin Laden's mother says video 'doctored'," In Brief, *USA Today* (Dec. 24, 2001)
314 German experts rip videotape: Christopher Bollyn, "Bin Laden Tape Dupes Public, Say Experts," *American Free Press* (Jan. 4–14, 2001)
314 Eric Margolis said bin Laden not the man in the tapes: Margolis, op. cit.
315 Wayne Madsen quote: www.thetruthseeker.co.uk/article.asp?ID=4075
316 BBC and tape: Matthew Davis, "Bin Laden threats may boost Bush," BBC News, (Jan. 20, 2006)
316 CIA admits faking bin Laden tapes: Jeff Stein, "CIA unit's wacky idea: Depict Saddam as gay," *Washington Post* (May 25, 2010)
316 Paul R. Pillar and modest purpose of tapes: blog.washingtonpost.com/spytalk/2010/03/osama_tape_has_intelligence_of.html
316 Fox News reports bin Laden death in 2001: www.foxnews.com/story/0,2933,41576,00.html
317 Madeleine Albright in 2003 on bin Laden's death: www.newsmax.com/archives/ic/2003/12/17/15126.shtml

317 CIA Officer Robert Baer on bin Laden's death: www.youtube.com/watch?v=Njp0XYO6EDw
318 Dr. Steve Pieczenik on bin Laden's death: www.prisonplanet.com/jones_report_042402_pieczenik.html
319 Osama bin Laden used to mobilize emotions: Ibid.
320 Bin Laden death photo a fake: www.boston.com/news/politics/articles/2011/05/05/senator_scott_brown_duped_by_bin_laden_photo
320 Obama and Clinton view mansion attack: www.dailymail.co.uk/news/article-1382859/Osama-bin-Laden-dead-Photo-Obama-watching-Al-Qaeda-leader-die-live-TV.html#ixzz1MT3uL7cL
320 Leon Panetta on 25-minute blackout: www.pbs.org/newshour/bb/terrorism/janjune11/panetta_05-03.html
320 Jason Reed on Obama's stage talk: www.ibtimes.com/articles/141463/20110504/obama-s-bin-laden-speech-photostaged.htm#ixzz1MT7DKjDY
321 FBI center warns of computer viruses: www.tulsaworld.com/business/article.aspx?subjectid=52&articleid=20110503_52_0_hrimgs864598
322 Republicans suppress Saudi information: pub12.ezboard.com/fnuclearweaponsnuclearweaponsforum.showMessage?topicID=282.topic
323 Motley suit: Tony Bartelme, "September 11 Suit Wins First Major Legal Battle," *Post and Courier* (Aug. 7, 2003)
324 Saudi princes immune: www.whitecase.com/alert_litigation_0908
325 9/11 Citizen's Complaint: releases.usnewswire.com/GetRelease.asp?id=39128
326 Deborah Jeane Palfrey: www.youtube.com/watch?v=tzvrgQ5hOM4
326 Sen. Bob Graham: Linda Robinson, "What's In The Report?" *U.S. News & World Report* (Aug. 11, 2003)
327 Saudi government sponsored charities fund al Qaeda: Editors of the National Commission on Terrorist Attacks Upon the United States, *The 9/11 Commission Report* (New York: W. W. Norton & Company, 2004), pp. 170–71
327 Saudi oil production tripled: Michael Field, "Good for business," *Financial Times* (Feb. 21, 1991)
327 CFR report on Saudis: George Gedda, "Report: Saudi Charities Back al-Qaida," Associated Press (Oct. 17, 2002); story.news.yahoo.com/news?tmpl=story2&cid=513&u=/ap/20021017/ap_on_go_ot/us_saudi_terror_
328 John Loftus explanation: www.john-loftus.com/press_release.asp
329 FBI Agent Steven Butler and the Saudis: Gloria Borger, Edward T. Pound and Linda Robinson, "The Road to Riyadh," *U.S. News & World Report* (Dec. 9, 2002)
329 Saudi bank connected to JP Morgan and Bank of America: Martin Mbugua, "Saudi Bank Tied To Terror Has US Banks," *Daily News* (Nov. 10, 2001)
329 Jeff Hershberger: Ibid.

## SOURCES

329 Salem bin Laden in Texas: Mike Ward, "Bin Laden relatives have ties to Texas," *Austin American-Statesman* (Nov. 9, 2001)

330 Close ties between bin Ladens and Bushes: Ibid.

331 James Bath: Ibid; Jonathan Beaty and S. C. Gwynne, *The Outlaw Bank: A Wild Ride into the Secret Heart of the BCCI* (New York: Random House, 1993); *American Free Press* (Oct. 15, 2001)

331 Ashcroft denies access: Ward, op. cit.

331 Bath's connection to Saudi bank: Pete Brewton, "The Mafia, CIA and George Bush," (New York: S.P.I.Books/Shapolsky Publishers, Inc. 1992)

331 Mahfouz and BCCI: J. H. Hatfield, *Fortunate Son: George W. Bush and the Making of an American President* (New York: St. Martin's Press, 1999)

333 Bill White: Beaty and Gwynne, op. cit.

333 Main Bank: Ibid.

333 John Mecklin's estimates: newsandviews9.tripod.com/news/timeline.html

334 Harken low-interest loans to Bush: Editors, "Bush Received Company Loans He Now Wants Banned," Reuters (July 11, 2002)

334 1990 Bahrain agreement for bases: Russell S. Bowen, *The Immaculate Deception* (Carson City, NV: America West Publishers, 1991)

335 Harken stock sale: Bowen, op. cit.

336 George H. W. Bush and Carlyle Group: Michael Ruppert, "Must Read: The Best Enemies Money Can Buy," *Guerilla News Network* (Oct. 11, 2001); www.guerrillanews.com/newswire/164.html

337 Bush and Prince Bandar: Unger, op. cit.

337 Larry Klayman of Judicial Watch: www.judicialwatch.org/archive/2001/863.shtml

337 Big pile of money: Ruppert, op. cit.

338 Two documents: Interviews, "Has someone been sitting on the FBI?" *News Night*, BBC News (June 11, 2002)

338 Constraints on investigating Saudis: Greg Palast, "FBI and US Spy Agents Say Bush Spiked Bin Laden Probes Before 11 September," *Guardian* (Nov. 7, 2001)

338 Al-Rajhi banking family: John Mintz and Tom Jackman, "Finances Prompted Raids on Muslims; US Suspected Terrorism Ties to N. Va. For Years," *Washington Post* (March 24, 2002)

339 Grover Norquist: Duncan Campbell, "FBI Raids pro-Republicans," *Guardian* (March 25, 2002)

339 Abdullah Noman: Associated Press, "Official Took Bribes for US Visas," *New York Times* (May 21, 2002)

339 Michael Springman: www.gregpalast.com/detail.cfm?artid=104&row=1

## PART III – THE 9/11 BACKLASH

342 Bush and Los Angeles plot: Deb Riechmann, "Bush Says Cooperation Thwarted 2002 Attack," Associated Press (Feb. 9, 2006)

342 Los Angeles Mayor: Michael R. Blood, "L.A. Mayor Blindsided by Bush Announcement," Associated Press (Feb. 9, 2006)

343 Doug Thompson's blog: www.capitolhillblue.com/blog/2006/02/intel_pros_say_bush_is_lying_a.html

343 Not leadership but fear-mongering: Jonah Goldberg, "Obama's fear-mongering," *Los Angeles Times* (March 10, 2009)

343 Steve Verdon on fear mongering: www.outsidethebeltway.com/obama_the_fear_monger

344 Michael Chertoff represents body scanners: www.pbs.org/ombudsman/2010/01/scanning_the_source_1.html

345 Kate Hanni critizes Chertoff: www.boston.com/news/nation/washington/articles/2010/01/02/group_slams_chertoff_on_scanner_promotion

345 Ben Wallace on scanners not picking up plastic, chemicals and liquids: www.independent.co.uk/news/uk/home-news/are-planned-airport-scanners-just-ascam-1856175.html

345 Boian Alexandrov and team on DNA damage: arxiv.org/abs/0910.5294

346 Office of Transport Security manager Cheryl Johnson: www.prisonplanet.com/admitted-airport-body-scanners-provide-crisp-image-ofyour-genitals.html

346 Marc Rotenberg on potential for misuse of scanning machines: cnn.org/2010/TRAVEL/01/11/body.scanners/index.html

347 Marshals Service and Rotenberg: news.cnet.com/8301-31921_3-20012583-281.html

347 Powell's comments: Frank Bruni, "Bush Taps Cheney to Study Antiterrorism Steps," *New York Times* (May 8, 2001)

348 Unnamed intelligence source: Jon Rappoport, "Briefing on Al Qaeda," *StratiaWire* (Sept. 5, 2002)

348 Al Qaeda as CIA database: Robin Cook, "The struggle against terrorism cannot be won by military means," *Guardian* (July 8, 2005)

349 Same ideology: Thom Hartmann, "Hyping Terror for Fun, Profit and Power, www.commondreams.org/cgi-bin/print.cgi?file=/views04/1207-26.htm

349 Model State Emergency Health Powers Act: Mimi Hall, "Many states reject bioterrorism law," *USA Today* (July 23, 2002)

350 FEMA plans tent cities: John O. Edwards, "FEMA Preparing for Mass Destruction Attacks on Cities," *NewsMax.com* (July 15, 2002)

351 History of repression in emergencies: Pamela Sebastian Ridge and Milo Geyelin, "Civil Liberties of Ordinary Americans May Erode—Legally—Because of Attacks," *New York Times* (Sept. 17, 2001)

351 Frank Serpico booed: Editors, "Serpico decries anti-terrorism measures,"

Associated Press (July 6, 2002)
351 Janet Reno's remarks: Jim Burns, "William Bennett Hopes to Shape Public Opinion of War on Terrorism," *Cybercast News Service* (March 12, 2002); www.snsnews.com/ViewPolitics.asp?Page=\Politics\archive\200203\POL20020312
352 Guantanamo prisoner information released: "US Discloses Names of 558 at Guantanamo," Associated Press (April 20, 2006)
353 Red Cross accuses US of torture: Neil A. Lewis, "Red Cross Finds Detainee Abuse in Guantánamo," *New York Times* (Nov. 30, 2004)
353 Sen. Patrick Leahy: Matthew Purdy, "Bush's New Rules to Fight Terror Transform the Legal Landscape," *New York Times* (Nov. 25, 2001)
353 Durbin's comments: www.senate.gov/~durbin/gitmo.cfm
356 Military as panacea for domestic problems: Matthew Carlton Hammond, "The Posse Comitatus Act: A Principle in Need of Renewal," *Washington University Law Quarterly*, (summer, 1997)
356 WWII vet Fred Hubbell arrested: Paul Marks, "Texan Learns to Rue Remark," *Hartford Courant* (Aug. 3, 2002)
356 GI Joe disarmed: Editors, "Soldier toy disarmed at airport," BBC News (Aug. 5, 2002)
357 Attack on Kingsville: David M. Bresnahan, "What happened in Kingsville, Texas, Monday night?" *World Net Daily* (Feb. 10, 1999)
358 Britt Snider and Garden Plot: Ron Ridenhour with Arthur Lubow, "Bringing the War Home," *New Times* (Nov. 28, 1975)
359 Marines in Indianapolis: www.infowars.com/fbi-homeland-security-behindmartial-law-exercises-in-indianapolis
359 Operation Diomedes: www.clarksvilleonline.com/2009/09/23/101st-airbornesoldiers-to-conduct-air-assault-training-into-troy-tn
359 Cable Splicer and reactions: Ridenhour with Lubow, op. cit.
360 New under secretary of defense for intelligence: Linda Robinson, "Moves that matter," *U.S. News & World Report* (Aug. 12, 2002)
360 Stephen A. Cambone: rightweb.irc-online.org/profile/1066
361 SSB and Stephen Cambone: www.cnn.com/2005/ALLPOLITICS/01/23/pentagon.intel
362 Strategic Support Branch's secret growth: Barton Gellman, "Secret Unit Expands Rumsfeld's Domain," *Washington Post* (Jan. 23, 2005)
362 Office of Strategic Influence closed: Editors, "US closes 'disinformation' unit," BBC News (Feb. 26, 2002)
362 Rumsfeld vows to continue disinformation: foi.missouri.edu/osi/osiisgone.html
363 $200 million to create dossiers: William Safire, "You Are a Suspect," *New York Times* (Nov.14, 2002)
364 Army plan to spy on Americans: Christopher H. Pyle, "Be afraid, be very

afraid, of spying by the US Army," *Hartford Courant* (Dec. 5, 2002)
365 Detention camps: Author's interview with retired Lt. Col. Craig Roberts, Sept. 22, 2009
367 John Brinkerhoff: www.homelandsecurity.org/journal/Articles/brinkerhoffposseecomitatus.htm
367 Bush's urgent need: news.bbc.co.uk/2/hi/americas/2031255.stm
367 Real losers are American people: Editors, "Sen. Lashes Out Over Ridge No-Show," Associated Press (April 30, 2002)
370 Statements in support of Homeland Security: Tom Ridge, written statement to the House Select Committee on Homeland Security (July 15, 2002)
370 DHS contractors outnumber federal employees: www.govexec.com/dailyfed/0210/022410e1.htm
370 Steven Aftergood on wall between government and public: Spencer S. Hsu, "Homeland Security Employees Required to Sign Secrecy Pladge," *Washington Post* (Nov. 16, 2004)
371 Clark Kent Ervin on dysfunction at DHS: abclocal.go.com/wls/story?section=news/national_world&id=5017688
371 Gregory Despres: www.outsidethebeltway.com/archives/2005/06/man_with_bloody_chain_saw_let_in_to_us_
372 Bills to stop laptop seaches at the border: Editors, "Congress must act to end electrtonic fishing expeditions at the border," *Los Angeles Times* (Sept. 13, 2010)
374 DHS Domestic Extremism Lexicon: www.webcitation.org/5gYPnOstE
376 ALIPAC, SPLC and MIAC: www.alipac.us/article4073.html
376 Hate crime numbers worthless: www.splcenter.org/intel/intelreport/article.jsp?aid=157
377 PA Homeland Security chief resigns: Brad Bumsted, "Pennsylvania Homeland Security chief quits," *Pittsburgh Tribune-Review* (Oct. 2, 2010)
378 Fusion center abuse, Rep. Lon Burnam and Bill Braumbach: Peter Gorman, "Fusing Fear and Data: A North Texas law-enforcement data-gathering center has some folks worried," *Fort Worth Weekly* (Aug. 25, 2010)
379 Oliver North's martial law plan: Alfonso Chardy, "Plan called for martial law in US," Knight-Ridder News Service (July 5, 1987)
379 EDxectuive Order 13489: www.presidency.ucsb.edu/ws/index.php?pid=76782
379 John Dean's concern: Ritt Goldstein, "Foundations Are In Place For Martial Law In The US," *Sydney Morning Herald* (July 27, 2002)
382 ACLU objections to Homeland Security: Timothy H. Edgar, Testimony before the House Select Committee on Homeland Security and others (June 25-28, 2002)
382 Sen. Joseph Lieberman: www.cnn.com/2002/ALLPOLITICS/11/25/homeland.security
383 Timothy Sparapani: Walter Pincus and Dan Eggen, "325,000 Names on

# SOURCES

Terrorism List," *Washington Post* (Feb. 15, 2006)
383 David D. Cole: Ibid.
383 Alberto R. Gonzales: Ibid.
383 Sen. Kennedy on list: Sara Kehaulani Goo, "Sen. Kennedy Flagged by No-Fly List," *Washington Post* (Aug. 20, 2004)
384 Reginald T. Shuford and David C. Fathi: Ibid.
384 Library incident: Cameron W. Barr, "Policing Porn is Not Part of Job Description," *Washington Post* (Feb. 17, 2006)
385 Dr. Robert Johnson: www.thenation.com/blogs/thebeat?pid=63406
385 Vietnam veteran writes: Jeffrey St. Clair and Alexander Cockburn, "Tom Ridge in Vietnam: Tarnished Star," *CounterPunch* (Oct. 1, 2001)
386 The Phoenix Program: Douglas Valentine, "US Terrorist Attacks: Homeland Insecurity," *Disinformation* (Oct. 9, 2001); www.disinfo.com/archive/pages/article/id1631/pg1/index.html
387 Open letter to Gen. Lawlor: Douglas Valentine, "Flight Of The Phoenix—From Vietnam To Homeland Security," *CounterPunch* (Aug. 25, 2002); www.counterpunch.org/valentine0824.html
388 Richard Armitage: Ibid.
389 Armitage major participant in narcotics: James "Bo" Gritz, *A Nation Betrayed* (Sandy Valley, NV: Bo Gritz, 1988)
390 Post office incident: Matthew Rothschild, "The New McCarthyism," *The Progressive* (Jan. 2002)
391 Operation TIPS: Citizen Corps website; www.citizencorps.gov/tips.html.
391 Cuba's Committees for the Defense of the Revolution: Isabel Garcia-Zarza, "Big Brother at 40: Cuba's revolutionary neighborhood watch system," Reuters (Oct. 12, 2000)
391 ACLU opposition to TIPS: Randolph E. Schmidt, "Postal Service Won't Join TIPS Program," Associated Press (July 17, 2002)
391 John Whitehead: Ellen Sorokin, "Bush Wants Letter Carriers, Meter Readers As Informants," *Washington Times* (July 16, 2002)
392 TIPS website changes: Editors, "Website for Operation TIPS Quietly Changes," The Memory Hole; www.thememoryhole.org/policestate/tips-changes.htm
392 Neighborhood Watch: Darragh Johnson and David A. Fahrenthold, "Watching the Homeland," *Washington Post* (March 8, 2002)
393 Mike German and iWatch program: www.usatoday.com/news/topstories/2009-10-03-197785316_x.htm
393 Informants pay, regulation and AFF: Dennis G. Fitzgerald, *Informants and Undercover Investigations: A Practical Guide to Law, Policy, and Procedure* (Boca Raton, FL: CRC Press, 2007)
394 A.J. Brown and the Secret Service: Rothschild, op. cit.

395 Dwight Scarbrough and bumper stickers: Matthew Rothschild, "Homeland Security Hassles Owner of Truck with Bumperstickers," *The Progressive* (Feb. 22, 2006)
395 Joe the comedian arrested by Homeland Security: Ralph Forbes, "Watch What You Post on 'Facebook'", *American Free Press* (Sept. 20 & 27, 2010)
396 Military recruiters denied, Rep. Vitter and Jill Wynns: David Goodman, "No Child Unrecruited," *Mother Jones* (Nov.–Dec. 2002)
397 Katie Sierra, Robert Jensen, Dan Guthrie and Tom Gutting: findarticles.com/p/articles/mi_m1141/is_1_38/ai_79965737
397 Richard Allen Humphreys: Robert Wilson, "Man Convicted of Threatening President Bush in Sioux Falls," *KSFY, Dakota First News* (Oct. 22, 2002)
398 Denver photographer Mike Maginnis: Editors, "Photographer Arrested For Taking Pictures Near Cheney Hotel," *2600 News* (Dec. 5, 2002)
398 Kindergartners disciplined: Editors, "'Gun-toting' tot loses suspension suit," Associated Press (May 1, 2002)
398 Ellen Schrecker and Nadine Strossen: Ibid.
400 Paul Craig Roberts: www.infowars.com/it-is-official-the-us-is-a-police-state
400 US Attorney Peter Smith on no privacy in public: www.wired.com/threatlevel/2010/09/public-privacy/#ixzz10OcxiGlS
400 Snooping is Un-American: Paul Proctor, "The War on Freedom," *News With Views* (July 17, 2002); www.newswithviews.com/war_on_terror/war_on_terrorism1.htm
401 Rep. Dennis Kucinich: Eli Pariser, editor, "Can Democracy Survive An Endless 'War'?" *MoveOn Bulletin* (July 18, 2002); www.moveon.org/moveonbulletin
401 Rep. Ron Paul: Kelly Patricia O'Meara, "Police State," *Insight Magazine* Nov. 9, 2001)
402 Rep. Bernie Sanders: Ibid.
403 ACLU statement: action.aclu.org/reformthepatriotact/whereitstands.html
404 Patriot Act expands FISA: Walter Brasch, "The fiction behind national security," *Online Journal* (July 25, 2002)
404 FISC rejects Ashcroft's guidelines: Ted Bridis, "Special Court Rejects Ashcroft's Rules," Associated Press (Aug. 22, 2002)
404 Internet users warned: Editors, "EFF Analysis of The Provisions of the USA Patriot Act," *Electronic Frontier Foundation* (Oct. 31, 2001); www.eff.org/Privacy/Surveillance/Terrorism_militias/20011031_eff_usa_patriot_analysis.html
405 Patriot Act provisions that cause concern: Editors, "Overview of Changes to Legal Rights," Associated Press (Sept. 5, 2002); www.newsday.com/news/nationworld/wire/sns-ap-sept-11-legal-rights-glance0905sep05.story
406 Global Relief Foundation faces secret evidence: Geoff Dougherty and Laurie Cohen, "US Using New Law on Secret Evidence: Patriot Act invoked to fight lawsuit by Muslim group," *Chicago Tribune* (March 15, 2002)
406 Global attorney Roger Simmons: Ibid.
406 Hany Kiareldeen and Niels Frenzen: Stephen Franklin and Ken Armstrong,

"Secret evidence bill raises concerns," *Chicago Tribune* (Sep. 30, 2001)
407 Dr. Al-Badr Al-Hazmi: Editors, "Saudi doctor returns to San Antonio, denounces terrorist attacks as having 'nothing to do with Islam'" Associated Press (Sept. 25, 2001); James R. Elwood and Jarret B. Wollstein, "Dictatorship At Your Door," *International Society for Individual Liberty* (May 2002); www.isil.org/resources/lit/dictatorship-at-doorstep.html
408 Robert Lee Lewis: Author's interviews, summer 2009
408 Reporter's quote: O'Meara, op. cit.
408 Ron Paul on sneak-and-peek: Ibid.
409 Sen. Frank Church: James Bamford, "The Agency That Could Be Big Brother," *New York Times* (Dec. 25, 2005)
409 Defense documents denied: Liz Halloran, "Everyone's Spinning The Spying," *U.S. News & World Report* (Feb. 13, 2006)
409 Unchecked, abused: Fein, op. cit.
410 Rep. Butch Otter: O'Meara, op. cit.
410 Editorial comment: Editors, "Another Cave-In on the Patriot Act," *New York Times* (Feb. 11, 2006)
411 Rep. Paul on "Know Your Customer": Ron Paul, "Privacy Busters: Big Bank is watching," *Ron Paul Newsletter* (Dec. 1998)
411 Walter Soehnge: Bob Kerr, "Pay too much and you could raise the alarm," *The Providence Journal* (Feb. 28, 2006)
411 ACLU's Nadine Strossen: O'Meara, op. cit.
411 Act used hundreds of times: Mark Mueller, "To catch a monster, using anti-terror law," *Star-Ledger* (Aug. 14, 2005)
412 Strossen's comment: O'Meara, op. cit.
413 Treading the razor's edge: Doreen Miller, "High Treason in the US Government," *YellowTimes.org* (July 4, 2002); www.yellowtimes.org/article.php?sid=444
414 Patriot Act is treason: Karen G. Schneider, "Patriot Act: Last Refuge of a Scoundrel," *American Libraries* (March, 2002); www.ala.org/alonline/netlib/il302.html
414 Arline Johnson: Brasch, op. cit.
414 Act trumps protections in 49 of 50 states: Adam Piore, "USA Patriot Act: Librarians Keep Quiet," *Newsweek* (Oct. 28, 2002)
416 David Goodman and freedom fighters: www.youtube.com/watch?v=LC9wLGNPZH0
416 A chilling effect on constitutional freedoms: Brasch, op. cit.
416 Elwood quote: James R. Elwood and Jarret B. Wollstein, "Dictatorship At Your Door," *International Society for Individual Liberty* (May, 2002)
417 FBI's telephone contracts: Ryan Singel, "FBI Tried to Cover Patriot Act Abuses With Flawed, Retroactive Subpoenas, Audit Finds," *Wired* (March 13, 2008)
417 Unprecedented powers for attorney general: Miller, op. cit.

418 Ashton Lundeby and his mother: www.wral.com/news/local/story/5049867
419 Alexa Gonzalez arrested and handcuffed: www.aolnews.com/2010/04/03/girl-arrested-for-doodling-sues-new-york-city
420 Dr. Debra H. Freeman: www.wlym.com/www.larouchepub.com/other/2001/2803_ashcroft_testimony.html
420 Ashcroft as clear and present threat: www.jewishworldreview.com/jonathan/turley082002.asp
421 Robert Doumar compares case to Star Chamber: www.wsws.org/articles/2004/sep2004/hamd-s30.shtml
422 Bill of Rights shattered: Mike Whitney, "Jose Padilla and the Death of Personal Liberty," *Dissidentvoice.org* (Sept. 11, 2005); www.dissidentvoice.org/Sept05/Whitney0911.htm
423 The Padilla Game: Carl Worden, "The Padilla Test Run," *Free American* (Aug. 2002)
423 That's not the American way: Nat Hentoff, "General Ashcroft's Detention Camps Time to Call for His Resignation," *VillageVoice.com* (Sept. 4–10, 2002)
424 Paul quote: O'Meara, op. cit.
424 Gonzales vs. Geneva Convention: www.americanprogress.org/site/pp.aspx?c=biJRJ8OVF&b=246536&printmode=1
425 Gov. Bush memos: Alan Berlow, "The Texas Clemency Memos," *Atlantic Monthly* (July/Aug. 2003)
425 Bush off jury duty: Joan Biskupic, "He could be the next Supreme Court justice Alberto Gonzales has become a rising star by defending President Bush's conservative policies. He also has alienated key Democrats whose support he would need to be confirmed," *USA Today* (March 18, 2002)
425 Gonzales and energy: www.americanprogress.org/site/pp.aspx?c=biJRJ8OVF&b=246536&printmode=1
426 Eric Holder on disrespect for rule of law: www.boston.com/news/politics/politicalintelligence/2008/11/holder_on_bush.html
428 Janet Napolitano on substitute for Real ID: www.cnn.com/2009/POLITICS/04/22/real.ID.debate
428 NYPD chips: policechiefmagazine.org/magazine/index.cfm?fuseaction=display_arch&article_id=127&issue_id=102003
429 National ID system: Frank Pellegrini, "The National ID Card That Isn't, Yet." *Time.com* (Jan. 8, 2002)
429 The long and short of it: Steven Yates, "'Your Papers, Please': National ID, 2002," *LewRockwell.com* (Oct.12, 2002); www.lewrockwell.com/yates/yates64.html
430 VeriChip: Press releases and website, Applied Digital Solutions, Inc. www.adsx.com/prodservpart/verichip.html.
431 Rep. Jane Harman and "smart card": Dee Ann Davis and Nicholas M. Horrock, "Ridge eyes new driver's licenses," *Washington Times* (May 2, 2002)

## SOURCES

431 D.C. Mayor Anthony Williams: www.dcwatch.com/issues/privacy07.htm
431 Echelon and Tempest: Jim Wilson, "Spying on Us," *Popular Mechanics* (Jan. 2001)
433 New Cyberspace security plan: Ted Bridis, "US Considers Cybersecurity Plan," Associated Press (Sept. 7, 2002)
434 Leslie Harris on cybersecurity threat: www.cdt.org/headlines/1196
434 Larry Selzer on direct control of the President: www.wnd.com/index.php?fa=PAGE.view&pageId=93966
434 Jennifer Granick on loss of privacy: www.motherjones.com/politics/2009/04/should-obama-control-internet
434 Key logger used by FBI: Ted Bridis, "Anti-Terror Tools Include High-Tech, " Associated Press (Oct. 28, 2001)
435 William Newman: Nat Hentoff, "The Sons and Daughters of Liberty," *Village Voice* (June 21, 2002)
435 GPS tracking: Julia Scheeres, "GPS: Keeping Cons Out of Jail," *Wired News* (Oct. 15, 2002); www.wired.com/news/privacy/0,1848,55740,00.html
436 Sheriff Don Eslinger: Ibid.
436 Siemens tracking device: Joe Queenan, "Electronic Leashes for Teenagers," *New York Times* (May 24, 2001)
437 Kevin Bankston on cell phones: www.gpsdaily.com/reports/That_Cell_Phone_In_Your_Hand_Is_A_Tracking_Device_999.html
437 Worst-case scenario: Russ Kick, "Machine Age—Gotcha!" *Village Voice* (Feb. 27, 2001)
438 Obama's unkept campaign promises: Editors, "What promises has Obama kept?" *Baltimore Sun* (Sept. 13, 2010)
438 Sean Reilly, "Open government group gives Obama administration a mixed grade," *Federal Times* (Sept. 7, 2010)
440 CBS News poll on Obama: www.cbsnews.com/htdocs/pdf/poll_obama_040210_7am.pdf?tag=contentMain;contentBody
441 Gen. James L. Jones on taking daily orders from Henry Kissinger: www.cfr.org/publication/18515/remarks_by_national_security_adviser_jones_at_45th_munich_conference_on_security_policy.html
442 Fredrick Palmer: Editors, "Did You Know?" *Sierra Magazine* (Sept.–Oct. 2002)
442 Jennifer Van Bergen: writ.news.findlaw.com/commentary/20060109_bergen.html
443 Obama's signing statements: www.coherentbabble.com/listBHOall.htm
445 Blanton, Claybrook, Nelson and Klayman quotes: Alan Elsner, "Bush Expands Government Secrecy, Arouses Critics," Reuters (Sept. 3, 2002)
445 Gary Bass and Steven Aftergood: Ibid.
446 Cheney inebriated: prisonplanet.com/articles/february2006/220206_b_drunk.htm
446 Zone of privacy: Kenneth T. Walsh, "Playing by His Own Rules," *U.S. News*

& *World Report* (Feb. 27, 2006)
448 Only executive branch represented: Barton Gellman and Susan Schmidt, "Shadow Government Is at Work in Secret," *Washington Post* (March 1, 2002)
448 Daschle comments: Ibid.
449 True conservatives don't act this way: Michael Ventura, "The Shadow of Totalitarianism," *Austin Chronicle* (March 22, 2002)
450 David Friedman (Dafydd Ab Hugh) on shadow government: hotair.com/greenroom/archives/2009/09/07/is-obama-forming-a-shadowgovernment

## PART IV – HISTORICAL PRECEDENTS

453 1968 gun law lifted almost verbatim: www.jpfo.org/GCA_68.htm
453 Douglas Reed's comments: Louis L. Snyder, *Encyclopedia of The Third Reich* (New York: McGraw-Hill Book Company, 1976)
454 Nazis as a great economic power: Paul Manning, *Martin Bormann: Nazi in Exile* (Secaucus, NJ: Lyle Stuart, Inc., 1981)
454 Nazis did not die: Jim Keith, *Casebook on Alternative 3: UFOs, Secret Societies and World Control*, (Lilburn, GA: IllumiNet Press, 1994)
454 Goering's quote: G. M. Gilbert, *Nuremberg Diary* (New York: Signet Books, 1947)
455 Bush like Hitler: John F. Dickerson, "Bush's Furor Over Der Fuhrer," *Time* (Sept. 30, 2002)
456 CFR-One World Money group: Curtis B. Dall, *FDR: My Exploited Father-in-Law* (Washington, D. C.: Action Associates, 1970)
456 Admiral James O. Richardson: Robert Anton Wilson, *Everything Is Under Control: Conspiracies, Cults and Cover-ups* (New York: HarperPerennial, 1998)
456 Japanese war preparations known: Carroll Quigley, *Tragedy and Hope: A History of the World in Our Time* (New York: Macmillan, 1966)
457 Marshall's message: Michael Litchfield, *It's A Conspiracy* (Berkeley, CA: Earth Works Press, 1992)
457 Australian intelligence and Popov reports: Vankin and Whaley, op. cit.
457 Toland's names: Perloff, op. cit.
458 Marshall and Knox in White House: Ibid.
458 Stimson's diary entry: Wilson, op. cit.
459 Germans intercept Roosevelt-Churchill conversation: Gregory Douglas, *Gestapo Chief: The 1948 Interrogation of Heinrich Muller* (San Jose, CA: R. James Bender Publishing, 1995)
459 Warning came on parallel level: Douglas, op. cit.
460 Battle of the New World Order: Jonathan Vankin and John Whalen, *Fifty Greatest Conspiracies of All Time* (New York: Citadel Press, 1995)

461 Glaspie and Saddam's conversation: Russell S. Bowen, *The Immaculate Deception* (Carson City, NV: America West Publishers, 1991); Tarpley and Chaitkin, op. cit.; Jonathan Vankin and John Whalen, *Fifty Greatest Conspiracies of All Time* (New York: Citadel Press, 1995)
462 Glaspie's summer vacation: Webster Griffin Tarpley and Anton Chaitkin, *George Bush: The Unauthorized Biography* (Washington, D.C.: Executive Intelligence Review, 1992)
462 Paul Adler: Warren Hough and Lawrence Wilmot, "Saddam: Bush-Whacked?" *Spotlight* (April 8, 1991)
463 Bobby Lee Cook: Warren Hough, "Iraq Policy No Accident," *Spotlight* (Oct. 5, 1992)
463 Kissinger Associates: Ibid.
463 Barr's impeachment: Mike Blair, "Gonzalez: Impeach Top Cop," *Spotlight* (Sept. 28, 1992)
463 Bush administration repayments: Mike Blair, "You Pay for Bad Loans to Iraq," *Spotlight* (April 27, 1992)
464 Loan guarantees enabled arms buildup: Bowen, op. cit.
464 Bush quote: Tarpley and Chaitkin, op. cit.
464 $4 billion secret payoff: Warren Hough, "Did George Bush Get a Big Payoff?" *Spotlight* (Aug. 30, 1993)
465 "Weapons of mass destruction": Jay Higginbotham, "Letters," *U.S. News & World Report* (Jan. 18, 1999)
466 Elite secret army: William M. Arkin, "The Secret War: Frustrated by intelligence failures, the Defense Department is dramatically expanding its 'black world' of covert operations," *Los Angeles Times* (Oct. 27, 2002)
467 P2OG: David Isenberg, " 'P2OG' allows Pentagon to fight dirty," *Asia Times Online* (Nov. 5, 2002); www.atimes.com/atimes/Middle_East/DI05AK02.html
467 Secret operations launched: Arkin, op. cit.
467 NSC to be in charge: Isenberg, op. cit.
467 An endless night of black ops: Chris Floyd, "Global Eye—Into the Dark," *Moscow Times* (Nov.1, 2002); www.themoscowtimes.com/stories/2002/11/01/120.html
468 CIA as facilitators: www.newyorker.com/archive/2005/01/24/050124fa_fact?printable=true
468 Gen. Smedley D. Butler: www.veteransforpeace.org/war_is_a_racket_033103.htm
469 Iron Mountain quotes: *Report from Iron Mountain on the Possibility and Desirability of Peace*, (New York: The Dial Press, 1967)
470 Iron Mountain Study not fiction: Radio interview transcript of Col. Donn de Grand Pre, "Former Pentagon Official Says 'No-Win Wars' Part of Plan for One World Government," *Spotlight* (April 23, 2001)
471 John McCain on war profiteering: Julian E. Barnes, "Cashing In on the Defense Buildup," *U.S. News & World Report* (May 13, 2002)

472 Rick Santorum: Ibid.
473 Lockheed bribery scandals: Christopher H. Schmitt, "Wages of Sin: Why lawbreakers still win government contracts," *U.S. News & World Report* (May 13, 2002)
473 Rep. Peter DeFazio: Ibid.
474 Fitts on missing trillions: Catherine Austin Fitts, "The Missing Money: Why the Citizens of Tennessee Are Working Harder and Getting Less," www.scoop.co.nz/stories/HL0207/S00031.htm
475 Engineered destruction of the dollar: See solari.com and Catherine Austin Fitts, "A Matter of Life or Death," Foreword to Ruppert's *Crossing the Rubicon*, p. xiii
475 Security and Prosperity Partnership: www.spp.gov; www.whitehouse.gov/news/releases/2005/03/20050323-4.html
475 North American Super Highway: www.nascocorridor.com
476 Concerns over Super Highway: www.imaja.com/as/environment/cars/SuperhighwaysThreatenNA.html
477 Hamilton Peterson learned things: Russ Kick, "Associated Press Story Change: The Flight 93 Tape," *The Memory Hole*; www.thememoryhole.org/911/ap-93tape.htm
478 Rep. Bernie Sanders on media control: baltimorechronicle.com/sanders_jun02.shtml
479 Project Censored Report: Bridget Thornton, Brit Walters, and Lori Rouse, "Corporate Media Is Corporate America"; www.projectcensored.org/newsflash/C2006_chap6.pdf
479 Uncritical passing of officials' opinions: Michael Parenti, *Inventing Reality: The Politics of the Mass Media* (New York: St. Martin's Press, 1986)
479 Brit Hume: Ibid.
480 Steering the ship of state: Martin A. Lee and Norman Solomon, *Unreliable Sources* (New York: Lyle Stuart Books, 1990)
481 CFR media members: *CFR/Trilateral Influence on the Carter/Reagan/Bush/Clinton Administration*, non-copyrighted material from the Fund to Restore an Educated Electorate, Kerrville, TX; obtained from *The United States Government Manual 1991/92*, Office of the Federal Register National Archives and Records Administration; Standard & Poor's *Register of Corporations, Directors and Executives*, 1991; *Annual Report 1991/92*, Council on Foreign Relations, New York City
481 Reed Irvine and AIM: Michael Collins Piper, " 'Watchdog' Won't Bite," *Spotlight* (May 7, 1990)
482 Walter Cronkite, Daniel Schorr and Morley Safer: Bill Kirtz, "Disgust within the ranks," *Quill* (May, 1998)
483 Robert McChesney on fewer professional journalists: www.socialistproject.ca/bullet/246.php
484 Michael H. Price on shallow news reporting: Interview with author, Jan. 28, 2010
484 Ann Bayefsky on the UN Human Rights Council: weeklystandard.com/

Content/Public/Articles/000/000/017/043ytrhc.asp?pg=1
486 Top 25 censored news stories of 200-2010: www.projectcensored.org/top-stories/category/two-thousand-and-ten-book
487 Digg site censorship: blogs.alternet.org/oleoleolson/2010/08/05/massivecensorship-of-digg-uncovered
487 "Invent a new history": Milan Kundera, *The Book of Laughter and Forgetting* (New York: HarperCollins, 1978)
488 Eric Margolis on Islamic terrorism: Margolis, op. cit.
488 Gore Vidal: Jon Vlements, "Gore Vidal: Oil Behind Bush's Afghan Fiasco," *Daily Mirror*, mirror.co.uk (July 10, 2002)
493 Foreign adventurisms listed: Editors, *The New Encyclopedia Britannica* (Chicago: Encyclopedia Britannica, Inc., 15th Edition, 1991)
493 We are hated because of our government: Robert Bowman, "The Security Charade," *National Catholic Reporter* (Oct. 2, 1998)
493 Robert Bowman on 9/11 as a pack of lies: Greg Szymanski, "9-11 Lies Under Fire," *American Free Press*, Sept. 16, 2005. www.americanfreepress.net/html/9-11_lies_under.html
494 Ho Chi Minh as agent: Lloyd Shearer, "When Ho Chi Minh was an Intelligence Agent for the US," *Parade* (March 18, 1973); *New Encyclopedia Britannica*, Vol. 5
495 Greatest myth of contemporary history: G. Edward Griffin, *The Creature from Jekyll Island* (Westlake Village, CA: American Media, 1994)
495 Trotsky and Wall Street: William T. Still, *New World Order: The Ancient Plan of Secret Societies* (Lafayette, LA: Huntington House Publishers, 1990)
495 Jacob Schiff's $20 million: Gary Allen, *None Dare Call It Conspiracy* (Seal Beach, CA: Concord Press, 1971)
495 No fear of communism: Allen, op. cit.
496 Goering's quote: G. M. Gilbert, *Nuremberg Diary* (New York: Signet Books, 1947)
498 The key to understanding world history: Texe Marrs, *Circle of Intrigue* (Austin, TX: Living Truth Publishers, 1995)
498 Another force wishes: Still, op. cit.
499 Mother of all coincidences: Margolis, op. cit.
501 An attack that failed: Philip Marshall, *False Flag 911: How Bush, Cheney and the Saudis Created the Post-911 World* (Murphys, CA: Pilots of 911, 2008), p. 130
505 Barry Jennings' death questioned: edwardrynearson.wordpress.com/2009/04/17/new-information-on-the-death-of-911-eyewitness-barry-jennings
505 Kenneth Johannemann's death: www.nydailynews.com/ny_local/2008/09/03/2008-09-03_911_claims_one_more_victim.html
505 David Graham's death: 911review.org/Media/whistle/Graham_Kahn.html
506 Christopher Landis at Pentagon: Pat Shannan, "Key 9-11 Witnesses Turning Up Dead, Others Scared to Tell What They Saw," *American Free Press* (May 10, 2010)

506 Paul Smith run down by taxi: www.nydailynews.com/news/2007/10/07/2007-10-07_channel_7_chopper_pilot_killed_by_runawa.html

506 Deborah Palfrey and her suicide: www.infowars.com/dc-madam-predicted-she-would-be-suicided

507 Maj. Gen. David F. Wherley's death in train crash: www.yorkblog.com/yorktownsquare/2009/06/-two-york-county-natives.html

507 Salvatore Princiotta's death: Andrew Strickler, "Firefighter, 9/11 responder slain in Ariz. Home," *Newsday* (May 25, 2007)

507 Beverly Eckert dies in plane crash: www.huffingtonpost.com/2009/02/13/planecrashes-into-house_n_166609.html

507 Ezra Harel and Menachem Atzmon: www.thebarrychamishwebsite.com/newsletters/detroit.htm

508 Yale Senior Suzanne Jovin: killtown.blogspot.com/2007/01/yale-students-98-murder-linked-to-911.html

509 Bertha Champagne crushed by car at Bush home: www.fromthewilderness.com/free/ww3/101003_bush_death.html

509 Normal security bypassed: L. Fletcher Prouty, "An Introduction to the Assassination Business," *Gallery* (Sept. 1975)

510 Michael Rivero quote: Robert Sterling, "Dubya Dubya Three—Are Americans The Victims Of A Hoax?" *Konformist* (Oct. 23, 2001)

511 Bush's blood ties: www.guardian.co.uk/uselections2004/story/0,13918,1284632,00.html

513 Great masses of people fall victim to a great lie: Adolf Hitler, *Mein Kampf* (New York: Houghton Mifflin Company, 1940), p. 313

# APPENDIX

## The Pentagon Attack Papers

### Seven Hours in September: The Clock that Broke the Lie

#### Barbara Honegger

The *San Francisco Chronicle* commemorated the 100th anniversary of the Great California 1906 Earthquake with front-page articles featuring a single iconic image—a charred clock frozen in time at 5:12 a.m.—the exact moment that "The Big One" hit.[1] A century after that devastating event, this stopped clock still serves as both the ultimate evidence and the historic icon that "captures it all."

Today, 100 years later, another series of clocks and watches frozen in time at the exact moment of the violent event at the Pentagon on the morning of September 11, 2001, also "capture it all" and serve as the ultimate evidence shattering the official conspiracy theory of what happened there that terrible morning—and who was really responsible.

**The Pentagon was first attacked much earlier than the official conspiracy theory and 9/11 Commission claim—and from the inside, not the outside:**

The Pentagon was first attacked shortly after 9:30 a.m.—almost 8 minutes before the official 'impact' time of 9:37:46, when the official conspiracy theory says a plane hit the building from the outside.

Both DoD and mainstream media first reported 9:43 as the time of alleged Flight 77 impact on the building; some early reports claiming to quote official sources were as late as 9:48). Over time, the time given by Pentagon officials for the claimed outside impact on the building moved earlier and earlier, until it finally 'settled' at about 45 seconds after 9:37 (as of the time of this writing). But the officially given time has never come close to the actual time of the first violent event at the Pentagon—shortly after 9:30 a.m. Clearly, if the official story that Flight 77 hit the Pentagon at almost 9:38 were true, Flight 77 could not have been the source of massive damage to the west wedge of the building which occurred as much as eight minutes earlier.

**Converging lines of evidence of a 9:30-to-9:32:30 a.m. violent event at the Pentagon on September 11, well before the official story says anything hit the building:**

Multiple standard-issue, battery- and/or electric-operated wall clocks on the walls of the area of the Pentagon attacked on 9/11—including one in the heliport just outside the west wedge—were stopped between 9:30 and 9:32-1/2 by at least two violent events, almost certainly bombs inside the building and/or in a truck or construction trailer parked immediately outside the west face. The first Associated Press report, in fact, stated that the Pentagon had been damaged by "a booby trapped truck." The Navy posted a photo of the stopped Pentagon heliport clock on an official website, and another of the building clocks stopped shortly after 9:30 was in the 9/11 display at the Smithsonian Institution.[2] These are just some of the west-section Pentagon clocks stopped between 9:30 and 9:32-1/2 on September 11.

In addition, there is April Gallop's stopped wrist watch.

April Gallop, an Army employee with a Top Secret clearance, was at her desk in the Army administrative offices in the west section of the Pentagon on 9/11, the area of the building most heavily destroyed and with the most casualties, when what she said sounded and felt "like a bomb" went off, soon followed by a second explosion. According to the Pentagon's own after action report, Gallop's desk was approximately 30 feet from the inside trajectory of the alleged plane impact. "Being in the Army with the training I had, I know what a bomb sounds and acts like, especially the aftermath, and it sounded and acted like a bomb," Gallop told the author in an under-oath videotaped interview.[3] "There was no plane or plane parts inside the building, and no smell of jet fuel."

In those two hours of under-oath videotaped testimony, Gallop states that the explosion went off at the *precise instant* that she hit the 'power on' button on her computer in the Army administrative area, to which she had just returned that morning after some months of pregnancy and childbirth leave, and that the first explosion stopped her wrist watch just after 9:30 a.m.[4] She has kept the stopped wrist watch in a safe deposit box as evidence of the exact moment of the initial explosion.

The FAA's [Federal Aviation Administration] timeline document "Executive Summary—Chronology of a Multiple Hijacking Crisis—September 11, 2001" includes the following entry: "0932: ATC [Air Traffic Control] AEA reports aircraft crashes into west side of Pentagon."[5] The earlier-than-official-time is the critical fact here, not the claimed cause which was taken from the official story and not the result of ATC eyewitnesses.

Denmark's soon-to-be Foreign Minister Per Stig Moller was in a building in Washington, D.C. on 9/11 from which he looked out, heard an explosion and saw the smoke first rise from the Pentagon. He immediately looked at his wristwatch, which read 9:32 a.m. He gave radio interviews to Denmark stations the next morning in which he stated that the Pentagon had been attacked at 9:32.[6]

On August 27, 2002, then-White House Counsel and former Attorney General Alberto Gonzales gave an audio-taped Secretary of the Navy Guest Lecture at the Naval Postgraduate School in Monterey, CA, a DoD university, in which he explicitly and clearly states that "The Pentagon was attacked at 9:32." A tape of this segment of Gonzales' talk was played at the 9/11 Emergency Truth Convergence at American University in Washington, D.C. in July 2005, and is on the public record.

**The Pentagon was attacked by explosives between 9:30 and 9:32 a.m., possibly followed by an impact from an airborne object significantly smaller than Flight 77, a Boeing 757.**

We have already seen that Army Pentagon employee April Gallop, whose wristwatch was stopped by the first violent event at the Pentagon shortly after 9:30, says that her military training and experience led her to immediately determine that the source of the initial explosion was a bomb.

I have interviewed an Army auditor from Ft. Monmouth, NJ, who was on temporary duty assignment at the Pentagon before, on and after 9/11. He was in the Army financial management spaces only minutes before the Pentagon explosion on the morning of 9/11. He had just returned to his temporary office on the ground floor of the adjacent south side of the Pentagon by the cafeteria when he heard an explosion and felt the building shake. Immediately afterwards, he said, hundreds of panicked Pentagon personnel ran by him down the corridor just outside his office and out the south entrance, yelling "Bombs!" and "A bomb went off!" The witness has requested that his name not be used in this evidence summary, but is willing to testify to a grand jury or independent official investigation; his name and contact information have been provided to Prof. Griffin as *bona fides* for the "Reports of Bombs" section of the chapter on the Pentagon attack, Chapter 2, in Griffin's book *The New Pearl Harbor Revisited*, as has the two-hour under-oath testimony-interview with April Gallop.

This Army financial management/audit area was part of or contiguous to the Army personnel office, and this general Army administrative area was one of the two west wedge functions most heavily damaged and with the greatest number of fatalities in the Pentagon attack—the other being the Naval Command Center, more of which below. The day before 9/11, on September 10, Secretary of Defense Rumsfeld publicly announced and acknowledged that the Pentagon was "missing"—that it allegedly could not account for and needed to "find"—$2.3 trillion dollars (other reports said $2.6 trillion). Were some of the auditors who could "follow the money," and the computers whose data mining could help them do it, intentionally targeted by the inside-the-building explosions at the Pentagon on Sept. 11? Professor Griffin states that this possibility, first suggested based on publicly known circumstantial evidence by the author, deserves serious investigation in his books. It is worth noting that the Pentagon's top financial officer leading up to and at the time of the attacks, Dov Zakheim, who also acknowledged the "missing" trillions, had a company specializing in aircraft remote-control technology. As a part found in the Pentagon wreckage has been claimed to be the front-hub assembly of the front compressor of a JT8D turbojet engine used in the A-3 Sky Warrior jet fighter,[7] and as Air Force A-3 Sky Warriors—normally piloted planes—were reportedly secretly retrofitted to become remotecontrolled drones and fitted with missiles in a highly-compartmented operation at an airport near Ft. Collins-Loveland Municipal Airport in Colorado in the months before 9/11,[8] the question further arises as to whether Pentagon auditors trying to "follow the money" and their computerized databases were intentionally targeted on 9/11.

Once it is realized that the real story at the Pentagon—as in the WTC in New York City—is inside explosives, the possibility that specific offices, functions or even individuals were targeted to be "taken out" becomes very real, whereas the cover story that a Boeing 757 hit the building leads immediately to the assumption—probably desired by the real perpetrators—that any specific deaths and destruction were random.

The Ft. Monmouth Army auditor and his two colleagues were also eyewitnesses to multiple teams of bomb-sniffing dogs and their K-9 handlers in camouflage uniform at the Pentagon metro station just outside the Pentagon at approximately 7:30 a.m. on 9/11. He said that K-9 bomb squads had not been at the Pentagon metro stop before 9/11, or since, but only that day. Since K-9 dog squads don't usually search for airliners, but bombs, a bomb attack was clearly anticipated. Ms. Gallop said she also saw the bomb sniffing K-9 teams that morning, from the top of the Pentagon Metro stop looking down.

As mentioned above, in addition to the Army administrative area, the second most-destroyed area of the Pentagon on 9/11 was the Naval Command Center (NCC). The official conspiracy theory contained in *The 9/11 Commission Report* and repeated by the mainstream media states that 44 Naval Command Center personnel were physically present in that space on the morning of 9/11, and that 43 of the 44 died. This author, however, was told a very different story by the military officer in charge of the Navy Anti-Terrorism Division in the NCC on the morning of 9/11, Coast Guard Reserve Rear Adm. Jeffrey Hathaway.[9]

After the attack on the USS *Cole* in Aden Harbor in Yemen, Hathaway was put in charge of Navy Anti-Terrorism Force Protection (ATFP) and was temporarily assigned to the NCC before the attacks. Upon hearing that the reported sole survivor of the Naval Command Center on 9/11 was Navy Lt. Kevin Shaeffer, Adm. Hathaway immediately responded that that wasn't the whole story, and that a secret 19-person intelligence cell in a hardened room at the NCC were also present and that all survived the attack. Given that everyone officially present in the Naval Command Center, except for Shaeffer, reportedly died—by far the greatest acknowledged fatalities-per-capita of any section of the Pentagon—the possibility immediately presents itself that this secret intelligence cell or function was intentionally targeted by the internal explosives. The author queried Army Reserve Lt. Col. Anthony Shaffer, author of the expose book *Operation Dark Heart* censored by the Defense Intelligence Agency (DIA) and a key operative in the pre-9/11 Special Operations Command (SOCOM) intelligence cell "Able Danger" that identified two of the three "al Qaeda" cells allegedly responsible for the 9/11 attacks including "ringleader" Mohammed Atta. The new Rumsfeld Pentagon shut down "Able Danger" in late January 2001, immediately after Bush and Cheney took control of the White House.

Shaffer, is no immediate relation to NCC sole official survivor Lt. Kevin Shaeffer, who, following months of surgery and therapy from sustaining 60 percent burns from the attacks went on to be the key staff member on the key 9/11 Commission subgroup on Pentagon/DoD response to the attacks. This subgroup censored not only "Able Danger" issue but the Pentagon inside-the-building explosions as well as NORAD's hijack scenario/counterterrorism exercises being "played" on the morning of 9/11. Asked whether this potentially-targeted NCC intel cell was part of "Able Danger," Shaffer said not to his knowledge, but that he would look into it further.

Survivor eyewitnesses from inside the west section of the Pentagon reported that the blast that morning caused its windows *first* to expand *outwards*, and then inwards.[10]

Multiple witnesses said they smelled cordite after the initial explosion at the Pentagon, an explosive which has a distinct and very different smell from that of burning jet fuel.[11] And as we have already noted, Ms. Gallop said there was no smell of jet fuel inside the most-damaged section of the west wedge, where she worked in the Army administrative area, shortly after the first violent event that stopped her watch there shortly after 9:30.

Even Secretary of Defense Rumsfeld told Sam Donaldson in an ABC News interview shortly after 9/11 that his first thought, being in the building when the initial attack happened, was that a bomb had gone off. Donaldson asked, "What did you think it was?" Rumsfeld replied, "A-bomb?"

It is important to note that bomb explosion(s) between 9:30 and 9:32 a.m. on the first and second floors of the west section of the Pentagon are *not* inconsistent with there having *also* been a later, or even near-simultaneous, impact by some kind of airborne object—a piloted plane, an unmanned drone, or a missile—into the same or nearby section of the building, which may have been the cause of the later collapse of the west wall section approximately 20 minutes after the initial violent event. Indeed, if a heat-seeking missile hit the building *after* the bomb(s) went off, the heat from the earlier explosion(s) would become the *target* for the missile. Recall that A-3 Sky Warrior planes were reportedly retrofitted shortly before 9/11, not only enabling them to be remotely controlled but also fitted with missiles.

This author has interviewed the then-Acting Assistant Secretary of Defense for Special Operations on 9/11 Robert Andrews—the top civilian official in charge of special operations under Secretary of Defense Rumsfeld—a former Green Beret whose office was on the second floor of the south section of the Pentagon, adjacent to the west section. Perhaps significantly, the pre-9/11 "al Qaeda"-tracking and data-mining operation "Able Danger" was a Special Operations Command (SOCOM) operation. While drawing the path that he took that morning on a sketch of the Pentagon, he revealed the following:

Immediately after the second World Trade Center attack of 9:03 a.m., Secretary of Defense Rumsfeld left his office on the Potomac side of the Pentagon and went (merely) across the hall on the same floor to his Executive Support Center (ESC), which is set up for teleconferencing. There, he joined the now-famous teleconference of top government officials run by White House NSC counterterrorism 'czar' Richard Clarke out of the White House Situation Room media room. Clarke, in his book *Against All Enemies*, confirms that Rumsfeld was among the first officials on this teleconference shortly after the second WTC tower was hit. Clarke's account and Andrews' confirmation are thus completely at odds with the official conspiracy theory and *The 9/11 Commission Report*, which claimed that no one could 'find' Secretary Rumsfeld until approximately 10:30 a.m. when he walked into the National Military Command Center (NMCC) in the Pentagon. The fact that Rumsfeld, the military's top civilian official, was on Clarke's teleconference with *the* top official of the Federal Aviation Administration, FAA Director Jane Garvey, also unmasks the total lie of the official cover story that Air Force interceptors weren't scrambled in time "because the military and the FAA couldn't talk each other" on 9/11. *The* topmost officials of the Pentagon and FAA were *talking to one another constantly* and being recorded on Clarke's teleconference from as early as 9:15 a.m. This videotaped Clarke teleconference is "The Butterfield Tape" of 9/11 which, not surprisingly, has never been released to the public. (During the 1970s Watergate scandal, secretly made tapes of President Nixon's Oval Office conversations revealed by Alexander Butterfield were the "smoking guns" which forced Nixon to resign or face certain impeachment by the House and trial in the Senate.)

According to Andrews, immediately after the second WTC tower was struck at 9:03 a.m., he and his aide left his office and ran as fast as they could down to the secretary of defense's west section Counterterrorism Center (CTC), arriving at approximately 9:10 a.m. While they were in the CTC, a violent event caused the ceiling tiles to fall from the ceiling and smoke to pour into the room. Andrews immediately looked at his watch, which read approximately 9:35 a.m. but which was set fast to ensure timely arrival at meetings, so the actual time was closer to 9:32. He and his aide then immediately evacuated the CTC with the goal of joining Rumsfeld in the secretary of defense's Executive Support Center (ESC) across the hall from Rumsfeld's main office. He said that Rumsfeld was already on Richard Clarke's White House teleconference when they arrived. En route to Rumsfeld's ESC, Andrews said when he and his aide entered the corridor on the *inside* ring of the west section, "we had to walk over dead bodies" to get to the inner courtyard. This is two rings *further in* towards the center from the *inner most* purported "exit" hole in the central "C"-Ring made by whatever allegedly impacted the Pentagon that morning.

Once in the inner courtyard, Andrews and his aide again ran as fast as they could to Rumsfeld's Executive Support Center, where he joined Rumsfeld as his special operations/counterterrorism adviser during Clarke's White House teleconference. Andrews also said that Secretary of Defense Rumsfeld *spoke with President Bush* while in the ESC. Whether this was via the Clarke teleconference or by phone or other means was not stated. The fact that Rumsfeld personally communicated with Bush on 9/11 while Rumsfeld was in his Pentagon ESC has been published on an official DoD website.[12]

In addition to the already legion evidence that Flight 77 did not hit the Pentagon—i.e. the small hole in the west side of the Pentagon being not nearly large enough for the plane's fuselage, let alone wing width; no damage to the lawn where Flight 77 allegedly struck and skidded before hitting the building; wrecked plane parts at the site identified as being from an A-3 Sky Warrior, a far smaller plane than that of Flight 77, a Boeing 757; Pentagon requests to TV media on the morning of 9/11 not to take up-close images, etc.—there is also *official* evidence that Flight 77 did not hit the building:

In the Air Force's own account of the events of 9/11, *Air War Over America*, the North American Aerospace Defense Command (NORAD) general who finally ordered interceptor jets scrambled on 9/11, although too late, Gen. Larry Arnold, revealed that he ordered one of his jets to fly down low over the Pentagon shortly after the attack there that morning, and that this pilot reported back that there was no evidence that a plane had hit the building. This fighter jet—not Flight 77—is almost certainly the plane seen on the Dulles Airport air traffic controller's screen making a steep, high-speed 270- to 330-degree descent before disappearing from the radar. (When a plane flies low enough to go undetected, usually at or below 500 feet, it is said to be flying "under the radar." Note: The Pilots for 9/11 Truth website and their "Pandora's Black Box" video have determined from official data released by the National Transportation Safety Board (NTSB) that the true altitude/height of the plane represented by the blip was 476 feet—*way too high* to have hit the Pentagon at all, let alone the ground floor, but, significantly, in *just* the height range to been seen by controllers to have *just gone off radar* so it could *be said* to have crashed into the building.)

Military pilots—like the one sent by Gen. Arnold on 9/11 to report on the Pentagon's damage—are *trained* to fly at approx. 500 feet above ground in order to evade radar detection. In fact, when the air traffic controller responsible for the plane and her colleagues watched the extremely difficult 330-degree maneuver (originally claimed to be a 270-degree maneuver, since updated) on her screen, they were certain that the plane whose blip they were watching perform this extremely difficult feat *was* a US military aircraft, and said so at the time. It almost certainly was.

Thus, the likely reason the Pentagon has refused to lower the current official time for "Flight 77" impact, 9:37, to 9:32 a.m.—the actual time of the first explosions there—is that they decided to pretend the blip represented by Arnold's surveillance jet approaching just before 9:37 was "Flight 77." As the official cover story claims that the alleged 9:37 impact was the *only* Pentagon attack that morning, yet by the time Arnold's surveillance jet arrived on the scene the violent event had already happened, the Pentagon cannot acknowledge the earlier 9:32 time without revealing an attack on the building *prior* to the alleged impact.

It is significant that the *The 9/11 Commission Report* ignores the testimony of Secretary of Transportation Norman Mineta to its own commission and did this *only* for the testimony of Secretary Mineta. The clear reason for this blatant and targeted censorship is that Mineta's eyewitness testimony is extremely dangerous to the official cover story. The portion of Mineta's testimony that is particularly dangerous is his claim that Vice President Cheney, in charge in the Presidential Emergency Operations Center (PEOC) beneath the White House since before Mineta arrived in the PEOC at 9:20, insisted to an incredulous "young man" that "the orders (given earlier by Cheney to this same individual) still stand" when the man told Cheney that the presumed plane they had been tracking as a blip on a screen was 50, then 30, and finally just 10 miles from Washington—orders which could only have been *not* to shoot down the plane. Otherwise there would have been no reason for the agent to ask Cheney if they "still" stood, despite the plane's being almost upon the Capital where Cheney himself was. This is critical because of the timing that can be inferred from Mineta's testimony: As Mineta arrived at the PEOC at 9:20 a.m., and as Mineta estimated the "still stand?" interaction between Cheney and the agent happened 5 to 6 minutes after that, or about 9:25, it can be inferred based on the officially given speed of the plane represented by the blip of 540 mph that whatever that fast-approaching blip represented, it arrived in the vicinity of the Pentagon at approximately 9:32—nowhere close to the original official cover story time of 9:43, or even the six-minute-earlier time the Pentagon finally officially settled on for an alleged impact time of 9:37.

**Significantly, all of this also happened at or about 9:32 a.m. (from "The Complete 9/11 Timeline" at www.HistoryCommons.org):**
- After an inexplicable delay during which they knew that both WTC towers had been attacked, the Secret Service suddenly acts as if the 9/11 attacks are "real," rushing President Bush out of the library at the Florida school where he had been allowed to continue to read to children as long as 10 minutes after being told the second New York tower had been hit.
- Firefighters are suddenly ordered out of WTC1.
- The New York Stock Exchange is ordered closed.
- The takeover of Flight 93 reportedly begins with the stabbing of a flight attendant and one of the alleged hijackers announces that there is a bomb on board, picked up by air traffic controllers.

But perhaps the most damning evidence for the Sept. 11 attacks being an inside job is that the actual attacks were mirrored by NORAD/Air Force *hijack-scenario*/counterterrorism "exercises" being conducted by NORAD/Air Force's North East Sector (NEADS) on the morning of 9/11 itself. This author's original research and analysis first revealed the NEADS hijack-scenario "exercises" that "went live" on 9/11 as the *modus operandi* for the planning, execution and cover-up of the attacks, credited as the "Holy Grail" of 9/11 research by author Michael Ruppert in his early 9/11 expose book *Crossing the Rubicon*.

Critically, this author has interviewed White House NSC counterterrorism "czar" Richard Clarke, who confirmed that NORAD was conducting hijack-scenario exercises in the Northeastern Air Defense Sector (NEADS)—where all three attacks (New York City, the Pentagon and Pennsylvania) took place—on the morning of 9/11 to an audience of 75, published on an official DoD website. Says Clarke, "Yes, this happened on 9/11, and it happened with TWA Flight 800, when the Navy was doing a sea search exercise in the very area where the plane went down...I wouldn't have been able to respond the way we did on 9/11 if we hadn't exercised it five times."[13]

Also most critically, the operational head of NORAD NEADS on 9/11, Bob Marr, has also now publicly acknowledged his agency was conducting a plane-hijack scenario/counterterrorism exercise on the morning of 9/11.[14]

It is impossible for the US government to have not been able to "imagine" using planes as weapons when its own military was practicing how to defend against exactly such a hijack-scenario attack on the morning of 9/11 itself. Impossible.

**Explosive revelations regarding the World Trade Center attacks:**

Millions in the US and around the world now contend, due to the efforts of Professor David Ray Griffin and Architects & Engineers for 9/11 Truth, that World Trade Center Towers 1 and 2, as well as WTC Building 7—not hit by any plane—fell due to controlled demolitions using super-military-grade *thermite* explosives *pre-planted* inside the buildings, to which "al Qaeda" could never have obtained access. Nearly 1,300 licensed architects and engineers have signed the Architects & Engineers' petition (www.ae911truth.org) calling for a new, truly independent investigation of the events leading up to and on 9/11.

Among the most explosive revelations of what really happened at the World Trade Center on Sept. 11 is WTC 7 owner and WTC 1 and 2 leaseholder Larry Silverstein's admission, in an interview on PBS that the New York City "Fire Department commander," after a discussion in a phone call with Silverstein late on the afternoon of 9/11, made the decision "to pull [the building, a professional term for triggering the *controlled demolition* of a structure with pre-placed explosives] and we watched the building collapse." This claim takes on sinister dimensions when combined with the below inside information received from American Helicopter Society executive director M. E. Rhett Flater, who knows many of the principals involved:

"The NYC Police [Department] has two Bell 412s [helicopters] equipped with hoists and rescuers in the air on 9/11 next to the WTCs. One of these was the same 412 and police crew which assisted with rooftop rescues when one of the buildings was attacked by al Qaeda bombers several years earlier [in 1993]. The NYC Fire Department, which has no love for the NYC Police Department, assumed jurisdiction and denied access to the roof by the NYC police helicopters. Complicating matters, the rooftop doors were [double] locked prior to 9/11 at the direction of the NYC Fire Department. As a result, there were no helicopter rescue attempts. When a fleet of Sikorshy U-60L Black Hawks arrived from Stratford with medics and supplies, they were ordered to a local airport and directed to stay away from the towers. The same was true of other rescue attempts by civil and military and para-military helicopters."[15]

Amazingly, the pilot of one of the New York Police Department helicopters who sent two of his crew members down to the WTC 1 roof to rescue survivors after the basement bombing of the building in 1993, Detective Greg Semendinger, was the official NYPD photographer in one of its four helicopters circling around the towers on 9/11, who expressed "surprise" that there was no one on the roof to rescue, though it was well known—even infamous—throughout the NY Police Department that the NY Fire Department had ordered the roof doors double-locked. Further, Semendinger's helicopter that morning was equipped with the same winch and foldable rescue seat he had used to rescue almost two dozen from the WTC roof eight years earlier. Semendinger took photographs from the NYPD helicopter on 9/11 which were provided to the National Institute of Standards and Technology (NIST) as background for their report, a report that *refused* to consider the controlled demolition hypothesis. NIST then provided these photos to the 9/11 Commission, which subsequently were given to ABC News as the result of its FOIA demand. Of the 2,770 photos taken by Semendinger, only 24 have been released to the public.[16]

The remaining 2,746 photos almost certainly contain literal "smoking guns" and must be forced into the public domain by a new, truly independent investigation of Sept. 11. Putting two and two together, the New York Fire Department commander(s) who ordered the WTC 1 and 2 rooftop doors to be double-locked—thus closing off the only hope of escape for victims caught above the point of the plane impacts and fires, many of whom were forced to jump to their deaths—also refused to allow NY Police Department helicopters equipped and ready to rescue anyone able to get to the roofs along with the other dozens of civilian, military and paramilitary helicopters that rushed to Manhattan ready to rescue them—to do so. And, after talking with WTC 7 owner Silverstein, it was ordered that Building 7 was to be destroyed by classic remote-controlled demolition.

And what's "good" for the goose (WTC 7), is "good" for the gander (WTC 1 and 2); i.e., it is almost certain that Silverstein and the Fire Department commander also made the decision to bring down WTC 1 and 2 by controlled demolition earlier in the day. This is a high evil forcing a devil's alternative on the victims caught above the plane impacts and fires that would make Hitler's SS jealous with rage.

To add fuel to the fire, Fox News reporter and former Gannett News journalist Jeffrey Shapiro has claimed that New York Police Department officials told him late on the afternoon of 9/11 that Silverstein also was on the phone with his insurance company trying to talk them into approving the controlled demolition destruction of WTC 7, the one WTC structure he owned outright, using language similar to that Silverstein told PBS he and the Fire Department commander had used as the pretext for "pulling" the building.[17]

Further, WTC janitor William "Willy" Rodriguez, the last person to leave the WTC alive on 9/11, has testified that he was in the first *basement* level of the WTC when an immense explosion went off *below* him in the yet-deeper *sub*basement level(s) of the building a few seconds *before* the plane hit the tower high above.[18] As Robert Andrews revealed that the west side *basement* level of the Pentagon was damaged at approximately 9:32 a.m. and as we know that the cause of the 9:32 Pentagon attack was not an impact event but explosives, there are thus eye- and ear witness reports of bombs going off in *both* the Pentagon *and* the WTC *underground* level(s) *before* both buildings were hit by *anything* from the outside.

As no "outside" terrorist, al Qaeda or otherwise, could have had access to either the Pentagon or the sustained advance access needed to pre-place explosives inside the WTC, *only* domestic insiders could have pre-placed the explosives in *both* the Pentagon *and* the WTC. Further, because the WTC1 deep-basement explosions(s) experienced by Willy Rodriguez happened *before* the tower was hit by a plane; as any incoming plane not controlled by the same party that triggered the sub-basement detonation(s) could have veered off from the building at the last second, ruining the plane-impact-as-cover-story for the later building collapse; and as the sub-basement explosions were necessary for the actual later collapse of the buildings by controlled demolition, *the same domestic-US insiders had to have controlled both the sub-basement detonations and the incoming plane(s).*

BARBARA HONEGGER

Thus, even if al Qaeda hijackers were on the incoming planes, they were *not* in final control of the impact of the planes into the buildings, which had to have been guaranteed by domestic/US insider controllers to ensure the sub-basement bombs didn't go off prematurely and destroy the plane-impact cover story. This fact is critical, as it takes jurisdiction for the mass murders at the WTC away from the Bush administration's FBI, which oversees crimes committed in the air, and places it squarely with the State of New York, as murder is a State crime and multiple/mass murders are the sum of individual State crimes. Because the controllers of the timing of the basement level explosives had to have also been the controllers of the final approach of the planes, and the former was clearly on the ground and not in the air, a Manhattan grand jury can suddenly pull jurisdiction for the Bush-Cheney Reichstag Fire out of their hands.

Because the *real* modus operandi at the Pentagon and WTC are so similar, it is logical to deduce that the same domestic-US terrorists were responsible for pre-placing and detonating the bombs—both inside the WTC and inside the Pentagon. That is, a single group of US-domestic conspirators—not al Qaeda or any other outside terrorists—must have planned both the WTC and Pentagon attacks *and* controlled both the approaching planes *and* the inside-the-building explosions in real time on 9/11.

**Other relevant Interviews:**

The author interviewed the famous "lone taxi driver" whose cab is the only car visible still parked on I-395 above the Pentagon lawn looking down at the west face after the other cars have left the freeway. This taxi can be seen in overhead photos taken on the morning of 9/11 and viewable on the Internet. The driver said his was the last car allowed onto that section of I-395 before police put up a barricade and that he decided not to immediately leave the scene like the others "because I realized this was history and I wanted to see for myself." He stated that he saw no evidence of a plane having impacted the building nor any visible plane pieces on the lawn at the time he arrived, which was after the first violent event had occurred at the building, as black smoke was already streaming up and to the right from inside-the-building fires. The taxi cab driver drew a diagram of what he saw that morning while overlooking the Pentagon's west face from I-395, which the author has retained.

The author has interviewed a Navy public affairs officer who was assigned to the Naval Command Center on 9/11, one of the two major Pentagon west section areas destroyed that morning, the other being the Army Financial Management/Audit area as mentioned earlier. This officer was not in the building that morning but was quickly assigned to be the deputy public affairs officer at the underground "back-up Pentagon" location in Pennsylvania close to the Maryland border, called "Site R." This eyewitness Navy officer inside Site R said Deputy Secretary of Defense Paul Wolfowitz and later Vice President Cheney were flown to the Site R underground bunker in response to Richard Clarke's officially declaring "Continuity of Government/Continuity of Operations" (COG/COOP) on the morning of 9/11. This is confirmed in Clarke's book, *Against All Enemies*, in which he reports that Secretary of Defense Rumsfeld chose Wolfowitz to be the designated COG/COOP official at Site R in his stead. Perhaps significantly, Site R and Camp David are not far from the "crash" site of Flight 93 is not far from Site R and Camp David, which early reports on the morning of 9/11, presumably taken from official sources, said may have been the flight's intended target. The airspace around Camp David, like around Washington, D.C., is a standing "shoot-down" area. Additional information about Site R, on and after 9/11, can be found in James Bamford's book, *A Pretext for War.*

On February 4, 2004, the author interviewed Air Force General Ralph Eberhart, Commander of NORAD on 9/11. To the author's knowledge, Gen. Eberhart has granted no other interview since the events of September 11. Before asking questions, Eberhart was given copies of all the mainstream press articles published as of that date on the subject of the confusion on 9/11 of his NORAD Northeast Sector (NEADS) personnel who were running NORAD's "Vigilant Guardian/Vigilant Warrior" emergency-response war-game exercises that morning. As of the date of the interview, therefore, the then head of NORAD was made aware of the initial confusion by his own NEADS "game" players on 9/11 between incoming exercise reports and incoming reports of the actual hijacks.

The author first asked Gen. Eberhart if there was any connection between NORAD's "Vigilant Guardian/Vigilant Warrior" exercise being run on 9/11 and the plane-crashing-into-tower emergency response exercise simultaneously being held at National Reconnaissance Office (NRO) headquarters outside Washington, D.C.[19] He replied, "No." This response was surprising, as a large percentage of NRO personnel are from his own agency, the Air Force. He was asked for reconfirmation, to which he again said, "No." Laying the ground for the next question, the author mentioned that NEADS' "game" director Lt. Col. Dawne Deskins had said that she was confused as to whether initial reports of the hijacked planes on the morning of 9/11 were "real world" or "part of the game." This, the author noted, showed that the NORAD exercises that morning had to have been on a hijack scenario *at least similar to* the actual attacks, as otherwise there would have been no grounds for confusion. After considering this for a moment, Gen. Eberhart refused to answer any further questions and abruptly ended the interview.

Significantly, subsequent to the initial publication of this white paper, NORAD officials have confirmed that their "exercise" on the morning of 9/11 did, indeed, include a hijack scenario, as originally first inferred and published by the author—see the book *Touching History*, published for the seventh anniversary of 9/11.

**In addition to the already well known and officially acknowledged evidence of Bush administration foreknowledge of the broad outlines of the September 11 attacks—advance warnings from the intelligence agencies of as many as 11 foreign countries and the content of the now-famous August 6, 2001 presidential daily brief (whose 10-page attachment still has not been made public), etc.—there is strong evidence that Bush administration insiders had near perfect—if not complete—advance knowledge of both the details and the date of the September 11 attack:**

(Note: That Bush administration insiders had advance knowledge of the date and details of an "outside" attack is not inconsistent with these insiders having facilitated and even orchestrated the attacks. That is, the plot behind the attacks of September 11 is similar to that of the *Reichstag* fire, through which Hitler rapidly consolidated power. Like the Nazi-facilitated *Reichstag* fire, there was a real though highly-unlikely-to-succeed "outside" plot about which administration insiders gained advance intelligence. They then secretly protected and enabled this plot to ensure that it not only succeeded, but succeeded *spectacularly* as the psychological operation needed to justify the entire subsequent Bush-Cheney global and domestic agenda.)

Shortly after September 11, *Newsweek* reported that *before* 9/11, the Bush administration initiated a Foreign Intelligence Surveillance Act (FISA) Court surveillance/tap of "up to 20" suspected al Qaeda-linked terrorists then in the US, but that then-FISA Court Chief Justice Royce Lamberth subsequently ordered the then-already-ongoing surveillance stopped. This can only mean one thing—that the Bush Justice Dept./FBI/NSA initiated the tap *before* asking the FISA Court for a warrant for it, as with the now-famous post-9/11 NSA taps initiated by the Bush administration without first applying for FISA warrants.

As "up to 20" is a clever way of saying "19" without making the link to 9/11 explicit, the Bush administration Justice Dept/FBI/NSA almost certainly initiated surveillance of all 19, or close to all 19, of the soon-to-be alleged 9/11 hijackers *before* 9/11. Though Judge Lamberth ordered the surveillance ended once the administration filed the formal warrant application, there is evidence that the Bush administration ignored his order to cease the tap and continued the surveillance of the alleged 9/11 hijackers up to and including the day of 9/11. Zacarias Moussaoui—the only person indicted by the Bush administration for anything even related to 9/11—has stated in court filings that both he "and my (al Qaeda) brothers" then in the US were surveilled by the Bush administration before 9/11 and that the Bush administration knows he can prove it. How could this be the case? If Moussaoui was one of the "up to 20" al Qaeda-linked terrorist suspects they surveilled before 9/11 without an advance FISA warrant as reported by *Newsweek*, then Moussaoui was also one of the "up to 20" whose taps Judge Lamberth ordered stopped. Moussaoui, after all, was originally named as the "20th hijacker" of the 9/11 plot. Amazingly, the FISA Act requires that, if the FISA Court rejects a surveillance initiated before a warrant has been applied for, as in this case, the court has to inform the "target" of the surveillance and give him the government's stated reason for the tap in the surveillance application. Moussaoui says that he can "prove" the Bush administration/FBI initiated surveillance on him before 9/11 because, it can be deduced, the FISA Court itself told him so after Lamberth ordered his— and those of the other "up to 20"—surveillance ended.

If this is the case, it opens the very real possibility that the FISA Court likewise informed most or all 19 of the "up to 20" alleged 9/11 hijackers before 9/11 that they were being surveilled by the Bush administration—and the reason for such surveillance. This also throws new light on the claims by the Pentagon's then-secret data mining task force, "Able Danger," to have tracked lead 9/11 hijacker Mohamed Atta and at least four of the other 19 hijackers beginning in January 2000, when Atta actually did enter the country according to Daniel Hopsicker in his book, *Welcome to Terrorland*. The FBI falsely claimed, and still falsely claims, that Atta did not enter the US until the summer of 2000, six months later. The likely reason for this intentional lie about when Atta first entered the country is what Atta is known to have done while inside the US between January and the Summer of 2000. Hopsicker reveals that, among other activities, Atta visited Portland, Maine, in March 2000, and perhaps even earlier. An abiding "mystery" of the official cover story is why Atta drove to Portland, Maine on September 10, the day before 9/11, and then flew from Portland to Boston early on the morning of September 11. The answer to this "mystery," which the FBI clearly already knows, is the link between what Atta was *doing* in Portland before the administration admits he was even in the country, as well as what he was doing there the day before 9/11 and early on the morning of 9/11. This may all have something to do with the fact that the CIA reportedly runs secret flights out of an airport in Portland, Maine, and that "rendition" detainees have said they were flown out of the country on special jets after first stopping at Portland's International *Jet* Port.[20]

The FBI's top bin Laden/al Qaeda hunter until shortly before 9/11, John O'Neill, "happened" to be at the same hotel in the same town near Tarragona, Spain in mid-July 2001 *just before* lead hijacker Mohamed Atta and 9/11 plot "coordinator" Ramzi Binalshibh. Some Bush administration officials now also believe that 9/11 "mastermind" Khalid Sheikh Mohammed (KSM) met there for what the 9/11 Commission calls "the Final 9/11 Planning Meeting." This cannot be—and is not—a coincidence. O'Neill, who was in close contact with German intelligence—recall that Atta led the "German cell" for the 9/11 attacks—and Spanish intelligence, had clearly been alerted to the upcoming meeting and was at the hotel to surveil/tap/bug the room where the meeting was about to be held. O'Neill and his agency, the Bush administration's FBI, thus knew every detail, or nearly every detail, of the planned 9/11 plot *at least two months in advance.*

Perhaps just as significantly, European media reported that bin Laden was in an American hospital in Dubai incapacitated for surgery during precisely this same mid-July 2001, period of the Spanish "final 9/11 Planning Meeting." Reportedly, bin Laden was visited in the hospital by the area's then CIA station chief. The question naturally arises as to whether bin Laden was telephoned by Atta, Binalshibh, and perhaps also KSM, or visa versa, while the latter were at the "final 9/11 planning meeting" in the hotel that O'Neill had pre-bugged. If so, then O'Neill, the FBI, and the highest levels of the Bush administration—including O'Neill's then boss, Attorney General Ashcroft, who suddenly stopped flying commercial aircraft about this time—knew not only every detail of the 9/11 plot as of that date, but almost certainly recorded all the key "outside" conspirators plotting their "final plans" including possibly bin Laden himself, *on tape*—clearly another "Butterfield" tape to be demanded by subpoena.

As noted above, on 9/11 *itself* the US military was conducting NORAD/Air Force emergency response exercises on scenarios involving multiple hijacks, and the NRO was conducting an emergency response exercise on the scenario of a plane crashing into one of the towers at its headquarters just outside Washington, D.C.—many NRO personnel being from the Air Force and CIA. It is next to impossible for this to have been the case unless the exercises, also referred to as war games, were intentionally scripted to *mirror* what had been learned from the above-mentioned detailed advance intelligence. That is, the purpose of the war games held on 9/11 was to practice how to defend against the very attacks that John O'Neill's Tarragona meeting surveillance, the Pentagon's "Able Danger" data-mining tracking, and the FBI's FISA-warrant-less surveillance of the "up to 20" ("19"?) suspected al Qaeda terrorists had already revealed. You don't practice something in a multi-million-dollar set of exercises that you "can't imagine." The date for the actual attacks—September 11—was then chosen to coincide with the Pentagon's exercises, which in turn mirrored the real attack plans.

Perhaps the most burning data point to prove Bush administration complicity in 9/11 is the fact that lead hijacker Mohamed Atta took to the mid-July "final 9/11 planning meeting" in Spain the information that "the date *has been* set" (i.e. set by someone else *other* than Atta), and that he, Atta, didn't yet know it, but would "know it" in five to six weeks, or by late August 2001.[21] Atta was clearly waiting to learn the date of "his own" attack. This last piece of the puzzle fell into place during the first phase of Zacarias Moussaoui's sentencing trial, in the 58-page transcript of 9/11"mastermind" Khalid Sheikh Mohammed's interrogation "testimony" read into the trial record by the Bush administration prosecution. In this KSM transcript, it is revealed that bin Laden and KSM "allowed *Atta* to choose" both the final targets for the attacks and the attack date."[22] From this, therefore, we know that neither bin Laden nor "mastermind" KSM nor "coordinator" Binalshibh set the September 11 attack date. However, from what Atta said to Binalshibh—and probably also KSM and even possibly bin Laden by phone link—at the "Final Planning Meeting" in Spain, *we also know that neither did Atta*. Atta was *waiting* to *learn* the date of his "own" attack five to six weeks *after* the mid-July "final 9/11 planning meeting," and that date did *not* come from any of his al Qaeda superiors. It must be the case then, despite KSM's claim that he "let" Atta choose the date, that *none* of the top "outside" terrorist conspirators set the date for the September 11 attacks, *including* Atta.

The key and central fact of the entire 9/11 plot is that the attack date Atta was "waiting for" *was* the date of the Bush administration's planned war games, which, in a vicious circle, were scripted to mirror the content of Atta's attack plan gleaned via advance intelligence obtained from O'Neill's surveillance of the "final planning meeting" near Tarragona, the Pentagon's "Able Danger" tracking of Atta, and the FBI's warrantless surveillance of Atta and other of the about-to-be alleged hijackers. Atta was thus the *sole* individual to whom the date the Bush administration finally chose for its war games—9/11—was leaked as soon as it was selected and he bought his one-way ticket as soon as he learned it, in late August 2001, just as he had predicted at the "final planning meeting." The No. 1 Bush administration conspirator, therefore, is whoever gave the administration's own war game scenario details and date—9/11—to Mohamed Atta.

Lt. Gen. Mahmoud Ahmed, then head of Pakistan's military intelligence agency ISI, is a prime suspect for the middleman who laundered this No. 1 Bush administration conspirator's insider war game information to Atta. On the morning of 9/11 he was having breakfast with future CIA Director Porter J. Goss and Senator Bob Graham, who co-chaired the joint House/Senate "investigation" of the 9/11 attacks, and had met with CIA Director George Tenet and with top officials at the Pentagon, about to conduct the war games, in the few days leading up to 9/11. He is most likely the person who was told the date and details of the Pentagon's emergency response exercises and communicated them, directly or via an intermediary, to Atta, as Ahmed also approved wiring $100,000 to Atta shortly before 9/11. Atta then confirmed 9/11 as the date for the war games—which *was* the date of the attacks—in his now-famous NSA-intercepted call with KSM of September 10, in which he related "The Match is about to begin. Zero hour is tomorrow." "Match" is a way of saying "exercise" or "war game." This critical September 10 intercept, by the way, was almost certainly made without an advance FISA warrant, putting the lie to now CIA Director and then-NSA Director Gen. Michael Hayden's patently false claim that the "first" warrantless taps were initiated in defensive response to 9/11, and thus came *after* the attacks.

Another abiding "mystery" of September 11 is why Gen. Eberhart, the commander of NORAD on 9/11, claimed to the 9/11 Commission that on the morning of 9/11 NORAD was conducting, among others, a preplanned "Soviet-era" emergency response exercise[23] in which US fighter jets were to defend against Russian nuclear bombers. After all, the Soviet Union had ceased to exist *ten years before.* He didn't say "Russian," he said "Soviet." This is very strange until one discovers that, despite repeated official and media claims that September 11 was "completely unique" and that the skies over America had "never before" been cleared of all commercial and private civilian aircraft, NORAD had conducted another emergency response exercise 40 years earlier, which completely cleared the skies over the mainland US. This was on October 14, 1961, in a war game called "Sky Shield II," which was based on a scenario of how to defend against an air attack by *Soviet* bombers on New York City.[24] The main difference between the 1961 exercise and September 11 is that the clearing of the skies was announced in advance to the public in "Sky Shield." This original Soviet-era exercise, which included 1,800 US and 15 Canadian military planes and was billed as "the greatest exercise ever conducted by Western air-defense forces," is mentioned in the Air Force's own account of the events of September 11, *Air War Over America.*

In fact, Gen. Larry Arnold, NORAD's commander for the continental US on 9/11 directly under Eberhart who finally ordered interceptor jets scrambled to belatedly meet the hijack threat, made a point of including the eerily similar 1961 Air Force war game in the book. Not only did both the 1961 and September 11 NORAD "Soviet-era" war game scenarios include attacks on New York City, in the 1961 exercise US military planes played the role of Soviet attack bombers. That is, the US military pre-scripted both the defense *and* the "attack" by its own planes pretending to be Soviet aircraft. If Gen. Eberhart's testimony to the 9/11 Commission is correct, NORAD may have been conducting a "Soviet-era" exercise much like the one in 1961, on 9/11.

In this light, it is significant that mainstream press stories contain intriguing reports that point to the possibility that there were *two* American Airlines "Flight 11s," leaving from two different gates at Boston Logan airport within a few minutes of one another on 9/11, as well as emerging evidence of other of the hijacked 9/11 flight numbers possibly being "twinned,"[25] or duplicated. The question thus naturally arises, were these "twin" planes US *military* planes "playing" hijacked airliner "attackers," similar to the 1961 scenario except substituting commandeered airliners for Soviet bombers? And could the 9/11 exercise have included a "trigger" event to clear the skies over the mainland US so that a realistic test of US air defenses could be conducted without interference from the thousands of civilian aircraft normally in the air?

Key quotes from *New York Times* articles during the 1961 NORAD exercise are eerily similar to stories appearing on 9/11 [text in parentheses and *italics* added]: "It is not so much the fear of collisions with military aircraft that has caused civilian planes to be ordered out of the skies, as it is the knowledge that *in*adequate [civilian FAA] electronic flight controls will be available during the exercise to guide them. Strategic Air Command (SAC) bombers, playing the role of the marauding forces, will seek to foul communications and radar. They will drop tinsel-like pieces of metal called "chaff" overhead [like the myriad small pieces of metal scrap found on the Pentagon lawn and Shanksville, Pennsylvania "crash" site on 9/11?]…that will throw radarscopes [including the FAA's] into a confusion of false signals"; "All the bomber missions were laid out ahead of time and fed into the NORAD computer"; "An automated shorthand running display of the entire battle was provided at NORAD combat center and in similar centers at Strategic Air Command headquarters [where President Bush was taken on 9/11] and in the Pentagon [which was attacked on 9/11]"; "A fight plan for every aircraft [private, commercial and military] is fed into the computer's memory beforehand. When a plane shows on the radarscope, a console operator picks up an aluminum electronic gun, points it at the blip, and squeezes the trigger. That brings the flight to the computer's attention. If the flight [plan] is filed in its memory, the computer automatically replies, 'Yes, I am aware of that [plane].' It does this by marking the flight with an F for Friendly. While the computer compares the flight with its memorized data, it marks the flight P for Pending. Finally, it may mark it H for Hostile. 'We have *two minutes* to identify a flight [as Friendly] before we scramble [interceptor jets]...to make a visual identification of an uncertain aircraft or to attack it'; 'We do not train [in exercises like the 1961 'Sky Shield II, or on 9/11] with Hostile symbology [showing on screens]; therefore, the Strategic Air Command's bombers playing the role of the attacking [Soviet Russian] force [on October 14, 1961] were marked K, for Faker'"; and "There are seventeen units of Army Air Defense Artillery with ground-to-air anti-aircraft missiles near New York [in 1961; how many more were there on 9/11, 40 years later, when none were used?]" The 1961 war game was directed by then-NORAD Commander, Air Force General Laurence Sherman Kuter from his combat operations center at NORAD's Colorado Springs headquarters, which in the mid-1960s moved to Cheyenne Mountain, Gen. Eberhart's command center on 9/11. It may also be significant that the Air Force's war games simulation center is at Maxwell Air Force Base in Alabama, which Gen. Kuter had earlier commanded and where lead 9/11 hijacker Mohamed Atta received training.

The Pentagon's "Able Danger" data miners claim that "Department of Defense lawyers"—almost certainly from the National Security Agency, then headed by Gen. Hayden, an officer in the Air Force, the same service that planned the 9/11 war games—blocked planned meetings with the FBI at which they wanted to tell the FBI that they had "tracked" Atta and other of the 9/11 hijackers prior to 9/11 and ask the FBI to initiate additional surveillance on them. The fact that the FBI *did* initiate exactly such a surveillance of the "up to 20 Al Qaeda linked terrorist suspects" before 9/11 is strong evidence that, despite its current claims to the contrary, the Pentagon's "Able Danger" team *did* communicate what they learned from tracking Atta and the others to the FBI before 9/11, and that the FBI then initiated FISA-warrant-less surveillances of Atta and others subsequently ordered stopped by then-Chief FISA Court Judge Lamberth—all *prior* to 9/11. The fact that initially-suspected "20th 9/11 hijacker" Moussaoui officially filed claims that he "and my brothers" *were* surveilled before 9/11 is further evidence that the FBI continued to watch all or most of the 9/11 hijackers right up until the attacks, despite Lamberth's order to cease and desist. FBI Headquarters supervisors David Frasca and his deputy Maltbie refused 70— *seventy*—urgent requests by Moussaoui's FBI interrogator for either a FISA Court warrant or an "ordinary" criminal warrant to get into Moussaoui's computer and surveil anyone mentioned therein. Doing so would have clearly stopped the plot, as Moussaoui now claims to have personally known 17—almost all— of the alleged 19 hijackers.[26]

In addition to all the evidence that plane-impacts-plus-fire was the carefully planned cover story for the cause of collapse of WTC 1, 2 and 7, as well as the west façade of the Pentagon, both of which were initially hit by inside-the-buildings bombs, not planes, the other overwhelming line of evidence for 9/11 being an "Inside Job" is the anthrax attacks.

Any evidence linking 9/11 to the anthrax letters—dated September 11 but sent in mid- October and only to Democratic leaders in Congress, no Republicans—is direct evidence of an inside job because that particular type of anthrax is known to have been of the highly controlled "Ames strain" developed by the US Army at Ft. Detrick, Maryland, and at the University of Iowa in Ames, Iowa. It was also high-spore-count, *military*-grade weaponized anthrax refined according to a trade secret reportedly held by William Patrick, former Ft. Detrick bioweapons expert, mentor of Steven Hatfill, the only "person of interest" stalked by the FBI as a suspect in the still "unsolved" anthrax case, and the close friend and colleague of Bush administration bio-counterterrorism expert Jerry Hauer, a signer of the PNAC manifesto calling for "a new Pearl Harbor."

On September 11, this same Jerry Hauer personally delivered anti-anthrax *Cipro* to Vice President Cheney's staff at the White House. Why? The conservative legal watchdog group Judicial Watch has filed a suit against Vice President Cheney and other Bush administration officials demanding to know why *Cipro* was delivered to the executive mansion—and only to the executive mansion—on the day of the attacks. So far the response has been deafening silence. On September 10, the day before 9/11, FEMA and other emergency response personnel arrived in New York City for a counter-bioterrorism exercise called "Tripod II," claimed by the Bush administration to have been scheduled to begin September 12. There is reason to believe that the bio-agent this drill was to practice defending against was anthrax, as Jerry Hauer was also a major planner of the New York City exercise. And there is also a strong possibility the true start date for the exercise was September 11, as many "exercise" personnel were already in place in New York City on September 10. As the Air Force's war game scenario had just "come to life" in real attacks on 9/11, were Hauer and Cheney worried that the same thing might be about to happen with their counter-bioterrorism "exercise" Tripod II? Is this why the anti-anthrax drug *Cipro* was distributed to the

White House, "just in case"? If so, it would be strong evidence that Tripod II was on the scenario of defending New York City against an anthrax attack. Was the "vector," or delivery vehicle, for that emergency response exercise scenario anthrax attack to have been by air via hijacked plane(s)?

Notably, in their book on bioterrorism, *Germs*, Judith Miller and William Broad claim, apparently from inside sources, that Ramzi Yousef's plans for the first World Trade Center attack in 1993 included explosively pushing large quantities of cyanide out into New York City. Khalid Sheikh Mohammed, the "mastermind" of 9/11, is Ramzi Yousef's uncle. Finally, former New York City mayor Rudolph Giuliani testified to the 9/11 Commission that when WTC7, the location of his emergency operations center, collapsed on 9/11, he moved those operations to the command and control center set up on Pier 92 for the "Tripod II" bio-terrorism exercise and that it worked even better than the original. Giuliani told the 9/11 Commission, "The reason Pier 92 was selected as a command center was because on the next day, on September 12, Pier 92 was going to have a drill. It had hundreds of people there—from FEMA, from the federal government, from the State [Dept.], from the [New York] State Emergency Management Office—and they were getting ready for a drill for biochemical attack. So that was going be the place they were going to have the drill. The equipment was already there, so we were able to establish a command center there that was *two and a half to three times bigger* than the command center that we had lost at 7 World Trade Center. And it was from there that the rest of the (9/11 and subsequent) search and rescue effort was completed."

## Conclusion

Covert elements of the US military and intelligence community, not al Qaeda, had the access to plant explosives inside its own most heavily defended world headquarters, the Pentagon. The US military and intelligence community, not al Qaeda, had the access to plant the explosives Willy Rodriguez heard and felt go off deep in the sub-basement of the World Trade Center. The US military and intelligence community, not al Qaeda, also had the sustained access weeks before 9/11 to also plant controlled demolition charges throughout the superstructures of WTC1 and WTC2, and in WTC7, which brought down all three buildings on 9/11. The US military and intelligence community, not al Qaeda, had access to the sulfur-enhanced military-grade thermite (*thermate*) detected in the sub-basement levels of the WTC needed to melt the steel found molten deep in its basements weeks later. The US military and intelligence community, not al Qaeda, would have chosen the least populated and most reinforced section of the Pentagon—its newly upgraded west wedge—to strike, minimizing casualties. Real terrorists would have maximized them. Real terrorists also would have also maximized casualties at the World Trade Center by placing explosives so as to allow the building to fall haphazardly on other buildings and streets around it, not bring it down neatly by controlled demolition into their own footprints, which minimizes casualties. A US military plane, not one piloted by al Qaeda, performed the highly skilled, steep, high-speed 270- to 330-degree dive towards the Pentagon that Dulles air traffic controllers on 9/11 were sure *was* a military plane as they watched it on their screens that morning. Only a military aircraft, not a civilian plane flown by al Qaeda, would have given off the "friendly" signal needed to disable the Pentagon's anti-aircraft missile batteries as it approached the building. Only the US military, not al Qaeda, had the ability to break all of its Standard Operating Procedures to paralyze its own emergency response system on 9/11. Only the US military, not al Qaeda, had access to the weaponized, military-grade US Army "Ames strain' anthrax contained in letters mailed only to Democratic congressional leaders. It is absurd to believe that al Qaeda would target only Democrats, especially as the US leadership at the time of the attacks was Republican. When he received the anthrax letter dated September 11, then-Democratic Senate Majority Leader Tom Daschle was calling for a congressional investigation of 9/11 and had already been warned off from "looking too closely at" 9/11 by personal calls from both President Bush and Vice President Cheney. When he received his anthrax letter, another Democratic leader, Senator Patrick Leahy, was leading the congressional resistance to the Patriot Act, a premeditated assault on *Americans'* privacy and civil liberties justified by "al Qaeda's" attack, clearly drafted by the Bush administration well *before* 9/11 and "in the can" awaiting its "New Pearl Harbor" trigger event.

And who in the US military, intelligence and military contractor chains of command and US civilian leadership are among the prime suspects for these acts of High Treason? First and foremost are the signers of the pre-9/11 Project for a New American Century (PNAC) manifesto calling for "a new Pearl Harbor" to catalyze its global domination agenda:

1. Vice President Dick Cheney.
2. Secretary of Defense Donald Rumsfeld and Deputy Secretary of Defense Paul Wolfowitz.
3. Richard Perle, head of Secretary Rumsfeld's Defense Policy Board.
4. Jerry Hauer, one of the government's top bio-terrorism experts who reportedly took anti-anthrax *Cipro* to the White House on 9/11.[27] Hauer had been director of NYC Mayor Rudolph Giu-

liani's Office of Emergency Management (OEM), whose personnel were moved to a New York pier on 9/11 just before its WTC7 offices were destroyed. A central player in scripting the biological/chemical terrorism attack scenario for the September 10–12 "Tripod II" exercise in NYC, Hauer is also an expert in the response to building collapses.[28] It was Hauer who insisted, despite the 1993 terrorist attack on WTC1, that Giuliani still locate his Office of Emergency Management, from which a response to another terrorist attack would have to be orchestrated, in WTC7. Hauer zealously pushed the "bin Laden did it and planes-and-fires brought down the towers" official story on CBS News on 9/11 in the immediate aftermath of the attacks before anyone without inside knowledge could have possibly determined the actual cause of the collapses—taking pains to state that explosives were not involved. The OEM opened on the 23rd floor of WTC7 in June 1999, where Hauer, its director, had his office. Hauer was also managing director of Kroll Associates before and on 9/11, the company that provided "security" for the World Trade Center, and thus had complete access to pre-place the explosive charges he adamantly insisted on national TV on 9/11 were not involved.[29] Hauer became a national security adviser to the National Institutes of Health on Sept. 10, from which he managed the Bush Administration's "response" to the imminent anthrax attacks.

5. Gary Bauer, the right-wing "family values" zealot who "happened" to be one of the "witnesses" to immediately claim publicly to have seen "Flight 77 hit the Pentagon."

6. National Security Council Middle East Adviser Zalmay Khalizad, soon to be the first US ambassador to Afghanistan after 9/11 and then US ambassador to Iraq—the very two countries whose invasions were rationalized as retaliation for the 9/11 attacks. During the Cold War, Khalizad was reportedly a liaison to then-CIA "bag man" Osama bin Laden in the CIA-Pakistani ISI covert war against the Soviets in Afghanistan, the crucible from which al Qaeda emerged. "Al Qaeda" was, in fact, originally the CIA-ISI list of anti-Soviet foreign fighters in Afghanistan.

Another key suspect is Air Force General Michael Hayden, former director of the CIA and then head of the National Security Agency (NSA), which tapped the calls of lead hijacker Mohamed Atta and 9/11 "mastermind" Khalid Sheikh Mohammed the day *before* 9/11, and surely on many other occasions before 9/11 as well—all almost certainly without FISA warrants as required by law. These pre-9/11 warrantless NSA taps put the lie to President Bush's claim that he initiated the program of warrantless NSA taps of al Qaeda suspects because of—and thus only after—9/11. Yet another key suspect is Army Lieutenant General William "Jerry" Boykin, the radical Christian fundamentalist Special Operations commando recently proposed to head the Army's Special Operations Command. Yet another is the Pentagon's POP2 office, which reportedly plans and scripts "false flag" operations—attacks orchestrated by the US military but made to appear perpetrated by an outside enemy to justify US military "retaliation." Yet another suspect is Defense Intelligence Agency Iran expert Lawrence "Larry" Franklin, who was "loaned" to Perle and Wolfowitz's neocon associate Douglas Feith and arrested for passing national security secrets to Israeli operatives at a meeting of top American-Israel Public Affairs Committee (AIPAC) personnel. Franklin also was and is an officer in the Air Force Reserve, which directed NORAD's "Vigilant Guardian/Vigilant Warrior" war game exercises on 9/11.

Scrutiny should also be leveled at the scriptwriters for the NORAD and NRO emergency response exercises planned for and held on 9/11, especially members of their lead "White Teams," which set the content and then oversee both "Red Team attackers" and "Blue Team defenders" on the actual day of an exercise, in this case on 9/11 itself. And every one of the as-yet-to-be-identified "top Pentagon officials" who on Sept. 10, the day before 9/11, according to *Newsweek*, suddenly canceled their already-booked flights for September 11.[30] Also National Military Command Center (NMCC) Commander Brig. Gen. Montague Winfield, who on that same day, September 10, asked his deputy, Navy Capt. Charles Leidig to take over for him the next morning between 8:30 and 10:30—precisely the time window of the "game" whose details and date had been given to Atta. Further investigation should be directed at the (government) "agency" the 9/11 Commission revealed, without identifying it by name (probably the CIA), took out the vast majority of the put options on American Airlines, United Airlines, Boeing and Morgan Stanley Dean Witter in the few days before 9/11. Also, Michael Chertoff, US Attorney for the District of New Jersey during the first 1993 attack on the World Trade Center who, as a private attorney, represented Egyptian-born US resident Magdy Elamir, under investigation for illegally diverting millions of dollars and whose brother, Mohammed Elamir, funded arms smugglers linked to al Qaeda.[31] Significantly, Mohamed Atta's name in his country of birth, Egypt, was *also* Mohamed Elamir. In other words, the very man President Bush put in charge of the entire 9/11 "investigation" and who is now director of Homeland Security—*the* top official charged with defending the US mainland from an attack by al Qaeda—may have himself been directly involved with al Qaeda and even with Mohamed Atta. In fact, Chertoff may well have been the top Bush-Cheney insider whom we know had to have been the source for Atta's finally being told what the date of "his own" attack was going to be. And FBI headquarters supervisor David Frasca and his deputy Michael Maltbie, who ignored 70 pleas by Zacarias Moussaoui's FBI interrogator to let him investigate the contents of Moussaoui's computer before 9/11. Attention should especially be directed to Philip Zelikow, NSC adviser along with Zalmay Khalilzad to then-NSC Adviser Condoleezza Rice before and on 9/11. Zelikow both orchestrated *The 9/11 Commission Report* cover up of the administration's inside job and, at Rice's personal request, rewrote the Bush administration's official national strategic plan draft to better match the global domination agenda of the pre-9/11 PNAC manifesto. Zelikow specializes in political mythologies, clearly the most important qualification for his selection as executive director of the official myth of Sept. 11—*The 9/11 Commission Report*. Only someone in the innermost circle of the actual criminal conspiracy would be trusted with this critical mission.

These are just *some* of the names being knit into the scroll of the September 11 Truth Revolution.

Barbara Honegger, M.S., is senior military affairs journalist with the Naval Postgraduate School (1995-present), DoD's graduate science, technology, national security and homeland security university. *This appendix, as is all of the author's research, publications and presentations on September 11, are solely in her capacity as a concerned citizen and do not imply official endorsement.* Honegger served as special assistant to the Assistant to the President and White House policy analyst (1981-83); was the pioneering Irangate author and whistleblower on the October Surprise (*October Surprise*, Tudor, 1989); was featured in the Iran-Contra expose documentary *Cover-Up*; and was called as a investigator and witness at both the October 23, 2004 and August 27, 2005 Los Angeles Citizens 9/11 Grand Jury hearings held at Patriotic Hall in Los Angeles, CA. Author David Ray Griffin has stated that any serious reinvestigation of 9/11 should include the information and analysis contained in this appendix. Honegger's two-hour, under-oath, videotaped interview of key Pentagon eyewitness April Gallop, cited below, provided the basis for a critical 9/11 lawsuit filed in Manhattan on Dec. 15, 2008.

### Notes:

1. The clock stopped at the moment the Great Earthquake hit San Francisco on April 18, 1906 is at sfgate.com/greatquake.
2. The clock at the Pentagon heliport just outside the west section, frozen at 9:31:40

a.m. by the violent event at the Pentagon, was posted on an official Navy web site at: www.news.navy.mil/view_single.asp?id=2480Pentagonclock_BBC. Note that whoever took this official Navy photo placed the clock in front of a poster of the controversial Marine Corps part-helicopter/part-fixed-wing plane, the Osprey, perhaps thereby suggesting what may have struck the building (after the inside explosions went off), if anything did. Though the Osprey officially existed only in prototype at the time, a prototype Osprey would be unique in that its military IFF transponder would have given off a "friendly" signal and it could have approached the Pentagon helipad in its helicopter mode and changed over into fixed-wing plane mode at the last second, taking defenses off guard. Yet another stopped Pentagon clock is—or was—in the September 11 exhibit at the Smithsonian Institution, originally posted at www.americanhistory.si.edu/september11/collection/record.asp?ID=19. The author was informed that, after this white paper was published on the Internet, the clock was removed from the Smithsonian 9/11 exhibit but is still in storage there.

3. Videotaped under-oath testimony of April Gallop to the author, Irvine, California, March 2007, approx. two hours.
4. April Gallop's watch, which was stopped just after 9:30 by the explosion that happened at the precise moment she hit the "power on" button on her computer on the morning of 9/11, is evidence that the actual time of the initial explosive violent at the Pentagon was closer to 9:30 than 9:32. As the information about Gallop's watch was obtained after the first version of this article was published, despite this, the author has retained the shorthand reference to the average time of stoppage of the Pentagon wall clocks and April Gallop's watch as 9:32 for simplicity of discussion.
5. Federal Aviation Administration (FAA) timeline document "Executive Summary Chronology of a Multiple Hijacking Crisis, September 11, 2001."
6. Danish Foreign Minister Per Stig Moller interview with Denmark Radio P3, September 12, 2001, 6:15 a.m. Denmark time. "...I saw smoke and fire rising from the Pentagon at 9:32...My first impression was that a bomb had been detonated at the Pentagon." The audio of this radio interview is in the 9/11 video documentary *Bomberne som Forsvandt* by Danish researcher Henrik Melvang, available at www.unmask.dk and at www.bombsinsidewtc.dk. See also 9/11 timeline by European researcher Jose Garcia in *Reality, Truth and Evil Facts, Questions and Perspectives on September 11, 2001*, Temple Lodge Publications, 2005.
7. *The 9/11 Conspiracy*, Catfeet Press/Open Court, James Fetzer, editor, 2006, chapter by Prof. James Fetzer; and photos of a JT8D turbojet engine and the remnant found at the Pentagon at www.simmeringfrogs.com/articles/jt8d.html.
8. Report by two civilian defense contractor employees at "Secret Global Hawk Refit for Sky Warrior," portland.indymedia.org/en/2005/05/318250.shtml.
9. "Context of '(Shortly After 9:03 a.m.) September 11, 2001: Admiral in Charge of Navy Anti-Terrorism Division Finally Realizes US is Under Attack But Does Not

KnowFromWhom,'" www.historycommons.org/context.jsp?item=complete_911_timeline_3229#complete_911_timeline_3229.

10. *9/11—Coup Against America: The Pentagon Analysis*, compilation of Pentagon eyewitness reports, photos and analyses with hundreds of references, by Pete Tiradera, 2006, available from petertiradera@yahoo.com.

11. Pentagon eyewitness Don Perkal to MSNBC: "Even before stepping outside, I could smell the cordite. I knew explosives had gone off somewhere." Also eyewitness account of Amtrak electrical engineer Samuel Danner who was at the site and said he smelled cordite (*American Free Press*, July 7, 2006, reporting based on audio report by Republic Broadcasting Network, summary at www.total911.info/2006/07/pentagon-eyewitness-ids-global-hawk.html).

12. Author interview with former acting assistant secretary of defense for special operations and low intensity conflict, Monterey, California; summary posted on Naval Postgraduate School web site www.nps.navy.mil, subsequently changed to www.nps.edu. Article no longer posted; hard copy available from the author.

13. Richard Clarke interview article at www.nps.edu/About/News/Counterterrorism-Czar-Richard-Clarke-Calls-for-New-National-Cyber-Defense-Policy-to-Prevent-a-Cyber-9/11-.html.

14. Lynn Spencer, *Touching History: The Untold Story of the Drama That Unfolded in the Skies Over America on 9/11*, Free Press, 2008, pp. 24–27.

15. Personal communication to the author by Rhett Flater, executive director of the American Helicopter Society.

16. "Chilling Aerial Photos of 9/11 Attack Released: Police Aerial Photos Show World Trade Center Collapse," abcnews.go.com/US/wireStory?id=9796098.

17. "Bombshell: Silverstein Wanted To Demolish Building 7 On 9/11," www.prisonplanet.com/bombshell-silverstein-wanted-to-demolish-building-7-on-911.html.

18. Videotaped testimony of William ("Willy") Rodriguez, former World Trade Center janitor and the last person to leave the WTC alive on September 11, in the 9/11 documentary "Loose Change—Second Edition," text in parentheses added: "All of a sudden we hear 'Boom!' in the basement. I thought it was a generator that blew up, and I said to myself, 'Oh, my God, I think it was a generator. And I was going to verbalize it, and when I finished saying that in my mind I heard (another, second) 'Boom!' right on the top (above), pretty far away. And so it was a difference (in space and time) between coming from the basement and coming from the top...and a person comes running into the office (in the first basement level, from a deeper basement level) saying 'Explosion!'...and he said '(it was from) The elevators!' And there were many (deep basement WTC1) explosions."

19. "Agency (NRO) Planned Exercise on September 11 Built Around a Plane Crashing into a Building," Associated Press, August 22, 2002; by Jonathan Lumpkin; "They Scrambled Jets, but It was a Race They Couldn't Win," *Syracuse Post-Stan-*

*dard*, January 20, 2002, by Hart Seely; "Rome Staff's Efforts on 9/11 Earn Praise, Commission Says Military Did the Best It Could with the Information It Had," *Syracuse Post-Standard*, June 18, 2004, by Hart Seely; Complete 9/11 Military Exercises Timeline, Cooperative Research, at www.cooperativeresearch.org/timeline.jsp?timeline=complete_911_timeline&before-9/11=militaryExercises; *Crossing the Rubicon*, by Michael Ruppert, Chapter 19: "Wargames and High Tech: Paralyzing the System to Pull Off the Attacks" and Chapter 20: "Q&A: Many Asked, Some Answered—and a Golden Moment," New Society Publishers, 2004. In the Acknowledgements to *Rubicon*, p. xi, Ruppert credits the author with what he refers to as "the Holy Grail of 9/11 research" (p. 336): "Thanks to Barbara Honegger, who kept hammering on the wargames until we all paid notice…you showed me the most important lead I needed to put it all together."

20. "Detainee's Suit Gains Support from Jet's Log," *New York Times*, March 30, 2005, p. A1. Key excerpt, text in parentheses added: "Mr. Arar (a "rendered" detainee) says he followed the (Gulfstream jet) plane's movements on a map displayed on a video screen (inside the plane), watching it as he traveled to Dulles Airport outside Washington, to a Maine Airport he believed was in Portland (Maine), to Rome, and finally to Amman, Jordan, where he was blindfolded and driven to Syria." Though the FAA claims its records show a plane on that date making the other stops but landing in Bangor, not Portland, Maine, the detainee's account may be accurate, as only Portland's airport is labeled an "International *Jet* Port," specializing in landings and takeoffs of just such private, corporate and government jets.

21. Ironically, at the final hearing of the 9/11 Commission, where its report was released to the press and public, commissioner John Lehman responded to the question, *What if anything remained unknown*, by noting that the commission still wasn't clear as to "how Atta chose the date for the attacks."

22. Summary interrogation of Khalid Shaikh Mohammed, claimed "mastermind" of the September 11 attack plot, read into the Zacarias Moussaoui sentencing trial record by the prosecution on March 27, 2006; the full text is part of the court proceedings transcript for that date available through Exemplaris.com.

23. *The 9/11 Commission Report*, note 116, p. 458, at www.9-11commission.gov/report/911Report.pdf. Key excerpt: "On 9/11, NORAD was scheduled to conduct a military exercise, Vigilant Guardian, which postulated a bomber attack from the *former Soviet Union*."

24. *Air War Over America: Sept. 11 Alters Face of Air Defense Mission*, by Leslie Filson, US Air Force account of the events of September 11. Also "Civilian Planes to be Grounded 12 Hours Today in Defense Test," *New York Times*, October 14, 1961, pp. 1 and 4; "Civilian Planes Halted 12 Hours in Defense Test: Joint Maneuvers Fill Air Over Canada and US with Military Craft, Cities 'Hit' by Bombers," *New York Times*, October 15, 1961, pp. 1 and 46; "Computer is Key to Area Defense: Ever-Alert Device in (New)

Jersey Joins in Air Exercises," *New York Times*, October 15, 1961, p. 46; and "US-Canada Test of Air Defense Rated a Success: President Receives a Report on Maneuvers, Search is Pushed for Missing B-52," *New York Times*, October 16, 1961, pp. 1 and 16.
25. For example, see "Flight 11: The Twin Flight," by "Woody Box" at new.globalfreepress.com/article.pl?sid=04/03/14/212247, and "Flight 11 and Flight 93 'Survived'" at inn.globalfreepress.com/modules/news/article.php?storyid=858.
26. "Moussaoui, Undermining Case, Now Ties Himself to 9/11 Plot," *New York Times*, March 28, 2006, pp. A1 and A14.
27. www.judicialwatch.org/1967.shtml.
28. "Jerome Hauer, 9/11 Suspect Awaiting Indictment," truthmovecom.blogspot.com/2008/07/jerome-hauer-911-suspect-awaiting.html.
29. Ibid.
30. *Newsweek*, September 24, 2001.
31. "Michael Chertoff—Where All the Questions Should Start," January 12, 2005, allspinzone.blogspot.com.

THE PENTAGON ATTACK PAPERS

# INDEX

Abbottabad, Pakistan, 319–320
Abd, Umar, 237, 285
Abdullah, Crown Prince, 128, 270, 337–339
Abdussattar Shaikh, 24, 328
Abidor, 372
Able Danger, 148–150
Abrams, Elliot, 174
Abu Dhabi National Oil Company, 332
Abu Ghraib, 29, 351, 353
Abu Sayyaf (ASG), 118
ACLU (American Civil Liberties Union), 371–372, 377, 379, 381, 383–384, 391–392, 398, 401–402, 411–415, 435
Adams Mark Hotel (Denver, CO), 397
Aden, Steven H., 398
Adler, Paul, 462
Advise and Assist, 250
Afghanistan, 24, 27, 40, 44, 74, 116–117, 143–145, 149–152, 169, 175, 179, 206, 223–228, 236, 245, 250–259, 266, 268, 277–278, 297–303, 306–311, 314–319, 335, 339–341, 348, 352, 413, 420–423, 439, 446, 449, 465, 493, 499, 502, 504
Aftergood, Steven, 370, 445
Ahmad, Mahmoud, 178
Ahmed Umar Saeed Sheikh, 317
Ahmed, Jamal, 127
Ahmed, Nafeez Mosaddeq, 239, 317
*Air Force One*, 10–11, 14, 22, 187, 333
Air Force, US, 4, 9–11, 14, 17, 22, 47, 179–180, 186–187, 189–190, 192, 201–202, 205–206, 211, 216, 304, 333, 361, 407, 452, 472, 505
Air France Flight 8969, 117
Air Traffic Controllers, 2–4, 9, 34, 53, 181–182, 185, 199, 204
Airborne Warning and Control System (AWACS), 17, 182, 190
Airbus Industries, 432
Airfone, 195, 197–199, 204
al Kabir, Fahd, 42
Al Qaeda, 5, 25–29, 40–44, 112–120, 127–129, 132–135, 139, 143–149, 151–156, 164–165, 171, 188, 223–224, 232, 235–238, 241–242, 261, 264, 273–274, 285, 288, 297, 300, 310–311, 315, 321, 324–327, 329, 331, 335–336, 339, 342–348, 351, 420, 423–424, 432, 476–477, 511–512
Al Rajhi banking family, 324, 338
al Suqami, Satam, 35
al-Banna, Hassan, 43
al-Ghamdi, Saeed, 26
Al-Hazmi, Al-Badr, 407
Al-Hazmi, Nawif, 113, 146, 185, 329
Al-Jazeera, 259, 314
al-Khidamat, Maktab, 44
al-Marashi, Ibrahim, 264
al-Midhar, Kahlid, 113, 146, 329
al-Omari, Abdulaziz, 26
al-Qadi, Yasin, 329
al-Sabah, Sheik Fahd Mohammed, 464
al-Saud, Sultan bin Abdul Aziz, 323
al-Saud, Sultan bin Faisal bin Turki, 42
al-Shehhi, Marwan, 289
al-Shehri, Waleed, 26, 240
al-Shibh, Ramzi bin, 19, 139, 171
al-Yemeni, Haitham, 143
al-Zawahiri, Ayman, 144
Alami, Murad, 313
Alamoudi, Abdurrahman, 270
Albert, Heinrich, 46
Alderman, Liz, 323
Aldrich, Gary, 131, 135
Alexander, Lamar, 355, 385, 455, 488
Alexandrov, Boian, 345
Alfa Group, 305–306
Alfred P. Murrah Federal Building, 59, 284
Alito, Samuel, 314
Alkadiri, Raad, 280
Allen, Gary, 161, 228, 397, 490, 495
Allende, Salvador, 228, 490
Allison Engine Co., 180
Altanmia Commercial Marketing Co., 281–282
Amalgam Virgo, 18–19
America Rebuilds, 104
American Airlines Flight 11, 2, 8, 17, 26, 35, 196–198, 208, 212, 215, 240, 507
American Airlines Flight 77, 2–4, 10, 12, 19, 32–35, 44, 50–56, 146, 183–185, 190–194, 201, 215, 242, 329
American Booksellers Foundation for Free Expression (ABFFE), 414
American Library Association, 413
American Muslim Council, 270
American Society of Civil Engineers (ASCE), 58–59
Americans for Legal Immigration Political Action Committee (ALIPAC), 374
AMR Corp., 158
Anarchist Club (Sissonville High School, WV), 395
Anderson, Harold, 481
Anderson, Jack, 218
Anderson, Maxwell, 293
Andrews Air Force Base,
Andrews, Robert, 8, 201
Angeles, Edwin, 118
Anthony, Bill, 149, 303, 371, 396, 431
Anti-Defamation League (ADL), 373
Antiterrorism and Effective Death Penalty Act, 284
Anthrax, 65, 42, 349, 400–401, 432, 488, 508
Applied Digital Solutions, Inc., 429
Arafat, Yasser, 174
Arbenz, Jacobo, 490
Arbusto Energy, 330, 332
Arctic National Wildlife Reserve National Park, 268
Arkin, William M., 195, 466–467
Armed Forces Institute of Pathology (AFIP), 32
Armitage, Richard, 174, 388–389
Army, US, 10, 17, 20, 36–38, 42–49, 53, 118, 121–122, 130, 147–148, 161, 171, 177, 190, 217–221, 228, 244, 247–250, 254, 260, 264, 278, 281–282, 302–303, 331, 354, 357–358, 361–364, 378, 384–386, 397, 457, 460, 466, 494, 508

# INDEX

Arney, George, 253, 256
Arnold, Larry, 18, 46, 54, 202, 436, 501, 511
Ashcroft, John, 124, 134–135, 138, 142, 176, 234–235, 238, 258, 324, 331, 381, 387, 392, 404–405, 415, 419–423, 445
Aspen Institute, 225
Atkins, James, 261
Atlanta, GA, 267, 270, 462–463
Atta, Mohamed, 19, 34–35, 39–40, 139, 148–150, 170–171, 176–178, 185, 240, 274, 289–290, 317
Atwan, Abdel-Barri, 121
Atzmon, Menachem , 507
Auerbach, Gerald, 330
Auster, Bruce, 263
Australia, 88, 179–180, 282, 291, 352, 388, 432
Avery, Dylan, 505
Awad, Mohammed, 307
Axis of Evil, 260, 466
Azad, Farhad, 259
Aziz, Ahmed, 323
Aziz, Turki, 41

Babbitt, Bruce, 488
Bahrain, 334, 352, 463
Baker, James, 318, 332, 336, 440, 460–461, 488
Baker, Jeremy , 239
Baker, Lisa , 376
Baker, Paul, 172
Baker, Raymond, 298
Baldwin, Chuck, 375
Balkans, 190, 278, 470
Ballard, Greg, 358–359
Balsamo, Rob, 184
Baltimore, MD, 161, 437
Banca Nazionale del Lavoro (BNL), 462
Bandar, Prince, 270, 336–337
Bank of America, 329
Bankers Trust Building, 98
Bankston, Kevin, 436
Barak, Ehud, 218, 444
Barksdale Air Force Base, 505
Barr, Bob, 375, 388, 463
Barr, Cameron, W., 375, 388, 463
Barr, William, 375, 388, 463
Bartley, Robert, 481
Bartmer, Craig, 102
Basmyiah, Iraq, 292
Basnan, Osama, 329
Bass, Gary, 445

Bath, James R., 330–333
Batista, Fulgencio, 490
Baton Rouge, LA, 304
Baumbach, Bill, 378
Baxter, Sheri, 33
Bay of Pigs, the, 161, 213, 465, 467, 490, 511
Bayefsky, Anne, 484
Bayoumi, Omar al, 323, 329
BCCI (Bank of Credit & Commerce International), 161, 229, 331–332, 334–335
Beaty, Jonathan, 332–333
Beck, Bud, 272
Bedard, Paul, 290
Beghal, Djamel, 151
Bellone, Mike, 38–39
ben Zui, Sar, 178
Ben-Veniste, Richard, 231, 234–235
Benevolence International, 406
Bennett, William, 150
Berg, Philip J., 325
Berger, Sandy, 441, 488
Berlet, Chip, 169
Bermas, Jason, 210
Bernard, Marcel, 33, 35, 425
Bernhard, Prince, 472
Bethesda, MD, 360, 384
Biblical, 217–218, 295, 429
Bilderbergers, 228, 455, 472, 475
Bill of Rights, 372, 413, 416, 422, 510
Bin al-Shibh, Ramzi, 19, 139, 171
Bin Laden, Abdullah, 337–338
Bin Laden, Carmen, 327
Bin Laden, Mohammed Awad, 307
Bin Laden, Omar, 337
Bin Laden, Osama, 5, 11–12, 23–27, 37, 41–44, 112–121, 127–134, 140, 143–147, 150–156, 160, 182, 188, 219, 224, 228, 236–237, 241, 245, 253–259, 266, 274, 285–289, 306–325, 335–339, 347–348, 400, 413, 468, 476–477, 487–488, 501–502, 507–508, 511–512
Bin Laden, Salem, 329–331
Bin Ladens, 23–24, 162, 241, 322, 335–337, 340
bin Laden virus, 321
Bingham, Mark , 195–196
Binladen Brothers Construction, 335

Blair, Tony, 28, 165, 262, 271–272, 450
Blanton, Thomas, 445
Blix, Hans, 263
Blood, Jack, 505
Bloomsburg, PA, 414
Blum, William, 315
Bodansky, Yossef, 115
Bodine, Barbara, 128
Body Scanners, 345–346
Boeing E-4 / E-4B, 186–188, 221
Bogdanos, Matthew, 295
Bojinka, Project, 117, 230, 288
Bollyn, Christopher, 52, 77, 227, 238, 294
Bolshevik Revolution, 495
Bolton, Alexander, 174
Bolton, John, 174
Bonior, David, 266
Booker Elementary School (Sarasota, FL), 3
Bordley, William, 346
Bormann, Martin, 454
Boston, MA, 2, 17, 23–24, 39–40, 169, 182–183, 207–209, 211, 213–214, 302, 317, 330, 383, 507
Bowen, Russell S., 464, 481
Bowen, William G., 464, 481
Bowie, MD, 33
Bowman, John, 48
Bowman, Robert, 21, 493
Boyce, Dan, 418
Bradley International Airport, 356
Brancaccio, David, 264–265
Brant, Jim, 206
Brasch, Walter, 403, 416
Brassman, Osama, 323
Bratton, William, 392
Breen, Kenneth, 157
Breitweiser, Kristin, 31
Bremer, Jerry, 163
Brewton, Peter, 334
Brinkerhoff, John, 366
Brinkley, David, 481
Brisard, Jean Charles, 252, 256
Britain, 27–30, 84, 275, 299, 323, 348, 356, 456, 460–461, 495
British Airways, 181
Broad, William, 370, 380, 404, 413–414, 478
Brokaw, Tom, 481
Brookhart, Linda, 188–189
Brooks, Jack, 463

Brown, A. J., 394
Brown, Bryan D., 361
Brown, Harold, 488
Brown, Herman, 278
Brown, Hyman, 78
Brown, Scott, 320
Brown, Willie, 124
Brzezinski, Zbigniew, 252, 254–255, 488
Bucca, Ronald P., 76, 82
Buchanan, Lyn, 217, 219
Buckley, William F., Jr., 481
Bunch, William, 39–40, 52, 264, 346, 486
Bundy, McGeorge, 468
Bureau of Alcohol, Tobacco, & Firearms (BATF/ATF), 76, 99, 133–134, 286–287, 399
Burgener, Clair, 359
Burien, Walter, 163
Burlingame, Charles, 33, 192
Burnam, Lon, 377–378
Burnett, Tom, 197–198
Burns, Jim, 49, 86
Burns, Margie, 49, 86
Bush, George H. W., 127, 229, 249, 269, 303, 327, 332, 336, 407, 440, 464, 488, 491–492, 512
Bush, George W., 3–15, 19–32, 42–43, 48, 60–65, 72, 74, 86, 111–115, 124–127, 131–137, 141–144, 148, 153–155, 160–166, 173–175, 178, 181, 188, 193–194, 201–202, 219–235, 238, 240–254, 258–284, 290–291, 296–297, 300–306, 311–367, 375, 378–379, 382, 386–403, 407–409, 413–415, 421–426, 429, 433, 437–451, 454–456, 460–464, 467–468, 471, 474–477, 487–493, 501–505, 508–512
Bush, Jeb, 32, 268, 304, 335
Bush, Marvin P., 86, 160, 242, 508
Bush, Neil, 335
Bussey, John, 69
Butler, Smedley D., 468
Butler, Steven, 328–329
Byrd, Robert, 261, 367

Cabal, Alan, 27, 193
Cable Splicer II, 359
Cacchioli, Louie, 66–67, 233
Cairo, Egypt, 43, 120
Calais, ME, 371

CALEA (Communications Assistance for Law Enforcement Act), 172–173
Callahan, David, 164
Cambone, Stephen A., 360–361
Cameron, Carl, 169–170, 450
Camp Anaconda, Iraq, 283
Campbell, Duncan, 359
Canada, 18, 159, 216, 236, 366, 392, 399, 432, 475
CanaMex, 475
cancer, 52, 99, 328
Caracas, Venezuela, 83–84
Card, Andrew, 3, 13, 35–36, 247, 304, 341, 363, 397, 411, 417, 424, 427–428, 430, 452
Carew, Tom, 302
Carlucci, Frank C., 336, 488
Carlyle Group, 162, 269, 330, 336–337
Carnahan, Mel, 419
Carnivore, 126–127
Carrier, Silvia, 21, 105, 192, 319, 390, 458
Carroll, Eugene, 261
Carter, Ashton B., 226
Carter, Chris, 125
Carter, Hodding, III, 481
Carter, Jimmy, 254, 318, 338, 442, 448
Casey, William, 145, 161, 229
Caspian Sea, 245–246, 250, 253, 258
Castro, Fidel, 213–214, 223, 391, 468, 490, 509
Cayman Islands, 116, 279, 283, 298, 333–335
CentGas, 250–251
Central Asia Institute, 253
Central Asian Gas Pipeline, 250–251
Century Group, 456
Cerf, Bennett, 150
Cessna 172, 32–34
Chaitkin, Anton, 461
Champagne, Bertha, 508–509
Chancellor, John, 452, 481
Chaney, Rick, 206
Chantilly, VA, 16
Chao, Elaine, 440
Charlesbois, David, 33
Chavez, Lauro "LJ", 17
Chechnya, 250, 310, 312, 455
Cheney, Dick, 3–4, 11, 13, 17–19, 21–23, 47, 54–55, 74, 113, 201–202, 205, 216,
219, 226, 231–233, 251–252, 276–281, 283, 296, 305–306, 319, 324, 348, 360, 398, 425, 437, 439–440, 445–446, 468, 488, 501–503, 506, 509
Chertoff, Benjamin, 238
Chertoff, Michael, 28, 40, 134, 238, 344–345
Chevron Oil, 279
Chicago, IL, 29, 117, 126, 128–129, 132, 134, 157–159, 167, 173, 293, 389–390
Chile, 228, 488, 490
Chin, Denny, 47–48
China, 58, 118–119, 190, 248, 260–261, 302, 456, 459, 472, 484, 512
ChipMobile, 430
Chossudovsky, Michel, 177–178
Christian, George, 414–415
Christison, William, 261
Christopher, Robert, 481
Church, Frank, 69, 218, 337, 355, 408–409, 417, 493, 497
Churchill, Winston, 458
CIA (Central Intelligence Agency), 7, 16, 27–28, 41–42, 44, 67, 102, 107–108, 113–118, 125, 128, 132, 142–157, 161–164, 171, 175–178, 182, 213, 217–226, 229–232, 237, 240–241, 254, 261, 285, 297–305, 309–310, 313–317, 320, 324, 330–332, 337–343, 348, 361–362, 375, 381, 386–388, 399–403, 409, 412, 432, 435, 459–460, 465–470, 487–494, 500–512
Cincinnati, OH, 430, 449
Cipro, 65
Citibank/Citigroup, 162, 298
Citizen Corps, 390–391
CitizensWatch, 325
CityWatcher, 430
Clapper, James R., Jr., 360
Clark, Richard, 303
Clark, Wesley, 355, 488
Clarke, Richard A., 3, 16, 24, 28–29, 127–128, 131–132, 205, 235–236, 261, 433
Claybrook, Joan, 445
Clean Break paper, 174–175
Cleland, Max, 232
Cleveland Hopkins International Airport, 207
Cleveland, OH, 204, 207–213, 216

# INDEX

Clifford, Clark, 161
Cline, Phil, 29
Clinton, Bill, 131-137, 143, 148, 151, 155, 172-173, 193, 230-231, 235, 240, 254, 257, 266, 284, 288, 303-306, 310-311, 355, 381, 410, 429, 433, 437, 440-444, 447-448, 464-465, 477, 493, 502-503, 512
Clinton, Hillary, 131, 320, 343, 440, 488
Coast Guard, US, 129, 368-370, 381
Cockburn, Alexander, 385
Cockpit Voice Recorders (CVR), 38
Cogan, Charles, 299
Cogitek Corp, 182
Cohen, Samuel, 100
Cohen, William, 478
COINTELPRO, 381
Coldren, Lee, 256-257
Cole, David D., 383
Cole, Jonathan, 90-91
*Cole*, USS, 128, 143
Collinwood, C. C., 481
*Columbia*, space shuttle, 39, 224, 244
Commerce Department, 119, 131, 434
Committees for the Defense of the Revolution (CDR), 391
Commodity Credit Corporation (CCC), 463
Computer Fraud and Abuse Act, 404
Comverse Infosys, 172
Connally, John, 224, 332
Conner, Ben, 33
Constitution, US, 136, 228, 248, 261, 266-268, 325, 352, 365, 379, 388, 395, 401, 403-405, 413, 418, 421, 434, 442-443, 448-449, 502, 510
Continental Flight 3407, 507
Continuity of Government (COG), 447
Contras, 491
Controlled Demolition, 63-65, 79, 81, 88, 103-107, 110, 241
Cook, Bobby Lee, 463
Cook, Robin, 27, 348
Coolidge, Archibald, 302
Coolidge, Joseph, 302
Cooney, Joan Ganz, 481

Corley, W. Gene, 59-60, 81-82
Corpus Christi, TX, 278, 357
Corpwatch, 282
Coulson, Danny, 288
Council on Foreign Relations (CFR), 57, 119, 132, 137, 172, 174-175, 220, 226-228, 247, 253, 255, 268, 291, 302, 324, 327, 366, 388, 440, 454, 459, 469, 475-476, 480-481, 488, 502-503, 512
Counterterrorism Command Center (CTC), 48
Cowen, Donovan, 77
Cramer, Glen, 200
Crawford, TX, 23, 28, 153, 270
Crescent Group of Pakistan, 251
Crogan, Jim, 289-290
Crone, Marcia, 407
Cronkite, Walter, 482, 500
Crossley, Richard, 158
Cuba, 213-214, 223, 278, 283, 351, 353, 420, 465-467, 484, 490
Cummings, John, 304
Curry, Andrew, 337
Curtis, Adam, 456
Customs House (WTC Building 6), 75-76, 107
Customs Service, United States, 76, 108, 368
Cybersecurity Act of 2009, 433-434

Dafydd Ab Hugh (David Friedman), 450
Dall, Curtis B., 456
Dallas, TX, 97, 123, 278, 280, 332, 377-378, 486
Damadola, Pakistan, 144
Danang, Vietnam, 387
Danner, Samuel, 52-53
Darman, Richard, 336, 488
DARPA (Defense Advanced Research Projects Agency), 180-181, 363
Daschle, Tom, 259, 448
Dasquie, Guillaume, 169, 252, 256
Däubler-Gmelin, Herta,
David, Felipe, 73, 96
Davidson, Ralph, 481
Davis, Jayna, 287
Daytona Beach, FL, 451
DCS-1000, 126
De Borchgrave, Arnaud, 481

De Grand Pre, Donn, 190, 469
Dean, John, 379
Dean, Lisa, 173
Dearlove, Richard, 271
Decatur, GA, 267
Decker, Dennis, 206
Dees, Morris, 376
Deets, Dwain, 111
DeFazio, Peter, 473
Defence Science and Technology Organisation (DSTO), 179
Defense Department (DoD), 56, 102, 107, 149, 172, 180-181, 194, 201-202, 282-283, 293, 322-324, 333, 355, 362, 438, 465-466, 474, 493
Defense Intelligence Agency (DIA), 217-218, 360
Defense Policy Board, 173-175
Dejka, Joe, 187
Del Giorno, John, 506
Delano, Frederic, 246, 456
Delray Beach, FL, 170
Delta Air Lines Flight 1989, 208-213
Delta Force, 361
Delta Oil Company Limited of Saudi Arabia, 251
DeMasi, Nicholas, 38-39
Denmark, 352
Denver, CO, 26, 392, 397-398
Deskins, Dawne, 17
Despres, Gregory, 371
Deutch, John M., 162, 226, 488
Deutsche Bank, 160-161
Devlin, John, 99
Dhahran, Saudi Arabia, 335
Diamandis, Alex, 166-167
Dintilhac, Jean-Pierre, 142
DNA, 274, 345, 404, 437
Doherty, David, 161
Dole, Robert, 355
Doran, Michael, 506
Downie, Leonard, Jr., 481
Downing Street Memo, 271, 273, 502
Dresser-Rand, 280
Drogoul, Christopher, 462-463
Drug Abuse Resistance Education (DARE), 392
Drug Enforcement Agency (DEA), 169-170, 173, 299, 303-304, 333, 393
Dubai, UAE, 150-151
Dulles International Airport, 2, 16, 86, 160, 184, 508
Dulles, Allen, 161, 228, 490

Dulles, John Foster, 161, 490
Duncan, Allan P., 133–134, 279
Durbin, Richard J., 353–354
Durenberger, David, 145

Eager, Thomas, 84, 178, 315
Eagleburger, Lawrence, 488
East Timor, 228, 490
Echelon, 11, 142–143, 165, 431–432
Eckert, Beverly, 507
Ecstasy, 169, 299
Edgar, Timothy H., 379–381, 457
Edinburgh Air Force Base, 179
Edmonds, Sibel, 135–138, 238
Edwards Air Force Base, 179
Edwards, John O., 179–180
Eglin Air Force Base, 9
Egypt, 43–44, 115, 134, 295, 308, 352, 399, 484
El Salvador, 491
El Sayyid Nosair, 38
Elamir, Magdy, 134
Elamir, Mohammed, 134
Elbaradei, Mohamed, 263
electromagnetic pulse (EMP), 93–96, 186–187, 190
Electronic Frontier Foundation (EFF), 402, 404, 434, 436
Electronic Privacy Information Center, 126, 346, 404
Elgindy, Amr Ibrahim, 157
Ellington Field, Houston, TX, 333
Elliott, Tom, 70–71
Ellner, Oded, 168
Elwood, James R., 416
Emad Salem, 37–38
Embassy Suites Hotel (Oklahoma City), 288
Enabling Act (Germany), 452
Enchanted Valley, TX, 329
enemy combatant, 418–422
Energy Task Force, 268, 280, 425, 445
England, 239, 271, 291, 346, 412, 431, 454, 456, 511
Enron, 23, 243, 268, 279–280, 333, 425, 441, 474, 503, 511
Erlanger, Phil, 157
Ervin, Sam, 358, 364, 371
Es Sayed, Abdelkader Mahmoud, 115
Eslinger, Don, 436
Evangelista, Lieutenant, 68
Evans, Steve, 70
Executive Orders (EO), 365, 369, 388, 447
Export-Import Bank, 75, 232, 305

F-15s / F-16s, 2–4, 8–9
F-35, 472
FAA (Federal Aviation Administration), 2–4, 6, 9–13, 17–18, 23, 25, 124, 129, 144, 154, 190, 194, 201, 208, 211–212, 230, 242–243, 305, 499
Facebook, 395
Fahd, King, 41–42, 309, 464
Faisal, King, 42, 307, 323, 329
Faisal, Princess Haifa bint, 42, 307, 323, 329
Faisal, Turki bin, 42, 307, 323, 329
Faisalabad, Pakistan, 40
Falls Church, VA, 337
Falmouth, MA, 2
false radar images, 18
Family Steering Committee (FSC), 6, 12, 325
Farben, I. G., 453
Fassbinder, Jorg, 292
Fathi, David C., 384
Faulkner, Larry R., 396
FBI (Federal Bureau of Investigation), 7, 10–12, 20, 24–26, 29–33, 35–42, 50–51, 58, 74, 105–107, 114, 118, 123–146, 149–150, 153–154, 157, 160, 164–173, 177–178, 189–194, 197–200, 203–210, 222–223, 234–241, 252, 270, 281, 286–290, 304–305, 317, 321, 328–329, 337–339, 347, 354, 358, 364, 375, 381–383, 391–393, 399, 401–409, 412–418, 427, 434–435, 457, 463, 500–505, 508
FCC (Federal Communications Commission), 478
Federal Reserve, 333, 456, 481
Federation of American Scientists, 370, 446, 467
Feegle, John, 206
Fein, Bruce, 409, 443
Feingold, Russ, 372
Feith, Doug, 174
Felt, Edward, 192
FEMA (Federal Emergency Management Agency), 18, 22, 58–61, 64, 75, 81–84, 90, 105–106, 110, 241, 350, 357, 364–366, 368, 370, 372, 378–379, 381, 390, 504
Ferguson, Gail, 219
Fichte, Johann Gottlieb, 497
Fielding, Fred, 230
Fine, Glenn , 7, 24, 35, 62, 339, 349, 362, 397, 415–416, 427, 429
Firefighters (FDNY), 38–39, 59, 66, 68, 76–77, 79, 81, 83
First Amendment, 129, 372, 381, 405, 407, 409, 479, 484
first responders, 66, 87, 91, 98–99
FISA (Foreign Intelligence Surveillance Act), 141, 403–404, 409
FISC (Foreign Intelligence Surveillance Court), 127, 403–404
Fisher-Rosemount, 280
Fisk, Robert, 294
Fitts, Catherine Austin, 474–475
Fitzgerald, Dennis G., 393
FitzSimmons, Dennis, 478
Fleischer, Ari, 40, 114, 312, 443, 477
Flight Data Recorders, 38
Flight Termination System (FTS), 57
Flowserve, 280
Floyd, Chris, 467
FOIA (Freedom of Information Act), 352, 380
Forbes, Scott, 86
Ford Motor Co., 478
Ford, Gerald, 225, 277, 318, 330, 348, 488
Foreman, Liz, 207
Fort Belvoir, VA, 363
Fort Bragg, NC, 38, 42, 316
Fort Campbell, 359
Fort Chaffee, AR, 365
Fort Detrick, MD, 508
Fort Hood, TX, 355
Fort Meade, MD, 142
Fort Sill, OK, 285
Fort Stewart, GA, 36–37
Fort Worth, TX, 198, 288, 377, 407
Foster, Vincent, 134
Fountain, Ben, 86
Fourth Amendment, 347, 372, 408–409
Fox, Mike, 252
Frankel, Max, 481
Frankfurt, Germany, 495

# INDEX

Free Congress Foundation, 173
Freeman, Dr. Debra H., 419
Freeway Airport, Bowie, MD, 33
French Intelligence Service, 141
Frenzen, Niels, 406
Fuller, Craig, 248
Fulton, Frederick, 371
Fulton, John, 16
fusion centers, 374–375, 377–378

G-8, 258
Gaffney, Mark H., 187–190
Gallop, April, 46–48
Ganci, Peter, 101
Garrick, Cassandra, 398
Garvey, Jane, 3, 154
Garza, Felipe, 357
Gayle, Frank, 77
Gelb, Richard, 481
Gellman, Barton, 361–362
General Accounting Office (GAO), 280, 339
General Electric (GE), 473
General Motors, 453
Geneva Conventions, 386, 424
Genoa technology, 363
Geostatic Imperatives, 255
Gergen, David, 481
German, Mike, 393
Germany, 20, 121, 158, 171, 176, 180, 226, 258, 291–292, 305, 313, 385, 420, 441, 452–455, 458, 495, 498, 511
Gerth, Jeff, 278
Gestapo, 385, 391, 458
Geyelin, Phillip, 481
Geyer, Georgie Ann, 481
Ghanem, Alia, 313
Ghazni Province, Afghanistan, 143
Ghent, Randy, 475
GI Joe toy, 356
Gibson, McGuire, 293–294
Gilgamesh, 292
Gillette, Guy, 457
Gingrich, Newt, 267
Giuliani, Rudolph, 18, 64–65, 100–101, 103, 242
Glaspie, April, 461–462
Glass, Randy, 71, 133–134, 294, 391
Glick, Jeremy, 199, 204
Global Guardian, 187–188
Global Hawk, 52, 179–182, 184–185, 200, 206
Global Options LLC, 123

Global Relief Foundation, 405
Glover, William E., Jr., 17
Goering, Hermann, 452, 454, 496
Goldberg, Jonah, 343
Golden Chain, the, 335
Golden Triangle, the, 247, 299, 388
Goldman Sachs, 438
Goldsmith, Gilah, 48
Gonzales, Alberto, 45, 383, 415, 424–426
Gonzalez, Alexa, 418–419
Gonzalez, Henry, 462–463
Goodman, David, 415
Gordon, Steven, 169
Gore, Al, 259, 318, 488, 495, 511
Gorelick, Jamie, 230
Gorman, Peter, 377
Gorton, Slade, 231
Goss, Porter, 161, 178, 315, 506
GPS (Global Positioning System), 64, 400, 431, 435–436
Graham, Bob, 24, 113, 178, 326
Graham, David, 505–506
Graham, Hugh, 444
Graham, Katherine, 481
Grand Prairie, TX, 333
Grandcolas, Lauren, 197
Grangier, Francois, 51
Granick, Jennifer, 434
Grassley, Charles, 138
Gray Fox, 361
Great Depression, the, 468
Great Game, the, 246, 464
Green Berets, 42
Greenberg, Hank, 162
Greenhouse, Bunnatine, 281–282
Greenspan, Alan, 488
Greider, William, 478
Gribbin, Dave, 306
Griffin, David Ray, 9, 14, 36, 38, 55, 83, 85, 147, 197, 205, 226, 240, 244, 461
Griffin, G. Edward, 495
Gritz, Bo, 388
Ground Zero, 7, 35, 39, 58, 67, 82, 85, 88, 92–93, 96, 98–99, 105–106, 108–109, 242, 508
Grune, George V., 481
Grunwald, Henry, 481
Guantanamo Bay, 278, 351, 353, 420, 437, 466
Gul, Hameed, 175–176, 178
Gulf of Tonkin, 247–248, 272

Gulf War, 147, 192, 195, 248–249, 263, 276, 278–279, 285, 293, 327, 335, 384, 459, 461–464, 492
Gunderson, Ted, 144–145
Guste, William J., Jr., 304
Guthrie, Dan, 397
Gutting, Tom, 83, 397
Gwozdecky, Mark, 262–263

Haas, Ed, 11
Hadith, the, 328
Haglund, Dean, 125
Haig, Alexander, 488–489
Haji, the, 53, 307
Halberstam, David, 481
Hall, Mimi, 420
Halliburton, 251, 277–284, 305–306, 350, 439, 473, 478
Hamas, 157, 260, 270, 285, 432
Hambali, 342
Hamburg, Germany, 171, 176, 258, 314
Hamdi, Yaser Esam, 420–421
Hamilton, Bill, 162
Hamilton, Lee, 55, 149, 196, 222, 228–233, 477, 503
Hammond, Matthew, 355
Hampton, VA, 4
Hanjour, Hani, 32–34, 53, 130, 185, 241
Hanni, Kate, 345
Hansen, Mark, 10
Hanssen, Robert, 140
Happyland Social Club Fire, 58
Harel, Ezra, 507
Harken Bahrain Energy Company, 334
Harken Energy, 279, 332–335, 439
Harman, Jane, 430
Harris, Katherine, 268
Harris, Leslie, 434
Hartmann, Thom, 30, 348
Hatfield, J. H., 331
Hauer, Jerome, 64–65, 306
Havana, Cuba, 391
Haver, Richard, 360
Hayden, Katherine S., 398
Hayden, Michael, 409
Heathrow Airport, UK, 286
Hegelian, 451, 496–497, 499
Heidenberger, Michelle, 183
Hentoff, Nat, 423
Hersh, Seymour, 175, 467
Hershberger, Jeff, 329
Hess, Michael, 103–104

Hess Oil, 228
Heyman, Jack, 389
Hezbollah, 270
Hightower, T. Mark, 96
Hijackers, 3, 5, 10, 12, 19, 24–43, 57, 114, 117–118, 123, 131, 146, 148, 155, 170, 176, 181–185, 191–199, 204–205, 240–241, 258, 270, 321, 323, 328–329, 347, 407, 477, 500, 505–507
Hill & Knowlton, 248
Hill, Eleanor, 114–115
Hilton Hotel (Sherman Oaks, CA), 144
Hilton, Stanley G., 144
Himmler, Heinrich, 453
Hinckley, John, 511
Hirsh, Michael, 155
Hitchens, Christopher, 228
Hitler, Adolf, 43, 247–248, 403, 420, 452–457, 464, 496–497, 511–512
Ho Chi Minh, 494, 496
Hoffman, David, 288–289
Hoffman, Jim, 61–62
Hoglan, Alice, 195
Holland, 458, 472
Holocaust, the, 183
Holy Land Foundation for Relief and Development, 406
Homeland Security Act, 370, 381–382
Homeland Security Advisory Council, 229
Homeland Security Department, 16, 28, 132–134, 229–231, 238, 283, 344, 347, 349–350, 354, 358, 366–386, 390–399, 411, 427–428, 440, 448, 502
Homer, LeRoy, Jr., 192
Honegger, Barbara, 4, 18–19, 22, 45, 48, 54, 205
Hoofard, Shirley, 97
Hookers, 39, 183
Hoover, J. Edgar, 381, 457
Hopsicker, Daniel, 31–32, 39–40, 303–305
Hotchkin, Sheila, 477
House, Karen, 481
Houston Gulf Airport, 330
Houston, TX, 24, 144, 211, 329–330, 332–334, 396, 407, 463
Howe, Carol, 287
Hoyos, Carola, 280

Hubbell, Fred, 356
Huffman Aviation, 32
Hufschmid, Eric, 82, 102
Hughes, Baker, 280
Hull, Cordell, 456
Hume, Brit, 479
Humphreys, Richard Allen, 397
Huntleigh USA, 507
Hussein, Saddam, 174, 195, 235, 248–249, 260, 262–266, 273, 278, 287, 291–292, 295–296, 308, 334, 337, 432, 459–465, 468, 496, 502–503, 511–512
Husseini, Abdel El M., 313
Hutchinson, Billy, 201–202
Hutchinson, John, 97
Hyundai Engineering & Construction Co., 251

Ibragimov, Rustem, 37
Idiatullin, Nail , 37
Idris, Saleh, 310
Ikle, Fred, 174
Illuminati, 451, 494, 497, 511
Imle, John F., 250
Immigration and Naturalization Service (INS), 368, 406
Inderfurth, Karl Rick, 256–257
India, 178, 231, 250, 253, 260, 337–338
Indianapolis, 358–359
Indonesia Petroleum Ltd, 251
Information Awareness Office (IAO), 363
Ingersoll-Dresser Pump, 280
Ingledue, Jim, 35–36
Inspector General (IG), 9, 113, 136, 148, 150–52, 229, 339, 370, 380–381, 393, 416–417, 474
Institute of Terrorism Research and Response, 376
Intelligence and Security Command (INSCOM), 46, 218, 363
International Atomic Energy Agency (IAEA), 262
International Center for 9/11 Studies, 88, 98
International Consultants on Targeted Security (ICTS), 507
Internet "kill switch", 433
Internet Service Provider (ISP), 167
Iran, 115, 120, 229, 245, 253, 258, 272, 283–285, 352, 363, 400, 460–462, 467, 488–491, 496, 499, 510
Iran-Contra, 130, 229, 305, 327, 363, 378–379, 388, 464, 467, 491
Iraq, 22, 24–25, 32, 40, 74, 120, 147, 165, 174–175, 201, 223–226, 235, 248–250, 258–269, 271–285, 290–297, 312, 327, 340–342, 352–353, 370, 385, 389, 394, 421, 438–439, 443, 446, 455, 459–465, 470, 499, 502–504
Iraq-Iran War, 460
Iraqgate, 327, 463
Iraqi National Museum, 293, 295, 465
Iron Mountain, 468–470
IRS, 411, 426–427, 444, 447, 485
Irvine, Reed, 481
Isaac, Paul, Jr., 67
Isenberg, David, 467
Isikoff, Michael, 155
Iskandar, Joseph, 35–36
Islamabad, Pakistan, 299
Islamic Institute, 338
Israel, 43, 57, 121–122, 165–178, 190, 249, 260, 312, 326–328, 421, 444, 460, 487, 491, 499–500, 507, 510
Israeli Herzliya International Policy Institute, 156
Italy, 115, 258, 352, 432, 462
ITOCHU Oil Exploration Co. Ltd, 251
Ivins, Bruce, 508
iWATCH, 392–393

Jackson, Jesse, 291
Jacksonville, FL, 36–37
Jansen, Brad, 173
Japan, 34, 158, 246, 251, 456–457
Java, Indonesia, 457
Jaylan, Phil, 214–216
Jeddah, Saudi Arabia, 307–308, 339
Jefferson, Lisa, 196
Jennings, Barry, 103–104, 505
Jennings, Peter, 100, 188
Jensen, Robert, 396–397
Jersey City, NJ, 123
Jerusalem, 165, 171
Jihad, 27, 41–42, 115, 236, 260, 285, 348
Johannemann, Kenneth, 505
Johnson, Arline, 414

# INDEX

Johnson, Cheryl, 346
Johnson, Larry, 42
Johnson, Lyndon B., 247–248, 272, 278, 432, 490, 509
Johnson, Robert, 384–385
Johnson Space Center, 211
Johnson, W. Thomas, 481
Joint Chiefs of Staff (JCS), 16, 38, 42, 56, 201, 214, 223, 264
Joint Intelligence Congressional Inquiry (JICI), 225
Joint Interagency Coordination Group, 295
Jones, Alex, 212, 318, 326, 506
Jones, Edwin, 506
Jones, James L., 440–441, 488
Jones, Steven E., 87–88
Jones, Van, 449–450
Jordan, 174, 352
Jovin, Suzanne, 507–508
JP Morgan Chase, 329
Judicial Watch, 280, 284, 337, 445, 448
Justice Department, 6, 26, 43, 76, 114–116, 135, 173, 196, 234, 375, 390, 400, 404–405, 411–412, 416, 420, 424, 443, 463

Kabul, Afghanistan, 117, 254, 258–259, 294
Kadi, Yassin, 129
Kahane, Meir, 38
Kalb, Marvin, 481
Kant, Immanuel, 497
Karzai, Hamid, 143, 252, 317
Katz, David, 117
Katzenbach, Nicholas, 481
Katzman, Kenneth, 112
Kean, Thomas H., 138, 154, 228–229, 232–233, 503
Keating, Frank, 286
Keith, Jim, 454
Keller, Amanda, 39
Kellogg, Brown & Root (KBR), 278
Kelly, Mick , 320, 399, 408
Kennard, William, 478
Kennedy, John F., 155, 213–214, 223–224, 244, 269, 278, 286, 365, 447, 465, 468, 503–504, 509
Kennedy, Patrick F., 344
Kennedy, Robert, 286
Kennedy, Ted, 383
Kenya, 145, 237, 310
Kerik, Bernard, 35
Kerrey, Bob, 231

Kerry, John, 511
Key, Charles, 286
Khalilzad, Zalmay, 174, 252
Khobar Towers (Saudi Arabia), 309, 335, 339
Khomeini, Ayatollah, 489
Khost, Afghanistan, 310
Kiareldeen, Hany, 406
Kick, Russ, 123, 437
Kimberly-Clark, 478
Kimmel, Husband, 247
Kinder, Chad, 192, 375
KinetX, Inc., 182
King, John, 188
King, Martin Luther, Jr., 286, 493
King, Rachel, 391
King, Rick, 204
Kingsland, TX, 330
Kingsville, TX, 357–359
Kinnucan, John, 159
Kinton, Tom, 24
Kissinger, Henry, 227–228, 318, 440–441, 462–463, 469–470, 488–490, 502–503
Klayman, Larry, 337, 445, 448
Kleinberg, Mindy, 12
Knox, Frank, 458
Koppel, Ted, 481
Koran, the, 34, 38, 217, 328
Korea, 115, 120, 251, 260, 272, 291, 502
Koryagina, Tatyana, 119–120
Kozyrev, Nikolai, 257
Kraft, Joseph, 478, 481
Kreindler, Jim, 285
Kroll Associates, 65
Krongard, A.C. Buzzy, 160–161
KSM (Khalid Sheikh Mohammed), 19, 147–148, 342
Kuala Lumpur, Malaysia, 146
Kubiak, Dan, 78
Kucinich, Dennis, 401
Kull, Steven, 275
Kundera, Milan, 487
Kurt, Baron, 105
Kurzberg, Paul and Sivan, 168
Kutler, Stanley, 444
Kuwait, 248, 282, 308, 327, 334–335, 352, 359, 459, 461–464
Kuwait Company for Process Plant Construction & Contracting (KCPC), 282
KuwAm, 86
Kwiatkowski, Karen U., 223

L3 Com, 180
La Nouvelle, 282
Lackland Air Force Base, 407
Lamberth, Royce, 127
Landis, Christopher, 506
Langdon, James C., Jr., 306
Langley Air Force Base, 4
Lansdale, Edward, 213
Larocco, Robert, 96
Las Vegas, NV, 39, 224, 244, 339, 356, 411
Lavello, Randy, 67
Lawlor, Bruce, 387
Lay, Kenneth, 441
Leahy, Patrick, 138, 353
Lebanon, 35, 308, 491
Lee, Doug, 359
Lee, Martin A., 480
Lehman, John, 230–231
Lehrer, Jim, 481
Lemkau, Kristin, 329
Lemnitzer, Lyman, 214
Lerner-Lam, Arthur, 80
Levin, Carl, 298, 376
Levin, Joseph J., Jr., 298, 376
Lewis, Robert Lee, 407
Libertarians, 353, 356, 371–372, 377, 385, 393, 401, 404–405, 409, 423, 427–428, 431, 436, 443
Liberty Tower / Library Tower, 342
Library Connection, 415
Libya, 120, 272, 352, 492, 510
Lieberman, Joseph, 113, 370, 382
Liebner, Lincoln, 53
Liman, Arthur, 378
Lincoln, Abraham, 53, 350–351
Lindh, John Walker, 420
Linowitz, Sol, 481
Little Falls Library, MD, 384
Litvinenko, Alexander, 455
Livingston, Neil, 123
Lockerbie, Scotland, 407
Lockheed Martin, 472–473
Loftus, John, 43–44, 328
Logan International Airport, 2, 24
Loizeaux, Mark, 79
London, England, 75, 112, 116, 121, 157–158, 167, 180, 272–273, 286, 297, 302, 310, 317, 327, 431, 455, 464, 472
*Lone Gunman, The*, 509
*Loose Change*, 6, 210, 505

Lopez, Joe, 279
Los Angeles International Airport, 236, 356
Los Angeles, CA, 2, 24, 27, 83, 114, 116, 184, 197, 208–209, 236–237, 297, 342–343, 356, 372, 392, 448, 466
Lott, Trent, 266
Lubow, Arthur, 358
Luftwaffe, 452, 454, 496
Lundeby, Ashton, 417–418
Luxor, Egypt, 115
Luzhetskiy, Evgeniy, 37

M. A. Bank, 298
Macover, Micha, 166
Madison, James, 267
Madison, WI, 414
Madrid, Spain, 83, 116
Madsen, Wayne, 314
Maginnis, Mike, 397–398
Magna Carta, 404
Mahfouz, Sheikh Kahlid bin, 228, 331–333, 335–336
Mahon, Dennis, 287
Major Cities Chiefs Police Association, 392
Maktab al-Khidimat (MAK), 308
Malaysia, 113, 171
Mandell, Andrew, 389–390
Manila, Philippines, 117–118
Mann, James, 71
Manning, Bill, 58
Manning, Paul, 454
Marco Polo, 245
Marcos, Ferdinand, 496
Maresca, John J., 252
Margolis, Eric, 222, 297, 314, 487, 499
Mariani, Ellen and Louis Neil, 324–325
Marines, US, 119, 294, 358–359, 468, 490–491
Marks, Paul, 179
Marmari, Omer, 168
Marr, Robert, 17
Marrs, Texe, 498
Marshall, George C., 457–458
Marshall, Philip, 130, 501
Marshals Service, US, 346
Martin, Al, 322
Martin, David, 262
Martin, Paul, 475
Marx, Karl, 414, 497
Match, the, 19
McCain, John, 113, 343, 442, 471–472
McCarthyism, 338, 398
McChesney, Robert, 482–483
McClellan, Scott, 262, 273, 296
McCloy, John J., 228
McCoy, Alfred, 299
McDaniel, Barry, 87
McDermott, Jim, 265–266
McDougal, James, 407
McElwain, Susan, 206
McFarlane, Robert, 488
McGovern, George, 261
McHugh, John, 385
McIlvaine, Bob, 325
McIntyre, Jamie, 45–46
McKinney, Cynthia, 267–270, 471
McMahon, Ed, 392
McNamara, Robert, 214, 468–469
McNeil, Robert, 481
McNiven, Timothy, 20
McRae, Ronald M., 218
McVeigh, Timothy, 286–290
Mearsheimer, John, 167–168, 173, 175
Mecklin, John, 333
Meese, Ed, 162, 304
Mena, AK, 303–304
Meridian Plaza fire, Philadelphia, 58, 82–83
Merrill Lynch, 158–159
Mesopotamia, 295
Metcalfe, Daryl, 377
Mexico, 65–66, 178, 194, 261, 269, 284, 345, 349, 366, 424, 475
Meyerowitz, Joel, 96
MI6, 116, 271, 317
Miami, FL, 29, 393, 466
Milanytch, Ross, 69
Military Commissions Act, 352, 417
Military Operations in Urban Terrain (MOUT), 359
Miller, Doreen, 413, 417, 421
Miller, Wallace E., 204
Milwaukee Deep, 215
Mindanao, Philippines, 288
Mineta, Norman, 3–4, 54–55, 205, 324
Minneapolis, MN, 126, 139–141, 223, 399, 508
Minto, New Brunswick, 371
Mir, Mushaf Ali, 41–42
Missile, 4, 50, 52–56, 97, 143–144, 179, 191, 205, 213, 236, 257, 311, 365, 492
Mission Accomplished, 297
Missouri Documents, 375
Missouri Information Analysis Center (MIAC), 375
Mitchell, Billy, 450, 458
Mohamed, Ali A., 42
Monbiot, George, 273
Moore, Michael, 119
Moran, Jim, 427
Morgan Stanley Dean Witter & Co., 159
Morris Corporation of Australia, 282
Moscow, Russia, 257, 306
Mosiello, Steve, 101
Mossad, 40, 43, 168, 171, 175–177, 179, 219–220, 502
Mossadegh, Mohammed, 489
Motley, Ron, 323–324, 331
Mount Anthony Union High School (Bennington, VT), 396
Moussaoui, Zacarias, 5, 10, 76, 138–141, 194, 196–198, 204, 289–290, 477
Moyers, Bill, 229, 447
Mubarak, Hosni, 120
Mueller, Heinrich, 458
Mueller, Mark, 411
Mueller, Robert, 20, 30–31, 38, 126, 129, 132, 136, 140, 142, 404
Muhalhal, Naeem Abd, 285
Mujahideen, 28, 44, 117, 145, 254, 299, 302, 308, 315, 335, 348
Muller, Daniel, 389–390
Munich, Germany, 292, 440
Murad, Abdul Hakim, 117, 288, 313
Murphy, Thomas S., 481
Murrah Federal Building, 59, 79, 118, 284–287, 289, 355
Murray, Chris, 51
Musharraf, Pervez, 317
Muslim Brotherhood, 43–44, 307
Muttawakil, Wakil Ahmed, 116–117
Muwafaq Foundation, 329, 336
*My Pet Goat*, 3, 15
Myers, Richard, 3, 17, 47, 201

NAFTA Superhighway, 475

# INDEX

Naik, Niaz, 253, 256–257
Nairobi, Kenya, 237
Napolitano, Janet, 347, 370, 399, 428, 440, 488
NarusInsight, 126
NASA Glenn Research Center, 210–211
Nasseri, Cyrus, 283
National Commerce Bank (Saudi Arabia), 329, 331, 333
National Construction Safety Team (NCST), 60
National Counterintelligence Center (NCIC), 170
National Flight Emergency Response System (NFERS), 182
National Geospacial-Intelligence Agency (NGA), 360
National Guard, 2, 250, 285, 308, 330, 332–333, 358, 378, 507
National ID Card, 427, 430
National Institute for Drug Enforcement Training, 393
National Institute of Standards and Technology (NIST), 60, 74, 77, 90, 505
National Intelligence Council (NIC), 146
National Military Command Center (NMCC), 56
National Reconnaissance Office, 16
National Security Act, 135, 367, 447, 500
National Security Agency (NSA), 11, 114, 142, 217, 408, 431–432
National Security Archives, 445
National Security Council (NSC), 174, 178, 226, 252, 272, 378, 441, 467, 491
National Security Letter (NSL), 415–416
National Security Strategy, 226, 503
National Security Whistleblowers Coalition, 138
National Transportation Safety Board (NTSB), 38, 184, 191, 199
National Urban Search and Rescue Team (FEMA), 18
NATO, 43, 190, 258, 301
Navy Command Center, 49
Navy, US, 32, 49, 64, 230–231, 261, 278–279, 318–320, 361, 394–395, 420, 456, 458, 492

Nayirah, 248
Nazis, 43–44, 354, 452–454, 511
NEADS (Northeast Air Defense Sector), 2–3, 17, 202, 208
Nebuchadnezzar, 295
Nelson, Brendan, 180
Nelson, Scott, 445
New Brunswick, NJ, 371
New Delhi, India, 250
*New Industrial State, The*, 470
New World Order, 365, 429, 456, 460, 511
New York Stock Exchange, 155
Newark Airport, 2
Newman, William, 435
Nicaragua, 229, 278, 363
Nichols, Terry, 118, 287–289
Nidal, Abu Nidal, 176
Niger, 315
Night Stalkers, the, 357
Nila Sagadevan, 33
*9/11 Commission Report, The*, 3–4, 6, 9, 15, 38, 43, 45, 55, 67, 85, 130, 135, 146–148, 154, 160, 164, 198, 205, 209, 221, 223, 233, 240, 243, 326
NIST Building and Fire Research Laboratory, 60
Nixon, Richard, 230, 272, 277, 297–298, 318, 322, 348, 364, 375, 379, 409, 432, 441, 445, 488, 492, 502
No Child Left Behind Act, 396
No-Fly List, 383–385
Nobel, Alfred, 246, 276
Nogeim, Gregory T., 414
Noman, Abdullah, 339
Nomura, Kichisaburo, 456
NORAD (North American Aerospace Defense Command), 1–3, 6, 8–9, 12, 16–18, 21–22, 46, 54–56, 112, 202, 230, 242–243, 501, 509
Norfolk, VA, 55, 351, 420
Noriega, Manuel, 492, 496
Norquist, Grover, 338
North Korea, 115, 120, 260, 272, 502
North Vietnam, 248, 353, 490
North, Oliver, 378
Northern Command, US, (USNORTHCOM), 366
Northern Guardian, 18
Northern Ireland, 251
Northern Vigilance, 18

Nosair, El Sayyid, 38
Novak, David, 198
Nuclear device, 93–94, 99
Nunn, Sam, 478
Nuremberg Trials, 496

O'Brien, Danielle, 53
O'Meara, Kelly Patricia, 408, 412
O'Neill, John, 127–129, 252
O'Neill, Paul, 235
Oasis technology, 435
Obama, Barack, 231, 249, 273, 297, 301, 319–320, 341, 343, 379, 392, 399–400, 426, 437–440, 443, 447–450, 454, 468, 484–486, 503, 512
October Surprise, 19, 229, 464
Odigo, 166–167
Office of Emergency Management (OEM), 64–65, 100, 103, 107
Office of National Preparedness (ONP), 22
Office of Strategic Influence (OSI), 362
Office of Strategic Services (OSS), 494
Offutt Air Force Base, 187
Ogonowski, Peg, 198
Oklahoma City Bombing, 118, 286, 289–290, 296
Olberg, Ralph, 145
Olmsted, Thomas R., 32
Olson, Barbara, 10, 184, 192–194, 197
Omar, Mullah, 254, 256, 273–274, 323, 329, 337
Ondrovic, Patricia, 93–94
One World Government,
OPEC (Organization of Petroleum Exporting Countries), 461
*Open Chemical Physics* Journal, The, 88–89, 91
Operation Desert Storm, 459
Operation Diamondback, 133–134
Operation Diomedes, 359
Operation Last Dance, 357
Operation Mongoose, 213
Operation Northwoods, 213–214, 223, 465–467
Operation Shamrock, 432
Operation TIPS, 390–392
Opium, 247, 251, 299–303
Organization of the Islamic Conference, 484

Organized Crime, 40, 169, 213, 298, 304–305, 324
Ortega, Daniel, 491
Orwell, George, 378–379, 381, 383, 391
Osman, Tim, 144–145, 224
Oswald, Lee Harvey, 511
Otis Air Force Base, 2, 4, 8, 17, 55
Otter, Butch, 409, 412

P2OG (Proactive, Preemptive Operations Group), 466–467
Padilla, Jose, 421–423, 425, 442
Paine, Thomas, 443
Pakistani Intelligence (ISI), 42, 133, 175, 177, 240, 299, 309, 319
Palast, Greg, 338
Palestine, 157, 312, 485, 491
Paley, William, 481
Palfrey, Deborah, 326, 506
Palisades, NY, 80
Palm Beach, FL, 429
Palmer, Fredrick, 441
Palmer, Orio J., 76–77, 82
Pan Am Flight 103, 407
Panama, 278, 458, 488, 492
Panetta, Leon, 297, 320
Parenti, Michael, 479
Paris, France, 117, 139, 151, 227, 229, 453, 489
Parker, Kathleen, 269–270
Patrick, William, 138, 344, 353, 404
Patriot Act, 21, 242, 314, 343–344, 398, 400–419, 424, 426, 430, 443, 453, 488
Patterson, Steve, 53
Paul, Ron, 266–267, 375, 401, 410–411
Pavitt, James L., 152
Peak Oil, 246
Pearl Harbor, 57, 74, 223, 227, 246–247, 252, 255, 259, 351, 455–458, 465, 509
Pecoraro, Mike, 71–72, 94
Pellegrini, Frank, 427–428
*PentaCon, The*, 506
pentaerythritol tetranitrate (PETN), 344
Pentagon, 3–9, 12, 16–18, 21, 25, 32–36, 44–57, 63, 98, 117, 124, 146–148, 157–158, 165, 176–178, 184–191, 195, 199–201, 210, 213–215, 224,

230, 241–242, 253, 258, 264, 270, 278, 282, 285, 290, 293, 302, 306, 313–314, 337, 358, 360–363, 461, 465–469, 500–501, 506
Perelman, Marc, 168
Perkal, Don, 48
Perle, Richard, 173–175, 502
Perloff, James, 456
Perry, Patricia, 325
Perry, Rick, 511
Perry, Steve, 141–142
Perry, William, 440
Persian Gulf, 119, 248–253, 334–335, 459, 464, 492
Peshawar, Pakistan, 308
Peterson, Derek Lawrence, 36–37
Peterson, Donald A., 477
Peterson, Hamilton, 196, 477
Peterson, Peter G., 324
Petroleum Finance Company, 280
Philadelphia, PA, 39, 74, 82–84
Philippines, 28, 118, 288, 338
Phillips, Noelle,
Phinney, David, 282
Phoenix Program, 385–388, 467
Pickard, Thomas, 234
Picocell, 193
Pieczenik, Steve R., 318–319
Pilots for 9/11 Truth, 184, 190
Piper, Michael Collins, 203, 481
Pipes, Daniel, 172
Pistole, John, 29
Pitt, Harvey, 159
Pitt, Williams Rivers, 159
Pittsburgh, PA, 5, 411
Plaugher, Ed, 46
Poindexter, John, 229, 363
Poland, 399, 453
Pollard, Jonathan, 171
Poole, Patrick S., 404
Popov, Dusko, 457
Popovic, Alex, 159
Port Arthur (Pinyun Lu-shun), 458–459
Port Authority of New York & New Jersey, 72, 76, 159–160
Porter, Richard, 109
Portugal, 352
Posner, Gerald, 40–42
Posner, Michael, 481
Posse Comitatus Act, 354,

358–360, 362, 364, 366
Postal Service, US, 390
Powell, Colin, 263–265, 347, 388, 424, 439–440, 488, 502
Powell, Jeremy, 2
Powell, Judy, 356
*Power of Nightmares, The*, 26–27, 348
Powers, James F., Jr., 376–377
POWs, 285, 388–389
Praimnath, Stanley, 77
Predators, 143–144, 492
President's Daily Brief (PDF), 126, 153
Presidential Emergency Operations Center (PEOC), 22
Price, Michael H., 483–484
Princiotta, Salvatore, 507
Problems Solutions Innovations, 219
Proctor, Paul, 399–400
Project Censored, 478, 485
Project for New American Century (PNAC), 252, 360
Project Government Oversight, 21
PROMIS software, 145, 162
Prouty, L. Fletcher, 447, 509
Public Citizen, 444–445
Put Options, 158–160, 164
Putin, Vlamidir, 119, 455
Pyle, Christopher H., 364

Qaddafi, Muammur, 492
Qatar, 119
Qiao Liang, 118
Qualcomm, 192
Queenan, Joe, 436
Quetta, Pakistan, 150–151

Rabia, Abu Hamza, 144
Racicot, Mark, 443
Radio Kabul, 258
Radlauer, Don, 162
Rand Corporation, 270
Ranneft, Johan, 457
RAO Gazprom, 251
Rapiscan Systems, 344
Rappoport, Jon, 25, 347
Rather, Dan, 64, 481
Ratigan, Dylan, 158
Razim, Mohammad Alim, 252
Reagan, Ronald, 19, 144–145, 162, 191, 229–231, 235, 241, 248, 266, 277–278, 303, 336–337, 348, 359, 363, 378–379, 388, 399, 409, 421,

# INDEX

437, 442, 445, 467, 492, 512
Rearing and Empowering America for Longevity against acts of International Destruction (REAL ID) Act, 427
Red Cross, 97, 352–353
Redden, Jim, 392
Reed, Douglas, 453
Reed, Jason, 320
Reed, Terry, 304
*Reichstag* fire, 403, 452, 465
Reilly, Tim, 407
Remote control, 125, 179–181, 190, 205–206
Remote viewing, 217–220
Rendell, Ed, 376–377
Reno, Janet, 124, 351
Resource Services Washington, 49
Ressam, Ahmed, 236–237
Reston, James, 481
Retinger, Joseph Hieronim, 472
Rewards for Justice, 393
Reynolds, Morgan, 63–64, 94, 97
Rhodes, Cecil, 497
Rice, Condoleezza, 20, 135, 226, 236–238, 252, 259, 300, 324, 440, 476, 489
Rich, Marc, 15, 247, 332, 444
Richardson, James O., 440, 456, 489
RICO (Racketeer Influenced and Corrupt Organizations Act), 74, 215, 324
Riconosciuto, Michael, 144–145
Ridenhour, Ron, 358
Ridge, Tom, 286, 351, 354, 367–370, 383, 385–387, 407, 448
Riechmann, Deb,
Risen, James, 275, 300
Riskus, Steve, 49–50
Ritter, Scott, 263
Ritz Hotel (Paris), 227
Rivera, Daniel, 68
Rivero, Michael, 510
Riyadh, Saudi Arabia, 292, 309
Roberts, Craig, 88, 285, 365
Roberts, Paul Craig, 399
Robertson, Mary, 282, 296
Robertson, Pat, 282, 296
Robinson, Linda, 360
Rockefeller, David, 462
Rockefeller, Jay, 433
Rockefeller, Nelson, 469

Rodman, Peter, 174
*Rodriguez v. Bush*, 74
Rodriguez, Paul, 170, 173
Rodriguez, William, 72–74, 97, 233, 325
Roemer, Timothy J., 231
Rogers, Arthur, 179, 357
Romer, Bruce, 384
Romero, Van, 65–66
Rommel, Erwin, 43, 247
Roosevelt, Franklin Delano, 246–247, 259, 442–443, 455–459
Root, Elihu, 129, 278, 391, 495
Rosenfeld, Stephen S., 481
Rosenthal, A. M., 419, 449, 481
Rosin, Hanna,
Ross, Andrew, 69, 449
Roswell, NM, 269
Rotenberg, Marc, 346–347, 404
Rothschild, Matthew, 246, 472, 511
Rotter, Gernot, 314
Rouse, Lori, 479
Rove, Karl, 226, 485, 511
Rowley, Coleen, 140–142, 223
Royce, Knut, 127
Royer, Jeffrey A., 157
Rubenstein, Howard J., 167
Ruby Ridge, ID, 286, 351, 407
Ruiz, Robert, 93–94
Rumaila, Iraq, 459
Rummel, Marsha, 414
Rumsfeld, Donald, 3, 27, 47, 49, 54, 56, 74, 125, 174, 201, 235, 259, 262, 277, 322, 324, 348, 360–363, 366, 439–440, 466, 502
Ruppert, Michael C., 22, 148, 158–159, 161–162, 337
Rusk, Dean, 468
Russell, Jerry, 56
Russell, Samuel, 301
Russian Revolution, 494
Russo-Afghan War, 255, 306
Russo-Japanese War, 459
Ryan, Kevin R., 77–78, 88, 180, 416

Sa, Kuhn, 388–389
Sabah Family, 461, 464
Sadat, Anwar, 42
Safer, Morley, 273, 275, 482
Salah, Muhammad A., 157
Saleh, Ali Abdullah, 128, 310
Salem, Emad, 37–38, 329–331
Salisbury, Harrison, 481

Samit, Harry, 138, 140
San Antonio, TX, 329–331, 407
San Diego, CA, 24, 89, 113, 157, 185, 329, 389
San Francisco, CA, 2, 38, 47, 117, 124, 160, 196, 396, 402
Sanchez, José, 74, 357
Sanchez, Tomas, 74, 357
Sanders, Bernie, 401, 478
Sands Motel (Oklahoma), 289
Sands, Philippe, 272, 289
Santorum, Rick, 472
Sarandon, Susan, 291
Sarasota, FL, 3, 13
Saud IV, King, 307
Saud, Prince, 31, 42, 307, 315, 327
Saudi Arabia, 24, 26, 31, 40–44, 228, 251–252, 254, 258, 261, 270, 307–310, 313, 322–324, 326–331, 333–340, 352, 421, 461, 464, 484, 487, 500
SAVAK police, 489
Sawyer, Diane, 481
Scahill, Jeremy, 161
Scarbrough, Dwight, 394–395
Scarry, Elaine, 205–206
Scheer, Robert, 27
Schiff family, 495
Schippers, David, 134–135
Schlafly, Andrew, 350
Schmidt, Howard, 433
Schmitz, Hermann, 453–454
Schneider, Karen G., 413
Schneider, Rene, 228
Schoomaker, Pete, 148
Schorr, Daniel, 481–482
Schrecker, Ellen, 398
Schroeder, J. Henry,
Schwarzenegger, Arnold, 436, 511
Scott, Alan, 211
Scott, William B., 18
Scottsdale, AZ, 185, 507
Scowcroft, Brent, 187, 337, 440, 489
Scranton, William, 481
Seal, Al, 387
Seal, Barry, 303–305
SEAL, Navy, 319–320,
SEAL Team Six, 361
Sears Tower (Chicago), 29, 117
SEC (Securities and Exchange Commission), 159–160, 164, 334–335
Secret Service, US, 3, 11,

13–14, 43, 102, 107, 121, 157, 176, 190, 369–370, 381, 394, 398, 407, 446
Secret Societies, 228, 243, 440, 451, 459, 470, 481, 497–498, 502, 510, 512
Securacom, 86, 160, 508
Seibert, Tom, 53
Selzer, Larry, 434
Senate Foreign Relations Committee, 388, 462
Senate Judiciary Committee, 136, 353, 383, 409, 419
Senyan, Qaed, 143
Serpico, Frank, 351
Shadow government, 378, 447–450
Shaffer, Anthony A., 149–150
Shah of Iran, 496
Shah, Wali Khan Amin, 288, 460, 489, 496
Shahawar Matin Siraj, 29
Shaikh, Abdussattar, 24, 147, 328
SHAMRC, 110
Shanksville, PA, 5, 202–204, 207, 507
Shannan, Pat, 303, 506
Shapiro, Jeffrey Scott, 104–105
Sharon, Ariel, 491
Shaw, Bruce, 287
Shearer, Lloyd, 494
Sheikh, Ahmad Umar, 19, 147–148, 178, 317, 331–332, 342
Shelby, Richard, 113
Shishkin, Philip,
Shmuel, Yaron, 168
Short, Walter, 247
Shuford, Reginald T., 384
Sierra, Katie, 280, 395–396, 441
Silverstein, Larry, 104–105, 110, 159–160, 167, 241, 425
Simmons, Roger, 406
Simons, Tom, 256–257
Skilling, Jeffrey, 441
Skousen, Joel, 238–239
Skull and Bones, 301, 468, 511
Slater, Mike, 48
Slatkin, Nora, 162
Smith, Charles R., 172
Smith, Ivan C., 131
Smith, Patti, 291
Smith, Paul, 506
Smith, Peter, 400
Smith, Walter Bedell, 490
Smith, William French, 378
Snider, Britt, 113, 358–359

Snowe, Olympia, 434
Sobel, David, 126–127
Soehnge, Walter, 411
Solomon, Norman, 480
Somalia, 278, 309, 311, 493
Sonnenfeld, Kurt, 105–109
South Bend, IN, 77–78, 418
Southern Air Transport, 305
Southern Law Poverty Center (SPLC), 373
Southwest Aviation Services, 333
Soviet Union, 21, 27, 44, 91, 144, 218, 227, 248, 250, 254–255, 277, 299, 302, 307, 315, 348, 431, 494, 496
Spain, 83, 116, 201, 291, 337, 352, 444
Sparapani, Timothy, 383
Special Operations Command (SOCOM), 148, 194, 357, 361
Special Supplemental Nutrition Program for Women, Infants and Children (WIC), 373
Specter, Arlen, 224, 442
Sperry, Paul, 131
Spinelli, Tom, 206
Spitzer, Eliot, 325–326
Springer, Jerry, 482
Springman, Michael, 339
SPS International, 57
Spying, 140–141, 172–173, 341, 364, 381, 391, 409–410, 412, 446, 476
St. Clair, Jeffrey, 385
Stafford, Ned,
Standard Oil, 246, 453
Standley, Jane, 5, 109
Star Wars, 21, 97, 100
Starr, S. Frederick, 253
State Department, 24, 42, 112, 128, 137, 146, 163, 174, 257–258, 264, 293, 323, 339, 344, 462
Statue of Liberty, 389–390, 428
Steensma, David K., 474
Stein, Jeff, 316
Steiner, Carl W., 194
Stewart, Jim, 124
Stewart, Payne, 9
Still, William T., 495
Stimson, Henry, 458
Stoffer, Irit, 169
Stoga, Alan, 462
Stoltz, Dick, 133
Stone, Oliver, 30, 214
Strasbourg, France, 20
Strategic Support Branch

(SSB), 360–361
Stratesec, 86–87
Strossen, Nadine, 398, 411–412
Stubblebine, Albert, 46
Sudan, 38, 43, 309–311, 352, 450, 485, 493
Sugg, John F.,
Sule, Gidikumo, 279
Sullivan, Louis W., 440
Sullivan, Martin E., 294
Sullivan, Thomas, 103, 110–111
Sultan, Prince, 42, 270, 323, 336
Sulzberger, A. Ochs, 481
Sunke, Salvador Gerson, 178
Super-thermite, 89
Supreme Court, US, 22, 106, 194, 281, 314, 351–352, 393, 396, 422, 424–425, 431, 503, 511
Suter, Dominick, 169
Sweeney, Madeline Amy, 40, 196–198
Sweeney, Mike, 198
Swinton, Stanley, 481
Switzerland, 354
Sydney, Australia, 282, 431
Syntek Technologies, 363
Syria, 120, 174, 308, 421, 510
Szymanski, Greg, 35–36, 212, 216

Taft-Hartley Act, 389
Talbott, Strobe, 481, 488
Taliban, 116, 133, 143, 149, 224, 251–259, 294, 299–302, 308–310, 316, 351, 420, 423–424, 501
Tanzania, 145, 237, 310
Tarpley, Webster Griffin, 14–15, 19, 38, 461
Teledyne Ryan Aeronautical, 180
Tempest, 431–432
Tenet, George, 113, 125, 152–153, 161, 178, 188, 230, 324
Terrorist Identities Datamart Environment (TIDE), 383
Thatcher, Margaret, 464
Thermate, 89–91
Third Reich, 43, 403, 512
Thomas, Helen, 272
Thomas, William, 9
Thomasson, Todd, 377
Thompson, Doug, 342–343, 446

Thompson, Jim, 231, 234
Thornton, Bridget, 479
Thorpe, Elliot, 457
Tibold, Laszlo, 282-283
Tikrit, Iraq, 282
Tillman, Pat, 302-303
Tinker Air Force Base, 17
Tisch, Laurence A., 481
Toland, John, 457
Tomb, Rex, 11, 292
Torture, 26, 29, 41, 106, 341, 353, 386, 424-426, 442
Trancredo, Tom, 366
Transamerica Tower (San Francisco), 117
Transponders, 2, 5, 9, 55, 185-186, 199, 213, 436
Trilateral Commission, 119, 220, 252, 255, 440, 455, 475, 481, 486
Tripod II, 18, 64
Trireme Partners, 175
Tritium, 99
Trotsky, Leon, 495, 498
Troy, Tennessee, 359
Truman, Harry, 389
Tucker, James P., 247
Tully, Peter, 79
Tunisia, 31
Turkey, 174, 282, 291, 308, 352, 432
Turki, Prince, 41-42, 323
Turkmenistan, 250, 252
Turley, Jonathan, 420-421, 423
TWA Flight 800, 471
Tyler, Patrick E.,
Tyndall AFB, FL, 18
Tyumen Oil, 305-306

UAL Corp., 158
Umar Farouk Abdulmutallab, 343
Unger, Craig, 25, 327-328, 337-338
United Airlines Flight 175, 2, 212
United Airlines Flight 93, 202, 212, 220
United Kingdom, 165, 271-272, 352, 432
United Nations (UN), 5, 117, 249, 263-267, 273, 278, 352, 460, 484, 489, 502
Unocal, 228, 250-252
Urban Moving Systems, 168
*US vs. Singleton*, 393

Utah, 87, 349
Uzbekistan, 253, 278

Valentine, Carol A., 183
Valentine, Douglas, 386-388
Van Bergen, Jennifer, 442
Van der Lubbe, Marinus, 452
Van Natta, Don, Jr., 278
Vance, Cyrus, 318, 481
Vankin, Jonathan, 249, 460
Veale, William, 47
Veliz, Teresa, 69
Venice Airport, 31-32
Ventura, Jesse, 64
Ventura, Michael, 448
Verdon, Steve, 343
VeriChip, 430
VeriTracks, 435
Vernon, Wes, 210
Verton, Dan, 187-188
Vialls, Joe, 180-181, 186, 192
Vidal, Gore, 259, 488
Vienna, Austria, 262
Vietnam, 21, 228, 247-249, 272-273, 277-278, 285, 291, 296, 302, 353, 357-358, 385-388, 432, 466-470, 490, 493-494, 504
Vigilant Guardian, 1, 16, 18, 22, 112, 215, 242
Vigilant Warrior, 17-18
Vilker, Lee, 339
Villaraigosa, Antonio, 342
Vitter, David, 396
Vlements, Jon,
Von Wedel, Franz, 463

Waco, TX, 183, 286, 351, 355, 407, 475
Wahhabi, 314, 322, 328
Wald, Matthew L., 9
Walker, John Mercer, Jr., 48
Walker, Wirt, III, 86, 242
Wallace, Ben, 204, 345
Walsh, Kenneth T., 277
Walt, Stephen, 5, 167-168, 173, 175, 477
Walter, Jimmy, 63
Walter, Mike, 53
Walters, Barbara, 481
Walters, Brit, 479
WAMY (World Assembly of Muslim Youth), 338
Warburg, Paul, 495
Ward, Ed, 99
Ward, Mike, 331
Warner, John, 261, 366,

477-478
Warren Commission, 110, 161, 221, 223, 225, 227-229, 231, 233, 235, 237, 239, 241, 243
Watergate, 231, 234, 272
Watson, Dale, 136, 317
Watson, Steve, 274
Weehawken, NJ, 169
Weijerman, F. G. L., 457
Weinberger, Casper, 489
Welch, John F., 481
Weldon, Curt, 148-149
Wellstone, Paul, 266
Welna, David, 124
Werthebach, Eckhardt, 176
Wessel, Vernon "Bill", 210-211
West Warwick, RI nightclub fire, 60
Whalen, John, 249, 460
Wherley, David F., Jr., 507
Whistleblowers, 7, 141, 237, 281, 380, 382, 474
White, Charles W., 332
White, Gary, 99
White, Michael R., 207
Whitehead, John, 391
Whitney, Mike, 422
Whittington, Harry, 446
Wilkerson, Lawrence B., 264-265
Will, George, 481
Williams, Anthony A., 130
Williams, Kenneth J., 431
Wilson, Jim, 431-432
Wingate, Lynn, 157
Wiretaps, 115-116, 127, 172-173, 404
Wise, David, 150
WMD (Weapons of Mass Destruction), 264, 271-272, 292, 450
Wolfowitz, Paul, 173-174, 201, 205, 264, 277, 502
Wood, Judy, 60, 94-95, 97-98, 300, 508
Wood, Richard, 481
Woodward, Michael, 198
Woolsey, James, 67
Worden, Carl, 422
Worden, Robert L., 146
World Trade Center Disaster Review Panel, 59
World Trade Organization (WTO), 118-119, 476
World War I, 351, 494-495, 498
World War II, 43, 137, 247-248, 253, 255, 294, 310, 351, 356, 364-365, 443, 453-455,

468, 472, 488–489, 496
WorldCom, 333, 503
Wright, Bill, 203
Wright, Lawrence, 127–130, 134
WTC (World Trade Center), 2–7, 11–13, 22, 26, 31, 35, 38, 42, 54, 59–72, 75–95, 98–101, 103–110, 117–118, 123, 129, 156–160, 165–168, 178–190, 200, 205, 215, 219–220, 223, 230, 240–242, 258, 306, 323–325, 337, 406, 465, 500, 504–508
WTC 1 (North Tower), 2–5, 12–13, 35, 63–75, 80–83, 97, 100, 106–108, 167, 240–241
WTC 2 (South Tower), 3–5, 11–13, 54, 63–77, 80–87, 93, 96, 102, 106, 188, 241, 324
WTC 5 (Building Five), 75–76
WTC 6 (Building Six), 75, 79, 104, 107–108
WTC 7 (Building Seven), 5–7, 63–64, 79–81, 86, 100–111, 205, 223, 230, 241–242, 505
WTC "bathtub," 95
Wurmser, David, 174
Wyatt, Nancy, 198
Wynns, Jill, 396

Xe Services LLC, 130
Xiong, Jing, 10

Yates, Steven, 429
Yemen, 128, 143–144, 308–309, 311, 339, 352
Yildash, Tahir, 117
Yonts, Jim, 300
Young, Ling, 77
Yousef, Ramzi, 117–118, 122, 127, 236, 288

Zakheim, Dov, 57, 174
Zarrillo, Richard, 100–101
Zebuhr, Michael, 508
Zelikow, Philip, 149, 222, 225–226, 503
Zim American Israeli Shipping Co., 167
Zogby, John, 271, 275–276
Zubaydah, Abu, 40–41, 147, 151, 237
Zuckerman, Mortimer, 481